PARENTING

Parenting

Third Edition

JANE B. BROOKS
KAISER PERMANENTE MEDICAL CENTER

Mayfield Publishing Company
Mountain View, California
London • Toronto

Library of Congress Cataloging-in-Publication Data

Brooks, Jane B.
    Parenting / Jane B. Brooks.—3rd ed.
      p.   cm.
    Includes bibliographical references and index.
    ISBN 0-7674-1797-6
      1. Parenting.   2. Child rearing.   3. Parent and child.   I. Title.
HQ755.8 .B748 2000
649′.1—dc21   00-055044

Manufactured in the United States of America

10   9   8   7   6   5   4   3

Mayfield Publishing Company
1280 Villa Street
Mountain View, CA 94041

Sponsoring editor, Franklin C. Graham; production editor, Julianna Scott Fein; manuscript editor, Andrea McCarrick; design manager and cover designer, Violeta Díaz; text designer, Claudia Smelser; art editor, Rennie Evans; illustrators, Judith Ogus and Emma Ghiselli; manufacturing manager, Randy Hurst. The text was set in 10.5/13 Minion by UG / GGS Information Services, Inc. and printed on acid-free 45# Chromatone Matte by Banta Book Group.

Text credits: p. 67, from *Between Generations,* by Ellen Galinsky. Copyright © 1981 by Ellen Galinsky. Reprinted by permission of Times Books, a Division of Random House, Inc.; pages 89, 98, from *Children: The Challenge,* by Rudolf Dreikurs, M.D., with Vicki Soltz, R.N. Copyright © 1964 by Rudolf Dreikurs, M.D. Used by permission of Dutton, a division of Penguin Putnam, Inc.

Photo credits: page 3, © Elizabeth Crews; page 25, © Russell Schleipman/Offshoot Stock; page 41, © Bob Daemmrich/The Image Works; page 60, © Elizabeth Crews; page 81, © Michael Newman/PhotoEdit; page 97, © Elizabeth Crews/Stock, Boston; page 105, © Elizabeth Crews; page 112, © Bob Daemmrich/The Image Works; page 147, © Frank Siteman/Jeroboam, Inc.; page 161, © Kent Reno/Jeroboam, Inc.; page 171, © Jose Carillo/PhotoEdit; page 182, © Robert Brenner/PhotoEdit; page 209, © Esbin-Anderson/Picture Quest; page 226, © Myrleen Ferguson Cate/PhotoEdit; page 248, © Lawrence Migdale/Photo Researchers, Inc.; page 254, © Nancy Sheehan/PhotoEdit; page 274, © Joel Gordon 1994; page 277, © Richard Hutchings/PhotoEdit; page 326, © Catherine Ursillo/Photo Researchers, Inc.; page 337, © Okoniewski/The Image Works; page 349, © Joel Gordon; page 354, © Joel Gordon 1998.

To my grandparents and parents,
my children and their children

Contents

Preface xvii

PART ONE   General Concepts, Goals, and Strategies of
Parenting

CHAPTER 1
Parenting Is a
Cooperative
Venture

Parenting Is a Process   1
The Role of the Child   2
   Children's Needs   2
   Parents' Needs of Children   3
The Role of the Parent   3
   How Parents Influence Children   4
   Influences on Parents' Behavior   4
The Role of Society   4
   The Environment   4
      Box 1.1 The Ecological Environment   6
   Social Influence   6
   Protective and Risk Factors   7
      Box 1.2 Generic Risk Factors   8
Interactions among Child, Parent, and Society   9
The Effect of Historical Time on Parenting   11
      Box 1.3 Trends in Family Values over the Past Fifty
      Years   15
The Effect of Individual Timing on Parenting   16
   The Decision to Parent   16
      Adolescent Parents   16
      Couples   17
      Single Mothers   18
      Unplanned Children   18
   Age and Pregnancy   18
   Age and Parenting   20
      Adolescent Mothers   20
      Parents over Thirty-Five   21
      Box 1.4 Guidelines for Older Parents   22
The Means of Becoming a Parent and Its Effect on
Parenting   22

How Much and What Kind of Influence Parents Have
   on Children   25

What Society Owes Parents   29
   Box 1.5 Parents' Bill of Rights   32

Main Points   33

Exercises   37

Additional Readings   38

CHAPTER 2

Learning to Be Parents

A Parent's Job Description   39

Parental Goals   40
   Physical Competence   42
   Intellectual Competence   43
   Emotional Competence   44
   Self-Esteem   45
   Social Competence   48
   Moral Competence   49
   The Role of Authoritative Parenting   50

Cultural and Socioeconomic Influences on Parenting   51
   Culture   51
   Socioeconomic Status   54

What Parents Learn from Their Families of Origin   56

The First Three Years of Parenting   59
   Advances in Neuroscience   59
   Factors to Consider   60
   The Importance of Experience in the Early Years   61
   The Modifiability of Early Experiences   64
   In Conclusion   66

How Parents Change as a Result of Parenting   67

Main Points   68

Exercises   70

Additional Readings   71

CHAPTER 3

Establishing Close Emotional Relationships with Children

Family Atmosphere   73
   Box 3.1 Adults' Reasons for Wanting Children   73
   Close Emotional Relationships   73
   The Power of Positive Feelings   76
      *Box 3.2 Eight Forms of Positive Parent-Child
         Communication*   78
   The Disruptive Effects of Negative Feelings   78
      Lack of Time   79

Everyday Negative Moods 80
Everyday Anger 80
Affective Processes in Parenting 82
Fostering a Harmonious Family Atmosphere 84
Communicating Feelings 84
Active Listening 84
I-Messages 86
Establishing Democratic Family Living 87
Providing Respect and Encouragement 88
Handling Mistakes 89
Emphasizing Importance versus Self-Sufficiency 90
Box 3.3 Dealing with Adversity 91
Providing Supportive Parenting 92
Providing Opportunities for Self-Expression 92
Coaching Children to Manage Emotions 93
Dealing with Negative Feelings 95
Creating Family Time 95
Developing a Support System 96
Maintaining Realistic Expectations 97
Managing Negative Feelings 98
Box 3.4 Eight Ways to Deal with Parental Anger 99
Increasing the Joys of Parenting 99
Main Points 100
Exercises 102
Additional Readings 103

CHAPTER 4
Modifying
Children's
Behavior

The Learning Process 104
Promoting Learning 106
Establishing a Collaborative Atmosphere 106
Setting Realistic Expectations 106
Helping Children Meet Expectations 107
Paying Attention to Positive Behaviors 107
Teaching Acceptable New Behaviors 109
Establishing and Enforcing Rules for Appropriate Behavior 109
Stating Limits Effectively 109
Enforcing Limits 110
Mutual Problem Solving 110
Natural and Logical Consequences 111
Punishments 111
Ineffective Forms of Discipline 113
The Controversy over Physical Punishment 113

How a Child's Temperament Influences Parenting
    Strategies   117

Socializing Boys and Girls   120

Selecting Individually Appropriate Problem-Solving
    Strategies   123

Main Points   124

Exercises   125

Additional Readings   126

PART TWO   **Parenting at Different Developmental
    Stages**

CHAPTER 5

**Infancy and
Early
Childhood**

Transition and Adjustment to Parenthood   127
    *Box 5.1 Recommendations to Couples for Easing the
      Transition to Parenthood*   128

Promoting Secure Attachments   129
    Bonding   129
    Early Parent-Child Relationships   129
    Forms of Attachment to Parents   130
    The Process of Attachment   131
    Social and Cultural Influences on Attachment   133
    Attachment to Both Parents   136
    Stability of Attachment   137

Attaining a Sense of Identity   137
    Box 5.2 Ways to Encourage Secure Attachments   138
    Gender Identity   140
    Ethnic Identity   140

Helping Children Regulate Their Emotions   141
    Infant Crying   143
    Anger   144
    Temper Tantrums   144
    Empathy   146

Promoting Self-Regulation   146
    Encouraging Compliance   147
    Establishing Rules   148

Cultural and Social Influences That Affect Parenting
    in Infancy   150

Parents Who Face Special Difficulties   153
    Adolescent Parents   153
    Adolescent Mothers   153

Adolescent Fathers 154
Help for Teenage Mothers and Fathers 155
Depressed Parents 156
Substance-Abusing Parents 157
Troubled Families 159

Creating a Positive Family Atmosphere 160

How Parents Change As They Raise Young Children 162

Main Points 164

Exercises 166

Additional Readings 166

CHAPTER 6
The
Elementary
School Years

Parent-Child Relationships 167

Development of the Self 170
Gender Identity 170
Ethnic Identity 170
Box 6.1 Four Basic Dimensions of Ethnic Differences in Children 172
Accuracy in Self-Perception 173

Development of Self-Regulation 174
Common Feelings of School-Age Children 174
Empathy 174
Aggressiveness 175
Fearfulness 175
Loneliness 175
Unhappiness 175
Coping with Stress 176
Strategies 176
Supportive People 176

Internalizing Rules and Values 178

Promoting Children's Achievement in School 179
Influences within the Home 180
Parents' Social Characteristics 180
Parents' General Beliefs and Behaviors 181
Parents' Beliefs about the Specific Child 181
Parents' Specific Behaviors 182
Influences within the School 183
Parents' Partnership with Schools 183
Parents as Advocates for Children 186
Cultural Factors 188

Encouraging Children's Positive Peer Relationships   188
  Peer Acceptance and Rejection   189
  Biological and Environmental Contributions
    to Social Skills   190
  Parents' Contributions to Social Skills   190
    Helping the Shy Child   191
    Helping the Aggressive Child   191
    Helping the Bullied Child   193

Managing the Television   194
  Television Use among Children   194
  The Effects of Television Violence   196
  Helping Children Use Television Effectively   196

Parents' Experiences during the Elementary
  School Years   197

Main Points   198

Exercises   200

Additional Readings   201

CHAPTER 7
Adolescence

A Time of Change   203
  Physical Changes   203
  Intellectual Changes   204
  Emotional Changes   205
  Changes in the Self   206
  Social Changes   206
  Dating   208
  School   209

Forming a Sense of Identity in Times of Change   210
  Gender Identity   210
  Ethnic Identity   211
    *Box 7.1 Methods to Enhance Identity Formation of Ethnic
      Minority Youths*   212

Parent-Child Relationships   213

Promoting Adolescents' Capacity for Emotional
  Regulation   216
  The Importance of Parents' Examples   216
  Helping Children Control Aggressive Feelings   217
  Helping Children Manage Feelings of Depression   219
    Causes of Depression   220
    Depression and Suicide   221
    Obtaining Professional Help   221

Promoting Healthy Behaviors   224
  Parents' Healthy Behaviors   225

Protective Factors 227
Parents' Awareness and Specific Actions 227
Promoting Later Sexual Activity 227
Discouraging Alcohol Use 228

Promoting Teens' Positive Peer Relationships 230
**Resolving Conflicts As Adolescents Move toward
Independence** 231
Parents' Experiences during the Adolescent Years 232
Main Points 234
Exercises 235
Additional Readings 235

PART THREE **Parenting: Varying Life Circumstances**

CHAPTER 8
Parenting and
Working

Dimensions of Participation in Work and Family Life 237
Typologies of Family 238
Children's Ratings of Parents 240
Divergent Realities 241
Divergences in Men's and Women's Perceptions 241
Divergences in Parents' and Children's Perceptions 242

The Flow of Work and Family Life 243
Parent-Child Interactions 243
Focusing on Children's Needs 243
Monitoring 245
*Encouraging Family Cooperation in Household
Work* 246
Spillover from Home to Work 248
Box 8.1 Moving to New Patterns of Household Work 249
Spillover from Work to Home 250

Strategies for Navigating Work and Family Life 252
Types of Day Care 255
Availability and Affordability of Day Care 256
Impact of Nonparental Care on Children 257
Nonparental Care during Infancy and Early Childhood 257
Nonparental Care during Later Childhood
and Adolescence 261
Gender Differences in Response to Nonparental Care 261
The Effects of Economic Hardship on Parenting 262
Who Are the Poor? 262
The Effects of Poverty on Children's and Adolescents'
Development 263

Birth Outcomes and Physical Health   263
Cognitive Development and School Achievement   264
Emotional and Behavioral Development   264
Pathways Accounting for the Effects of Poverty   264
Ways to Intervene   266
The Care of Both Partners   267
Main Points   268
Exercises   269
Additional Readings   269

CHAPTER 9
Nontraditional
Families

The Heterogeneity of Single-Parent Families   271
**The Experiences of Unmarried Mothers
and Their Children**   272
Unmarried Mothers at the Time of the Child's
Birth   272
Unmarried Mothers in the Years following the
Birth   272
Outcomes of Children Born to Unmarried
Mothers   273
Marital or Partner Conflict   275
The Process of Divorce   276
Telling Children about Divorce   276
Children's Reactions to Divorce   278
Parents' Reactions to Divorce   279
Factors Affecting Adjustment to Divorce   280
*Box 9.1 Out of Harm's Way: Protecting Children
from Parental Conflict*   281
Protective Factors for Children   282
Family Changes over Time   283
Children's Behavior over Time   284
**Should Parents Stay Together for the Sake
of the Children?**   286
Before the Divorce   286
After the Divorce   287
Fathers' Role in Children's Lives   287
Father Absence   287
Fathers' Contributions to Children's Lives   288
Encouraging Fathers' Participation   290
When a Parent Dies   291
Telling Children   291
Dealing with Children's Reactions   292

Remarriage 294

Challenges of Stepfamilies 294

Family Changes over Time 295

Children's Behavior over Time 299

Box 9.2 Eight-Step Program for Strengthening Ties in Stepfamilies 300

Typologies of Stepfamilies 301

Lesbian and Gay Parents 303

Divorced Lesbian and Gay Parents 303

Lesbian and Gay Couples' Transition to Parenthood 304

Children of Lesbian and Gay Parents 305

Parenting Tasks at Times of Partner and Marital Transitions 305

The Power of Authoritative Parenting 306

Main Points 306

Exercises 308

Additional Readings 309

CHAPTER 10
Parenting at
Times of
Trauma

Victimization of Children 310

An Ecological/Transactional Model of Community Violence and Child Maltreatment 313

Dealing with Child Abuse and Violence 316

Exposure to Family Violence 316

Prevalence 316

Effects on Children 317

Interventions 317

Sexual Abuse 318

Prevalence 318

Effects on Children 319

Interventions 324

Physical Abuse 325

Prevalence 325

Effects on Children 327

Interventions 328

Neglect 328

Prevalence 328

Effects on Children 329

Interventions 329

Other Forms of Personal Abuse 331

Community Violence 331

Prevalence 331

Effects on Children   332

Coping Resources   333

Common Themes in Abuse and Violence   334

Prevention of Violence   335

The Challenge Model   336

Keeping Children Safe   338

*Box 10.1 Some "What If?" Questions for Young
Children*   339

Main Points   340

Exercises   342

Additional Readings   343

CHAPTER 11
**Supports for
Parents and
Children**

Social Supports   345

Support within the Family   346

Supportive Family Members   346

Siblings   346

Grandparents   347

Other Relatives   347

Family Rituals   348

Support outside the Family   352

People outside the Family   352

Teachers   352

Other Nonrelatives   353

Parenting Programs   354

Workplace Supports   356

Governmental Supports   357

Community Programs   359

Box 11.1 A Family-Friendly City   360

Church Support   362

The Power of a Single Individual   366

Main Points   367

Exercises   368

Additional Readings   368

Notes   369

Index   406

Preface

AMERICANS REPORT THEY GAIN their greatest satisfaction in life from relationships within the family. For example, after testing and interviewing men and women about the impact of parenthood on their lives, psychologist David Gutmann writes, "For most adult humans, parenthood is still the ultimate source of the sense of meaning. For most adults the question 'What does life mean?' is automatically answered once they have children; better yet it is no longer asked."

Do people get training to succeed in this central life activity? No! Anyone who cuts hair for pay or drives a car must have a license and demonstrate a certain level of skill before being permitted to engage in these activities independently. But nowhere does society require systematic parenting education, which may matter most of all.

This book attempts to fill this educational gap. Like earlier editions, the third edition of *Parenting* shows how parents and caregivers can translate their love and concern for children into effective parenting skills. The book strives to bring to life the child's world and concerns, so parents can better understand what their child may be thinking and feeling. The book also describes the myriad thoughts and feelings—positive and negative—that accompany parenting so parents can better understand themselves.

The book is divided into three broad sections. The first section, consisting of Chapters 1 through 4, focuses on general concepts, goals, and strategies of parenting. The second section, Chapters 5 through 7, discusses parenting children of different ages. The third section focuses on parenting in varying life circumstances.

Each chapter in the three sections presents a brief overview of information and then examines four or five specific topics in greater depth. In Chapter 1, for example, we briefly discuss the definition and process of parenting as well as the ecological/transactional framework for understanding parenting. We then explore in greater depth such topics as the influence of historical time on parenting, the nature and importance of parents' influence on children, the influence of the means and timing of parenting on the process of parenting, and the support that society provides parents as they rear the next generation. In Chapter 2, we examine parents' basic goals in parenting and how they learn specific parenting behaviors to achieve their goals. We explore what parents learn from their cultural and social groups, what they learn from their personal experiences with their parents, and the degree to which these early learning experiences are modifiable. We discuss whether parenting in the first three years is the most important for children, and finally we look at how parents change in the course of parenting.

Chapters 3 and 4 focus on the two main tasks of parenting—establishing close emotional relationships with children (Chapter 3) and modifying their behavior (Chapter 4). In Chapter 3, we look at such topics as how parents foster closeness and harmony among family members and ways parents coach their children to identify their feelings accurately and express them appropriately. We identify sources of stress and negative feelings in family life and ways to minimize the effects of anger and stress so that family satisfactions and enjoyment increase. Chapter 4 presents strategies for modifying children's behavior and looks in detail at the effects of physical punishment. We examine how a child's temperament influences parents' choices of strategies and the different challenges in socializing boys and girls. Finally, guidelines are established for selecting strategies appropriate for individual parents and children.

Chapters 5, 6, and 7 give brief overviews of children's development in infancy and early childhood (Chapter 5), elementary school years (Chapter 6), and adolescence (Chapter 7). In Chapter 5, we also examine how social and cultural influences affect early parenting. An extended section looks at parents who have particular difficulties in the early years with children—adolescent parents, depressed parents, substance-abusing parents, and parents who get into a vicious cycle with children. We describe help that is available for these parents. In Chapter 6, we focus particularly on how parents work with children and with the schools to promote children's academic success. In Chapters 6 and 7, we discuss ways parents help children form and maintain positive relationships with peers and deal with problems such as aggressiveness, shyness, victimization by bullies. In Chapter 6, we look at how parents handle external influences like TV and media on children, and in Chapter 7, ways parents promote physically and emotionally healthy lifestyles amidst all the changes of this period.

Chapters 8, 9, and 10 present information on parenting in varying life circumstances—parenting when parents are employed or unemployed (Chapter 8), when parents and children live in less traditional families (Chapter 9), and when children have been abused or traumatized in some way (Chapter 10). In all these chapters, the emphasis is on understanding the nature of the special circumstances and challenges involved in each situation and promoting effective functioning in parents and children—on navigating the worlds of family life and work, on finding good substitute care for children when parents are employed outside the home, on dealing with the stresses of poverty, on establishing effective same-sex-parents and single-parent homes, maintaining single fathers' involvement with children, easing the transition to blended families. In Chapter 10, we look at the distinctive features of the different forms of abuse and useful forms of treatment for children. We discuss ways to minimize the risks of community violence and abuse and help children feel safe in a world that is sometimes unsafe.

Throughout, the book describes programs that support parents, but Chapter 11 presents a systematic framework for understanding the roles supportive people and programs play in the process of parenting. As in previous editions, the book discusses cultural and social factors as they pertain to specific topics such as identity formation and bicultural identity. I do not have a separate chapter on specific ethnic groups individually, in terms of particular beliefs and practices. Individuals and subgroups within larger ethnic groups vary so widely that it is difficult to construct a composite portrait that does justice to both individuals and the group.

In selecting topics for more detailed discussion, I have focused on questions that parents ask themselves, and most of these are new to this edition: How important are parents in children's lives? Are only the first three years important for parenting? Are we bound to repeat our parents' behavior with our children? Do we need to treat sons and daughters differently? When in conflict, should parents stay together for the sake of the children? What are the effects of father absence and nonparental care?

There is a new section in Chapter 8, "Parenting and Working." The results of a new survey provide insights on how children evaluate working mothers and fathers and the qualities that matter most to them in their relationships with their parents. New information also gives parents suggestions for how to navigate the worlds of family life and work most effectively. Chapter 9, "Nontraditional Families," presents new material on never-married parents and children and successful strategies for effective parenting. Chapter 10 includes new discussions on domestic violence and neglect of children. Chapter 11 contains a new section on ways to incorporate family rituals into everyday life.

I write this book from the point of view of a parent, a clinician, a researcher, a teacher of parenting. I have the firm conviction that anyone who wishes to invest attention and effort in becoming a competent, caring parent can do so in his or her own way. The single prerequisite is the desire to succeed along with the willingness to invest time and energy, and the results are well worth the effort. My experience as a clinician has shown me that children face many difficult situations; with a loving, supportive caretaker, children can live life fully and happily even if temporarily engulfed by trauma.

Children are not the only ones enriched by adults' efforts to be effective parents. Helping children grow is an intense, exciting experience that brings special meaning for parents. Our physical stamina, agility, and speed increase as we care for infants and toddlers. Our emotional stamina grows as we deal with our own intense feelings with our children and help children learn to express and modulate their feelings. Our intellectual skills grow as we answer young children's questions and, later, help them master school subjects. In helping new life grow, we gain for ourselves an inner vitality and richness that affects all our relationships.

Acknowledgments

Writing the acknowledgments is one of the pleasures of completing a book; and as one reads galleys and page proofs, there are constant reminders of all the people who have helped make the book a reality.

I thank all the clinicians and researchers who gave generously of their time not only for the interviews themselves but also for their additional time reviewing the excerpts and clarifying points. They are Jay Belsky, Andrew Billingsley, Susan Harter, Sylvia Hewlett, Barbara Keogh, Jacqueline Lerner, Richard Lerner, James Levine, Susan McHale, Emily Visher, John Visher, Jill Waterman, Emmy Werner, and Steven Wolin.

Special appreciation goes to Dr. Robert Kremers, chief of the Department of Pediatrics of Kaiser Medical Center, for his willingness to give questionnaires about the joys of parenting to parents in the waiting rooms. I thank the many anonymous parents who completed them there and in parenting classes. Most particularly, I express my gratitude to all those parents I interviewed about the joys of parenting and the ways they changed and grew through the experience. I gained valuable insights about the process of parenting, and their comments enliven the book immeasurably. These parents are Wendy Clinton, Mark Clinton, Judy Davis, Robert Rosenbaum, Linda Dobson, Douglas Dobson, Jill Fernald, Charles Levine, Outie Gould, Warren Gould, Caryn Gregg, Robert Gregg, Jennifer Lillard, Michael Hoyt, Henrietta Krueger, Richard Krueger, Patricia Landman, Steven Tulkin, Chris McArtor, Robert McArtor, Kathy Malone, Jean Oakley, Susan Opsvig, Paul Opsvig, Sherry Proctor, Stewart Proctor, Iris Yotvat-Talmon, Moshe Talmon, Raymond Terwilleger, Patricia Toney, Anthony Toney, Barbara Woolmington-Smith, Craig Woolmington-Smith.

I also thank the late Paul Mussen for his suggestions and interest in my writing over the years. He recommended using comments from researchers to make material more vivid for students. His concern with the social forces impinging on parenting has continued to influence my thinking.

Coworkers at Kaiser Medical Center at Hayward were supportive and helpful throughout. Pediatricians and pediatric advice nurses have provided helpful information about parents' concerns. My coworkers on the Child and Family team in the psychiatry department were encouraging and enthusiastic about the work. I am most appreciative of the leadership at Kaiser. Dr. Paul Jewett, recent physician-in-chief, Dr. Anabel Anderson Imbert, present physician-in-chief, Dr. Jerome Rauch, chief of psychiatry, and Dr. Paul Opsvig, head of the Child team all promote an atmosphere that stimulates creativity.

The staff at Mayfield Publishing Company deserve special appreciation for the care and diligence they exercised in transforming the manuscript into a book. Franklin Graham, the sponsoring editor, has brought his enthusiasm and critical skill to the task of improving the book so it will be more informative and useful for students. His assistant, Kate Schubert, has solved many practical problems. Julianna Scott Fein, production editor, has given the book the care and attention that warm an author's heart. She assembled an outstanding production staff and no detail has escaped her attention. Violeta Diaz, design manager; Claudia Smelser, designer; and Rennie Evans, art editor, have made the book not only more attractive but also more readable and comprehensible to students. Andrea McCarrick has been a dream copyeditor; she has improved the organization and structure of the book and with a few words and reordered sentences has given greater clarity to the writing. I have learned a great deal from her and have nothing but praise and admiration for her work. Martha Granahan, permissions editor, has given thorough and helpful directions in this area.

Finally, I wish to thank my family and friends for their thoughtfulness and their company. I thank my patients for sharing their lives and experiences with me. I hope they have learned as much about life from me as I have learned from them. Finally, I want to thank my children, who are now grown and live away from home. They are very much in my mind as I write and as I relive experiences with them in the different developmental periods. I find that I have learned the most important truths of parenting from our interactions. I believe that when I have paid attention, they have been my best teachers.

1

Parenting Is a Cooperative Venture

PARENTHOOD TRANSFORMS PEOPLE. AFTER A BABY comes, parents are no longer the same individuals they were. A whole new role begins, and they start a new way of life. What does parenting really mean? What are the joys and responsibilities of being a parent? How has being a parent changed over the past fifty years? How does society help or hinder parents? This chapter explores parenting as a cooperative venture between parents, between parents and their children, and between parents and society. It defines parenting, describes the roles of parents and the environment in rearing children, and focuses on how society can help both parents and children.

Four million babies are born in the United States each year.[1] The challenge for parents and society is to rear children to attain their full potential in adulthood. How parents do this under varying family and social conditions is the subject of this book. The aim of the book is to open up the potential of parenthood for all adults by giving information on how children grow and develop and how parents' actions influence children's feelings, behavior, and growth.

Parenting Is a Process

The word *parent* has several definitions—a mother, a father, one who generates new life, a guardian, a protector. Summarizing these definitions, one can say a parent is an individual who fosters all facets of a child's growth, who nourishes, protects, guides new life through the course of development.[2]

In our society, parents usually provide the biological beginnings of new life—the egg and sperm—and also serve as caregivers for the child after birth. But this is not always the case. Adoptive parents become parents through actions of the court. Through assisted reproductive technology, a child can have as many as five parents. Jaycee Louise Buzzanca had five parents. Her two intended parents, the Buzzancas, wished to have a child but could not conceive even after undergoing fertility treatments. They sought sperm and egg donors, unrelated to each other, who contributed the genetic material for Jaycee, and a gestational mother carried the fertilized egg to term in her womb.[3] (In a later section, we consider how assisted reproduction influences parenting.)

We emphasize that parenting is a process that brings about an end result. Although the relationship between each parent and child is unique, parenting, in general, can be described as a series of actions and interactions on the part of parents to promote the child's development.[4] Parenting is not a one-way street in which parent influences child but rather a process of interaction between the two that is influenced by cultural and social institutions. Jay Belsky describes three major influences on the process of parenting: (1) the child's characteristics and individuality, (2) the parent's personal history and psychological resources, and (3) the social context of stresses and supports.[5]

The Role of the Child

Children bring to parenting their individual needs, gender, birth order, temperament, and patterns of growth. All of these factors influence parents' behavior and are, in turn, influenced by parents and their larger social context.

Children's Needs

Children's immature state at birth requires that parents and society nurture them and meet their needs so they can survive. Meeting these needs reorganizes parents' lives and makes demands on society as well.

According to Urie Bronfenbrenner and Pamela Morris, a child grows through "progressively more complex reciprocal interaction [with] persons, objects, and symbols in its immediate external environment." Further, "to be effective, the interaction must occur on a fairly regular basis over extended periods of time." A father feeding a baby and a child exploring a toy are just two examples of such interactions. There must be "one or more other persons with whom the child develops a strong, mutual, irrational attachment, and who are committed to the child's development, preferably for life." The maintenance of the caregiver-child relationship depends on the attachment and involvement of a second adult "who assists, encourages, spells off, gives status to, and expresses admiration and affection for the person caring for and engaging in joint activity with the child."[6]

Bronfenbrenner and Morris believe these interactions must continue on a regular basis so the activities can become more complex and stimulate further development. The child need not be biologically related to his or her parent nor live in a two-parent family, but the caregiver must have a long-term, "irrational" attachment and love for the child and receive the emotional support and respect of at least one other adult.

Parents are interactive partners with their children from the first days of life.

Parents' Needs of Children

Accustomed as we are to thinking about parents' importance to children, most of us fail to recognize children's importance to parents. Children, however, meet many of their parents' basic psychological needs.

In recent surveys, two-thirds of men and women report that their families and love life are the most satisfying parts of their lives.[7] Parents of all ethnic backgrounds cite the love and emotional closeness they experience as the most important reason for having children.[8] Further, parents talk about the special quality of this love. Bronfenbrenner and Morris refer to an "irrational attachment."[9] Tracy Gold announces her feelings about her baby on the cover of *People* magazine: "You never imagined you could love someone this much."[10] Parents also enjoy watching and helping their children grow and develop. Children give parents a sense of being responsible, mature adults; link their parents to the rest of the community; and can even provide a sense of immortality.[11]

The Role of the Parent

Parents bring a complex personal history and a richly patterned social life to the parenting process. When they become parents, they have to adapt their individual qualities to meet the demands of their new role. Further, they need to adjust to the changes in this role that social change brings.

Ross Parke and Raymond Buriel believe parents meet role expectations and socialize children in three ways: (1) as an interactive partner with the child, (2) as a direct instructor, and (3) as a provider of opportunities that stimulate children's growth.[12] We can classify parents' behaviors as having direct or indirect influences on children's behavior.[13] For example, instructing children on oral hygiene and healthy eating habits has a direct influence on children's physical health. Indirect influences consist of parental actions that affect the child in general and increase the likelihood of competent behavior in a given area. For example, when parents use reasoning to influence children's behavior—that is, give pertinent information and reasons for following parental requests—children are more likely to develop self-reliance and a sense of responsibility, which are in turn associated with the learning of healthy behaviors.

While past research has focused on how parents directly teach and socialize children, current research indicates that many parent-child interactions previously unrecognized as significant may greatly affect children's growth and development. For example, the kinds of fantasy play that parents engage in with children help children learn to regulate and control their emotions.[14] The form of the questions parents ask and the style of their comments also influence children's language development and later cognitive functioning.[15] So, children learn from all kinds of interactions with parents.

Influences on Parents' Behavior

Many factors shape parents' behavior. Children's temperaments and individual qualities shape what parents do, but many other influences also come into play. As we shall see in Chapter 2, parents' early interactions with their own parents mold how they interact and respond to their babies and to the other parent. A person's marriage, work, and overall support network also affect his or her parenting behaviors.[16] Finally, parents' cultural background and social heritage influence their goals and how they go about accomplishing them. (We will explore this in greater detail in Chapter 2.)

The Role of Society

Parenting occurs in a social context. Children live in families, and families belong to social groups in a larger society that, in turn, influences how parents carry out their tasks. In this section, we look at the social context in terms of (1) the levels of interaction the child has with the environment, (2) the various forms of social influence on parenting, and (3) protective and risk factors in the social context.

The Environment

Earlier in this chapter, we discussed Bronfenbrenner's view that children's development requires daily interactions with persons and objects that stimulate increasing complexity in behavior. Here, we examine Bronfenbrenner's analysis of the environment and relate it to the material that will be presented in the rest of the book.[17]

"At her christening party, we had a tape recorder, and each guest taped a little message into the recorder. When she began to sing, she would sing into the recorder, and when her grandmother was alive, she sang the old Norwegian songs into the recorder so we have that on tape. And every year at various times, at birthdays or holidays, we would all talk into the tape recorder about what our lives had been like and what had gone on since the last time we did it. We have her singing 'Silent Night' with all the words wrong, and that has been a real thread. We have a sort of oral history, and it's a real pleasure for us." —*Mother*

"Thomas Wolfe wrote *You Can't Go Home Again*, but James Agee said you do go home again in the lives of your children. It is a sort of reexperiencing what you experienced when you grew up—they're reading the same books you read, the conflicts they have are the ones you remember having with your parents, or issues that mattered to you as a child are issues for them. When you have time to reflect on them, they bring you back over and over again to issues in your own childhood that I guess you have a second opportunity to resolve. You have a different perspective on them than you did before." —*Father*

"One of the interesting things was when we took our children back to Ohio. Before she could crawl, one used to scoot around on her rear end and tuck one knee under the other, and she wore out all the seats of her pants. Her great-grandmother was alive then and said, 'Oh, that is just the way her grandfather did it.' We never knew that and it was just amazing. One of our girls is so like her great-aunt who never had any children of her own and was such a lovely woman. It would have pleased her so much to see my daughter grow up. Our son looks like my father and is so much like him in every way. He has his build. My father always had a joke at dinner every night and our son has always loved jokes. As soon as he could read, he had a joke book and was always telling us jokes at dinner. Our other son looks just exactly like his father and his grandfather." —*Mother*

"One of my great joys was the first time my parents came to visit us, very proudly handing my son to my father and saying, 'Here's my boy!' That was a real highlight, a great thrill. I get choked up saying it now." —*Father*

"I like having my family around. For the first time in my life, I want my mother to be here. There is a basic need to have your family around you. My husband's family and cousins are here, and I have a really strong urge to have everyone around. I was not really prepared for that." —*Mother*

"Being a parent has helped me to see into myself. It's very illuminating in a personal way. It brings back a lot of memories, good and bad." —*Father*

BOX 1.1

The Ecological Environment

Microsystem*	Immediate settings in which a child develops and patterns of daily activities or interactions a child has in those settings (e.g., at home, at school, in the neighborhood)
Mesosystem*	Interrelationships between two or more settings in which a child participates (e.g., interrelationships between parents at home and teachers at school)
Exosystem*	Agencies and institutions that influence a child but with which the child does not directly interact (e.g., parent's work, government agencies)
Macrosystem*	Broad cultural contexts in which mesosystems and exosystems exist—culturally shared blueprints about how things are done (e.g., how children are cared for)
Chronosystem†	Changes and continuities over time that influence a person's development (e.g., school entry, puberty, marriage)

*From Urie Bronfenbrenner, *The Ecology of Human Development: Experiments by Nature and Design* (Cambridge, MA: Harvard University Press, 1979).
†From Urie Bronfenbrenner, "Ecology of the Family as a Context for Human Development," *Developmental Psychology* 22 (1986): 723–742.

The pattern of activities and daily interactions children experience with objects and with people—parents, caregivers, teachers, coaches, peers—Bronfenbrenner calls the *microsystem* (Box 1.1). This is what we will explore in most chapters—the daily interactions children have with other people and objects. The *mesosystem* consists of the interactions and interrelationships between parents and other people who care for children—parents and teachers (see Chapter 6), parents and day care providers (see Chapter 8), and so on. The *exosystem* includes agencies and institutions that influence children's daily life but do not include children as participants—parents' work (see Chapter 8) and community and government agencies (see Chapter 11). For example, parents' work can promote positive parent-child relationships by allowing time off for children's illnesses or activities. The *macrosystem* is the broad cultural context in which children, parents, institutions, and agencies exist. The social system provides a set of beliefs about what parents must do and how they must do it. The *chronosystem* refers to major changes occurring over time that influence development, such as entering school, leaving home, or getting a job.

Social Influence

Community influences on parenting consist of such factors as a neighborhood's safety and the number of services the community provides. We will discuss these influences from time to time throughout the text and particularly in Chapter 11.

Culture provides a set of beliefs about (1) the importance of parenting, (2) the roles of extended family members and the community, (3) the goals of parenting, (4) approved methods of discipline, and (5) the roles of children in society. Our diversified culture has many ethnic groups with varying beliefs on these topics.[18]

Ethnicity "refers to an individual's membership in a group sharing a common ancestral heritage based on nationality, language, and culture. Psychological attachment to the group is also a dimension of ethnicity, referred to as ethnic identity."[19] Culture includes shared views of the world, values, and conduct that are passed down from one generation to the next. Each cultural group has its own social system based on some combination of parents' occupations, education, and income. Like culture, social position influences parents' goals and ways to achieve them, as we shall see in the next chapter.

Protective and Risk Factors

Researchers have noted that both individuals and the environment have qualities that can be labeled protective or risk factors.[20] *Risk factors* are variables significantly associated with poor outcome of some sort—poor health, poor growth, poor cognitive or social growth. Poverty, for example, is a risk factor. (Box 1.2 lists other risk factors residing within the individual or the environment.) *Protective factors* are conditions or qualities related to positive outcome even in the face of increased risk. Arnold Sameroff suggests that these be termed *promotive factors* as they promote development whether or not there is risk.[21] Recognizing that these factors are promotive even when there is no risk, we continue nonetheless to use the term *protective factors,* as these factors also can prevent a risk or buffer the individual against the effects of a risk. Protective factors are such individual qualities as easy temperament and good health and such environmental qualities as good schools and high-quality day care.

Examining the environment in terms of risk and protective factors can help us understand continuities in children's behavior. The Rochester Longitudinal Study investigated the effects of the social environment on children's intellectual and social-emotional competence from birth through adolescence.[22] The researchers selected ten environmental risk factors to relate to child competence—maternal mental illness, high maternal anxiety, rigid beliefs about development, few positive maternal interactions, minimal maternal education, unskilled parental occupation, disadvantaged minority status, single parenthood, stressful life events, and large family size. Paternal qualities were not included in the findings, as only a small number of men participated in the study.

The research yielded several important findings, which were confirmed in a subsequent study in Philadelphia. First, no one particular risk factor led to a poor outcome. Second, the accumulation of risks led to poor outcome; the more risks, the less competent the child's functioning. Children with no risks scored thirty points higher on intelligence tests than children with eight or nine risks. Children with more risk factors had more clinical problems as well. Third, the continuity of risk factors across childhood (a correlation of .77 between risk factor scores at ages four and thirteen) was as great as or greater than any continuity in the child's characteristics. Thus, the environment had a

BOX 1.2

Generic Risk Factors

1. ECOLOGICAL CONTEXT

Neighborhood
disorganization
Racial injustice
Unemployment
Extreme poverty

2. CONSTITUTIONAL HANDICAPS

Perinatal complications
Sensory disabilities
Organic handicaps
Neurochemical imbalance

3. FAMILY CIRCUMSTANCES

Low social class
Family conflict
Mental illness in the family
Large family size
Poor bonding to parents
Family disorganization
Communication deviance

4. SKILL DEVELOPMENT DELAYS

Subnormal intelligence
Social incompetence
Attentional deficits
Reading disabilities
Poor work skills and habits

5. EMOTIONAL DIFFICULTIES

Child abuse
Apathy or emotional blunting
Emotional immaturity
Stressful life events
Low self-esteem
Emotional dyscontrol

6. INTERPERSONAL PROBLEMS

Peer rejection
Alienation and isolation

7. SCHOOL PROBLEMS

Academic failure
Scholastic demoralization

From John D. Coie et al., "The Science of Prevention: A Conceptual Framework and Some Directives for a National Research Program," *American Psychologist* 48 (1993): 1022. Copyright © 1993 by the American Psychological Association. Reprinted with permission.

consistently negative or positive effect on the child. Only one child in a sample of fifty went from living in a low-risk environment (zero or one risk) at age four to a high-risk environment (four or more risks) at age thirteen, and only one child went from a high-risk environment at age four to a low-risk environment at age thirteen.

Fourth, the environment greatly limited or expanded the range of the child's competencies. The least resilient or resourceful child in a low-risk environment scored higher on measures of competence than did the most resilient and resourceful child living in a high-risk environment. "The negative effects of a disadvantaged environment seem to be more powerful contributors to child achievement at every age than the personality characteristics of the child."[23]

Fifth and finally, there was no single change that could be made—increased income, a change in marital status from single to married—that would eliminate the risks for children. Researchers concluded that efforts to improve high-risk environments must focus on making changes in a broad constellation of factors—improving mothers' mental health, encouraging positive parent-child interactions, improving occupational status. "We can maximize the efficiency of intervention efforts when we realize it is not being poor alone, or living in a bad neighborhood alone, or having a single parent alone that places children at risk, but rather the combination of these factors that saps the lives of families."[24]

Investigators in the Rochester Longitudinal Study also identified protective factors that were related to positive changes in cognitive and social-emotional functioning in high-risk children between four and thirteen years of age.[25] Protective factors in the child, measured at age thirteen, were self-esteem, a sense of social support, and a sense of predictability about the world.

More protective factors were identified in parents' qualities. A mother's teaching style that encouraged thinking and reflection, measured when children were age four, was a protective factor. When children were age thirteen, protective factors in the mother centered on her feeling positive about herself and the child. Mothers who voiced fewer dissatisfactions, scored lower on a depression measure, and made supportive rather than critical comments to children promoted children's positive development. Protective factors also included mothers' having a confidante and social support and their encouraging values of self-direction for children rather than conformity.

Protective factors in the environment included fewer negative events and social support for families. There were no gender differences in the protective factors. As we shall see throughout the book, and especially in the next chapter, these really are what Sameroff termed promotive factors because they encourage positive development in all children.

Interactions among Child, Parent, and Society

We have seen that children, parents, and society play their own vital role in the process of parenting, and each is affected by the actions of the other two. A further level of complexity exists because the effect of one of the participants may depend on the relationship between the other two participants—what Bronfenbrenner and Morris call *interaction effects*.[26] We need to consider these effects because they indicate that what may be quite important for understanding a certain group of children and families may have little relevance to other families. For example, low birth weight and birth complications are developmental risk factors when parents are poor and have few resources to deal with these problems. In more advantaged families, however, these factors have little effect on later development because parents have the emotional and financial resources to handle them.

Jay Belsky and his colleagues provide a model of how children, parents, and society interact to predict the probability of child competence—a combination of

TABLE 1.1   Relative Probability of a Child's Developing Competently

Probability of Child Competence	Conditions of the Parental Subsystems*		
	Parent's Personal Resources	Subsystems of Support	Child's Characteristics
High	+	+	+
	+	+	−
	+	−	+
	−	+	+
	+	−	−
	−	+	−
	−	−	+
Low	−	−	−

From J. Belsky, E. Robins, and W. Gamble, "The Determinants of Parental Competence: Toward a Contextual Theory," in *Beyond the Dyad*, ed. Michael Lewis (New York: Plenum, 1984), p. 253. Reprinted by permission.
*(+) stands for supportive mode; (−) stands for stressful mode.

abilities reflected in the child's emotional security, capacity for independent behavior, demonstration of social skills with peers, and intellectual achievement at school (Table 1.1).[27] When all factors are supportive, the probability of child competence is high. When two of the three factors are supportive, there is still a good probability of child competence. For example, if a child has a learning disability but the parents' personal resources are strong and the school personnel provide practical help and emotional support, the probability of child competence is high.

Conversely, even when the child has many skills and positive qualities, a lack of social support and parental involvement lowers the probability of child competence. Belsky and his colleagues believe that even when all goes wrong, if the parent brings his or her personal resources to bear on behalf of the child, there is a good chance that the child will develop average competence.

Figure 1.1 presents a schematic diagram summarizing the relationships of the participants in the process of parenting, the activities and institutions, and the social, cultural, and historical factors that influence these relationships. At the heart of the process are the mother and father, who are usually married to each other. They form a *parenting bond* that continues even if the *marital tie* dissolves and each marries someone else. Sometimes, a single parent has no ties to another partner.

Brothers and sisters develop what is called a *sibling bond*. When a marriage dissolves, the relationship, or bond, between siblings may provide the most continuous, steady family relationship for children who go back and forth between parents.

As shown in Figure 1.1 by the two-way arrows, parents form direct relationships with each child. They also engage in parenting behaviors to care for their child—the one-way arrows extending from the parenting bond to the children. Children respond to these behaviors in turn.

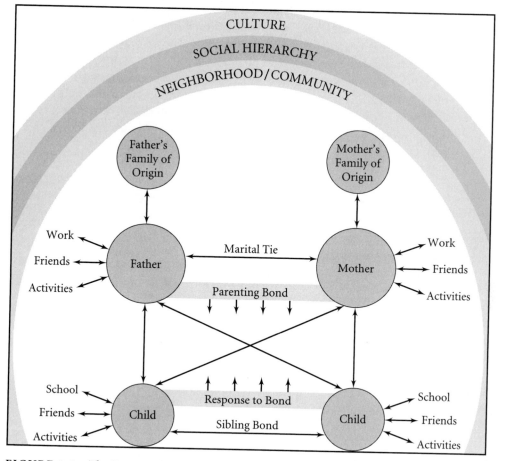

FIGURE 1.1   The Process of Parenting in a Particular Historical Time

Parents are also connected to their families of origin—parents, siblings, and other relatives—who are in turn connected to them and to their children. (Space and clarity did not permit arrows from families of origin to children, but they should be there.)

Parents relate to work, friends, and activities in the neighborhood/community that surrounds the family. The neighborhood/community is part of a social hierarchy within a specific cultural context within a particular historical time. Thus, the family is nested in several social layers that provide support for the family, which, in essence, serves as the vital nucleus of society.

The Effect of Historical Time on Parenting

As shown in Figure 1.1, historical time serves as a framework for parenting. Historical time provides specific social and economic conditions that, in turn, present challenges and supports for parents. For example, rearing children during times of war generates particular worries and strongly shapes parenting behaviors in the direction of focusing on children's protection and safety to a greater degree than would be the case in times of peace. To better understand the challenges that historical time presents to modern-day families, we examine here family life in the nineteenth century and in the mid-twentieth century, highlighting the kinds of social and economic forces that influenced families.

In early-nineteenth-century America, nuclear families consisting of parents and children lived on farms or in small towns.[28] Extended family members lived close to one another, forming a supportive social network. Although the average life span then was shorter than it is today, marriages occurred later than they did throughout much of the twentieth century and the average family size was larger. Mothers, for example, had an average of eight children, and both men and women spent most of their adult years as active parents. Fathers were the heads of their families, authorities who had responsibility for providing financially for family members and seeing that their children were established in work and marriage. All family members worked together as economic producers, with women and children turning over the money they earned from products, such as eggs, or from their labor to fathers.

The family was the center of life activities—the place of work, prayer, and entertainment. It was also the reformatory. Government provided no general services except public education, and in times of trouble, family members were the main source of support and help. Life was not easy at this time. Because (1) life expectancy was shorter, (2) the parenting years were longer, and (3) the death of mothers in childbirth was more frequent than it is today, many families were disrupted by the death of a parent. Epidemic and unpreventable illness, economic hardship, and discrimination against women and minorities also took their toll. Family members, however, retained strong feelings of closeness and interdependence, and family needs took precedence over individual needs. For example, children often postponed marriage to run a farm or take care of ailing parents or growing brothers and sisters.

Following the Industrial Revolution, which occurred gradually in this country during the nineteenth century, nuclear families lived in more urban settings.[29] Fathers left their families to go to a workplace that was nonfamilial and bureaucratic. Women's and children's labor decreased in the middle class, where it was a sign of a father's success that the mother could stay home and focus on childrearing. If additional money was needed, children went to work or families took in boarders before mothers went to work. Working-class minority and immigrant families faced more difficulties. Economic times were hard, and all members of the family worked to survive, sometimes together in factories. In African American families, mothers more often went to work than did children, perhaps because there was more work for them or because families wanted to keep children in school.

Households of all classes were no longer places where members produced but places where they consumed services and nurtured children. The home was seen as a retreat from an impersonal world, a place where family members could enjoy strong bonds to one another. Families were child-centered and concerned with children's advancement in the world. Although public education was available, family members continued to provide supportive services needed throughout the life span—help for orphaned children, widows, aging parents. Private settlement houses in large cities sought to help immigrant families with services.

Life in the nineteenth century posed such physical challenges as surviving illnesses, epidemics, and harsh physical conditions without the technological help of heating, transportation, and health care that is available today. It also presented the challenge of surviving in uncertain economic times without the safety net of job protection or unemployment benefits. There was little assistance outside the family in the event of other emergencies. A person's greatest support at this time was strong family ties and strong relationships with extended kin.

In the mid-twentieth century, the United States had emerged from World War II. The family flourished because of a happy combination of events. The average life span had lengthened, and infant and child mortality had decreased; thus, families were rarely disrupted by death in the parenting years. Following the war, the economy expanded; good-paying jobs were available, and unions obtained legislation for job protection and yearly cost-of-living increases. A single job, even one of unskilled labor, paid a wage that could support a family. In fact, a factory worker could earn in one day the closing costs of a $10,000 home (today, a factory worker would need to work eighteen weeks to afford the closing costs of the same home, currently valued at $100,000).[30]

The government and private businesses also provided support to families.[31] The government offered assistance to families in the form of the G.I. Bill, which paid veterans to go to college or for further technical training that led to job advancements, and V.A. mortgage loans eased the difficulties of buying a home. Government programs also provided assistance to aging parents so adult children did not have to make sacrifices to care for them. In addition, corporate businesses assured workers that they would be kept on in slow times and have secure work for life.

Child-centered, nuclear families continued to predominate. Families typically had three or more children. Marriages were stable and less frequently disrupted by divorce than in the decades preceding or following the period between 1950 and 1970. Women remained the heart of the family, staying at home to care for children and to support husbands emotionally in their work. Most homes had telephones and radios, but television had not yet become a central influence on family life.

So, mid-twentieth-century America provided many supports to parents as they raised children. Government-assisted adult education, government loans to buy homes, economic security with lifelong jobs that could support a family, and government programs that helped support aging parents all made life easier.

During this period, however, women were restricted in job opportunities, and minorities continued to experience discrimination that prevented them from participating fully in the growing economy and in all aspects of social life, from education to housing to recreational pursuits. Nonetheless, in this time, there was a trickle-down effect of prosperity. Between 1947 and 1973, the median paycheck more than doubled, and the poorest 20 percent of the population made the greatest gains.[32]

The two decades beginning in about 1973 saw many economic and social changes that affected families. First, the nature of work changed. Jobs became less secure as companies went through periods of "downsizing," reducing the entire workforce in that business. In addition, many manufacturing jobs were sent overseas. Single jobs frequently did not support a family. In fact, many middle-class families had to depend on two, sometimes three, jobs to meet monthly expenses.[33] Women entered the workforce in greater numbers, in part because economic changes required their paychecks to support families and in part because raising children occupied a smaller segment of the life span and women had the time and interest to work and to seek higher-status occupations. (Box 1.3 summarizes the major changes in family values over the past fifty years.)

As these economic changes occurred, family life changed. Both the divorce rate and the number of children born to unmarried women increased; today, more than 50 percent of children can anticipate living in a single-parent home for a period of time in their development.[34] Because both parents in many families work outside the home, children spend a significant amount of time in others' care. And even when the family remains intact and members are at home, they spend less time in direct interaction with one another because television absorbs their time.[35]

Another change in family life during the 1970s was the pursuit of self-development.[36] Adults, assuming they would continue to enjoy the economic prosperity of their parents and relying on the fact that many families had two paychecks, turned to self-development. Two-thirds of adults felt they should be free to pursue their own lives even if it meant less time with their children. As these attitudes changed, adults no longer expected that their children would make sacrifices for them later in life. Nonetheless, although adults searched for self-fulfillment, 96 percent of those surveyed sought the traditional ideal of two people sharing their lives with each other. Statistics since 1980 indicate that rates of marriage, birth, and divorce have stabilized. The contemporary family is now dealing with all the changes that have occurred from the 1970s to the 1990s.

As we enter the twenty-first century, what are the challenges and supports for parents? It is important, first, to recognize that the army of parents rearing children at this time are a very diverse group of individuals. Nuclear families of two parents and one or two biological children predominate (68 percent of families), and 32 percent are single-parent families that take many forms. Women most often head single-parent families (27 percent of families are headed by women and 5 percent by men).[37] Single parents include those who have been divorced and those who never married. Some single-parent families are headed by same-sex partners who live in committed relationships that have lasted decades; their children may have been adopted or are the result of artificial insemination. The need for homes for less frequently adopted children means that older adults and individuals with disabilities—individuals who would not have been approved as adoptive parents in the past—are now parents rearing children.

Although parents form a diverse group, they have common needs in rearing children: (1) the need to earn money to purchase basic necessities in an insecure economy that requires two to three incomes to meet monthly expenses; (2) the need to have adequate childcare when single or dual-earner parents are at work; (3) the need to give children feelings of security and attachment when time with parents is

BOX 1.3

Trends in Family Values over the Past Fifty Years

TRADITIONAL FAMILISM (MID-1940s TO MID-1960s)

1. Couples with children dominated.
2. Birthrates were high.
3. Divorce rates were low.
4. The degree of marital stability was high.
5. Economic factors affecting the family included a strong economy with a high standard of living and an expanding middle class.
6. Cultural values emphasized conformity to social norms, different gender roles for men and women, and idealization of family life.

INDIVIDUALISM (MID-1960s TO MID-1980s)

1. The population was more diverse.
2. The single lifestyle was created.
3. Marriage was postponed.
4. The birthrate declined.
5. The divorce rate rose.
6. Economic factors affecting the family included women's increasing participation at work and the idealization of work.
7. Cultural values emphasized self-expression as the source of meaning in life and a decline in definite gender roles for men and women.

NEW FAMILISM (MID-1980s TO PRESENT)

1. The birthrate increased.
2. The divorce rate leveled off.
3. Economic factors affecting the family included a leveling-off of women's participation in the workforce but a decrease in the number of adequate-paying jobs.
4. Cultural values included a shift from self-expression to greater attachment to family but with less conformity than in the traditional period.

Barbara Dafoe Whitehead, "The New Family Values," *Utne Reader*, May–June 1993.

limited by work and/or by the child's dividing time with biological parents who do not live together; (4) the need to help children feel secure in a world that seems scary; (5) the need to monitor and deal with the influences of external social forces, such as movies and television, that present values contradictory to those of the family; and (6) the need to find time to do all these tasks while balancing the responsibilities of work and the family.

The Effect of Individual Timing on Parenting

With an earlier onset of menstruation and the development of assisted reproductive technology, girls and women can become parents from early adolescence into their sixties—a fifty-year span of time—and boys and men can become fathers from adolescence through life. Physical ability, however, is not the only requirement for parenthood. Education and employment, both social characteristics, enable parents to support a child. Parents' psychological characteristics are important as well. Reviewing research, Christoph Heinicke identifies three qualities that provide "an optimal parenting environment": feelings of self-esteem, the capacity for positive mutuality in relationships, especially with the partner, and the capacity for flexible problem solving.[38]

There is no magical age at which one is ready to become a parent. Although age is an indicator of one's ability to become pregnant and take on the parent role, the way one decides to become a parent is an indication of problem-solving skills and psychological maturity. Let us examine that area first and then look at how age affects pregnancy and parenting.

The Decision to Parent

About two-thirds of children are planned, and when they are unplanned, parents have to decide whether to continue the pregnancy. The decision to initiate or continue a pregnancy reflects parents' psychological maturity and problem-solving skills, which are, in turn, related to parent effectiveness.

ADOLESCENT PARENTS   About 85 to 90 percent of adolescent pregnancies are unplanned.[39] Many girls who do get pregnant as teens are identifiable as early as third grade. Following a sample of low-income children, researchers found that eight-year-old girls who were more frequently described by peers as aggressive or aggressive and withdrawn engaged in a series of behaviors that made them more likely to become teen mothers than were girls who were low or average on aggressiveness and withdrawal.[40] Aggressive girls had more peer problems and experienced more social rejection. They were more likely to have school problems and to drop out before graduating. They had deviant friends, engaged in high-risk sexual activity, and had more gynecological problems and sexually transmitted diseases.

Studies comparing adolescent mothers with teens who did not have babies have found that adolescent mothers are less independent, less certain of themselves, and less trusting of others. They have a diffuse sense of identity and greater susceptibility to depression.[41] They have also experienced more sexual abuse; in one study, 65 percent of adolescent mothers had been sexually abused in childhood or early adolescence, 61 percent by numerous perpetrators.[42]

Most studies of adolescent parents have focused on mothers because fathers of their babies, in about 50 percent of cases, are in their twenties or older.[43] More recent work, though, has followed samples of boys to determine the markers of those who become adolescent fathers. In many instances they share the qualities of the mothers.[44] They are from low-income families in which parents often have problems with antisocial behavior. Parents use ineffective disciplinary techniques, and the boys are not well monitored. By early adolescence, these boys are engaged in deviant, rule-breaking activities. They also have little academic success. Another study identified similar risk factors—lower socioeconomic status, poor school performance, early sexual activity, and drug use as individual factors—but concluded it was the accumulation of risks that was most predictive of adolescent fatherhood.[45]

Other longitudinal studies looking at the antecedent qualities of adolescent parents, both boys and girls, find that these teenagers have experienced less involved, less affectionate relationships with parents as well as less monitoring. With supervision, however, those headed in the direction of deviant behavior are able to stay involved in school and avoid pregnancy.[46]

We can see that both adolescent boys and girls come to parenthood having experienced many hardships and few successes. Once pregnant, they have to decide whether to continue the pregnancy. About half decide to terminate the pregnancy, and those most likely to make such a decision come from middle-class families. They feel support from family and friends for their decision.[47] Adolescent mothers who release a child for adoption—in one study, 4 percent—come from small, financially stable families. They have had academic success and see other alternatives for themselves. They have positive views of adoption and believe their mothers support their decisions.[48]

COUPLES   When couples become parents, the most important factor is whether the partners agree on the decision to have or not have a child. Carolyn Cowan and Philip Cowan studied couples through the period of becoming or not becoming a parent and identified four decision-making groups.[49] Planners, about 52 percent of their couples, discussed having a child and made a definite decision to have or not have a child. Acceptance-of-fate couples, 14 percent, became pregnant without planning and quietly or, in many cases, enthusiastically accepted the pregnancy. Ambivalent couples, about 26 percent, expressed both positive and negative feelings about having a child, with the parents leaning in opposite directions. A yes-no group, 10 percent, were in marked conflict about having or not having a child.

The decision-making process regarding pregnancy is related to later marital satisfaction, and marital satisfaction is related to satisfaction and effectiveness in parenting. When couples plan the decision, regardless of whether they do or do not have a child, their marital satisfaction remains high after the birth of a child or an equivalent time period. Couples who accept an unplanned pregnancy have a drop in marital satisfaction, but their initial level is so high that they are still as satisfied as parents who plan the decision.

Marital dissatisfaction is most marked among couples who are ambivalent or in conflict but still have a baby. Ambivalent couples are not as high as other couples in their initial satisfaction levels, and these levels drop when they have a baby. Ambivalent couples who do not have a baby retain their initial satisfaction level. Of nine couples who were in conflict about having a child and had a child, seven divorced by the time the child entered kindergarten. In all seven cases, the husband did not want a child. The two women who did not want to have a child and had one seemed better able to adjust, and their marriages continued.

SINGLE MOTHERS   An increasing number of women are making the conscious choice to have a child alone.[50] About half the women in general surveys say they would consider having a child alone if they did not have a child with a partner by the time they reached their late thirties or early forties. The percentage of educated business and professional women who have chosen to have a child alone has risen from 3 percent in 1980 to 8 percent in 1990.[51] These women are older and have achieved occupational stability. Strong desires for a child along with the feeling that they have lost the opportunity to do this under the ideal circumstances of marriage to a loved partner spur women to consider this option.

We do not know precisely the stages single mothers go through in making their decision to have a child. Merle Bombardieri, a social worker who holds workshops and counsels prospective single mothers, believes that a third of the women later decide not to have a child.[52] She believes that feelings of loss may cause the desire for a child, and she encourages women to discover and mourn unresolved grief from deaths of family members such as a parent or from not having a child in marriage. When the loss is mourned, the desire for a child may well decrease.

A national organization, Single Mothers by Choice (SMC), holds sessions for prospective mothers and urges them to consider a variety of issues: their ability to support a child financially, their ability to mesh family life and work, their psychological ability to rear a child on their own, and their conviction that they can provide a loving home for a child in the absence of a father.[53] Like Bombardieri, the group also urges women to mourn the loss of the ideal pregnancy prior to conception. One study in the 1970s indicated that single women are most likely to become parents when they can build a support system that enables them to combine work with rearing children.[54]

UNPLANNED CHILDREN   Although most unplanned children are welcomed by the time of the birth, unwanted children have a more difficult time.[55] In one study, children whose mothers had twice requested abortions to terminate the pregnancy had significantly more problems and less enjoyment in life than children whose parents wanted them.[56] In elementary school, the unwanted children had fewer friends, more behavior problems, and poorer school performance even though they had equally high intelligence. In adolescence, the differences between the two groups widened, and in young adulthood, individuals unwanted before birth were less happy with their jobs and their marriages. They had more conflict with coworkers and supervisors and less satisfaction with friends. They were discouraged about themselves and their lives, but many took the positive step of getting help for their problems.

In sum, when parents can plan a pregnancy with people who support their decision, they and their children are off to a good start.

Age and Pregnancy

A mother's age influences the biological aspects of conception, the pregnancy, and delivery. Being either very young or over thirty-five is related to increased difficulties.

Although teenage mothers experience few difficulties becoming pregnant, they suffer more pregnancy complications and have babies with problems more often than do mothers in their twenties or early thirties. Prematurity and low birth weight, which increase the likelihood of cerebral palsy, mental retardation, and epilepsy in babies, occur most often in the babies of teenage mothers. Two explanations have been given. One is the physiological immaturity of the mother and the other is the mother's psychosocial circumstances, such as having a less healthy lifestyle and poorer access to prenatal care. Prenatal care improves the outcome, but age still appears to be a factor.[57]

Biological risk depends somewhat on the ethnic background of the mothers. Whereas early childbearing age is related to greater risk in European American mothers, later childbearing (meaning from ages eighteen to thirty-four) is related to greater risk in African American mothers, perhaps because their health declines as they get older.[58]

The age of first-time mothers has been increasing. In the past, women over thirty-five having babies were usually having the last of their children; now, many mothers are having their first. In 1996, 425,000 babies were born to women over thirty-five.[59] Factors that account for the growing numbers of older first-time mothers include feminism, a general postponement of childbearing, the large number of baby boomers in childbearing age, advances in contraception, better health among women, advances in reproductive technologies, and better obstetrical care.

With first pregnancies, conception difficulties can arise, particularly for women thirty-five and older. Although the overall rate of infertility, defined as failure to conceive after a year of unprotected sexual intercourse, is about 8 percent, it is 25 percent for women ages thirty-five to thirty-nine and 27 percent for women ages forty to forty-four.[60] A thorough medical checkup can often identify the source of the problem. Interventions range from intrauterine insemination to surgery and the highly complex methods of assisted reproductive technologies. Initially help takes the form of supporting natural processes by insemination and by chemically stimulating the ovaries to produce more eggs. In a more advanced method, the egg can be fertilized in a petri dish and then implanted in the uterus; this technique is used for women who have blocked fallopian tubes.

Women can now freeze their eggs, just as men can freeze their sperm. Fertilized eggs can be frozen for use at a later date if conception has not taken place, or the eggs can be given to another woman. This is an important advance, because research reveals that it is the age of the egg that limits a woman's fertility, not the age of the uterus. Infertile women who receive an egg from a young woman greatly improve their chances of conception. For example, a forty-four-year-old woman has a 3.5 percent chance of conceiving with her own egg but a 50 percent chance if she uses a donor egg.[61]

Mothers over thirty-five have higher rates of genetic abnormalities in the fetus, so screening for such abnormalities is routine. Furthermore, spontaneous abortions increase with age, from 25 percent at age thirty-five to 50 percent at age forty-five.[62] Like teenage mothers, older mothers have a greater likelihood of pregnancy complications such as diabetes and low-birth-weight babies, but these conditions can be treated as they can be with younger women.

Age and Parenting

Having children during adolescence presents many risks to parenting. Postponing parenthood until the twenties confers benefits on both parents and children.

ADOLESCENT MOTHERS   Girls who become teenage mothers generally have psychological and economic problems before the birth of the child. They are more economically disadvantaged than are older mothers, and they encounter more problems with fewer resources for meeting them than does the average parent. Birth to a teenage mother becomes one factor in a chain of events that predict long-term difficulties.[63]

As noted above, babies of adolescent mothers are born with more problems than are those born to older mothers, and teenage mothers are less psychologically mature than are their age-mates and less effective in parenting, as we shall see in Chapter 5. Compared with older mothers, they are less able to provide stable living arrangements, so their children experience more moves and changes in caretakers and male support figures.[64] Further, adolescent mothers and their children are more likely to live in poverty (see Chapter 8 for a detailed discussion of the effects of poverty on children). Single parenthood increases the risk of poverty, but adolescent single motherhood confers an additional disadvantage to mother and child.[65] The exact reasons are not known, but lower educational attainment and the smaller likelihood of entering a stable, supportive marriage are two important factors. Ethnic origin also makes a difference. One study found that delaying parenthood to age twenty-five resulted in economic gain for European American women but not for African American women.[66] Further studies comparing African American mothers with Hispanic American mothers found that African American mothers receive more support from family and friends than do Hispanic American mothers.[67]

It is not surprising, then, that children of adolescent mothers are at greater risk for problems in development even if they are later-born children of teenage mothers. They are more likely to suffer from illnesses and to be seen in emergency rooms, even when families have medical coverage.[68] Infants and toddlers of teenage mothers do not differ from children of older mothers in cognitive measures; however, by the time they reach preschool age, differences begin to emerge and continue into the elementary school years, when they face a greater likelihood of academic difficulties, school failure, and behavior problems.[69] Teens of adolescent mothers are more likely to become teen parents (in one study, 40 percent of girls and 21 percent of boys); still, the majority of children of teenage mothers do not themselves become teen parents. Even when they delay marriage, however, they are not as competent and well adjusted in early adulthood as are children of mothers who delayed pregnancy until their twenties.[70]

Although adolescent mothers and their children have many problems, diversity of outcome is a striking finding of many studies. Table 1.2 lists the protective factors that increase success for these mothers, along with risk factors that impede success. Indeed, many adolescent mothers overcome their problems.

Risk Factors

1. Living in poverty with attendant problems of frequent residence changes, of living in high-crime and high-violence areas, and of experiencing changes in caretakers and male support
2. Birth complications: prematurity, low birth weight
3. Poor parenting from mothers
4. Behavior and school problems
5. Less social support from relatives/friends

Protective Factors

1. Being a boy
2. Having an easy, adaptable temperament
3. Having intelligence and problem-solving skills that lead to better coping
4. Mother continuing her education
5. Mother limiting number of subsequent children
6. Mother entering a stable marriage
7. Mother having high self-esteem

Adapted from Joy D. Osofsky, Della M. Hann, and Claire Peebles, "Adolescent Parenthood: Risks and Opportunities for Mothers and Infants," in *Handbook of Infant Mental Health*, ed. Charles H. Zeanah, Jr. (New York: Guilford Press, 1993), pp. 106–119.

The invidious stereotype of the adolescent childbearer underestimates young mothers' chances of recovery. . . . Ironically, part of the handicap of being a teenage mother may come from a widespread perception that failure is virtually inevitable—a belief that may become a self-fulfilling prophecy.[71]

PARENTS OVER THIRTY-FIVE   Although older mothers face difficulties in conception, they have many advantages as parents. Compared to younger mothers, they have more education, higher-status jobs, and, as a result, greater incomes with more money available to spend on childcare and other child-related items.[72] Further, older parents tend to be in more stable marriages and to be more attentive and sensitive parents. Yet older parents' work and community responsibilities make it more difficult for them to incorporate an unpredictable, time-consuming young child into their lives.

In the late 1980s, Andrew Yarrow collected information from 1,800 respondents who were raised by older parents.[73] The respondents were primarily adults of different ages who were raised by older parents thirty to eighty years prior to Yarrow's study. Many reported appreciating their parents' greater patience, broader outlook on life, and more comfortable, settled lifestyle. Many, however, expressed worries about their parents' becoming ill and dying, feelings of being isolated from a large extended family

> **BOX 1.4**
>
> ## Guidelines for Older Parents
>
> 1. Be open with children about your age and reasons for postponing children. Lying and avoiding the issue cause children to feel shame or embarrassment about your age.
> 2. Make a special effort to understand your children's world, as it may seem very different from the one in which you grew up.
> 3. Connect your children to extended family members. If this is not possible, provide an extended support network of friends who serve as uncles, aunts, grandparents.
> 4. Stay physically fit and energetic so you can share physical activities such as hiking and camping with your children. If you cannot participate, then see that children join friends and other adults in these activities.
> 5. Most important, balance the time you spend on work and nonfamily commitments with your family's needs so children feel they are important parts of your lives.
>
> ---
>
> Adapted from Andrew Yarrow, *Latecomers* (New York: Free Press, 1991).

as their grandparents were dead, and feelings of being isolated from peers whose parents were younger and more active with them. Some felt cheated out of childhood because they were around adults so much, and some resented having to take responsibility for aging parents when they were entering young adulthood. Children with older parents today might not have the same experiences, as there are more older parents and they are active and in better health. (Box 1.4 lists some suggestions for older parents.)

The Means of Becoming a Parent and Its Effect on Parenting

In the past, there were two ways that couples could become parents. They could conceive their biological child, or they could adopt a child. In the past twenty years, assisted reproductive technologies and more liberal adoption policies have increased the number of pathways to parenthood so that a variety of people who were excluded from parenting in the past can now become parents. Here, we examine the influence of the means of becoming parents on parenting itself and on children's development.

There are a host of studies on the functioning of adoptive children.[74] Aside from the fact that this legal procedure has existed for many decades, there are several reasons why adopted children are overrepresented in samples of psychiatric inpatient and outpatient groups. First, adoptive parents may seek counseling for problems more quickly because they are sensitized to the possibility of problems and are more used to working with social service professionals. They also may find psychological difficulties a greater threat to family unity and therefore get help earlier. Other factors perhaps accounting for increased problems are genetic predispositions passed on from of the biological parents and biological and psychological vulnerabilities caused by the prenatal and immediate postnatal environments.

In nonclinical samples, research has found little difference in the behaviors of infants, toddlers, and preschoolers of adoptive and nonadoptive parents. Some studies of elementary school children have found that teachers rate adoptive children as less socially, emotionally, and academically mature than peers, but these differences seem to decrease in adolescence. Further, a recent British study found that elementary school children of adoptive parents were as well adjusted as children of biological parents.[75] Because differences tend to appear when children become aware of the meaning of adoption, problems may be triggered not by the adoption itself but by the children's feelings of loss with regard to the biological family and feeling different from their peers.

Adults previously excluded from adoption—older, single, gay or lesbian, disabled, or poor adults—are now approved for adoption. Research indicates that these adoptive parents experience great satisfaction in their roles as parents and have good placement outcomes. Children adopted by single parents do as well as those adopted by young couples even though single parents adopt more difficult children. We should be cautious in drawing conclusions here, though, as few longitudinal studies have yet been completed on single-parent adoptions.

In considering children conceived through assisted reproduction therapies, we should be aware that artificial insemination and in vitro fertilization (fertilization outside the body with implantation of the fertilized egg inside the body) result in parents' having children who may or may not be genetically related to them. Artificial insemination and in vitro fertilization enable a couple to have a child genetically related to both of them, to one of them, or to neither, depending on whether donor eggs and sperm were involved. Single and lesbian women who become pregnant by donor insemination will bear children who receive half their genetic characteristics. In the case of in vitro fertilization involving donor eggs and donor sperm, the child may not be genetically related to the parents.

A British study compared (1) adoptive parents, (2) parents relying on donor insemination or in vitro fertilization, and (3) parents who naturally conceived a child. The study found that parents who relied on assisted reproductive technology and adoptive parents were warmer and more emotionally involved and committed than were parents relying on natural conception, perhaps because such parents tend to be older and older parents tend to be more responsive to children.[76] Both parents and teachers rated children of all parent groups as competent and socially accepted with strong attachments to their parents. Thus, there were no differences among children related to the means by which pregnancy occurred.

Studies indicate that parents' living in different family structures at the time of conception and birth—for example, in single-parent or in two-parent families, with heterosexual or lesbian parents—appears to have no ill effects on the functioning of elementary school children who live in financially secure families.[77] The results concerning the effective functioning of children from single-mother homes may be surprising but most likely are due to the mothers' financial stability and the lack of conflict with a male partner, as the conception was the result of donor insemination.

What did predict the functioning of this sample of children was the amount of parental stress and interpersonal conflict with a partner. Children functioned well when parenting stress was low and there was warmth and harmony between partners, regardless of their sexual preference. So, it is the process of family life rather than its structure that influences children's functioning as judged by parents and teachers.

Although parents who adopt are encouraged to tell children about their adoption from an early age, children born of donor eggs or donor sperm often are not told. In the British study, all but one child knew that he or she was adopted, whereas none of the children conceived by means of assisted reproductive technology knew this, though they were still only in early elementary school and their parents may have been waiting to tell them when they were older. In some instances, this was not necessary as the child was genetically related to both parents. But when donor eggs and/or donor sperm are used, the child does have at least one other biological parent. Many adults who have learned later in life that their conception was the result of donor insemination have reported feeling angry at being deceived about their biological roots and wanting to find the donor.[78]

The American Fertility Society recommends telling children about their origins. In England, the law permits children to request nonidentifying information about the donor at age eighteen, and in Sweden, individuals conceived by donor eggs or donor sperm have the right to identifying information at age eighteen and can contact the donor if they wish. In the United States, the tendency in the past has been not to tell children, and records have been destroyed. But currently there is a move to adopt the policies of Sweden. The Sperm Bank of California, for example, already requests permission from donors to give children identifying information when they are eighteen, and 80 percent of donors have agreed. It will be at least five years before the first children reach eighteen, so we will need to wait to see how this works out.[79]

The desire for greater openness is supported by studies of open adoption (adoptions in which the birth parents continue to have contact with the child and the adoptive parents) that reveal that a lack of secrecy and a better understanding of one's biological parents have improved the adjustment of adoptive children.[80] The situation of children of donor eggs and donor sperm is not exactly comparable to that of adoptive children, as a biological parent did not "give them up" but instead helped create them for their rearing parents. Still, knowing about a donor and the fact that one can have contact with this person later in life may eliminate the anger and the feeling of a missing biological connection that some adults of donor sperm or donor eggs feel.

So, these studies indicate that genetic ties between parent and child are not necessary for satisfying, committed parenting and the effective functioning of children. In addition, the feelings of loss that parents experience when they cannot conceive a biological child do not interfere with later satisfying and effective parenting. Indeed, these parents appear more committed, more emotionally involved with and appreciative of their children perhaps because they have had a more difficult time becoming parents. As one mother said, "Every night I stand in each of my children's rooms for a

25

*How Much
and What
Kind of
Influence
Parents Have
on Children*

Families today are more varied than ever before—married couples with children, same-sex couples with children, and nonrelatives raising children.

few minutes, watching them sleep, and recall the terrible childless years. I came so close to never having them. I am humbled by, and deeply thankful for, the miracle of my children."[81]

How Much and What Kind of Influence Parents Have on Children

In 1998, Judith Rich Harris captured national attention with the publication of her book *The Nurture Assumption: Why Children Turn Out the Way They Do.* The book included such provocative statements as, "Parenting has been oversold. You have been led to believe that you have more influence over your child's personality than you really do."[82] She contends that parents' importance to children's growth and adult personality is an assumption—the nurture assumption—that is not supported by research evidence.

If parenting is not central to children's development and subsequent adult personality, what does count? In brief, genes and peer relationships are what shape children's growth. Harris, a writer of developmental psychology textbooks, arrived at these ideas as she was reading an article about juvenile delinquency. The author of the article made the point that adolescents try to take on adult behaviors when they drink and smoke. Harris suddenly had the thought that adolescents are not interested in parents' standards but instead want to please and gain acceptance from their peers. She immersed herself in research in social psychology, anthropology, and sociology and considered the influence of peers in cultures around the world. Harris became convinced that once children reach school age, they learn about culture, society, and themselves from their interactions with peers.

Although Harris believes that peers, not parents, shape and modify children's behavior as they develop their adult characteristics, she does not completely rule out parental influence. She agrees with attachment theorists that the mother-child relationship is very important in the first five years of life. Parents teach moral and religious values, interests, and attitudes about life. But she believes that children would be foolish to enter the larger social world with expectations that others will treat them as their parents have.

Harris does not deny that parents and children resemble each other, and she acknowledges that some psychologists interpret the resemblance as evidence that parents' behavior has fostered these qualities in their children. However, Harris attributes most parent-child resemblance to genetic factors. She cites behavior geneticists' estimates that 50 percent of the variations in people's personality characteristics can be attributed to genetic factors (some believe the figure is 20 to 60 percent, depending on the particular quality) and 50 percent to environmental factors.

While Harris agrees that the environment plays a role in children's development, she contends that the environment itself may be the result of genetic factors. For example, intelligent parents may provide an enriched and stimulating environment for their children. The relationship between stimulation and children's intellectual success may not be due to the stimulation but to the genes bright people pass on. Or, individuals' impulsiveness and poor control, temperamental qualities influenced by genes, may lead to job and financial insecurity due to more frequent job dismissals; as a result, such individuals may live in more unstable conditions with partners who often share their lifestyle. Their poor control is not the result of unstable factors in their lives but rather the cause of them.

Yet another way that genetic influences determine the environment is through the effect that children's genetically determined behaviors exert on parents' behavior toward children. The easygoing, adaptable baby who evokes a positive response from the parent and the aggressive toddler who elicits a negative parental response are just two examples.

Those who claim the importance of parents in children's lives have rarely argued that parents are the only influence, nor have they denied that children can shape parents' behavior. Like Harris, they often believe that peers have great influence in children's lives. They are quick to admit that unpredictable events such as natural disasters or serious accidents can profoundly affect a child's life. What they do argue is that given adequate living conditions, parents, on average, are the most important influence in children's lives. Here is the evidence they cite that Harris does not mention.

First, they refer to the fact that genes only exist in an environment, and at the time of conception and pregnancy, parents provide that environment. Whereas most parents lead lifestyles that safeguard the possibility of conception, women who expose the fetus and growing baby to alcohol or cocaine during pregnancy irreparably damage the

27

*How Much
and What
Kind of
Influence
Parents Have
on Children*

genetic contributions to the child.[83] New research indicates that a prospective father's work environment and alcohol, smoking, and drug habits can affect the quality of the sperm and the coming baby as well.[84] So, parents are important, if only as transportation for genes, because if they are not careful, they can destroy the genes' potential.

Second, they point out that parents' responsive behavior after birth can ameliorate negative factors at birth. For example, Bronfenbrenner and Morris graph data from a seven-year longitudinal study of premature infants' development and show that poor school achievement at age seven (measured by children's performing below the level of their score on ability tests) was related to early behavior problems that interfered with performance.[85] If, however, mothers provided responsive, sensitive caretaking when children were young, the children had fewer behavior problems and better school achievement later. These results were consistent in upper, middle, and lower socioeconomic families and in children of normal, low, and very low birth weight. So, regardless of a child's birth weight or the living conditions of the parents, sensitive caretaking reduced behavioral difficulties and, in turn, promoted school achievement.

Responsive parenting can modify a baby's temperamental qualities even though these are genetically determined. Jerome Kagan's longitudinal research documented that highly reactive infants showing fretful crying and much motor activity at four months were less fearful as toddlers when mothers were firm and set reasonable limits with their babies.[86] Mothers who were responsive to the child's fretting and did not set limits had toddlers who continued to be fearful. Such responsiveness did not have the same effects with low-reactive infants. This finding has been confirmed in another longitudinal study.[87] Researchers speculate that parents who did not reinforce crying enabled their highly reactive infants to learn other coping strategies when they were upset so that in new situations they were less likely to cry and fuss.

Changes in parenting behavior can help reverse children's behavioral difficulties even if parents and grandparents have the same behaviors. Gerald Patterson and Deborah Capaldi document how abusive and irritable parents whose disciplinary techniques involved explosive behavior tended to rear antisocial children.[88] When such children grew up, they had less education, got lower-paying jobs, and experienced more life stress because of unemployment and divorce. As parents, they were relatively poor disciplinarians and monitors of children's behavior, so their children had problems as well. Harris might argue that this is all the result of genetic influence, and that may well be. Still, the children's difficulties decreased when the parents learned to discipline effectively and monitor their children more consistently.

Further, many studies demonstrate the importance of parents' stimulating influence on children's intellectual achievement. It is true, as Harris points out, that intelligent parents pass on intelligent genes. Nonetheless, when children of low-income parents with less education have consistent access, over years, to toys and stimulating activities—similar to those provided to children of parents with more education and higher income—they perform better on measures of intellectual ability and school achievement than do peers of low status who do not have exposure to such experiences.[89]

At the same time, parents can also socialize children for lower achievement. Parents' expectations predict academic success more accurately than do children's ability scores.[90] Parents who view their children as less capable of academic success than test scores indicate have children who develop an illusion of incompetence despite their initial success with tasks. These children, aware of their parents' negative views of their abilities, underestimate their own abilities, see school as harder, and have lower expectancies of success. As a result of their low confidence, they avoid more challenging tasks that would demonstrate their abilities. They give up more quickly, thus perpetuating a vicious cycle of feeling lowered confidence, attempting less, achieving less success, and thus ensuring their low confidence. It is not clear how parents develop inaccurate views of their children's abilities, but it is evident that children's self-perceptions incorporate parents' views, which in turn shape how children act in school.

We also know that parents influence children's achievement through research that examines the role parents play in the development of individuals of outstanding achievement. Benjamin Bloom and his coworkers studied 120 young men and women who achieved international recognition for high levels of performance in a variety of fields.[91] The researchers interviewed the individuals, their family members, and teachers and coaches to understand the process by which the children achieved such excellence. Few of the individuals, the researchers noted, were identified as special in the beginning. It was the combination of individual commitment, family support, and outstanding instruction that led to accomplishment.

What is our role as parents? It shifts over time. In the beginning, it is one of selecting a teacher or coach, scheduling practices, providing support and encouragement, emphasizing the ethic of hard work and doing one's best. After children attain initial success, parents find more advanced teachers and coaches, making financial and time commitments not only to provide instruction but also to attend recitals, games, meets. In fact, the entire family's schedule may change to accommodate the child's training and performance schedule. As children continue to advance, parents continue to be both emotionally and financially supportive. Studies of talented and world-class achievers emphasize that enormous effort on the part of many people goes into the gradual development of superior accomplishment. When families are unable to provide the finances and time to support potentially talented youth, schools and communities may have to step in to provide the additional resources needed. So, even when children have the potential for superior accomplishment, parental support is essential along the way.

A final example serves to illustrate parents' importance in their children's lives. Parents have a profound impact on children's lives because as primary caregivers, there from the beginning, they set up ways of interacting with people and the world that children take with them when they enter the larger social world.[92] One study found that when mothers expressed positive affect in interactions with preschoolers, when they were warm and supportive in advice giving, then preschoolers gained greater social competence and acceptance with peers. Conversely, highly active preschoolers who were impulsive and poorly controlled were perceived negatively by teachers and peers.[93] They were restless, fidgety, dominant, competitive, and aggressive. When parents did not act to modify these behaviors, the behaviors continued into elementary school, and at age seven the high activity level was also linked to poor performance on intelligence tests. Of interest is that peers were unable to socialize these children to adopt more positive behaviors, as Harris might predict they would.

Harris's book received praise for helping parents understand that they are one of several influences on children and that they are not totally responsible for their children's subsequent development.[94] It also, however, received criticism for supporting the kind of self-absorption that discourages the extra efforts parents must often make in rearing children.[95] Although it was not the intended purpose, the book also discourages politicians from taking steps to support parents' efforts in rearing children by suggesting that "parenting does not matter" in children's growth.

As we shall see throughout the book, there are many influences on children's development—historical time, the child's temperament, social living conditions, peers. On average, though, parenting matters most of all.

What Society Owes Parents

As we have seen, parents make a profound contribution to their children's growth, but so does the social system, as Sameroff and his colleagues have documented. Here we discuss society's obligations to parents and children.

A comparison of the supportive services available to children and parents in the United States with those offered in other countries provides a broad background for understanding what options society has for supporting parents. Let us start with what the United States currently offers children and parents. The government provides to all children free public education from ages five to eighteen and to all parents a specific tax exemption for each dependent child and a tax credit for childcare or preschool expenses. Further help is extended only when a child has a specific disability or the family lives below the poverty level.

By contrast, other industrialized countries offer all children free public education beginning at age three and health care. Families are given an allowance or direct cash benefit up to 5 or 10 percent of the family income per child.[96] Many countries are adding a guaranteed minimum child support payment if an absent parent does not pay. In addition, most countries require government or business employers to provide paid maternity leave of twelve weeks. In fact, the United States is one of only six countries in the world (the others are Australia, New Zealand, Lesotho, Swaziland, and Papua New Guinea) that do not provide paid maternity leave.[97] The Family and Medical Leave Act in the United States permits a parent to take twelve weeks of unpaid leave.

The treatment of children living in poverty illustrates how the United States differs from other countries in supporting children and parents. In the United States, 20 percent of children live under the poverty level, and 70 percent of these poor children live in families in which one adult is working.[98] Further, another 20 percent of children live under twice the poverty level.[99] Britain and France have higher poverty rates than does our society (26 percent and 21 percent, respectively), but government policies provide benefits to poor children, reducing the overall rate of poverty in Britain and France to

8 and 4 percent, respectively. In our country, benefits to poor children reduce the overall poverty rate 2 percent—from 22 percent to 20 percent.[100] As a result, the living conditions of poor children in this country rank fifteenth of eighteen industrialized countries.[101]

Not only do we fail to give financial support to children and families, but we fail to give psychological support as well. Jay Belsky and John Kelly, summarizing observations from Belsky's study of new parents, write of society's failure to acknowledge parents' contribution to society:

> As I watched our couples cope with financial concerns and with all the other challenges of the transition, I found myself deeply moved. The quiet dignity and courage of our new fathers and mothers—especially our employed mothers—was inspiring to behold. But as I watched them, I also found myself deeply troubled by how little public acknowledgment, how little public support and gratitude they and other new parents receive for their selflessness and devotion.
>
> In its better moods our society now treats the family with benign neglect; in its darker moods, as a source of parody. None of our participants complained about the lack of public support for their family building, but it affected them—in many cases by making the routine sacrifices of the transition that much harder. It is difficult to sacrifice oneself when the larger society says the overriding purpose in life is devotion to self, not devotion to others. And in a few cases it made those sacrifices too far to go. The rising divorce rate, falling school grades, widespread drug use—all ills that plague the American family today—are complex and have many sources. But I think one major source is that our society no longer honors what I witnessed every day of the Project—the quiet heroism of everyday parenting.[102]

Survey data support Belsky and Kelly's observations. A 1996 survey of 2,600 adults (nonparents and parents of European American, African American, and Hispanic American backgrounds) reveals that only a small percentage (12 to 17 percent) describe children and adolescents as friendly and respectful.[103] A much larger percentage (30 to 50 percent) see them as wild, disorderly, disrespectful, undisciplined, and uncontrolled in public. Nonparents and parents alike blame parents for children's and teens' problems. They believe parents have children before they are ready for the responsibility, and half the respondents believe parents spoil children and fail to give them appropriate discipline. Only 22 percent of nonparents and 19 percent of parents feel it is common for parents to be good role models for children. All recognize, however, that a parent's job today is more difficult than in the past, because children face problems with drugs and alcohol, more sex and violence in the media and the world outside the home, and more gangs in school.

In 1997, concerned that parents fail to receive support from the surrounding environment, social scientists Sylvia Hewlett and Cornel West commissioned a national survey of European American, African American, and Hispanic American parents with incomes ranging from $20,000 to $100,000 to determine what parents want from government and employers.[104] They also conducted focus groups with a subset of the sample. In their sample, 86 percent of men and 73 percent of women had paid employment, with most of the men (70 percent) and fewer women (43 percent) working full-time. Twenty percent reported that they held two jobs to support the family; only 18 percent of women were stay-at-home mothers. Many parents (62 percent) reported at least some community activities with children.

The parents surveyed were also asked their opinion of what government and employers do and can do to support parents in rearing children. Only 6 percent of the sample think either government or employers were doing a great deal to help parents; 84 percent believe that government could help parents, and 76 percent think that employers could act to support parents. Further, parents believe that government can take a variety of actions to ease their financial burdens and offer services to children, such as providing health care for the 9 million children who do not already have it,[105] tripling the dependent tax exemption to $7,500, doubling the tax credit for childcare and preschool expenses to $1,000 per year, eliminating sales taxes on necessities for children (such as diapers, car seats, and school supplies), providing employers tax incentives to encourage family-friendly policies (such as part-time and flex-time hours), requiring businesses with more than twenty-five employees to give twelve weeks of paid maternity or paternity leave at times of birth or adoption, and extending school hours each day and throughout the year to better match parents' work schedules. Parents also want government to require gunmakers to install safety devices to prevent firearm accidents among children. Finally, parents believe that employers can adopt policies that give parents more time with family, such as allowing parents to take two additional weeks of leave without pay each year and ensuring three days of paid leave for family needs such as school conferences or doctors' visits.

Although these parents' wishes may sound impractical, a 1996 national survey reported that over 70 percent of adults favored spending tax money on children's programs.[106] The proposed actions have the advantage of being primarily extensions or increases in existing practices and not new, untried measures to support parents.

Believing that neither government nor employers are giving parents the supports they require, Hewlett and West have organized the National Parenting Association to assist in lobbying for what they want. Hewlett and West point to the success of the AARP (American Association of Retired Persons) in organizing voters and focusing the attention of government and business on the needs of older Americans. The decline in the poverty rate among people over 65 illustrates the effects of AARP lobbying that began in 1958. In 1960, the poverty rate of people over 65 was 35 percent; in 1995, the comparable figure was 11 percent, just about half the poverty rate of children. The poverty rate among children dropped from 27 percent in 1960 to a low of 14 percent in 1969 but then rose to its present figure of 20 percent in 1984 because there was no strong voting block to ensure protection of children's interests. Organizing an effective voting block would not be easy as the proportion of parents in the electorate has dropped from 55 percent in 1956 to 35 percent in 1996 because of the general aging of the population.

Still, Hewlett and West point to the success of government programs benefiting families after World War II. A Parents' Bill of Rights (Box 1.5) is based on the G.I. Bill of Rights that so effectively supported the educational and occupational advancement

BOX 1.5

Parents' Bill of Rights*

I. TIME FOR CHILDREN

    A. Paid Parenting Leave—24 weeks that either parent can use in the child's first six years

    B. Family-Friendly Workplaces—tax incentives for companies offering flexible hours and home-based work

    C. A Safety Net—income support for poor parents with children under six; teen mothers would live with experienced mothers

II. ECONOMIC SECURITY

    A. Living Wages—$7.00 per hour minimum wage and subsidies for low-wage workers

    B. Job Opportunities—programs that improve job skills

    C. Tax Relief—eliminating payroll taxes for parents; extended childcare credit

    D. Help with Housing—mortgage subsidies; rent vouchers

III. PRO-FAMILY ELECTORAL SYSTEM

    A. Incentives to Vote

    B. Parents' Voting in Behalf of Children

IV. PRO-FAMILY LEGAL STRUCTURE

    A. Stronger Marriage—tougher standards for marriage and greater obstacles to divorce

    B. Support for Fathers—paternity leave; generous visiting for noncustodial parent

    C. Adoption Assistance—benefits to people adopting children

V. SUPPORTIVE EXTERNAL ENVIRONMENT

    A. Violence-Free and Drug-Free Neighborhoods

    B. Quality Schooling; Extended School Day and Year

    C. Childcare and Family Health Coverage

    D. Responsible Media

    E. Organized Voice—creation of organization to promote parents' interest

VI. HONOR AND DIGNITY

    A. Index of Parental Well-Being—measure reflecting parents' wages, time for children, affordable housing, and health care

    B. National Parents' Day

    C. Parent Privileges—education for parent who cares for child; reduced costs for certain family activities

of parents and the housing needs of families in the 1950s. The benefits were available for all veterans and represented an investment that boosted the economic well-being of everyone.

The G.I. Bill was an expression of gratitude to men and women who performed incalculable service to their country by risking their lives in the war. Parental rights would also be an expression of gratitude to parents who perform service for their country by rearing the next generation. They spend enormous amounts of time and money to rear children who will grow into healthy, competent adults whose work and taxes will support an ever increasing older population of adults. Creating and rearing such children is indeed a great service to the country.

Main Points

Parenting is

- nourishing, protecting, and guiding new life
- providing basic resources, love, attention, and values

The process of parenting involves

- ongoing interaction among children, parents, and society
- children who have their own needs and temperaments and at the same time meet important needs of parents
- parents who have responsibilities to rear their children and meet their children's needs
- society as a source of support or stress for children and parents
- risks and protective factors within individuals and the social environment

Historical time

- influences parenting through the social and economic conditions that shape family life
- presents challenges and supports to parents

Parenting

- is more difficult for adolescent parents, who have little education and few resources, and more effective when parents are older and have a more settled, stable lifestyle
- gets off to a better start when parents are in agreement about becoming parents
- is more involving and appreciated when parents have had difficulties becoming pregnant

Parents are

- the single most important influence and resource in a child's life
- not the only influences on children's behavior; peers, media, communities, and social events outside the family all affect children's behavior and development

Interview
with Sylvia Hewlett

Sylvia Ann Hewlett is a fellow at Harvard University's Center for the Study of Values in Public Life. She is chairman of the National Parenting Association and, with Cornel West, coauthor of *The War against Parents*.

Of all the items listed in the Parents' Bill of Rights, what would you say are the most important things to push for parents?

I think generous, gold-plated parenting leave is enormously important because it concerns the beginning of a life. I think that if new parents get their heads in the right place, many struggles downstream will be easier, as they have already gotten their priorities set, right at the beginning. Besides which, we know that a good start is important for the child's development. It is not that you don't continually have to create good conditions for a child, but we know that if the start is compromised by lack of attachment or poor developmental progress, then it is very hard to catch up.

So, birth is an enormously important time to get right, as a nation, and we do such a very poor job of it right now. We discovered at the Parenting Association that when Clinton passed the Family Leave Act in 1993, something like 33 percent of women did not qualify for family leave because they worked for small companies; in 1998, 41 percent did not qualify for unpaid leave because they worked for small companies. Most of the growth in the economy is in small companies. Increasingly, we are creating a situation in which almost half of women do not even qualify for unpaid leave, and three-week-old babies are in day care. That's a wretched scenario.

So, in practical terms, one of the things we can do to enhance the developmental outcomes for children is to allow parents to be with their children for the first four to six months. Symbolically, we would be telling these parents, "We have laws in place to make sure you can spend this time with your child because we as a nation feel this is important." Right now, however, we tell parents, "We cannot afford parental leave as a nation. It is not very important." That is not the signal that parents get in other countries. Parents elsewhere understand that their nation feels it is essential for the country's well-being for parents to spend that time with their children.

I pick parental leave not because it is enormously practically significant but because the symbolism is so important. Our policies create a public morality that people absorb, and our public morality around birth is just awful. We don't support prenatal care in the way we should. So, I would put the funding policies around birth right up there in terms of their importance because it sets the tone for how men and women will parent for the rest of their lives, and it is supremely important for the baby to get off to a good start.

Also very high on my list is a living wage. I have gotten very angry with the media about this in the last two or three years. You would think from the relentless good news in the newspapers that the economy was wonderful for everyone. It is actually wonderful for the top 15 percent, most of whom don't have children. In this country, there are big divides between blacks and whites, between old and young. But equally as big as these two known cleavages in our society is the cleavage between families without children and families with children. We have not reduced the poverty rate at all amongst families with children; it is still at 20 percent, which is where it was thirty years ago.

Poverty results in these families' struggling to have access to health care and other services. The other consequence is that parents are working one and a half jobs each, resulting in three-job families. That means that little Johnny's homework is not supervised; Jane does not see her father until Sunday morning because he works two shifts a day. And that is the scenario for a two-parent family. When a single mom is working two jobs, as is often the case for a mom going off welfare, kids get creamed.

So, you have to understand that a living wage, where one wage earner working full-time can keep a family of three people living above the poverty level, is only a beginning goal. I think the figure is that 33 percent of all young men working full-time cannot keep a family of three above the poverty line. Since men's salaries are higher than women's, the figures for single moms are worse.

A living wage should not be such an ambitious target in a country that is so very prosperous and where wealth is being created and budget surpluses exist at all levels of government—city, state, and federal. We debate whether a tax cut is the way to go. The issue of a living wage is not even being talked about. Kennedy has a proposal to raise the minimum wage a very modest amount, a little bit more than the Clinton plan, but no one is talking about it. It would be very easy to create incentives for companies to pay all of their workers some multiple above the poverty wage. We have incentives in place for exports, for putting a plant in Kentucky, why not incentives for paying your workers a living wage?

So, if you were to ask me to choose the most important, I would choose these two. But they are both huge. We have failed totally to do these things, so I am not saying that it is easy. I think for a different set of reasons, they are both monumentally important to families. Also, they are important to the majority of families with children; a living wage would help most of the lower middle class of America who are struggling, working these crazy, crazy hours because they cannot afford their mortgage without a third job or they cannot afford to keep their twelve-year-old car running. We are not talking about greedy yuppies. The comment I often have thrown at me is, "Surely people have a lot of choice, and if they want to work very long hours and go abroad three times a year, it is their choice." But people are working hard for necessities.

It is hard to understand why we in this country are so indifferent to the needs of families.

The thing that surprises me is that even Federal Reserve Board chairman Alan Greenspan, who is not a raving radical, got indignant about what is happening to the compensation of senior executives, which went up 86 percent this year when workers got only a 2 percent increase in wages. This is inequality, and it is such a travesty of what this country is supposed to stand for. This country's tradition is that of an egalitarian society. When I came to America twenty-five years ago, this country was still

(continued)

(continued)

more equal than the United Kingdom. Today, it is twice as unequal as the United Kingdom, and that has happened in one generation. The United Kingdom has not changed much, but there has been such galloping polarization here. The United States is more unequal than any of the western European countries. The people are working their one and a half jobs and feeling like hamsters in a wheel, running harder and harder to stand still. Why don't people look at this and say, "This is wrong," and look for political leaders who will do something about it? But it doesn't happen. It is not a sensitive issue.

The variation of the living wage that I like is the four-thirds solution. It is a Stanley Greenspan idea, and I snuck that into the Parents' Bill of Rights. Greenspan, a developmental psychiatrist, suggests that parents, particularly parents of young children, hold two-thirds of a job. Together, two parents work four-thirds of a job, two-thirds each, and that creates a work week that allows them to be good parents. You couldn't make the arithmetic work unless parents were paid more per hour. You need a living wage plus a great deal of flexibility in the ways careers are constructed so that working slightly less than full-time did not shunt the parent into a cul de sac for the rest of their work life. Management needs to do more creative thinking about what a normal career should look like for both sexes.

And having a place for parents is important. There is no place for parents in our public life. That is so easy to change, and the symbolism of those changes is so powerful. It shows that we are supporting and celebrating parents' doing things with children. One of the ridiculous examples of how shortsighted our public places are is the newly designed children's center in Central Park. I think it opened about two years ago. It is a beautiful place for the under-five crowd. It has all kinds of wonderful hands-on stuff—little story-time corners as well as the petting zoo.

But look at the fee structure going in; it is typical of many children's museums and children's parks around the country. If you are over two, you have to pay three dollars—not an insignificant amount—a parent pays seven dollars, but senior citizens get massive discounts. So what you see outside on any nice afternoon is a row of mothers having designated one mother to go in with the children because they cannot all afford to go in. If we are serious about encouraging parent-child recreational time, the first

- in strong agreement that government needs to be more financially supportive of parents and that employers need to allow parents more time with families

U.S. society

- offers parents fewer supports than are given to parents in European countries
- provides fewer benefits to children than do European nations
- may respond to parents' and children's needs only when parents organize and vote to obtain what they need

thing you have to do is make the fee structure reflect that. We should be encouraging single parents to take their children there. It is educational and absolutely something mothers should be doing with children. Yet when it is ten dollars a visit, they cannot do that. You stand there and look at the fees, and your jaw drops, because the group that does not need the subsidy in this context at all is the one that is privileged.

Another thing that makes me crazy in this city and is typical of other cities is that there is no place on buses for parents and young children and their strollers and other equipment. I take the bus across town to get one of my children at school. I go with my toddler, and there is no place to sit, no place to put the stroller. Now, buses have learned to recognize the needs of the elderly and the disabled. Right up front there are nice seats for them but no seats for pregnant mothers or parents with babies or young children. You get on a New York City bus, clutching your toddler, your equipment, and a stroller, and the first thing you do is feel apologetic about being there. The bus driver scowls at you, and no one wants to sit near you. It's a ridiculous situation, and it doesn't happen in other countries.

I also think there should be a parents' room in every school. At present there is no place to go, to hang out, to have coffee and read a little literature about developing reading skills or something. I think the whole thing about having a place for parents, an honored place in our public squares and in our schools and on our transportation system is so critical. There is a tiny movement to create parking spaces in suburban malls for mothers with young children, but the efforts for programs like that are few and far between. That could spread like wildfire if a few communities did it. You need leadership. You need political leaders to take the issues seriously.

I am at Harvard Divinity School now on a sabbatical, writing a book to get communities of faith involved in many of these issues. For example, no church is involved in the Paid Parenting Leave Coalition. What I am trying to do is to write about family values that go beyond political philosophy. I begin with celebrating the miracle of life, because the way that family values are currently focused on abortion—pro-life or pro-choice—is so narrow. I want to get churches and a wide variety of groups beyond the abortion issue and focus instead on affirming and celebrating the miracle of life and doing the best we can for the children we choose to have.

Exercises

1. From the year you were born, trace the social influences acting on your parents as they raised you. For example, for the 1980s, such influences might have included the high rate of women's participation in the workforce, the high rate of divorce and remarriage, the drop in skilled-labor jobs, and the instability of jobs in corporate America. Show the effects of social change on your daily life and the ways your parents cared for you—for example, if your mother's working resulted in specific day care, if divorce led to your being in two homes, if remarriage introduced more adults into your life, if violence affected your family life.

2. Based on the material in this chapter, write a job description for a parent. You may want to revise the job description as you read future chapters.

3. Suppose that parents had to obtain a license in order to have a child, much as they do to get married or drive a car. What would you require for such a license?

4. Read the newspaper for one week, and cut out all the articles of interest to parents, including news and feature articles. Describe what these articles tell you about the parenting experience today. The articles might focus on solving certain kinds of behavioral problems or providing opportunities for children's optimal development (certain play or educational activities). Or they might consider laws relating to parents' employment benefits or to the rights of parents and children in courts when parents divorce or must pay penalties because of children's behavior.

5. In California, a surrogate mother petitioned the court for the baby she bore even though the child was not genetically related to her. Who are the parents of the child—the genetic parents or the parent who carried the child in utero?

Additional Readings

Hamburg, David A. *Today's Children*. New York: Times Books, 1992.

Harris, Judith Rich. *The Nurture Assumption: Why Children Turn Out the Way They Do*. New York: Free Press, 1998.

Hewlett, Sylvia Ann, and Cornel West. *The War against Parents*. Boston: Houghton Mifflin, 1998.

Konner, Melvin. *Childhood: A Multicultural View*. Boston: Little, Brown, 1991.

Louv, Richard. *Childhood's Future*. New York: Doubleday, 1991.

Skolnick, Arlene. *Embattled Paradise: The American Family in an Age of Uncertainty*. New York: Basic Books, 1991.

2

Learning to
Be Parents

PARENTS FACE THE DAUNTING RESPONSIBILITY OF caring for children and promoting their healthy growth. It's a big job. In this chapter we present a job description for parents and examine the many ways parents learn to carry out these complex tasks. We look at how culture and families of origin influence parental behaviors. We consider whether parenting is most important in the first three years of a child's life. And we see how children change parents. Because parents go through their own stages while their children develop, parenting is a process that changes both parents and their children.

A Parent's Job Description

In the first chapter, we defined a parent generally as a nurturer, a protector, and a guide for children. Here we become more specific about what this means in terms of day-to-day activities. In the past, a parent would have been described first as the creator of a new life, but as we learned in Chapter 1, many parents are not involved in the creation aspect of their child's life. So, we focus on the behaviors of a parent following birth.

According to social scientists,[1] a parent's main tasks are to provide children:

the physical necessities of life—food, shelter, and clothing

the emotional necessities of life—love, affection, attention, and sensitive and responsive care

protection and safety

the appropriate stimulation and opportunities for developing physical, intellectual, and social skills

39

values and a moral code

a model of a happy and contributing member to family and community

Using a recently developed questionnaire designed to understand individuals' perceptions of the parent role, researchers found six dimensions of parenting that shift in importance over the course of childhood.[2] The six dimensions are bonding, protection, sensitivity, responsivity, education, and discipline. Bonding was seen as very important throughout childhood but dropped slightly in adolescence. Protection, responsivity, and sensitivity were seen as equally important behaviors in infancy, with education and discipline farther down on the list of behaviors at that age. With toddlers, education and discipline were perceived to be more important parental behaviors than they were in infancy, but responsivity, sensitivity, and protection remained very important. In adolescence, there was less distinction between the different dimensions of parenthood, and all were seen as important. We can see, then, that the tasks of parenting change as a child ages.

Understanding the tasks of parenting is the first step in understanding what parents do. Now we turn to the goals of parenting. What is it parents are trying to achieve?

Parental Goals

Parents have three broad goals in rearing children: (1) ensuring the physical health and survival of the child, (2) preparing the child to become an economically self-sustaining adult, and (3) encouraging positive personal and social behaviors—for example, psychological adjustment, intellectual competence, and the ability to establish social relations with friends.[3]

The desire to protect children from harm and ensure survival is the strongest long-term goal for parents and perhaps the clearest.[4] In socializing children to be responsible and economically productive members of society, however, parents seek a broad array of competencies. The priority given to competencies depends on parents' social and ethnic backgrounds. For example, parents in the majority culture in U.S. society emphasize goals of academic achievement and cognitive skills, whereas several minority cultures emphasize goals of social skills, harmony, sharing, and cooperation within the extended family.

Parents typically encourage the development of several forms of competence in their children: self-esteem and physical, intellectual, emotional, social, and moral competence. Before examining how parents encourage competencies, we need to be aware of three key points.

First, as we saw in Chapter 1, parenting is a process influenced by the contributions of parent, child, and society. Here, we focus on what parents do to encourage growth in a variety of areas.

Second, as we also saw in Chapter 1, parents exert both direct and indirect influences on children.[5] In this chapter, we discuss these influences more fully. For example, indirect influences tend to be highly similar for all the competencies.[6] Parents who form secure attachments with children; who provide a home atmosphere free of unre-

Lev Vygotsky believes that what children learn, they first experience at the social level in a social interaction with someone and then internalize it at the individual psychological level.

solved conflict, intense anger, or severe stress; who use reasoning and positive rewards to increase valued behaviors; and who avoid physical and harsh discipline indirectly encourage all forms of competent behavior.

Third, we can view the development of competencies as a complex interaction of constitutional factors within children and environmental forces in their daily lives.[7] Genes provide one major source of constitutional differences within the child. Events during pregnancy, labor, and delivery can also result in physical or physiological characteristics that influence development. Environmental forces include characteristics of the parents and other caregivers as well as of the larger social system.

Some social scientists emphasize that one factor—either constitutional or environmental—is more important than the other. Here and throughout the book, we emphasize the view many developmentalists espouse—namely, that the interaction of these two factors is complex and may differ depending on the behavior of interest.[8] Thus, in understanding any particular behavior, the question centers on how these two factors interact to affect jointly the development of a specific behavior.

We turn now to parents' contributions to particular forms of competence. In later chapters, we will look in greater detail at the parent-child interactions of specific age periods.

Physical Competence

Physical competence has two aspects—physical health/well-being and motor competence. In their direct role, parents model healthy behavior—eating nutritious meals, exercising, avoiding harmful habits such as smoking and excessive alcohol consumption, and getting preventive health care in the form of routine checkups. They also teach healthy behaviors—dental hygiene, proper diet, and so on. Further, they provide resources for healthy behavior, making sure their children get checkups, immunizations, and dental care.[9]

In addition to ensuring physical health, parents provide experiences so children develop motor competence and motor skills. Exciting research suggests that motor competence develops as a result of real-life experience rather than maturation of inborn abilities.[10] Infants and children integrate sensory perceptions and motor movements and form a multisensory map of experience. From their experience, they select and retain movements that help them accomplish their goals. For example, young infants who seek an object across a room use whatever movements—rolling, pulling themselves, crawling, crabbing, walking—are available to them depending on their size and strength. Successful movement patterns that achieve goals are strengthened and, with use, lead to further refinements. Neuroscientists now hypothesize that the brain provides a "rough palette" for human experience but that experience determines the selection and retention of certain neural connections.[11] The brain makes certain behaviors possible, but the actual connections among brain cells are made and strengthened by experience.

Thus both the environment and parents play a more important role in promoting motor competence than was once believed. Parents provide opportunities for experience in the world that leads to neural change and motor competence. Some may question the importance of motor abilities, but motor competence, particularly in the early years, fosters cognitive and social development. Increasingly skilled movements enable infants and children to explore their world in greater depth. They share their discoveries with others who give their discoveries a name and thereby add to their knowledge. Exploration also triggers social interactions. With greater ability to move, infants and toddlers can initiate social interactions with parents. Older children expand their social world as they move around even more independently, and they can enjoy social interactions centered on games and sports.

As yet, little research has examined exactly how the environment and caregivers can intervene to promote motor competence. We have learned, though, that interventions are most successful when behaviors are in transition and the child "has sufficient flexibility to explore and select new solutions."[12]

Intellectual Competence

Like motor competence, cognitive development arises from repeated cycles of perception, action, selection, and retention. Jean Piaget, the Swiss psychologist, deepened our understanding of how children's minds grow and develop when he emphasized the importance of the child's active construction of knowledge.[13] Intellectual competence is a dynamic process in which the child explores the world, takes in information, and organizes it into internal structures called *schemes*. The process of taking in and organizing information is termed *assimilation*. Further, as children obtain new information, they find their internal schemes inadequate and modify them to account for the new information, a process called *accommodation*. Intellectual growth is a constant interplay of taking in new information (assimilation) and modifying it (accommodation) to achieve balance, or equilibrium, between the individual's structure of the world and the world itself. *Equilibration* is the active process by which the individual achieves this effective balance.

Piaget believed that intellectual growth is not just a matter of adding more and more refined schemes. Growth also results from new ways of responding to experience and organizing it. Piaget described intellectual growth in terms of four major periods, each with its own substages. In the first two years, the *sensorimotor stage*, perceptions and motor activity are the sources of knowledge, and schemes consist of action patterns. In the *preconceptual period*, from two to seven years of age, symbols such as language and imitative play lead to knowledge. The child reasons intuitively but not logically. In the period of *concrete operations*, from seven to about eleven years of age, the child structures knowledge symbolically and logically but is limited to concrete objects and events that are seen and manipulable. In the last stage, the period of *formal operations*, from age twelve through adulthood, the individual reasons logically and can go beyond what is present to consider hypothetical and abstract situations.

While Piaget emphasized individual action and maturing capacities, the Russian psychologist Lev Vygotsky, working at the same time as Piaget, emphasized the social aspect of intellectual growth.[14] He believed that knowledge, thought, and mental processes such as memory and attention all rest on social interactions. Whatever children learn they first experience at the social level in a social interaction with someone and then internalize it at the individual psychological level. For example, an infant watches how an adult shakes a rattle or plays with a toy and then carries out the same action. Later, the child independently performs the activity.

Social interactions rest on the organization of the individual's culture and society. Every culture has a view of the world and the way to solve problems. Language, writing, art, and methods of problem solving all reflect this social worldview. Adults use these societal forms in interacting with children, and children internalize them.

Social interaction not only conveys societal knowledge of the world but also plays an important role in stimulating children to learn that knowledge. Vygotsky described a unique concept called the *zone of proximal development.* According to this concept, a child can perform a range of actions alone, demonstrating a capacity that is clearly internal. This is what most of us would consider the child's level of ability. But Vygotsky pointed out that the child's behavior in this area can improve. When a more experienced person guides or prompts the child with questions, hints, or demonstrations, the child can respond at a more mature level not achievable when the child acts alone. So, the child has potential that emerges in social interaction. For example, a child learning how to talk may use a particular number of words spontaneously. That would be the child's verbal ability. A mother, however, might increase the number of words by prompting the child to remember what she called an item previously or by waiting for the child to add an action to an object he just identified, saying, "The doggie?" and waiting for "runs" or "goes bow-wow."

This zone of behavior, extending from what the child can do alone to what the child has the potential to do when guided, is the zone of proximal development. Vygotsky's interest went beyond what the child can do to what the child's learning potential is. Teaching has the greatest impact, he believed, when it is directed to the child's potential at the high end of the zone of proximal development. The experienced person helps the child do alone what he or she can initially do only with guidance.

Language plays a significant role in mental development. Language develops from social interaction and contact and initially is a means of influencing others. Adults talk to children, influencing their reactions or behavior. Children initially guide their own behavior with external language similar to that already heard. They talk to themselves as others have and guide their behavior with their speech. A toddler will say "No, no" to herself as a way of stopping forbidden action, with varying degrees of success. As the child matures, she internalizes the speech that guides her behavior. Such inner speech is thought rather than spoken in the older child.

The theories of Piaget and Vygotsky suggest that parents' roles are (1) to provide opportunities for independent exploration and action in the world and (2) to interact with children, serving as a model and guide in the world to help them reach their potential.

Emotional Competence

In his best-selling book *Emotional Intelligence,* Daniel Goleman argues that learning to modulate and control the arousal and expression of feelings is now more important to both individuals and society than is intellectual competence.[15] He points to the relationship between the capacity to deal with emotional feelings and success at work and in relationships with family and friends. He expresses concern over the increase in such psychological problems as depression, eating disorders, and anxiety attacks that ensue when individuals cannot effectively modulate their feelings and the effect of these problems on work and family life. Of equal importance is the cost to society. Poorly controlled individuals can react in aggressive and destructive ways that harm others as well as themselves.

Psychologists use the term *emotional regulation* to refer to "the ability to respond to the ongoing demands of experience with the range of emotions in a manner that is socially tolerable and sufficiently flexible to permit spontaneous reactions as well as the ability to delay spontaneous reactions as needed."[16] Emotional regulation underlies moral development. Robert Emde and his colleagues believe that the moral self, present in the child by age three, grows out of reciprocal relations with parents in the first year of life.[17] Responsive caregivers appropriately regulate the child's feelings—encouraging interest in the surrounding world, maintaining positive affect, and soothing the child when upset. These interactions give the child a sense of how things happen in the world, of how people interact with one another. The child internalizes these routines and rules, which then guide his or her behavior.

Parents play a crucial role in directly helping children develop emotional regulation. First, research suggests that parents' physical presence serves as an external regulator of young children's physiological functioning.[18] When a caregiver leaves, physically or emotionally, one can see changes in children's physiological functioning, in their eating and sleeping patterns, in their play patterns, and in their moods. These changes last until the parent returns. Similar responses to parents' absence have been observed in the young of many other species as well.[19] Second, parents' sensitive, accepting, and responsive caregiving minimizes the arousal of negative affect, helps infants shift from negative or neutral moods to positive and engaged ones, and prevents children from being overwhelmed by intense feelings.[20] Third, parents provide, and then encourage children to develop, strategies for controlling their feelings once aroused. They model ways to handle frustration and anger as well as love and caring. As children develop their own strategies, parents provide support and encouragement in refining the strategies. In subsequent chapters, we examine precisely how they do this.

Just as parents can help children develop emotional regulation, so parents who expose children to atypical levels of stress put them at risk for being overwhelmed by feelings they cannot control.[21] Conflict in the home, extreme and abusive discipline, parents' severe psychological problems—all present children with stress that not only disorganizes their behavior but requires stronger coping skills at a time when they have fewer resources.

Recent evidence suggests that positive early parent-child interactions are critical for still another reason. In promoting the child's emotional regulation, parents also promote the development of certain connections in the frontal area of the brain that, in turn, increase the capacity for emotional control. So, these early experiences have a powerful impact on later emotional control.[22]

Self-Esteem

Parents want children to feel good about themselves, to have self-esteem. Susan Harter describes the domains of the self-concept at each stage of development;[23] Table 2.1 outlines these domains. Across the life span, the self-concept becomes increasingly differentiated though the basic dimensions remain surprisingly similar. Young children do not verbalize global feelings of self-worth, but they do express them in behavior.

Global feelings of self-worth are related to two independent factors: (1) one's feelings of competence in domains of importance and (2) the amount of social support

TABLE 2.1   Domains of the Self-Concept at Each Period of the Life Span

Early Childhood	Middle/Late Childhood	Adolescence	College	Adult
Cognitive competence	Scholastic competence	Scholastic competence	Scholastic competence	
			Intellectual ability	Intelligence
			Creativity	
		Job competence	Job competence	Job competence
Physical competence	Athletic competence	Athletic competence	Athletic competence	Athletic competence
	Physical appearance	Physical appearance	Physical appearance	Physical appearance
Peer acceptance	Peer acceptance	Peer acceptance	Peer acceptance	Sociability
		Close friendship	Close friendship	Close friendship
		Romantic relationships	Romantic relationships	Intimate relationships
			Relationships with parents	
Behavioral conduct	Behavioral conduct	Conduct/morality	Morality	Morality
			Sense of humor	Sense of humor
				Nurturance
				Household management
				Adequacy as a provider
	Global self-worth	Global self-worth	Global self-worth	Global self-worth

From Susan Harter, "Causes, Correlates, and the Functional Role of Global Self-Worth: A Life-Span Perspective," in *Competence Considered*, ed. J. Kolligian and Robert Sternberg (New Haven, CT: Yale University Press, 1990), p. 73. Reprinted by permission.

one receives from others. Those highest in self-worth feel good about the abilities they value and also feel that others support and accept them. Those lowest in global self-worth feel they lack competence in domains deemed important and report that they receive little social support. Harter notes that no amount of social support can directly counteract one's perception of incompetence; conversely, no amount of competence can completely overcome feelings of lack of social support. So, to increase self-esteem, one has to increase both social support and feelings of competence in valued domains.

High-self-esteem children, ages three to seven, have two qualities—confidence in approaching situations and resilience when frustrated or upset.[24] These are also the qualities of children securely attached to their caregivers. Parental experiences that foster secure attachment are most likely those that help develop high self-esteem. Parental

Interview

with Susan Harter

Susan Harter, a professor of psychology at the University of Denver, has spent twenty years studying the development of the self and self-esteem and has written numerous articles and chapters on the subject.

You have done a great deal of research on self-esteem. More than any other quality, I would say, parents hope to help children develop self-esteem. What can they do to promote it in their children?

We have identified two broad themes that impact children's self-esteem. First, the unconditional support and positive regard of parents and others in the child's world are particularly critical during the early years. What do we mean by support? It is communicating to children that you like them as people for who or what they are.

That sounds relatively easy but is in fact extremely difficult. Most of us as parents are far more skilled at providing conditional regard or support for children even though we are unaware we are doing it. We approve of our child if he cleans up his room or shares or doesn't hit his brother. So our support is conditional on his conduct. However, it isn't perceived by children as supportive at all. Basically it specifies how the child can please the parents. That does not feel good to children.

Unconditional regard validates children as worthy people and lets them know they are appreciated for who they are, for their strengths and weaknesses. It also involves listening to them, which is very validating to children as well as adults. So many well-meaning parents, and I make the same mistake, preach at their kids because we think we have a lot to say. We think we're teaching when we are really preaching. We don't refrain from talking; we don't shut up, listen well, and take the child's point of view seriously.

With unconditional support early on, children internalize positive regard so that when they are older, they can approve of themselves, pat themselves on the back, give themselves psychological hugs—all of which contribute to high self-esteem.

Another major part of self-esteem, beginning at about age eight, is feeling competent and adequate across the various domains of life. One does not have to feel competent in every domain in order to experience high self-esteem. Rather one needs to feel competent in those domains that he or she judges to be *important*. Profiles of competence for two children in the different areas of athletic, social, and intellectual competence can look very similar, but one child can have high self-esteem while the other can have low self-esteem. They both can feel competent in the same areas and feel inadequate in the same other areas. What distinguishes the *low*-self-esteem child is the fact that areas of incompetence are very important to one's feeling of being worthwhile; thus the child doesn't feel good about himself or herself. The *high*-self-esteem child feels the low areas are very unimportant and so still feels good about himself or herself.

support, then, is a more important determinant of early self-esteem than is competence per se. In later childhood, both support and feelings of competence are important in determining self-worth.

The specific areas of competence that contribute most to feelings of self-worth are physical appearance and social acceptance by others—namely, parents and peers. Surprisingly, physical appearance and social support continue to be salient across the life span for individuals from eight to fifty-five years of age.

Which comes first—do children and adolescents base their self-esteem on others' social approval and others' perceptions of their attractiveness, or do children and adolescents high in self-esteem believe that others like them and find them attractive?[25] According to questionnaire responses, about 60 percent of children and adolescents say their self-esteem depends on others' views of them and about 40 percent say they like themselves and feel others approve of them. Those in the first category have lower self-esteem because they depend on the shifting regard of others. Those who like themselves and assume others do too have higher self-esteem that is more stable because it is an internal quality.

Although self-esteem depends on the early positive regard given by parents and caregivers, this regard does not fix it for life. Levels of self-esteem can increase over time as individuals become more competent in areas of importance to them or as they receive increased support from others. Self-esteem decreases under the reverse conditions.

Times of change and transition—entrance into kindergarten or junior high or college, moves to new schools or new neighborhoods—can trigger changes in self-esteem. New skills to develop, new reference groups for comparison, and new social groups for support provide the stimulus for change. People maintain self-esteem most successfully when they join or create positive social support or when they increase in other areas of competence.

Social Competence

Parents take a direct role in encouraging social competence when they choose residential neighborhoods where playmates are available and where flat areas, parks, and playgrounds make play possible.[26] Parents promote social skills when they organize both informal and play group activities for their children and supervise them to ensure that positive interactions occur. A parent's role is both direct and indirect when she or he creates a family atmosphere conducive to positive interactions with people in general. Creating secure attachments with children, modeling positive interactions with family members, arranging and reinforcing pleasurable sibling interactions—all promote children's trust in other people, their skills in understanding and dealing with others, and their overall enjoyment of social activity.

Research suggests fathers' behavior may be particularly important in promoting children's social development.[27] For example, physical play with their fathers may help children learn to use signals to regulate others' behavior. A father's ability to accept his children's anger and sadness and to help them cope with these feelings at age five are related to his children's social skills at age eight. When fathers respond to children's negative feelings with anger, their children will more likely be aggressive and avoidant of others than will children of more accepting fathers.

Children from families under chronic stress are less socially skilled than are those not under stress. Poverty, for example, exerts a negative impact on social competence. Children in low-income families have a great need for social group activities, but both the physical environment and parental resources restrict access to play. Low-income neighborhoods often are not safe for outdoor play, and parents have less time to organize peer contacts, so there are fewer of them.

Other stressors that decrease social competence include parental unemployment, marital conflict, and divorce. Parental abuse, depression, and alcoholism further decrease children's abilities to interact positively with others.

Moral Competence

Moral competence refers to several aspects of children's behavior: (1) carrying out positive acts that are voluntary, helpful, and beneficial to others; (2) avoiding disruptive or negative behaviors that are harmful to others, such as lying, stealing, and physical aggression; (3) developing a conscience or internal standards that direct behavior; and (4) acquiring the capacity to make moral judgments.[28] Moral competence rests on the capacity for self-control and concern for others and thus is related to emotional and social competence.

Helpful behavior springs from early caregiving experiences. In his book *The Moral Sense*, James Q. Wilson, like Robert Emde, points to the important contribution of early parent-child relations to moral development:

> Our moral senses are forged in the crucible of this loving relationship and expanded by the enlarged relationships of families and peers. Out of the universal attachment between child and parent, the former begins to develop a sense of empathy and fairness, to learn self-control, and to acquire a conscience that makes him behave dutifully at least with respect to some matters. Those dispositions are extended to other people (and often to other species) to the extent that these others are thought to share in the traits we find in our families.[29]

Parents also exert a direct influence on children's helpful behaviors by encouraging empathy for others. Parents verbalize concern for others and induce children to understand others' points of view with statements such as, "See, you made Joey cry." They also take an active role in modeling and teaching children how to be helpful and in conveying standards of behavior that they hope children will meet. Warmth and nurturance in the absence of moral standards are less effective than such actions in promoting helpful behavior.[30]

The emotional climate of the home influences children's level of sympathy and concern for others.[31] In homes where parents fight, children have sympathy for mothers and siblings but less concern for peers outside the family. When mothers express tension, sadness, and fear at home but help their children understand these feelings, the children's sympathy increases.

Children tend to be more sympathetic and prosocial when they have parents who help them with their negative feelings. Listening to children's negative emotions, talking about them, and helping children find ways to manage them are all related to children's being more sympathetic to others' distress and more likely to take action to comfort others.

Parents increase children's hurtful behaviors when they enforce harsh discipline, show little concern for their children's needs, and reflect inconsistent and fleeting interest in their children's behavior. When parents fail to supervise and monitor children's actions consistently, the children are more likely to be aggressive toward and unconcerned about others.[32]

We know more about parents' influence on helpful and hurtful behaviors than about their role in promoting the internalization of rules and moral reasoning. Toddlers do not develop internal standards of accomplishment until about age three. At that time, they take pride in their successes and feel sadness at their failures. But not until the elementary school years do children feel guilt, a sense of having done something wrong and wanting to make amends for it. Parents help children internalize family values by conveying standards of behavior and making nonpunitive, supportive statements to help children understand others' points of view and act in accordance with what is best for all.

The capacity to reason about moral issues and make moral judgments depends, in part, on the child's cognitive skills, but parents can help this capacity develop in several ways. When parents are supportive of children's opinions and views of situations, when they ask questions and elicit children's opinions in real-life situations, and when they present higher levels of moral reasoning for consideration, then children achieve more advanced levels of moral reasoning. Criticizing children's opinions, challenging their views, and correcting them with new information are not associated with children's moral growth.[33]

The Role of Authoritative Parenting

The parental behaviors associated with competencies in several areas center on what Diana Baumrind terms *authoritative parenting*. In studying children in the preschool years and following their development, she identified three parenting styles.[34]

Authoritative parents exercise firm control over the child's behavior but also emphasize independence and individuality in the child. Although the parents have a clear notion of present and future standards of behavior for the child, they are rational, flexible, and attentive to the needs and preferences of the child. Their children are self-reliant and self-confident and explore their worlds with excitement and pleasure.

Authoritarian parents employ similar firm control but in an arbitrary, power-oriented way without regard for the child's individuality. They emphasize control without nurturance or support to achieve it. Children of authoritarian parents, relative to other groups of children, are unhappy, withdrawn, inhibited, and distrustful.

Permissive parents set few limits on the child. They are accepting of the child's impulses, granting as much freedom as possible while still maintaining physical safety. They appear cool and uninvolved. Permissive parents sometimes allow behavior that angers them, but they do not feel sufficiently comfortable with their own anger to express it. As a result, the anger builds up to unmanageable proportions. They then lash out and are likely to harm the child more than they want to. Their children are the least independent and self-controlled and could be best classified as immature.

So, respecting individuality, providing warmth and nurturance, establishing standards of behavior, monitoring and supervising children, and actively teaching desired behaviors are all related to competencies in several areas.

Cultural and Socioeconomic Influences on Parenting

In Chapter 1, we described parent-child relationships as being nested in social and cultural influences (see Figure 1.1). Here, we discuss what parents learn from their culture about parenting.

Because of our country's growing ethnic diversity, parents draw from many different traditions as they go about rearing their children. Immigration and higher reproductive rates in some ethnic groups have brought about an increase in the numbers of various ethnic groups. The main ethnic groups in this country are European Americans (72 percent), African Americans (12 percent), Hispanic Americans (11 percent), Asian Americans (3 percent), and American Indians (.7 percent).[35] Just as European Americans trace their origins to different European cultures with different values, so other ethnic groups consist of several subgroups, each with its own set of values. For example, Hispanic Americans from Mexico differ from Hispanic Americans from Cuba. In addition, families from the same ethnic group may have different values, depending on their length of residence in this country. For example, third-generation ethnic Americans tend to have values more similar to those of mainstream American culture than to those of their ethnic group of origin.[36]

Culture

Social scientists Sara Harkness and Charles Super believe that culture provides a "developmental niche" in which children develop. This niche includes (1) the physical and social settings the culture provides for parents and children, (2) the childrearing practices the culture recommends, and (3) the psychological characteristics of the caregivers.[37] So, culture shapes a broad range of parental behaviors, from the more general values parents teach to the concrete aspects of daily life such as where children eat and sleep.

To illustrate how culture influences parental behaviors, let us look at a study in which samples of American mothers and Italian mothers of infants four to sixteen months were interviewed and observed in their homes with their babies to determine mothers' conceptions of development, their goals, and their practices with their infants.[38] The participants were all members of nuclear families of parents and children.

American mothers' long-term goals for their children were that they develop (1) economic and emotional independence, (2) a sense of well-being and happiness that did not depend on financial success, and (3) honest and respectful interpersonal relationships. A short-term goal was to provide sufficient stimulation for the child's growth, which mothers worried they were not providing. Italian mothers' long-term goals focused on social relationships and physical and economic well-being.

All of the Italian mothers mentioned good health, financial security, and a good family life as important. Their definition of a good family life included a spouse and children. These mothers felt much less pressure than the American mothers because they did not feel responsible for the outcome of the child's development. Italian mothers considered all mothers adequate by virtue of being mothers and believed that children turn out as they will.

This study found that goals and attitudes determined how infants and mothers spent their days. American infants spent their time in one-on-one interactions with mothers (about one-third of the time) or in isolation in their rooms, sleeping or playing with toys. Although other people came in and out of the home, they, including siblings, did not participate much in the care of the child. In Italy, infants had little direct interaction with mothers (10 percent of the time) and were almost never alone. They slept in the same room as their parents, often until the second birthday, and were regularly in the company of two or three people. For all but one infant, at least one grandparent lived nearby and visited daily.

As infants began to get around the environment, American parents babyproofed the environment and let the child crawl about; at ten months, infants spent 52 percent of observation time in crawling and exploring on the floor freely. Mothers taught infants at this age preliminary safety rules, as they felt it was important for the child to explore and accept some responsibility for safety. Mothers felt reassured that their children were developing well when they were active and curious. Italian mothers, on the other hand, believed free exploration was too dangerous—too cold, even in the summer, and involving too many hazards. Their ten-month-old infants spent about 26 percent of observation time in crawling on the floor. When it was time to walk, infants were always supported by adults who held their hands. None of the Italian mothers felt concern that their children were not more independent.

American mothers placed great emphasis on establishing good sleep patterns. By four months of age, most infants slept in their own beds, often in their own rooms, though several shared a room with a sibling but none with their parents. Getting enough sleep was very important, and mothers established schedules and rituals for helping children get enough sleep, even when children resisted naptime or bedtime. In contrast, Italian mothers rarely held to any sleeping schedule, and babies often dropped off to sleep in the midst of family activity without bedtime rituals or songs. One mother had no schedule because she felt it was cruel to deprive the child of family time.

With regard to eating behaviors, however, the attitudes of the two groups of mothers were reversed. American mothers felt their children could regulate their food habits. Infants ate on demand and often at times different from the family's, so eating was an activity involving mother and child, with the mother talking while she fed the infant. As children got older, they were encouraged to feed themselves. Italian infants, in contrast, were required to eat on 4-hour schedules and to come to family meals, even if they had to be awakened to do so. Solid foods were begun at four months, and infants had to eat certain amounts. They were expected to get used to eating rituals even if they did not like them.

TABLE 2.2   Contrasting Cultural Models of Parent-Child Relations

	Developmental Goals	
	Independence	Interdependence
Developmental trajectory	From dependent to independent self	From asocial to socially responsible self
Children's relations to parents	Personal choice concerning relationship to parents	Obligations to parents
Communication	Verbal emphasis	Nonverbal emphasis (empathy, observation, participation)
	Autonomous self-expression by child	Child comprehension, mother speaks for child
	Frequent parental questions to child	Frequent parental directives to child
	Frequent praise	Infrequent praise
	Child negotiation	Harmony, respect, obedience
Parenting style	Authoritative: controlling, demanding, warm, rational	Rigorous and responsible teaching, high involvement, physical closeness
Parents helping children	A matter of personal choice except under extreme need	A moral obligation under all circumstances

From Patricia M. Greenfield and Lalita K. Suzuki, "Culture and Human Development: Implications for Parenting, Education, Pediatrics, and Mental Health," in *Handbook of Child Psychology*, ed. in chief William Damon and vol. ed. Irving E. Sigel and K. Ann Renninger, vol. 4, *Child Psychology in Practice*, 5th ed. (New York: Wiley, 1998), p. 1085. Reprinted by permission of John Wiley & Sons, Inc.

Overall, then, American mothers put primary emphasis on independence—in play, exploration, eating, and sleeping alone at bedtime. Italian families enveloped their infants in complex social interactions, which required adaptation on the part of the babies and gave few opportunities for independence.

Patricia Greenfield and Lalita Suzuki have surveyed differences among many ethnic groups and describe two cultural models—the independent and the interdependent models—that provide a framework for organizing and understanding what parents think matters and what they do with children.[39] Table 2.2 outlines these two models, which apply to many different cultural and social groups rather than any ethnic group in particular.

In the independent model, parents help children become self-sustaining, productive adults who enter into relationships with other adults by choice. The child receives nurturance to develop autonomy, competence, and a freely chosen identity that in adulthood merges with others outside the family.

In the interdependent model, parents help children grow into socially responsible adults who take their place in a strong network of social relationships, often within the family, that place obligations on the adult. Parents indulge the young child, but as children grow older, they are expected to internalize and respect the rules of parents and other authorities. Parents and relatives are respected and obeyed, and family and group needs matter more than individual ones.

Although cultural beliefs and values are deeply ingrained and often invisible, they are not fixed and unchangeable. The anthropologist Jean Briggs writes,

> The notion that meaning inheres in culture and that people receive it passively as dough receives the cookie cutter, is rapidly being replaced by the idea that culture consists of ingredients, which people actively select, interpret, and use in various ways, as opportunities, capabilities, and experience allow.[40]

James Youniss describes a series of studies showing that immigrant parents can identify the cultural values of their new country and socialize their children to fit in while the parents maintain their more traditional beliefs.[41] Youniss reviewed studies of two groups who emigrated from Croatia to the United States. One group lived very much as a self-contained community, stressing their traditional values, customs, and language. The other group became assimilated into the new culture. Both groups, however, socialized their children to be more independent, questioning, and self-directed than the parents had been raised to be, thus helping their children fit into their new culture.

Many children in our multicultural society are exposed to two sets of cultural values and develop what is termed a *bicultural identification,* an identification with the values of two groups. For example, one can harmonize the values of the independent and interdependent models and become an independent adult who belongs to a strong family network. One can both respect parents, showing consideration for their needs, and become an achievement-oriented, self-sustaining person. For this reason, Ross Parke and Raymond Buriel warn against making overly sharp distinctions that only promote stereotypes. Parke and Buriel emphasize the importance of considering both individual and collectivist features when one tries to understand childrearing in any type of family.[42]

Cultural models influence not only what parents do in their homes but also the qualities children take with them into the larger society.[43] Children more easily adapt to the larger culture when the home culture is the same as that of the larger society. For example, problems can arise when the home culture conflicts with that of the school. U.S. teachers and schools operate on the independent model, emphasizing individual effort to achieve knowledge. Questions and expressions of opinion are encouraged and seen as signs of intellectual curiosity. Children's quiet acceptance of the teachers' statements may be interpreted as a lack of interest or a lack of intelligence. So, we need to recognize that children may live in a home culture that differs from the culture in school and the larger society. Throughout the text, we will further explore cultural influences on parenting.

Socioeconomic Status

Every cultural group contains a social hierarchy. Erika Hoff-Ginsberg and Twila Tardif state that socioeconomic status (SES), like culture, provides a developmental niche for children.[44] Social position partly prescribes the settings children live in, their parents' childrearing practices, and the psychological characteristics of their parents.

Three variables—parents' occupation, education, and level of income—make up SES. Because the three variables, though correlated, can vary, SES is a complicated concept. Thus, one middle-class family may have an average income, education, and occupational status, while another middle-class family of average income and occupational status may have a higher educational status. Even if the two families had different values, both would be considered middleclass.

Although income at or below the poverty level affects parenting (see Chapters 1 and 8), income above the poverty level appears less influential in shaping parenting beliefs than are education and occupational status. One study in China indicates that people with the same income may exhibit values that differ greatly. In the United States, too, studies indicate that values may remain the same though income varies.

The influence of social status, like that of culture, is not fixed. For example, parents' occupations may change as the result of increased education, or a family may find great success in some endeavor and their income may rise sharply. Conversely, income and social status may drop as a result of unemployment. Further, parents change their ideas about parenting as a result of new information.

Hoff-Ginsberg and Tardif, in their comprehensive review of research, cite one study in which mothers of all educational levels provided their young children with books and read to them, most likely because of a widespread public campaign to read to children. However, the mothers with only a high school education had fewer children's books and read far less to their children than did college-educated mothers.

Reviewing the influences of SES on parenting, Hoff-Ginsberg and Tardif point to three significant findings. First, whether one compares college-educated and high school–educated parents or middle-class and working-class parents, the higher the SES, the more likely the parents will have a child-centered orientation to parenting. Parents with this orientation seek to understand children's growth and development, to understand children's feelings and motivations, and to use reasoning and negotiation to solve problems. Such parents approach children in an egalitarian manner. The lower the SES, the more likely parents will be parent-centered in their approach to children and want obedience and conformity to the rules without discussion or explanation. Such parents seek to direct and control activities rather than to understand them or negotiate with their children. Melvin Kohn speculates that working-class parents are more likely to stress obedience and conformity because their jobs require these qualities, whereas higher-status occupations permit more autonomy, initiative, and independence.[45]

A second major finding is that differences in SES correlate with more differences in verbal than nonverbal interactions between parents and children. A third finding is that higher-status parents talk more to children and elicit more speech from them. They also show more responsiveness when children do speak, and they encourage the development of verbal skills by supplying more labels that describe what children see and do.

The description of such differences may sound uninteresting and unimportant, but an unusual study has documented the profound impact of these differences in young children's lives. Betty Hart and Todd Risley recorded the words spoken to and by children in their homes from the ages of one to three years.[46] Investigators visited the homes of forty-two families of professional, working-class, and welfare background for an hour each month. The children in the study were European American and African American. Results indicated no gender or racial differences in language acquisition, but they did reveal large differences based on social group.

All children in the study experienced quality interactions with their parents; all heard diverse forms of language spoken to and around them; and all learned to speak by the age of three. However, the differing amounts and kinds of language heard in the homes surprised the investigators.

First, professional parents spoke about three times as much to their children as did welfare parents and about one and a half times as much as did working-class parents. Children in professional families heard about 487 utterances per hour; children in working-class families, 301; and children in welfare families, 178.

The emotional tone of the conversations also reflected startling differences. In professional families, children received affirmative feedback (confirming, elaborating, and giving explicit approval for what the child said) about 30 times an hour, or every other minute. In working-class families, children received affirmative feedback 15 times an hour, or once every 4 minutes. In welfare families, children received positive feedback 6 times an hour, or once every 10 minutes. Professional parents gave prohibitions about 5 times an hour, and welfare parents about 11. Children in welfare families heard twice as many negative comments as positive ones, whereas children in professional families heard primarily positive comments and rarely any negative ones.

These findings have important implications for the development of self-concept and general mood as well as for language development. Language differences in the home strongly predicted vocabulary growth and intellectual development for the next five years. The most important predictors of vocabulary and intellectual competence were the emotional tone of the feedback and the amount of linguistic diversity the child heard.

Encouragingly, the study shows that all parents have the capacity to promote language and intellectual development, because they already have the ability to speak and interact with children effectively. Of course, some parents need to increase certain kinds of behavior—namely, their verbal interactions with their children—and provide more positive feedback to them.

What Parents Learn from Their Families of Origin

If you ask parents how they are rearing their children, they usually say they are doing or definitely not doing what their parents did with them. Certainly Gerald Patterson and Deborah Capaldi's research described in Chapter 1 confirms that parents draw on their childhood experiences in caring for their children.[47] So, our relationships with our parents provide guideposts that we may or may not wish to follow.

In the early twentieth century, Sigmund Freud pointed to the kinds of childhood experiences that were important. In 1950, Erik Erikson, a psychoanalyst with a strong interest in cross-cultural research, expanded Freud's ideas and identified social and cultural influences that have an impact on development. Erikson described growth as a

TABLE 2.3   Erik Erikson's Eight Stages of Life

Ages	Crisis	Virtue
0–1	Trust versus Mistrust	Hope
1–3	Autonomy versus Shame/Doubt	Will
3–5	Initiative versus Guilt	Purpose
5–12	Industry versus Inferiority	Competence
12–19	Identity versus Identity Diffusion	Fidelity
19–	Intimacy versus Isolation	Love
20–	Generativity versus Stagnation	Care
	Integrity versus Despair	Wisdom

Erik H. Erikson, *Childhood and Society,* 2nd ed. New York: W. W. Norton. 1950, 1963.

series of eight stages.[48] In each stage, the individual has specific physical and psychological needs and a developmental crisis that must be met and resolved. People have positive and negative experiences in satisfying needs, and both kinds of experiences are important for optimal development. If we receive only positive gratification, we never learn how to cope with difficulties. However, for healthy growth, the balance should favor the positive side. Table 2.3 lists the stages by age, the developmental crisis that arises in each stage, and the positive virtue that develops when the balance of experiences is on the positive side.

Erikson did not believe that we solve a developmental crisis once and for all. Later experiences can change earlier resolutions for better or worse. For example, stress during adulthood can disrupt mature ways of coping, so that for a brief time, an individual may seem immature. By the same token, positive experiences in adulthood can reverse mistrust or doubt developed in childhood.

When children experience trustworthy care that encourages independence, competence, and a positive sense of identity unburdened with excessive shame and guilt, then as adults they can commit themselves to partners and rear the next generation. From these childhood experiences, parents internalize a working model of how people relate to one another, how trustworthy others are, and how much control one has over interactions with other people. This internal model influences how parents perceive their children and interact with them.

Interviews with parents about their feelings concerning childhood experiences with their parents yield information on parents' current state of mind regarding their attachment to their parents.[49] Securely attached parents, even those who experienced traumatic events, value these early attachments and place negative childhood events in perspective so they can think about and understand the effects of these events on their life. Insecurely attached parents who also dismiss the importance of these early events and attachments minimize the influence of these events on their present life. They see themselves as independent and strong adults. Insecurely attached parents preoccupied with past events seem confused about their experiences with early attachment figures.

They remain entangled in feelings of anger, helplessness, conflict, or fearfulness, and they cannot gain insight or closure regarding these early experiences.

Securely attached parents are direct and open in their dealings with others and are not inclined to misperceive situations. Toward their children, they are emotionally supportive, sensitive, and responsive, yet they can set clear and consistent limits.

Insecurely attached, dismissive parents emphasize their independence and strength in the face of parental rejection, and they remain cool and remote from their children. As they do not believe their parents mattered in their life, they do not try to help or support their children emotionally. Confident of their abilities, they have few doubts about their parenting effectiveness. They report few negative thoughts about children in difficult childrearing situations.

Insecurely attached, preoccupied parents behave in a confusing and inconsistent manner with their children. Warm and gentle at times, they become angry and forceful with children at other times. They have many negative thoughts about children in difficult childrearing situations, blaming the problems on the child's personality. Clearly, parents' views of children and their styles of relating to them stem from a general way of perceiving and relating to people based on early life experiences.

Additional studies of parents' attachment to their own parents reveal that the group of securely attached parents consists of two subgroups—those with continuous secure attachments and those with "earned security."[50] Continuously securely attached parents are those who report early positive relationships with parents and have a current secure working model of attachment. Parents with earned security are those who describe difficult early relationships and hardships with parents but who, nevertheless, are able to gain distance from the hard times, put those experiences in perspective, and develop a secure working model of attachment. Their childhood experiences were as difficult as those of the group of parents who have insecure attachments with their parents, and they have as many sad, depressed feelings as insecurely attached parents. Parents with earned security, however, differ from parents with insecure attachments in that they have worked through their painful feelings from harsh childhood experiences. They are then able to develop a flexible, warm style of parenting similar to that of parents with continuous security. Even during stressful times, parents with earned-security attachments are able to maintain warmth and positive relationships with their children. Nevertheless, even those parents who have not worked through their difficult childhood experiences are insensitive parents only when they are stressed.

Another study of parenting across three generations looked at the influence of genetic factors on the similarity of parents and children in their childrearing behaviors.[51] Parents of adult female-female identical or fraternal twins described their parental behaviors on three dimensions: parental warmth, protectiveness, and amount of control. The twins also rated how their parents treated them and their cotwins and how they, in turn, reared their children.

Although parents said they treated their children the same regardless of the genetic relationship of the twins, identical twins reported more similar levels of warmth from parents than did fraternal twins. Further, in describing their own parenting, identical twins were more similar in reporting warm parenting behaviors than were fraternal twins. When it came to variables such as protectiveness and control, parents' reports of their behavior indicated less influence from genetic factors.

We do not yet know the mechanisms of the transmission of parenting behaviors from one generation to the next, though, as we have just noted, research indicates some genetic contribution to parent-child similarity in parenting.[52] Adopting a parenting strategy may be the outcome of coaching, modeling, or some other cognitive process.

We do, then, derive many parenting behaviors from our early experiences with our parents. It is clear, however, that we are able to modify the childhood legacy either by working through feelings about these experiences or by getting parenting training of the kind Patterson and Capaldi offered to parents in their studies, which we discussed in Chapter 1.

The First Three Years of Parenting

Recent studies in neuroscience and brain development have heightened concerns about the kind of environmental stimulation children receive early in life. The question arises, Are the first three years the most important years in parenting?

Advances in Neuroscience

Brain development determines how we interact with the world.[53] We used to think that genes determine how the brain develops. Although some scientists considered the effects of nutrition and other environmental events on brain development during pregnancy, people generally thought that apart from extreme circumstances, genetic determiners account for brain development.

Recent advances in research tools, such as imaging techniques, have taught us, however, that much supposedly genetically determined brain development actually involves input from the environment. Beginning with conception, environmental factors such as nutrition, physical surroundings, care, and stimulation influence "how the intricate circuitry of the human is 'wired.'"[54] After birth, environmental input and stimulation establish and strengthen connections among brain cells, thus shaping the architecture of the brain. Daniel Siegel summarizes this new emphasis on the plasticity of the brain:

> An infant is born with a genetically programmed excess in neurons, and the postnatal establishment of synaptic connections is determined by both genes and experience. Genes contain the information for the general organization of the brain's structure, but experience determines which genes become expressed, how, and when. The expression of genes leads to the production of proteins that enable neuronal growth and the formation of new synapses. Experience—the activation of specific neural pathways—therefore directly shapes gene expression and leads to the maintenance, creation, and strengthening of the connections that form the neural substance of the mind. Early in life, interpersonal relationships are a primary source of the experience that shapes how genes express themselves within the brain. . . . Experiences lead to an increased activity of neurons, which enhances the creation of new synaptic connections. This experience-dependent brain growth and differentiation is thus referred to as an "activity-dependent brain process."[55]

Mothers' smiles increase babies' good humor, smiling, and laughter and increase the likelihood babies will approach others in a positive, smiling way.

This new emphasis on the plasticity of the brain and the importance of early experience has attracted public attention. It sparked a 1997 White House conference, Early Childhood Development and Learning: What New Research on the Brain Tells Us about Our Youngest Children. Major magazines and newspapers featured articles on the topic, and *Newsweek* devoted a special edition to children's development in the first three years of life.[56] Political action in California, based on this new emphasis, sponsored and helped to pass a 1998 proposition allocating all cigarette tax money to programs for children under five years of age.

Some observers have drawn broad conclusions from this work and insist that if children do not receive certain kinds of stimulation in the early years, they will not develop their full potential. Such interpretations of the research have increased parents' anxieties as to whether they are providing sufficient and appropriate stimulation for their children. Research on infants' incredible capacities for observation, exploration, and learning has added to parents' anxieties about the adequacy of the stimulation they provide their infants and toddlers. Here, we look at the impact of parents' behavior with children in the first three years and address two questions: Does parenting matter more in these years? If so, what should parents be doing?

Factors to Consider

There are several factors to consider as we ponder these questions. First, although there is evidence of the plasticity of the brain throughout the life span,[57] early experiences shape the architecture of the brain and thus influence not only what information is absorbed but the ways in which the mind develops to process that information.[58] So, early experiences may be especially important because they influence how the brain organizes and handles stimulation.

Second, our knowledge of environmental factors in brain development is limited. Environmental factors such as nurturant caregiving, good nutrition, good health care, and avoidance of toxins such as lead are known to be important. But a far wider array of environmental factors may also be involved in brain development. For example, recent findings from space research demonstrate that gravity may play a role in the physiological functioning of all cells and in the migration of nerve cells to the outer cortex during brain development.[59] Moreover, the use of the hands may be especially important in brain and cognitive development. In his book *The Hand*, neurologist Frank Wilson speculates that our society may change as more and more preschoolers are seated in front of computers to learn passively about the world. According to Wilson, failure to use our hands to explore the world may have serious consequences as

> The hand speaks to the brain as surely as the brain speaks to the hand. Self-generated movement is the foundation of thought and willed action, the underlying mechanism by which the physical and psychological coordinates of the self come into being. For humans, the hand has a special role and status in the organization of movement and in the evolution of human cognition.[60]

Third, early environmental factors may have important effects on later behavior without changing the brain. Experiences in the earliest years could have highly significant effects because they set in motion ways of interpreting the world and responding to others that are reinforced by others' responses and are thus self-perpetuating. For example, an infant whose mother smiles readily increases a baby's good humor, smiling, and laughter.[61] When the child toddles off and approaches others in a positive, smiling way and receives a smiling, friendly response, the likelihood of the child's positive mood increases. Thus, the mother has set in motion a positive way of responding to others that continues. So, let us now look at the kinds of early experiences known to be important.

The Importance of Experience in the Early Years

Parental care in the first months of life is critical for the child's survival and well-being. Close physical contact with the mother serves to regulate the infant's hormonal levels, sleep patterns, eating patterns, heart rate, and vagal tone.[62] (Vagal tone refers to the neural control of increases and decreases in the heartbeat and is considered a measure of individual differences in the expression and regulation of emotion.) In the first few weeks of life, infants who receive extra carrying and physical closeness cry less than babies who are not carried as much, and they are more visually and aurally alert.[63] As we noted earlier, when mothers are away or unavailable because of hospitalizations or trips, babies do not eat, sleep, or function physically and socially as well as they did before the mothers' absence.[64]

Parents' closeness and caring support infants' physical growth and well-being. As we saw in Chapter 1, parents' care can also help physiologically overreactive infants stabilize their responses to stimulation and, thus, avoid fearful and inhibited behavior in later childhood.[65] Effective parenting for these infants involves setting limits and enabling infants to find coping strategies when they are upset.

The complex forms of communication and interaction that are established between parent and child in the early months of life can, when supportive, promote positive emotional moods and a positive approach to the world.[66] When parents are responsive caregivers who read a baby's signals and provide optimal levels of stimulation for the infant by following the baby's rhythm or by modifying the baby's behavior, then a secure attachment grows between infant and parent, and such an attachment provides many positive benefits for the growing child.

As we noted in the previous section on parents' attachment to their parents, children incorporate their experiences with attachment figures and form an internal model of how people relate to one another. When attachment is secure, babies are able to soothe themselves, explore the world more freely, and develop positive interactions with others. These positive attachments are related to effective functioning in the preschool years and on into elementary school. Children with secure attachments in infancy appear more able to form close interpersonal relationships with others, although the exact reasons for this—perhaps more sensitive parenting, greater social skills, more positive social expectations—are not known.

Further, early positive attachments with parents may buffer the child against difficulties.[67] In a sample of poor families, children with positive attachments with mothers in the infant/toddler years showed better adaptation in the elementary school years than did those who had insecure attachments, even though both groups of children had displayed problems in the preschool years. The early positive experience may have given the children an advantage by providing early models of care and self-worth that stimulated these children to seek out similar experiences in later years.

In addition to promoting security, parents' behavior in the first few years of life is associated with intellectual growth through childhood and adolescence. Longitudinal research following a sample of middle-class children found that parental qualities and family patterns of interaction, assessed when children were twenty-one months of age, predicted intellectual growth.[68] Investigators controlled for parents' intellectual ability and found that a mother's energy, tension, and concern for the child predicted a son's intellectual level from age two to eighteen and a daughter's intellectual development from age eight to thirty. Mothers with energetic qualities were thought to do more things with their children and perhaps were more responsive to them. The study also found that a son's intellectual growth was related to the father's satisfaction with his work, and a daughter's above-average intellectual level was associated with the parents' marital compatibility and the father's interest and closeness with his daughter. The results of the study could not determine whether the effect of the environment occurred before, during, or after the first two years of life. But the important finding is that—even with parents' intellectual ability controlled for—the family emotional milieu, as measured at twenty-one months, had predictive significance for the intellectual performance of boys and girls from early childhood into adulthood.

One more finding illustrates the importance of early experience. Recall our earlier discussion of language use in the homes of toddlers. The emotional tone of the parents' verbal feedback, the diversity of the parents' language, and symbolic emphasis in the years from one to three predicted vocabulary at ages nine to ten and children's overall language development. Although early language stimulation was not related to other academic skills or school grades, it was speculated that as children proceeded in school, vocabulary and language development would predict grades as verbal skills become more salient.

Hart and Risley summarize their conceptual view of the importance of these early experiences. They do not believe these years are *the* most important in children's development, "only that the first three years are a time when children are uniquely susceptible to the culture," because children have not yet encountered the influence of peers and other institutions outside the home.[69] Hart and Risley write:

> Given the nature of babies and their interactions, the very first years of life establish an entire general approach to experience. A vocabulary of how things are done is laid down in interactions with an adult about things that matter. Children learn through words and actions what the world means, who they are, and what is valued. Children learn what it means to be a social being, how to use language, and the patterns of what people do interpersonally.[70]

Just as positive experiences can predict later well-being, early negative experiences have importance as well. The babies of depressed mothers show less affectionate behavior with their mothers, touching them less, and they are more likely to be angry, irritable, and poorly controlled than babies of nondepressed mothers. The negative behavior of babies of depressed mothers is associated with changes in frontal cortical brain activity as measured by EEG recordings.[71] Longitudinal follow-ups with these babies will determine the long-term significance of these early differences. Infants who experience violence have elevated hormone levels, and there is speculation that the chronic experience of traumatic violence may lead to hyperarousal of the sympathetic nervous system and the physiological responses related to the fight or flight response.[72]

Positive experiences in early life, nonetheless, do not guarantee healthy development throughout childhood. Secure attachments can change to insecure attachments and vice versa, and many events can intervene. Michael Lewis assessed the psychological adjustment of one hundred middle-class eighteen-year-olds who had been observed at age one and assigned an attachment classification at that time.[73] He found no relationship between attachment at one year and psychological adjustment at eighteen. Adjustment at eighteen was related instead to the adolescents' current model of attachment relationships rather than that of infancy, illustrating that many events intervene between age one and age eighteen to shape children's adjustment.

Lewis believes that it is the biological and social forces in the present that influence children's behavior. Children modify their behavior to meet the demands of the social situations they confront. He writes, "Social control and biological imperatives can be seen not as controlling forces but rather as input that informs children about their own nature and the nature of the environment. With this knowledge, children then are capable of constructing how to behave and what to think."[74] Although this may be true of middle-class children with many social resources, recall the results of the Rochester Longitudinal Study in which children's individual resources were less powerful than the accumulation of social risks they faced.[75]

Examining this sampling of studies indicating the important effects of parents' early behavior, we see that parents' positive emotional involvement is a main influence on children's emotional, intellectual, and verbal development. In their book *The Scientist in the Crib*, Alison Gopnik, Andrew Meltzoff, and Patricia Kuhl write that infants are drawn to relationships with parents. Parents, they believe, already know many of the behaviors needed to foster babies' growth:

> For babies and young children, care and teaching are inseparable. The very actions
> that nurture babies give them the kind of information they need. . . . The scientific
> research says that we should do just what we do when we are with our own babies—
> talk, play, make funny faces, pay attention. We just need time to do it.[76]

The Modifiability of Early Experiences

Brain research indicates that infants are born with most of the nerve cells they will ever have. The connections between the cells (*synapses*) increase from about 2,500 per cell at birth to about 15,000 per cell at age three, many more than in the adult brain. As young children reach puberty, they begin to get rid of old, little-used connections in a process termed *pruning*, and the number of synaptic connections is reduced to that found in adult brains.[77]

As noted earlier, some observers believe that if children do not receive stimulation early in life, they will not be able to develop certain capabilities. While research indicates that there may be critical windows for the development of perceptual and motor abilities in animals, such critical windows for the development of human behaviors are few and greatly extended in time. John Bruer, reviewing the evidence concerning critical periods in the development of human behaviors, concludes:

> The odds that our children will end up with appropriately fine-tuned brains are
> incredibly favorable, because the experiences the brain *expects* during critical periods
> are the kinds of stimuli that occur everywhere and all the time within the normal
> developmental environment for our species. It is only when there are severe genetic or
> environmental aberrations from the normal that nature's expectations are frustrated
> and neural development goes awry.[78]

Thus, stimulation need not occur at a specific time for an ability to develop, yet it may be easier to develop that ability early.

We have described the positive behaviors associated with early secure attachments and are concerned about identifying the kinds of events and factors that can maintain or change parent-child attachments over time. Even though Lewis found that secure attachments at age one did not predict security of attachment relationships at age eighteen, still, most research indicates that stability of attachment classification is greater for secure than for insecure attachments.[79] Presumably the positive cycle of mutual and self-perpetuating satisfaction of parent and child maintains the secure attachment.

Stressful life events that exceed the capacity of the parent's coping strategies (such as parental separation from the child and residential changes) predict changes from secure to insecure attachments. For example, one study found that the security of firstborns' attachment to mothers decreased following the birth of a sibling.[80] The decreases were greatest when firstborns were between the ages of two and five (as opposed to being under two), when mothers became depressed or anxious, and when mothers lacked support from a husband. In other studies, changes from insecure to secure attachment occurred when mothers became more sensitive and understanding caregivers. So, clearly, early attachments are not forged in steel but are affected by other life events and the personal qualities of mothers.

What about the modifiability of early cognitive functioning? Let us look first at language development. Here there appears to be a critical period that may last as long as ten years. Studies of children who have been deprived of language stimulation find that a child deprived of language until age six can, with time, learn to speak with correct grammar. If the child has been deprived until age thirteen, the child can learn only a few words and no grammar.[81]

It has long been known that babies are born with the ability to make all the sounds of all the languages in the world, but that they lose that capacity over time. They become limited to the sounds of language they hear routinely. Thus, if a child learns a foreign language before the age of ten, he will unlikely speak that language with an accent; after the age of ten, however, he will tend to speak with an accent. His brain will have become hardwired to produce the sounds heard routinely.

Until recently, the inability to make the sounds of other languages easily was thought to be irreversible. Recent research, however, shows that adults can be retrained to produce sounds not found in their native language. Using a computer that slows and elongates speech sounds enabled Japanese adults to carve out new neural circuits to distinguish the English-spoken sounds *L* and *R*, which in Japanese form a single sound.[82] Natural speech alone resulted in little or no improvement in the Japanese adults' ability to make these distinctions, but the exaggerated speech of the computer, as speech might be heard in infancy, followed by gradual training toward conversational speech produced results. So, under the right conditions, changes can occur in behavior thought to be irreversible.

When it comes to more general cognitive abilities, as noted in Chapter 1, early intervention programs improve cognitive and social functioning in children from poor families. But what about later interventions? Three examples of later stimulation are given here.

The first example involves a junior-senior high school on Long Island that initiated a program titled Success Through Academic Readiness (STAR) for twenty-seven ninth-graders who were failing.[83] The school was one of Long Island's very poorest, and the program, funded by the nonprofit Institute for Community Development, provided money for the additional staffing of a full-time psychologist, social worker, career and college coordinator, program director, and outreach worker. These people worked together to provide a level of attention and consistency that these students lacked in everyday life. These students received two additional hours of daily activities, including workshops on peer pressure, trips to museums, and tutoring. School counselors were assigned for the four-year period and were also available to students. Observers attribute the success of the program to the staff's emotional involvement and the relentless encouragement and support they gave the students. Help was always available, and when students missed class, phone calls were made to the home to inquire about problems, difficulties, and plans to return to school.

Four years after the inception of the program, twenty-five of the twenty-seven students were college-bound. In a comparable group of twenty-five students who did not accept the invitation to join the program, twenty-three had dropped out of school. Although the program cost $5,000 per year per pupil in addition to the $9,380 the district spent on each pupil, the total cost of $14,380 was still less than the $16,000 per year per pupil spent in wealthier neighboring districts. One can see here that the same emotional involvement and concern that predicted intellectual growth in middle-class toddlers helped to produce academic success in this group of economically impoverished, low-achieving students.

The second example involves an army program that provided educational opportunities for recruits despite their low scores on entrance tests.[84] Follow-up of 7,000 low-scoring recruits who remained in the army found that although only 66 percent had completed high school at the time of entrance, 96 percent had completed high school at the time of follow-up twelve to seventeen years later. At entry, only 1 percent had scores above the thirty-first percentile; at the time of the follow-up, however, 27 percent had achieved this score. So, learning opportunities extended to young adults also have benefits.

The third example comes from a longitudinal study of a representative sample of children followed from birth in the 1920s through childhood and adolescence and into middle age (thirty-six to forty-eight years of age).[85] Comparing late adolescent IQs with IQs obtained in middle age, researchers found that the group as a whole made modest gains in verbal, performance, and overall IQ scores. Eleven percent of the sample gained more than thirteen IQ points, and 11 percent decreased six or more IQ points. The group that decreased in IQ points contained many individuals who were heavy alcohol users and persons with debilitative illnesses. Those who increased in IQ points tended to be married to spouses whose IQs were ten points more than that of study members when they were adolescents. The researchers conclude that the results "encourage us to believe that means can be found to promote intellectual growth among adults, as they have for young children."

In Conclusion

Early experiences have significance because they shape the way the brain processes information, and they can set in motion self-perpetuating ways of responding to people and the world. There are few fixed windows of critical development unless deprivation is extreme and sustained. Stimulation, however, at any time in development leads to learning and accomplishment, and exciting results of new research, such as the computer-based retraining of adults' language discrimination, may help us find ways to increase individuals' development throughout life.

Parents continually develop new behaviors as they rear their children and as they deal with their frustrations as parents. So, it is not surprising that creating these new responses leads to permanent changes in parents themselves. However, there has been relatively little research on parents' changes as a result of parenting.

Ellen Galinsky, a consultant and lecturer on child development, found herself changing after her children were born. Curious about the meaning of her feelings, she consulted books and research reports to see what other parents were describing. Finding little information, she began forming groups of parents of young children. She then interviewed 228 parents with different experiences of parenthood, including married, divorced, step-, foster-, and adoptive parents. These parents did not represent a random sampling but were a broad cross-section of the population.

Galinsky has divided parenthood into six stages in which parents focus their emotional and intellectual energy on a given task.[86] These stages differ from most in that a parent can be in more than one stage at a time with children of different ages. The first stage, occurring in pregnancy, she terms the *image-making stage*. It is a time when parents prepare for changes in themselves and in their relationships to others. The *nurturing stage* goes from birth to the time when the child starts to say "no," about eighteen to twenty-four months. As parents become attached to the new baby, they arrange their lives to be caregivers, balancing their own and their child's needs and setting priorities. The *authority stage* lasts from the time the child is two to four or five. Parents become rule givers and enforcers as they learn that their love for their child goes hand in hand with structure and order. From the child's preschool years through adolescence, parents are in the *interpretive stage*. The child is more skilled and independent, and parents establish a way of life for the child, interpret outside authorities such as teachers, and teach values and morals. In brief, they teach the child what life is all about. During the child's adolescence, parents enter the *interdependent stage*. They form new relationships with the child, and, though they are still authorities, their power becomes shared with the child in ways it was not in past years. In the sixth stage, the *departure stage*, parents evaluate themselves as their child prepares to leave home. They see where they have succeeded and where they might have acted differently.

Galinsky summarizes her views of how parenthood changes adults:

> Taking care of a small, dependent, growing person is transforming, because it brings us in touch with our baser side, it exposes our vulnerabilities as well as our nobility. We lose our sense of self, only to find it and have it change again and again. We learn to nurture and care. We struggle through defining our own rules and our own brand of being an authority. We figure out how we want to interpret the wider world, and we learn to interact with all those who affect our children. When our children are teenagers, we redefine our relationships, and then we launch them into life.
>
> Often our fantasies are laid bare, our dreams are in a constant tug of war with realities. And perhaps we grow. In the end, we have learned more about ourselves, about the cycles of life, and humanity itself. Most parents describe themselves as more responsible, more accepting, more generous than before they had children.[87]

The Joys of Being A Parent

"It has changed my priorities, my perspective. I am much more protective. If I see someone driving like an idiot, I get much more upset. I feel more like a regular person, more grown up." —*Father of toddler*

"Now I'm officially grown up. It's kind of funny because I am a forty-year-old person who is just feeling grown up. For me, it's being less caught up in myself, more unselfish, I don't do everything I want to do all the time, and that's changing and it's okay. I used to resent that. I am less self-centered, less concerned with myself and how I'm doing, how I'm feeling, what's up. Now I am thinking more about him. For both my husband and me, I don't know whether this is going to change, but we are more oriented toward the future." —*Mother of toddler*

"My own personal sense of the meaningfulness of life, in all aspects, has really gone through a dramatic change. It's just been so gratifying and meaningful and important to have this other little life, in a sense, in my hands, to be responsible for it." —*Mother of toddler*

"It has changed my sense of the past. I appreciate more of what my parents must have gone through for me. No matter what their problems or shortcomings, gee, they had to do all this for me." —*Father of toddler*

"It's that overused word, *maturity*. It happened for both of us, my husband and me. We look back on how our lives were before our son and afterwards. Our whole lives were what we wanted every hour of every day. Along came the baby and, by choice, there was a reverse, almost 100 percent. We don't get to go out like we used to. It seems like an agony sometimes, but we are growing as a couple and as a family. It's very enriching." —*Mother of toddler*

Main Points

Parents' job involves providing

- physical and emotional care and protection
- education, values, and discipline

Specific competencies of children

- include physical, intellectual, emotional, social, and moral competence as well as self-esteem
- depend on parents' direct involvement in providing opportunities for growth in each competency
- stem from parents' own competency and modeling
- are affected by parenting style: authoritative, authoritarian, or permissive

"It has changed me for the better. It matured me, really at the core. I am much more responsible because I want to be a good example for them, provide stability for them. It has helped me to see into myself. I recall things I did as a child, and I understand better what was happening then. It has changed the kinds of things I think of as fun." —*Father of elementary school child and early adolescent*

"I wish I could say it has made me more patient, but it has intensified my emotions; and if something really difficult has happened, as it did today when she destroyed something I took a lot of time to make for her, because she didn't follow a simple rule, then I am amazed at how furious I feel. Yet a little while later, the great love I have for her made forgiveness easy, and I sat down and started to make the whole thing over. So now I have extremes of feeling from great love to great anger." —*Mother of elementary school child and early adolescent*

"Having children makes you more patient, more humble, better able to roll with the punches because life is not so black and white. You can't just base your life on platitudes. You have the experience of having things go not the way you would have them go, having your children do things you would not have them do; and you have to roll with that. You learn it; it either kills you or you go on, and you have a different view of life. You become more patient and, I think, more kind." —*Mother of early and late adolescents*

"I want to be a good father so it makes me evaluate what I do and say; I look at mistakes as you would in any important and intense relationship, so it certainly makes me more self-examining and more aware of myself and how I am being experienced by the other person. It is also a challenge to be tolerant when I don't feel very tolerant. So in developing certain interpersonal skills, I think being a parent has helped me to become a better person." —*Father of elementary school child*

Parents encourage children's competencies in all areas when they

- model competent behavior themselves
- form positive attachments and maintain a harmonious home atmosphere in which feelings are expressed in a regulated way
- provide opportunities for independent exploration and action in the world
- guide children's actions so children achieve their goals
- provide emotional support for children's efforts
- arrange appropriate experiences to stimulate social and moral development
- use reasoning and positive rewards and avoid harsh, physical punishments

Parents learn parenting behaviors from

- culture, which provides parents with values, goals, and strategies
- early experiences with their own parents that establish ways of relating to others and interpreting their behavior

Sensitive, responsive parenting in the very early years of life

- helps regulate the child's physical system
- influences ways the child's brain organizes and handles stimulation
- can set in motion for the child self-perpetuating ways of relating to the world and others
- does not predict functioning throughout childhood

As they raise children, parents go through the stages of

- being the image-makers, nurturers, and authorities in their children's lives
- interpreting the world to and being interdependent with children
- preparing for their children's departure from home

Exercises

1. Erikson's theory of life span development focuses on the importance of positive experiences and strengths. Review your own life in terms of positive experiences you have had and the strengths you feel you have developed. For example, you may have developed a love of the outdoors from camping activities with your family. Temporarily sacrificing the luxuries of home and having to provide for your needs may have given you the strengths of independence and responsibility.

2. Rate yourself on the dimensions Susan Harter says college students use to describe themselves. (See Table 2.1.) For each dimension, rate yourself on a seven-point scale (1 = low; 7 = high) in terms of where you want to be on these dimensions and where you think you are. Note where you have strong feelings of competence. Also rate yourself on global self-worth on a seven-point scale. What dimensions seem to be most strongly related to your feelings of global self-worth?

3. Describe how you think you and your siblings have changed your parents as individuals. If possible, interview your parents about how they changed in the course of rearing you and your brothers and sisters.

4. To get an idea of the range of values in rearing children, interview a classmate or interview parents of different ethnic groups in the community to determine their values in childrearing: (a) What kind of child do they want to raise? (b) How much help do they anticipate from family and friends? (c) Will caregivers outside the family be used? (d) How much contact will there be with different generations? (e) What disciplinary techniques do they think they will use? (f) Do they have very different expectations about raising boys and girls? (g) How much independence will they encourage in their children?

5. Interview classmates about the three competencies they most want their children to develop. Why do they think these are the most important qualities to have? Do they think other competencies will be more valuable later? What are they?

Additional Readings

Erikson, Erik H. *Childhood and Society.* 2d ed. New York: Norton, 1963.

Galinsky, Ellen. *The Six Stages of Parenthood.* Reading, MA: Addison-Wesley, 1987.

Goleman, Daniel. *Emotional Intelligence.* New York: Bantam Books, 1995.

Guarendi, Ray, with David Eich. *Back to the Family.* New York: Simon & Schuster, 1991.

Wilson, James Q. *The Moral Sense.* New York: Free Press, 1993.

3

Establishing Close Emotional Relationships with Children

THE FIRST PARENTING TASK—ESTABLISHING A CLOSE emotional relationship with a child—sounds easy enough. But how do parents create close ties with their children? How do they help children to understand and express their feelings? What do parents do when they feel angry? How do they reduce stress and maintain harmony in the family?

When you ask adults why they want to have children, parents and nonparents of all ethnic backgrounds cite the love and emotional closeness that comes with parenting as the most important reason for having children.[1] Box 3.1 lists the seven major reasons adults give. When parents speak of the love they have for their children, they speak of its special quality. One father says, "It's the first time in my life I know what the term 'unconditional love' means. The wonder of this little girl and nature, I have never experienced anything like that. It is 'Yes' without any 'Buts.'" Psychologists Urie Bronfenbrenner and Pamela Morris refer to the "irrational attachment" that parents have with children.[2] Close emotional relationships involve strong positive feelings, but there are negative feelings too—stress, anger, frustration. This chapter describes the many ways families form and strengthen the emotional ties that are so essential for parents and children and how they foster love and caring and manage stress and anger.

BOX 3.1

Adults' Reasons for Wanting Children

1. Love and satisfying, close relationship with others
2. Stimulation and excitement of watching children grow
3. Means of self-development—becoming more responsible, more sensitive, more skilled in relationships
4. Way of achieving adult status—parenthood is "proof" of being mature
5. Sense of creativity and achievement in helping child grow
6. Expression of moral, religious belief
7. Utility—belief that children will care for parents when parents are older

Adapted from Lois Wladis Hoffman and Jean Denby Manis, "The Value of Children in the United States: A New Approach to the Study of Fertility," *Journal of Marriage and the Family* 41 (1979): 583–596.

Family Atmosphere

Here, we look at what parents can do to build the close relationships they want and to manage the factors that interfere with that closeness.

Close Emotional Relationships

Parents begin to form a positive parental relationship when they love the child as a special person. Dorothy Briggs describes the psychological climate that enables children to feel their parents' love: "Nurturing love is tender caring—valuing a child just because he exists. It comes when you see your youngster as special and dear—even though you may not approve of all that he does."[3] Children are loved simply because they exist—no strings attached, no standards to meet. This is the "unconditional support" that Susan Harter refers to in her interview in Chapter 2.

Loving attention to a child creates a close relationship in which the parent and child share experiences, understandings, joint intentions. Shared reciprocal interactions lead to mutual understanding and a state of intersubjectivity, or shared meanings.[4] Parent and child create a relationship in which both participate; they form a unit that one cannot reduce to separate individuals.

Parents form close relationships with children of all ages in two basic ways—by providing sensitive, responsive care that meets the child's needs and by becoming an interactive social partner who shares the child's response to life's experiences. Sensitive, responsive care fosters the child's feelings of security and closeness to the parent. Sensitive care changes with the age and individual qualities of the child, as we detail in later chapters.

Becoming a social partner who provides appropriate stimulation and shares the child's experiences and pleasures in life takes many forms depending on the age of

74

CHAPTER 3
*Establishing
Close
Emotional
Relationships
with Children*

Interview
with Emmy E. Werner

Emmy E. Werner is research professor of human development at the University of California, Davis. For three decades, she and her colleagues Jessie Bierman and Fern French at the University of California, Berkeley, and Ruth Smith, a clinical psychologist on the Hawaiian island of Kauai, have conducted the Kauai Longitudinal Study, resulting in books such as *Vulnerable but Invincible*, *The Children of Kauai*, *Kauai's Children Come of Age*, and *Overcoming the Odds*.

From your experience of watching children at risk grow up on Kauai, what would you say parents can do to support children, to help maximize their child's potential? From your work with children at risk, what helps children survive and flourish even when faced with severe problems?

Let me say that, in our study, we studied the offspring of women whom we began to see at the end of the first trimester of pregnancy. We followed them during the pregnancy and delivery. We saw the children at ages one, two, and ten, late adolescence, and again at thirty-two and forty years. We have test scores, teachers' observations, and interview material at different times on these people. We have a group of children who were at high risk because of four or more factors. They were children who (1) experienced prenatal or perinatal complications, (2) grew up in poverty, (3) lived in a dysfunctional family with one or more problems, and (4) had a parent with alcohol or mental health problems.

You ask me to comment on parenting and what parents can do, but first I would like to urge that we redefine and extend the definition of parenting to cast a wider set and include people who provide love in the lives of children. I like to talk about *alloparenting*, the parenting of children by alternate people who are not the biological parents—they can be relatives, neighbors, siblings.

In our study of vulnerable but invincible children, we found that a major protective factor was that at least one person, perhaps a biological parent, or a grandparent, or an older sibling, accepted them unconditionally. That one person made the child feel special, very, very special. These parent figures made the child feel special through acts. They conveyed their love through deeds. They acted as models for the child. They didn't pretend the child had no handicap or problem, but what they conveyed was, "You matter to me, and you are special."

Now, another theme in our findings is that the parent figure, whoever he or she was, encouraged the child to reach out to others beyond the family—to seek out a friendly neighbor, a parent of one of their boy or girl friends, and, thus, learn about normal parenting from other families.

the child. In infancy, the parent engages the child, smiling, laughing, talking, tickling. The parent matches his or her behavior to the baby's rhythm and tempo and gives the baby opportunities to initiate or withdraw from activity, so the baby is a true partner in the interaction. This partnership continues throughout childhood and adolescence.

The resilient child was temperamentally engaging. He or she encouraged interaction with others outside the home and was given the opportunity to relate to others.

I had no preconceptions about this protective factor, but what came through was that somewhere along the line, in the face of poverty, in the face of a handicap, faith has an abiding power. I'm not referring to faith in a narrow, denominational sense, but having someone in the family or outside of it who was saying, "Hey, you are having ups and downs, this will pass, you will get through this, and things will get better."

Another thing was that these children had an opportunity to care for themselves or others. They became nurturant and concerned, perhaps about a parent or a sibling. They practiced "required helpfulness."

Now, another protective factor is whether the children were able to develop a hobby that was a refuge and gave them respect among their peers. One of our study members said later, "If I had any doubts about whether I could make it, that hobby turned me around." The hobby was especially important as a buffer between the person and the chaos in the family. But it was not a hobby that isolated you from others; it nourished something you could share with other people.

As many of the children looked back, they describe how a positive relationship with a sibling was enduring and important. As adults they commented with surprise how supportive the relationship was and how these relationships were maintained despite great distances and despite dissimilarity in life and interests.

What did adults say they wanted to pass on to their own children?

Looking back as an adult, they felt that some sort of structure in their life was very important. Even though the family life was chaotic, if a parent imposed some reasonable rules and regulations, it was helpful.

They emphasized faith as something to hang on to and make this clear to their children. As parents now they are quite achievement motivated. They graduated from high school, and some went back and got additional training. They encourage their children to do well in school.

The main theme that runs through our data is the importance of a parent figure who says "you matter" and the child's ability to create his or her own environment. The children believed they could do it, someone gave them hope, and they succeeded against the odds.

As the baby grows, parents join the child in playing with toys and exploring the world; they respond to the child's pleasure, curiosity, and growing skills. The child's ability to talk brings an added dimension to the closeness. Alexander Luria has written that words enable human beings to deal with objects that are not physically present or directly perceived and with events in which they did not participate.[5] Words enable

76

CHAPTER 3
Establishing
Close
Emotional
Relationships
with Children

parents and children to understand each other's feelings more clearly and to share events that only one of them experienced directly. Words also allow greater mutual understanding as parents and children describe their individual reactions to an event they both experienced. As children grow more skillful, parents and children engage in more activities together—both recreational and work-related. Joint participation in a great variety of activities and events deepens closeness.

Thus far we have looked at close relationships from the point of view of how a parent promotes them. Let us look at the qualities children of different ages say they want in the "good parent" or "good mother." These qualities fall into the two broad categories of sensitive caregiver and social partner.

Preschoolers interviewed about the qualities of a good and a bad mommy and daddy suggest that good parents are physically affectionate and nurturant, especially in the area of providing food for children. In addition, good parents like to play games with their children and read to them, and they discipline them—that is, they keep children from doing things they should not, but they do not spank them or slap them in the face. Bad parents have the opposite qualities. They don't hug or kiss, don't fix food, don't play games. They hit and don't let children go outside. Bad parents are also described as generally irresponsible—they go through red lights, throw chairs at people, and don't read the newspaper.[6]

As children grow older, they continue to value nurturance and affection, but they also appreciate qualities reflecting psychological nurturance. Mothers' good qualities include "understanding feelings and moods," "being there when I need her," and "sticking up for me." Children continue to emphasize the limit-setting behaviors in a good mother—"She makes us eat fruit and vegetables," "She yells at me when I need it"—but they want their mother to consider their needs and wishes in setting the rules. Older children still enjoy mutual recreational time—playing, joking, building things together. Finally, as children get older, they appreciate the teaching activities of the good mother.[7]

The Power of Positive Feelings

In Chapter 2, we saw that positive attachments are powerful stimulants of competent behavior in parents and children. When parents have positive attachments to their own parents and to their partners, they are more likely to have secure attachments to their children. These secure attachments promote children's competent behavior in a variety of areas. When people are happy with each other, they are more likely to be understanding and sympathetic.[8]

Good feelings come from one's own actions and successes as well as from relationships. Kirk Felsman and George Vaillant, following the development of a sample of men from early adolescence to late middle life, identified boyhood competence as an important forerunner of adult mental health. Boyhood competence—a summary measure of working part-time, having household chores, participating in extracurricular activities, getting school grades commensurate with IQ, participating in school activities, and learning to make plans—generates feelings of effectiveness. Felsman and Vaillant write, "Perhaps what is most encouraging in the collective portrait of these men's lives is their enormous capacity for recovery—evidence that the things that go right in our lives do predict future successes and the events that go wrong in our lives do not forever damn us."[9]

We do not always have a recent accomplishment to treasure, but studies reveal that if children simply think of some pleasant event for a short time, their performance improves and their behavior becomes more friendly, responsive, and responsible. These children resist temptation more successfully and respond to unfair treatment with fairness and generosity.[10]

Happy feelings serve as an inoculation against the effects of negative events. These good feelings are not just fleetingly helpful. Longitudinal research shows that how one spends leisure time, how one has fun in childhood, is more predictive of later psychological health than is the presence or absence of problems in childhood.[11]

Experiencing positive feelings not only helps family members enjoy life and function more effectively; it also helps them handle problems. A program designed in Holland to reinforce potential family strengths focused on eight areas of positive parent-child communication (which are listed in Box 3.2).[12]

Increasing these positive forms of communication enabled families to improve their behaviors in all areas. For three to four months, social workers in Israel went into the homes of welfare families in which parents were having difficulties with preschool children. For the first ten or twenty minutes of the weekly hour-and-a-half visit, they videotaped family interactions. At the next visit, the workers and the family members watched the tape that workers had already reviewed for positive interactions. Workers identified and reinforced one form of positive parent-child interaction at each visit. Occasionally, the workers modeled a positive interaction not yet observed in the family.

Prior to the intervention, few of the families interacted positively with their children—rarely making positive comments to children about their behaviors or sharing pleasurable times with them. The families receiving the intervention went from a mean of 1.83 on an index of positive parent-child communication at the start of the program to a mean of 8.04 at the end of the visits, and they maintained these changes six months after the program ended. The mean index of a group of control families who did not receive visits was unchanged over a comparable period of time.

The intervention concentrated on positive behaviors, but an index of negative interactions—shouting at children, hitting them, and ignoring their attempts to get close—declined as well. There were nonsignificant declines in shouting and hitting but significant declines in ignoring children's bids for closeness. When children cried or sought attention for a problem, parents were more likely to pick them up or give them some other form of attention. So, focusing on the positive did not increase the family closeness that was maintained over time.

Although closeness is enjoyable for and helpful to children, some parents do not feel good about themselves or some of their own qualities, causing them to wonder if their children might not be better off remaining distant from them. They fear their children will pick up their bad qualities. Research on close and nonclose relation-

78

CHAPTER 3
*Establishing
Close
Emotional
Relationships
with Children*

BOX 3.2

Eight Forms of Positive Parent-Child Communication

1. *Naming with approval.* The parent provides a positive verbal description of what is occurring when the parent and child interact so the child understands the significance of the interaction.

2. *Taking turns.* All family members have an opportunity to express themselves and gain the appropriate attention from other members; no one is left out.

3. *Strengthening the weak link.* Any family member who is less interactive and assertive, be it child or adult, is encouraged to be more active.

4. *Following.* The parent makes verbal and nonverbal responses following an interaction with the child. The parent comments on the interaction and looks at the child.

5. *Saying yes.* The parent phrases all directions to the child in terms of what the child is to do—"Carry your coat," not "Don't drag your coat on the floor."

6. *Supporting initiative.* Any initiative the child makes to learn something receives a positive response from the parent.

7. *Taking the lead.* The parent takes action and guides the child's behavior so the child knows what is expected and that the parent is in charge.

8. *Sharing pleasant moments.* The parent takes time to enjoy the child and share in pleasurable moments.

These eight activities are sufficiently broad that they can be adapted to interactions with growing children of any age, though there might be less saying yes and taking the lead with teenagers or older children than with younger ones.

Adapted from Anita Weiner, Haggai Kuppermintz, and David Guttmann, "Video Home Training (The Orion Project): A Short-Term Preventive and Treatment Intervention for Families of Young Children," *Family Process* 33 (1994): 441–453.

---

ships among adolescents and their parents revealed that children who feel close to their parents are less likely to take on the parents' negativism than are children who feel distant. Parents' negativism is a more potent influence on children when parents and children are not close.[13] Thus, even when parents have many self-doubts and self-criticism, closeness with them and all their failings is still a positive experience for their children.

The Disruptive Effects of Negative Feelings

We have long known that emotional extremes in parents, such as violent anger or clinical depression, affect children's behavior. We are increasingly aware as well that negative moods in the course of daily life—such as those caused by limited free time and the overall challenges of parenting—can also have adverse effects on parents' interactions with children and on children's behavior.

LACK OF TIME   Parents identify the lack of time with family as the greatest source of stress in family life.[14] The economic need for parents to work—and for some parents to have two jobs—means that in about two-thirds of families or more, both mothers and fathers are balancing home and work responsibilities. Adults, particularly parents of young children, feel rushed and starved for time, yet studies of time diaries over a thirty-year period and survey data on time use yield provocative findings. John Robinson and Geoffrey Godbey, summarizing their extensive work in *Time for Life*, point out that according to time diaries recorded by participants, adults overestimate the number of hours they work.[15] They also underestimate the amount of free time, defined as that time not spent in essential activities such as work, self-care, and family and household activities.

Robinson and Godbey argue that of the 168 hours available each week, about 68 go to sleep and necessary self-care such as eating and grooming. Of the 100 remaining hours, about 53, on average, go to work and direct family care, about 7 to discretionary self-care, and about 40 to free time. Parents of young children have less free time than do adults in other age groups—about 30 hours per week, occurring mostly on weekends, as compared to 40 hours for the average adult—but they still have about an hour more of free time than was available to parents in 1965. Single parents, Robinson and Godbey believe, have considerably less time with their children—about 3 hours less per week—so their children lose time with them and daily time with the absent parent in the case of divorce.

Many would argue with these conclusions, but Robinson and Godbey's data and analysis of others' data do point to the fact that people may have more free time than they realize and that feelings of "time-famine" have other causes. Robinson and Godbey believe that Americans feel rushed not because of extra work but because of the accelerated pace of life. They write,

> Speed and brevity are more widely admired, whether in serving food, in the length of magazine articles, or in conversation. As the pace of life has speeded up, there has been a natural tendency to assume that other time elements have been reshaped as well. Primary among these assumptions is that hours of work (duration) are increasing and that those who feel most rushed must work the longest hours.[16]

Feelings of lack of time may also come from the fact that Americans spend about 40 percent of their free time in an activity that gives them less satisfaction than most other leisure activities—namely, watching television. Thus, they do not take the time they have for more satisfying social activities and pursuits with family and friends. We discuss ways to decrease the stress of lack of time later in this chapter.

Interestingly, studies of time diaries reveal that children have increasingly less time for activities and conversations with parents.[17] A University of Michigan study found that in 1981, children had about 63 hours per week for discretionary activities—free time when they were not eating, sleeping, in school, or engaged in self-care. In 1997, they had only 51 hours, a 16 percent decline in free time. Time in school increased from 21 hours per week to 29 hours per week, and time spent in self-care and getting ready to go places increased as well. But time spent talking to parents decreased

80

CHAPTER 3
*Establishing
Close
Emotional
Relationships
with Children*

100 percent. In addition, parents and children have less time with each other because about 50 percent of children experience divorce, and many go back and forth between two households and thus see less of each parent. So, time pressures exist for both parents and children.

EVERYDAY NEGATIVE MOODS   Minor daily hassles at work or with children contribute to parents' negative moods, which in turn affect parenting and children's behavior. Negative moods bias what parents recall about children's past behaviors, shape parents' interpretations of current behavior, and cause parents to discipline children more harshly.[18]

Hassles do not have to be intense or prolonged. In one study, even a briefly induced negative mood reduced mothers' positive comments and verbal interactions with their children during play and laboratory tasks.[19] And in another study, being distracted by a simple task involving anagrams resulted in parents' being less positive, more irritable, more critical of and more interfering with their preschoolers.[20]

The hassles that generally trigger a negative mood are the daily challenges of parenting rather than major difficulties with children.[21] Hassles fall into two broad categories: (1) the effort required to rear children—continually cleaning up messes, changing family plans, running errands to meet children's needs—and (2) the challenge of dealing with irritating behaviors such as whining, sibling fights, and constant demands.

Parents' personality characteristics, their coping styles, and the amount of support available to them can intensify or decrease stress.[22] Outgoing, sociable, optimistic parents are less likely to respond to hassles with negative moods. Parents who use avoidant coping styles, who wish stress would go away so they wouldn't have to deal with it, experience increased stress. Parents who use positive reappraisal of the situation, who feel they are learning from the situation and becoming more skilled, experience decreased stress and retain their self-confidence.

EVERYDAY ANGER   Many researchers have documented that when children are exposed to different forms of anger, they respond with emotional arousal that triggers changes in heart rate and blood pressure,[23] as well as the production of hormones.[24] Whether the angry interaction is actually observed or only heard from another room or whether only angry silence is observed, young children react in a variety of ways.

A majority of children show signs of anger, concern, sadness, and general distress that can disrupt play, lead to increased aggressiveness, or result in attempts to end the conflict or comfort the participant.[25] Almost half of children primarily feel distress with a strong desire to end the fight. Slightly over a third of children are ambivalent, revealing both high emotional arousal and upset but at the same time reporting that they are happy. A small percentage (15 percent) give no response. The ambivalent child is the one who becomes more aggressive in behavior.

Not surprisingly, then, children exposed to parents' fighting at home have strong physiological and social reactions to anger.[26] They are more likely to comfort the mother if she is involved in an angry exchange in a laboratory setting. With their friends, they characteristically play at a less involved level; and when anger occurs, they find it very hard to handle.

When parents achieve a fair compromise to a conflict, children feel minimal stress.

Children are particularly upset when arguments center on child-related issues or when parents imply children are to blame for the argument.[27] If parents reassure them that they are not to blame, children are less distressed. But when children feel conflict is their fault, they are likely to intervene to try to stop it. Even children as young as four believe they can reduce parental anger, and, in part, they are right.[28] Parents say they are more likely to stop fighting when young children ages four to six intervene. Older children believe there is less they can do to stop parents from fighting—and they are right, because parents pay less attention to their pleas.

Does this mean that parents should never fight or disagree in front of children? No. Conflict is a natural part of life when people live closely together, and children may need to observe how conflicts are settled to learn these skills themselves. In their work, Mark Cummings and his associates discovered that children who viewed angry adults who found a compromise to a situation had emotional reactions that were indistinguishable from their responses when viewing friendly interactions.[29] They had the most negative reactions to continued fighting and the "silent treatment." Their responses to submissions or changes in the topic indicated that they did not consider the situation resolved. So, what is most important to children is whether adults achieve a fair compromise to settle conflicts after they erupt.

Even when there is no particular distress, family members, both parents and children ages five to fifteen, see themselves as major causes of angry feelings in others.[30] Fathers (for whom there is limited information because they were not questioned in as much detail) and children of all ages saw themselves as the major cause of mothers'

82

CHAPTER 3
Establishing
Close
Emotional
Relationships
with Children

anger. Although mothers cited more general reasons such as violence and poverty, when asked to keep diaries of what made them angry on a daily basis, they most often cited the noncompliance, destructiveness, and demanding nature of children. Thus, the children's perceptions appear accurate.

Children cited the family as the major source of their own anger and saw their happiness as coming from experiences outside the home with friends and personal accomplishments. In contrast, mothers thought children's happiness comes from the family and their anger from other experiences. This is how mothers attributed their own feelings—they saw the family as a major source of positive feelings and other experiences as a source of anger—and they assumed children view life in the same way.

Equally important, all family members believed they could change other members' feelings even when anger was involved. The majority of children believed they could alter their mothers' feelings—68 percent said they could make happy mothers angry, 68 percent said they could make sad mothers happy, and 63 percent said they could make angry mothers happy. Here there is agreement. Mothers said children could change their feelings dramatically, but they believed that they could alter children's feelings as well. Behavioral and verbal strategies were most frequently used by adults and children, but children also reported material reward strategies.

All family members saw anger as very much a part of family life. Children appeared the most accurate in seeing their behavior as a major cause of family anger—though on any given occasion they could be mistaken—and the family routines and demands as the major source of their own irritations.

Affective Processes in Parenting

As we have seen, family life involves strong positive and negative feelings on the part of parents and children. Children feel love and anger toward parents, and they arouse love and warmth, but they also trigger stress and conflict when they are young as often as fifteen times an hour.[31] For this reason, Theodore Dix presents a model of parenting that gives a central role to emotions in organizing parents' behavior with children.[32] He believes that parents' feelings determine how they view their children's behavior and how they respond to it. When parents are in a positive mood, they are more likely to be patient, understanding, and controlled with children than when they are in a negative mood. When feeling positive, parents are less threatened by children's noncompliance and resistance to rules, and they are likely to stay focused on the children's behavior that needs changing.

Parents' emotional states also determine the type, consistency, and effectiveness of the discipline they use. When angry, they may resort to physical punishment and carry it out more forcefully than they would otherwise. Dix concludes,

> Thus, perhaps more than any other single variable, parents' emotions reflect the health of parent-child relationships. They are barometers for the quality of parenting, the developmental outcomes that are likely for children, and the impact that environmental stresses and supports are having on the family.[33]

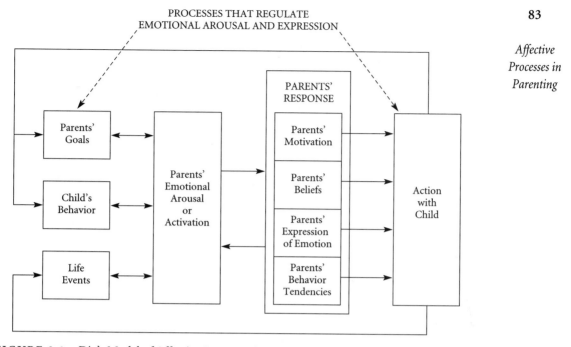

FIGURE 3.1 Dix's Model of Affective Processes in Parenting

Dix identifies three sources of parents' emotions: (1) parents' concerns and goals, (2) children's behavior, and (3) life events and social factors. The emotions, in turn, influence parents' motivations and beliefs about children and organize and energize parental behavior. Parents regulate and modulate emotional reactions so they are appropriate to the situation. Figure 3.1 depicts this model of affective parenting.

The following example illustrates Dix's model. A father has goals of raising an independent, curious child. On a particular day, however, he is frustrated and angry because his boss ignored his suggestions and gave impractical orders. When his four-year-old son asks numerous questions and insists on answers, the father, in his frustrated mood, views the child's behavior as defiance of his request to wait until later for the answers. He then punishes the child and feels worse because now he feels inadequate as a parent.

He talks his work situation over with his wife, makes positive plans, and feels better. When his persistent four-year-old returns in a few hours with new questions, the father, in a good mood, interprets the behavior as curiosity about the world and goes to the encyclopedia to look up the answers. The father feels good about taking the time to help his child. In each of the two situations, the father's goals and the child's behavior were the same. But the father's mood, negative in one instance and positive in the other, influenced his interpretation of the boy's behavior and his own response to it.

Fostering a Harmonious Family Atmosphere

CHAPTER 3
*Establishing
Close
Emotional
Relationships
with Children*

Strategies for creating the positive relationships with family members that are so important for development and well-being include (1) communicating feelings, (2) maintaining
a democratic family, (3) providing respect and encouragement for children, (4) providing
supportive parenting and (5) providing opportunities for self-expression. We turn first to
strategies for communicating feelings, which is at the heart of the parenting process.

Communicating Feelings

In a comprehensive survey concerning people's feelings about family life, participants
described their families as loving and caring. They reported, however, that they themselves lacked the skills to communicate these feelings to other family members and, as
a result, felt their families were not as close and supportive as they could be. The ways
to communicate feelings described in this section give parents the tools for expressing
their positive as well as their negative emotions.[34]

Haim Ginott describes emotions as follows:

> Emotions are part of our genetic heritage. Fish swim, birds fly, and people feel.
> Sometimes we are happy, sometimes we are not; but sometimes in our life we are sure
> to feel anger and fear, sadness and joy, greed and guilt, lust and scorn, delight and
> disgust. While we are not free to choose the emotions that arise in us, we are free to
> choose how and when to express them, provided we know what they are. That is the
> crux of the problem. Many people have been educated out of knowing what their
> feelings are. When they hated, they were told it was only dislike. When they were
> afraid, they were told there was nothing to be afraid of. When they felt pain, they were
> advised to be brave and smile. Many of our popular songs tell us "Pretend you are
> happy when you are not."
>
> What is suggested in place of this pretense? Truth. Emotional education can help
> children to know what they feel. It is more important for a child to know what he feels
> than why he feels it. When he knows clearly what his feelings are, he is less likely to
> feel "all mixed up" inside.
>
> How can we help a child to know his feelings? We can do so by serving as a mirror
> to his emotions. A child learns about his physical likeness by seeing his image in a
> mirror. He learns about his emotional likeness by hearing his feelings reflected by us.[35]

When parents feed back children's feelings, children feel understood, important, and
valuable as individuals. As their responses receive attention, their self-esteem grows.
How does one go about feeding back feelings? First, one pays attention and listens to
hear what the feelings are and then restates those perceptions in simple language.

ACTIVE LISTENING   *Active listening* is Thomas Gordon's term for what parents do
when they reflect their children's feelings.[36] Parents listen to children's statements, pay
careful attention to the feelings expressed, and then frame a response similar to the
child's statement. If a child says she feels too dumb to learn a school subject, the parent
might feed back that she feels she is not smart enough. In contrast, Ginott might feed

back a response about the child's fear, worry, or frustration. Gordon gives examples of feeding back responses about deeper feelings, so the difference between the two strategies is minimal. Following are Gordon's examples of active listening.

CHILD: I don't want to go to Bobby's birthday party tomorrow.

PARENT: Sounds like you and Bobby have had a problem maybe.

CHILD: I hate him, that's what. He's not fair.

PARENT: You really hate him because you feel he's been unfair somehow.

CHILD: Yeah. He never plays what I want to play.

CHILD: (Crying) I fell down on the sidewalk and scraped my knee. Oh, it's bleeding a lot! Look at it!

PARENT: You're really scared seeing all that blood.[37]

If the parent's response is accurate, the child confirms the feedback with a positive response. If the parent's interpretation is wrong, the child indicates that and has a chance to correct the misinterpretation by expanding on his feelings. The parent can continue active listening and gain greater understanding of what is happening to the child.

Active listening has many advantages. First, it helps children express feelings in a direct, effective way. As feelings are expressed and parents accept them, children feel understood and learn that they are like everyone else. When parents talk about feelings and help their children pay attention to others' feelings, their children understand and get along better with people.[38]

Second, as feelings are expressed, parents and children together learn that the obvious problem is not necessarily the real or basic problem. Like the rest of us, children use defenses and sometimes start by blaming a friend, a parent, or circumstances for what they are feeling. Sometimes, they initially deny that they are upset. As parents focus on the feelings, children gradually come to identify the underlying problem and discover what they can do about it.

Third, listening to children's feelings is sometimes all that's needed to resolve the problem. Often when we are upset, frustrated, sad, or angry, we simply want to express the feeling and have someone respond, "Yes, that's frustrating" or "It is really painful when a friend walks off with someone else and leaves you behind." The response validates the feeling as being justified and important, and frequently that is all we want.

What must parents do to become active listeners? First, Gordon warns parents not to attempt active listening when they are hurried or when they are preoccupied. Active listening should not be started if a parent is too busy to stay with it and really hear and respond to the child's feelings. Active listening requires persistence, patience, and a strong commitment to attend to both the child's words and accompanying behavioral clues. Furthermore, there are times when active listening is not appropriate. If a child asks for information, give the information. If a child does not want to talk about her

86

CHAPTER 3
Establishing
Close
Emotional
Relationships
with Children

feelings, respect the child's privacy and do not probe. Similarly, if active listening and the dialogue have gone as far as the child is willing to go, then a parent needs to recognize that it is time to stop.

One of the mothers in Ginott's group raised the question of reflecting back feelings of great sadness over a loss.[39] Is this wise? Does it help children? Might not such feelings overwhelm them? Ginott responded that parents must learn that suffering can strengthen a child's character. When a child is sad in response to a real loss, a parent need only empathize, "You are sad. I understand." The child learns that the parent is a person who understands and sympathizes.

I-MESSAGES   When a parent is angry, frustrated, or irritated with a child, the parent can communicate his or her feelings constructively with an *I-message* rather than nagging, yelling, or criticizing. The I-message contains three parts: (1) a clear statement of how the parent feels, (2) a statement of the behavior that has caused the parent to feel that way, and (3) a statement describing why the behavior is upsetting to the parent. For example, a parent frustrated with a teenager's messy room might say, "I feel upset and frustrated when I look at your messy room because the family works hard to make the house look clean and neat and your room spoils our efforts."

Parents need to spend time analyzing their feelings and becoming more aware of exactly how they feel. Gordon points out that, often, when a parent communicates anger at a child, the parent may actually be feeling disappointment, fear, frustration, or hurt. When a child comes home an hour late, the parent may launch into a tirade. The worry that grew into fear during the hour of waiting is transformed into relief that the child is safe, and that relief is then translated into angry words intended to prevent a recurrence of this disturbing behavior. Similarly, a parent may complain about a child's behavior when, in reality, what is disturbing the parent is a problem at work. The parent who has learned to use accurate I-messages is less likely to misplace anger and use a child as a scapegoat.

What should a parent do if a child pays no attention to I-messages? First, be sure the child can pay attention to the I-message. Don't try to communicate feelings when the child is rushing out of the house or is already deeply immersed in some other activity. If an I-message is then ignored, send another, more forceful message, in a firm tone of voice.

Sometimes, a child responds to an I-message with an I-message. For example, when a parent expresses distress because the lawn is not mowed, the daughter may reply that she feels annoyed because mowing interferes with her afterschool activities. At that point, the parent must "shift gears," as Gordon terms it, and reflect back the child's frustration by using active listening.

I-messages have several benefits. First, when parents use I-messages, they begin to take their own needs seriously. This process benefits all family relationships because parents feel freer—more themselves—in all areas of life. Second, children learn about the parents' reaction, which they may not have understood until the I-message. Third, children have an opportunity to engage in problem solving in response to I-messages. Even toddlers and preschoolers have ideas, not only for themselves but also for others.

Siblings often have good ideas about what may be bothering another child in the family. They think of things that might have escaped the attention of parents.

I-messages not only express parents' frustrations and unresolved feelings but also can convey appreciation—"I feel pleased when you help me with the dishes because then we have time to go to the store for your school supplies." I-messages are also useful in heading off problems and in helping children see that their parents have needs, too. These messages, termed *preventive I-messages*, express parents' future wants or needs and give children an opportunity to respond positively. For example, if a parent says, "I need quiet so I can drive the car," the child learns what to do to be helpful.

Although parents use I-messages most often to describe their feelings about children's behavior, parents can also use such statements to describe their reactions to other events. This does not mean discussing intimate details of adult life that may upset children; rather, it means discussing parents' reactions to important daily concerns. In the discussion of moral competence in Chapter 2, we saw that when parents describe their own feelings and what causes them, children are more sympathetic to others. Parents' honesty and openness may help children better understand and be more involved with others.

Establishing Democratic Family Living

Thomas Gordon and Rudolf Dreikurs both emphasize the importance of a democratic family atmosphere, but each gives a slightly different meaning to the concept. In *Teaching Children Self-Discipline*, Thomas Gordon describes his great concern about authoritarian families, in which parents control children through rewards and punishment.[40] He is highly critical of parents who manipulate children in order to change them into what the parents think is desirable. He dislikes the concept of praise because it implies that the parent is judging and evaluating the child in terms of some external standard. He also disapproves of punishment because it allows a powerful person to take advantage of a less powerful person, and he especially condemns physical punishment for children because it belittles them, makes them angry at and fearful of the parent, and does not work. Gordon also criticizes a permissive atmosphere as disorganized and even chaotic.

What Gordon does encourage is a democratic atmosphere in which children are accepted as they are, with important needs and wishes that at times conflict with others' needs. When there is a problem, parents send I-messages, reflecting their own thoughts and feelings, and engage in active listening to get the child's point of view. If a solution does not arise, then parents and children move on to mutual problem solving, which we will discuss in the next chapter.

According to Gordon, parents should never dictate solutions but should work cooperatively with children to form a plan that meets everyone's needs. Working together this way frees children from feeling judged, evaluated, or manipulated. Children and parents become partners in solving the hassles of life.

Dreikurs, too, believes that democratic family living provides an encouraging atmosphere in which the needs of children and parents receive equal respect and consid-

88

CHAPTER 3
*Establishing
Close
Emotional
Relationships
with Children*

eration, and in which responsibilities are shared.[41] Parents provide food, shelter, clothes, and recreation for children. Children, in turn, contribute to family functioning by doing chores and running errands. Material rewards are not given for doing a particular number of chores. When mutual respect among equal individuals is the rule in a family, members work together to do the jobs that are necessary for the welfare of all. To deny children the opportunity to do their share is to deny them an essential satisfaction in life. Democratic living ensures freedom for family members but does not imply an absence of rule. Dreikurs strongly favors structure in family life and believes that providing boundaries gives a child a feeling of security.

To help children follow routines, parents serve as models. They also teach children how to do routine tasks. Parents often expect children to be able to learn self-care and do household chores without any instruction, so they do not spend the time needed to teach children. How many parents have taught a child, step-by-step, how to make a bed or how to get dressed and then observed as the child increased in skill, giving added coaching as needed? An encouraging parent helps children to be both self-sufficient and involved with other people.

Providing Respect and Encouragement

Dreikurs believes that children have built-in capacities to develop in healthy, effective ways.[42] Because children seek to be active and competent, a parent's main task is to provide an environment that permits this development. The child's strongest desire is to belong to a group. From infancy the child seeks acceptance and importance within the family, but each child develops a unique path to family acceptance. The child accomplishes this task by using innate abilities and environmental forces to shape dynamic relationships with other family members.

Do parents usually help children discover their own strengths and abilities? No, says Dreikurs. Most often, parents tear down children's confidence with such comments as "What a mess you make" or "I can do it for you faster" or "You are too little to set the table." Dreikurs recommends that parents use encouragement to help children develop their abilities. He defines encouragement as a "continuous process aimed at giving the child a sense of self-respect and a sense of accomplishment."[43] Encouragement is expressed by word and deed.

A parent's facial expressions, tone of voice, gestures, and posture all tell children how the parent feels about them. In many different ways—warm cuddling, active play, gentle nurturing—a parent can communicate that children are worthwhile and capable of participating in social living. How does a parent provide encouragement for development? First, by respecting the child and, from infancy, permitting self-sufficiency in all possible situations. Babies, for example, are encouraged to entertain themselves; they are left alone at times to explore their fingers and toes, play with toys, and examine their surroundings. As soon as possible, they learn to feed themselves. Children as young as one or two are included in family chores and responsibilities as soon as they show any interest in helping. Even a toddler can empty a wastebasket and carry small, nonbreakable items to the dinner table.

Second, parents foster development by giving verbal encouragement, telling children specifically what they do well—"I like your painting with all the bright colors" and "You certainly picked up all your toys quickly, and that helps Daddy when he vacuums."

Third, parents offer encouragement when they teach children to ask for what they want. Children need to learn that parents cannot read their minds and that they must take an active role in saying what they want. As children try out new activities, parents should wait until children ask for help before giving it. If children ask for help, parents can start off by helping, or they can encourage children to begin without them and say they will be available later if the children cannot proceed. When parents give encouragement, they call attention to the challenge of the task—"It's hard practicing now, but you'll master the keys and really enjoy playing the piano as you get more experience."

Finally, parents encourage development when they emphasize children's gains. They show children how far they have come since starting the activity. Encouraging comments often refer to the completed task. But children soon learn that enjoyment comes from the process as well as from final success.

HANDLING MISTAKES   In all families, children make mistakes. Dreikurs describes parents' tendencies to overemphasize the errors children make. Parents want so much for children to grow up and do well that they sometimes point out every minor mistake and continually tell children what they must do to improve. Under such a regime, children may feel they have to be perfect to be accepted. That fear may immobilize the child. As Dreikurs observes,

> We all make mistakes. Very few are disastrous. Many times we won't even know that a given action is a mistake until after it is done and we see the results! Sometimes we even have to make the mistake in order to find out that it is a mistake. *We must have the courage to be imperfect*—and to allow our children also to be imperfect. Only in this way can we function, progress, and grow. Our children will maintain their courage and learn more readily if we minimize the mistakes and direct their attention toward the positive. "What is to be done now that the mistake is made" leads to progress forward and stimulates courage. Making a mistake is not nearly as important as what we do about it afterward.[44]

When children learn a healthy attitude toward mistakes early on, they are freer to explore and act; as a result, they learn and accomplish more. A healthy attitude consists of believing that mistakes are an expected part of life; though often accidental, they do have causes and many times can be prevented. So children and parents can learn to look at mistakes carefully and find out what to do differently the next time. Mistakes are proof that the child is trying to do something but may not be quite ready to achieve the goal. Mistakes are incompletions, not failures. The child can take more time learning the activity or perhaps practicing to achieve the goal.

Though unfortunate in the sense that they take up time and sometimes cost money, mistakes are rarely disastrous or damaging. To the contrary, they are very often valuable experiences because a child learns what is not effective. In addition, many warm family memories center on mistakes that were overcome.

90

CHAPTER 3
Establishing
Close
Emotional
Relationships
with Children

Research supports Dreikurs's advice on handling mistakes and documents the power of parents' explanatory style in shaping children's way of thinking about themselves and their abilities.[45] Some children, at a very early age, show vulnerability to criticism. After receiving criticism about a single mistake, they generalize the criticism to their overall ability and feel helpless and inadequate. Vulnerable children five to six years of age who lack a clear concept of ability interpret the criticism as a comment on their goodness or badness as a person. When children feel helpless and inadequate, they give up and find it very hard to improve. Sensitive children are more likely than confident children to report that parents make critical comments about their mistakes. Sadly, even very young children internalize these comments and feel helpless and inadequate when they make a mistake.

Martin Seligman, who has studied the widespread effects of optimistic and pessimistic attitudes toward adversity, advises parents to teach children how to dispute global, pessimistic beliefs or interpretations of mistakes and difficulties.[46] Parents can teach children that a negative event has many causes, some beyond their control. For example, a student may get a poor grade on a test because she did not study enough, the test was unusually hard, the class has many bright students and the test was graded on a curve, the teacher came late and allowed less time for the exam, or the student was nervous and could not organize her answers as well. The student might blame herself, saying she is stupid, is going to fail the class, and won't be able to take more courses in that area. She is "latching onto the worst of these possible causes—the most permanent, pervasive, and personal one."[47]

Parents can teach their children to dispute pessimistic interpretations with such questions as, "What is the evidence for my belief?" "What are other, less destructive, ways to look at this?" "What is the usefulness of this belief?" Seligman advises, "Focus on the changeable (not enough time spent studying), the specific (this particular exam was uncharacteristically hard), and the nonpersonal (the professor graded unfairly) causes."[48] Then parents and children can generate alternative explanations and future actions. Seligman calls his method the ABCDE—Adversity, Belief (usually negative), Consequences (usually negative), Disputation, Energization—method. This method is illustrated in Box 3.3.

EMPHASIZING IMPORTANCE VERSUS SELF-SUFFICIENCY   When children feel discouraged and unable to make positive contributions to the social group, they seek other ways to feel important and competent. Misbehavior results from the pursuit of goals that give feelings of importance instead of feelings of self-sufficiency and social integration. Dreikurs identifies four "mistaken" goals of behavior—mistaken because they do not bring genuine feelings of competence and participation. These goals are attention, power, revenge, and inadequacy. The parent's task is (1) to understand which of the four mistaken goals is motivating the child's behavior and (2) to act so that the purpose is no longer achieved. Thus, the parent must understand the child's underlying feelings, but instead of reflecting back feelings, Dreikurs advises action to modify the child's behavior.

BOX 3.3

Dealing with Adversity

Adversity:	My teacher, Mr. Minner, yelled at me in front of the whole class, and everybody laughed.
Belief:	He hates me and now the whole class thinks I'm a jerk.
Consequences:	I felt really sad, and I wished that I could just disappear under my desk.
Disputation:	Just because Mr. Minner yelled at me, it doesn't mean he hates me. Mr. Minner yells at just about everybody, and he told our class we were his favorite class. I guess I was goofing around a little, so I don't blame him for getting mad. Everyone in the class, everyone except for maybe Linda but she's a goody-goody, but everyone else has been yelled at by Mr. Minner at *least* once, so I doubt they think I'm a jerk.
Energization:	I still feel a little sad about being yelled at, but not nearly as much, and I don't feel like disappearing under my desk anymore.

Martin E. P. Seligman, *Learned Optimism* (New York: Pocket Books, 1990), p. 241.

A child is seeking mistaken goals when his or her behavior conflicts with the needs of the situation. For example, a child may seek *attention* by being talkative and charming. This behavior can be pleasant and endearing rather than annoying, but when such behavior prevents others from talking, it becomes misbehavior.

When attention is denied, a child may hunt for an issue to use in the struggle for *power*. For example, a three-year-old may insist that he does not have to go to bed at 7:30 p.m. If he persists, running around the house and causing his mother to spend time chasing him down, the child is struggling for power. Sometimes, parents find it hard to tell whether a child is seeking attention or power. Dreikurs points out that children usually stop the mistaken behavior after the first request if they are seeking attention but not if what they want is power. Attempts to stop the behavior only aggravate children's attempts to gain power.

When problems continue, children may intensify the power struggle and seek *revenge* and retaliation. Here, children have lost hope of getting approval through positive behavior and feel they have nothing to lose, so they seek revenge as a means of feeling important. Children are determined to feel important even if they have to hurt others physically.

Dreikurs notes that this form of misbehavior is particularly sad because the children who need the most encouragement are the ones most likely to be punished. Parents need to offer warm understanding and sympathetic acceptance so that children can express their own positive qualities. Unfortunately, punishment intensifies anger and guilt, leads to further attempts to provoke the parents, and sets up a vicious cycle.

92

CHAPTER 3
*Establishing
Close
Emotional
Relationships
with Children*

Children who claim *inadequacy* to explain poor performance in some activity also pursue a mistaken goal. Dreikurs gives the example of an eight-year-old boy who was having school difficulties. The teacher told the mother he was a poor reader, was slow in all subjects, and showed no improvement despite the teacher's extra efforts. She asked the mother what he did at home. The mother replied that he did not like chores and did them so poorly that she had stopped asking him. The child had developed a low opinion of his abilities over a period of time and found it easiest to claim incompetence. Feelings of helplessness exaggerate any real or imagined problem. In such a situation, a parent can demonstrate the chores and work with children until they feel competent to function alone. Encouragement helps children persist until they are able to finish a job independently.

Providing Supportive Parenting

Researchers have identified several dimensions of positive and supportive parenting that predict children's effective functioning.[49] An extensive study carried out family assessments when children were about to enter kindergarten. Researchers looked at parents' behavior with their children, their use of harsh punishment, and the quality of mother-child interactions. Using teachers' ratings and school records, they assessed children's adjustment as measured by children's social skills, academic performance, and behavior problems when children were in kindergarten and in sixth grade.

The researchers identified four dimensions of supportive parenting: mothers' warmth (because one-third of fathers were not interviewed, only mothers' ratings were used), proactive teaching, positive involvement with the child's social activities, and discipline based on reason and calm discussion. They found that early supportive parenting predicted children's academic success and social skills in kindergarten and six years later. Although the individual measures of supportive parenting were unrelated to one another, they all predicted some aspects of later adjustment even when the effects of harsh punishment were controlled for. Not only did supportive parenting predict greater success for the child; it seemed to buffer the child from the effects of adverse family situations such as low social status, single-parent status, or stressful family events that were often related to the development of behavior problems. Researchers speculate that supportive parents select from a wide variety of positive behaviors that are all related to positive outcomes.

Providing Opportunities for Self-Expression

Family relationships are most harmonious when both children and parents have outlets for expressing feelings. Activities such as daily physical exercise, drawing, modeling clay, painting, and cooking all serve as outlets to drain off tensions and irritations and provide individuals with additional sources of pleasure and feelings of competence. Wise parents provide children with a variety of outlets so that they develop many skills. Research indicates that childhood leisure activities, especially a wide variety—such as painting, reading, and participating in athletics—are more predictive of psychological health in adulthood than are the child's own personality characteristics in childhood. These activities promote self-confidence and self-esteem, which increase psychological health.[50]

Coaching Children to Manage Emotions

Recent research indicates that when parents coach their five-year-old children in how to deal with feelings, the children function better physically and psychologically when they are eight years old. They perform better academically and are socially more competent with peers. They are physically healthier as well, perhaps because coaching helps children modulate their emotional reactions, which, in turn, helps their physiological system function better.[51] Coaching involves all those behaviors recommended by Ginott and Gordon—listening to children's feelings, accepting and validating them, using I-messages regarding one's own feelings, and helping children solve problems while maintaining acceptable limits concerning the expression of feelings.

A study by John Gottman and his associates finds that parents differ in their attitudes and thoughts about how important feelings are in life. Some parents have heightened awareness of their own and their children's feelings and a strong conviction that feelings are a central part of life. Feelings signal that change is required. Anger serves to initiate action in frustrating situations, and sadness slows a person down to have time to cope with loss. These parents feel comfortable with their feelings, and they consider that a major parental task is to help their children live happily with their own emotional reactions. They do this by coaching children to label their reactions, validating the importance of their feelings whatever they might be, and teaching their children strategies for expressing the feelings appropriately. Feelings do not frighten these parents. Rather, parents see such feelings as opportunities to become closer to their children through sharing the strong reactions and teaching ways to handle them.

Other parents feel uncomfortable with feelings and seek one of three ways to handle the discomfort.[52] *Dismissive* parents minimize the importance of feelings, making light of or ignoring them because they believe the feelings may make matters worse. *Disapproving* parents criticize, judge, and punish children for the expression of feelings. These parents do not usually disapprove of all feelings, just a subgroup such as anger and sadness or just those feelings that arise under certain conditions such as a "minor event." Children of dismissive and disapproving parents have a hard time trusting their own judgment. By learning that their feelings are wrong, they come to believe there is something basically wrong with *them* for having the feelings. Because they have little experience in acknowledging and dealing with their feelings, they often have difficulty controlling them and solving problems. Finally, *laissez-faire* parents accept all feelings and often comfort the child when the child experiences a negative emotional reaction, but they do little to teach or guide the child in how to express feelings appropriately. These parents seem to believe that expressing the feelings in any form—whether appropriate or inappro-

94

CHAPTER 3
*Establishing
Close
Emotional
Relationships
with Children*

priate—will take care of the problem. Their children do not learn to cope with feelings constructively and have difficulty concentrating and learning in school and in making friends.

So, the three types of response—ignoring or criticizing feelings so they occur as little as possible and accepting all expressions of feeling without providing guidance for expression—lead to similar kinds of problems for children, such as the inability to regulate feelings and to feel comfortable with themselves and others. Coaching children not only helps them deal better with their feelings and with social and cognitive endeavors; it also frequently brings parents and children closer together because parents feel they really understand their children.

On the basis of their research, John Gottman and his colleagues describe five key steps in emotion coaching:[53]

Step 1: Parents recognize when they are having a feeling, what that feeling is, and when others are having feelings.

Step 2: Parents consider feelings opportunities for intimacy or teaching. When the child is upset, happy, or excited, parents see this as an opportunity to be close to the child and to teach the child how to express feelings appropriately.

Step 3: Parents listen empathically and validate the child's feelings. They use active listening skills and validate what the child feels without trying to argue the child out of the feeling.

Step 4: Parents help the child verbally label the feeling. The child may be confused about what he or she is feeling. Labeling the feeling is identifying the feeling, giving the child a word for the strong emotion; it is not telling the child how to feel. Labeling a feeling while the child is experiencing it appears to have a soothing effect on the child's nervous system. Labeling feelings also helps a child see he or she could have two feelings at the same time.

Step 5: Parents set limits while helping the child solve the problem. Parents limit the way feelings are expressed; they do not, however, limit the child's having the feeling itself. Anger, for example, is acceptable, but hitting a sibling is not. Parents help the child think of possible actions to express feelings and ways to achieve his or her goals in the situation.

Several additional strategies help parents implement the five steps. First, parents avoid criticism, sarcasm, mockery, or humiliation when they talk to children about feelings. The importance of this advice cannot be overemphasized. In one study, parents' negative reactions (minimizing, becoming distressed, assigning punishment) in response to children's emotional reactions predicted poor emotional regulation and poor social functioning in children two to six years later.[54] No doubt there was a bidirectional influence with children's poor emotional regulation intensifying parents' negative responses. Still, parents' negative reactions predicted children's problem behaviors six to eight years later even when effects of early problem behavior and emotional regulation were controlled.

Second, in emotion coaching, parents use scaffolding and praise in teaching. *Scaffolding* is giving basic information or help to start the child out in problem solving. Parents give specific positive feedback to the child at the beginning and then let the child take over and handle the situation. Third, parents focus on the child's agenda, not on their own. If a child is upset while the parent is paying bills, the parent puts away the checks and focuses on the child. Parents' use of these steps and strategies enables children to feel comfortable with their emotions and to find appropriate means of expressing them.

Dealing with Negative Feelings

Active listening and I-messages help parents and children deal with negative feelings once they are aroused. But preventing stress is a major way to decrease negative feelings. Strategies to minimize hassles and negative feelings in the family include (1) creating family time, (2) developing a support system, (3) maintaining realistic expectations, and (4) learning ways to manage negative feelings.

Creating Family Time

As we noted earlier in this chapter, parents experience a time crunch. So what can parents do to feel less pressured and create more family time? Robinson and Godbey make several suggestions.[55] First, they suggest that parents might feel less pressured if they realized that their feelings of time-famine, although genuine, are not related to the actual number of free-time hours available to them. Keeping weekly time diaries will help parents see those blocks of time, mainly on weekends, during which they can fit valued activities. Free time is available in small chunks during the week, but parents must plan carefully to make good use of it. They write, "Free time requires commitment, imagination, reflection, and discipline if we are to use it wisely."[56]

Second, they advise parents to spend free time in activities that give them satisfaction. Television, as noted earlier, absorbs 40 percent of people's free time, despite the fact American adults do not rate it as satisfying as most other activities they engage in and list it as the first activity they would give up in a time crunch. What is the charm of television? "As an activity, television viewing requires no advance planning, costs next to nothing, requires no physical effort, seldom shocks or surprises, and can be done in the comfort of one's home—with pizza only a call away."[57] And as we noted, satisfying use of free time does require planning. But certainly a first step toward engaging in more rewarding activities might be to turn off the television.

Third, Robinson and Godbey voice their concern for what they term *time-deepening activities*—that is, doing two or more things at the same time to get maximal use of time. They believe that this contributes to people's feeling stressed and rushed. They describe a friend who wrecked the car while talking on the car phone as the audiotape was playing and the friend ate lunch from a McDonald's bag. Eating dinner while listening to the television and reading the newspaper is another example of such time-deepening activities that may only add to feeling rushed.

96

CHAPTER 3
Establishing
Close
Emotional
Relationships
with Children

Instead, Robinson and Godbey recommend efforts at time-savoring rather than time-saving.

> We need to reexamine our consciousness of everyday life—to become more aware of and thankful for the good things in life as they occur. Instead of time-saving skills, we need to cultivate time-savoring skills, in order to appreciate the simpler delights of life as they are occurring: the taste of good food, the presence of good company, and the delights of fun and silliness. To be happier and wiser, it is easier to increase appreciation levels more than efficiency levels. Only by appreciating more can we hope to have a sustainable society. While efficiency, at least as envisioned in American society, always starts with wanting more, appreciating may start both with valuing more what is already here and with wanting less.[58]

The authors find evidence in their survey data since 1995 that Americans may have begun to slow down. The percentage saying they had less free time than they did five years earlier dropped from 54 percent in 1991 to 45 percent in 1994/1995. The proportion saying they had about the right amount of free time increased from 35 percent in 1993 to 42 percent in 1995. Although it is unlikely that parents of young children fall in this group, parents can begin to chronicle what they do and how they can shift to do more truly satisfying activities with family members and others.

Developing a Support System

When parents get support from friends, relatives, and each other, they experience less stress and fewer negative moods. The support may come from organized parenting groups such as those attended by the couples in Carolyn Pape Cowan and Philip A. Cowan's study.[59] Those groups, which included both husband and wife, met over a long period and were shown to decrease couples' stress.

Joseph Procaccini and Mark Kiefaber outline an extended program to provide parents with varied kinds of support to prevent *parent burnout*, defined as "a downward drift toward physical, emotional, and spiritual exhaustion resulting from the combination of chronic high stress and perceived low personal growth and autonomy."[60] Parents feel worn out by meeting seemingly endless family needs, especially those of children, and they lose enthusiasm for parenting.

Enthusiastic, devoted parents actually are the ones most likely to burn out because they invest so much of themselves in the parenting process and want to be perfect. Procaccini and Kiefaber propose a six-week program of daily exercises to deal with burnout by substituting positive attitudes for negative ones and by changing behavior slowly. Woven into the program are eight important ingredients for reducing burnout: (1) getting information about children and parenting skills from books, (2) connecting with a significant other for support (spouse, relative, friend, minister), (3) becoming part of a small social group, (4) engaging in some goal-oriented activity (athletics, artistic pursuit, hobby), (5) gaining knowledge of oneself, (6) having access to money or credit, (7) developing spiritual or intellectual beliefs that provide meaning to life, and (8) maintaining self-nourishing activity. All eight are needed to buffer a parent against burnout. Note that only one ingredient, the first, bears directly on rearing chil-

When parents describe their own feelings and what causes them, children are more sympathetic and understanding of others.

dren. All the rest focus on helping the parent to become a competent, integrated person and on forging interpersonal connections with other people.

Research supports the findings of Procaccini and Kiefaber.[61] Parents who receive training in parenting skills and in techniques to reduce parental distress were more effective in managing their children's behavior than were parents who received information only on parenting skills.

Maintaining Realistic Expectations

We all approach new experiences with expectations. Expectations are built from what authorities tell us and what we and other people we know have actually experienced. If expectations are realistic, they can help us prepare for the event, function at our best, and elicit the most positive results for all who are involved.

Realistic expectations prevent the stress that results when the experience differs vastly from what was expected. Violated expectations lead to self-questioning and self-doubt. For example, for new parents, violated expectations are associated with lowered energy and lack of confidence as a parent.[62]

Parents' expectations also play a role in defining a hassle. For example, parents who grew up with siblings and have a realistic view of how much arguing siblings do are less stressed when their own children squabble. Having realistic expectations of children based on an understanding of their individual qualities and needs pre-

98

CHAPTER 3
*Establishing
Close
Emotional
Relationships
with Children*

vents parents from feeling stress, because children do not perform as the books say they should or as the parents did as children.[63] Parents develop realistic expectations from reading, from observing their own and other children, from talking to other parents and sharing problems with them, and from their own experiences as a parent.

Managing Negative Feelings

Because anger, stress, frustration, and guilt are all part of rearing children, parents need to find their own strategies for controlling the expression of these feelings. When these feelings lead to criticism, nagging, yelling, and hitting, both parents and children suffer. Children are hurt and discouraged; parents feel guilty and inadequate.

Nancy Samalin, who runs parent groups on dealing with anger, suggests that families compile lists of acceptable and unacceptable ways for parents and children to express anger.[64] Acceptable ways include such actions as crying, going for a walk, and yelling, "I'm mad." Unacceptable ways include destroying property, hitting, spitting, and swearing.

Of course, I-messages are the most direct way to express anger, but sometimes people want more physical outlets such as work or exercise. Box 3.4 lists a variety of ways to deal with anger.

To parents who feel guilty about or frustrated with the mistakes they have made, Jane Nelson, using Dreikurs's guidelines, suggests following a three-step recovery program: (1) recognize the mistake, (2) reconcile with the child by apologizing, and (3) resolve the problem with a mutually agreed-on solution.[65] Nelson advises parents to view mistakes as opportunities for learning. Seeing mistakes in that way reduces parents' self-criticism and their resistance to recognizing them. Apologizing is a behavior children can emulate when they have made a mistake. It also enables parents to experience children's quickness to forgive.

Dreikurs emphasizes that, like children, parents must develop the courage to be imperfect. He writes,

> The importance of courage in parents cannot be overemphasized. Whenever you feel dismayed or find yourselves thinking, "My gosh, I did it all wrong," be quick to recognize this symptom of your own discouragement; turn your attention to an academic and impersonal consideration of what can be done to make matters better. When you try a new technique and it works, be glad. When you fall back into old habits, don't reproach yourself. You need to constantly reinforce your own courage, and to do so, you need the "courage to be imperfect." Recall to your mind the times that you have succeeded, and try again. Dwelling on your mistakes saps your courage. Remember, one cannot build on weakness—only on strength. Admit humbly that you are bound to make mistakes and acknowledge them without a sense of loss in your personal value. This will do much to keep your courage up. Above all, remember that we are not working for perfection, but only for improvement. Watch for the little improvements, and when you find them relax and have faith in your ability to improve further.[66]

BOX 3.4

Eight Ways to Deal with Parental Anger

1. Exit or wait—taking time out is a way of maintaining and modeling self-control.
2. Make "I," not "you," statements to help the child understand your point of view.
3. Stay in the present—avoid talking about the past or future.
4. Avoid physical force and threats.
5. Be brief and to the point.
6. Put it in writing—a note or letter is a way of expressing your feelings in a way that the person can understand.
7. Focus on the essential—ask yourself whether what you are arguing about is really important and worth the energy involved.
8. Restore good feelings—talk over what happened calmly or give hugs or other indications that the fight is over.

Adapted from Nancy Samalin with Catherine Whitney, *Love and Anger: The Parental Dilemma* (New York: Penguin Books, 1992).

Increasing the Joys of Parenting

The challenges, hassles, and frustrations of parenting often obscure the real joys in rearing children. Yet it is the joys that compensate for, and at times completely eliminate, all the negative feelings. Despite their importance, little has been written about the joys of parenting. In a remarkable study fifty years ago, Arthur Jersild and his colleagues interviewed 544 parents about the joys and problems of childrearing. They introduce the book with the following comments:

> There has been relatively little systematic study of the cheerful side of the ledger of childrearing. Studies of characteristics that bring headaches to a parent have not been matched by surveys of characteristics that warm a parent's heart. . . . The fact that the emphasis has been so much on the negative side is perhaps no more than one should expect. Behavior that is disturbing to the parent or to others usually calls for action or for a solution of some sort, and as such it also attracts the research worker. On the other hand, what is pleasant can be enjoyed without further ado.[67]

Parents have many opportunities to be happy and to enjoy their children. In the interviews, parents reported 18,121 satisfactions, far more than the 7,654 problems described. The most common joys are easy to guess: the child's special qualities as a person, companionship and affection, parents' feelings of satisfaction in helping another person grow, and pleasure in watching the child's growth. What is not so easy to guess is that parents' joys, reported in Jersild's study and in this author's interviews with parents, relate to everyday experiences, everyday interactions—not outstanding achievements—that are readily available to all parents.

100

CHAPTER 3
*Establishing
Close
Emotional
Relationships
with Children*

Parents need not be interacting with children to experience pleasure. Parents can enjoy watching children in their daily lives—having fun with a playmate or a grandparent or exerting effort to accomplish a goal. Even disciplining a child can bring satisfaction in doing the right thing for the child. A father describes such a feeling:

> Another great joy is like painting a good picture or taking a good jump shot. It's doing something that is just right for your kids. It just hits the target. It might be, after reprimanding him and sending him to his room, going up and talking to him, telling him you love him and to come downstairs now. Just knowing how good a thing that is, how appropriate it is. It may be buying the fishing rod for a child that he desperately wanted. It is the pleasure of pleasing someone you care about and pleasing him on the basis of personal knowledge you have about him.

But Jersild and his coworkers were wrong that these pleasures can be enjoyed without further ado. Parental action is required to savor the daily joys often lost in the rush of life. Enjoying everyday interactions requires two rare commodities—parents' time and attention. Consider an out-of-town visitor's remark to a resident that she thought the town's greenery was really beautiful. The resident replied, "Oh, I never really notice it." That is what happens often with parents and children—the special and pleasurable qualities are overlooked. As Robinson and Godbey point out, savoring experiences brings richness to lives. When we do this, we get the rewards Jersild and his colleagues describe in concluding their study. About parenthood, they write, "Perhaps no other circumstance in life offers so many challenges to an individual's powers, so great an array of opportunities for appreciation, such a varied emotional and intellectual stimulation."[68]

Main Points

Close emotional ties rest on the parent's love for the child

- as a unique person
- expressed in sensitive daily care and in becoming a social partner
- and the mutual expression of feelings and thoughts

Positive feelings have power:

- happy people are more understanding and sympathetic
- childhood competencies and satisfactions contribute to later psychological health
- paying attention to positive interactions improves parent-child relationships

When parents listen to their child's feelings and reflect them,

- the child becomes increasingly able to identify feelings and to understand what their causes and consequences are
- the child learns that his or her own feelings are important
- the parents and child learn that the obvious problem is not always the real problem

When parents express their feelings, they send I-messages that

- help clarify their own feelings
- state how they feel, what behavior aroused the feelings, and why the behavior affects them
- convey a message about a problem, convey appreciation for a good act, or express their future wants or needs
- help their child understand their wishes and points of view

Emotion coaching

- involves the behaviors recommended by Ginott and Gordon
- is avoided by parents who instead are dismissive, disapproving, or laissez-faire
- involves five steps of identifying, labeling, and validating feelings and helping the child find appropriate ways to express them

Close relationships grow when parents

- encourage the child and give the child a sense of self-respect and accomplishment by allowing as much independence as possible
- avoid criticism that discourages the child and instead help the child deal with mistakes
- teach children to communicate their needs
- create a democratic family atmosphere of mutual respect and cooperation in accomplishing family tasks and resolving problems that arise

Dix presents a model of the process of parenting that describes

- emotion at the center as an organizing, directing force in parenting
- the child's characteristics, parents' goals, and life events as the main activators of parents' emotions
- emotion as a determiner of parents' view of the child's behavior and the parents' response to it
- regulatory processes that modulate and control parents' emotions

Disruptive negative feelings include

- stress from lack of time with family members
- daily hassles
- family anger

When adults express unresolved anger in the presence of a child, the anger

- produces feelings of sadness, anger, and guilt in the child
- makes it hard for the child to learn to express his or her own anger—some children become overly passive and others become overly aggressive
- makes the child assume blame for the anger and feel responsible for fixing the situation
- has minimal impact when parents resolve conflict fairly

102

CHAPTER 3
*Establishing
Close
Emotional
Relationships
with Children*

Strategies for dealing with negative feelings include

- creating family time
- developing a support system
- maintaining realistic expectations
- learning to deal with negative feelings

Exercises

1. Imagine a time when you were a child and felt very close to one of your parents (if you like, you can do the exercise for each of your parents), and describe your parent's behavior with you. What qualities did your parent show that created the closeness? Share these qualities with class members. Is there a common core? If you do this exercise with each of your parents, note gender differences. Do your mother and father at times show different qualities of closeness with you? Do your classmates experience differences in their mothers' and fathers' behavior toward sons and daughters?

2. Imagine a time when you were a child and felt very distant from one of your parents (again, you may do this for each of your parents), and describe your parent's behavior with you. What qualities did your parent show that created distance? Again, share these qualities with class members, and find the common core. Are these qualities the opposite of qualities that lead to closeness, or do they represent a variety of dimensions? Do the qualities you discovered in Exercises 1 and 2 support what clinicians and researchers say is important?

3. Take turns practicing active listening with a classmate. Have a partner active-listen as you describe one or several of the following situations, and then you active-listen as your partner does the same: (a) Describe a time when you were upset as a child. (b) Describe negative feelings in a recent exchange. (c) Describe scenes you have witnessed between parents and children in stores or restaurants. (d) Follow directions your instructor hands out for what one child in a problem situation might say.

4. With a classmate, practice sending I-messages. Again, choose from a variety of situations: (a) Recall a situation when a parent was angry at you when you were growing up and describe I-messages your parent might have sent. (b) Recall a recent disagreement with a friend or instructor and give appropriate I-messages. (c) Describe public parent-child confrontations you have witnessed and devise appropriate I-messages for the parents. (d) Devise I-messages for problem situations presented by your instructor.

5. (a) Select one of your minor faults or weak points. When did you first become aware of this fault? In many instances, it goes back to what your parents said to you when you were a child. Use Martin Seligman's ABCDE method of dealing with negative beliefs to give different interpretations to that quality. (b) Recall a recent example, no matter how minor, in which you confronted adversity and felt negative emotions. Follow Seligman's recommendations for dealing with them.

Additional Readings

Briggs, Dorothy. *Your Child's Self-Esteem.* Garden City, NY: Doubleday, 1970.

Faber, Adele, and Elaine Mazlish. *How to Talk So Kids Will Listen and Listen So Kids Will Talk.* New York: Rawson Wade, 1980.

Ginott, Haim G. *Between Parent and Child.* New York: Avon Books, 1969.

Gordon, Thomas. *P.E.T.: Parent Effectiveness Training.* New York: New American Library, 1975.

Gottman, John, with Joan DeClaire. *The Heart of Parenting: Raising an Emotionally Intelligent Child.* New York: Simon & Schuster, 1997.

Robinson, John P. and Godbey, Geoffrey. *Time for Life.* University Park, PA: Pennsylvania State University Press, 1997.

Seligman, Martin E. P. *Learned Optimism.* New York: Pocket Books, 1990.

4

Modifying Children's Behavior

MODIFYING A CHILD'S BEHAVIOR WITH FAIR AND firm limits challenges parents. Deciding what is "fair" is no simple task. What are realistic expectations for that particular child of that particular age? What behaviors are appropriate? Getting the child to meet the expectations that are set can be even more difficult. How do parents effectively communicate what they expect and what the limits are? What if expectations are clear but the child fails to meet them? To establish firm boundaries, parents must enforce limits by using appropriate problem-solving techniques to modify behavior.

Children do not naturally do all the things parents want them to do. When children are infants, crying and whining and fussing are their only means of drawing attention to what they need—food, a dry diaper, a burp, a hug. Their crying brings caregivers who satisfy their needs, thus reinforcing the crying. As children's skills increase, they develop more positive means to get what they want—asking, gaining cooperation from others, doing it themselves. Their parents' task is to encourage new behaviors to replace the coercive (forcing or pressuring) behaviors so natural to the infant.[1] In this chapter, we look at the many steps parents take to do this. We also focus on parenting strategies for children of different temperaments and different genders.

The Learning Process

As we saw in Chapter 2, parents have many different goals in helping their children become members of their social group. They want children to learn specific behaviors (staying out of the street, making requests with polite language), and they want children to learn values and morals (being kind to others, avoiding physical or psychologi-

Parents structure situations to prevent problems when they show children how to be helpful
in stores.

cal harm to others).[2] These values may vary somewhat according to the particular social group of the parents. But whatever their goals, parents take many actions to encourage children to adopt approved behaviors. The term *socialization* refers to the
process by which adults in a society help children acquire and refine the skills to meet
the demands of the social group.

Children learn in several ways. They learn by observing models and imitating
them. Models may be parents, siblings, or playmates. Children tend to imitate models
who are warm, nurturant, and powerful. When such models are unavailable, children
will imitate a cold, rejecting model.

Children also learn by the consequences of their actions. A reward or positive consequence increases the chance an action will occur again. Rewards may be pleasurable
internal feelings that are not observable. Often, rewards are external—getting attention, earning privileges, achieving a goal. When behavior leads to no reward or a negative consequence, then the behavior is less likely to occur than is a positively reinforced
action. Consequences are most effective when they immediately and consistently follow the behavior.

When parents use low-power strategies such as reasoning and helping children understand the consequences of their actions, their children are more likely to internalize
parents' rules and values than are children of parents who use high-power strategies
such as threatening and spanking.[3] Low-pressure strategies also enable children to learn

the procedures and behavioral scripts of everyday life. Children can then more easily think through the outcomes of different actions; they can run through a mental simulation of what will happen and make appropriate choices. As a result, children increase their understanding of their own behavior and others' reactions to them.[4]

In contrast, when parents use high-power strategies, children may conform quickly, but they are less likely to internalize the rules and more likely to follow them only as long as a powerful external authority is present. Further, they are likely to become angry and resistant to high-power strategies.

A new focus in learning emphasizes learning as a collaborative process.[5] Instead of looking at learning as a process in which children acquire information from experts and gradually approach competence, the collaborative process emphasizes the dynamic process in which individuals gain new behaviors and understandings in the course of adjusting to ongoing events and people. Learning is seen not in the acquisition of bits of knowledge but in the changing nature of the child's participation in activities.

The collaborative process of learning emphasizes that the child actively initiates learning, as seen in many of Jean Piaget's observations of children and, more recently, in an observational study of toddlers who initiated 82 percent of the interactions with a caregiver.[6] Parents provide support for learning, structuring the learning environment, engaging the child's interest and effort, tailoring the task to the child's level of ability, and providing support and guidance as the child learns to master the task. In many ways, the parent is a supportive coach who helps the child learn in the zone of proximal development, which we discussed in Chapter 2.

Promoting Learning

Parents take many actions to create a positive climate for the child's learning in a collaborative way. They establish a positive emotional climate, set realistic expectations of the child, structure the environment so the child can easily do what is asked, provide encouragement and support, and actively teach the child what they want them to do.

Establishing a Collaborative Atmosphere

Parents create an atmosphere of *receptive compliance*, defined as a "generalized willingness to cooperate with (or perhaps, 'exchange compliances with') a partner."[7] Sensitive parents, responsive to their children's needs, form secure attachments to their children and create a climate in which children tend to comply because their parents attend to their needs and wishes. The children act out of their commitment to the relationship with their parents. Throughout the learning process, parents give children the encouragement and support needed to persevere in the learning process that oftentimes can be frustrating.

Setting Realistic Expectations

Parents establish realistic expectations based on the child's age, temperament, and the family's needs and values. We discuss how parenting changes with the age of the child throughout the book. In a later section of this chapter, we describe how a child's temperament shapes parenting. The family's needs and values influence what parents expect. For example, when both parents are employed outside the home, it may be more important to finish chores before school, or if the family lives on a busy street, more emphasis may be placed on safety rules. Social and cultural values, as noted in Chapter 2 and discussed throughout the book, also shape many expectations about behaviors, such as independence, sociability, and respect for elders.

Helping Children Meet Expectations

Having established realistic expectations, parents help children meet them in several ways. First, they structure the child's physical environment. Parenting is easier when the family house can be arranged to meet children's needs, with play space available outdoors and furniture, rugs, and decorations selected with an active family in mind. Putting dangerous substances out of the way, having locks on drawers containing knives, clearly marking sliding glass doors—all these changes minimize the opportunities for children to harm themselves and help children lead safe, healthy lives. Figure 4.1 presents additional suggestions for childproofing a house.

Second, parents help children meet parental expectations by establishing a regular daily routine. A regular routine makes a habit of certain behaviors that children learn to do automatically. Most of us, in fact, function better with a regular routine of eating, sleeping, and exercising. Here again, however, children's individual tempos must be taken into account. For example, some children are slow to wake from sleep and so need more time in the morning to get started. Other children need more time to wind down at night, so their bedtime routines may have to be started earlier than usual.

Third, parents help children meet expectations by monitoring the amount of stimulation children receive. They schedule their children's activities in such a way that their children do not become overly tired or overly excited. For example, parents do not take a preschool child shopping all morning and then send the child off to a birthday party in the afternoon.

Fourth, parents prepare children for difficult situations or changes in routine. They may calmly rehearse a visit to the dentist, letting the child practice with a doll or stuffed animal, so the child will be much less likely to feel overwhelmed when the real event occurs. Parents can use rehearsal to prepare children for other changes in routine, such as a vacation or a change in day care.

Paying Attention to Positive Behaviors

As we noted earlier, when behaviors result in a positive consequence, the behavior is likely to occur again. Positive consequences can include internal pleasurable feelings. Children run and jump because it is fun. They draw and build because these activities are pleasurable. Parents have to do little to promote these behaviors.

But many times, parents provide the positive consequences that ensure a particular behavior will continue. Rewards or external positive consequences fall into two

Bedroom
1. Install devices that prevent windows from opening and child from getting out or falling out.
2. Cover electrical outlets.
3. Inspect toys for broken and jagged edges.

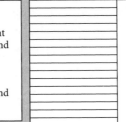

Stairs
1. Block off tops and bottoms of stairs.
2. If necessary, mark top and bottom steps.

Kitchen
1. Keep vomit-inducing syrup on hand.
2. Store soaps, cleaners, all poisonous chemicals in locked cabinet.
3. Have guard around burners or use back burners on stove so child cannot pull contents onto self.
4. Unplug all appliances when not in use.
5. Store sharp knives in safe place.
6. Store matches out of child's reach.

Bathroom
1. Keep safety caps on all bottles.
2. Keep medicines, aspirin, rubbing alcohol in locked cabinets.
3. Adjust water heater so water is not scalding hot.
4. Use rubber mats in bath and shower.
5. Keep bathmat next to tub and shower.
6. Do not allow young child alone in bath.

Dining Room
1. Cover electrical outlets.

Living Room
1. Cover electrical outlets.
2. Check safety of plants.
3. Put rubber-backed pad under small scatter rugs.
4. Pad sharp edges of tables.
5. Have screen for fireplace.

Garage/Workroom
1. Keep tools out of child's reach.
2. Keep poisons locked up.
3. Store paints and other toxic materials out of child's reach.
4. Store nails and screws in safe place.

Have lock for door.

General
1. Install smoke alarms in house.
2. Have fire extinguishers.
3. Plan fire escape routes.
4. Keep poison-control, fire, police-department numbers by telephone.

FIGURE 4.1   Childproofing the House. Adapted from *Working Mother*, October 1985.

broad categories—*social rewards* of attention, smiles, and approval, and *material rewards* of special gifts or purchases or special privileges and activities, such as an outing or having a friend over. Learning theorists encourage parents' use of social rewards, as they bring families closer together and create an atmosphere of trust.

Attention is the most positive consequence for children and often for adults as well. Parents are advised, then, to pay positive attention to the many ways in which their children change and conform their behavior to meet parents' requests. In the rush of everyday life, parents are quick to rush from one problem behavior to another and pay attention only when the child's behavior needs modifying. Thus the child hears only what requires changing and rarely hears appreciation for his or her positive actions. Parents are more successful when they attend to the positive more often than they make requests for change.

Sometimes positive attention alone is not sufficient to establish appropriate behaviors. Parents must actively teach children what they want them to do. Teaching approved behaviors and values is a two-pronged process: (1) parents send a clear, direct message to the child of what they want, its importance to the parents, and the expectation the child will comply with the request; and (2) children accept the message, consider the request fair, and fulfill it without feeling a loss of autonomy or self-respect.[8]

The most effective way to teach children is to have parents model the desired behavior. Because children may not spontaneously do what parents want them to do, parents show the child what they want done. They move very young children through the necessary steps, verbalizing each step as they go—"This is how you put on your shirt." Parents can break the task into separate units and describe what is being done while the child does it. Parents offer encouragement and praise after each step. After the child has thoroughly learned the behavior, only occasional praise is needed.

In some situations, the child is not able to carry out the behaviors the parents want to reward, so the parents must *shape* the child's existing behavior. For example, suppose a parent wants her five-year-old to begin making his bed and he does not know how. The first step for the parent is to decide what behaviors come closest to the specific behavior she wants the child to learn, such as pulling up the sheets and bedspread. She then rewards these behaviors. As the behaviors increase in frequency, she demands a higher level of performance—such as tucking in the sheets and smoothing the bedspread—before the reward is given.

Shaping behavior is also a useful approach with schoolchildren who get poor report cards. Parents can reward the highest passing grade on the first report card. They can then contract with children for rewards after the next report card if there are specific improvements. Because grading periods are usually six weeks long, parents may reward good test performance during that period or contract to give small regular rewards for teachers' weekly reports of acceptable work.

Establishing and Enforcing Rules for Appropriate Behavior

Theoretically, it is possible to raise children using only rewards and ignoring all misbehavior, which subsequently becomes extinguished for lack of reward. In everyday life, however, parents usually must deal with behavior that violates rules. When the child actively does something not approved, parents have two tasks before them: (1) stating limits effectively and then (2) enforcing them.

Stating Limits Effectively

When rules are clearly, specifically, and firmly stated, children are more likely to follow them than they are to comply with vaguely worded or implied rules. Say, "I want you to play outside for a while," not, "Be good this afternoon." Phrase the rule, if possible, in positive form, also stating its purpose. For example, say, "Carry your coat so it stays clean," not, "Don't drag your coat on the floor." Children respond well when rules are phrased in an impersonal way. "Bedtime is at eight" or "Dinner at six" is more likely to result in compliance than "You have to go to bed now" or "You have to be home for dinner at six."

When possible, give the children options—"You can have hot or cold cereal." Having choices gives children some control over what is happening. Parents can also give options when they prepare for changes in behavior. For example, they might say, "In five more swings, it is time to leave the park." This gives children a chance to get ready to follow the rule.

Parents might like to see many changes in their children's behavior, but parents are most effective when they prioritize rules. Health and safety rules are most important—staying out of the street, always letting parents know their whereabouts. Next are what might be called rules that ease social living—rules that make being together easier. This category includes rules against destroying other people's property and rules of general consideration such as being quiet when others are sleeping or being helpful with chores. Third in priority come conventional rules—how to use a napkin and silverware. Even young preschoolers are more impressed with the importance of kindness to others than with social conventions.[9] Last on the list are rules governing behaviors than involve the child's choice. What clothes to wear, what games to play, and so on are, in most cases, matters of the child's individual preference, unless a safety issue is involved. Parents need not expend enormous energies getting children to do things just as they would like them to in these areas of individual preferences.

Enforcing Limits

When rules have been stated clearly but children do not follow them, then parents need to enforce them. Before acting, however, parents must do two things. First, they must ask themselves whether their children continue to break the rule because, in some subtle way, parents are rewarding the rule-breaking behavior. Parents sometimes tell children to stop running or to stop teasing but then undermine themselves with a chuckle and a shake of the head to indicate that the child has a lot of spirit and that they admire that spirit. So the child continues.

Second, parents must be sure they are in general agreement about enforcing the rules. Parents who have big differences on enforcing rules should negotiate the differences with mutual problem-solving techniques. If parents frequently disagree, they may want to delay setting the consequence for a particular behavior until they have a chance to talk with each other, because children view such parental conflicts as justification to do what they want to do.

Parents have many options in enforcing limits, as the following sections explore.

MUTUAL PROBLEM SOLVING   Using Thomas Gordon's *mutual problem-solving technique* is a useful first step for enforcing limits.[10] Employing this approach, parents identify the rule breaking as a problem to them, a problem they want children to help them solve so that children, too, will be satisfied with the outcome. Parents solicit their children's opinions and work together to find a win-win solution agreeable to all concerned. For example, when children are consistently late for dinner or do not come to the table when called, parents present this as a problem they all must solve. The underlying assumption is that the family's working together can find an alternative that satisfies everyone. There are six steps to the problem-solving process: (1) defining the problem, (2) generating possible solutions, (3) evaluating possible solutions, (4) deciding on the best solution, (5) implementing the decision, and (6) doing a follow-up evaluation.

When an agreed-upon solution is followed, parents must send a strong I-message of disappointment and surprise as soon as possible. Perhaps the child can be helped to keep the agreement. Or perhaps another problem-solving session is needed. Gordon advises against the use of penalties to enforce agreements. Parents should assume children will cooperate instead of starting with a negative expectation expressed in the threat of punishment. Children frequently respond to trust.

Just as parents have behaviors they want children to perform, so children have objects, activities, and privileges they wish to attain. Using the behavioral system of *contracting*, parents offer desired rewards in exchange for the performance of certain activities. For example, if a child does her chores (making her bed, clearing the table) without reminders, she earns an extra fifteen minutes of time for playing. Likewise, an older child may be given use of the family car on the weekends if he maintains acceptable school grades and arrives home at the prescribed times.

NATURAL AND LOGICAL CONSEQUENCES The terms *natural consequences* and *logical consequences*[11] are used jointly and interchangeably but have slightly different meanings. Natural consequences are the direct result of a physical act. For example, if you do not eat dinner, you experience hunger. If you stay up late, you become tired. Logical consequences are those events that follow a social act. For example, if you lie, other people will not believe you. If you misuse the family car, your parents will not trust you with it. Natural and logical consequences are directly related to the act itself and are not usually imposed by others. Exceptions exist, however. A natural consequence of running out into a busy street is being hit by a car. To prevent such a consequence, parents generally use a logical consequence. If a child starts toward the street, the child's movements are restricted such as having to play in the house.

Logical consequences differ from punishment in several ways. Logical consequences are directly related to what the child has done—if children do not put their clothes in the laundry, they have no clean clothes. A punishment may have no logical relationship to what the child has done—a spanking is not the direct result of being late for a meal but is the result of the parent's authority. The method of logical consequences does not place moral blame or pass moral judgment on the child. The child has made a mistake and pays the price. The parent stands by as an adviser rather than a judge.

PUNISHMENTS If the preceding methods do not work, parents use punishments. Punishment means giving a behavior a negative consequence to decrease the likelihood of its recurrence. Punishments require varying degrees of effort on the parents' part. Before describing these, let us look at six general principles for using punishments: (1) Intervene early. Do not let the situation get out of control. As soon as the rule is violated,

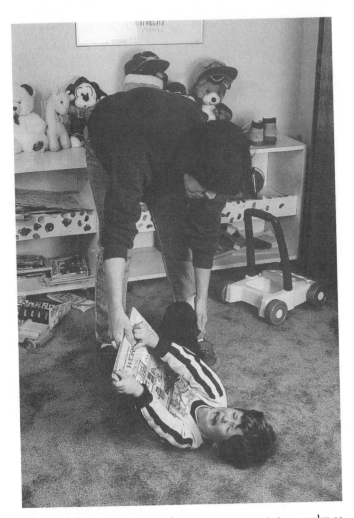

When children have anger outbursts, parents must stay as calm as possible so they can deal effectively with the children's behavior.

begin to take action. (2) Stay as calm and objective as possible. Sometimes, parents' upset and frustration are rewarding to the child. Parents' emotions can also distract the child from thinking about the rule violation. (3) State the rule that was violated. State it simply, and do not get into arguments about it. (4) Use a *mild* negative consequence. A mild consequence has the advantage that the child often devalues the activity itself and seems more likely to resist temptation and follow the rule in the future. (5) Use negative consequences consistently. Misbehaviors continue when they are sometimes punished and sometimes not. (6) Reinforce positive social behaviors as they occur afterward; parents do not want children to receive more punishments than rewards.

The following punishments range from mild to severe. First, *ignoring* might seem the easiest punishment in that the parent simply pays no attention to what the child says or does. It requires effort, however, because the parent must keep a neutral facial expression, look away, move away from the child, and give no verbal response or attention to what the child says or does. Ignoring is best for behaviors that may be annoying but are not harmful to anyone. For example, children's whining, sulking, or pouting behavior can be ignored.

A second punishment is *social disapproval.* Parents express in a few words, spoken in a firm voice with a disapproving facial expression, that they do not like the behavior. When children continue disapproved behavior, parents can institute a *consequence*—removing a privilege, using the time-out strategy, or imposing extra work. When families have contracts, children agree to carry out specified chores or behaviors in exchange for privileges. When certain behaviors do not occur, children lose privileges.

Finally, *time out* is a method best reserved for aggressive, destructive, or dangerous behaviors. It serves to stop the disapproved behavior and to give the child a chance to cool off and, sometimes, to think about the rule violation. There are variations on the time-out method. The child can be requested to sit in a chair in the corner, but many children get up. If the child is required to face the corner, parents can keep the young child in the corner for the stated time. With older children, parents may want to add the rule that if the child does not comply with time out for one parent during the day, making the presence of both parents necessary, then the child will spend twice the amount of time in time out. The time need not be long. For young children, the number of minutes in time out should equal the number of years in age.

It is best to have only two or three behaviors requiring time out at any one time. Otherwise, a child may spend a great deal of time in the corner for too many different things. Further, it is important that both parents and all caregivers agree on the two or three things that will lead to time out so the child gets consistent punishment.

When children get older and have many toys and recreational pleasures in their rooms, such as stereos and computers, restriction to their room is not an effective punishment. For these children, it is better to substitute extra work or chores that have a constructive outcome such as cleaning the garage or devoting time to a community activity.

INEFFECTIVE FORMS OF DISCIPLINE   A review of over three hundred studies[12] identifies four kinds of problems in disciplining children: (1) inconsistent discipline, referring to inconsistency both on the part of one parent and between two parents; (2) irritable, harsh, explosive discipline (frequent hitting and threatening); (3) low supervision and low involvement on the part of the parent with the child; and (4) inflexible, rigid discipline (use of a single form of discipline for all transgressions regardless of seriousness). All four forms of ineffective discipline are related to children's aggressive, rule-breaking behavior that frequently leads to social difficulties with peers.

THE CONTROVERSY OVER PHYSICAL PUNISHMENT   No issue so separates social scientists from parents as the acceptability of physical punishment as a form of discipline. Physical punishment is often subdivided into two categories: (1) mild physical punishment, defined as a slap or two with the flat of the hand on the buttocks or extremities without causing any physical injury to the child and normatively used with young children; and (2) abuse (including beating, kicking, punching) that results in injury to the child.[13]

Most social scientists advise against the use of mild physical punishment as the major form of discipline even when they accept it as an action to enforce a safety limit or respect for parents. None, however, advocate harsh or abusive discipline. In their view, physical punishment presents a model of an adult's using physical force on a smaller person, and that is not a model we want children to imitate. Experiencing physical punishment is thought to increase children's aggressiveness. Further, spanking and hitting do not encourage children to develop internal controls, the goal of discipline. Instead, physical punishment is associated with the child's behaving well only when a punishing adult is present. Finally, an angry parent can lose control and abuse the child.

Although the use of spanking has decreased over the past three decades, the vast majority of parents report that they spank their children.[14] In a study begun in the 1960s, 148 of 150 middle-class families reported using spanking.[15] In another study, teachers-of-the-year from around the country were asked to nominate families who they felt stood out in terms of the overall quality of their family life. Researchers then interviewed the parents of these families and found that 70 percent used spanking to get children's attention for a serious misbehavior such as a dangerous act.[16] Parents give a variety of reasons for spanking: "Nonphysical punishment is not effective."[17] "Children learn better from punishment than rewards." "Young children don't understand reasoning." "Physical punishment builds character and prepares children for the outside world, which can be cruel if children have not learned the consequences of their behavior." A common reason is "It worked for me when I was growing up."

In a 1993 survey of middle-class families, 83 percent of parents reported using physical punishment.[18] Although most spanked a few times a month or less at only mild to moderate intensity, researchers were concerned that about a third of parents were reported by their children (who were interviewed separately from their parents) to use objects to hit them, and many said this occurred in about half the punishments. About 17 percent of children said they were hit a few times a week, and 4 percent said they were hit daily.

Parents in this study were most likely to use spanking and hitting when children were out of control, disobedient, or disrespectful. Four factors related to parents' use of physical punishment: (1) parents' belief in its usefulness, (2) parents' own experience with it as a child, (3) an authoritarian style of parenting, and (4) children's problems of aggressiveness and acting out. Although 93 percent justified its use, 85 percent of those who used it said they would rather not. They felt they were angry when they did it and that it upset the children; they wished they had alternatives. Even though most children in the sample were hit infrequently and at low levels, all children reported that physical punishment hurt and made them angry and upset. Nonetheless, although the children did not like it, they felt parents had a right to use physical punishment. Children in other surveys also report they believe parents have that right.[19]

Researchers concluded that because both children and adults were angry when physical punishment was used, it is doubtful that this form of discipline helped children learn and internalize rules. Of concern to the researchers was the fact that parents continued its use despite their discomfort with it and its doubtful value. Parents seemed to rely on it as a continuation of their own childhood experience of physical punishment rather than institute change and learn new methods. The investigators were concerned that the children in the sample would continue the practice for the same reason.

Because of the potential for abuse and because physical punishment is related to aggressiveness among children and to a more violent society, social scientist Murray Straus wishes to ban physical punishment in schools and at home.[20] He cites statistics from a national, representative sample of children that revealed that the more corporal punishment a child received in middle childhood and early adolescence, the greater the probability of the child's being a delinquent. In another longitudinal study of delinquency, those boys who experienced corporal punishment were more likely later to be convicted of a crime. Straus recognizes that not all physical punishment results in adult criminality, but he says that even if spanking increases adult violence by 10 percent, it is worth eliminating to decrease violence by that amount.

Other social scientists such as Diana Baumrind believe that research does not support a blanket injunction against spanking.[21] She believes that the effects of spanking, which she defines as a slap or two with the flat of the hand on the buttocks or extremities, depends on the context of the parent-child relationship. When a parent uses spanking in the context of a warm parent-child relationship and uses reasoning as well, then there are "no documented harmful long-term effects."[22] Further, she points out that in Sweden, where physical punishment was outlawed at home and at school in 1974, there was an increase in parental physical abuse of children and an increase in violent acts by teenagers.

An extensive review of studies from 1974 to 1995 on the effects of nonabusive or customary physical punishment supported Baumrind's contention that the effects of spanking depend on the parent's overall relationship with the child.[23] The review of 35 studies found that with abusive discipline excluded, nonabusive spanking led to a decrease in noncompliant behaviors. Physical punishment was associated with no detrimental effects when it was not severe, when it did not involve any implement, when it was used less than weekly, when it was used with young children two to six and possibly with children seven to twelve, when it was accompanied by reasoning, when it was used as a backup measure to other strategies, and when parents were not violent with other family members. Parents had the best results when they were positively involved with children, were acting in terms of children's needs rather than their own motivations, did not arouse fear in children, were consistent in discipline, did not use verbal put-downs, and changed their main discipline to grounding as children got older.

A longitudinal study of the development of children's externalizing (aggressive, hostile) conduct problems, as measured by teachers' reports, also supported Baumrind's conclusions.[24] Assessing punishment in the first five years of life and following children for a period of six years in school, the authors found that the relationship of nonabusive physical punishment with externalizing behavior problems depended on the severity of the punishment, the child's cultural group, and the context of the parent-child relationship. Physically abusive punishment in the first five years predicted externalizing problems through the sixth grade of school, regardless of the child's cultural group or the nature of the parent-child relationship. When punishment was mild, was accompanied by reasoning, and occurred in the context of a positive parent-child relationship, then there was a negligible relationship with children's externalizing problems.

In the African American subsample there was no relationship between mild physical punishment and children's externalizing problems, whereas in the European American subsample there was a significant relationship between mild punishment and externalizing behavior problems. In explaining this result, the authors speculated that in the African American group, nonabusive physical punishment is a more accepted disciplinary technique, although physical abuse is no more accepted than in any other group. The use of nonabusive physical punishment is more normative than in the European American group and may occur when parents are calm and controlled. Thus, African American children may interpret a spanking as a sign of caring and responsible parenthood. In the European American community, physical punishment is less accepted as a parenting strategy and may occur when parents are less controlled. Children may see it as rejection and become angry. Summarizing the implications of this and other studies of physical punishment for parents, psychologist Hugh Lytton concludes,

> Physical punishment tends to reduce normal children's misbehavior, but for them other, more rational methods would be equally effective. It tends to exacerbate aggressive children's problem behavior. Hence, physical punishment is useless where a corrective effect is more needed.[25]

All social scientists, whether they accept the use of mild physical punishment or wish to ban it, emphasize the importance of the steps described in Chapter 3 and earlier in this chapter to encourage approved behaviors through teaching and positive rewards. Discouraging the use of physical punishment, while a useful first step, does not automatically put in place the strategies of supportive parenting described earlier. Pediatrician Robert Chamberlin, for example, identifies the use of physical punishment as just one risk factor related to poor outcome for children. Because it is the accumulation of risk factors that causes the most damage, he believes communities and professionals need to join with parents to promote the "affectionate and cognitively stimulating types of parenting behavior that appear more directly related to positive developmental outcomes rather than focus on whether or not parents use physical punishment."[26] Baumrind also cautions professionals,

> It should be the concern of professionals who work with parents to respectfully offer them alternative disciplinary strategies, using carefully evaluated intervention programs, rather than to condemn parents for using methods consonant with their own, but not with the counselor's beliefs and values. Parents who choose to use punishment often seek guidance in using it efficaciously. Efficacious punishment is contingent upon the child's misbehavior, as well as upon the parents' responding in a prompt, rational, nonexplosive manner and with knowledge and consideration of the child's developmental level and temperament.[27]

In Chapter 1, we discussed the effects of genetic contributions to parenting. A major way that genes are thought to influence parent-child relationships is through a child's temperament. Temperament is defined as "constitutionally based individual differences in emotional, motor, and attentional reactivity and self-regulation."[28] The specific neurophysiological processes thought to underlie temperament are not yet known. Differences in temperament among newborns appear hours after birth in such behaviors as the amount of crying, ability to soothe oneself and be soothed by a caregiver,[29] and enjoyment of being hugged and cuddled.[30]

Although investigators differ on the specific dimensions of temperament, a thorough review of studies indicates six basic aspects of temperament: (1) *fearful distress*, emphasizing the baby's fearfulness and poor adaptability to new situations; (2) *irritable distress*, emphasizing fussiness, irritability, and distress at limitations; (3) *positive affect*, including laughing, smiling, and approaching objects and stimuli; (4) *activity level*; (5) *attention span*, or persistence; and (6) *rhythmicity*, or predictability of behaviors.[31] Parents are curious to know to what degree these differences persist. Some children showing certain temperamental qualities early on do not continue to show them later, but others do. For example, vigorous neonatal movements in the nursery were related to high activity levels at ages four and eight,[32] and activity level at twelve months predicted activity level and extroverted behavior at six and seven years.[33] High physiological reactivity (as measured in high motor activity and crying) to novel stimuli at four months was related to inhibition in behavior in the toddler years, which, in turn, was related to being less outgoing and expressive in early adolescence.[34]

Although early crying and fussiness did not endure, irritability at seven months tended to endure for the next year or two. Difficult temperament (which included negative affect, lack of rhythmicity, and persistence in behavior) measured at six months predicted difficult temperament at thirteen and twenty-four months and behavior problems at age three.[35] Stability from infancy to ages seven and eight has been found for such qualities as approachability and sociability, rhythmicity, irritability, persistence, cooperativeness and manageability, and inflexibility.[36] Behavioral differences in impulsivity at age three have been linked to measures of impulsivity, danger seeking, and aggression at age eighteen.[37]

Research shows that temperament influences parenting, but the relationship is inconsistent.[38] For example, difficult temperament stimulates greater parental involvement and attention in some mothers who later become frustrated and uninvolved and in other mothers a negative and uninvolved approach from the start. Early high reactivity stimulates in some mothers a very soothing and solicitous approach but in other mothers a firm insistence that the infants learn to soothe themselves.[39] There are, however, no studies showing that a positive, sociable baby stimulates a negative reaction in parents.[40]

Temperament also influences how children respond to parents' disapproval and how easily they can regulate their feelings and their behavior. Furthermore, parents' behavior in establishing rules and shaping behavior has different outcomes

Interview

with Jacqueline Lerner and Richard Lerner

Richard Lerner holds the Anita L. Brennan Professor of Education position at Boston College, and Jacqueline V. Lerner is a professor of education at Boston College.

Parents are interested in temperament and what this means for them as parents. What happens if they have a baby with a difficult temperament that is hard for them to deal with? Is this fixed? Will they have to keep coping with it?

R. Lerner: We don't believe temperament necessarily is fixed. We believe that temperament is a behavioral style and can, and typically does, show variation across a person's life. We're interested in the meaning of temperament for the person and the family in daily life.

J. Lerner: Although we know temperament is present at birth, we don't say that it is exclusively constitutionally derived. Temperament interacts with the environment. We find children who do seem to stay fairly difficult and children who stay fairly easy. Most children change, even from year to year. Given this, we can't possibly believe that temperament ever becomes fixed unless what happens in the family becomes fixed.

R. Lerner: What we are concerned with are individual differences. They are identifiable at birth, but they change, we believe, in relation to the child's living situation. We find that what one parent might call difficult is well below the threshold of another parent's level of tolerance for difficulty. What some people find easy, others find quite annoying.

In fact, you can find in our case studies examples of how difficult children ended up developing in a particular context that reinterpreted their difficulty as artistic creativity. One girl picked up a musical instrument at age thirteen or fourteen and began playing. She had a gift for that. Prior to that, she had a difficult relation with her father, who found her temperamental style totally abhorrent to him. As soon as she had this emerging talent, he said, "Oh, my daughter is an artist. This is an artistic temperament." They reinterpreted the first thirteen years of their relationship, believing they had always been close.

We believe the importance of temperament lies in what we call "goodness of fit" between the child's qualities and what the environment demands. The child brings characteristics to the parent-child relationship, but parents have to understand what they bring and how they create the meaning of the child's individuality by their own temperaments, and their demands, attitudes, and evaluations. Moreover, I think parents should understand that both they and the child have many other influences on them—friends, work, or school.

When you think about the fit with the environment, how do you think about the environment, what is it?

R. Lerner: We have divided demands from the environment into three broad categories: physical characteristics of the setting, the behavioral characteristics of the environment, and the behavioral and psychological characteristics of the other important people in the child's life.

J. Lerner: The setting has physical characteristics, and the people have behavioral characteristics and demands, attitudes, and values.

R. Lerner: Parents need to understand the demands of the context (the living situation) they present to the child by means of their own values and behavioral style. Even the features of the physical environment the parents provide can affect the child's fit with the context. Parents need to understand there are numerous features of the context; and because of the child's individuality, a better or lesser fit will emerge. For example, if your child has a low threshold of reactivity and a high intensity of reactions, you don't want to put that child's bedroom next to a busy street. If you have a choice, you'll put that child's bedroom in the back of the house or won't let the child study in any part of the house where he or she will get distracted.

A poor fit also occurs if you have a child who is very arrhythmic and you demand regularity, not necessarily as a verbal demand but perhaps in the way you schedule your life. You begin to prepare breakfast every morning at 8:00, the bagel comes out at 8:05 and disappears at 8:15, and some days the child makes it and some days not. The parents have to see how they may be doing things that create poorness of fit. It's not just their verbal demands but also their behavioral demands and the physical setup of the house.

J. Lerner: Some parents don't see what they are reinforcing and what they are teaching their child through their demands. There has to be consistency between the demands and the reinforcements. Sometimes you don't want to be too flexible. I learned this the hard way. My nine-year-old tells me about what I have done in the past. "But when I did this last week, it was okay and now it isn't."

In actively trying to get the child to behave or in trying to change a temperamental quality, parents need to focus themselves on what behaviors they want reinforced and what ones they don't. They need to be perceptive on both ends of the response—the demands they are setting up and what they are actually reinforcing. If you know a child is irregular in eating in the morning and you want to change the pattern because you know he'll get cranky and won't learn well if he doesn't have a full stomach, be consistent. "You don't walk out the door unless you have had at least three bites of cereal and a glass of juice." But if you let it go one morning, you can expect the child to say, "Well, yesterday you didn't make me do that."

From your research, do you see areas that can be supports for children as they are growing up?

R. Lerner: More and more children experience alternative-care settings, and this has to become a major support. The socialization of the child is moving out of the family more and more, and we are charging the schools with more of the socialization duties. Throughout infancy and childhood, the alternative caregiving setting is the day care, the preschool, and, obviously, the school. These settings have to be evaluated in terms of enhancing the child's fit and the ability to meet the demands of the context.

depending on the child's temperament. For example, infants' emotional regulatory ability appears to be the forerunner of behavior control in toddlerhood.[41] One study found that five-month-old infants who were able to regulate their emotions in response to frustration were at age two and a half able to conform to parents' requests. Experiencing frustration in infancy may be essential to developing regulatory skills. If infants do not experience frustration, perhaps because of general low reactivity, they may not experience sufficient emotional arousal to develop and practice regulatory skills.

Other research suggests that toddlers who are relatively reactive and responsive to others' behavior, who are relatively fearful and quick to feel bad at their own wrongdoing, respond well to gentle discipline; so, parents need to do little to help these children learn to internalize the rules.[42] Toddlers who are relatively fearless and have little reaction to their own wrongdoing do not benefit from gentle low-power techniques, nor do they benefit from high-power strategies that arouse their anger. Instead, they learn rules most easily when parents establish a positive, initially cooperative partnership based on a secure attachment. More securely attached, fearless children comply with what the mother wants because of the relationship, not the specific disciplinary techniques she uses.

How much can parents influence temperamental qualities? Research shows that sensitive parenting can help children overcome early temperamental difficulties.[43] Sensitive, responsive caregiving can help irritable babies (who are more likely to have insecure attachments) develop positive attachments to parents. Early limit-setting can help highly reactive infants learn self-soothing strategies and become less inhibited as toddlers.[44] Clearly, no one set of interventions will help all children. Rather, parents should be sensitive, flexible caregivers who target their behaviors to provide a "good fit" with their child's temperamental qualities. Sybil Escalona uses the term *effective experience* to describe what parents provide each child—the kind of experience that helps the child develop optimally.[45]

Socializing Boys and Girls

Here, we examine the way a child's gender influences parenting strategies. In the next chapter, we talk about how children form gender identities (that is, how they develop a sense of self as a boy or girl). First, let us review what we know about the different ways boys and girls are socialized.

Babies are born into a gender-typed world. In the days prior to routine ultrasounds during pregnancy, the baby's sex was usually the first fact known about a baby after birth. Today, however, the fetus's sex is often the first fact known during the pregnancy. Once delivered, babies enter an environment in which gender shapes the furniture, colors, clothing, and toys available for the child. Parents select dolls and pastel-colored bedding and clothing for girls and sports equipment, vehicles, and blue clothing for boys.[46] Adults perceive babies identified as boys as tough and sturdy and the same babies identified as girls as frail and sweet.[47]

Parents encourage different interests and activities for boys and girls, and fathers are more likely to emphasize these differences than are mothers.[48] Parents encourage boys to build more and to be more physically active and competitive. They encourage girls to play more with dolls and to pursue artistic activities. Parents are warm and nurturing with girls, engage in more verbal communication with them, and encourage girls' nurturing and cooperative behavior. Boys are permitted more independence than are girls, but they are more frequently punished.

Although parents channel children's activities and interests according to gender, they tend to treat boys and girls alike in day-to-day interactions.[49] This observation is in line with the general finding that the more familiar a person is with the child, the more the individual's characteristics shape his or her response to the child. Parents are equally attached to sons and daughters and use authoritative strategies and similar teaching styles with them. When certain behaviors occur, however, parents and adults outside the home may treat boys differently than girls. For example, parents and preschool teachers both tend to ignore boys with insecure attachments to parents even when they seek help but help girls with insecure attachments when they request it. So, even when boys' and girls' behavior is identical, adults respond differently depending on the child's gender.

Prior to about eighteen months of age, boys and girls show no differences in such behaviors as aggressiveness, toy play, large motor activity, and communication attempts, all of which exhibit gender differences at later ages.[50] As development proceeds, however, boys and girls are at risk for different kinds of problems for a variety of reasons. Boys are at risk for developing problems with aggression, hyperactivity, impulsiveness, and poor attention. Girls are at risk for developing feelings of low self-esteem and depression in adolescence. Carolyn Zahn-Waxler refers to the gender issues here as the problems of the warriors and worriers.[51]

Jack Block's longitudinal study following middle-class children from age three to eighteen confirmed these differences.[52] He found that at age eighteen, boys who rated themselves as depressed described themselves as angry with the world, undercontrolled, and hostile. Depressed girls described themselves differently. They said they lacked self-esteem, brooded and blamed themselves for problems, and felt their lives were out of control. Characteristics in early adolescence and, in some cases, childhood predicted depression for both boys and girls. Girls who were shy, reserved, oversocialized, and focused on the needs of others rather than on self-assertiveness were more likely to be depressed in adolescence. Boys who were undercontrolled and stretched limits were more likely to be depressed in adolescence. Block commented in an interview, "Simplistically, it seems to me that the developmental problem for girls is to move away from overcontrol, while boys have to move away from undercontrol."[53] Clinical psychologists who work with boys and girls agree with Block that both boys and girls have special needs as they develop.

Mary Pipher, working closely with adolescent girls, believes that in the teenage years, girls lose their sense of themselves as individuals and become overfocused on the needs, feelings, and approval of other people. Girls have to develop "identities based on talents or interests, rather than appearance, popularity or sexuality. They need good habits for coping with stress, self-nurturing skills and a sense of purpose and perspective."[54] She believes that homes that offer both protection and challenges help girls find and sustain a sense of identity.

Parents need to listen to daughters and encourage independent thought and rational decision-making skills and to encourage friendships with boys and girls and a wide variety of activities that build skills in many areas—artistic, athletic, intellectual, and social. As a therapist, Pipher teaches adolescent girls to separate thinking from feeling and to combine these two aspects of experience in making decisions. She also teaches girls to manage pain in a positive way.

> All the craziness in the world comes from people trying to escape suffering. All mixed-up behavior comes from unprocessed pain. I teach girls to sit with their pain, to listen to it for messages about their lives, to acknowledge and describe it rather than run from it.[55]

She also encourages altruism to counter the self-absorption that is characteristic of adolescence. Helping others leads to good feelings and to greater maturity.

Clinical psychologist William Pollack believes that boys are socialized from childhood to conform to what he calls the Boys Code.[56] This code requires boys (1) to be strong, tough, and independent, even when they may feel shaky and in need of support; (2) to be aggressive, daring, and energetic; (3) to achieve status and power; and (4) to avoid the expression of tender feelings, such as warmth and empathy. He believes that boys are forced to separate from parents too early and that if they protest, they are ridiculed and shamed. He writes,

> I believe that boys, feeling ashamed of their vulnerability, mask their emotions and ultimately their true selves. This unnecessary disconnection—from family and then from self—causes many boys to feel alone, helpless, and fearful. . . . Over time, his sensitivity is submerged almost without thinking, until he loses touch with it himself. And so a boy has been "hardened," just as society thinks he should be.[57]

Pollack advises parents to get behind the masks that boys develop by (1) becoming aware of signs that sons are hiding their feelings, (2) talking to sons about feelings and listening to what they say, (3) accepting sons' emotional schedules for revealing feelings (boys may be slower than girls), (4) connecting with sons through joint activities that can bring parents and sons closer together, and (5) sharing their own growing-up experiences with their sons. He calls for the development of "a New Boy code that respects what today's boys and men are about—one that will be based on honesty rather than fear, communication rather than repression, connection rather than disconnection."[58] Boys need to stay connected to those who love and support them and encourage them to express all their feelings. "They need to be convinced, above all, that both their strengths and their vulnerabilities are good, that all sides of them will be celebrated, that we'll love them through and through for being just the boys they really are."[59]

So, parents need to help both boys and girls find and express their own true selves. This means staying more closely connected to sons than in the past and encouraging more independence of thought and action in girls than in the past.

Selecting Individually Appropriate Problem-Solving Strategies

123

*Selecting
Individually
Appropriate
Problem-
Solving
Strategies*

Parents often wish they had a single solution to each kind of problem they encounter in childrearing—one way to handle temper tantrums, one way to deal with teenagers' rebelliousness. Unfortunately, there is no one formula that all parents can use to raise all children. Each child, as well as each parent, is a unique individual.

When parents have difficulties, a seven-step problem-solving approach—combining Gordon's mutual problem-solving method and Dix's attention to parental emotions (see Chapter 3)—seems most useful. The approach allows parents to choose interventions (actions to change a problem behavior, such as holding a mutual problem-solving session or setting up a reward system) that take into account the child's age and temperament and the family's social values and living circumstances. It also enables parents to encourage the qualities that they and their ethnic group value. Here are the seven steps:

1. Spend pleasurable time daily with the child.
2. Specifically identify any problem; observe when and how often it occurs.
3. Question yourself on the reality of the problem.
4. Get the child's point of view.
5. Carry out an intervention.
6. Evaluate the results of the intervention.
7. Start over again if necessary.

How do parents select interventions? Most use a combination of the techniques described earlier in this chapter to enforce limits, but parents develop beliefs about the effectiveness of low-power, authoritative methods as opposed to high-power, authoritarian methods.[60] Often, parents react in terms of these beliefs.[61] As noted in Chapter 3, however, a parent's affect is perhaps a more important determiner of the choice. When parents are under stress, angry, or upset, they tend to assert power. This is true of depressed mothers as well. According to one study, even though many such mothers believed in the importance of low-power techniques, their resentment of the child and the parenting role determined the choice of their parenting behaviors, not their beliefs.[62]

The complexity of using childrearing strategies increases when we realize that children may not be learning by the strategy parents are using. Jane Loevinger, in a perceptive and humorous article, illustrates this problem with the example of a five-year-old who hits his younger brother.[63] The parent who punishes the older child with a spanking may actually be teaching that child that it is permissible to use physical aggression to obtain one's ends. The parent who uses reason and logic in dealing with the older boy may find that the child, seeing that no punishment follows hitting, is likely to do it again.

So why use a strategy? Why not just do whatever comes to mind at the time? Because, says Loevinger, those children who have the most difficulties growing up and functioning are raised by parents who are impulsive, self-centered, and unable to follow a set of guidelines. "The chief value of a parental theory," writes Loevinger, "may well be in providing a model for the child of curbing one's own impulses out of regard for the future welfare of another."[64]

When we combine the problem-solving approach with the parental qualities and behaviors all strategies advise—modeling desired traits, respecting the child's and parents' own needs, having confidence that the child can learn what is necessary, and sharing problems and solutions in family meetings—then parents can effectively foster the growth and development of their children. Each individual has a unique potential to discover and develop. Arnold Gesell and Frances Ilg state it well:

> When asked to give the shortest definition of life, Claude Bernard, a great physiologist, answered, "Life is creation." A newborn baby is the consummate product of such creation. And he in turn is endowed with capacities for continuing creation. These capacities are expressed not only in the growth of his physique, but in the simultaneous growth of a psychological self. From the sheer standpoint of creation this psychological self must be regarded as his masterpiece. It will take a lifetime to finish, and in the first ten years he will need a great deal of help, but it will be his own product.[65]

Parents have the privilege of serving as guide and resource as their child creates a unique "psychological self."

Main Points

Parents set the stage for learning by

- establishing a collaborative relationship
- developing realistic expectations of the child
- helping children meet expectations
- rewarding approved behaviors consistently
- setting limits with clear, positive statements of what they want

To enforce rules, parents can

- use mutual problem solving
- let natural or logical consequences of the act teach the child
- use punishments to decrease the disapproved behavior

Nonabusive spanking as a punishment

- is used by most parents at one time or another and its effects depend on the cultural group
- may or may not have detrimental effects, depending on the context of the parent-child relationship
- is best supplanted by other forms of negative consequence

Ineffective forms of discipline include

- inconsistent discipline
- harsh, explosive discipline
- low supervision of the child

- rigid, inflexible discipline

Temperament

- is the individual's constitutionally based way of responding to the world
- influences the usefulness of parenting strategies

In socializing their children, parents

- encourage different interests and activities in boys and girls
- in many ways treat boys and girls the same
- are more effective when they encourage greater emotional closeness with sons than in the past and greater independence of thought and action for daughters than in the past

The advantages of the seven-step problem-solving approach are that

- parents can take into account the child's individuality
- parents can retain their own goals and values for their children's behavior

Exercises

1. Write a description of the disciplinary techniques your parents used with you in the elementary and high school years. How would you characterize your parents' methods and your response to them?

2. Choose some behavior you want to improve upon—for example, regular exercise—and work out a reward system to encourage that behavior. Chart the frequency of the desired behavior before and during the reward period. If time permits, observe the frequency for a week after you stop the reward system. Share your experiences with classmates. What kinds of rewards have most successfully helped you and other students improve upon desired behavior?

3. Choose some behavior you want to eliminate. Chart the occurrence of the behavior before any intervention. Then, choose a negative consequence that will occur after every repetition of the undesired behavior. If you wish, choose to reward the opposite of the undesired behavior at the same time. Then monitor the occurrence of the undesired behavior. If time permits, observe the frequency of the behaviors after you have stopped the consequences. For example, you may decide you want to stop procrastinating going to the library. Decide that every time you postpone going to the library for 5 minutes or longer, you will have to stay at the library an extra 30 minutes. If you go to the library on time, permit yourself to leave 10 minutes early.

4. Observe parents and children together at a playground, in the grocery store, or at another public place. Select pairs of children of approximately the same age and contrast how their parents treat them. Do the parents show similar behavior? What theories of learning do they appear to be using? What parental behaviors seem effective with the children? Observing each child for five minutes, time how often the parent intervenes to maintain or change the child's behavior.

5. Select a friend's behavior that you wish to change. For example, you might decide to change a friend's habit of being late for meetings or of not calling when she says she will. Devise a system of rewards or a system of positive/negative consequences to change the behavior. Carry out your plan for five weeks and note the change.

Additional Readings

Chase, Stella, and Alexander Thomas. *Know Your Child.* New York: Basic Books, 1987.

Dinkmeyer, Don, and Gary D. McKay. *The Parent's Handbook.* Circle Pines, MN: American Guidance Service, 1989.

Nelson, Jane. *Positive Discipline.* New York: Ballantine Books, 1987.

Pipher, Mary. *Reviving Ophelia.* New York: Ballantine Books, 1994.

Pollack, William. *Real Boys.* New York: Henry Holt, 1998.

5

Infancy and Early Childhood

INTRODUCING AN INFANT INTO A HOUSEHOLD CRE-ates a true full-time job—24 hours a day, 365 days a year. How can couples prepare for the parenting task? What adjustments must they make in their lifestyle? How do they interact with their child to promote a secure attachment, a positive self-concept, and competent behaviors?

This chapter focuses on how parents make the transition to becoming parents and how they shape their behaviors to enhance the parent-child relationship. It describes the many activities parents carry out to establish secure attachments with their child and to foster his or her physical and cognitive development, emotional regulation, and social and moral competence.

Transition and Adjustment to Parenthood

The arrival of a baby changes every aspect of married life, from a couple's finances to their sex life, sleeping habits, and social life. Although many first-time parents report that nothing could have adequately prepared them for the experience, knowing what to expect in advance is the first step in helping parents cope with their new role.

Parents give each other crucial support during this transitional period. In one study, new mothers reported a number of problems, including (1) tiredness and exhaustion, (2) loss of sleep, especially in the first two months, (3) concern about ignoring the husband's needs, (4) feelings of inadequacy as a mother, (5) an inability to keep up with housework, and (6) feelings of being tied down.[1] The mothers did not anticipate the many changes that would occur in their lives when their babies arrived, in part because they did not realize how much work is involved in caring for an infant. Fathers gave a similar list of complaints: (1) loss of sleep for up to six weeks, (2) the need to

BOX 5.1

Recommendations to Couples for Easing the Transition to Parenthood

1. Share expectations.
2. Give yourselves regular checkups on how each partner is doing.
3. Make time to talk to each other.
4. Negotiate an agenda of important issues; if one partner thinks there is a problem, there is.
5. Adopt an experimental attitude; see how solutions work and make modifications as necessary.
6. Don't ignore sex and intimacy.
7. Line up support for the early stages after the birth.
8. Talk with a friend or coworker.
9. Find the delicate balance between meeting your needs and the baby's needs; children grow best when parents maintain a strong positive relationship.

Carolyn Pape Cowan and Philip Cowan, *When Partners Become Parents* (New York: Basic Books, 1992), pp. 206–209.

adjust to new responsibilities and routines, (3) disruption of daily routines, (4) ignorance of the amount of work the baby requires, and (5) financial worries (62 percent of the wives were employed prior to the child and only 12 percent afterward). Husbands made such comments as, "My wife has less time for me" and "Getting used to being tied down is hard." Parents most at risk for difficulties are those who have unrealistic expectations of what the birth will bring, who have negative views of their partners, who are disappointed in their marriages and pessimistic about improving them, who are unable to talk over these problems, and who cannot arrive at mutually agreeable ways of dividing family responsibilities.[2]

Carolyn Cowan and Philip Cowan and Jay Belsky write movingly about the difficulties young couples face as they have babies, and all these researchers agree on what produces the problems. First, our society is in a state of transition regarding men's and women's roles.[3] Economic factors require most women with infants and young children to work outside the home, so couples must share childcare and family responsibilities as well as work responsibilities. There are no agreed-on rules about how this should be done, and there are few role models to teach couples how to work out such conflicts. Second, society does little to give young parents support by providing or subsidizing high-quality day care. And third, young parents often live far from their families of origin, so their parents and other relatives are often not around to help. These young people have fewer social supports and resources. Thus, they have more to do than parents did in the past, with fewer guidelines and less help. (Box 5.1 lists some suggestions for easing the transition to parenthood.)

Promoting Secure Attachments

Attachment is defined as "an enduring affectional tie that unites one person to another, over time and across space."[4] In Chapter 2, we described the many positive benefits associated with a secure parent-child attachment. For example, children with secure attachments in infancy and toddlerhood were described in preschool years and later childhood as being more independent and socially competent and having a positive mood and higher self-esteem than children with insecure attachments. Parents who describe secure, autonomous attachments with their own parents are warmer and more supportive with their children than are parents who have insecure attachments with their parents.[5]

Thus, a primary goal of parenting is to promote secure attachments. The question is, How do parents do this? To answer the question, let us first review how parent-child relationships develop after birth.

Bonding

The first meeting between parents and child is an important occasion. In the first hour after birth, babies are more alert and visually attentive than they will be for the next three or four hours. During that first hour, they may be most responsive to contact with parents.[6]

While recognizing that early contact is pleasurable and starts the relationship between parents and child on a positive note, Michael Rutter is critical of the concept of bonding that suggests physical contact is essential to strengthen the attachment.[7] He points out that relationships are multifaceted and not dependent on a single sensory modality such as skin contact. Relationships develop over time, and strong attachments can be formed with caregivers even if the early bonding is not possible for some reason.

Early Parent-Child Relationships

Babies come into the world preprogrammed to respond to human beings.[8] They see most clearly at a distance of 8 to 10 inches, the average distance of a parent's face from the baby when being held. Babies show an early preference for objects that in any way resemble a human face—even a circle with a dot or two where the eyes would go. They hear best in the range of the human voice. Infants a few hours old respond to the cry of another newborn and often cry themselves. Babies also move in rhythm to human speech. They are capable of social behaviors—such as crying and smiling—that motivate adults to care for them. Adults appear preprogrammed to respond to babies. Babyish features (big eyes, small nose, large forehead) elicit special reactions from adults, such as pleasure and tenderness. Further, adults around the world speak in a special way to infants, using higher-pitched voices, short phrases, and elongated words.

In the earliest weeks of life, as we noted in Chapter 2, physical contact with parents soothes babies and regulates the child's physical system.[9] Babies cry, frown, kick, and later smile to make their feelings known. When these communications receive positive responses from parents (for example, crying leads to being fed) babies learn that communication gets results and is worthwhile.

In their early interactions, parents shape infants' emotional reactions, encouraging positive moods and smiling and discouraging negative moods with phrases such as, "Don't cry," or "Don't fret."[10] Babies respond to parents' emotional reactions and pattern their own after what they see parents do. Infants as young as ten weeks mirror mothers' emotional expressions; they respond with joy and interest to mothers' happy faces, with anger and a form of fear to mothers' angry faces, and with sadness to mothers' sad faces.[11] Babies pattern their moods after mothers' moods on a more ongoing basis as well. Over time, mothers' positive expressions are related to increases in babies' smiling and laughter.[12]

As the infant's system settles down in the first two to three months of life, parents begin to engage their baby in a social dialogue during face-to-face interactions.[13] Sensitive parents adjust their behavior to the rhythm and tempo of the baby, looking for periods of alertness and readiness to respond. In face-to-face interactions, parents wait for their baby to look at them before they talk, tickle, or play games. Parents often imitate the baby's behavior, and the baby may imitate parents' behavior. In vocalizing and social play, babies learn to capture parents' attention. They also learn the rules of communication—one person speaks at a time, and each gets a turn. In these interactions, babies get a sense of themselves as active doers and initiators of others' social behavior. Babies as young as three months develop expectations about how interactions proceed, and they become distressed if these expectations are not met. For example, when a parent of a three-month-old adopts a still, impassive facial expression, the baby responds negatively and often tries to elicit the anticipated reaction by smiling or vocalizing.[14] If this does not work, the baby turns away. Similarly, if a parent arrives when the baby is distressed over a routine such as a diaper change and does not attempt to soothe the child, the baby protests.

Influencing the behavior of others who respond in return establishes babies as social partners with parents. At the same time, parents recognize babies' increasing role as active participants who have individual preferences and unique behavioral preferences. As partners, parents and babies interact and adjust to each other; they create mutual understanding and *intersubjectivity*, or a shared state of meaning.[15] In the state of shared meaning, the baby uses the parent as a *social reference* for responding to experience. For example, babies will not play with a toy if the mother has looked at the toy with disgust.[16]

Babies' temperaments and emotional reactivity influence the social dialogue between parent and child. When babies adjust well to change and are easily soothed when upset, parents can regulate the babies' environments and conditions reliably and consistently. However, when babies are fretful, easily upset by change, and difficult to soothe, parents find it harder to provide this consistent regulation, and both partners in the dialogue are frustrated.

By seven to eight months, face-to-face interactions decrease, in part, because babies become mobile and interested in active exploration of objects and the world.

Forms of Attachment to Parents

By seven or eight months, babies show attachment to parents. Attachment is a strong psychological bond to a person who is a source of security and emotional support. The baby seeks out the parent, is fearful when the parent leaves or strangers come, and uses the parent as a safe physical base from which to move into the world. Attachment is usually measured in a laboratory setting by the quality of the mother-infant interactions and the infant's reactions to the mother's leaving the room and then returning.

In middle-class families, about 60 to 70 percent of babies are described as having *secure attachments;* they feel comfort in the parent's presence, fearful when he or she leaves, and happy at the parent's return.[17] Infants with secure attachments explore more and are more persistent in tasks than are those with insecure attachments.

Insecure attachments are revealed in one of three ways. When parents are intrusive and overstimulating, babies form *anxious avoidant attachments* (about 15 to 20 percent of babies) and avoid parents after separation. When parents are insensitive to babies' cues and often unavailable, babies form *anxious resistant attachments* (about 10 to 20 percent of babies) and alternately cling to the parents and push them away.

More recently, a third form of insecure attachment has been identified as *disorganized/disoriented attachment* (ranging from 13 to 82 percent of babies, depending on the sample). Babies with such attachments show unpredictable alterations in their behavior with the parent. At times, they happily approach the parent as a securely attached infant would, and at other times they avoid the parent. Thus, their attachment is considered disorganized. They show signs of conflict by "freezing" or "stilling" when they are near the parent. They appear confused as to how to respond; thus the term *disoriented* is used to describe them.[18]

Such attachments are found in families in which a parent appears frightened or traumatized and, as a result, may appear frightening to the child. These classifications are made for a small number of babies in low-risk families (13 percent), but the percentage increases in babies in high-risk families—28 percent in multiproblem families receiving supportive services, 54 percent in families of low-income depressed mothers, and 82 percent in families whose members mistreat babies.[19] Other groups at risk of insecure attachments include adolescent and depressed mothers (of all incomes).

The Process of Attachment

John Bowlby, who was a pioneer in research on the concept of attachment, identified parental sensitivity as the crucial ingredient for forming a secure attachment with a baby.[20] *Sensitivity* is defined as the ability to perceive the infant's signals accurately and respond appropriately and promptly to his or her needs. An analysis of sixty-six studies on infants' attachments to mothers (as mothers were the focus of most studies) found that sensitivity was indeed an important but not the only contributor to the security of an infant's attachment.[21] *Mutuality* (positive harmony and mutuality in relationship), *synchrony* (coordinated social interactions), and *positive attitude* (emotional expressiveness, acceptance, and delight in the child) were all related to the formation of secure attachments. So, when parents are sensitive, responsive to the child, warm, accepting, and attentive to the rhythm of the child's behavior and individuality, they create a state of mutual understanding that contributes to the formation of a secure parent-infant attachment.

Psychologists believe that experiences in attachment relationships provide a framework for babies' understanding of the world.[22] From these relationships, babies build internal models of how people relate to one another. Babies develop expectations

The Joys of Parenting in Infancy and Early Childhood

"I love babies. There is something about that bond between mother and baby. I love the way they look and smell and the way they hunker up to your neck. To me it's a magic time. I didn't like to babysit particularly growing up, and I wasn't wild about other people's babies, but there was something about having my own; I just love it. And every one, we used to wonder, how are we going to love another as much as the one before; and that is ridiculous, because you love every one." —*Mother*

"I think it's wonderful to have a baby in the house, to hear the baby laugh, sitting in the high chair, banging spoons, all the fun things babies do. They seem to me to light up a household. When there's a baby here, a lot of the aggravations in the household somehow disappear. Everyone looks at the baby, plays with the baby, and even if people are in a bad mood, they just light up when the baby comes in the room. I think there is something magical about having a baby in the house." —*Mother*

"I've heard of this, and it's true; it's rediscovering the child in yourself. Sometimes, it's the joy that he and I hop around the couch like two frogs on our hands and knees. Or we're in the bathtub pretending we are submarines and alligators. Sometimes he likes to ride around on my shoulders, and I run and make noises like an airplane or a bird. And I am not just doing it for him, but we are doing it together, playing together." —*Father*

"When she was four, she was the only girl on an all-boy soccer team. Her mother thought she was signing her up for a coed team, but she was the only girl, and she enjoyed it and liked it even though she is not a natural athlete. She watches and learns and gets good at it, and we got a lot of joy out of watching her." —*Father*

"He's four, and he's so philosophical. He's always thinking about different things, and sometimes he'll tell me, and I am amazed. One day we were driving and he said, 'Can God see me riding here in the car?' Or one night at dinner, he was watching his little sister who's one, and he said, 'Do you think when she gets to be a big girl she'll remember what she did as a baby?'" —*Mother*

of how well others will understand and respond to them, how much influence they have on others, and what level of satisfaction they can expect from other people.

From these relationships, babies also develop a sense of their own lovability and competence. When others respond positively to their overtures, babies feel valued and influential and anticipate similar responses from adults in new situations. When babies are ignored or rejected, they may develop a sense of unworthiness and helplessness.

When interactions follow a consistent pattern, babies acquire a sense of order and predictability in experience that, in turn, generalizes to daily activities and to the world at large. Babies develop expectations about family routines and activities, and, as we have seen, they pattern their interest in toys and in exploration on their parents' emotional reactions.

As children become toddlers, parents maintain a state of mutual understanding through continuing sensitivity and availability as a secure base for exploration. In this state of mutual understanding, parents go on to teach and guide children, balancing support and guidance with increasing independence for the child. The effective parent observes the child's level of interaction in a situation and stays, in a sense, one step ahead. When the child confronts a new barrier, the parent steps in to give just the amount of help that enables the child to solve the problem and move on. Jutta Heckhausen terms this behavior "balancing the child's weakness" in order to stimulate a new level of skill.[23] This behavior is sometimes referred to as scaffolding, as parental help provides the structure to compensate for the child's lack of skill with the task.

A final essential quality in parenting during toddlerhood is the parent's ability to match his or her behavior to the child's personality and particular needs. What is most helpful for one child is not necessarily best for another. For example, highly active toddlers will explore the environment most widely when parents give little stimulation or direction and let the child control the activity. Less active toddlers require just the opposite behavior and explore most widely when parents are more stimulating.[24]

During the preschool years, sensitive, involved, flexible parenting promotes feelings of security in children. As in infancy and toddlerhood, shared play with parents brings enjoyment and opportunities for learning. But with children's increased understanding of others, wider spheres of interaction, and growing language skills, much of what children learn about parents' reliability and trustworthiness comes from observing parents' behavior with each other, with siblings, and with other relatives, as well as through conversations about the present and the past and about what is approved of and disapproved of.[25] Feelings of security stem also from the ways parents negotiate conflicts with the preschooler—with their willingness to seek compromise and respect the child's autonomy while still providing limits that give security.

In this period, then, children's secure attachments to parents come from a wide variety of behaviors. Because preschoolers have greater cognitive skills and thus can more accurately understand parents' behavior, their views of their parents are more realistic than those of toddlers and lead to greater predictability of parents' behavior.[26]

Four-year-olds tend to look at family interactions in ways that confirm the underlying dimensions that researchers propose. Four-year-olds' stories depict family interactions that focus on engagement/disengagement among family members, the amount of cooperation or conflict that exists, and the degree to which family members are equal or dominant. Their stories describe families' emotional tone as reassuring, rational, helpful, affectionate, gratifying, angry, aggressive, and punitive, showing that children focus on the very aspects of family life that researchers find salient.[27]

Social and Cultural Influences on Attachment

When living conditions are difficult, because of either economic stress or marital tensions, the proportion of insecure attachments rises.[28] Moreover, when unusual circumstances exist, parents' sensitivity as a means of promoting secure attachments can be overridden. For example, in Israeli samples of infants, 80 percent of those infants

Interview

with James Levine

James Levine is the director of the Fatherhood Project at the Families and Work Institute in New York City. He served as a principal consultant to Vice Present Al Gore in drafting the federal initiative on fatherhood, created by executive order in 1995.

As a result of your work regarding fathering, do you think that, on average, fathers bring special qualities to parenting?

That's a difficult question in the field. Do they bring something different, and if they do, is this culturally or biologically determined? I think what fathers bring that is different centers on two dimensions. First, there is a fair amount of research that fathers' interactive style with young children is different from mothers'. With young children, they have a more rough-and-tumble style. On average, dads whoop it up with little kids. They chase them, throw them up in the air, roll around with them. Ross Parke has a theory that this type of interaction has some relationship to how children relate to the social world outside the family.

The second dimension I think is really important is that the father is a man and knows what it is like to be a man in this society, what it takes. While my wife and I can guide our children in terms of basic values, there are some ways I can talk to my son about what the world expects of him and what it has felt like to me to be a man in this society, what the expectations are of men and women. I also share that perspective with my daughter. So my wife and I bring a different storehouse of experience to parenting, different ways of being in the world based on the way the world expects us to play roles as men and women.

What are the best ways to get men involved in parenting?

There are several issues. I think the absolute key is the couple's expectations of what the father's role will be. If the mom doesn't expect the dad to be involved, and the dad doesn't expect to be involved, that's a prescription for noninvolvement. If Mom doesn't expect dad to be involved and Dad might want to be involved, he won't be involved. The mother is the gatekeeper in the relationship. Many women say they want husbands to be involved, but in effect, they want them to be involved as sort of mom's subordinate or assistant. Mom's the manager, telling Dad how to be involved as opposed to assuming Dad will be involved and will learn the skills to be a father. It is important for mothers to back off and be in the background, and let fathers be with children.

So, one key to involvement is the couple's dynamics. I don't mean to blame Mom, but there is a system here—men and women as a system—and one starts here in terms of making a supportive system for fathers' involvement.

Then let's look at men in terms of men and the system outside the couple. All the research we've done shows that men today define success on two dimensions—being a good provider and equally important is having good relationships with children. So if you look at the values men bring to parenthood, there are generally agreed-upon desires to have close relationships with their children. But, aside from the couple relationship, there are two obstacles. Men sometimes feel incompetent as to how to do this; they need skills. And, second, their work sucks them up in spite of their best intentions to give time to relationships with children. They spend a lot of time working, not to avoid forming relationships with children but as a way of caring for children.

A key to change is changing the cultural cues men get about being fathers. Looking at this from an ecological and systems point of view, we can ask, "What are the cues that men get about parenting across the life cycle?" The expectations others have about them have a lot to do with shaping their behavior. For example, prenatally if men get expectations from the health care system that they are expected to be at pre-natal visits, they will be there. Mostly, however, they get the message that they have no role during the pregnancy. Yet, research has shown that one of the best predictors of good prenatal care for the mother is whether the partner is involved with prenatal care.

We have found in our work with low-income men that when men understand how vital their role is even before the child is born, they can change their level of involve-ment. Knowing how important their role is with their babies increases the motivation of low-income men to be involved.

So at the time of birth and afterwards, if the pediatrician sends messages that he or she wants both parents at visits—"I need to know both of the baby's parents. I want to see you both, not just the mother"—that message shapes the father's behavior. Same thing at preschools or day care. They can also send messages that they want both parents, not just mothers, to be involved.

So it is the expectations that are embedded in daily interactions that are the real keys to fathers' involvement. If you look at the face-to-face interactions with mater-nity nurses and pediatricians, embedded in dialogues with doctors, health care providers, and teachers are messages about expected involvement. If more messages expect fathers to be involved and daily interactions offer support for fathers' involve-ment, fathers will be involved.

To give a specific example, West Virginia wanted to increase the rate at which fa-thers established paternity of children born to single mothers, and the question was how to do that. One could think about a big public-information campaign with mes-sages to encourage involvement, but the key was the maternity nurse, who had the most influence on both the young man and the young woman. The father would come and look at the baby, and if the nurse assumed he was some bad guy and chased him away, if she did not invite him in to be involved with the baby, he would disen-gage and disappear. They increased the rate of paternity establishment by increasing the dialogue with fathers and also by changing what the nurse said to mothers. The nurse told mothers it is important for children to be involved with their fathers even if mothers decide not to marry the fathers. In two years, the rate of establishing pater-nity went from 15 percent to 60 percent of fathers who claimed paternity of babies born to single mothers.

The overall message to fathers was we want you here, we want you to establish pa-ternity and be fathers to your children. Changing expectations encoded in daily inter-actions are the important elements in increasing fathers' involvement with their children.

who slept at home at night were securely attached, whereas only 48 percent of infants who slept in a communal arrangement were securely attached.[29] The two groups of infants did not differ, however, in temperament and early life events.

Cross-national comparisons of the proportions of secure/insecure attachments reveal that broad cultural influences shape the responses of infants to the laboratory situation measuring attachment and that the percentages of infants in different classifications differ from those in middle-class samples in the United States. In Germany, where early independence is strongly encouraged once babies are mobile, about 49 percent of babies show anxious avoidant attachments, 33 percent show secure attachments, and 12 percent show anxious resistant attachments.[30] When encouraged to spend time separated from the mother, babies show less protest at mothers' going and less clingy, dependent behavior on her return than do American babies.

In Japanese culture, where a close relationship between mother and child is encouraged and separations from the parent rarely or never occur, babies almost never demonstrate anxious avoidant attachments but are much more likely than babies in other cultures to protest mothers' leaving and find it so stressful that they cannot adjust easily to their return. Japanese babies have about the same rate of secure attachments as U.S. babies, but anxious avoidant attachments are rare or absent, and anxious resistant attachments occur in about 30 percent of babies.[31]

Separation history, then, appears to affect children's responses to mothers' leaving and returning. Within U.S. culture, babies of working mothers are less likely to protest their leaving the room and less interested in their return, presumably because they have had more experience with temporary separations and adjust to them. In Japan, babies of working mothers show attachment patterns similar to those of U.S. babies, presumably because their experience of separations is similar to that of babies in this country.[32]

Attachment to Both Parents

Until recently, the mother-child bond was considered the only attachment of importance in infancy. As researchers have observed parent-child interactions and attachments more carefully, however, they have found that babies become attached to both parents. The quality of the relationship with each parent determines the attachment. Although it is possible to be securely attached to one parent and insecurely attached to the other, attachment classifications are most often the same for both parents. Yet even when attached to both parents, babies still seek comfort from mothers when they are distressed.[33]

Research has shown that parents interact differently with babies. First, even though a high percentage are employed in the workforce, mothers spend more time with infants. Studies indicate that even in families with fathers staying at home at least part of the time and mothers going off to work, mothers spend more time with children than do fathers.[34]

Mothers and fathers differ not only in the quantity of time but also in the way they spend time with babies.[35] Mothers, even when working, are significantly more engaging, responsive, stimulating, and affectionate. They are more likely than fathers to hold babies in caregiving activities and to verbalize. Fathers, on the other hand, are more likely to be attentive visually and to be playful in physically active ways than are mothers. Although fathers spend less time than mothers with infants, they are sensitive caregivers and are as perceptive as mothers in adjusting their behavior to babies' needs. Fathers are most likely to be highly involved in caregiving and playing when the marital relationship is satisfying and wives are relaxed and outgoing. Both fathers and mothers give mostly care and physical affection in the first three months, when babies are settling in. As babies become less fussy and more alert at three months, both parents become more stimulating and reactive.[36]

Although mothers and fathers interact differently with babies, recent observations indicate that parents do not treat sons and daughters differently in routine caregiving activities at home during this early period. When mothers and fathers are observed at home interacting with their infants, they give sons and daughters equal amounts of affection, stimulation, care, and responsiveness. We cannot rule out possible differences in narrower measures of parent-child interaction (such as touching, frowning, physical closeness), but in these wide-ranging measures, including overall engagement with the child, parents treat their sons and daughters equally.[37]

Stability of Attachment

Secure attachments are more stable over time than are insecure attachments, perhaps because satisfying relationships tend to keep going. Unstable attachments are often associated with mothers' having stressful life experiences that they find hard to manage, changes in availability of mothers because of employment, and changes in mothers' personality.[38]

When attachment classifications were first studied in the 1970s, researchers found a 70 to 80 percent rate of stability in attachment from twelve to eighteen months. In recent large-scale studies, however, the rate has dropped to about 50 percent.[39] Many changes in the patterns of infant lives may account for the lower stability today. Many more mothers of infants work, more fathers are involved in childcare, and more tensions exist because of the greater instability of parents' employment. See Box 5.2 for ways parents can promote secure attachments in the face of these changes.

Attaining a Sense of Identity

We have just seen how others' reactions to babies and young children give them a sense of themselves. Even as they experience a growing closeness and connectedness with parents, babies and young children develop a sense of who they are from their own actions in the world. They get a sense that they can do things—grasp things with their hands, mouth objects, make noise. As they interact with objects, they form intentions about their activities. Out of their actions, they form a sense of themselves as being separate from others, as persons who can act and will.[40]

From ten to fifteen months, babies become increasingly differentiated from parents and develop an *I-self;* they see themselves as the doer, the active agent.[41] Al-

BOX 5.2

Ways to Encourage Secure Attachments

Because early attachments are so important for babies, we want to do all we can to encourage their formation. When parents support each other, they make a positive contribution to themselves, to their marriage, and indirectly to their babies, who flourish in a happy marital atmosphere. Parents get practical help and support from meeting regularly with other parents, as we noted in Chapter 3.

The encouragement of early physical contact between mother and infant has proven highly successful in promoting secure attachments.[42] The day after the birth of their children, one group of low-income, inner-city mothers was given Snugglies in which to carry their babies; a control group of mothers was given infant seats. The mothers used the Snugglies and infant seats regularly, and at three and thirteen months, mother-child interactions were assessed. At three months, mothers who had used Snugglies were more vocally responsive with their infants, and at thirteen months, most of their infants (83 percent) had secure attachments to them; only 38 percent of the control group infants had secure attachments. Insecure attachments were observed in 61.5 percent of the control group infants but in only 17 percent of infants who had increased physical contact with their mothers.

The increased carrying helped mothers to become more sensitive and responsive to their babies. The mothers had the capacity to be caring, and the increased contact gave them all the information they required to respond appropriately. These mothers received no extra teaching, coaching, or demonstrations.

Studies show that teaching programs given in hospitals at the time of birth can also increase parents' competence in caring for their babies.[43] The information focuses on babies' states and their repertoire of behaviors, the ways they send signals to parents, and the ways parents learn to understand and respond to the signals. Especially helpful are tips on when to "engage" babies (when they are fed and alert), when to "disengage" (when they turn away or fall into a drowsy state), how to feed infants, and how to deal with crying.[44]

though babies remain attached to their parents, they move off, using parents as a secure base for exploration. During this time, babies also develop a *we-self*, internalizing their relationships with their parents. The we-self may be what sustains infants in parents' absence.

From fifteen to eighteen months a *me-self* develops. Toddlers begin to internalize how others respond to them—that is, they start to react to themselves as others do. Children at this age recognize themselves in a mirror, identify photographs of themselves, and respond strongly to others' responses to them.

From eighteen to thirty months, toddlers develop a greater understanding of what influences others to act; as a result, they gain a greater sense of the separation between the self and others. Developing language enables toddlers to describe themselves and what they do. By age two, they use pronouns such as *I, me,* and *mine* and describe their physical appearance and actions—"I run," "I play," "I have brown hair." Besides re-

Workers in extended visiting programs have gone into high-risk homes to promote appropriate parenting skills and have had success in establishing secure attachments between mothers and infants. One intervention program for lower-social-status mothers with irritable infants consisted of only three sessions with mothers and infants to increase mothers' sensitivity and responsiveness to their babies. These two-hour interventions occurred at three-week intervals when babies were six to nine months old.[45]

At six months, irritable infants were less attentive and less responsive to their mothers, smiled less, and fussed more than nonirritable babies. Mothers responded to their irritability by withdrawing and becoming passive and inactive, not wanting to initiate fussiness. Mothers were guided to attend to their babies' signals, make accurate interpretations of them, and respond appropriately. Mothers were encouraged to play with their infants, using toys and games to promote interaction.

When the infants were nine months old, the mothers were significantly more stimulating, attentive, and interactive than a control group of mothers who did not receive training. The intervention infants were more sociable and more exploring, more self-soothing, and less irritable than the control babies. At twelve months of age, 62 percent of intervention infants had secure attachments with their mothers, as compared to only 22 percent of the control infants. This powerful intervention required only six hours of training.

Two extensive reviews of such programs indicate that they help both low- and high-risk parents become more effective caregivers.[46] Although some of the programs are intensive and expensive in terms of time and level of professional help, many, such as those advocating the use of Snugglies, those giving information in hospitals, or those sponsoring parenting groups, are highly effective without being costly. A third extensive review of such programs found that the short-term interventions had greater success than the longer programs.[47]

flecting a growing self-awareness, describing one's looks and actions also actually increases self-awareness.

Toddlers develop internal standards for their behavior and are very responsive to parents' reactions to their behaviors. When they feel successful, they look happily at parents, but when they feel they have failed, they turn away or drop their heads. They show distress and try to make repairs for misdeeds.[48] Although they clearly look for approval or disapproval, they are still more concerned with their own pleasure and delight in things, and they maintain positive views of themselves.

In the preschool years, children continue to describe themselves in terms of physical characteristics and actions but also begin to organize their self-perceptions. Because they have internal standards, they see themselves in dichotomous terms such as good or bad, smart or dumb.[49] Still, they are optimistic as they approach new tasks and believe that when they want something, they will be able to achieve it and ignore any failures along the way. When success is important to them, they believe they will be able to exert whatever effort is necessary to achieve it.[50]

Gender Identity

An important part of one's self-concept is gender identity. *Gender identity* is an individual's personal experience of what it means to be a boy or girl, man or woman.[51] In early childhood, the child begins to evolve a sense of gender identity that grows in stages. First, children learn to give gender labels to boys or girls, men or women. This occurs at about age two. They then learn to associate gender labels with objects, activities, tasks, and roles. They develop a *gender schema*, or organized body of knowledge of what it means to be a boy or girl. This occurs over a much longer time.

From age two to two and a half, a child proudly announces, "I am a boy," or "I am a girl." Children gradually learn that their gender is stable across time—they will always be a boy/man or girl/woman. They also learn that gender is stable across situations—they are a girl whether they have short or long hair, wear pants or a dress, drive a truck or take care of a baby.[52] John Money says that by age four, children would find changing their gender identity as difficult as it would be for an adult.[53]

Money states that gender differentiation results from an interaction of physical, social, and psychological forces. Physical influences include genes, which, in utero, trigger hormones that lead to the development of internal and external sexual characteristics. Societies and subcultures within societies pass on beliefs about what is appropriate for boys and girls.

Even in these early years, children have an established gender identity and know that this is an unchanging part of them even if their appearance or activities change.[54] During these years and well into the elementary school years, children learn what is associated with being a boy or girl. They learn first about their own gender and then about the other. Girls have a greater gender knowledge than do boys. Because children appear most prone to gender stereotyping while they are in the process of learning, the preschool years may show a peak in stereotyped activity.[55]

Even in these years, preschoolers will approve of themselves when they play with gender-appropriate toys and feel self-critical when they do not.[56] Standards frequently come from parents, but not always. When given a truck to play with, one little girl commented, "My mommy would want me to play with this, but I don't want to."[57] She apparently derived her standards outside the family. This illustrates clearly what two social scientists found in reviewing gender development: "Gender is not simply something that is imposed on children; at all points of development, children are actively constructing for themselves what it means to be female or male."[58]

Ethnic Identity

Ethnic identity begins to be laid down in the preschool years, when children first learn to identify themselves as members of an ethnic group. They initially use skin color as a marker. In one study, African American and Native American preschoolers could correctly identify pictures of their racial groups, but when shown dolls, they preferred and identified with white dolls. Although these same children measured high in self-esteem, researchers speculated their preference for white dolls showed they were aware white figures are preferred, and feeling good about themselves, chose white dolls.[59]

As they proceed through these early years and on into school, children gradually learn what is distinctive about their own ethnic group. Ethnic identity becomes more firmly established by age seven, when children of different groups realize they cannot change their ethnic identities.[60] We will discuss ethnic identity formation in greater detail in Chapters 6 and 7.

Helping Children Regulate Their Emotions

Feelings are a part of life from the beginning and are newborns' and infants' primary tools for communicating what they need. In this section, we focus on what feelings children have in early childhood, how they deal with these feelings, and how parents can help them manage their feelings. As we noted in Chapters 2 and 3, regulation of emotions underlies children's abilities to control their behavior and function competently in many areas.

Parents can most effectively help children learn to live comfortably with their feelings when they understand the emotional life of young children. By the end of the first year, babies express interest, surprise, joy, anger, fear, and disgust. As self-awareness grows, toddlers express embarrassment, pride, guilt, and empathy.[61]

Mothers begin to guide babies to control their emotional reactions in the first few months of life. They do this with both nonverbal and verbal techniques. They avoid negative facial expressions that the baby can copy; and, as mentioned, they emphasize the positive emotions.

Although babies are clearly responsive to others' feelings, they are not totally dependent on parents' emotions. When confronted with negative stimulation, babies can cope and soothe themselves.[62] In fact, a basic task of infancy is to begin learning to regulate feelings.[63] Babies soothe themselves by sucking hands or fingers, manipulating themselves, and finding a neutral scene to fix upon.[64] Babies take an active role not only in soothing themselves but in giving themselves pleasure as well. Babies smile when they can make something happen.[65] Babies just a few months old get pleasure from making a mobile go or a rattle shake.

As soon as toddlers can talk, they talk about feelings. By age three, toddlers talk about positive feelings such as being happy, having a good time, feeling good, and being proud. They talk about negative emotions as well—being sad, scared, and angry. And they talk about uncomfortable physical states—being hungry, hot, cold, sleepy, and in pain. Words play an important role in helping toddlers learn how to handle negative feelings by enabling them to communicate these states to parents, get feedback about how appropriate the feelings are, and think about how to manage them.[66]

Toddlers also use objects to handle negative feelings. They frequently have transitional objects such as stuffed animals, blankets, pieces of cloth, and dolls to provide comfort in times of distress. The use of such objects reaches a peak in the middle of the second year, when as many as 30 to 60 percent of children use transitional objects.[67]

What I Wish I Had Known about Infancy and Early Childhood

"I remember when we brought him home from the hospital, and we had him on the changing table for a minute, and I realized, 'I don't know how to keep the engine running.' I wondered how could they let him go home with us, this little package weighing seven or eight pounds. I had no idea of what to do. I kind of knew you fed him, and you cleaned him and kept him warm; but I didn't have any hands-on experience, anything practical. In a way I would have liked them to watch me for a day or two in the hospital while I changed him, to make sure I knew how to do it. It's kind of like giving me a car without seeing whether I could drive it around the block." —*Father*

"I wasn't prepared for all the decisions. Is it okay if he does this or not? He's trying to do something; shall I step in so he doesn't hurt himself or shall I let him go? It's making all those choices, making sure what I feel." —*Mother*

"I wish I had known how much time they needed between one and two. They are mobile, but they are clueless about judgment. I think it was one of the most difficult times. Even though she did not get into a lot of trouble sticking her finger in light sockets, still she takes a lot of time and watching, so the transition to two was great." —*Mother*

"I wish I had known how much frustration comes just because kids are kids and you have to be tolerant. They don't have the attention span for some things. They might want to do something with you, but they can only do it for about fifteen minutes. You have to go places prepared with all his things or with things to keep him entertained. In the car on a trip, we have a lot of things for him to do. When you plan ahead, you can still be spontaneous at times. You learn that if you are prepared, things really don't have to be a hassle." —*Father*

Toddlers also enlist the help of parents and other caregivers to resolve negative feelings and situations beyond them. They call or pull parents to what they want remedied. As they move beyond age two, toddlers seem to have a greater understanding of when they need the extra help and call for it more quickly.[68]

Toddlers are aware, too, of others' feelings, and they develop ideas about what actions cause feelings and what actions change feelings. Following are examples of comments from twenty-eight-month-olds: "I give a big hug. Baby be happy." "Mommy exercise. Mommy having a good time." "I'm hurting your feelings 'cause I mean to you." "Grandma's mad. I wrote on wall." "You sad, Mommy. What Daddy do?" Toddlers also learn that one person's feelings can stimulate another person's actions: "I cry. Lady pick me up." "I scared of the shark. Close my eyes."[69]

Preschoolers become increasingly accurate in understanding the connections between feelings and the events and social interactions that produce them. While they at first believe that feelings are temporary, by the end of the preschool period, they recognize that feelings can persist and are influenced by what one thinks.[70]

Children are accurate in identifying what triggers emotions, especially when there is a social cause for the feelings. In one study, preschoolers agreed 91 percent of the time with adults in giving reasons for other preschoolers' feelings as they occurred in the course of everyday activity.[71] Preschoolers were most accurate in understanding anger and distress and less accurate in understanding happiness and sadness.

We turn now to how parents help children handle specific feelings.

Infant Crying

All babies cry, yet crying distresses parents and can create strain in the growing relationship. There are great differences, however, in the amount of crying among individual babies. According to one study, in newborn nurseries, babies cried from 1 to 11 minutes per hour. The average daily total per baby was about 2 hours of crying. Researchers who classified reasons found hunger to be a significant cause, as were wet or dirty diapers. The largest single category, however, was "unknown reason." It may be that crying expressed a social need for cuddling, warmth, or rhythmic motion.[72]

Babies' crying increases to an average of about 3 hours at six weeks and decreases to an average of 1 hour per day at about three months. Although hunger seems a predominant reason, unknown causes remain the second highest category during this period. As crying increases at six weeks, it becomes concentrated in the late afternoon or evening hours, with little during the day.

What strategy is most effective in terminating crying? In one study, picking up and holding the baby stopped the crying in 80 percent of situations. Feeding, which involves physical contact, was almost as effective. The least effective method was to stand at a distance and talk to the child.[73] Judy Dunn reviewed ways of comforting crying babies and found that caregivers around the world soothe by "rocking, patting, cuddling, swaddling, giving suck on breast or pacifier."[74] Effective techniques provide continuous or rhythmic—as opposed to variable—sensations for the child. For example, constant temperatures, continuous sounds, and rhythmic rocking at a steady rate reduce the amount of time the infant cries. Effective soothing techniques also reduce the amount of stimulation the baby receives from his or her own movements. Thus, holding and swaddling reduce sensations from the child's flailing arms and legs and thus decrease crying.

Monitoring the crying of babies from age three weeks to twelve weeks, investigators found that the supplemental carrying in a Snuggly for three extra hours per day eliminated the peak of crying that usually occurs at six weeks, reduced crying overall, and modified the daily pattern of the crying so there was less in the evening hours.[75] Equally important, babies who were carried more were more content and more visually and aurally alert. The supplemental carrying provides all the kinds of stimulation that we know soothe babies—rhythmic, repetitive movement with postural changes. Close physical contact with babies also gives mothers a better understanding of their infants' needs and reactions so that caregiving is more sensitive and responsive.

Pediatrician William Sammons provides another suggestion. He observed many different kinds of babies and gradually developed the belief that babies have the ability to calm themselves but that they must be given the opportunity to develop this skill.[76] Babies suck on their fingers, wrist, or arm; get into a certain body position; or focus on certain visual forms such as walls or objects or light to soothe themselves. In his pediatric practice, Sammons has encouraged parents to engage in a mutual partnership with babies so that the infants can find their own ways of self-calming.

Anger

Parents most want to help children deal with anger. In one study, Florence Goodenough found that many factors influenced the occurrence of anger.[77] Outbursts peaked in the second year and were most likely to occur when children were hungry or tired (just before meals and at bedtime) or when they were ill. Thus, when physical reserves were low, tempers flared. Outbursts were usually short-lived—most lasted less than 5 minutes—and with young children under three, the aftereffects were minimal. With increasing age, children tended to sulk and to have hard feelings. From age one to three, the immediate causes of anger seemed to be conflict with authority, difficulties over the establishment of habits (at mealtime, bathtime, and bedtime), and problems with social relationships (wanting more attention, wanting a possession someone else had). With older children, social and particularly play relationships triggered more outbursts. After the second year, boys seemed to have more outbursts than girls.

The parents of the children who had the fewest outbursts used a daily schedule to achieve a more tolerant, positive home atmosphere. They were consistent and fair in the rules they established. They had realistic expectations that children would be independent, curious, and stubborn; they anticipated problems and found ways to prevent them. These parents tried to help children conform by preparing them for changes in activities. They announced mealtimes or bathtimes in advance so children had 10 minutes or so to get ready. In these homes, parents focused on the individuality of the child. When a real conflict arose, however, they were firm.

In contrast, parents of children with many outbursts were inconsistent and unpredictable, basing decisions on their own wants rather than the children's needs. These parents tended to ignore children's needs until a problem forced them to respond. In some of these families, parents imposed a routine regardless of the children's activity of the moment and forced the children to act quickly in terms of the parent's desire. Criticism and disapproval characterized the home atmosphere.

In short, when children are tired, hungry, or sick, they are likely to respond with anger. Parental behaviors that reinforce attachment—acceptance, sensitivity to children's needs, and cooperativeness—minimize angry outbursts.

Temper Tantrums

With Goodenough's study in mind, let us examine what parenting advisors Haim Ginott and Thomas Gordon (who both stress the importance of communicating feelings) and Rudolf Dreikurs (whose focus is on changing behaviors) suggest about parental management of children's temper tantrums. Ginott recommends accepting all angry feelings but directing children's behavior into acceptable channels.[78] Parents can do this by saying, "I see you are angry, but people are not for hitting. If you want to hit, use this pillow." Neither parent nor child is permitted to hit another person. If children's tantrums are not ended by verbal statements, parents take action, even in public, returning home if a child has a tantrum in a store.[79]

Gordon suggests finding substitute activities to head off trouble. If no jumping is permitted on the sofa, parents can allow children to jump on pillows on the floor. When anger arises, Gordon recommends mutual problem solving to find a solution agreeable to both parent and child. But when a compromise is not possible, Gordon suggests that parents listen actively and provide feedback about the frustration and irritation the child feels. Sometimes a child needs nothing more than acceptance of what he is feeling.[80] Gordon cites the example of a child who was unable to go swimming because he had a cold. When the child's mother commented that she understood it was hard for him to wait until the next day, he calmed down.

Dreikurs recommends many of the techniques that Goodenough found were used by parents whose children had few tantrums.[81] When tantrums occur, Dreikurs recommends further that parents ignore children and leave the room. Ignoring a child is appropriate in public as well as at home.

Behaviorists John Krumboltz and Helen Krumboltz use a similar method of ignoring. They tell of a little boy who learned that if he cried and had a tantrum, his parents would pick him up instead of paying attention to the new baby.[82] When the parents realized that their actions were creating the tantrums, they agreed to ignore the outbursts. When the boy learned that he gained nothing by banging his head and demanding what he wanted, the tantrums stopped. The behaviorists insist that parents must be firm and consistent. Otherwise, tantrums will continue, and each time children will hold out longer because they have learned that they can win by outlasting the parents.

Stanley Turecki and Leslie Tonner, who work with difficult children, draw a distinction between the *manipulative tantrum* and the *temperamental tantrum*.[83] Children who want their way use the tantrum to manipulate the parents into giving them what they want. Turecki and Tonner recommend firm refusal to give in to such tantrums. Distracting children, ignoring their outbursts, and sending them to their rooms are all techniques for handling that kind of tantrum.

In the more intense temperamental tantrum, however, children seem out of control. They are reacting to some aspect of their temperament that has been violated. For example, the less adaptable child who is compelled to switch activities suddenly may have an outburst, or a child sensitive to fabric may have a tantrum when he or she has to wear a wool sweater. In these instances, Turecki and Tonner advise a calm and sympathetic approach. Parents can reflect the child's feelings of irritation or upset—"I know you don't like this, but it will be okay." Parents can then put their arms around the child or just be a physical presence near the child. No long discussion of what is upsetting the child takes place unless the child wants to talk. If the situation can be corrected, it should be. For example, if the wool sweater feels scratchy, let the child remove it and wear a soft sweatshirt. This is not giving in but just correcting a mistake. All parents can do then is wait out the tantrum.

Throughout a display of the temperamental tantrum, parents convey the attitude that they will help the child deal with this situation. Even though parents change their minds when good reasons are presented, they are generally consistent in waiting out the tantrum and insisting on behavior change when necessary.

Empathy

At the same time that the expression of anger is on the increase during early childhood, so expressions of affection and empathy increase as well. In the second year, babies begin to give signs of affection—love pats and strokes—to parents, particularly mothers. They are also affectionate to animals and younger children.

Empathy develops in stages during toddlerhood.[84] At ten to twelve months, babies respond to other children's distress by crying with agitation. In the second year, however, they take action—touching, cuddling, or rubbing the injured party. An eighteen-month-old girl, upset by her baby brother's crying, may bring him a diaper to hold because she likes to carry a diaper for comfort. Between eighteen months and two years, children begin to imitate the emotional reactions of the hurt individual, mimicking facial expressions of pain. Many go through a process of referring the pain to themselves. If a mother bumps her arm, the child rubs the mother's elbow and then his own. Compassionate action follows the self-referencing behavior. Investigators suggest that true kindness may depend on the ability to relate the other's distress to oneself.

Preschoolers appear more able than toddlers to adopt the perspective of another person and respond to him or her. Because they are better able to understand the sources of emotional reactions, their strategies for making things better go more directly to the source of the problem. When another child is angry, they are likely to share some material thing with the child.[85] When another child is sad or distressed, they are more likely to do something positive for the child, such as playing with or comforting the child.

Sharing and giving among friends occurs most frequently in an atmosphere of comfort and optimism. Best friends continue to share when happy, appreciative responses follow. Even when one friend will not share with another friend, as long as he or she remains happy and smiling, conflict will be averted and sharing will resume.[86]

Promoting Self-Regulation

In children's first eight or nine months of life, parents are actively involved in nourishing and giving physical care to babies, meeting their needs, and helping them regulate their functioning. Babies cooperate in the care, but parents are the more active partners, relying on their own sensitivity to understand what babies want. Now we turn to a task that parents find challenging and demanding—helping children develop the ability to control their own behavior.

Parents do many things to encourage children's compliance; they persuade and guide the child in what to do.

Encouraging Compliance

Toward the end of the first year, babies' increasing motor and cognitive skills enable them to plan and carry out actions that do not meet parents' approval, so even in the first year, parents begin guiding and modifying children's behavior. Babies also have the capacity to comply with simple requests. The way parents go about shaping children's behavior to meet standards establishes behavioral patterns that children use in interactions with others.

In the second year of life, toddlers gain increasing control of their behavior. The goal is not simple compliance with rules but autonomy, or self-regulation—the capacity to monitor and control behavior flexibly and adaptively even when an adult is not present.[87] Self-regulation is achieved by age three to four.

Parents take many actions to encourage children's cooperation with parental requests. First, they create an atmosphere of receptive compliance, described in Chapter 4.[88] When parents have secure attachments to children and are sensitive and responsive to their needs, they create a climate in which children are more likely to comply. Noncompliance is low, but when it occurs, parents use reasoning and explanations—low-power techniques—that result in a sharing of power. Sharing power with children has a strong impact because it communicates essential respect for the child as a person.[89]

In addition to creating an atmosphere for receptive compliance, parents often take preventive actions to head off conflicts before they arise. Parents divert children's attention from tempting but forbidden activities by suggesting interesting substitutes. For example, in grocery stores, they suggest that children pick out items or they make a game of identifying products or colors or items to prevent whining for candy.[90]

Establishing Rules

Parents generally introduce rules that dovetail with the toddler's increasing abilities;[91] Table 5.1 lists sample behavioral standards. A detailed study of mothers' rules and toddlers' compliance reveals that the major rules at thirteen months center on safety issues—safety for the child, safety for other people (no hitting, kicking, or biting), and safety for possessions. At about eighteen months, the rules expand to include behavior during meals, requests to inhibit behavior and delay activity, and early self-care. At about twenty-four months, more is expected in terms of polite behavior and helping with family chores (putting toys away). By thirty-six months, children are expected to do more self-care, such as dressing oneself.[92]

Children's compliance with safety rules is high and increases with age. Overall compliance appears to increase up to thirty months, and after that, children increasingly are able to comply without help from parents. Still, by age four, parents remind or guide about 40 percent of the time.

Resistance to parents' requests continues for years, but children adopt varying strategies for expressing their resistance.[93] Initially, toddlers rely on direct, often angry defiance and passive noncompliance. These methods decrease somewhat with age as toddlers develop more skill in bargaining and negotiating. Despite a change in resistant strategies as the child ages, there is "modest stability" in children's general choice of behavior. Those children who use the most unskilled forms of resistance as toddlers use the most unskilled forms as five-year-olds. Those who use simple refusal and negotiating as toddlers are most likely to use bargaining at age five.

Children often adopt similar methods in resisting parents and in influencing them to get their own way. Children who use outright defiance to resist parents use forceful methods such as demanding and whining to get what they want. Children who resist by bargaining and negotiating use persuasion to influence parents.

Defiance occurs most frequently when parents use high-power strategies such as commands, criticisms, threats, and physical punishments to control children's behavior. Suggestions and guidance in the form of explaining, persuading, directing, and verbally assisting the child to do what is wanted all increase compliance. Giving feedback about difficulties is also helpful.[94] Verbal methods make requests clear to the child. When children understand what is wanted, compliance is high; noncompliance occurs most frequently when requests are not understood.[95]

The time and involvement required for promoting self-regulation is enormous. In one study, mothers of two-year-olds intervened every 6 to 8 minutes to make a request or stop a behavior.[96] Parents must realize, however, that children most often comply

TABLE 5.1   Specific Behavioral Standards, by Category

Category	Category Items
Child safety	Not touching things that are dangerous Not climbing on furniture Not going into the street
Protection of personal property	Keeping away from prohibited objects Not tearing up books Not getting into prohibited drawers or rooms Not coloring on walls or furniture
Respect for others	Not taking toys away from other children Not being too rough with other children
Food and mealtime routines	Not playing with food Not leaving table in the middle of a meal Not spilling drinks, juice
Delay	Waiting when Mom is on the telephone Not interrupting others' conversations Waiting for a meal
Manners	Saying "please" Saying "thank you"
Self-care	Dressing oneself Asking to use the toilet Washing up when requested Brushing teeth when requested Going to bed when requested
Family routines	Helping with chores when requested Putting toys away Keeping room neat

J. Heidi Gralinski and Claire B. Kopp, "Everyday Rules for Behavior: Mothers' Requests to Young Children," *Developmental Psychology* 29 (1993): 573–584. Copyright © 1993 by the American Psychological Association. Reprinted with permission.

with requests. In fact, they take pleasure in matching their actions to the words of another. The pleasure of accomplishing a goal is a powerful incentive for toddlers' obeying commands. In another study, toddlers who were asked to do easy and interesting tasks happily repeated the tasks when no adult was involved.[97]

Positive feelings increase children's compliance. In one study, mothers were trained to play with children for 10 to 15 minutes per day for a week in a nondirective, responsive manner—following the child's lead, when possible being a partner in the play, avoiding comments and questions.[98] In the laboratory, the children had more positive moods after playing in this way with mothers than did children whose mothers were given no special play instructions.

In another part of the same study, when children were instructed to recall a happy, positive mood for 15 seconds, they were more compliant in picking up blocks than were children who were instructed to recall a negative mood such as anger or fear for 15 seconds. Although we cannot conclude from this study that responsive play leads directly to compliance—as the differences in positive mood between the two groups of children were not significant after a week of play—we can say that responsive play leads to pleasurable feelings and that a pleasurable, good mood leads to compliance.

Cultural and Social Influences That Affect Parenting in Infancy

In Chapter 2, we described interdependent and independent models of caregiving. The differences between the two models are seen clearly in infancy. The interdependent model emphasizes close physical contact and a very close relationship between parent and child.[99] The infant is held or carried much of the time, is nursed often, and at night frequently sleeps in the same bed with the mother. Mother and child are considered a unit, and babies grow with an intuitive understanding of what parents want.

The independent model emphasizes the child's growing independence and interest in the world. There is less carrying, less holding, more toys to manipulate, and more devices, such as strollers and playpens, that emphasize separation between parent and child. Children are more likely to be bottle-fed and at night are expected to sleep alone in their own cribs, often in their own rooms.

As examples of the independent model, parents in the United States present an interesting contrast to parents in Japan, who follow the interdependent model.[100] The contrast is especially revealing because both countries are child-centered and industrialized, with similar standards of living. Japanese mothers focus on closeness and dependency within the parent-child relationship. They indulge infants and encourage social responsiveness and interaction. When they play with their infants, they focus on being social partners. Japanese mothers encourage early emotional control, social sensitivity, and responsiveness to others.

Although parents in the United States rely on the independent model of caregiving, there is a growing emphasis on behaviors characteristic of the interdependent model. Many U.S. mothers are following the recommendations of the medical community by breast-feeding their babies for at least a year. And more parents are using Snugglies and slings to carry their children, as parents do in other parts of the world. Changes are occurring in sleep patterns as well. In most parts of the world, infants sleep with a parent (cosleeping), and most toddlers and older children sleep with or near a parent. Surveys reveal that in the United States, infants in middle-class families sleep alone or in bassinets or cribs near a parent, and by six months of age, most sleep in their own rooms.[101] In families of lower social status, however, a significant number of babies cosleep with parents—in one sample, 80 percent of African American infants and 23 percent of European American infants slept with their parent or parents.[102] And now a growing number of middle- to upper-class parents are sleeping with their babies, perhaps to make breast-feeding easier at night, to reduce babies' crying, or to stay connected with the child at night.

As we noted in Chapter 2, babies' sleep is a matter of great importance to American parents. There are two general approaches to helping babies sleep. The first and more traditional one in the United States was put forth by Richard Ferber in 1985[103] and by Athleen Godfrey and Anne Kilgore in 1998.[104] This approach stresses that babies wake up several times at night and that as they mature, most learn to put themselves back to sleep. So, babies need to develop habits of going to sleep that they can duplicate in the middle of the night to put themselves back to sleep. If they develop the habit of falling asleep while nursing or being rocked, they will be unable to duplicate those conditions in the middle of the night and will cry. Parents' job is to develop a regular routine that soothes the child, who is then put in the crib to fall asleep alone. Parents respond to crying with verbal soothing but no picking up. Parents then increase the length of time each night before providing the soothing, and the child's crying gradually decreases. When mothers in other countries are told of this method, they consider it abusive or neglectful to leave the child alone to sleep.[105] The other approach to helping babies sleep is that followed by the rest of the world—namely, having babies sleep with mothers or both parents. The babies may fall asleep near the parents or in the parents' bed, but they sleep most of the night with the parents.

Controversy exists about the wisdom of cosleeping. A recent report identified over 800 deaths associated with cosleeping over the past eight years, either because of the parent's rolling over on the child or the child's being wedged between the mattress and the wall or the headboard.[106] The counterargument is that many more babies die of sudden infant death syndrome (SIDS) when sleeping alone and that by cosleeping a nearby parent could perhaps detect breathing difficulties before death. Moreover, when babies cosleep with mothers, they nurse more, and breast-feeding is thought to be protective against SIDS. Thus, environmental factors that promote breast-feeding are thought to reduce infant vulnerability to SIDS.[107] Those parents who want to cosleep are advised to use an attachment to their bed where the child can sleep without risk of rollover or being wedged.[108]

Although Ferber is considered by many to be a staunch supporter of sleeping alone, he stated in a recent interview that his children slept in the same bed with him and his wife and had to be trained to sleep in their own beds.[109] In general, his feeling is that children can sleep with or without parents. "What's really important is that the parents work out what they want to do."

James McKenna, a biological anthropologist and director of the Mother-Baby Behavioral Sleep Laboratory at Notre Dame, believes that cosleeping regulates the infant's physiological system. "Biologically and psychologically, infants, children, and their parents are designed to sleep close."[110] He acknowledges that there are no systematic studies of the relationship of sleeping arrangements to children's developing personality characteristics, but studies are beginning to produce evidence of the benefits of cosleeping. Cosleeping children were described in one study as less fearful and better behaved than children who slept alone. A study of adults who, as children, coslept with their parents suggested the adults had a feeling of satisfaction with life. They came from Hispanic American and African American families in New York and Chicago. The study, however, found no simple outcome of cosleeping; rather, cosleeping as a child was seen as part of a relationship embedded in a cultural and social system related to adult characteristics.

In contemporary society, cosleeping is one facet of a larger system of *attachment parenting*, which incorporates many aspects of the interdependent model of caregiving. Pediatrician William Sears encourages parents to accept their babies' dependency needs and meet them appropriately. He describes the five Bs of attachment parenting in infancy: (1) bonding with the infant at birth, (2) breast-feeding, (3) bed sharing (cosleeping), (4) baby wearing (carrying the baby in a Snuggly or a sling), and (5) belief in the baby's cry as an important signal. The five Bs keep baby and parents physically connected so parents can learn who their child is and be able to respond in a sensitive, caring way.[111]

Sears raised his own children this way and has been counseling parents for twenty-seven years about attachment parenting. The number of attachment-parenting advocates is on the increase, perhaps because as more mothers work outside the home, they want to find ways to stay connected to their infants and young children. Advocates of attachment parenting believe it (1) simplifies life (parents have no bottles, cribs, or strollers to manage); (2) increases parents' sensitivity and responsiveness as they get to know their babies better; (3) promotes gentle discipline because children's natural tendencies to independence and self-control are allowed to develop slowly and gradually over time; and (4) focuses on the family's needs, not just the needs of parent or infant.[112]

> With attachment parenting, parents and children find their needs met in cooperation with one another, thus creating a family-centered lifestyle. A key benefit of this responsive style of caregiving is that both parents and children feel that they are getting their "cup filled" as some parents say. Children feel whole and secure, while parents feel more relaxed and confident.[113]

Attachment parenting does not require that a caregiver be at home full-time, and there is much advice on how to combine attachment parenting and working. Parents are advised to create a community of caregivers who share the parents' values and will behave in the same way toward the baby when the parents are not there. Parents are advised to select caregivers who will give breastmilk the mothers have pumped, will carry the children during the day, and will respond quickly and attentively to children's cries.

Advocates believe that "experienced attachment parents who have seen their children through early childhood and beyond describe this gentle nurturing style as a completely fulfilling way of life."[114] Research evidence certainly supports elements of attachment parenting—the importance of sensitive, responsive care and the decrease in crying that comes from increased early carrying—but it is not clear that cosleeping and prolonged carrying of the child are beneficial, nor is it clear that immediate gratification of desires is essential or wise for all babies. Recall that soothed fearful and inhibited children maintained those behaviors when firm support to learn self-soothing appeared more useful in helping them overcome these behaviors (see Chapter 1).

Who are the parents who have the most difficulty in parenting infants and young children? In this section we look at (1) the special difficulties adolescent, depressed, substance-abusing, and troubled parents face as they rear their young children and (2) the ways to help these parents.

Adolescent Parents

As we noted in Chapter 1, adolescent parents, whether fathers or mothers, are more likely to have difficulties parenting for a variety of reasons. First, they come to parenthood with a history of many difficult experiences such as poverty, school failure and dropout, sexual abuse, and conflicted relationships with parents and partners. Second, adolescent parents are still in childhood themselves and have not gained the educational, social, financial, and psychological stability that will enable them to invest energy in caring for the next generation. On average, they have experienced fewer positive successes, and they face demanding challenges that would stress the sturdiest adult.

ADOLESCENT MOTHERS Adolescents' psychological immaturity creates difficulty in caregiving. Although they can be as warm as older mothers, adolescent mothers view their infants as more difficult, and they are less realistic in their expectations of children.[115] They foster premature independence in their infants, pushing them to hold their bottles, sit up too early, and scramble for toys before they can get them; however, as infants become toddlers, these mothers reverse their behavior and become overly controlling, not letting toddlers explore freely or have choices in activities.[116] Adolescent mothers also fail to provide a stimulating home environment conducive to learning, and they offer less verbal stimulation.[117]

Joy Osofsky and her coworkers explore how a mother's ability to regulate feelings affects her children.[118] They note that adolescent mothers are often depressed and emotionally unstable. These feelings can lead to the negative interpretations of their children's behavior and the mothers' inability to respond in a controlled way. These mothers are less available to their children in both infancy and toddlerhood, and the lack of nurturing sensitivity and availability to their children may account for the lower levels of secure attachments found in children of adolescent mothers.

Infants and toddlers of adolescent mothers do not differ from children of older mothers in cognitive measures; however, by the time such children reach preschool age, differences begin to emerge and continue into elementary school years.[119] Children of adolescent mothers face a greater likelihood of academic difficulties, school failure, and behavioral problems. Teens of adolescent mothers are also more likely than their peers to become teenage parents. Factors that promote positive development include the mothers' improved circumstances. If a mother goes off welfare between her child's preschool and adolescent years, she reduces the risk of her child's being retained a grade. When a male figure is present, adolescent offspring have fewer behavioral problems than those with no such figure.

The child's sex and temperament interact with other risk/protective factors to influence parenting.[120] Adolescent mothers appear more involved with sons than with daughters. When babies have easy, adaptable temperaments, adolescent mothers are more successful with them and feel better about themselves as parents. Conversely, if the child has a difficult temperament, does not adjust well, and is hard to soothe, adolescent mothers may have a more difficult time because it is hard for them to be patient.

Although these findings come largely from studies of African American teenage mothers, work with other samples yields similar findings. Judith Musick has studied samples with a broader representation of poor adolescent mothers of African American, Hispanic American, and European American backgrounds living in small towns and rural areas as well as urban areas in the Midwest and Southeast. In these samples, she finds similar difficulties in the maturity level of all the mothers and in their abilities to translate their love for their children into supportive, nurturing care.[121] She too finds diversity of outcome, with some mothers making heroic efforts to raise their children under very difficult circumstances.

Perhaps more important, her work has uncovered problems of a different sort—namely, that 65 percent of the adolescent mothers surveyed in one study were sexually abused in childhood or early adolescence and that 61 percent were abused by numerous perpetrators. She believes that these young girls feel helpless, unprotected, inferior, and unworthy of care; as a result, they fail to develop self-protection skills and are vulnerable to predatory or uncaring men. Further, they carry these feelings and difficulties into their role as parent and often cannot protect their own children from sexual abuse. In Chapter 10, we will explore the effects of sexual abuse in greater detail.

Other studies, comparing African American adolescent mothers with Hispanic American mothers, find that in both groups teenage mothers are more depressed, engage in less childcare, and provide less stimulating environments than do older mothers of the same ethnic backgrounds. However, African American adolescent mothers receive more support from family and friends and are less strict than Hispanic American mothers.[122]

Although they undoubtedly face many problems, adolescent mothers are often committed to their children, and many raise them successfully. Unfortunately, we pay less attention to the successes. For example, 75 percent of teen mothers studied in Baltimore were employed and not involved with social services, yet we focus on the 25 percent who received services.[123]

Who are the successful adolescent mothers? They are those who use contraceptives and control their fertility. They stay in school or return to school and complete their education. They maintain a high level of motivation and high educational goals for themselves. The most successful of them enter stable marriages with men who provide support and help.

ADOLESCENT FATHERS Discussions of adolescent parenthood have focused primarily on the mother, in part because a significant number of fathers (estimated at 50 percent) are older and are not teenagers. Although they are typically less involved with their children, adolescent fathers are often not completely absent. About 25 percent of adolescent fathers live with their infants, and a national survey suggests that about 57 percent visit weekly in the first two years of life. The percentage of those visiting drops as the children grow older—40 percent when the child is between two and four and a half, 27 percent when the child is four and a half to seven, and 22 percent when the child is over seven.[124]

African American fathers are more likely to be involved than are European American and Hispanic American fathers. Only 12 percent of African American fathers have no contact with their children, whereas 30 percent of European American fathers and 37 percent of Hispanic American fathers have no contact.[125]

Adolescent fathers are more likely to be involved when other people in the environment support their involvement. (See the interview in this chapter with Dr. James Levine.) When adolescent fathers do remain involved, however, they, like adolescent mothers, use many directives and negative comments. Adolescent fathers were observed in one study while solving problems and tasks with their children. The fathers offered strategies for completing the tasks, but they also gave many commands and made many negative comments as the children worked on the tasks. The fathers' negative ways of relating to their children encouraged negativity and resistance in their children, thus creating a vicious cycle of parents' negativity triggering children's negativity, which in turn intensified parents' negative views of their children. Researchers conclude, "Through their fathers' early entry into parenting and their parents' lack of resources and use of negative control, these children may be shaped, like their parents before them, into the next generation of antisocial children."[126]

HELP FOR TEENAGE MOTHERS AND FATHERS   Two kinds of programs attack the problems of teenage pregnancies: (1) those that postpone the birth of the first child by means of effective education and birth control and (2) those that help parents once they have had children. Both programs emphasize effective birth control while encouraging teens to develop a sense of confidence about their ability to make and carry out future goals for themselves.[127]

Although help for adolescent mothers includes help with parenting, continuing education, and meeting responsibilities, research suggests that these mothers also benefit from programs that help them sustain positive relationships with their children and their families. Because adolescent mothers tend not to trust others, they need help in developing trust both in themselves as competent caregivers and in the relationships they form with their children. They require help in building their own self-esteem to help them survive the irritations and frustrations of rearing children. They also need practice in empathizing with their babies so they can read babies' cues and better meet their needs. Videotaping interactions helps mothers recognize their powerful role in their babies' lives.[128] Joy Osofsky and her coworkers conclude, "We feel that an emphasis on positive mental health—that is, a focus on what may go right rather than wrong with adolescent mothers and their infants—will lead us forward toward the development of more effective preventive interventions."[129]

There are also programs to encourage active parenting for adolescent fathers. In Cleveland, for example, Charles Ballard has founded a private National Institute for

Responsible Fatherhood and Family Development.[130] Having grown up without a father and with anger because of his lack of a positive male role model, Ballard has established programs to help men learn responsibility so they can care for their children and be positive forces in their lives. As a social worker helping single adolescent mothers, he decided to go out on the streets and look for the fathers. He organized groups to discuss paternal responsibility. He raised money to support a small staff and formed the Teen Father Program. Fathers in his program have three requirements: they must (1) legitimize the child, (2) be in school or a general education development (GED) program, and (3) have a job. With the exception of the first requirement, these are the same actions that mothers are encouraged to take. This program has been extended to young mothers and grandparents, with the aim of strengthening the entire family. Now it is expanding to other cities, and Ballard believes there are applications to other social groups as well. "The problem is not exclusive to African-Americans and to poor people. A lot of men who have children in their homes—doctors, lawyers, politicians—are not taking care of their kids. When fathers get closer with their children, communities will become safer for all of us."[131]

Depressed Parents

Studies of depressed parents have focused on mothers, as they are the ones who interact most frequently with their babies.[132] As a group, depressed mothers look at their infants less often, touch them less often, have fewer positive facial expressions, and vocalize with infants less often than do nondepressed mothers. They are also less affectionate and play less with their babies. They see their babies in a more negative light than do nondepressed mothers. In addition, depressed mothers rate themselves more positively than others see them.

Depressed mothers' affect seems contagious because their babies' affect is negative as well. Babies of depressed mothers are fussier, more irritable, and less active than are babies of nondepressed mothers. Further, babies of depressed mothers show these behaviors with adult nondepressed strangers, who, in turn, respond with negative affect, setting up a vicious cycle. Depression in babies is observed at birth. They have higher sensory thresholds and need more stimulation to respond. They already have flat affect and low activity levels. They also have some of the same physiological characteristics that distinguish their depressed mothers from nondepressed mothers, such as elevated levels of norepinephrine and cortisol, which contribute to irritability. Moreover, by three months of age, they have EEGs that show right frontal activation similar to their mothers'.

Babies of mothers who are successfully treated for depression show no long-term adverse effects of their infant experience. Preschool children of mothers who continue to be depressed, however, show the same physiological characteristics as earlier. Further, depressed mothers continue to report having more behavior problems with their children than nondepressed mothers report with their children.

Because the effects of mothers' depression on infants' behavior are reversible when mothers are treated, interventions to help depressed mothers and their infants are essential. Effective interventions are directed to the mother and the child and their patterns of interaction.[133] In addition to the usual psychiatric treatments of medication and psychotherapy, interventions to alter mothers' mood include massage therapy and relaxation therapy, which have been found to lower mothers' scores on measures of anxiety and depression. Further, music therapy sessions, during which mothers listen to their preferred music, appear to temporarily reduce right frontal EEG activation.

Massage therapy—provided by mothers and professional therapists—is also an effective intervention for infants of depressed mothers. Massage therapy reduces infants' fussiness, improves their sleep patterns, increases their ability to soothe themselves and their activity level, and results in more positive patterns of interaction with mothers. In one study, just rubbing an infant's legs while the child gazed at the still face of the mother reduced the infant's distress. In another study, an adult's rubbing the infant's legs while smiling and cooing increased the infant's eye contact more than smiling and cooing alone.

Coaching also improved the interaction patterns between mothers and children. Withdrawn, depressed mothers were encouraged to keep their infants' attention. When mothers played more games and had more positive facial expressions, their babies responded with more activity and more positive moods. Depressed mothers who were intrusive and overstimulating were thought to be more effective when they imitated their infants' behavior. Imitating babies seemed to slow mothers' responses and enabled them to react more appropriately to their infants.

Interventions that seek to change depressed mothers' lifestyles have also been effective in decreasing depression. Becoming more active and returning to school or work improves mothers' interactions with their babies; they are less negative than depressed mothers who remain at home. In one study, mothers who were encouraged to return to school where infants were cared for in a center improved in mood and positive interactions with their infants. While there, infants received optimal stimulation and regulation of moods for significant periods of time during the day and were better able to relate to their mothers.

Substance-Abusing Parents

Although systematic research has not yet detailed the specific ways in which substance abuse affects parent-child interactions, we can make general observations on how parents' substance abuse affects children. It is difficult, however, to disentangle the effects of the substance abuse itself from the effects of the preexisting psychological and social problems of the parents and the poor living conditions that often accompany substance abuse once the child is born.

Substance abuse is associated with pregnancy and birth complications. Pregnant women who abuse substances are less likely to be in good health and less likely to seek prenatal care, compounding potential problems with pregnancy and delivery. Their babies may be born prematurely and be small for their gestational age. Substance abuse during pregnancy affects children's prenatal development directly and can lead to fetal damage and to ongoing health problems after birth.[134]

Infants born to heroin and morphine addicts are born addicted to substances, further complicating the process of nurturing these children. Definitive answers are not available on the long-term consequences of mothers' drug abuse because these children have not yet been followed through adolescence to adulthood. But there are indications that these children are more likely to have impairments in arousal, activity level, attention modulation, and motor and cognitive development. The kind and severity of impairment depends on the type, amount, and timing of the substance abuse during pregnancy.[135]

Fetal alcohol syndrome (FAS) serves as an example of the kind of damage a substance, even a legal one, can do. FAS is a congenital condition acquired by some children of alcoholic mothers. These babies are stunted in growth and development and are hyperactive. Their faces may be deformed, with asymmetrical features, low-set eyes, and small ears, and their intellectual growth is retarded. Worst of all, the damage is not reversible. When FAS was first identified, experts believed that a steady, daily consumption of 3 to 6 ounces of alcohol by the mother was necessary to produce abnormalities. But more recent research suggests that smaller doses have been related to such problems as low birth weight, sucking difficulties, and developmental delays.

Observational studies of substance-abusing mothers and their infants indicate that these mothers are more negative and are at times more withdrawn but at other times more interfering and directive than non-substance-abusing mothers.[136] They have difficulty being sensitive, responsive, caregivers, and insecure attachments are more likely between substance-abusing mothers and their infants and toddlers than between non-substance-abusing mothers and their children. One of the few studies of substance-abusing fathers and their young children yields a similar finding. Alcoholic fathers are more negative in interactions with their one-year-olds and more directive than fathers who have few or no alcoholic problems.[137]

Parents' substance abuse can not only produce long-lasting physical and intellectual impairments in children but also put them at risk for other problems.[138] Parents who abuse substances are more prone to violence—toward both adults and children. They are more likely to physically or sexually abuse, neglect, or abandon their children. Even if their behavior is not that extreme, they have more angry arguments in their families; and high levels of anger, as we noted in Chapter 3, are damaging to children.

Programs to help parents eliminate substance abuse must pay attention to the needs of the children of these parents as well.[139] First, drug-exposed infants with vulnerability to stress may be especially affected by parents' chaotic living arrangements. Effort must be directed to helping these parents establish stable and nonviolent households. Second, because their arousal and regulatory systems are altered, these children need help on a continuing basis. They experience difficulties as they enter group situations and the demanding environment of school. More information is needed on the medications and educational interventions that would help children stabilize their emotional reactions and identify pertinent stimulation in an effective way. Third, psychological assistance must be available to parents and children on an ongoing basis to help them cope with a variety of everyday problems that are only compounded by their circumstances. Children of substance-abusing parents are at increased risk for developing mood problems as well as substance-abuse problems themselves. Mental health professionals, however, must be aware of the complicated interactions of biological, genetic, and environmental factors. All these factors must be kept in mind in order to break "the continued cycle of substance use, poverty, and environmental chaos that so often tracks the lives of so many children from substance-using homes."[140]

It is noteworthy that non-substance-abusing adults who grew up in a home where a parent was a substance abuser tend to have difficulties as a parent. Philip Cowan and Carolyn Cowan report that, to their surprise, 20 percent of the parents in their study of couples becoming parents grew up with an alcoholic parent. Although none reported current problems with alcohol, "on *every* index of adjustment to parenthood—symptoms of depression, self-esteem, parenting stress, role dissatisfaction, and decline in satisfaction with marriage—men and women whose parents had abused alcohol had significantly greater difficulty."[141]

Even more distressing was the generational legacy of the children (the grandchildren of the alcoholics) in their study. Parents saw their preschoolers as less successful, though objective measures suggested that these children functioned as well as others. "This suggests that parents who grow up with troubled and ineffective parenting develop unrealistic expectations of what they can expect of their children, and as a result, have difficulty seeing their children's behavior in a positive light."[142] (In Chapter 11, we look at how parents have dealt with growing up in homes of substance-abusing parents.)

Troubled Families

The challenges facing adolescent, depressed, and substance-abusing parents are substantial. Equally significant are problems that are sometimes encountered within the range of average families. Problem behaviors can evolve over time into significant difficulties.

In a longitudinal study of children ages one to three, researchers identified a cluster of families in which the parents had particular difficulties controlling sons' behavior.[143] In these families, toddler sons defied parents' requests, and the interactions quickly escalated into angry power struggles with parents. Parents' responses were to express irritation at the children's behavior and to use simple prohibitions and directives with no attempt to guide the behavior or give reasons for what to do.

One cluster of troubled families had difficulties over the entire two-year period of observation, and by age three, these boys were more likely to have aggressive behavior problems. In these consistently troubled families, parents initially became angry *after* the child defied them, but by the end of the third year, they were angry with and critical of their children at the *beginning* of their attempts to control them. Parental anger was highly likely to trigger resistance in the child. A subgroup of the troubled parents seemed to overpower their children, so that by age three, the boys no longer defied the authoritarian control.

Measures of the family at the end of the child's first year of life significantly predicted families that would and would not have difficulties in the second and third years. Those families with the greatest economic, social, and psychological resources had the fewest difficulties. These resources appeared to buffer parents so that they did not respond to children's increasing self-assertiveness with anger and irritability.

In these studies, temperamental qualities such as infant emotionality at ten months and negativity at age one did not directly predict the child's behavior at age three.[144] Nevertheless, the child's negativity at age one in combination with parenting practices did predict those children who would have problems with aggressive and impulsive behaviors and those who would have difficulties with shy, inhibited behaviors. When male infants were highly negative and mothers were negative and less positive in dealing with them, as boys they were more likely to have aggressive, hostile behaviors. When boys were highly negative at age one and fathers were more positive and less negative, the boys were more likely to be shy and inhibited at age three. As in other studies of inhibited behaviors, high parental support does not seem to help the child change the behavior and become more expressive and outgoing.

In looking at the special problems some parents face in rearing children in these early years, it is important to note that parents can have more than one of these special problems. For example, adolescent mothers are more likely than other mothers to suffer depression. One can see also that a common feature of parents' difficulties is their negative, critical approach to children. Second, parents often have difficulty responding in appropriate ways to children, such as withdrawing or being overstimulating. Interventions can help these parents. In addition to the interventions mentioned in the preceding sections and in Box 5.2, strategies described in both Chapters 3 and 4 are helpful in dealing with these problems.

Creating a Positive Family Atmosphere

Siblings are usually born within a few years of each other, so during the early childhood of many a child, parents are incorporating another child into the family. Parents have a strong desire for children to love and care for each other. The question is, How do parents promote positive relationships within the family?

Although most firstborn children show signs of upset and frustration after a sibling's birth and misbehave, particularly when the mother is interacting with the baby, the vast majority (82 percent) of two- to four-year-old firstborns have positive feelings about being a brother or sister. At the end of the first year, 63 percent report wanting another sibling.[145]

Parents use different strategies to integrate a new child into the family.[146] In some families, fathers attend to the needs of the firstborn and mothers care for the newborn; in other families, the father takes on more household tasks, leaving the mother time to care for both children; and in a third group of families, parents become interchangeable, and both do all tasks. When parents are warm and responsive with both children and have secure attachments to each child, the children are more

The vast majority of two- to four-year-old firstborns have positive feelings about being a big brother or sister.

likely to get along with each other. When parents have a positive relationship with each other, there is less sibling conflict. Conversely, when parents have more conflict with each other or when parents use physical punishment with children, then sibling conflicts increase.

When parents maintain high standards for behavior and have warm and caring relationships with their children, they help young children adopt kind and helpful behavior to others' suffering.[147] Parents not only model kindness but also teach children how to do what is expected. Mothers expect children to control aggression, and they show disappointment when they do not. They make clear but nonangry comments such as, "Children are not for hitting," or, "Stop, you are hurting him."

In Chapter 3 we examined many strategies for creating positive, supportive relationships among all family members. Here, we describe a new one—reinforcing positive relationships through the stories we tell each other every day. "Babies are surrounded by the stories parents, siblings, and friends tell one another, and them, a captive audience. By the time children are 2 and 3 years old, they begin adding their own voices to the stories that surround them."[148] Stories initially consist of only a few words about an event—"Played house. I was baby." Observations reveal that mothers and toddlers tell about nine stories each hour.[149] In addition to telling stories to others, young children, as they play, often construct ongoing stories of what they are doing, monologues that will later develop into thoughts and day-dreams. By the time children grow up and are in college, they tell as many as five to thirty-eight stories each day.

Stories serve several purposes.[150] Stories shape our views of ourselves, other people, and events in our lives. We often discover more about what we think, feel, or know in the course of telling someone about an experience. We gain information about the world and our culture from the narratives told each day. In Chapter 4, we discussed that children develop scripts about daily routines and activities. Stories contribute to the evolving scripts that, in turn, shape the child's behavior.

As the emphasis in understanding children's development has broadened to include the social context of their lives, increasing interest has focused on understanding the family atmosphere and environment that are more than the sum of the individuals involved. Analyzing the stories family members tell each other is one way of understanding patterns of family interactions and the family culture. Stories are "naturally occurring accounts of life experiences, organized, stored, and recounted in personally meaningful ways."[151]

A group of family researchers has formed the Family Narrative Consortium (FNC) to develop a common coding system for analyzing parents' stories and has presented preliminary data on the reliability of the system and its usefulness in understanding family functioning.[152] The researchers looked at such dimensions as the organization of the stories, the behavior and affect of the people telling them and the match of the affect with the content, the way husbands and wives worked together in constructing the stories, and beliefs and expectations about social relationships expressed in the stories. In early analyses, the researchers found that mothers' negative affect expressed in criticism and conflict with family members at the story times and fathers' negative beliefs about relationships expressed in their stories are related to children's aggressive, hostile behavior problems. So, the content and affect of stories has a significant influence on family functioning.

Susan Engel gives parents tips for encouraging children to participate in story-telling. Children tell stories when they feel "confidence and joyousness in telling stories,"[153] and parents give that confidence when they listen attentively, expressing interest with smiles, gasps, facial expressions, repetitions. Parents collaborate in the stories by asking open-ended questions that encourage elaboration, and they expose children to a variety of stories and poems that stimulate children's stories. "Families that are able to make sense of their experiences, pleasant or challenging, however, provide their children with a meaning-making system that can better prepare them for an unpredictable world."[154]

How Parents Change As They Raise Young Children

Ellen Galinsky describes the first year of an infant's life as the *nurturing stage* of parenthood.[155] Parents focus on forming an attachment to the new baby, caring for the child, and accepting their new roles as parents. As they care for the child, they continue to question themselves: "Am I doing okay?" "Am I the kind of parent I want to be?" Although they devote most of their energy to the child during the first few months, parents gradually incorporate the other parts of their lives into caregiving activities. Relationships between mother and father and work activities are expanded to include the baby; relationships with other children and relatives are redefined. A great deal goes on during these early months.

From the child's second to fourth or fifth year, parents enter what Galinsky calls the *authority stage*. Parents must deal with their own feelings about having power, setting rules, and enforcing them. Parents have to decide what is reasonable when children mobilize all their energy to oppose them and get their own way. In the nurturing stage, parents were primarily concerned with meeting babies' needs and coordinating their own needs with caregiving activities. Usually, the appropriate childcare behavior was clear—the baby had to be fed, changed, bathed, put to bed. Although judgment was required in deciding whether to let the child cry or in timing sleep patterns, still the desired aim was clear. In the authority stage, however, parents must develop clear rules and have the confidence not only to enforce them but also to deal with the tantrums that follow. Parents require self-assurance so they can act calmly and neutrally when they meet with opposition from their children. Many parents, bogged down in battle with their toddler, find themselves doing and saying things they vowed they never would—the very words they hated to hear from their own parents when they were children. Parents are shaken and upset as their ideal images of themselves as parents collide with the reality of rearing children.

Parents' images of themselves undergo revision in light of the way they actually behave. This can be a painful process because it involves change. Parents must change either their ideal image or their behavior to come closer to living up to their own standards. Parents' images of children are revised as well. Parents discover that children are not always nice, loving, cooperative, and affectionate. Children can be extremely aggressive and destructive—breaking things, hitting parents, pulling their hair.

One father described how he coped with these feelings by revising the kind of parent he wanted to be and by finding new ways to relate to his eighteen-month-old child so that he met the image he wanted to keep of himself as parent.

> In my family, growing up, when someone got angry at someone, they'd stop loving them—which made me feel abandoned as a child.
>
> When my son gets angry, the easiest thing for me to do would be the same—walk out and slam the door.
>
> But when you've suffered that yourself you don't want to see it repeated. What I do is to stay and let the rage go through my ears and try to think clearly about what's going on.
>
> I tell him that even though I've said no, I still love him. I hold him while he's having a temper tantrum, and I tell him it's okay for him to be angry with me.
>
> Being able to do this is recent, new, and learned, and it's hard work. In the past, I couldn't see beyond my own feelings. What I've now learned is that I have to see past them.
>
> Another thing I've learned is that if I've gotten angry at my son or if I've done something that I feel I shouldn't have, I'm not the Loch Ness monster or the worst person in the world. I learned the reparability of a mistake.[156]

Parents must also deal with each other as authorities. It is wonderful if both parents agree on how and when to enforce rules. But this is rarely the case. One parent is often stricter or less consistent; one may dislike any physical punishment, and the other may believe it is the only technique to handle serious rule breaking. Communicating with each other and finding ways to handle differences is important for parents. Parents sometimes agree to back each other up on all occasions. Other times, they agree to discuss in private any serious misgivings they have about the other's discipline; then the original rule setter is free to revise the rule. Still other times, one parent may decide to let the other handle discipline completely. This is the least desirable solution because it means one parent is withdrawn from interaction with the child. Parents need to find ways to resolve differences so they can give each other the support they need in childrearing. Mutual support is the most important source of strength in parenting.

Single parents and employed parents must work with other authority figures, such as day care providers or relatives who provide major care, to develop consistent ways of handling discipline. Again, communicating with other caregivers helps provide consistent solutions to problems. When authorities do not agree, children become confused and are less able to meet expectations.

As parents become aware of their personal feelings about being authorities and learn to deal with them, they can put these misgivings aside and deal as neutrally with rule enforcement as possible. A range of preparations, such as reading books, gaining information from groups, taking parenting courses, and talking with other parents, helps parents handle the demands of conflicting feelings in the authority stage.

Main Points

As they make the transition to parenthood, parents

- often do not anticipate the stress produced by all the changes
- learn to set priorities and make decisions accordingly
- are able to be more competent when they receive support from their spouse, relatives, and friends
- use active listening and mutual problem-solving techniques to handle stress

Attachment

- is secure when parents are accepting and sensitive in meeting the baby's needs
- is insecure when parents are unavailable and uninvolved, intrusive and controlling, or frightened and traumatized
- develops between babies and both parents
- is the basis for the baby's sense of being lovable and worthwhile
- in infancy relates to social competence in the toddler and preschool years
- provides a model to young children about how people relate to each other
- can be promoted by interventions

Mothers and fathers
- interact with babies in different ways; mothers tend to be nurturing caregivers and fathers stimulating playmates
- can be partners in childrearing when mothers and other child specialists recognize that fathers are important figures in the process of parenting

Children's emotional control increases when parents
- provide models of controlling their own feelings
- listen to children's feelings and accept them as valid
- put children's needs ahead of their own
- use low-power parenting strategies to promote children's emotional control
- use mutual problem-solving techniques to settle differences

Parental techniques that encourage autonomy and self-regulation include
- creating an environment of receptive compliance
- using low-power parenting strategies of reasoning, suggesting, persuading, and guiding to control the child's behavior
- sharing power with the child
- decreasing defiance by clearly explaining what is wanted

Children develop a sense of identity that includes
- a sense of being an active agent, of being an active doer
- a sense of gender identity that is initially based on parents' positive and negative emotional responses to gender-appropriate activities
- a burgeoning sense of ethnic identity that begins with the child's awareness of the distinctiveness of ethnic groups

Cultural and social forces
- influence specific caregiving practices in infancy and early childhood
- are shifting to encourage a more interdependent model of caregiving among U.S. parents

Parents who are more likely to have trouble establishing secure attachments with infants and young children
- are those who have a negative, critical approach to children because of age (specifically adolescent parents), depression, substance abuse, or limited social resources
- have difficulty effectively timing responses to children—by either withdrawing or being overstimulating
- can be helped with interventions that provide education, opportunities for the parent to get to know the child, and support

Positive relationships among family members
- reduce sibling rivalry
- are promoted in many ways, including storytelling

Exercises

1. Discuss in class the father's comment, on page 142, that he knew so little about babies that he should not have been permitted to take one home from the hospital. In small groups, devise an exam that would be taken by all new parents, and then compare suggestions among the entire class.

2. Go to a toy store and spend an imaginary $150 on toys for an infant or toddler. Justify your choices.

3. In small groups, discuss the role of siblings in your lives. (a) What have been the positive and negative contributions of having siblings? (b) If you were having children now, how would you discourage sibling rivalry?

4. In small groups, make a list of your early experiences of gender-type learning. (a) Do the memories relate to activities, appearance, or feelings? (b) Who was teaching you about gender-appropriate behavior—parents, siblings, peers, relatives, teachers? (c) Were you more likely to accept the teachings of adults as opposed to peers? (d) Are similar experiences occurring today?

5. In small groups, survey each other on their parents' use of physical punishment. (a) Did parents use physical punishments? (b) If so, which ones—spanking, hitting? (c) How often? (d) For what misbehavior? (e) What feelings did it engender then and now? (f) Would some other punishment have been more effective? (g) If so, what and why? (h) Do you now or do you intend to use physical punishment with your child or children? (i) Why or why not? Report by group to the class at large and tabulate the overall responses.

Additional Readings

Bing, Elizabeth, and Libby Colman. *Laughter and Tears: The Emotional Life of New Mothers.* New York: Holt, 1997.

Eisenberg, Nancy. *The Caring Child.* Cambridge, MA: Harvard University Press, 1992.

Levine, James, with Edward W. Pitt. *New Expectations: Community Strategies for Responsible Fatherhood.* New York: Families and Work Institute, 1995.

Schatz, Marilyn. *A Toddler's Life.* New York: Oxford University Press, 1994.

Turecki, Stanley, and Leslie Tonner. *The Difficult Child.* New York: Bantam, 1985.

6

The Elementary School Years

THE FIRST DAY OF SCHOOL LAUNCHES A CHILD ON A SEA OF opportunity to increase his or her competence. Additional stresses accompany the greater independence. How does a child manage in this expanded world away from the protection of the family? Parents' roles change dramatically as they encourage independence, continue to guide the child's behavior, and, at the same time, take on the task of interpreting the outside influences the child is confronting. How do parents foster the child's development at school? How do they promote reliable habits and self-regulation? How do they help the child deal with upsetting experiences and disappointments that are beyond parental control?

The years from five to eleven are a time of expansion for children. They have learned the routines of living—eating, dressing, toileting—and can take care of many of their own needs. They have mastered language and can express themselves easily. Their world enlarges as they go off to school, meet new friends, and adjust to more demanding tasks. However, at the same time they are growing in competence, they experience increased stress in their lives. Because they are able to compare themselves to others and to external standards, they worry about their competence in many areas and feel vulnerable to embarrassment and feelings of inadequacy. Parents have a powerful role in helping children cope with these new demands. In this chapter, we examine the expanding dynamics of the elementary school years.

Parent-Child Relationships

Parents spend half as much time with elementary school children as with preschoolers and give them less physical affection than they did when their children were preschoolers.

167

Even so, parents enjoy parenting as much as in earlier years, and they report as much caring and regard for their children as earlier.[1]

Parents' acceptance of, involvement in, and sensitivity to children's needs continue as major forces in helping children become responsible, competent, happy individuals. Parents are still the number one figures in the lives of schoolchildren, whose greatest fear is of losing their parents.

Parent-child relationships during the elementary school years are related to both earlier and later behaviors.[2] Children who experienced positive attachments to parents in infancy and toddlerhood, versus those with insecure attachments, are more socially and personally competent at age ten. Individuals who had warm and affectionate relationships with parents at age five show strong psychological well-being at age forty-one; as adults, they are accomplished at work, feel less strain in their personal lives, and use many adaptive coping strategies. So, the quality of parent-child relationships has long-term impacts on later behaviors.

Because parents of school-age children no longer have exclusive control of their children, who spend several hours a day under the control of other adults, one can see changes in parent-child relationships. Specifically, parents tend to permit children to make decisions that the parents monitor, supervise, and approve. This coregulation, or sharing of control, with children serves as a bridge to the preadolescent and adolescent years, when children will assume more control.

Conflicts between parents and children center on children's interpersonal behavior with others (fighting, teasing), children's personality characteristics (irritability, stubbornness), and parents' regulating activities such as television watching, chores, bedtime, and curfews.[3] Parents tend to justify their point of view in terms of conventionality, practicality, and health issues. Children tend to listen to parents' rules that prevent harm and psychological damage to others. Children report that they have more conflicts with fathers than mothers. Rather than physical punishment, effective discipline involves the removal of privileges.

In the elementary school period, mothers and fathers continue to relate to children in different ways.[4] Mothers take major responsibility for managing family tasks—scheduling homework and baths, for example. Mothers are both more directive with children and more positive in their reactions to them. Fathers, though more generally neutral in affect, continue to engage in more physical play and give more affection to both boys and girls. Men who have high-status jobs have less time to spend with their children due to the demands of work, as compared to men who have less job involvement and are thus more likely to be involved with children, both playing with and caring for them.[5] Men are most likely to be involved as fathers when mothers do not take on all the caregiving and managing, thereby closing fathers out. Nevertheless, the more skillful the mothers are with children, the more skillful fathers become. Both parents are similar in being more demanding of boys than girls and more disapproving of boys' misbehavior.[6]

Although mothers and fathers have different roles, children see them as having many qualities in common.[7] Both parents are described as loving, happy, honest, responsible, self-confident individuals. Fathers are more interested in learning and creativity than mothers, and mothers are more concerned about others' feelings than fathers. Children describe themselves less positively than they describe their parents but still see many similarities between themselves and their parents. They are loving, happy, and interested in learning and creativity, but they are far below parents in self-confidence, cooperativeness, responsibility, and honesty. Children describe "having good family relationships" as the most important family goal of mothers and themselves but feel fathers' most valued goals are "educational/vocational."

Parents' behaviors contribute to their children's development of skills and abilities that are necessary for school and social success.[8] For example, children who have secure attachments with parents feel free to explore the world, and on all measures of cognitive functioning, they are more advanced than children with insecure attachments. Children who have learned cooperation in work and play with parents adapt more easily to school than do children who have patterns of resistance or domination in their relationships with their parents. When parents are warm and sensitive to children's feelings, child-oriented in their approach to parenting, and authoritative in reasoning with children to induce cooperation, their children tend to be popular and skilled with peers.

If problems occur, parents' actions can help improve behavior. In one study, when parents modeled appropriate social behaviors and gave positive reinforcement for skillful social behaviors or made extra efforts so children could be with peers, then children who experienced social rejection were able to gain in social skills and friendships.[9] Children's cognitive and social-emotional competence increased in the school-age years for a sample of high- and low-risk children assessed at ages four and thirteen.[10] Mothers who valued children's thinking for themselves and not conforming to others had high-risk children who gained in cognitive status. For both high-risk and low-risk children, mothers' lack of depression and lack of criticism and dissatisfaction were related to children's increase in social-emotional competence. Mothers' positive statements were also related to high-risk children's growth in social-emotional competence.

Parents' behaviors contribute not only to positive success but to negative outcomes as well. Mothers' harsh discipline, rated by interviewers and spouses and reflected in parents' statements of choice of discipline methods, predicted children's aggressive, impulsive behavior problems at school from kindergarten through grade four.[11] Even when the initial level of problem behavior was controlled, harsh discipline—seen in yelling, threatening, pushing, and spanking—predicted increases in aggressive behaviors over the four years. These relationships are not explainable solely on genetic grounds, that is, that aggressive parents pass on these traits to children and then have to use harsh discipline. A study of adoptive parents and children found that genetic factors play a role in that children at risk for aggressive behaviors (based on the behaviors shown by their biological parents) tended to evoke negative parenting, which in turn increased aggressive behavior.[12] Many children, however, who were not at risk for aggressive behavior developed aggressive behaviors when parents used harsh discipline. Thus, genetic risk is not necessary to develop aggressive behaviors when parents use harsh discipline.

So, even though parents spend less time with school-age children, when they make positive comments, model positive behaviors, and ensure that children get the benefit of additional activities, they help children grow in cognitive and social-emotional competence.

Development of the Self

In elementary school, children become capable of integrating behaviors and forming a more balanced view of themselves that takes into account both positive and negative qualities.[13] They are no longer limited to thinking of themselves in extreme terms—instead of smart or dumb, they think of themselves as smart at some things and not so smart in others.

Children also begin to evaluate their behavior in comparison to their peers. In the early grades, comparisons may be overt and direct ("I can finish the work faster than you"), but as children grow older, comparisons become more subtle and indirect ("I have more friends than other girls in my class"). With the ability to rank the performance of peers and compare it with their own, children become more vulnerable, because only the most competent ones will feel they are doing well, and many will feel they fall short.

Because children think of themselves in relatively general terms, they may let negative aspects of their behavior color their overall evaluations of themselves or feelings of self-worth. Children over eight evaluate themselves in terms of four dimensions: (1) physical competence, (2) cognitive competence, (3) social competence with peers, and (4) overall feelings of self-worth.

Gender Identity

Psychologists used to think gender role development was largely completed in the preschool years. Studies of older children now reveal that a gender role develops over a long span of time and is never complete.[14] Stereotyped gender behavior peaks in the later preschool years, when children are rapidly acquiring gender knowledge. In the school years, children are more flexible in their preferences for activities, chores, and future careers, with girls being more flexible than boys. Children's tolerance of non-stereotypical activities in peers increases as well over the school years.

The most flexible and tolerant children come from families where parents and same-sex siblings are flexible in their activities. Same-sex peers also play an important role in promoting flexibility and tolerance.

Ethnic Identity

Children learn about their own ethnic identities in a process similar to that involved in gender identity.[15] First, children learn to identify their ethnic group (label themselves white, African American, Hispanic American). This occurs in the preschool years for white and African American children and a little later on for other groups such as Asian American children. Children then learn what is distinctive about their own eth-

Minority group children learn what is distinctive about their culture and form a sense of their ethnic identity.

nic group. Children of all groups can do this by about age seven. Finally, again at about age seven, children learn ethnic consistency and constancy and realize they cannot change their ethnic identity.

During this period, minority group children learn what it means to be part of their culture. By age ten, they know their identity and prefer their own group. Mary Jane Rotheram-Borus and Jean Phinney suggest that children show ethnic differences on the four basic dimensions of behavior listed in Box 6.1.[16]

Although variations exist within groups, many studies find that Mexican American children tend to be more group-oriented, eager to share and cooperate, and more adaptable to others' demands on them than either European American or African American children. They rely on adult figures for advice and offer them great respect. If someone else is angry or aggressive toward them, be it child or adult, Mexican American children feel sad and blame themselves. Compared with both European American and Mexican American children, African American children are more emotionally expressive, action-oriented, and assertive with peers. They too respect adults but, if scolded, apologize and do not feel bad about themselves. Little is known about how Asian American children differ from the majority culture.

Parents have an important role to play in the formation of their children's ethnic identity. School-age children reason more logically and better understand parents' statements about ethnic issues. Because children spend more time outside parents'

BOX 6.1

Four Basic Dimensions of Ethnic Differences in Children

1. An orientation toward group ties, interdependence, and sharing versus an orientation toward independence and competition

2. An active, achievement-oriented approach that changes a situation versus a passive, fatalistic approach that insists on self-change to remedy the situation

3. Acceptance of, respect for, and belief in powerful authorities versus an egalitarian view that allows questioning of authority

4. An overtly expressive, spontaneous style versus an inhibited, formal style

Adapted from Mary Jane Rotheram-Borus and Jean S. Phinney, "Patterns of Social Expectations among Black and Mexican-American Children," *Child Development* 61 (1990): 543.

---

direct control, in school functions or other activities, they are more likely to experience prejudice or, at least, confusion at the different values other people hold.

Parents serve as a buffer between children and the larger society. As in so many areas, they interpret social experiences for their children and help them deal with the situations. To socialize children with regard to racial and ethnic issues, parents first teach children (1) their own cultural values, (2) the values of the majority culture, and (3) the realities of being a member of their own group in the majority culture and the ways people cope with the realities.[17] Successful socialization goes beyond these steps to teach pride in one's ethnic group and the importance of one's own self-development.

We focus here on how African American parents socialize children because more research is available on this group; other groups may experience a similar process.[18] African American parents think teaching about their ethnic identity is important but not *the* most important information to pass on to children. A primary goal of African American parents is to teach their children how to deal with prejudice, to feel pride and self-respect, to value a good education, and to recognize that their fair and moral behavior is not always reciprocated.

Many parents do not discuss ethnic issues with their children. In a national sample, over one-third of parents reported having never discussed ethnic issues with their children, and few of the two-thirds who reported discussing ethnic issues touched on more than one area. Parents who are most likely to talk to their children about ethnic issues include older, married parents who live in racially mixed neighborhoods with a sizeable white population. Mothers are more likely to socialize children than are fathers. And parents living in the Northeast are more likely to discuss racial matters, perhaps because, as in mixed neighborhoods, there is more contact among ethnic groups.

Table 6.1 summarizes socialization messages African American parents share with their children. Only about 22 percent teach ethnic pride and a positive self-image, yet this is the area parents are most uniquely fitted to address. Both majority and minority

TABLE 6.1   Socialization Messages African American Parents Impart to Children*

Message	% Parents
Achievement and hard work: *"Work hard and get a good education."*	22
Racial pride: *"Be proud of being black."*	17
Themes of black heritage: *"Taught what happened in the past and how people coped."*	9
Focus on intergroup relations: Summary category of many responses—*"Accommodate to whites."* *"Use collective action to help blacks."*	9
Presence of racial restrictions and barriers: *"Blacks don't have the opportunities whites have."*	8
Good citizenship: *"Be honest, fair."*	7
Awareness and acceptance of racial background: *"Realize you are black."*	7
Fundamental equality of blacks and whites: *"Recognize all races as equal."*	6
Maintenance of a positive self-image: *"Stay away from whites."*	5 3†

From Michael C. Thornton et al., "Sociodemographic and Environmental Correlates of Racial Socialization by Black Parents," *Child Development* 61 (1990): 405–406.

*Information from the National Survey of Black Americans, a representative national sample of 2,107 men and women. Statements tabulated from the answers to two questions: "In raising children, have you told them things to help them know what it is to be black?" and "What are the most important things you have said?"

†Remaining categories of 1 or 2 percent include a variety of responses having to do with emphasizing religious principles, discussing personal traits, stressing general self-acceptance.

children evaluate themselves as others close to them do, and so what parents convey strongly affects self-esteem. Because a minority child may get inaccurate and negative messages from other children, the media, and authority figures such as coaches or teachers, it is even more important for minority parents to encourage a positive self-image and ethnic pride. When parents emphasize awareness of social restrictions and barriers and at the same time encourage self-development and ethnic pride, children are happier, higher in self-esteem, and more successful in school.[19]

Accuracy in Self-Perception

As children begin to compare themselves with other children, parents may want the comparisons to be accurate. Evidence suggests that it is better to overrate your abilities and to see yourself more positively than objective tests or ratings might warrant. For example, children who overrate their abilities in school are more likely to respond to failure by getting help, finding out what they did wrong, and remedying the situation because it does not fit with their view of themselves.[20]

Albert Bandura, who has written on the importance of believing in one's own abilities to take effective action (self-efficacy), states that in hazardous situations, accuracy in self-perception of abilities is essential; for example, if you overestimate your ability to swim in heavy surf, you may not have a chance to correct the perception. In many nonhazardous situations, though, people prove more effective when they overrate their abilities.[21]

Life is full of problems; to overcome them, we have to persevere. People are most likely to persist when they believe in themselves. Optimistic views of the self, then, help people make the most of their talents. Young children appear naturally optimistic as they enter school and as they look ahead in life. Parents need to encourage and nurture this beneficial optimism.[22]

Development of Self-Regulation

Elementary school children understand their feelings better than preschoolers do and realize that feelings depend, in part, on what led up to an event and how the event is interpreted.[23] For example, at ages six and seven, children are pleased with their success whether it comes from luck or effort; in contrast, when they are nine and ten, children feel proud only if they believe their effort produced the success.

Children are most likely to express their inner feelings when they are alone or with another person who they believe will respond in a positive, understanding way.[24] Unfortunately, as children—particularly boys—grow older, they anticipate a less positive response from others, even from parents. Thus, older boys are much less likely to express their feelings than are girls or younger boys.

Children's ability to regulate their emotions appears related to temperamental qualities.[25] Children with highly intense emotional reactions have difficulty modulating their emotions and, as a result, become overwhelmed by them. Children with mid-range emotional reactions can manage feelings better. Ability to regulate feelings at the age of four is related to early elementary school students' ability to sympathize with the plight of others and respond to them compassionately.

Common Feelings of School-Age Children

Elementary school children reflect many common feelings that parents must help them handle. Understanding the specific emotional tendencies of their children will help parents avoid misunderstandings and allow them to guide their children to emotional satisfaction and harmony in social settings.

EMPATHY   We have discussed the parental behaviors—nurturing, modeling, reasoning, and explaining the benefits of prosocial behavior—that create sympathy and helping behavior in children. Because elementary school children's awareness of others' feelings has increased, they are better helpers and are more likely to offer social strategies rather than material ones to change distress in other people. When asked how to help distressed four- and five-year-olds, older children suggested giving verbal reassurance that the situation will pass, giving suggestions on how to solve the problem (such as advice on how to retrieve a lost object), or providing social activity to compensate for the unhappiness (having someone over to play, staying with a crying child).[26]

Children are most likely to help others when they feel happy, competent, and effective themselves. They are also most likely to help if they like the person and if that person has helped them in the past. So, positive feelings about oneself and others lead to generosity at this age.[27]

AGGRESSIVENESS   Aggression decreases during the elementary school years. When it does occur, children usually express it verbally rather than physically.

Consistent individual differences emerge and are likely to persist over time. Further, aggressive children often have problems such as poor peer relations and difficulty in acquiring academic skills. From the toddler years, boys are more frequently aggressive than girls. This sex difference in aggression is seen in cultures around the world and in animal species. The reasons for it are complex. Because such differences appear early and consistently in so many cultures, they may well have a biological basis that is not specifically known at this time.

FEARFULNESS   With age, children grow less fearful. Many of the fears of the preschool period—fear of animals, of the dark—decrease. Some specific ones remain, however—fear of snakes, of storms. These fears appear related to temperamental qualities involving general timidity. Up to age five, fears are equally prevalent in boys and girls, but beginning with the school-age years, sex differences increase. Fears and phobias are more prevalent in girls at all ages.

LONELINESS   For a long time, social scientists thought that children could not experience loneliness prior to adolescence, when they become more separate from the family. Research, however, finds that five- and six-year-old children have conceptions of loneliness as clear as those of adults.[28] They describe feelings of being sad and alone, having no one to play with. The remedy, they report, is to find a playmate. Older elementary school children give even more poignant descriptions of loneliness—"feeling unneeded," "like you're the only one on the moon," "always in the dark," "like you have no one that really likes you and you're all alone."

Extreme loneliness is related to lack of friends, shy and submissive behavior, and a tendency to attribute social failure to one's own internal inadequacies. Such loneliness, in turn, prevents the child from interacting with others, which intensifies the problem.

UNHAPPINESS   In one study, parents and teachers described 10 to 12 percent of a representative sample of ten-year-olds as often appearing miserable, unhappy, tearful, or distressed.[29] The children themselves reported similar depressive feelings. Boys and girls were equally as likely to report such feelings.

Children around the world, regardless of sex or socioeconomic status, agree with one another on what is upsetting even more than the adults and children within the same culture do.[30] The loss of a parent is the most devastating occurrence, and the birth of a sibling the least upsetting. Parental fights are highly stressful. Children reveal their distress at embarrassing situations—wetting their pants, being caught in a theft, being ridiculed in class. Although many students like school, it also causes them anxiety, frustration, unhappiness, and concern over grades, being held back, and making mistakes. Adults may be surprised at children's sensitivity to embarrassing situations and their worries about school. The data emphasize that children have a perspective on life that may be quite different from that of their parents and often not immediately apparent to parents.

Daily journals of elementary school students in the United States reveal that boys are more likely to cite external situations and demands such as school, chores, interruptions, and environmental factors as sources of stress.[31] Girls report disappointments with self and others and failure to live up to responsibilities as sources of stress in their lives.

Coping with Stress

In facing stress, children adapt in many ways. First, they use their own resources and the tools their parents give them. Second, they turn to trusted people for further support and guidance.

STRATEGIES   When children ages six to twelve are asked how to handle stressful situations—such as having a friend move away or having a parent angry at them—their solutions generally attack the source of the problem to change the upsetting circumstances.[32] They are most likely to strike at the roots of the difficulty when the problem focuses on peers or school, where they feel they have more control. Children tend to use distraction strategies to adjust to situations they cannot control, such as doctors' visits.[33]

Those children whose parents outwardly accept and comfort them tend to have a greater variety of strategies to use in confronting stressful situations. They disengage from situations in which they lack control.[34] Children also seek generally to buffer themselves from stress by turning to a fun activity such as having a friend over or some other special treat. Athletics, being at home with families, and special treats of food or surprises all help children feel good so they are better able to deal with stressors.[35]

SUPPORTIVE PEOPLE   When dealing with stressful or negative situations, children often seek out others to help them. Children "perceive mothers as being the best multipurpose social provider available, in contrast to friends and teachers, who are relatively specialized in their social value."[36] Friends provide companionship and emotional support second only to parents. Teachers provide information but little companionship. Fathers are excellent providers of information but are generally less available for direct help. Figure 6.1 illustrates where children of different ages and ethnic groups seek support.[37] Until early adolescence, parents and extended family provide the primary sources of support. Extended family are more important for African American and Hispanic American children than for European American children.

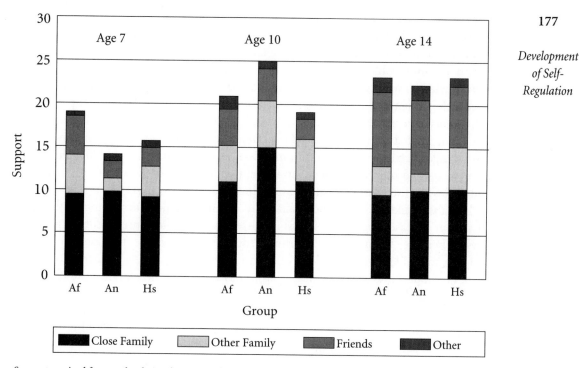

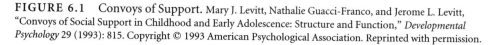

Support received from each relationship category by age and ethnicity. (Af = African American, An = Anglo/European American, Hs = Hispanic American.)

FIGURE 6.1 Convoys of Support. Mary J. Levitt, Nathalie Guacci-Franco, and Jerome L. Levitt, "Convoys of Social Support in Childhood and Early Adolescence: Structure and Function," *Developmental Psychology* 29 (1993): 815. Copyright © 1993 American Psychological Association. Reprinted with permission.

Parents play a powerful role in helping children cope with fears of tragic events and worries about school. Although parents cannot control the occurrence of these events, they can help children cope with them. Parents' interpretations of the events shape children's attitudes about difficulties and adversities. Recall Martin Seligman's views (described in Chapter 3) on the importance of teaching optimistic attitudes about life.[38] Optimistic attitudes motivate individuals to exert effort to get what they want.

Seligman has documented the nature of pessimistic attitudes that lead to discouragement and withdrawal from challenging tasks. Pessimistic individuals consider difficulty a pervasive, permanent problem that is one's personal fault and is unchangeable. Pessimistic children see a poor math grade as the result of their own stupidity and inability to do math. They sometimes avoid studying because they are discouraged and feel they are no good at the subject.

As outlined in Chapter 3, parents can supply new interpretations of the problem. Perhaps the child needs to study more. Perhaps the child has a special difficulty with math and a tutor can be obtained. Or perhaps the teacher gave a very hard exam or did not allow enough time; a child has no control over these factors but can deal with them by being overly prepared for the next test.

Parents can help their child to see that the outcome of any school or social event is determined by multiple causes and that the child never solely determines the events. Children must, however, work on those factors within their control. By taking a broad view of various problems, parents can help children see that most situations can be improved with effort. Parents can also encourage children to use their time and energy selectively. When children have reached the maximum benefit of effort, parents can help them move on to other activities. For example, when a child feels rejected because she is not invited to a peer's birthday party, parents can suggest ways she might be a more outgoing friend. If new techniques do not work with that friend, the child needs to move on and make new friends to be happy. Parents should remain optimistic that children will either remedy a situation or find pleasure elsewhere.

Because children adapt their reasoning about difficulties according to their parents' ways of reasoning, parents must be careful how they interpret events in their own lives. When they see a problem as unremediable and pervasive, they predispose their children to similar interpretations of events. When parents rely on derogatory criticism, no matter how accurate the criticism may be or how helpful the parent wants to be, the child becomes self-blaming and discouraged. Negative words—"You'll never have any common sense"; "You never learn anything. You just fool around"; "You don't care about anybody but yourself"—can last a lifetime; some children never escape the impact of such discouraging messages.

Internalizing Rules and Values

To control behavior, children need to (1) monitor their own behavior, (2) compare their behavior with some standard or ideal, (3) then, when a discrepancy appears, modify their behavior to come as close to the standard as possible, and (4) develop new behaviors. In this area, researchers know the most about how children learn an internal standard with which they compare their behavior; however, they know the least about how children monitor themselves and go about modifying their behavior on their own, before the involvement of an adult.[39]

Children begin to learn simple family rules when they are about one year old. It is during the elementary school period, however, that they internalize family and social values—that is, make them part of their own internal system of thinking. Sigmund Freud used the term *superego* to describe the internalized values that direct an individual's behavior. The child adopts the same-sex parent's values and beliefs, which then govern the child's conduct. Freud believed that the superego arouses pleasure or anxiety or guilt about possible actions and that these feelings permit or prevent the anticipated behavior.

Elementary school children can distinguish between guilt (feeling you did something naughty, feeling very sorry, wanting to make amends, fearing others won't like you) and shame (feeling afraid of being laughed at, feeling embarrassed, wanting to run away).[40] Guilt comes when children feel they have broken a moral rule, whereas shame is related to both moral and social blunders.

By about the age of eight, children become more self-critical, and their self-esteem is related to their ability to control verbal and physical aggression and other negative emotions. They feel ashamed when they violate a rule, and they take pride in being able to regulate their behavior and do what is approved. This is a good reason for parents to help children meet approved standards. Children do not feel good about themselves when they engage in behaviors they know others their age do not do.[41]

By the age of nine or ten, children can talk about how they use self-instructional plans to control anger, aggression, and other negative behavior to do what is correct. What works, though, varies with age. In one study, younger boys, ages six or seven, were most able to delay behavior when they simply verbalized not doing the forbidden act. Older boys were more successful when they verbalized while directing their attention elsewhere.

In describing why they follow household routines they do not like—brushing teeth, going to bed on time, doing chores—children between six and twelve initially focus on external rewards of approval or disapproval and the importance of following a rule. As they get older, they focus on more internal reasons—cleaning their room to find things more easily, going to bed to feel better the next day. So, there is a progression from external reasons for self-control to internal ones.[42]

Children are most likely to develop a strong conscience when parents use low-power techniques of discipline and begin early to help children comply with the rules.[43] Early toddler compliance predicts conscience development six years later in the elementary school years and supports Robert Emde's belief that moral development is based on early, everyday disciplinary encounters between parent and child.

Boys and girls are equally concerned about issues of justice and fairness in interpersonal relations.[44] Lawrence Kohlberg describes three levels of moral reasoning.[45] At the earliest (*premoral*) level, individuals act to avoid punishments and gain pleasure or reward. They show little concern for the rights of others. At the second (*conventional*) level, individuals act to conform to the rules or regulations laid down by powerful authorities such as parents or the law. At the most advanced (*principled*) level, individuals act to satisfy a set of internal standards of fairness and justice.

During the early elementary school years, until about age seven or eight, children reason at a premoral level and act to avoid punishments and gain rewards. By about age ten, conventional moral reasoning has developed, although premoral thinking still occurs. Very few children at this age display principled reasoning about moral problems. By the age of thirteen, a small percentage of children rely on principled reasoning; conventional reasoning still prevails. Even at this age, however, many children still reason in terms of avoiding punishment and gaining rewards. Clearly, parents of elementary school children need to give praise and social recognition of approved acts and, at the very least, give punishments by ignoring disapproved acts.

Promoting Children's Achievement in School

School is a major organizing force in parents' and children's lives. School provides opportunities for new activities and the development of knowledge and new competencies; however, it also places demands and stress on both parents and children. School occupies five to six hours of children's day throughout much of the year, and it determines their evening activities as well. Children must function in large groups of initially unknown children and adults. They also must meet standards of behavior and achievement. And neither parent nor child has a choice about schooling; the law requires that parents ensure that children get an education, though the form of education is a matter of personal choice—public, private, or home schooling.

In the United States, many tend to think that a child's innate abilities determine success or failure in school. We find added weight for this view in social scientists' attention to the genetic contributions to variations among individuals' performance on intellectual measures, even though behavior geneticists also recognize the importance of environmental factors. At present, behavior geneticists believe that genetic factors account for about 50 to 60 percent of variation among individuals on intellectual measures and environmental factors about 40 to 50 percent.[46]

Certainly, studies of individuals who have developed world-class abilities in athletic, artistic, and intellectual pursuits point to the importance of family and coaching support. Recall the study, cited in Chapter 1, of 120 young men and women who achieved international levels of performance in their special areas.[47] Researchers found that talent development takes twelve to fifteen years of commitment and is the result of a combination of individual commitment, family support, and outstanding instruction. Parents' support consists of early encouragement, the selection of appropriate teachers and coaches, financial support, and time commitments for driving to lessons, competitions, and so on.

Before discussing what parents can do to help children succeed, let us emphasize that school success is important for several reasons.[48] First, it gives children academic skills that will help them function effectively throughout life. Second, school success in the early elementary school years appears to serve as a protective factor against the development of high-risk behaviors in adolescence—delinquency, substance abuse, teen sexuality, and violence. Third, competence in school activities is related to social acceptance and social competence, which in turn reinforce academic success.

Influences within the Home

Jacquelynne Eccles, Allan Wigfield, and Ulrich Schiefele list four parental factors that contribute to children's motivation and outcomes in school—parents' social characteristics, their general beliefs and behaviors, their specific beliefs about their child, and their specific behaviors.[49]

PARENTS' SOCIAL CHARACTERISTICS   Parents' education, income, marital status, and number of children, as well as neighborhood characteristics, determine the resources available to parents to encourage their children's achievement at school. Two parents with a good income and education and one or two children have time, money, and neighborhood resources they can draw on to help their children. Compare these parents to a single, adolescent mother whose own experience in school success is limited and whose limited income must support two or three people; she is likely to live in a neighborhood with few school and community programs for her children. Thus, the broader social context of parents' lives provides resources to help children's achievements.

Nonetheless, a parent's limited resources need not determine what happens with children. Ben Carson, an internationally recognized African American pediatric neurosurgeon at Johns Hopkins University describes how his mother reared him and his brother.[50] Married at thirteen years of age to a man who, she later learned, had another family, Carson's mother raised her two sons alone. She worked as a domestic, sometimes holding two or three jobs to make ends meet. When Ben was in the fifth grade, he was at the bottom of his class and nicknamed "Dummy." Very concerned, his mother insisted the two boys turn off the television. She required that they read two books per week from the Detroit Public Library and give her a written report on each book. The boys did not know for some years that she could not read the reports.

Ben read books about animals, plants, and rocks. Later that year, he was the only student in his class able to identify a particular rock. He suddenly realized, "The reason you knew the answer was because you were reading those books. What if you read books about all your subjects—science, math, history, geography, social studies? Couldn't you then know more than all those students who tease you and call you a dummy?"[51] Within a year and a half, he went from the bottom of his class to the top. With relatively few resources, his mother took action that promoted her son's success.

Cultural values about the sources of achievement influence what parents expect of children and themselves. In the United states, European American parents view the child's innate ability as the main determiner of achievement. They consider it their role to give children emotional support in schoolwork. Failure is seen as a sign of limited ability. Asian parents, however, believe hard work and effort determine success. They take an active role in seeing that their child exert the necessary work and effort to achieve high standards. Failures are seen as remediable with increased effort.

PARENTS' GENERAL BELIEFS AND BEHAVIORS   Parents' general beliefs and behaviors create an emotional climate in the home that influences children's achievement. By forming secure attachments with their children, balancing their children's needs for independence with their needs for structure, and providing appropriate adult models for learning, parents help their children develop competence and motivation to achieve. Diana Baumrind, whose work we reviewed in Chapter 2, believes parenting strategies that balance an insistence on high standards and attention to the child's individuality and needs help children develop the self-reliance and confidence that contribute to school success.

Parents' general beliefs about gender-appropriate behaviors shape what they provide for their sons and daughters. For example, they provide boys with manipulative toys that develop spatial abilities. They are less likely to enroll daughters in computer programs and competitive athletics, and they are more likely to direct sons toward gifted programs. These parental behaviors in turn influence their children's achievement.

PARENTS' BELIEFS ABOUT THE SPECIFIC CHILD   Parents' beliefs about a child's skills and abilities and reasons for success shape children's achievement. Parents can encourage or discourage academic work by saying a child has ability or, conversely, has no skill at a task. They can soften a failure by identifying it as remediable through further work.

Parents play an active role in helping children master basic skills.

Parents' expectations regarding school achievement predict children's academic success more accurately than the child's ability scores.[52] For example, one group of students in third and fifth grades (with an equal proportion of boys and girls) underestimated their abilities. They thought they were incompetent even though tests indicated they had ability. Their self-perceptions came from parents who inaccurately saw them as lacking in ability. These children accepted their parents' assessments and acted accordingly; they attempted less challenging work, were less persistent, and, as a result, experienced less success than other children. In contrast, parents with positive expectations encourage children's achievement. Children feel they have ability and are more likely to do well because they are willing to work harder and persist until they meet the challenge.

PARENTS' SPECIFIC BEHAVIORS   Parents act in many specific ways to encourage achievement from the earliest days of life. Providing stimulating toys and opportunities for exploration, reading to children, encouraging conversation, verbal expression, and curiosity, providing lessons and activities that develop children's skills—all contribute to children's academic success.

We do not often think of emotional regulation as an important skill for school success,[53] but it is essential if children are to deal with the frustrations of mastering new material and getting along with others. Forming secure attachments, as described in Chapter 5, and learning to regulate feelings, as outlined in Chapter 3, prepare children to cope with such frustrations.

Parents also organize the home and structure the daily routine so the child has a regular time and place to do homework and projects. Of great importance is the daily interest and attention parents give to the child's work. For example, giving weekly spelling words, listening to the child read, or talking over a plan for a project helps the child maintain an interest in his or her work. Parents can skillfully help their child master material by asking pertinent questions and by guiding the child to a deeper understanding of the material.

Influences within the School

Within reason, the physical characteristics of a school are less predictive of success than is the staff's orientation toward achievement.[54] For example, the number of students, the size of the school, the number of books in the library, and the annual per-pupil expense do not appear strongly related to students' school achievement. The staff's expectations of students, the organization of the school, the cohesiveness of the staff, the staff's sensitivity to students' needs, and the staff's recognition of performance do appear important for student achievement. Further, teachers' skills in managing conflict can reduce or increase children's behavior problems such as aggressiveness.[55]

Children who develop a strong attachment their teachers and school have greater academic success.[56] Schools encourage a strong bond by (1) providing opportunities for active student involvement in the learning process, (2) helping children develop skills and competencies for active participation, and (3) giving rewards and recognition for competencies. Successful classroom interventions include good classroom management to minimize disruptions so learning can occur.

Effective teachers have clear, fair, and realistic expectations for children's social and academic behaviors.[57] Their teaching approach stresses mastery-based learning, in which students are given instruction and extra help until they grasp new material. Although schools have traditionally favored learning through individual competition, research shows that cooperative learning, in which students work as a group to learn material, may serve students better. In this approach, a team member may learn part of the material and then teach it to other team members. Such cooperation results in children's learning as much as through individual work and competition. Equally important, students like one another better in cooperative learning situations.

Parents' Partnership with Schools

In the past, people looked on the school as having the primary responsibility for educating children. Parents played a secondary role—raising funds, volunteering in the school, and enriching the curriculum with their input and values. Recently, a partnership model of family and school relationships has been advanced.[58] Acknowledging the powerful impact of parents' involvement and encouragement on children's

Interview

with Barbara Keogh

Barbara K. Keogh is professor emeritus of educational psychology at the University of California at Los Angeles. Her research interests include the role of children's temperament in children's adjustment to school.

For many parents with children in the elementary school years, issues concerning school have a very great importance—how to get children ready for school on time, how to help them behave in school, how to get them to do schoolwork. You have done a great deal of research on children's temperament and school, and I think temperament plays a role in many children's adjustment.

It intrigued me when I started work in this area, a long time ago, that most of the work with temperament had been done with interactions in families, and yet when you think of the number of interactions that teachers have with children per hour, per day, in a classroom and add that up over the school year, temperament is an enormous potential influence.

When we began our research, we found that teachers have a very clear picture of what teachable children are like. One of the very important contributors to teachability is the stylistic variables or temperament variables that characterize children. Some children are easy to teach. They settle down better, they are not as active, they are not as intense, their mood is good, they adapt well, they like novelty, they are curious. All those things make teachers think, "Gee, I am a great teacher," when they have a whole classroom full of children with those characteristics.

So we are really operating on the assumption that children's experiences in school are influenced by individual variations in temperament. We have tried to document and understand the kind of impact these variations have on the teachers. We have used the concept of "goodness of fit" in a loose way.

I am convinced, and this is not a new idea, that teachers do not operate at random. They make decisions based on how they attribute the reasons for the behavior. They may think that active, distractible children are mischievous and need to be restricted and punished, and that children who are very slow to warm up or are withdrawn are lazy and uninterested. When we work with teachers and make them aware of temperamental characteristics, we get a very consistent response: "Oh, I never thought of that." Making teachers sensitive to temperament variations helps them reframe the child's behavior, and it makes the behavior much less upsetting to teachers.

It also carries planning implications. If you know a youngster is very distractible, very active, and very intense, then you can predict that every time you have a long wait in line, there's going to be a problem with him. It's predictable.

When teachers begin to think of the individual variations on a temperamental rather than motivational basis, they begin to manipulate the environment more effectively. Temperament helps teachers reframe the problem behavior so it is not viewed as purposeful. This is true for both temperamentally "difficult" and "slow to warm up" children.

Another example I like is that most of the youngsters in an elementary class are delighted by novelty. The teacher says, "Oh, we are going to have a wonderful surprise today. At ten o'clock the fire department is coming." Most of the kids are excited. There will be a few little "slow to warm up" youngsters who will say, "But at ten o'clock we are supposed to do our reading." They are upset because the usual routine is not followed. The teacher thinks, "What's the matter with that child? Why isn't he interested?" The child has a need for routine and a tendency to withdraw from newness or change. These children can profit from advance preparation. If they know a day in advance, they get a little forewarning.

Do you have any advice for parents as to how to help their children adjust to school?

Certainly parents have to be advocates for their child. That is absolutely necessary even if it means being confrontational, which is often not too productive. But certainly parents need to be aware when their child is unhappy at school, when their child is having problems, and address the problem with school people.

It has to be recognized that when we are working on a ratio of twenty-five youngsters to one teacher, there are going to be good matches and very poor matches in any class. In no sense does that demean the quality of the teacher or the nature of the child. But there are differences in style, and some styles match better than others.

One thing parents can do is to provide teachers with some recognition that their child might not be a good match for this classroom. It helps the teacher to know that the parents are aware of that so they can direct their mutual efforts to modify the class so the demands are more reasonable, or they can give the child extra help in modifying his or her behavior so it is more compatible with what is going on in that class.

Do you feel most teachers are willing to change?

Yes, I do. We have worked with a lot of teachers in our research, and I think it helps them to think of ways that they can structure the situation so it is more compatible with the student without loss of educational goals. Yes, we have found teachers to be very open, and they were able to relate what we were saying to different children they have known: "Oh, yes, that's like Joey."

educational progress, the partnership model seeks to forge a strong link between parents and the schools. This model rests on six major kinds of involvement:

1. Parents are obligated to provide a home that allows children to (a) be healthy and attend school, (b) be calm and confident enough to pay attention in class and do their work, (c) receive encouragement to perform well, and (d) do homework and educational projects in a supportive setting. Schools may provide families with information on effective parenting and school-related issues; they may also provide supportive programs or workshops.

2. Schools are obligated to communicate and keep parents informed of students' progress and behavior, including students' current performance and any difficulties that may arise. Schools are also responsible for providing information on school matters such as school programs, school needs, and opportunities for parental involvement in projects. Parents must encourage students to bring these communications home. Effective communication also involves channels for parental input on programs.

3. Parents and other interested community members can volunteer in classrooms to promote children's educational progress. To further volunteer opportunities, schools can arrange ways for working adults to participate in school programs by varying program schedules and expanding the kinds of participation possible for adults. For their part, families can find ways to contribute their special skills and knowledge to school programs—painting equipment, giving special lessons or presentations, introducing cultural practices of interest. Children can also find ways to meet their school's needs by volunteering.

4. Teachers can help parents monitor them and help children learn at home. Schools can make educational goals and curricula available, show parents how to assist their children, and even give joint assignments that parents and students carry out together. For example, parents can show children how to apply math skills in grocery shopping or purchasing a large appliance; students may teach parents a history lesson they learned. In these and other ways, schools facilitate parents' education efforts.

5. Parents can participate in school organizations. Schools can encourage parents to join formal or informal groups that advise educators on school priorities, school improvement programs, and parents' and students' perceptions of problems in the school environment.

6. Finally, parents and schools can collaborate with the wider community to meet the needs of students and schools. This includes involving business organizations, local governmental agencies, and volunteer groups to form partnerships to meet children's overall needs, such as providing outdoor exercise and play equipment.

Parents as Advocates for Children

Parents also serve as advocates for their children at school. In the course of their education, most children confront academic or social difficulties requiring some form of parental intervention. A child may have a problem in learning a basic skill—reading,

> "I wish I'd known how much you need to be an advocate for your children with the school. When we grew up, our parents put us in public school and that was it. Then it was up to the teachers. Unless there was a discipline problem, parents did not get involved. Now, you have a lot more options, and the public schools aren't always great; so you realize how active you need to be in order to ensure a good education for your children." —*Mother*

> "The main thing, I think, is how important temperament is. I knew about temperament, but I did not know how important it is to go with the child's temperament. My daughter was in one school that was very noncompetitive; that's a wonderful philosophy, but it wasn't right for her. She is very competitive, and in that atmosphere she did not do as well. So with the second child, we are going to be more careful to see that there is a good fit between her temperament and what she is doing." —*Father*

> "I was surprised that even though the children are older, they take as much time as when they were younger; but you spend the time in different ways. I thought when they started school, I would have a little more time. Instead of giving them baths at night and rocking them, I supervise homework and argue about taking baths. Instead of taking them on Saturday to play in the park, I take them on a Brownie event. Knowing that things were going to take as much time would have made me less impatient in the beginning, and I would have planned better." —*Mother*

math, writing—or in paying attention or controlling overly social or aggressive behavior in class. In each case, parents form a coalition with the teacher to find a solution. Sometimes, additional testing reveals a learning disability or a need for special instruction. Parents may then seek out additional professional help for the child.

Sometimes a child has to work more consistently to complete assignments, pay attention, or control behavior. Having a daily or weekly contract that targets approved behaviors and the accompanying positive consequences can be helpful. For example, a student's school behavior can be monitored in terms of completing homework, staying on task, and controlling classroom behavior during each period of the school day. If the student gets 75 percent positive checks in these three areas, then the student earns television time. It is important that target behaviors reflect realistic expectations for the child; otherwise, the contract is unlikely to work.

Another group of students who face difficulties in school are those who react strongly to any experience of failure or criticism.[59] When these children fail a task or receive criticism, they feel bad, blame themselves, and see themselves as bad people who deserve punishment, even at young ages. They feel unworthy and inadequate, helpless to change the situation. Such children see failure as a sign that they lack some innate quality. Because they believe that no amount of effort or hard work will lead to achievement, they abandon any attempts to improve. They avoid challenging tasks, and they give up at the first signs of difficulty. In contrast, those children who do persist see criticism or failure as signs to look for a different solution or ways to improve some aspect of their work. They feel good about what they have done and anticipate that others will appreciate their efforts as well.

Some training programs work to give helpless-feeling children new ways of looking at difficulties so they can surmount their helpless reactions and proceed with learning.[60] Giving them strategies for goal-setting and interpreting failure in different ways (which we discussed earlier in this chapter and in Chapter 3), as well as encouraging these children to enjoy the process of learning rather than focusing on the achievements of learning, can reduce their feelings of helplessness.

Cultural Factors

Children from different cultural backgrounds with different values may feel at a loss to achieve in what seems a strange environment.[61] They may be used to working in cooperative ways, focusing on the effects of objects on people, learning from traditions, obeying standards. The school atmosphere, with its emphasis on competition, objective knowledge gained from reference books, and teachers as questioners, requires adjustment from many children.

Despite the cultural differences, minority children share their mothers' enthusiasm for education. They enjoy school, feel good about themselves and their achievements, and expect to do well in the future. They work hard and are self-disciplined.[62]

Although minority students' level of achievement in the elementary years differs from that of children from the majority culture, the differences are minimal when social status is taken into account. Investigators do not understand why the high rates of failure and school dropout occur in the later years, when indicators at the fifth-grade level seem to predict future achievement for minority students. One speculation is that families may be so positive that they do not help children isolate those areas where they need improvement. Inappropriate curriculum content seems a factor in lowering minority children's reading level and also may play a role in their later decrease in achievement.

The important point here is that minority elementary school students are as motivated and excited about learning as their peers in the majority culture are. So, we have to look at the curriculum and teaching strategies that maximize students' abilities, because the present ones may interfere with learning.

Encouraging Children's Positive Peer Relationships

During the elementary school years, children have more contact with peers. They spend 30 percent of their time with peers in many different settings—school, sports, interest groups—with less supervision than during the preschool years.[63] Good relationships with other children during the school-age years predict academic success, emotional well-being, and psychological adjustment. Conversely, withdrawn and rejected behaviors and an inability to establish satisfying relationships predict later difficulties in academic performance and emotional well-being. Summarizing research on peer interactions, relationships, and groups, Kenneth Rubin, William Bukowski, and Jeffrey Parker write, "knowledge of a child's peer rejection or lack of friendships in childhood should raise a warning flag for teachers, parents, and professionals."[64]

Social skills include many behaviors: (1) understanding others' thoughts, feelings, and intentions; (2) understanding the consequences of one's actions; (3) expressing positive feelings and inhibiting negative ones; (4) knowing how to start and continue conversations; (5) having good verbal and nonverbal communication skills that clearly convey feelings and intentions; (6) having positive and altruistic behaviors and control of negative behaviors; and (7) complying with a partner's requests.[65] These skills begin to develop during infancy and early childhood with the parent or caregiver as the social partner who models behaviors and creates a state of mutual synchrony and regulation. In these relationships, children learn to regulate their feelings and behavior.

Peer Acceptance and Rejection

Children are attracted to peers similar to themselves in interests and social behavior.[66] Relationships grow when children can express thoughts and feelings clearly and when interactions are positive. Friends negotiate so that both individuals' needs are met, and the relationship continues. Such experiences increase children's social competence as they learn to compromise and achieve solutions that balance individual and social goals.

When friends, compared with nonfriends, work on projects together, their interactions involve more smiles, laughter, and fun; even so, they stay task-focused and are more effective in their collaboration, perhaps because they know what to expect of one another.[67]

During the elementary school years, children begin to compare their social behaviors with those of peers.[68] Some children are identified as popular and are sought after as friends. These children are socially skilled and enter new activities or relationships in quiet ways, not drawing attention to themselves. Friendly, cooperative, sensitive to others' needs, and helpful, they rarely interfere with others' actions or plans.

Some children are rejected. This occurs mostly when they show aggressive behavior that disrupts the flow of activity or is verbally or physically hurtful to others. Rarely aware of their contribution to social difficulties, such children tend to blame others for their problems. A second group of children are rejected because of withdrawn behavior. Although peers do not notice this trait in the preschool years, during the elementary school years they notice this deviant behavior and dislike it. Aware of rejection, withdrawn-rejected children feel incompetent and lonely.

Neglected children make up still another group. They are neither accepted nor rejected but are overlooked. It is not clear why this happens, but these children do not appear to suffer the loneliness or dissatisfaction of withdrawn children.

There is a small group of controversial children who are liked by some children and rejected by others. These children have the traits of both popular and rejected children. They are helpful, cooperative leaders who are, at times, disruptive, aggressive, and noncompliant. Little is known about this group.

Biological and Environmental Contributions to Social Skills

We know that babies come into the world preprogrammed for social behaviors.[69] In the hospital nursery, they respond to the cries of other newborns; they also respond to stroking, holding, and rocking. Most babies form attachments to caregivers. In this sense, there is a biological contribution to positive early social behaviors, and biological factors may play a role in individual differences among children in empathy and helping behaviors, but none are known at the present time. As we will see in the next section, temperament plays a role in attachments and in later social behaviors, although there is no necessary relationship between temperament and later social behavior.

There is a more definite role attributed to biological factors in the development of aggressive behaviors. We can point to only a few findings here.[70] Research shows that genetic factors play a role, as identical twins are more similar in aggression than are fraternal twins. But environment also plays a role, as seen in a Swedish study of adopted males. Forty percent of adopted males with both biological and adoptive criminal parents were arrested for a petty crime; 12 percent of adopted males with a criminal biological parent and a noncriminal adoptive parent were arrested; 7 percent of adopted males with a noncriminal biological parent and a criminal adoptive parent were arrested; and 3 percent of adopted males with noncriminal biological and adoptive parents were arrested. Similar findings exist for females as well.

Environmental factors related to aggressive behaviors include parents' behavior, as we will discuss in the next section, but also social conditions such as poverty. Poverty brings with it hardships and risks. There is greater family instability and greater exposure to traumatic events such as physical abuse and neighborhood violence. (We will discuss poverty and abuse and violence in greater detail in Chapters 8 and 10.) Thus, poor children of all ethnic backgrounds are at risk for developing aggressive behaviors. Increase in income reduces the risk of aggressive behaviors for European American children but not for African American children. "Being black brings numerous social hardships in American society and, with these hardships, relative risk for aggressive behavior."[71]

Parents' Contributions to Social Skills

Parents' behavior in combination with the child's temperament may set up pathways that lead to varying levels of social skills.[72] When babies have adaptable, easy temperaments and when parents are warm and sensitive to their children's feelings, child-oriented, and authoritative and use reasoning to induce cooperation, children develop secure attachments, feel social relationships are trustworthy and rewarding, and are skilled with peers. Parents believe that social skills are learned, and they coach their children in expressing feelings and resolving problems. These children tend to be well liked and socially competent.

When infants have a low threshold for arousal and are hyperaroused and difficult to soothe and comfort, they are at risk for developing insecure attachments with parents. Feeling anxious and inhibited, they are likely to withdraw from groups of peers and focus on a relationship with an adult such as a preschool teacher or day care worker. During the early elementary school years, they show inhibited and withdrawn behavior, which in turn keeps them from developing social skills.

When infants have a difficult, irritable temperament and when parents are less responsive, perhaps because of stressful life circumstances or psychological problems such as depression, children develop insecure attachments marked by anger and resistance. When they are older and relate to peers, they express aggressiveness toward them. Peers avoid them and reject them, and these children do not then have opportunities for learning negotiating skills that would lead to acceptance.

HELPING THE SHY CHILD   Shy children hesitate to approach others, are often uncertain of what to say to others, and are uncertain how to join games. They worry about rejection. They are the neglected children described earlier. Philip Zimbardo and Shirley Radl offer many suggestions for the parent of the shy child. These measures focus on increasing the child's expressiveness (smiling, talking more), interactions with others (starting conversations), and opportunities for social contact.[73] All these actions are designed to increase self-esteem, confidence, and socially outgoing behavior. This behavior, along with coaching about group interactions, minimizes the likelihood of a child's being bullied and enables the child to deal more effectively with bullies (we will discuss the bullied child shortly).

Behaviorists have focused on ways of helping children make friends. Sherri Oden and Steven Asher devised a system of coaching children in interpersonal skills.[74] They gave children verbal instructions about effective ways of interacting and provided opportunities to apply the rules in play sessions. Instructions covered four topics: (1) participating in group activities (getting started, paying attention to the game), (2) cooperating in play (sharing, taking turns), (3) communicating with the peer (talking or listening), and (4) validating and supporting the peer (giving attention and help). The benefits of the instruction persisted and were measurable a year later.

Research looking at children who were rejected in the fourth grade but improved in social status by the end of the fifth grade found several factors related to improved status.[75] Children who got involved in extracurricular activities improved in social status. Whether it was the development of new skills, the opportunities for making new friends, or increased confidence and self-esteem that led to improved social status is not known. Children who took some responsibility for peer difficulties and whose parents believed good social skills were important, modeled them, and gave appropriate rewards for skillful actions also improved in status. Boys who felt self-confident and socially skilled improved their status.

HELPING THE AGGRESSIVE CHILD   Aggression takes many forms. Children may physically hit or hurt others, or they may be verbally assaultive—taunting, teasing, humiliating others. This type of aggression is overt, noticeable, and more characteristic of boys than of girls.[76] Another form of aggression, termed *relational aggression*, is more subtle, not easily detectable, and more characteristic of girls. It consists of acts designed to deprive children of friends—spreading untrue rumors about a target child, organizing other children to reject the target child, refusing to be a friend unless the target child does favors. These behaviors are considered aggressive because they are meant to hurt or damage the target child.

In one study, about 27 percent of boys were described as aggressive, and of those boys 93 percent were overtly aggressive.[77] About 22 percent of girls were described as aggressive, and of those girls 95 percent were engaged in relational aggression. Only about one-quarter of aggressive children used both forms to hurt children; most relied on one or the other. It is important to note that when relational aggression is assessed, girls are almost equal to boys in aggressive behavior.

Because both forms of aggressive behavior lead to peer rejection, ongoing social problems, feelings of loneliness, and low self-esteem, interventions are important so children can gain acceptance and avoid the problems of adolescence and adulthood associated with aggressiveness in childhood.[78] A major form of intervention is to help aggressive children develop positive social skills. Much like group programs for shy children, behavioral programs for aggressive children focus on positive behaviors. These programs encourage cooperation, offer positive techniques to support peers, develop verbal skills to make requests and suggestions, teach positive techniques for anger management, and provide opportunities for children to rehearse the skills that increase social competence and peer acceptance. In follow-up studies, children who have attended such programs have achieved greater peer acceptance and reduced their aggressive responses.

Because parents sometimes reward children's aggressive behaviors, Gerald Patterson and his coworkers have developed an effective program for parents.[79] Patterson describes the coercive, or forcing, process the child uses to try to get family members to do what he or she wants. To change these behaviors in the child, all family members must change. The program, developed at the Oregon Research Institute, involves an intake interview with the whole family. At this time, parents specify behaviors they wish to change. A trained team observes the family at home for two weeks to record and understand patterns of interaction in the family.

Parents then read either *Families*[80] or *Living with Children*,[81] books that introduce them to behavior modification techniques. After they pass a brief test on the ideas in the book, parents attend sessions at the institute to pinpoint exactly the behaviors they wish to change. They are then trained in procedures for recording the behavior. In order to get an idea of exactly what is happening before interventions are made, parents record the occurrence of negative and positive behaviors before making any changes.

In the next step, the parents and child draw up a contract. It is important that the child get points or tokens daily for behavior. For example, a child could accumulate 2 points for making his bed, 2 points for making a school lunch, 3 points for completing his homework by a specific time, 2 points for picking up his bedroom, and 1 point for brushing his teeth without being reminded. The child could then use the points for an extra 30 minutes of television time (5 points), an extra story (2 points), and the delay of bedtime by 30 minutes (3 points). The child loses points, however, for fighting with his siblings (2 points) or yelling at his parents (2 points). Parents deduct points without nagging, criticizing, or scolding. Each day, the points are added up and rewards are given. Psychologists from the institute contact families at certain times to note their progress in changing their child's behavior.

The Oregon Research Institute treatment has the following effects: (1) significant and persistent changes in the child's behavior, (2) modest decrease in coercive behavior of all family members, (3) increased positive perception of the child by parents, (4) no further unconscious parental rewards for negative behavior, (5) more effective punishments, (6) a more active role by fathers in controlling children's behavior, and (7) mothers' perception of their whole family as happier.

HELPING THE BULLIED CHILD   Bullying occurs when an aggressive child targets a single child or a small group and, though unprovoked, pursues the child(ren) and uses force in an unemotional way, divorced from conflict or disagreement. About two-thirds of aggressive children are overt bullies, and 10 to 15 percent of all children are victims of overt bullying.[82] As we noted earlier, almost all aggressive girls engage in relational aggression, and about 8 percent of all girls are victims of relational aggression.[83] Victims of both forms of bullying share certain characteristics. They tend to be quiet, inhibited children with low self-esteem. They are sometimes physically weaker. A small subgroup of victims are impulsive, disruptive children who invite negative reactions from others. Victims accept the aggression, withdrawing or responding with immature behavior such as crying, thus rewarding the bully's behavior. As victims continue to experience bullying, their self-esteem decreases further, and over time they become depressed and develop behavior problems at home and at school.[84] When followed up in young adulthood, victims have as many social skills as young adults who were not bullied, but bullying has left its mark. Former victims are prone to feelings of depression and low self-esteem.

Research on ways to combat bullying indicate that those children who have confidence in their social skills and resist bullying with self-assertion are able to end the victimization, even if they are initially inhibited or physically weaker children.[85] They need not be physically aggressive, but they do not tolerate the attacks. Parents can help children combat bullying by enrolling children in social skills programs that teach and rehearse self-assertion. Victimization requires intervention to help both the victim and the bully, as both suffer in the present and the future. Unfortunately, bullying rarely fades away on its own.

Dan Olweus, who has studied bullying extensively in Norway and developed a school-based program to decrease it, believes that "it is a fundamental democratic right for a child to feel safe in school and to be spared the oppression and repeated, intentional humiliation implied in bullying. No student should be afraid of going to school for fear of being harassed or degraded, and no parent should need to worry about such things happening to his or her child."[86] His program is a whole-school program that requires the involvement and commitment of school administrators, teachers, parents, and students. Adults create at school, and hopefully at home, an environment in which children experience warm, positive attention and firm limits against negative behaviors. Negative behaviors receive consistent, nonhostile, non-physical consequences, and monitoring occurs in and out of school. Olweus's interventions at the school level are similar to the interventions Diana Baumrind found so effective when parents used them in the home.

Interventions occur at the school, class, and individual level and include the formation of a coordinating group, meetings with staff and parents, better supervision during recess, class rules against bullying, and class meetings. At the individual level, parents, teachers, and students meet to discuss specific incidents and to develop strategies to handle them. Emphasis is on developing effective forms of communication and positive behaviors in all students, not just in bullies or victims.

Evaluated by 2,500 students and their teachers, the intervention program was found to reduce bullying by 50 percent and decrease other antisocial acts as well. Moreover, there was no increase in bullying away from the school. The program had other positive benefits. Students expressed greater satisfaction with their schoolwork, and their social relationships with children increased. The benefits were in some instances more marked after two years than after one year.

In all areas of social difficulties—shyness, aggressiveness, victimization—taking action to learn social skills, to engage in activities that increase confidence, and to assert oneself when attacked help children improve their social status. Parents play an important role here—to ensure that children have opportunities to increase their social competence and to ensure that the school atmosphere is a safe place for all children.

Managing the Television

At the same time that children encounter new social and cultural influences at school, they also have increasing exposure to societal values projected into the home via television. Parents, however, have control over the invading forces of television, video, and computer games.

Television Use among Children

"Television and other media occupy more time than any other activity except sleeping."[87] Infants react to what they see and hear on television; toddlers attend to and imitate what they see. Viewing increases through the preschool years, so that by late childhood, children watch television 3 to 4 hours a day. Viewing then decreases during adolescence. Although television joins the family, school, and church as a major socializing influence, it is the only such influence that is primarily a commercial enterprise.

The exact impact of television depends on the characteristics of the viewer, the amount of viewing time, the general family and social circumstances, and, most important, the content of the programs. Educators have been concerned that television decreases cognitive skills and academic achievement, yet the effects of television depend on the nature of the programs watched. When children watch educational programs, they can acquire literacy and number skills and increase their knowledge of science and history. Important for children in all income groups, educational programs especially serve children whose families have limited educational resources.

Television can also change social attitudes by breaking down social stereotypes and providing models of positive social actions. The day after Fonzie got a library card on *Happy Days*, the number of children applying for library cards increased fivefold.[88] Television, however, most often "presents a social world emphasizing violence, frightening events, and somewhat impersonal and casual sex."[89] Researchers suspect that such television messages do have an impact, for they may fill the void resulting from lack of discussion with parents.

The passive nature of television watching concerns social scientists; however, they recognize that it does require mental effort to understand and process programs. Still, watching television appears to decrease creativity and to color the nature of daydreaming. Viewing educational programs is associated with positive themes in daydreams and viewing aggressive programming with aggressive daydreams.

In general, little research has examined new technologies such as computers and the Internet, but reviewers summarize their contributions as follows:

> The new technologies, like television itself, have been exploited to deliver entertainment of questionable taste and value at considerable cost to children and profit to the industry. The vast educational and prosocial potentials of the media have been touched, sampled, proved valuable, but not yet developed to even a fraction of that potential.[90]

Television viewing is inversely related to social background. Families with more education and more income watch less television, perhaps because they have income to pursue other activities.[91] When social status is controlled, European Americans watch less television than do African Americans or Hispanic Americans. Hispanic Americans watch significant amounts, perhaps as a way to improve their English and better understand U.S. culture.

Television viewing needs to be considered in light of family and social contact. Children's viewing appears less related to the child's development/cognitive level or other personal qualities than to the family context and daily routines—how much parents watch, the television habits of older and younger siblings, preschool attendance, mother's work schedule.[92] Families socialize young children's television use early on; by the age of three or four, a child's consistent patterns are established.

Television, in turn, affects family life. Studies have found that when they are not watching television, family members talk more to each other and engage in more stimulating activities.[93] When they are watching television, family members are in close physical proximity and are more relaxed. An interesting finding is that adolescents who watch television with their families report feeling better during time spent with their families than during time spent with their friends.

Heavy television viewing has negative effects. The more television adults watch, the worse they report they feel; yet they do not give up the habit. "One of the few consistent findings cited across many studies was that children who used television heavily, especially violent programming, had more difficulties in impulse control, task perseverance, and delay of gratification."[94] Further, heavy television use deprives children of time they could be spending in more active pursuits such as sports, studying, or interacting with other people.

The Effects of Television Violence

"Perhaps no greater cultural influence on children's aggressive development can be found than the effects of viewing violence on television. Laboratory studies over the past quarter-century demonstrate that viewing televised aggressive models leads immediately to increased aggressive behavior, whether assessed by 'Bobo' dolls or toward peers. . . . The effect is fairly linear: the more a child watches TV violence, the more aggressive that child becomes."[95] These findings hold even when initial levels of aggression are controlled. These controls are especially important, as it is known that aggressive children watch more television. Without controlling for initial levels of aggression, we would not know whether the children being studied were more aggressive at the outset or if the television viewing was an effect rather than the cause of later behavior.

Repeated viewing of violent television programs has even greater effects over time. In one study, boys' preference for aggressive programs at age eight predicted aggression and seriousness of criminal arrests at age thirty, even when social class, parenting, intelligence, and initial aggression at age eight were controlled for. Reviews of the most carefully controlled studies "indicate that the effects of televised violence are robust and account for about 10 percent of the variance in child aggression, which approximately equals the magnitude of effect of cigarette smoking on lung cancer. This finding appears to be one of the most rigorously tested and robust effects in all of developmental psychology."[96]

Children are more influenced by television violence than are adults, perhaps because they attend to the dramatic effects of the programs and have less understanding of the moral significance of the behaviors they see. In addition, they are more likely than adults to believe that television violence is real. Educational programs to decrease aggressive behavior in frequent viewers of television violence help children understand that the violence is staged and not real. These educational efforts show children how television fools them and how violence is not useful in settling everyday problems. Children actively participate in passing this information on to other children by giving talks or making videos to show how television fooled them. Follow-up studies of such programs find that fewer participants are identified as aggressive than are children who did not participate in the intervention.

Helping Children Use Television Effectively

Parental example is the most significant way to influence children's television use.[97] Parents provide a model of how to use television for education, discussion, and relaxation. In addition, children also view parents' television choices; so, from the beginning, the content of parents' selections influences their children. Second, parents can monitor the amount of time children watch and encourage educational programs. Third, parents can watch programs with their children and make television viewing a social occasion by discussing the content of what they see. Fourth, parents can take community action. They can lobby television stations to follow the guidelines of the Television Violence Act of 1990 and the Children's Educational Television Act of 1990. Finally, parents can lobby schools to teach critical viewing skills. Schools in Canada and Europe have organized media literacy training for all students, and some require students to pass a media literacy test.

197

*Parents'
Experiences
during the
Elementary
School Years*

Aimee Dorr and Beth Rabin suggest that, in addition to these direct interventions, parents organize the household and children's activities around other interests and pursuits.[98] They believe that emphasizing other activities may be a more successful way to curb television use than regulating the amount of time children watch. They also recommend that parents become active socializers of their children by promoting core values that children internalize and rely on to counteract the messages that television provides.

Parents' Experiences during the Elementary School Years

Children's entrance into school marks a new stage in parenthood. Children spend more time away from their parents in school and with peers. They are absorbing new information and are exposed to new values. Ellen Galinsky describes this parental stage as the *interpretive stage.*[99] Parents share facts and information about the world, teach values, and guide children's behavior in certain directions. They decide how they will handle the child's greater independence and involvement with people who may not share similar values.

At this point, parents have a more realistic view of themselves as parents than before and a greater understanding of their children as individuals. Parents have been through the sleepless nights and crying of infancy, the temper tantrums of toddlerhood, and the instruction of their children in basic routines and habits. They have a sense of how they and their child will react in any given situation. Although some have a very negative view of themselves as parents, most have developed a sense of their strengths and difficulties and a confidence that, by and large, they and their children are okay. Children, however, leave the parents' control and enter a structured environment with rules and regulations. Children are evaluated in terms of their ability to control their behavior and learn skills that will help them as adults. For the first time, external standards and grades compare children with one another. Parents must deal with, and help their children deal with, these external evaluations, which may differ from those parents have formed at home.

For parents, bridging the gap between the way they treat their children and the way their children are treated by teachers, group leaders, and peers may be a constant struggle. Parents will develop strategies for dealing with adults outside the home who may not see the child as they do. An attitude that stresses cooperation seems most effective. When parents share their knowledge about their child, when they seek to understand the child's behavior that demands change, they can form a coalition with adults outside the home to produce a positive experience for their child.

Children's needs draw parents out of the home and into the community. Parents, for example, may get involved with school personnel to reduce bullying or to increase

The Joys of Parenting Elementary School Children

"I love watching them become little people who can take responsibility for chores, and also every now and then want to cook me dinner. Now they use the microwave; they can heat something up. They'll make tuna fish and raw vegetables." —*Mother*

"It's really fun learning more about girls. She is a lot like her mother in her interests and her understanding of people. I wasn't a reader; I was out on my bike, and I really like that she is such a big reader and enjoys many of the books her mother had as a girl." —*Father*

"This is the time when I can start instilling my values, why I do what I do, how people become homeless. When they were younger, you just had the rule, 'No play guns in the house,' and now you can talk about why you have the rule, and you are interacting on a whole new level." —*Mother*

"He's nine, and for the last several months, maybe because I'm the dad, he's come and said, 'Now there's this girl who's written me a note, what do I do?' Or, 'I have an interest here, how do I act?' I never heard any of this from my daughters. Then he says, 'What were you doing in the third grade? How would you deal with this when you were in the third grade?'" —*Father*

"One of the joys is you are learning or relearning through your children, whether it's actual subject matter or reexperiencing things and seeing the way they handle something versus the way you did. It gives me insight into their independence that they think of different solutions for things. There's always another way besides 'Mom's way.'" —*Mother*

educational resources. Parents may become involved in community organizations to expand recreational programs. We discuss such participation in greater detail in Chapter 11, but here we emphasize that parents change during the elementary school years as they come to see themselves and their children as interdependent parts of a larger society.

In the process of explaining the world and people's behavior, parents refine their beliefs and values, discarding some and adding others. Children often prompt changes when they discover inconsistencies and hypocrisies in what parents say. If lying is bad, why do parents tell relatives they are busy when they are not? If parents care about the world and want to make it a safer place, why are they not doing something to help? In the process of answering these questions, parents grow as well as children.

Main Points

Parenting tasks during the elementary school years include

- monitoring and guiding children from a distance as children move into new activities on their own

"Every night we have a talking time just before he goes to bed, either he and his dad or he and I. He's a real deep thinker, and he likes to get advice or get a response, and he just needs that verbal connection. So a few years ago when he was five, he was talking about being afraid of death and that he might not be married and he might not have children and that would be the worst. I can hear parts of what he might hear at church or other places like school, and he takes it all very seriously; when it collides, he wants to know what the answer is. They are always things we don't know the answer to, either." —*Mother*

"I enjoy the rituals we have developed. I don't know how it started, but every night we eat by candlelight. One lights the candles, and one turns down the dimmer, and it's a very nice touch after a day at work." —*Mother*

"I can say as a father of two girls between five and ten that to be a father to girls is delightful. It's nice being looked on as a combination of God and Robert Redford. They have a little glow in their eyes when they look at Dad, and it's great. The younger one said, 'When I'm ticklish, you know why? Because I love you so much.'" —*Father*

"He does well in school because he's willing to put in time on things. It is fun to work with him on projects. He wanted a Nintendo, and we said no because it is addictive and you spend too much time on it. He had a science fair project at school, and he decided to make up a questionnaire on how kids used their Nintendo, which he handed out to everyone. I helped him analyze the answers; and he proved the longer kids had it, the less they used it, and so it wasn't addictive. When his birthday came, we got it for him. He proved he was right." —*Father*

- interacting in a warm, accepting, yet firm manner when children are present
- strengthening children's abilities to monitor their own behavior and develop new skills
- structuring the home environment so the child can meet school responsibilities
- serving as an advocate for the child in activities outside the home—for example, with schools, with sports teams, in organized activities
- providing opportunities for children to develop new skills and positive identities
- becoming active in school and community organizations to provide positive environments for children

Children's competence increases during these years, and by the end of this period, they have

- learned greater understanding of their own and others' emotional reactions
- gained greater control of their aggressiveness and become less fearful
- learned to remedy situations they control and adjust to situations others control

- come to value themselves for their physical, intellectual, and social competence, developing an overall sense of self-worth
- learned to rely on parents as models and advocates

Schools

- are the main socializing force outside the family
- create stress in children's lives because children worry about making mistakes, being ridiculed, and failing
- promote a strong bond with children by encouraging active participation in learning and activities
- promote learning when they provide a calm, controlled environment and teachers are gentle disciplinarians with high expectations for students
- often do not reward the values of ethnic groups that emphasize cooperation and sharing among its members

Social relationships

- when positive, predict academic success and psychological adjustment
- when negative, predict later difficulties in academic performance and emotional well-being
- develop, in part, from the quality of the parent-child relationship
- can improve by the child's willingness to take responsibility for problems and learn new skills
- can be improved by having a whole-school policy to reduce bullying and relational aggression and to increase positive interactions

Children's television viewing

- can reinforce negative social stereotypes and takes time from growth-enhancing activities
- when parents regulate and monitor its use, yields such benefits as providing information, changing attitudes, and creating positive feelings
- of violent programs is as strongly related to child aggression as smoking is to lung cancer

In Galinsky's interpretive stage, parents

- achieve greater understanding of themselves as parents and of their children
- develop strategies for helping children cope with new authorities such as teachers

Exercises

1. In small groups of four or five persons, take turns recalling (a) how your parents prepared you for school, (b) how you felt the first days you can remember, (c) what your early experiences were, (d) how confident or shaky you felt about your abilities. Then, identify ways your parents and teachers could have helped

more. Share your group's experiences with the class and come up with recommendations for parents and teachers.

2. In small groups, take turns recalling the pleasurable events you experienced during the years from five to ten. Then, come up with a class list of twenty common pleasurable events for that period.

3. Take the list of twenty pleasurable events developed in Exercise 2 and rate each event—as you would have when you were a child of nine or ten—on a scale of 1 to 7, with 1 being least pleasurable and 7 being most pleasurable. What were the most pleasurable events? How did parents contribute to them? (Recall from Chapter 3 that children six to fifteen saw friends as major sources of pleasure and parents as major sources of frustration.)

4. In small groups, recall the fears you had as a child from five to ten. How could parents or teachers have helped you cope with those fears?

5. In small groups, discuss major activities that built self-esteem during the elementary school years. Were these athletic activities? group activities such as Scouts or Brownies? school activities? Come up with recommendations for parents as to the kinds of activities children find most confidence-building.

Additional Readings

Armstrong, Thomas. *Awakening Your Child's Natural Genius.* Los Angeles: Jeremy T. Tarcher, 1991.

Comer, James P. *Waiting for a Miracle: Why Schools Can't Solve Our Problems—And How We Can.* New York: Plume, 1998.

Damon, William. *The Moral Child.* New York: Free Press, 1988.

Dunn, Judy. *Sisters and Brothers.* Cambridge, MA: Harvard University Press, 1985.

Ehrensaft, Diane. *Spoiling Childhood: How Well-Meaning Parents Are Giving Children Too Much—But Not What They Need.* New York: Guilford, 1997.

Seligman, Martin E. P. *The Optimistic Child.* New York: Houghton Mifflin, 1995.

7

Adolescence

AS CHILDREN EXPERIENCE THE PHYSICAL AND PSYCHO-logical changes that launch them into adulthood, both they and their parents face exciting challenges. Adolescents must integrate all these changes as they encounter new school and social situations. Relationships with peers absorb more time and attention, yet close relationships with parents protect adolescents as they move toward greater independence. What parenting strategies are effective when teens assert their independence? How do parents help teens manage their intense feelings? How do parents help adolescents develop healthy behaviors and avoid high-risk behaviors? Balancing the freedom teenagers want with the guidance they need, parents broaden their roles as nurturers and monitors to also serve as supporters and consultants.

The adolescent years are a turning point for children. They leave the early childhood years of stable and steady growth to experience all the stresses of rapid physical growth, a changing hormonal system, and physical development that results in sexual and reproductive maturity. As their bodies and hormones change, children's emotions often become more intense and harder to control. Their thinking changes; they become more aware of possibilities, and they think more abstractly. At the same time that children undergo these physical and cognitive changes, they are reaching out socially to peers and becoming more independent of their parents. They are beginning to search for their own identity—who they are, what they like, what goals they will set for themselves.

As adolescents seek a sense of who they are, they question parents' authority, rebel against restrictions, and argue their own point of view. Parents must encourage the growth of their children's independence and self-esteem and help them become more competent, yet parents must not permit so much freedom that children get into situations they cannot handle. Although adolescence is taxing for parents, it is an exciting time to watch children blossom as they take their first steps out of childhood into a new life. In this chapter, we trace the joys and the potential pitfalls in this process.

A Time of Change

The years from eleven to eighteen are years of profound change in the areas of physical, intellectual, emotional, self-, and social functioning. Further, during this time, children develop interests in dating and encounter various changes in the school environment.

Physical Changes

The rapid physiological changes of adolescence take place over several years—for girls, on average, from about age nine to seventeen and for boys from eleven to twenty.[1] The timing of the changes is important. Early-maturing girls have greater difficulties than later-maturing girls.[2] They experience more conflict with parents, and they are out of sync with the development of age-mates—both boys and girls—because their bodies and interests are advanced. They sometimes lose interest in school and in classmates, preferring older friends. In contrast, early-maturing boys have an advantage because they develop the muscular strength valued in athletics.

Learning to live in new bodies is stressful. Adolescents have new physical concerns—acne, obesity, menstruation, sexuality, sexually transmitted diseases.[3] During the high school years, girls give themselves a poorer health rating than do boys their age and girls ten to fourteen.[4] Statistics suggest they are correct. They exercise less and diet more. Girls are more likely to make physicians' visits and be hospitalized than are boys, primarily because of reproductive health needs.[5] Although boys give themselves a better health rating than girls do, boys are twice as likely to die because they are more often involved in motor vehicle accidents.

All these physical changes impact self-esteem. Across the whole life span, physical appearance is the factor most closely related to self-esteem. An adolescent's physical appearance not only changes, but receives more intense scrutiny from others.[6] Girls, particularly, are subject to very rigid standards of physical attractiveness, and many girls come to hate their bodies and their appearance, as we will discuss shortly.

Of all the changes teenagers experience, their emerging sexuality is one of the most profound physical developments of adolescence. Before they become sexual with a partner, adolescents engage in self-stimulating sexual activities, such as fantasizing and masturbation. These may occur separately or together—half of all teens fantasize while masturbating. Masturbation, which often begins between ages twelve and fourteen for boys and girls, is the most common form of orgasm in both sexes during the adolescent years.[7]

TABLE 7.1   Adolescents' Reasons for Having or Waiting to Have Intercourse

Reasons to Have Intercourse

Girls	Boys
Peer pressure (34%)	Peer pressure (26%)
Pressure from boys (17%)	Curiosity (16%)
Curiosity (14%)	Everyone does it (10%)
Everyone does it (14%)	Sexual gratification (10%)

Reasons to Wait

Danger of sexually transmitted diseases (65%)

Danger of pregnancy (62%)

Fear of discovery by parents (50%)

Fear of ruining reputation with friends (29%)

Adapted from Herant Katchadourian, "Sexuality," in *At the Threshold: The Developing Adolescent*, ed. S. Shirley Feldman and Glen R. Elliott (Cambridge, MA: Harvard University Press, 1990), p. 344.

Heterosexual activity usually proceeds from kissing, to petting above the waist, to petting below the waist, and then to intercourse.[8] Figures vary for the exact percentages of adolescents engaging in sexual intercourse. The most recent figures indicate that in 1993, about 50 percent of high school seniors had had intercourse.[9]

Boys are more sexually active than are girls. In one study, almost 30 percent of boys reported having had intercourse by age sixteen, but only 13 percent of girls.[10] At age eighteen, the comparable figures are 64 percent of boys and 44 percent of girls. Ethnic groups vary. African American boys and girls tend to be more advanced than European American and Hispanic American boys and girls. For example, 92 percent of African American boys report having had intercourse by age seventeen, whereas only 50 percent of Hispanic American and 43 percent of European American boys make similar reports. Forty percent of African American girls report having had intercourse by age seventeen, compared with 25 percent of European American and 24 percent of Hispanic American girls. Table 7.1 lists adolescents' reasons for waiting or not waiting to have intercourse.

Among sexually active teenagers, intercourse may occur infrequently and with a limited number of partners.[11] According to one survey, most teens had intercourse again with the first partner, but the relationships were not long-lived. The typical teen had zero to one partner with whom he or she had sex, usually less than a couple of times a month. About two-thirds of adolescents in one study experienced their first intercourse in the homes of parents or friends. Their partners were most often people they knew well—a steady date or close friend.

Intellectual Changes

Adolescents think more abstractly than they did as younger children. They can analyze problems and can freely speculate about possibilities.[12] Because they can think abstractly about their own thoughts and reactions, they become more introspective. They imagine the future and what they might be doing. They also think about others' reactions and evaluate their behavior accordingly. Adolescents are often idealistic and criticize themselves and others for not meeting high standards.

Although adolescents have the capacity for abstract thought, their own theories about the way things are can interfere with their taking in new information and reasoning.[13] For example, teens sometimes have fanciful ideas about sexuality that prevent their absorbing new information. Some believe you can only get pregnant if you have sexual relations lying down or if you love the boy, and they will block out important facts on contraception. Therefore, parents are wise to get adolescents to talk about their theories and assumptions before parents provide new information.

Emotional Changes

Emotional life becomes more intense and complex during adolescence. Elementary school children rarely experience two different feelings at the same time; they rarely worry about the future or brood about others' reactions to them.[14] They live in the present, and when a difficult situation passes, they cease to think about it. So, they are more likely than early adolescents to describe themselves as very happy.

Although early adolescents' overall mood is the same as that of their parents, they tend to have more emotional variability—more highs and more lows—than their parents.[15] Part of their emotional variability stems from their heightened self-consciousness and concerns over how they appear to others. In one study, about a quarter of normal fourteen-year-olds reported feelings of being looked at, laughed at, or talked about.[16] David Elkind believes that the early adolescent "is continually constructing or reacting to an imaginary audience."[17]

Despite all the physical, social, and psychological changes of adolescence, as well as the heightened sensitivity, two-thirds of early teens report low to medium stress. The one-third who report high levels appear to be dealing with additional stress from family events such as marital arguing and divorce.[18]

Depressed and negative moods also increase over the early adolescent years. Although the increase seems slight for the majority of young teens, 10 to 20 percent of parents say their children have experienced some depressed mood—sad, unhappy feelings—in the past six months, and 20 to 40 percent of early adolescents report the same.[19] Depressed mood increases from age thirteen to fifteen, peaks at seventeen to eighteen, and then drops to adult levels. Girls are more likely than boys to report depressed mood, particularly early-maturing girls. European American and Asian American teens report more depressive symptoms than do African American and Hispanic American teens, even when the level of stress is controlled for. Gay and lesbian youth have a twofold to threefold risk for suicide and are most likely to experience more depression.[20] We take up depression in greater detail later in this chapter.

Positive experiences can serve as a buffer against the effects of stress. Such experiences provide an "arena of comfort" in which early teens can escape stress, relax, and feel good.[21] When early adolescents from various ethnic backgrounds were asked about their sources of support, all pointed to the importance of close family relationships as the main support.[22] As we saw in Figure 6.1, friends are very important as well.

Changes in the Self

Early adolescents describe themselves more abstractly in terms of general traits, such as cheerfulness, moodiness, kindness.[23] They are aware that their behavior shifts in different situations and with different people. They observe that they can be kind with friends and mean to parents, but the contradictions do not bother them. When asked why she ignored such a contradiction, an early teen replied, "That's a stupid question. I don't want to fight with myself."[24]

Mid-adolescents, however, speak of the many different me's—the self with my mother, the self with my father, the self with my best friend, the self with my boyfriend. Seeing their behavior change with circumstances intensifies mid-adolescents' concerns about "the real me." They feel they express their true selves when they discuss their inner thoughts, feelings, and reactions to events; they express false selves when they put on an act and say what they do not mean. Teens report acting falsely (1) to make a good impression, (2) to experiment with different selves, and (3) to avoid others' low opinions of them. When they believe they have parents' support, adolescents can voice their opinions and express their true selves. The higher the level of support, the more adolescents can express themselves and the higher their self-esteem.

In late adolescence, teens come to terms with contradictory qualities by finding a more general abstraction that explains the contradiction. For example, they explain changes in mood—cheerfulness with friends and discouragement with parents—by describing themselves as moody. They also come to accept the contradictions as normal—"It's normal to be different ways with different people." As they observe their changing behaviors, late adolescents note the situations in which they show the traits they value and in which they feel support, and they come to seek out these situations.

Social Changes

In early adolescence, boys and girls report having fewer friends than do elementary school children, but they gain more support from their relationships with their friends.[25] In early adolescence, children form cliques, small groups of five to nine members who choose each other as friends.[26] The most common activities are hanging out, talking, walking around school, talking on the phone, watching television, and playing physical games. Girls spend more time than boys talking and shopping, and boys spend more time than girls playing contact sports. Group activities serve several purposes: they provide sociability and a sense of belonging, promote exploration of the self and achievements, and provide opportunities for learning and instruction. Hanging out and talking promote closer social relationships, whereas competitive games promote achievements and greater understanding of the self. Both kinds of activities contribute to psychological growth and give children the kinds of experiences they need to form a stable sense of identity.

Peers play many important roles in the psychological development of adolescents. As in previous age periods, they provide opportunities for developing social skills, but they also provide support and understanding in the process of separating from parents. In Japan and the Soviet Union, adolescents spend 2 or 3 hours per week with peers.[27] In the United States, in a typical week, high school students spend twice as much time with peers (29 percent) as with parents (13 percent).[28]

During the adolescent years, other changes in peer relationships take place as well.[29] First, peer interactions are generally unsupervised by adults. Second, they are more likely to include larger numbers of peers who form crowds. Finally, peers gravitate to members of the opposite sex.

In adolescence, friendships become more intimate.[30] In addition to joint activities, friendships involve more self-disclosure, expression of feelings, and support for friends as needed. Friends are expected to tell each other their honest opinions and to express satisfactions and dissatisfactions with the other person. Friends also have to learn to resolve conflicts as they arise. So, friendships promote the development of social skills that, in turn, enrich friendships. Intimacy in friendships is related to adolescents' sociability, self-esteem, and overall interpersonal competence.

Adolescents feel quite loyal to their friends; they continue friendships despite parental disapproval and will not reveal details of the relationships to others. Although overall 56 percent would report if a friend was considering suicide, far fewer (17 to 20 percent) would break a confidence about drugs and alcohol, and almost none (6 percent) would tell if a friend was shoplifting.[31]

Peer groups that form in later adolescence are larger than the cliques of the early adolescent years. Bradford Brown refers to these as *crowds*.[32] Cliques form out of mutual choice; crowds, though, are based on judgments of personal characteristics, and a person must be invited to join. Through time we have seen slight shifts in the kinds of crowds, but generally studies find groups of "jocks" (athletes), "brains," popular kids, and "druggies" (delinquents).

A recent study, conducted over a year's time, describes peer groups formed on the basis of members' feeling upset and distressed.[33] Individual adolescents seek out peers with similar levels of distress. Boys tend to be influenced by the mood of peers, growing more similar to the mood of the group; girls tend to maintain their own personal level of distress. Although feeling distressed does not prevent teens from having friends, it does shape the kind of friends they will have.

At the same time that peers become important, time spent alone increases and takes on a new significance in adolescence.[34] Although solitude in early childhood may be a negative experience because it is not voluntarily chosen, in adolescence, children seek solitude in their rooms and spend about as much time alone as with peers and more time alone than with parents.

A moderate amount of solitude appears to have benefits for teens. Although they do not rate their mood level as highly when alone, their mood following time alone improves. Solitude provides a retreat from social relationships and gives teens time to reflect on their own qualities and the kind of person they want to be. Adolescents who spend intermediate amounts of time alone are rated as better adjusted by parents and teachers and rate themselves as less depressed than those who spend no time alone or large amounts of time alone.

Dating

Dating serves many important functions in adolescence. It is a way to learn how to relate to people of the opposite sex; it provides a structure for meeting people, exploring compatibility, and terminating a relationship with a minimum of embarrassment. Finally, dating gives practice in developing feelings of trust and enjoyment with the opposite sex. Because there are almost no studies of same-sex dating, we will discuss heterosexual dating here.

Although the sexual revolution has brought many changes, the concerns of adolescents who date remain much the same as those of their parents. "Will he like me?" "Will she go out with me?" "What do I say on a date?" Girls still wait for boys to call, and almost two-thirds of a national sample of girls say they have never asked a boy out. Boys rather enjoy being asked out, and only 13 percent said it would "turn them off."[35]

What qualities do boys and girls seek in each other? Over 90 percent of girls ages sixteen to twenty-one said the important qualities in boys are a good personality, kindness, good manners, and a sense of humor. Over 70 percent said compassion, good looks, and charm are important. The least popular qualities are heavy drinking, inability to communicate, drug use, and profanity, followed by indecisiveness, being a "super jock," and not being affectionate. Boys said they are initially attracted by a good figure and good looks, but for them, too, the most important qualities are personality and a good sense of humor—then beauty, intelligence, and psychological warmth. So, even though boys place an initial emphasis on physical qualities, they are basically seeking the same qualities in girls that girls seek in them.[36]

Most girls begin dating at about fourteen and boys between fourteen and fifteen. By their senior year in high school, about half of adolescents date more than once a week, and one-third between two and three times a week. It is widely held that boys are oriented toward sexual activity more than girls are. But even though adolescent boys desire physical intimacy early in the dating relationship, they want increasing affection and intimacy as the relationship progresses, just as girls do.[37]

About one-quarter of adolescent boys and one-third of adolescent girls say they are going steady. Going steady occurs most frequently among older adolescents sixteen to eighteen; 30 percent of boys and 40 percent of girls of this age say they are going steady. Over half the adolescents say they have been in love, with girls reporting this more frequently than boys. The intensity of these feelings and the pain that comes when the relationship ends rival anything any adult feels in such a situation. Some love relationships of adolescence develop into more committed relationships, but frequently the feelings fade.[38]

Adolescents who have definite educational and vocational plans and who wish for marriages like those of their parents go steady less often and report being in love less

Dating provides opportunities for developing trust and confidence in relationships with the opposite sex.

often during adolescence than the norm. When girls have high self-esteem, they date more often but go steady less often. Those who are most likely to be going steady do not want marriages like their parents have. In general, involvement in dating too early and too intensely may block opportunities for same-sex relationships or more casual opposite-sex relationships that develop the capacity for intimacy and closeness at later ages.

School

At the same time that adolescents' bodies, emotions, thought patterns, and social relationships are changing, society places added stress by moving adolescents to ever larger schools that demand independence and provide minimal individual attention to students. There is what Jacquelynne Eccles calls a "mismatch" between the developmental needs of early adolescents for support and the demands that schools place on them.[39]

Nonetheless, although school settings and the demands on students change during adolescence, schools that support competence continue to have the same qualities as effective elementary schools.[40] When students view teachers as academically and emotionally supportive, then they experience less stress and less alienation at school; conversely, when they view teachers as unfair or biased, students' stress increases. When schools focus less on competition and, instead, encourage students to focus on effort, self-improvement, and task mastery, students feel increased motivation and well-being. Students' needs for autonomy are met when schools encourage choice whenever possible—such as in choice of seating and work partners—and emphasize active participation in learning.

Forming a Sense of Identity in Times of Change

As mentioned earlier in this chapter, adolescents are in search of "the real me." Erik Erikson spoke of this sense of identity as a distinct, differentiated person.[41] The process of achieving a sense of identity occurs gradually over several years. Adolescents explore new experiences and ideas, form new friendships, and make a commitment to values, goals, and behavior. During this process, conflict and crisis can arise as the choices get worked out. There are, however, some adolescents who choose traditional values without even considering for themselves what they want to do with their lives. They face no crisis or conflict, because they do not want to deal with issues. James Marcia terms commitment without exploration *identity foreclosure* to indicate that possibilities have been closed off prematurely.[42]

A different path is taken by adolescents who experience a *moratorium*. These adolescents are in a crisis over what they want to do. They have ideas they explore, but they have not yet made a commitment. So, a moratorium is exploration without commitment. Finally, some adolescents experience *identity diffusion*, in which they can make no choices at all. They drift without direction.

One study found that adolescent boys who rank high in identity exploration come from families in which they can express their own opinions and at the same time receive support from parents even when they disagree with them.[43] Boys are encouraged to be both independent and at the same time connected to family members. Adolescent girls who rate high in identity exploration come from families in which they are challenged and receive little support from parents who are contentious with each other. Girls may need this slightly abrasive atmosphere in order to pursue a heightened sense of individuality rather than follow the path of intensifying social relationships. However, these girls do have at least one parent with whom they feel connected.

Gender Identity

Differences in gender identity appear mainly in the content of the identity, not in the process by which identity is formed. In the past, boys' identity has been linked with independence and achievement at work and girls' identity with close relationships with others. Boys have been socialized to get ahead and girls to get along.[44] These traits are expressed in their self-descriptions. Boys see themselves as more daring, rebellious, and playful in life than girls and, at the same time, more logical, curious, and calm.

211

*Forming a
Sense of
Identity in
Times of
Change*

Girls see themselves as more attuned to people than boys are (more sympathetic, social, considerate, and affectionate) and more emotionally reactive (more worrisome, more easily upset, more needing of approval).[45]

Adolescent girls are socialized both to have close relationships with others and to succeed at work. Like ethnic minority youth (whom we discuss shortly), they may have a more difficult time as they attempt to integrate their identities in a greater number of roles—wife, mother, worker—whereas boys focus on their work roles.[46]

In adolescence, a small percentage of teens identify themselves as gay, lesbian, or bisexual.[47] For boys, the mean age of awareness of same-gender attraction is thirteen, with self-description as "homosexual" occurring between fourteen and twenty-one. For lesbians, the average age of awareness is sixteen, with self-description occurring around twenty-one years of age.

Society's negative view of homosexuality and lesbianism creates pressure and self-doubt in adolescents attracted to same-sex partners. In one study, adolescents reported strong negative reactions from parents (43 percent) and friends (41 percent) on revealing their same-sex preference. They reported discrimination by peers (37 percent), verbal abuse (55 percent), and physical assault (30 percent).[48] Because such discrimination and rejection create additional psychological problems, it is not surprising that gay adolescents are two to three times more likely to attempt suicide than are other adolescents and may make up as much as 30 percent of all completed youth suicides.[49]

In spite of others' negative views, homosexual and lesbian adolescents can evolve a positive self-concept of themselves as lovable, respectable, competent individuals. As with ethnic minority youth, support from family and others may be especially critical in forming a positive self-concept and combating the social disapproval they may encounter.

Ethnic Identity

Achieving a sense of identity is a more complicated task for ethnic minority youth than it is for youth of the majority culture.[50] They have two cultures to explore, understand, and integrate in their quest for identity. They begin with a diffused view of their ethnic background. They talk to parents, family friends, and other adults about ethnic issues. They read books and share experiences with friends. They are aware of prejudice and think about its effects on their work and life goals. In the eighth grade, about a third of African American students are actively involved in this exploration. By age fifteen, about half of minority students are actively exploring their cultural roots and traditions, and an additional one-fourth have already achieved a sense of identity. By late adolescence, most have achieved a sense of ethnic identity. Sense of ethnic identity and high self-esteem are related to each other in an interactive fashion. High self-esteem promotes exploration of ethnic identity, and ethnic identity promotes a sense of self-esteem.[51] Box 7.1 lists methods for enhancing identity formation in ethnic minority youths.

Studies of African American and Mexican American adolescents in schools where they were the major groups and had positive status found that all students formed a valued sense of ethnic identity, but they differed in the degree to which they valued and identified with the broader American culture.[52] *Blended bicultural* students

BOX 7.1

Methods to Enhance Identity Formation of Ethnic Minority Youths

1. Methods should be proposed to keep minority youths in school and academically oriented, because lack of education increases the risk of poverty and disadvantage.

2. Efforts are required to heighten health consciousness, because poor health interferes with identity processes. The physical health of many minority youths lags behind that of majority youths.

3. The importance of social networks should be affirmed. Churches and extended families are important resources for minority families, as they socialize children.

4. Methods should be proposed to support parents as cultural transmitters. Many ethnic group parents do not discuss their distinctive values and experiences, and parents must receive support as they begin to do this.

5. Proposals are needed to offer a media-focused, cultural emphasis that affirms positive group identity for all youths to combat the negative stereotyping that occurs.

6. Methods are needed to promote teaching of native languages and cultures, particularly for American Indians who are at risk for losing their cultural heritage. Creativity is required to encourage biculturalism at the same time one preserves cultural traditions.

7. Programs are required for the special training of teachers so that they will be sensitive to cultural traditions, communication patterns, and sometimes the language of minority students.

8. Childrearing support by way of teaching parenting skills is required to promote parents' sense of ethnic pride and enhance the home-school partnership.

9. Improved training is required for mental health workers serving ethnic minority populations.

Margaret Beale Spencer and Carol Markstrom-Adams, "Identity Processes among Racial and Ethnic Minority Children in America," *Child Development* 61 (1990): 305–306.

positively identified with both the majority and their own ethnic group. For example, they saw themselves as African and American and saw no conflict between the identities. *Alternating bicultural* students identified with the majority culture when at school or at other places but primarily identified with their own ethnic group. A third, smaller group were termed *separated* students, as they did not identify at all with the majority culture, which they felt rejected and devalued them. Among African American students, slightly over half were classified as blended biculturals, about a quarter as alternating biculturals, and 17 percent as separated. Among Mexican American students, about one-third were classified as blended biculturals, almost two-thirds as alternating biculturals, and only 2 percent as separated.

A positive identification with both cultures is thought to be important for personal adjustment, yet the three groups of students did not differ on measures of self-concept, academic grades, and level of anxiety. Thus, there appear to be three pathways to integrating the experience of having two cultures, and the pathways all seem to be equally related to measures of effectiveness.

Parent-Child Relationships

As teenagers go through adolescence, they spend increasingly less time with their families, dropping from 25 percent of their time during their first year of high school to 15 percent during their senior year.[53] Further, what time they do spend with parents may be spent in what Reed Larson and Maryse Richards term *divergent realities*. For their research, Larson and Reed gave electronic pagers to parents and their children ages nine to fifteen and systematically beeped and asked them to write about their activities and feelings. After analyzing the data, Larson and Richards wrote, "Once we go inside family life we find that it is an illusion to talk about 'the family,' as though it were a single entity. The family is the meeting ground of multiple realities."[54] The authors believe that parents' and offspring's inability to understand and deal with their different realities creates problems for all family members.

In these researchers' Midwestern working and middle-class sample, fathers worked hard and viewed time at home as leisure. They brought home their work stress, which affected all family members. Mothers—about one-third of whom were full-time homemakers, one-third part-time workers, and one-third full-time workers—felt they should be able to create a harmonious home atmosphere; when frustrated, they sought pleasure in activities outside the home. Early adolescents, as noted, experience stress from many sources. When parents are available and responsive, negative feelings decrease.

Parents and children agree that the mundane, routine behaviors cause most conflicts. Schoolwork and grades become a more frequent topic as early adolescents move into junior high school. As they move into high school, chores become a focus and remain a major topic during later adolescence.[55]

Although they understand parents' insistence on following conventions, young adolescents simply do not agree with them. Early adolescents insist that many of these issues should be matters under their personal control. Parents are aware of their children's point of view, but they do not accept it as valid. Early adolescents do recognize that certain behaviors have important effects on other people; they, like parents, consider these moral issues that they do not challenge—for example, hitting others, not sharing.

Parents and children agree that most of the time conflicts end because children follow parents' wishes. In only 18 percent of conflicts do parents follow children's requests, and joint discussion and decisions settle only 13 percent of the disagreements. So, although there are conflicts, children tend to acquiesce.[56] The basic relationship between parents and children remains solid.

Mothers, however, bear the burden of the increasing disagreements,[57] perhaps because they are more involved than fathers in routine household management and scheduling. It also may be that mothers are more emotionally reactive with adolescents, so both boys and girls argue with them more. When fathers are present as a third party in disagreements, boys are more respectful and mother-son relations improve. Father-adolescent relations are more open and interactive when mothers are not present as a third party.[58] Mothers tend to dominate in parent-child relationships, and fathers tend to withdraw.

Although teens are in the process of maturing and seeking greater freedom and independence, the dimensions of parenting that predict adolescents' competence are the same dimensions that predicted competence beginning in the preschool years. Authoritative parenting, defined as balancing responsiveness to children's needs and individuality with demands for meeting behavioral standards, is related to adolescent self-confidence, competence, self-reliance, avoidance of delinquent activity, and general good mood.[59] These findings apply to all groups, regardless of sex and socioeconomic and ethnic background. All large-scale studies of adolescents have found that teens from authoritative homes function more effectively than do teens from nonauthoritative homes. Even if only one parent is authoritative and the other is not, adolescents achieve better grades than those growing up in families with two nonauthoritative parents.[60]

Trying to determine what aspects of authoritative parenting make it so effective, Marjory Gray and Laurence Steinberg established three core dimensions: acceptance and involvement, strictness and supervision, and psychological autonomy granting.[61] *Acceptance and involvement* reflects parents' responsiveness to children's needs and individuality. *Strictness and supervision* involves parents' monitoring and supervising teens' behavior so it conforms to family rules. *Granting autonomy* involves allowing children freedom to express their individuality and contribute to family decision making.

A self-report questionnaire administered to 10,000 students, fourteen to eighteen years of age, of diverse socioeconomic and ethnic backgrounds revealed that the three dimensions of parenting have distinct effects on adolescents' adjustment. Results were similar in all four ethnic groups—European American, African American, Hispanic American, and Asian American. Parents' acceptance and involvement were related to adolescents' reports of academic achievement, a positive identity, and adoption of appropriate roles. Parents' acceptance and involvement also appeared to be related to adolescents' general feeling of personal well-being. The researchers wrote, "We believe that teens excel in most areas of their lives when they simply feel they come from a loving home with responsive parents, regardless of whether they perceive other shortcomings in their parents."[62] Parents' strictness and supervision were related to students' developing a strong sense of self-control and discipline. Teens developed good study habits and the capacity to avoid drug use, school absence, and delinquent behaviors. Parents' granting of autonomy promoted feelings of self-confidence and competence in teens, which enabled them to act in socially appropriate ways.

The greater the parents' involvement, supervision, and autonomy-granting, the more teens reported competence and psychological well-being. Medium amounts of supervision appeared most predictive of school achievement. Parents' involvement and autonomy-granting were related to lack of psychological distress and worrying.

"Seeing him care for younger children and babies is a great pleasure. He's a great nurturer with small children. He has endless patience." —*Mother*

"I like that he does things I did, like play the trumpet. He started at the same age I did and since he took it up, it has rekindled my interest and I started practicing again. This last weekend, we played together. He also brings new interests too. Because he likes sailing I have started that and really like it." —*Father*

"I was so impressed and pleased that after the earthquake, he and a friend decided to go door to door and offer to sell drawings they made of Teenage Mutant Ninja Turtles. He raised $150 that he gave for earthquake relief. I was very proud that he thought this up all by himself." —*Father*

"I was very happy one day when I found this note she left on my desk. It said, 'Hello!!! Have a happy day! Don't worry about home, everyone's fine! Do your work the very best you can. But most important, have a fruitful life!!!' I saved that note because it made me feel so good." —*Mother*

"Sometimes the kids have friends over, and they all start to talk about things. It's nice to see them get along with their siblings as well as their friends. It gives you a good feeling to see them enjoying themselves." —*Father*

"I really like to see them taking responsibility. Yesterday they had a school holiday, and I was donating some time at an open house fundraiser. They got all dressed up and came along and helped too. The older one coaches a soccer team of four-year-olds, and the younger is a patrol leader in the Scouts, so they both have responsibility for children. They complain sometimes that it's hard to get the little kids' attention to show them things, but I think they like it." —*Mother*

"I enjoy that she is following in the family tradition of rowing. I rowed in college, and my brothers did, my father and grandfather did, and she saw a city team and signed up. She does it all on her own and has made a nice group of friends through it." —*Father*

"I enjoy his honesty and the relationship he has with his friends. He is real open with his feelings, and his friends look up to him. He's a leader." —*Mother*

When parents were described as providing all three aspects of authoritative parenting, teens reported the most effective functioning and greatest sense of well-being. If parents provided either high involvement or autonomy, teens' internal psychological distress was reduced.

Other research supports Gray and Steinberg's conclusions. Brian Barber identified three dimensions of parental behavior similar to those described by Gray and Steinberg—connection, regulation, and autonomy.[63] Barber studied adolescents' perceptions of these three dimensions in four contexts—family, peers, school, and neighborhood—

and their relation to academic grades, degree of depression, and aggressive behavior problems. Experiences in the family and with peers appeared most predictive of adolescents' functioning:

> The importance of family experience to the lives of these young people was evident in several results, including . . . the consistent correlations of family experiences to positive social experiences in the other contexts under study; the unique role of family relationships to the mental health of the youth; and, for a subset of the sample (young females), the predominant role of family experiences in predicting antisocial behavior.[64]

With these studies as background, let us discuss how parents promote adolescents' ability to regulate feelings, to develop healthy behaviors, and to establish positive peer relationships.

Promoting Adolescents' Capacity for Emotional Regulation

Recall in Chapter 4 that we discussed the particular stresses boys and girls experience in growing up. Carolyn Zahn-Waxler described the difficulties of the warriors and the worriers[65] that are most clearly seen during the adolescent years, when boys are at high risk for poorly controlled aggressive behavior and girls are at risk for depression.

The Importance of Parents' Examples

Before describing actions parents can take to help teens regulate their feelings, let us emphasize that the way parents regulate their own feelings and solve their own emotional dilemmas has a profound impact on children's development of aggressive and depressed feelings. So, parents' management of their own feelings is the first step in helping teens.

Parents' behavior affects children in at least two ways. First, parents' handling of feelings serves as a model to children as to how or how not to regulate feelings. Second, the level of emotional arousal in the home, resulting in part from parents' handling of feelings and conflict with each other, may promote or interfere with teens' ability to manage their feelings. Teens may develop problems if they are so highly aroused that they cannot deal effectively with their own emotions. Conversely, parents' modulation of feelings at home may enable teens to develop appropriate ways of handling feelings.

We must recognize, first, that parents' ways of handling emotion are, in part, determined by experiences with their parents. Using survey and observational data from three generations of 451 intact families, researchers demonstrated a cycle of transmission of feelings from one generation to the next.[66] The grandparent generation was rejecting of their children, who felt uncared for, criticized, and blamed for problems. The second generation developed depressed feelings. As adults, they had low energy, worried about things, and felt hopeless and discouraged about the future. When they became parents, they too rejected their children, criticizing them and blaming them for their problems. Their children also became depressed. Depressed feelings were modeled for the child and also intensified by the parents' rejection and criticism.

Research indicates that parents' ways of managing conflict, rather than the frequency of conflict, predict children's problem behavior.[67] When parents deal with conflict in hostile, subtle, covert ways, adolescents are at risk for worrying and anxiety. Other research indicates that the relationship between parents' behavior and children's behavior is complex.[68] For example, when marital distress leads to mothers' depressive symptoms, then adolescents are more likely to be angry and aggressive. When mothers' depressive symptoms lead to marital distress, then adolescents are more likely to develop depressive feelings. So, the sequence of feelings can lead to different reactions in teens. Nonetheless, the point is that parents' affect and ways of handling their feelings do play a role in children's development of emotional regulation.

217

*Promoting
Adolescents'
Capacity for
Emotional
Regulation*

Parents' individual personality characteristics also predict outcomes as well. In a study of adolescent boys' behavior, a measure of fathers' self-restraint and self-control in early adolescence predicted academic achievement, personal competence, conflict resolution skills, and good morale four years later.[69] Conversely, fathers' low self-restraint predicted adolescent drinking and drug use, poor peer relations, low grades, multiple sexual partners, and symptoms of depression. Fathers' self-restraint was predictive, even controlling for sons' self-restraint in early adolescence.

Helping Children Control Aggressive Feelings

James Garbarino, an internationally recognized expert on the impact of violence on children, became concerned about the epidemic of youth killings, often in inner cities, and determined to discover the causes to help parents and society prevent them in the future. Between 1996 and 1998, he interviewed young murderers and summarized his conclusions in *Lost Boys: Why Our Sons Turn Violent and How We Can Save Them.*[70] He compared his own early temperamental qualities to those of the boys who eventually killed and described all the supports and resources he had in gaining control over his early feelings.

> I myself was a difficult infant and toddler—cranky, troublesome, willful, and aggressive. At two I was found standing on the wall of the balcony outside our sixth-floor apartment and talking to the cats in the courtyard. When my mother ordered me in, I refused. That same year, I ran away from home one night and was found wandering the streets in my pajamas. When I was three, the neighbors routinely came to my mother to complain that I was beating up their six- and seven-year-old children. When I was six I would stand at the top of the monkey bars on the playground, let go with my hands and challenge other children to try to shake me off.[71]

Garbarino describes himself as being impulsive and subject to sudden inner rages. At age twelve he cruised the neighborhood on his bike, wondering what it would be like to commit the perfect crime, perhaps a murder. By later adolescence, however, he was president of the student council and editor of the yearbook. In 1964, the Lions Club of his city sent him to Washington, D.C., as a model youth.

Garbarino attributes his success to the tremendous help and support he got from his two loving parents, a safe neighborhood, and demanding schools.

> My mother devoted her every minute to me, literally "taming" me as one would a wolf pup. My father was there for me, a positive force in my life. When I started elementary school, I was assigned to strong and effective teachers in the early grades who took charge of me and the rest of their students and made sure we behaved in a civilized manner.[72]

Although he lacked inner controls, Garbarino lived in a world "filled with people who cared for me, with opportunities to become involved with positive activities at school and in the community, and with cultural messages of stability and moral responsibility. And I believed in God. In other words, while I was still living with a stormy sea inside, I was solidly anchored."[73]

In *Lost Boys*, Garbarino contrasts his own early experiences against the accumulation of stresses that many young murderers confront in their childhoods—the lack of connection with parenting figures, the lack of caregivers' positive regard and reasonable limit setting, and the presence of stresses such as poverty, physical and sexual abuse, and family or community violence. As we noted in Chapter 1, it is not any one stress but rather the accumulation of stresses that leads to difficulties.

Garbarino believes that successful programs for violent boys are those that provide (1) a safe, secure environment at home or in a community facility with people who can offer the supportive care and positive daily messages that children require to learn to conform to adult standards, (2) techniques for promoting social skills and overall psychological development, and (3) discussions focused on moral reasoning and responsibility. Such programs have to be ongoing and continuous so children have opportunities to learn positive social skills and emotional regulation, which take years to lay down.

The average aggressive adolescent boy with conduct problems does not murder someone or go to jail; still, aggressive, rule-breaking boys do continue to have problems through adolescence and into adulthood.[74] They are more apt to abuse substances, to drop out of school, to find it difficult to get and keep a job, and to have trouble with driving infractions. Further, they tend to date girls who are also aggressive and start families early. "It is hard to overemphasize the importance of childhood conduct problems for adjustment failures in young adulthood for males. These failures are pervasive and severe, and the consequences for the young man, his intimate partners, and the children whom he fathers are profound."[75]

What do researchers recommend? As we noted in earlier chapters, attentive, fair, supportive, consistent parenting helps boys learn new behaviors to replace the forcing, irritating, negative behaviors learned at home. Social skills programs with age-mates also have good success in decreasing the aggressive, disruptive behaviors that drive others away.

A third kind of intervention focuses on helping boys learn emotional regulation. In one study, aggressive boys who were emotionally volatile—irritating, disruptive, and inattentive to others—had far more problems with peers than those boys who were only aggressive.[76] Adolescents are willing to accept the teen who is only aggressive and seeks what he wants. They reject, however, the aggressive boy who fails to pay attention to others and interferes with others' activities. Thus, this boy must learn to control overreactivity and attend to others' needs. Anger management and communication skills programs can help here.

A longitudinal study of rule-breaking boys noted that about 45 percent of boys with aggressive problems also had symptoms of depression that were likely to persist into adulthood.[77] The boys who were both angry and depressed were at risk for more severe problems in adulthood than were boys who were either angry or depressed. Thus, help must deal with both sets of problems for a large number of aggressive, rule-breaking boys.

Helping Children Manage Feelings of Depression

Depression among adolescents is often a hidden problem. Many teens experience it, but few want to talk about it with parents or with friends. In addition, others often do not detect depression because many depressed teens are high achievers who seem to have everything. Teenager Sara Shandler edited a book of girls' essays about their important experiences in adolescence. She describes her own feelings of depression, common to many girls and some boys as well:

> The worst night of my life I envisioned my own funeral, my death by suicide. I curled up in a tight ball, paralyzed by my imagination. Scene after self-destructive scene reeled through my consciousness. My parents were the only people who cried at the service.
>
> Writing here is only the third time I've confessed those deathly images. The next day, I tearfully told my tenth-grade boyfriend. Later, I confided in my journal. Now, I tell you.
>
> Although I crashed that one night, I had been falling for months. Since the end of my tenth-grade year, self-judgment had tugged at the corner of my lips—that's why my smile looked forced, and my bottom lip often quivered. I didn't like myself. I only saw my weaknesses. I heard only the abrasive tone of self-criticism.[78]

The child of a therapist, Shandler insisted on rebuilding her self-worth through her own efforts, by developing a "support group" of talented women writers "who didn't insist that I smile back." Maya Angelou, Virginia Wolfe, and Alice Walker became her trusted advisers. She read their works and sat in coffee houses, writing her reactions in a journal. There was no one she had to please.

> Alone, nameless to others, I could concentrate on my own self-healing. That was the semester of Me. I learned a lot about myself, by myself. . . . With the benefit of hindsight, I can honestly say I shouldn't have done it alone. I did find strength in my solitude, in my gratingly close proximity to myself without the comfort of companionship. Still, I think recovering from my depression would have been easier with a therapist.[79]

Depression varies along a spectrum. At the one end are depressed moods—feeling down, being unhappy over an upsetting event such as failing a test or fighting with a friend.[80] The feelings may last a brief or extended time.

At the most serious end of the spectrum is clinical depression. The essential features of clinical depression are depressed mood and loss of interest or pleasure in usual pursuits. The depressed person may feel blue, down in the dumps, hopeless, or helpless in dealing with the mood. Disturbances in sleep, eating, and activity patterns may or may not accompany the depressed mood. Sometimes people awake early in the morning and cannot return to sleep. Their appetite decreases (some may eat compulsively and gain weight). Their energy level drops, and they move more slowly and accomplish less than they did formerly. Sometimes clinical depression is accompanied by loss of concentration and poor memory, so school performance may drop. Because they feel less interested and withdraw, depressed children may have fewer friends. These are the main markers of clinical depression.[81]

Estimates of clinical depression range from 1 to 4 percent for children and 1 to 15 percent for adolescents.[82] The lifetime prevalence estimate for major depression for adolescents is 15 to 20 percent, a rate comparable to that seen in adults, indicating that adult depression may begin in adolescence. Before puberty, boys and girls are equally likely to be depressed; after puberty, girls' rate doubles.

In some cases, depression is a normal response to a loss—the death of a parent, the divorce of parents, the loss of an important pet, moving to a new location. Children may show signs of depression off and on for months following the event, depending on the severity of the loss. But gradually the depression will lift. Early adolescent years are times of mood changes, and many boys and girls are occasionally blue. These moods are temporary and do not involve the global retreat from other people and decline in schoolwork that clinical depression does.

In early childhood and, to a greater extent, in adolescence, depression can be accompanied by angry, rebellious, acting-out behavior that masks the underlying condition. Some children who are serious discipline problems in school and become involved in drugs, alcohol, and risk-taking behavior are depressed. They lack self-esteem and feel helpless about themselves and helpless to change.[83]

CAUSES OF DEPRESSION   Many factors are thought to cause depressive states, including biological factors. For example, a family history of depression in parents and close relatives indicates greater susceptibility to the disorder.[84]

As reviewed in earlier chapters, children of depressed mothers are at risk for difficulties in several areas:[85] for avoidant or distressed behavior as infants, for out-of-control and dysregulated behavior as toddlers, for self-critical and self-blaming feelings as they become older, and for overly sensitive responses with peers. Although these reactions may be the forerunners of a childhood depression related to biological predisposition, they are certainly related to interactions with depressed mothers.

Life events also contribute to depression. The loss of loved ones through death, divorce, or separations; family stresses that result in neglect, abuse, or rejection of the child; pressure on the child to perform in school; and emotional deficits in the family that prevent the child from learning to identify and express feelings in a healthy way are all possible factors contributing to depression.[86]

Nevertheless, no one kind of circumstance produces depression. Some depressed children come from disorganized families that have experienced multiple stresses. Some depressed children lack friends and do poorly in school, but, as we stated earlier, other depressed children are highly successful and seem to have many friends and enjoy much success.

221

Promoting
Adolescents'
Capacity for
Emotional
Regulation

DEPRESSION AND SUICIDE   As a result of any combination of factors, children can become depressed and develop the hopeless feeling that they are confronted with an unresolvable problem that will continue. They blame themselves as incompetent, inadequate, and unworthy in some way.[87]

Prior to puberty, suicide attempts are rare, but after puberty, the rate of suicide attempts skyrockets. An estimated 90,000 adolescents attempt suicide each year, and approximately 6,000 kill themselves.[88] Suicide is the third leading cause—and is occasionally tied as the second leading cause—of death in teenagers. More girls than boys attempt suicide, but more boys actually die. Suicide is the second leading cause of death among European American boys.[89] Although rates of suicide among African American boys have been much lower, recent statistics indicate that their rates are rising at a rapid pace and may soon equal the rates of European American boys.[90] Further, 24 percent of high school students report they have thought seriously of suicide, 19 percent made a plan, and about 9 percent attempted suicide.[91]

Susan Harter and her coworkers have isolated the significant factors they believe account for the depression and suicidal ideation seen in some adolescents.[92] They believe that when adolescents feel incompetent in areas important to them and to others, as well as feel lack of support from important others such as parents and friends, they feel hopeless. Hopelessness leads to a "depression composite," consisting of low self-esteem, general hopelessness, and depressed mood. Depression then leads to suicidal ideation. Harter writes,

> There are powerful implications for *prevention* as well as *intervention*. For example, our findings suggest that intervening at the front end of the model, by influencing self-concept and social support, will have the biggest impact, since it is here that the chain of causal influences appears to begin. Thus, we can intervene to improve self-esteem, by helping the individual to become more competent in areas in which he/she has aspirations, or by aiding the individual to discount the importance of domains in which high levels of success are unlikely. Self-esteem can also be improved by intervening to provide more opportunities for support and approval from significant others. Such interventions should not only enhance the individual's self-esteem, but prevent the more insidious cycles that involve hopelessness, depression, and associated suicidal thoughts and gestures that may serve as the ultimate path of escape.[93]

OBTAINING PROFESSIONAL HELP   When parents notice the signs of depression mentioned earlier in this section, they should seek qualified professional help. At the

Interview
with Susan Harter

Susan Harter is professor of psychology at the University of Denver and has carried out extensive studies on self-esteem. This interview is continued from Chapter 2.

Self-esteem seems very important because it gives the person a kind of confidence to try many new activities. How important is it to have self-esteem?

One of the things that I began to fret about was that we had spent a lot of government money examining what feeds into self-esteem. I bolted upright one day and said to myself, "What if self-esteem doesn't do anything? What if it doesn't have any ramifications for everyday lives and happiness? We know what creates it, but if it does not really impact our lives, who cares?"

So, this is how we got interested in depression. We looked at the dimensions of depression, and mood is the most cardinal aspect of depression. To make a long story short, self-esteem has powerful implications for mood. The correlation between how much you like yourself as a person and your self-reported mood on a scale from cheerful to depressed is typically about .80.

Low self-esteem is invariably accompanied by depressive affect. We have extended these findings in developing a model that helps us understand suicidal thinking in teenagers. We included Beck's concept of hopelessness and have measured specific hopelessnesses corresponding to the support and self-concept domains. We ask, "How hopeless are you about getting peer support, parent support, about ever looking the way you want in terms of appearance?" "How hopeless are you about your scholastic ability?" There are various separate domains.

The worst consequences occur if you feel inadequate in an area in which support is important and feel hopeless about ever turning that area around. Moreover, if you don't have support and feel there is nothing you can ever do to get that support, this feeds into a depression composite of low self-esteem, low mood, plus general hopelessness. Thus, the worst case scenario is the feeling that I am not getting support from people whose approval is important, I am not feeling confident in areas in which success is valued, I am hopeless about ever turning things around, I don't like myself as a person, I feel depressed, and my future looks bleak. That, in turn, causes kids to think of suicide as a solution to their problems, as an escape from painful self-perceptions leading to depression.

There is another scenario that may also lead to suicidal thinking, namely, the teen who has done extremely well in all these areas. Then they experience their first failure, for example, scholastically (they get their first B), athletically (they feel they are re-

present time, there are several forms of help for depression.[94] Family therapy, individual therapy, and group therapy aimed at helping the child change the negative self-evaluations are useful. Medications are often used as well. Recently, medications have become more effective, but we have few long-term studies of them. If parents are uncertain whether their concerns about their child are justified, they can always

223

*Promoting
Adolescents'
Capacity for
Emotional
Regulation*

sponsible for a key loss), or socially (they don't get invited to a major party). As a result, they consider suicide as a solution to their humiliation. These teens seem so puzzling, but we think that conditional support plays a role here. We saw kids whose support scores were reasonable, but when we interviewed them, they would say, "Well, my parent only cares about me if I make the varsity team or if I get all As" or whatever the formula is for that family. So conditionality of support is important.

Another aspect about suicide is the co-occurrence of symptoms. People have talked about internalizers and externalizers as though you are one or the other. Most people have both qualities. When you look at measures of internalizing and externalizing symptoms, a correlation is about .65. Typically, you don't have a separate group of internalizing people who only engage in behaviors directed against the self. In clinical samples, it is often difficult to predict whether problem adolescents will act out against themselves or take it out on someone else. It may depend on the specific circumstances. Is the other person actually there when the adolescent is distressed or is the adolescent alone? Is there a weapon available? These factors partially determine whether one acts against the self or against the others.

That leads to another point. We asked teenagers who reported depressed affect which specific emotions comprise depression for them. We all suspect it is sadness of some kind, but are there other feelings that are part of the depressive experience? Eighty percent of adolescents tell us it is sadness plus *anger*. Who is the target of that anger—are they angry at themselves (the classic view of depression), or are they angry at someone else? We found that the majority of teens are angry at someone else. They have not yet internalized the anger against themselves. They will tell you, "Yeah, I am really, really sad, and I am angry at my mom. She got divorced and isn't paying attention to me or she is on my case."

Typically, adolescents view the causes of depression to be actions of others against the self. Other people have rejected them or are in conflict with them or aren't treating them the way they want to be treated. A few of them will admit they are angry at themselves, but most anger is directed at others.

I think it is important to point out that the reason people are spending so much energy and money on studying self-esteem is that low self-esteem has so many consequences, such as depressed mood, lack of energy to get up and do age-appropriate tasks and be productive, and, for some, thoughts of suicide. Most parents want their children to be happy, and self-esteem is an important pathway to happiness and the ability to function in today's world.

consult a therapist by themselves to determine the severity of the depression and the need to bring the child in.

Once help has been obtained for the child and the family, parents can listen and accept all the child's feelings about being depressed. Many parents, eager to see their children feel better, try to argue the child out of the depression, pointing out all the reasons the child should not be depressed—"These are the best years of your life. Enjoy them." Trying to argue someone out of depression, however, can make the individual even more depressed. He or she comes to believe that the other person is right: "I must be really weird for feeling this way."

Further, some parents minimize the importance of talk about suicide, believing that those who talk about it don't do it or that they simply want attention. Never consider such talk only an attention getter. Even attention getting can be fatal, as those attempting to get attention sometimes kill themselves by mistake.

In addition to getting professional help, parents can help depressed children in several ways. First, they can help children with negative thinking by encouraging optimistic thinking, as outlined in Chapter 3. Parents can encourage problem solving when difficulties arise and express confidence that children will find acceptable solutions to problems. Programs that help prevent depressive symptoms in at-risk children rely on teaching children to view difficulties as temporary problems they can actively manage. Children's symptoms decrease when they feel competent to handle whatever conflicts or problems arise. In *The Optimistic Child*,[95] Martin Seligman describes how parents can carry out such a program.

Parents can also follow Harter's suggestions to boost children's self-esteem and enjoyment in life. Arranging pleasurable outings with a parent or the whole family or arranging a special treat can help. Parents need not expect an overwhelmingly positive response, but it is worth carrying through even in the face of protest. Pleasurable activities bring family members closer together. If teenagers are not interested in any special activity, they may well be open to conversation with parents on all manner of things, provided parents are available and forgo advice, criticism, or guidance. Just sitting and listening to the adolescent, reflecting love in their interest in what is said, are positive steps parents can take during treatment.

Promoting Healthy Behaviors

Starting from the birth of their child, parents have been concerned about the child's health and safety. They have provided a healthy diet and opportunities for exercise, taken the child for vaccinations and medical and dental checkups, and done all they could to achieve this primary goal of parenting. In adolescence, parents' concerns about health and safety issues increase, as three of five deaths in the second decade of life are related to social factors such as unintentional injuries, homicides, and suicides.[96] Parents, however, lack the power to take direct action to ensure children's well-being; they must rely on teens' ability to avoid high-risk behaviors. So, adolescence is a time of worry and limited responses. Nonetheless, parents can rely on information and awareness as their most effective deterrents of high-risk behavior in teens.

Figure 7.1 reports questionnaire data on high-risk behaviors obtained from 3,000 high school students in 1996 and 1997.[97] More worrisome figures about alcohol use indicate that in a large-scale study of high school seniors in 1992, one out of three boys

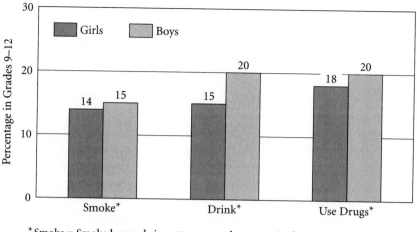

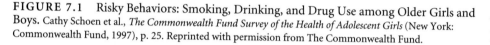

* Smoke = Smoked several cigarettes or a pack or more in the past week
Drink = Drink at least once a month or once a week
Use Drugs = Used illegal drugs in the past month

FIGURE 7.1 Risky Behaviors: Smoking, Drinking, and Drug Use among Older Girls and Boys. Cathy Schoen et al., *The Commonwealth Fund Survey of the Health of Adolescent Girls* (New York: Commonwealth Fund, 1997), p. 25. Reprinted with permission from The Commonwealth Fund.

and one out of five girls had consumed five or more drinks in a row in the past two weeks.[98] Dangerous in and of itself, such behavior is also related to both injuries and deaths from automobile accidents.

Adolescents also correctly consider mood problems as health concerns. As noted, depressive symptoms increase during adolescence. High-risk behaviors are related to current mood and life experiences. For example, girls who have depressive symptoms are twice as likely as those with no or few depressive symptoms to smoke, drink, or take drugs and three times as likely to have eating disorders.[99] Girls who have been physically or sexually abused or forced to have sex on dates are at risk in the same ways.

Parents' Healthy Behaviors

As parents seek to promote teens' healthy behaviors and discourage high-risk behaviors, they need to turn first to their own behaviors. When parents promote healthy behaviors—good nutrition, exercise, good dental care, and abstinence from smoking—and when they use reasoning and grant children autonomy, their children have good health.[100]

On the negative side, when parents use substances such as alcohol, cigarettes, and marijuana, children are likely to adopt these behaviors as well, especially if there is a good relationship between parent and child. In one longitudinal study, all teens modeled mothers' cigarette use and fathers' marijuana use. Older adolescents modeled mother's marijuana use, and younger adolescent girls and older adolescent boys modeled fathers' alcohol use.[101]

Parents model appropriate behaviors for teenagers—exercising, not smoking, not drinking excessively.

In two other longitudinal studies following children from the preschool years to young adulthood, the most serious use of alcohol and drugs was related to serious psychological problems both in adolescence and in early and middle childhood, while casual or experimental use was related to teens' competence and effectiveness in several areas.[102] Substance abusers came from families in which parents abused substances as well. It is important in helping children to recognize the long-standing nature of the serious substance abuser's problems and their need for extensive help.

So, a first step for parents in promoting adolescents' healthy behaviors is to adopt such behaviors themselves. Then, it is important for parents to reinforce the children's behaviors that serve as protective factors against high-risk behaviors.

Protective factors in the family, the individual child, and the social environment can increase the likelihood of healthy behaviors and reduce the likelihood of high-risk behaviors. In a national sample of 12,000 high school students, adolescents who said their parents cared about them and spent time with them in joint activities reported fewer high-risk behaviors.[103] Parents' supervision and granting autonomy have also been found to predict fewer health problems and adolescents' avoidance of drug use, with parents' supervision of teens' behavior being the single most powerful predictor of drug avoidance.[104] These findings occur in other studies as well; both parents' involvement and interest in their teens predict avoidance of smoking, drinking, and drug use. So, parents' involvement, interest, supervision, and granting psychological autonomy are primary protective factors in avoiding high-risk behaviors.[105] There is also evidence that parents' expectations about socially acceptable behavior in other arenas such as school serve as protective factors.[106]

Adolescents' personal qualities can serve as protective factors against problem behaviors such as drug use and drinking. When teens have a positive orientation to school, a commitment to socially approved activities and avoidance of deviancy, and good relationships with adults, they avoid problem behaviors.[107]

Social influences such as peer groups, school atmosphere, and religious affiliation also serve as protective factors against high-risk behaviors. Of the 88 percent of high school students who reported an affiliation with a religion, those who said religion and prayer were important to them reported a later age of first sexual intercourse and were less likely to use substances of any kind.[108]

Parents' Awareness and Specific Actions

To deal effectively with potential high-risk behaviors, parents must be aware of what their child is doing and feeling in order to both provide information and monitor behavior effectively. Here, we focus on early sexual activity and drinking.

PROMOTING LATER SEXUAL ACTIVITY   As we noted earlier, about 50 percent of ninth-through twelfth-graders indicate they have had sexual intercourse. When parents express disapproval of adolescent sexual activity and disapproval of contraceptive use, children are less likely to engage in early sexual activity.[109] Adolescents who feel connected to schools at which student attendance is high also delay sexual activity. Further, higher grade point averages are related to sexual activity delay.

Religious values also play a significant role. Students who attend parochial schools, who say religion and prayer play a role in their lives, and who take a pledge to remain virgins are at lower risk for early sexual activity. Adolescents who (1) look older than peers, (2) work more than 20 hours a week, (3) feel or act on a same-sex attraction, and (4) feel they have a risk of an untimely death all report earlier sexual activity.[110]

In a sample of 12,000 seventh- through twelfth-graders, about 20 percent of girls reported having gotten pregnant. Girls who did not get pregnant reported that they shared more activities with their parents and viewed their parents as disapproving contraceptive use. They themselves recognized the many negative consequences of pregnancy and were more likely to use effective contraception at their first and most recent intercourse.[111]

Although many teens are sexually active, many mothers underestimate their teens' sexual activity.[112] Older mothers who have good relationships with their teens, who are strongly opposed to their having sexual relations, and who do not talk to them about sex are most likely to underestimate their teens' sexual behavior. Although they are very responsive to perceived parental values, teens often misperceive the strength of their mothers' disapproval of sexual activity, in part because they share few conversations about sex.

It is important for parents to recognize that children need to hear parents' personal views expressed, that they do not automatically know what matters to parents. When they do know, many are willing to conform. Half of adolescents who do not have sexual relations say that the main reason they do not is that they fear their parents would find out about it.

Recognizing the strong possibility of sexual activity and having discussed their own values with their children, parents must also share information about birth control and sexually transmitted diseases. In a 1996 telephone survey of 1,500 teens, 69 percent said their parents had talked to them about AIDS, but only 46 percent had had a conversation about birth control.[113] More than two-thirds said their parents gave information too late and were not specific enough about where to get and how to use birth control devices. Twenty-two percent said they needed more details on how girls get pregnant; 24 percent of sexually active teens wanted more information on pregnancy. About 36 percent of teens said they sought information from parents, and about 40 percent sought it from teachers and schools. Only about 9 percent reported getting information from doctors and nurses.

Having expressed their values and shared information with their children, parents must act to minimize the possibility of early sexual activity by monitoring and supervising their children's time spent alone with the opposite sex. The most frequent place for first intercourse is the home of the parent or a friend. If pregnancy occurs, parents must get professional help. There are no easy answers, and parents and teens must work together to find solutions they can live with. Supportive communication with teens and medical and religious professionals can aid families in working out solutions that meet their needs.

DISCOURAGING ALCOHOL USE   Although parents often are more concerned about their children's use of marijuana and other drugs, alcohol is the substance most frequently used. In 1994, alcohol was implicated in 29 percent of motor vehicle deaths of fifteen- to seventeen-year-olds, and 44 percent of deaths of eighteen- to twenty-year-olds.[114]

Awareness of teens' alcohol use is essential for parents' effective management of this high-risk behavior, yet in one study, only about a third of mothers and fathers whose children reported regular alcohol use said it was possible that their child used alcohol.[115] Seventy-one percent of mothers and 69 percent of fathers were unaware their children drank. Over 50 percent of mothers and fathers were aware that their children's friends drank. Parents seemed to be saying, "Other teens drink, but not my kid."

When parents were aware of their teens' alcohol use, they were available and responsive in ways that tended to discourage episodes of drinking and driving. Aware mothers were more likely to talk about risky behaviors and more likely to worry about their teens' involvement in high-risk behavior. Aware fathers were less likely to have disapproving values about drinking.

When aware, parents can take action. Minimizing household access to alcohol reduces the risk of teens' drinking. When teens are connected to parents and family members and when parents are active and available participants at home, there is less frequent alcohol use among teens.[116] Teens are more likely to use alcohol when they have low self-esteem, earn low grades, work more than 20 hours per week, and experience or act on same-sex attractions. Religious beliefs and prayer also serve as protective factors that reduce the risk of teen drinking.

When parents are involved and monitor teens' behavior, there is less alcohol use. Should problems arise, however, parents must seek help. Miller Newton's experience with his son provides an illuminating example. Newton served as the executive director of the state association of alcohol treatment in Florida, and his wife was a supervising counselor at a treatment agency. Both parents were knowledgeable about the use of at least one drug. Their two older children, nineteen and twenty, were both happy and competent people. The first time their fifteen-year-old son Mark came home drunk, the family rallied around him, gave him information about alcoholism in the family, and began to monitor his behavior more closely. He was a bright, curious boy with many interests and a passion for healthy living, so the family was unprepared for the next drunk episode, two months later. Mark was violent and threatening with his father and brother. At that time he admitted he was using some pot as well.

Close family supervision followed, and Mark was allowed to go to only certain places and had to be home at certain times. His parents said that if there were recurrences, Mark would go into a treatment program. When a fight erupted a few months later, the parents found evidence of much drug use. Mark entered a residential treatment program and has been free of drugs for four years.

In their book *Not My Kid: A Parent's Guide to Kids and Drugs*, journalist Beth Polson and Miller Newton outline actions parents can take to promote a healthy, drug-free adolescence.[117] They insist that how families live day by day is the most important factor. Parents need to be involved family members who know what their children are doing and who their friends are. Then, they must make clear to adolescents that theirs is a drug-free family in which there is (1) no use of illegal drugs or misuse of any legal drugs or prescriptions, (2) no routine use of alcohol by parents, (3) no intoxication by adults, (4) no alcohol use by underage children, and (5) no use of drugs to lose weight, sleep, relax, or wake up. Every family member agrees to this contract. If a child is found to be using drugs, parents call the parents of all the child's friends to discuss ways of promoting organized student activities.

If a child tries drugs, the family contract is repeated. If the behavior continues, the child is taken to some additional form of counseling that deals with the child and the family. Because family members can help drug-oriented children, family counseling is important in addition to any individual therapy prescribed. As in many other areas, the family joins with other families to provide support and actions to promote a healthier, safer adolescence.

Promoting Teens' Positive Peer Relationships

As we noted earlier in this chapter, friends provide teens with great satisfaction because they exchange intimate thoughts and feelings. Teens feel they get emotional support from those who really understand. Friends also help teens feel normal because they share the experience of change during adolescence.

Nonetheless, friends in adolescence are a source of both help and temptation. About 60 percent of early adolescents and 70 percent of mid-adolescents list friends as a source of help in dealing with an alcohol problem.[118] Research shows, however, that teens engage their friends in substance use. A study over time found that similarity in drinking behavior among friends was more related to processes of peer influence than to processes of peers' selecting friends who had similar drinking patterns.[119]

Peer relationships are indeed very important to peers and contribute to self-esteem, yet parents must recognize that peer relationships also involve conflicts, though less frequent than conflicts with parents.[120] Conflicts center on issues of interpersonal behavior and relationship difficulties. When the conflicts cannot be resolved and friendships end, teens feel socially incompetent.

Teens who report conflicts with friends describe themselves as more aggressive and isolated than teens who report no conflicts with friends. Teens who report no conflicts with friends have high self-esteem, more socially approved behaviors, and greater academic competence than those who report conflicts with friends. Those teens who are able to resolve conflicts when they arise and continue relationships are more adaptive and friendly than those teens who end relationships and feel angry. Teens in this latter group have lower grades, lower self-esteem, and fewer social skills than those who can resolve conflicts in a friendly way.

Research points parents in three directions to promote the positive peer relationships that are so gratifying and important to teens' feelings of well-being. First, the quality of parent-child relationships influences the teens' orientation to peers.[121] When teens feel they have good relationships with parents and feel that parents allow them a growing role in decision making, teens are better adjusted, less likely to report extreme orientations toward peers, and less likely to seek peers' advice than are teens who feel parents retain power and control. This latter group of teens seems to seek with peers the egalitarian relationship and mutuality they do not feel with parents. Relationships between fathers and teens are especially predictive of peer relationships, perhaps because fathers and children engage in many recreational activities, and skills learned there transfer to relationships with peers.[122]

Second, parents can foster positive peer relationships by promoting teens' ability to regulate their feelings and resolve conflicts positively. Helping children develop communication skills and ways to manage anger so it does not spill out in uncontrolled ways with peers enables teens to have fewer conflicts and to resolve the ones they have in positive ways.

231

*Resolving
Conflicts As
Adolescents
Move toward
Independence*

Third, parents' behavior indirectly influences the kinds of group friendships adolescent children form.[123] Parents' discipline and monitoring predict teens' behavior, which in turn affects teen peer relationships. In one study, members of four groups—"brains," the popular crowd, "jocks," and "druggies"—described their parents' child-rearing practices. When parents stressed achievement and monitored children closely, children tended to get high grades and belonged to the brains group. When parents stressed achievement but failed to monitor children closely and did not encourage joint decision making, children tended to become part of the popular crowd and/or were exposed to the drug crowd. When parents stressed achievement but were moderate in monitoring, teens tended to become jocks. Peer group norms were most likely to reinforce those behaviors that parenting strategies had encouraged.

Different ethnic groups were more likely to belong to certain groups. European American students tended to be part of the popular crowd or the druggies. Asian American students were more likely to belong to the brains, and African American students were more likely to belong to the jocks.

Resolving Conflicts As Adolescents Move toward Independence

While parents provide information, positive models, and encouragement, they are also involved in resolving conflicts. As mentioned earlier in this chapter, conflicts between parents and adolescents center most frequently on mundane issues such as chores and school grades. Later adolescents understand that some activities are done because they benefit the whole family. Although conflicts about everyday issues continue, late teens accept and respect their parents' conventional views on situations and thus try to please their parents. Teens do not necessarily give in, but parents are more likely to grant their requests now, perhaps because teens seem to understand their reasoning.[124]

When adolescents struggle less over power with their parents, they become more self-governing and independent without giving up warm family relationships. Parents and adolescents then form a partnership directed toward establishing such autonomy.[125] When attachments are secure, parents and teens can regulate emotional responses and engage in problem-solving behaviors with relatively little anger and frustration.[126] With secure attachments, both parents and teens can discuss differences and arrive at compromises. Anger appears to motivate securely attached family members to overcome differences and restore harmony. When attachments are secure, a balance exists between the needs of the individual and the needs of the relationship.

When attachment relationships are insecure, one partner may try to dominate the other, refusing to listen or to compromise. Anger in these relationships serves to create greater distance. When separation occurs in the context of family misunderstandings and emotional distance from parents, teens report loneliness and feelings of dejection.[127] When issues of power are settled, about half the respondents in a large survey reported positive relationships with parents, which they wanted to continue as they moved through later adolescence.[128]

Childhood behavioral problems intensify the usual problems of adolescence. If parents have been overprotective or neglecting, children will have difficulty making and carrying out independent decisions. If teenagers have never had satisfying friend-ships with important emotional interchanges, they will be poorly prepared to handle the difficulties of achieving peer acceptance, and they may acquiesce easily to peer pressure. When control of impulses and physical activity has always been hard, teenagers will find it hard to cope with the excessive push to action that many feel dur-ing these years.

David Elkind points out that adolescents may try to pay parents back for treat-ment they felt was unfair when they were younger.[129] As young people achieve an in-creasing capacity to earn their own money, physical equality with parents, and freedom to drive and do things for themselves, many feel that they have at least some-what equal footing with parents. If they have felt mistreated, now they are capable of redressing the imbalance between what parents have demanded and what they have given. Nevertheless, most teenagers *do* want good relationships, and family ties can be strengthened during these years.

Parents' Experiences during the Adolescent Years

Parents report that they do not feel ready to have teenage children. The childhood years have gone so fast, it seems too soon to have a daughter with a mature figure and sons with bulging muscles and low voices. Although physically and sexually mature, teenagers are not psychologically mature, and they still need the guidance parents can give. Ellen Galinsky calls this the *interdependent stage* of parenting to highlight the greater freedom and control teenagers have.[130] Parents have several years to work through these issues be-fore their children leave home. When parents can become more separate from their chil-dren yet be available to help them grow without stifling them in the process, then parents' and children's relationships take on a new dimension and richness.

Laurence Steinberg observed 204 families for three years to understand how par-ents react and adapt to the changes and turmoil of their children's adolescence.[131] He found six aspects of a child's adolescent behavior that trigger parents' emotional reac-tions: puberty and the associated physical changes themselves, maturing sexuality, dat-ing, increasing independence, emotional detachment, and increasing de-idealization of the parent.

Parents with the following risk factors were most likely to experience difficulty: (1) being the same sex as the child making the transition, (2) being divorced or remar-ried, especially for women, (3) having fewer sources of satisfaction outside the parental role, and (4) having a negative view of adolescence. Protective factors that eased par-ents' adjustments to their teens' adolescence were having satisfying jobs and outside interests and happy marriages. The positive supports buffered parents so that in times of difficulty with children, they had other sources of satisfaction and self-esteem.

Steinberg found that about 40 percent of parents experienced difficulty. He termed them *decliners* because their well-being, life satisfaction, and self-image de-creased and they experienced nervousness, depression, and physical ailments. About 20 percent of the parents, *thrivers*, reported greater well-being, self-esteem, and life sat-isfaction. They enjoyed their children but relished greater freedom for themselves.

What I Wish I Had Known about Adolescence 233

*Parents'
Experiences
during the
Adolescent
Years*

"They seem to get caught up in fads in junior high. They do certain things to the max to be part of the crowd. I wish I'd known how to handle that. At what point are these fads okay, because it's important to identify with your peer group, and at what point do you say no? If they are really dangerous, then it's easy; but with a lot of them, it's a gray area, and I wish I'd known what to do better." —*Father*

"I wish I had realized that she needed more structure and control. Because she had always been a good student and done her work, I thought I could trust her to manage the school tasks without my checking. But she lost interest in school, and I learned only very gradually that I had to be more of a monitor with her work than I had been in the past." —*Mother*

"I wish I had known more about the mood swings. When the girls became thirteen, they each got moody for a while, and I stopped taking it personally. I just relaxed. The youngest one said, 'Do I have to go through that? Can't I just skip that?' Sure enough, when she became thirteen, she was moody too." —*Mother*

"This may begin earlier, but it goes through adolescence. I had always heard they look for their own independence, their own things to participate in; but until you really experience it with your own, it's hard to deal with it. When you read about independence, it sounds like it's carefully planned out. When it actually happens, all of a sudden they want to do something that they have never done before and which you firmly believe they have no idea how to do. It can be driving for the first time or suddenly announcing they want to go somewhere with friends. I knew it was going to happen; but exactly how to handle it myself and handle it with them so they got a chance to do something new without its being dangerous has been a challenge to me." —*Father*

"I wish that I had known that I had to listen more to them in order to understand what they were experiencing. I sort of assumed that I knew what adolescence was about from my own experience, but things had a different meaning to them. What was important to me was not that important to them, and I wish I had realized that in the beginning." —*Mother*

About 40 percent of the sample, *survivors,* responded to their children, but children's changes did not affect them personally.

Based on his research, Steinberg makes the following suggestions to parents for handling this stage of family development: (1) have genuine and satisfying interests outside of being a parent; (2) don't disengage from the child emotionally; (3) try to adopt a positive outlook about what adolescence is and how the child is changing; and (4) don't be afraid to discuss feelings with mates, friends, or, if need be, a professional counselor.

Parents often feel overwhelmed by cultural forces that do not support their efforts to rear children well. For example, the media bombard teens with messages about sexuality that do not conform to families' values. William Damon has developed the

"Youth Charter" program to combat cultural forces that make rearing children more difficult.[132] Parents can initiate this program to organize teachers, clergy, police, and all who care about children to develop community practices and standards that promote children's healthy development. Parents' childrearing efforts serve as a bridge to connect children to community activities at school, with peers, and in the neighborhood. But communities have to be organized to support parents' goals.

In this book *The Youth Charter: How Communities Can Work Together to Raise Standards for All Our Children*, Damon outlines a way of organizing concerned adults to identify children's specific needs and work together to find ways to meet them. Standards and expectations are drawn up for children and for the community so that parents and concerned citizens and youth can control teen drinking, vandalism, and early pregnancy and build a community more supportive of children and families. Damon writes:

> Beneath the sense of isolation that has divided our communities, we all share a deep well of concern for the younger generation. If we can find a way to tap into that well, child rearing can become the secure and fulfilling joy that it should be, rather than the risky and nerve-wracking challenge that it has become for too many parents.[133]

Main Points

Adolescents

- undergo changes in physical, intellectual, emotional, self-, and social functioning
- form a sense of identity that develops over many years
- of different ethnic groups achieve a bicultural identity in many different ways
- seek support and pleasure from friends

Parents' role during adolescence is to

- accept the child's individuality and maintain involvement with the child
- monitor the child's behavior and insist on the child's meeting certain standards of acceptable behavior
- grant psychological autonomy and share decision making with the child
- encourage the child to separate with a sense of well-being

Parents help their adolescent modulate and control feelings and avoid high-risk behavior by

- providing appropriate models of healthy behaviors and emotional regulation
- providing acceptance, support, monitoring, and autonomy
- seeing that their child is involved in socially approved activities
- getting professional help if problems develop

Parents' reactions to adolescence are more positive when they

- have satisfying jobs and outside interests
- adopt a positive outlook about all their child's changes
- remain involved with their child

1. Watch the following videos: *To Sleep with Anger, Avalon,* and *Parenthood.* Compare the portrayal of parenthood in the majority culture with parenthood in different ethnic groups. What are the roles of grandparents and parents in each culture? How does each culture socialize the young to be part of that culture?

2. Break into small groups, and describe the kinds of experiences that increased your self-esteem when you were teens. Then, with the whole class, write suggestions for parents who want to increase the self-esteem of their teens.

3. Divide into pairs. First, have one partner take the role of a parent who wants to talk about appropriate sexual behavior for the teen while the other partner plays the role of the teen who wants more freedom. Then reverse roles, and have the second "parent" try to convey values about the appropriate uses of substances to the second "teen." Practice active listening and sending I-messages.

4. Break into small groups, and discuss ways parents can talk to teens about responsible sexual behavior, including the use of condoms. How can parents increase the use of condoms to decrease sexually transmitted diseases?

5. Break into small groups, and take turns describing the kinds of enjoyable experiences you had with your parents as teens. Then, as a whole class, devise a list of highly enjoyable experiences you could have with your own future teens. Are there common elements in what makes for a good time?

Additional Readings

Garbarino, James. *Lost Boys: Why Our Sons Turn Violent and How We Can Save Them.* New York: Free Press, 1999.

Larson, Reed, and Maryse Richards. *Divergent Realities: The Emotional Lives of Mothers, Fathers, and Adolescents.* New York: Basic Books, 1994.

Shandler, Sara. *Ophelia Speaks.* New York: HarperCollins, 1999.

Steinberg, Laurence, and Ann Levine. *You and Your Adolescent.* New York: HarperCollins, 1990.

Steinberg, Laurence, with Wendy Steinberg. *Crossing Paths: How Your Child's Adolescence Triggers Your Own Crisis.* New York: Simon & Schuster, 1994.

8

Parenting and Working

COMBINING WORKING AND PARENTING IS A MAJOR challenge for today's men and women. The majority of mothers work from the time their children are infants, and more fathers than ever before are involved in childcare. How do parents solve the common problems that arise in integrating work and family lives? How do they find childcare that promotes children's development? How do they adjust routines to enhance the quality of time they spend with children? How do they adapt to their many responsibilities and maintain a sense of well-being?

This chapter examines the impact of working on parents, on their parenting, and on their children. In Chapter 1, Urie Bronfenbrenner described parents' work as part of the exosystem that exerts a major influence on children's development.[1] Children do not participate directly in parents' work settings, but what parents experience there affects parents' behavior at home, their relationships with their children, and, as a result, children's development.

Our understanding of the relationship between parents' work and family life is limited for many reasons. First, parents' work is not a unitary phenomenon but a multifaceted experience that varies in many ways from parent to parent—number of hours worked, level of job satisfaction, amount of stress. So, conclusions regarding parenting and work have to be generalized cautiously, because they may apply to only subgroups of parents. Second, families may experience several work and childcare patterns over even a short time in response to the family's economic and childcare needs, so it is difficult to identify one pattern that can be related to parents' and children's functioning. Third, research suggests that parents' work may have different effects on different children in the family, depending on birth order and personal characteristics.[2] Fourth, the relationship between parents' work and family life may change as the nature of work itself changes and society makes further adaptations to parents' work.

In our present society, most parents work. In 1996, both parents were employed in 64 percent of two-parent families with children under eighteen; only fathers were employed in 28 percent; only mothers were employed in 4 percent; and neither parent was employed in 4 percent. In families maintained by women, 65 percent of women were employed, and in families maintained by men, 84 percent of men were employed.[3]

In this chapter, we look at how men and women integrate working and parenting, the day care options available when neither parent can care for the child, the impact of day care on children, and what happens to children and families when family income is diminished.

Dimensions of Participation in Work and Family Life

Graeme Russell describes six domains of parental involvement in family life and two levels of activity—involvement and responsibility.[4] The six domains that apply to either mothers' or fathers' participation are

1. Employment and financial support
2. Day-to-day care and interaction with children (physical and psychological availability to the child)
3. Child management and socialization (looking after basic needs for health care, social experience, emotional connections, cognitive stimulation)
4. Household work (cleaning, shopping, preparing meals)
5. Maintaining relationships between caregivers (exchange of information about the child, raising and resolving areas of conflict)
6. Parental commitment and investment (amount of time spent with the child relative to paid work and leisure time and the degree to which the child's needs have priority over parents' needs)

The roles in each of these areas will be different for each parent depending on whether the person is involved or takes primary responsibility for the area. Men may care for children for a specified number of hours, but there is a different feeling when one takes responsibility for the child's well-being—arranging doctor visits, social activities. Similarly, women may work and provide income but not feel the responsibility of being the financial provider for the family.

In 1960, fathers were the primary financial providers and put in 1 hour of work at home for every 4 hours worked by mothers who cared for the children and the house. In 1996, with the work patterns of parents as described in the introduction to this chapter, women spent about 3.7 hours per day on household chores and childcare, and men spent about 3 hours per day.[5] Men, however, worked an average of 48 hours per week at full-time jobs, and women worked 42. So, women did about 55 percent of the work at home, and men worked longer hours at a job. Although fathers in dual-earner families participate more than fathers in single-earner families, mothers in both families perform more childcare.

Typologies of Families

There is no one way for parents to meet work and family needs. One study identified three family types in terms of work and parenting characteristics.[6] In *high-status families*, both parents had high levels of education and occupational status. Both parents were highly involved in their work and earned more money than the other two groups of families. In addition, the couples held less traditional ideologies on sex-role activities and shared tasks on an egalitarian basis. They experienced a great deal of work overload and stress, however, and as a result had more marital conflict, less marital satisfaction, and less love between the spouses than the other two groups. Parents confined tension to the marital relationship, and children in the families were not aware of the marital problems because the stress did not affect the ways parents treated the children.

In *low-stress families*, both parents reported low levels of work overload, high levels of marital satisfaction and love between the spouses, and low levels of conflict. Parents were available to take an active role in monitoring children, and such monitoring improved children's functioning.

In *main-secondary families*, fathers were the primary financial providers, and mothers provided a small supplementary income, frequently through employment in lower-status occupations. These families had the lowest incomes of the three types of families and the most traditional ways of organizing family activities. Girls in main-secondary families were more likely to engage in feminine tasks than were girls in other families. Marital satisfaction fell between that of the other two groups—higher than that of high-status families and lower than that of low-stress families. Their level of conflict also fell between the two groups—higher than that of low-stress families but lower than that of high-status families.

Based on interviews with 150 families, Francine Deutsch identified four patterns of working and parenting, which she termed *equal sharers, 60–40 couples, 75–25 couples,* and *alternating shifters*.[7] She found that families sometimes moved between these patterns. When children were infants, some families were unequal sharers, becoming equal sharers after children were older. Even within the types of families, there were many variations. Equal sharers could be providing all the day care with flexible work hours, or they could have childcare and work the same hours outside the home. Alternating shifters tended to have working-class occupations, as it is these types of occupations that offer daytime and evening shifts. Women's income in alternating-shift families was often very important, and women felt they had power and received appreciation for their contributions.

Deutsch found that these patterns of work influenced parents' ways of being with children but not the total amount of time they spent with children. Equal-sharing couples spent the same amount of time with children as the other three groups of couples, but equal-sharing mothers were alone with children less frequently than were the other mothers. Equal-sharing fathers compensated for this, as they were alone with children more often than were fathers of the other groups. Further, equal-sharing parents were more often together with children than were parents of the other groups.

Deutsch found that the couples in the four groups did not differ markedly in politics, education, or class, but they did vary in how they negotiated the everyday issues of childcare and household tasks. Couples who wanted equal sharing of parenting and working made every effort to distribute both kinds of tasks equally and to find friends who supported their decisions.

An interview study of middle-class men and women in dual-earner families looked at families at different points in the life cycle—some before or after having children but most in the childrearing stages of life.[8] This study focused on middle managers and professionals, as these people not only determine their own fates but also tend to shape the work lives of people they supervise. Sampling couples from upstate New York rather than those from an urban area may have resulted in an overrepresentation of families who have scaled back working demands.

In this sample, few participants were part of dual-career families in which both parents were highly involved in work and both were single-mindedly pursuing work goals. Dual-career couples usually had no children at home or hired help to meet many of the family demands. The vast majority of couples relied on one of three strategies for scaling back work demands to carve out time for the family. Although most couples had an egalitarian gender ideology, choices in day-to-day behaviors often resulted in traditionally gendered roles for men and women.

The three work-family strategies were termed *placing limits, job-versus-career,* and *trading-off.* Couples who placed limits (about 30 percent) turned down jobs or promotions that required relocation or traveling, refused overtime hours, and limited the number of hours worked. Women often did this when a child was born, and men sometimes did this when careers became established and parenting involvement grew. Job-versus-career strategies (relied on by about 40 percent) involved one parent's having an absorbing career and the other parent's having a job that produced income but was subordinated to the needs of the family and the parent with the career. In about two-thirds of these families, men had the career and women had the job, but in one-third, the wife had the career and the man the job. Often it was a matter of chance or early advancement or opportunity that determined which parent had the career. In the trading-off group, parents shifted back and forth between jobs and careers, depending on family needs and career opportunities.

Of concern to researchers Penny Becker and Phyllis Moen was the fact that couples' scaling-back strategies appeared to be private solutions to public workplace problems. They believe that private solutions do not challenge the underlying assumptions that work can make demands on parents—such as 60-hour weeks— while doing little to help them meet family and work needs. The couples appeared to make few demands for formal policies of flextime, job-sharing, or on-site day care and instead sought informal arrangements to meet family needs. Unfortunately, workers at lower levels in the employment hierarchy might not get such benefits without formal policies.

TABLE 8.1 Students'* Letter Grades for Parents' Behaviors

Letter Grade	A		B		C		D		F	
Parents' Behavior	M†	F‡	M	F	M	F	M	F	M	F
Being there for me when I'm sick	85	58	8	20	4	12	2	7	1	3
Appreciating me for who I am	72	69	15	16	6	8	4	5	3	2
Making me feel loved for who I am	72	66	16	18	8	9	4	4	1	2
Attending important events in my life	69	60	18	20	7	12	3	4	3	5
Being someone I can go to when I'm upset	57	48	18	19	11	14	6	8	8	10
Being involved in what's happening to me at school	55	45	22	24	11	15	7	10	5	6
Spending time talking to me	48	47	31	25	12	16	5	8	4	4
Controlling their temper when I do something wrong	28	31	31	28	19	18	11	11	11	12

From: Ellen Galinsky, *Ask the Children: What America's Children Really Think about Working Parents* (New York: Morrow, 1999).
*Students in third through twelfth grades
†M indicates percentage of students giving mother that grade
‡F indicates percentage of students giving father that grade

One can see that there are many ways to meet work and family needs and that families use more than one strategy to meet these needs over time. In a later section, we will discuss ways parents can minimize stress in using these strategies.

Children's Ratings of Parents

Regardless of the strategies used by parents to meet their family and work responsibilities, children give their parents high marks. Ellen Galinsky, cofounder and president of the Families and Work Institute, has long studied family-work issues but has been concerned that the opinions of children have not been included in the discussions of the effects of parents' work on children and family life. In 1998, Galinsky interviewed a representative sample of 605 employed parents with children under eighteen and surveyed a representative sample of 1,023 third- to twelfth-grade children.[9] The sample of children varied with respect to the parents' work status—employed or nonemployed—and number of hours worked. Children's attitude toward their mother and their assessment of the parent-child relationship did not depend on the work status of the mother or the number of hours the mother worked. Nonemployed fathers were rated lower than were employed fathers in the areas of (1) making their children feel important and loved and (2) participating in important events in their children's lives. Children tended to give parents higher grades when the family was seen as financially secure. We will discuss the influence of economic factors on parenting in greater detail in a later section.

Seventy-four percent of children felt mothers were very successful in managing work and family life, and 67 percent of children felt fathers were very successful. As shown in Table 8.1, parents received high marks for making children feel important and loved, being understanding, appreciating children, and being there for conversation. Although mothers were overwhelmingly seen as the parent who was there for children at times of sickness, more frequently involved than fathers in school matters, and someone children could go to when upset, the ratings for fathers on other qualities were similar to those given to mothers. Fathers were seen as being appreciative of who the child really was, as spending time in conversation, and as controlling their temper with the child as well as the mother.

Parents gave themselves equally high marks in these areas. Children's ratings of parents were higher when they spent more time with parents and when the time with parents was not rushed. About 40 percent of mothers and children and 32 percent of fathers, however, felt that their time together was somewhat or very rushed.

Divergent Realities

Mothers, fathers, and children do not always share the same views of experiences. It is important to highlight the divergences; otherwise, we make false assumptions about the meanings of events.

DIVERGENCES IN MEN'S AND WOMEN'S PERCEPTIONS   Recall the study in Chapter 7 in which mothers, fathers, and early adolescents carried pagers for a week. When beeped, family members wrote down their activities and their feelings. That study found that men and women experienced different levels of stress at work and at home.[10]

Mothers who worked did not have exciting jobs, by and large. Some were nurses and teachers, but many were office workers and service workers in low-paying jobs. These women worked longer hours than their husbands and had as much work conflict and stress as men in the study, yet their average emotional rating at work was higher than that of men and that of women who were not employed. Although these women had less control and autonomy at work than their husbands, they reported a friendlier work atmosphere and better relationships with their coworkers. In addition to social rewards at work, these women felt appreciated for their contributions.

When they came home, however, they were overwhelmed by household tasks—preparing dinner, cleaning up, supervising homework—and their moods dropped. They felt committed to caring for their families, yet they felt emotionally depleted from all the demands placed on them. Although they enjoyed feelings of self-esteem and competence from work, their overall rating of emotional well-being was only slightly higher than that of women who did not work because they had feelings of responsibility for everyone's well-being. When work made extra demands—longer hours, extra shifts—their emotional ratings dropped below those of nonworking mothers. In contrast, mothers who did not work lacked the stimulation and feelings of accomplishment of work, but they had time for friends and leisure activities, and their overall mood ratings were only slightly lower than those of working mothers without special stresses.

Regardless of the nature of their job, fathers were absorbed at work. When beeped at work, they almost always reported being focused on the task at hand. They felt alert, competent, and in control. They reported feeling more competitive at work than mothers felt. Because of their absorption and involvement in the work, they were highly frustrated if things went wrong. Their investment at work may have been so strong because they identified highly with being the main financial provider for the family.

Fathers left work tired from their effort and eager to get home to relax. Their moods rose when they got home, just as working mothers' moods dropped. If fathers had a stressful day, they brought the irritations home with them, but their feelings of irritation gradually dissipated. Home life was "an emotional antidote to their jobs," in part, because it was a place of leisure activities and leisurely work. It was not, on average, the place of many additional demands and responsibilities as it was for mothers.

So, work appears more socially and emotionally rewarding for mothers than for fathers, though both are highly involved in that area, and home appears more relaxing for fathers than for mothers. Thus, fathers and mothers feel more relaxed in the area traditionally assigned to the opposite sex.

DIVERGENCES IN PARENTS' AND CHILDREN'S PERCEPTIONS   The survey responses Galinsky obtained from children revealed discrepancies between parents' and children's perceptions.[11] Children were more satisfied with the amount of time parents spent with them than parents were. About 44 percent of mothers and 56 percent of fathers felt they spent too little time with their children, whereas only 28 percent of children felt mothers spent too little time, and 35 percent of children felt fathers spent too little time. The survey asked children to name one wish that would change the effects of parents' working on the family. Parents expected children to say they wanted more time with parents. Children, however, had three more important wishes. They wished that parents could earn more money, that they could return from work less stressed, and that they felt less tired. Fourth in frequency of response was the wish that parents could spend more time with children. Also, when asked if they worried about their parents, approximately one-third of children ages eight to eighteen said that they often or very often worried about their parents, and another third said they sometimes worried. So, about two-thirds of children worry about parents at least some of the time. Children said they worried because they were part of a caring family, but they also worried because they felt their parents had a lot of stress from work. Thirty percent of children ages twelve to eighteen said the worst thing about having working parents was that they were stressed out from work. Given their concern about parents' stress level, one suspects that children wanted them to make more money so they would feel less stressed.

Further, children saw their parents as less emotionally available to them than parents believed they were, and children were more concerned about parents' anger than parents were. Ninety-six percent of mothers and 90 percent of fathers gave themselves As and Bs for being emotionally available when their children were upset, but only 75 percent of children gave mothers As and Bs, and 67 percent gave fathers As and Bs. Only 4 percent of mothers and 5.5 percent of fathers gave themselves Ds and Fs for controlling their tempers, whereas 22 percent of children gave mothers Ds and Fs, and 23 percent gave fathers Ds and Fs.

So, parents are sometimes not aware of children's wishes and priorities. Children want parents to be happier and less stressed and available for them emotionally without being angry.

The Flow of Work and Family Life

Galinsky believes that words such as *balancing, integrating, combining* do not describe how parents deal with working and family life, as they imply that these two spheres of activity are separate. From her research and interviews, she believes work and family life flow together to form a stream of experience that adults navigate rather than balance or combine, as illustrated in Figure 8.1. Experiences at home carry over to work, and experiences at work spill over to feelings at home.

> Let's think of ourselves as navigating the stream. To steer through these waters, we need to understand the many outside forces affecting our passage—some of which are beyond our control; others of which are not. And we need to know ourselves: our life priorities and where we really want to go. We are at the helm, with at least some control over the course of our voyage.[12]

Parent-Child Interactions

Meeting children's basic psychological and physical needs absorbs parents' time at home. Galinsky describes eight basic needs children have that parents must meet—loving the child, responding to the child's cues, appreciating the child's individuality while also expecting success, providing values, providing constructive discipline, establishing structure and routine, helping with the child's education, and being emotionally available to the child. Parents meet children's needs in many ways.

FOCUSING ON CHILDREN'S NEEDS   A major strategy for employed parents is to focus their energy on meeting children's needs, especially their needs for relationships with parents. Fathers who engage in much childcare when children are little maintain strong involvements in daily activities with children across the childhood years and into adolescence.[13] Such fathers play more games and share educational activities during the week, spending equal time with sons and daughters. The children of involved fathers are more socially mature at age six and more academically successful at age seven than are children of uninvolved fathers.

Employed mothers who work more than 20 hours a week spend less time with their infants and preschoolers than do nonemployed mothers. Mothers with a higher education compensate for time at work by spending more time with children in the evenings and on weekends. Children appear to become willing partners in this arrangement. They sleep more during the day care hours and remain awake and play for longer periods in the evening. In single-earner families, evening time is reserved for fathers, but in dual-earner families, mothers use this time to relate to children, giving them verbal stimulation. Although fathers are "crowded out" in these early family interactions, they have their own time alone with children and, in fact, spend more time with their children than do fathers in single-earner families.[14]

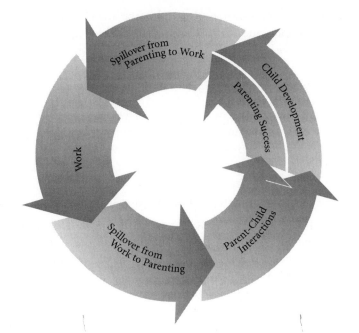

FIGURE 8.1 A Model of Work and Family Life. From Ellen Galinsky, *Ask the Children: What America's Children Really Think about Working Parents* (New York: Morrow, 1999), p. 205. Copyright © 1999 by Ellen Galinsky. Reprinted by permission of HarperCollins Publishers, Inc., William Morrow.

Although employed mothers spend less time with their infants, they are as sensitive and responsive as nonemployed mothers.[15] Mothers who are satisfied with their work and feel they get support are more responsive with their toddlers than are unemployed mothers; they give more guidance and use lower power-assertive techniques.[16]

Once children reach school age, mothers spend more time in single activities[17] with children than fathers do (90 minutes per week for mothers as compared with 60 minutes for fathers). Although no significant differences exist between single- and dual-earner fathers in the amount of time spent with children, they allot the time differently. Dual-earner fathers spend 60 minutes per week with sons and 60 minutes with daughters. Single-earner fathers spend 90 minutes per week with sons and 30 minutes with daughters. Researchers speculate that daughters of working mothers may do well in part because they have more time with fathers. (See the interview with Susan McHale.)

Time with children fluctuates seasonally for some mothers, with nonemployed and seasonally employed mothers spending more time in activities with children in the summer than in the winter.[18] Mothers who are employed the same number of hours throughout the year do not show this seasonal variation. Parenting of seasonally employed mothers becomes more traditional in the summer, as they have more involvement with children at that time than do fathers. Parenting becomes more egalitarian when mothers return to work.

Maintaining mother-child activities is important because such activities may buffer the child against possible negative effects from maternal absence.[19] When mothers with full-time employment or an increase in work hours maintain their time in shared activities with their children, the children show no decrease in social and cognitive functioning, as compared with children of nonemployed mothers. When mothers' hours of employment decrease and activities shared with the children increase, the children's functioning improves; if activities do not increase when work hours decrease, there is no improvement.

In the early adolescent years, the overall amount of time children spend with parents does not differ in single- and dual-earner families, but again, the difference is in *how* the time is spent. Full-time employed mothers spend more time doing homework with children and less time in leisure activities.[20] Children of mothers employed part-time report more time spent playing sports with parents.

MONITORING   A major task of parenting is monitoring and supervising children's activities. Although working parents are often not home after school, they can monitor what school-aged children do and make certain children are engaged in approved activities. Studies have found that parents in dual-earner families monitor as carefully as parents in single-earner families.[21] This is important because less well monitored boys have lower school grades and less skill in school-related activities, regardless of whether mothers are employed. Studies have not found girls' behavior as clearly related as boys' behavior to monitoring.

In a recent study of afterschool experiences and social adjustment of early adolescent boys and girls, Gregory Pettit found that parents' careful monitoring of their early adolescents was related to a lack of externalizing problems such as disobeying and fighting.[22] Careful monitoring counterbalanced the effects of living in an unsafe neighborhood and having a lot of unsupervised activities with peers, two other predictors of externalizing problems. As children progress through adolescence, parents' lack of monitoring is also associated with both boys' and girls' engaging in disapproved activities such as drinking.[23]

Galinsky uses the term *intentional parenting* to refer to the time, energy, and focus that working parents must bring to the process of meeting children's needs.[24] Parents feel good about their parenting when they spend time eating meals together and engaging in such activities as exercising, having fun together, or doing homework. They feel successful as parents and less stressed. Having supportive family and friends, having good day care, and having confidence that they are raising their child the way they want to also contribute to parents' feelings of success.

Despite the many demands these family activities make on parents, parents feel much less stress in caring for children than they do at work. Only 6 percent of parents say they feel a great deal of stress in caring for children, and an additional 36 percent say they feel a moderate amount of stress. By comparison, 24 percent experience a large amount of stress at work, and 45 percent experience a moderate amount.

To feel successful, though, parents have to make maximum use of time with family members. Family time need not be considered only as time for leisure or relaxation but also as time for accomplishing tasks. When families work together, parents not only spend time with children, but they create more time for other activities as household work decreases for parents.

Interview
with Susan McHale

Susan McHale is an associate professor of human development at Pennsylvania State University and codirector of the Pennsylvania State University Family Relations Project.

From your experience in studying dual-earner families, what kinds of things make it easiest for parents when both work?

We look at how the whole family system changes when mothers work, and we found very interesting changes in how fathers relate to children between nine and twelve years old when their wives are employed. We collect a measure of "exclusive" or dyadic time—how much time the father spends alone with the child doing some fun activity like attending a concert or school activity. In single-earner families, fathers spend about 90 minutes a week with boys in "exclusive" (dyadic) activities and about 30 minutes with girls, so there is quite a sex distinction in these families. In dual-earner families, fathers spend equal amounts of "exclusive" time with boys and girls—about 60 minutes per week—so mother's working may enhance the relationship between *father* and daughter and decrease involvement between father and son.

We do not get any straightforward sex differences in the effects of mother's working—that is, boys do not necessarily do less well—unless these are mediated by some other process. For example, we have just finished a paper on parental monitoring of children's activities. To collect data on monitoring, we telephone both the parent and the child and ask specific questions about what has happened that day: Did the child do his homework? Did he have a special success at school that day? Our measure of monitoring is the discrepancy between the children's report and the parent's report. (We presume the children are right.) We thought that monitoring might be related to children's adjustment. We do find that in families where the child is less well monitored, boys are a little bit more at risk for problems in conduct and school achieve-

ENCOURAGING FAMILY COOPERATION IN HOUSEHOLD WORK   Although women usually retain primary responsibility for household management, men's participation in traditionally female household chores serves as a positive example for boys and girls, who do less stereotyping when fathers perform such chores.[25] Further, children who participate routinely in chores that benefit the family tend to show concern for others' welfare.[26]

Although women have traditionally borne the major responsibility for meeting the household needs, they are shifting the responsibility to the family as a whole. Jacqueline Goodnow and Jennifer Bowes's interviews with parents and children concerning the distribution of household work reveal that the meanings people attach to particular jobs (men's/women's work, Dad's/Mom's responsibility), the feelings they have about the jobs (like/dislike, feel competence/incompetence), and underlying principles of fairness shape how families distribute work.[27]

Several recommendations emerge from the discussion with families. First, a problem-solving approach that focuses on the specific question of "Who does this particular job?"

ment. This is independent of who does the monitoring; as long as you have at least one parent who is a good monitor, you do not get these effects.

When we look at what helps families function well when parents work, we find one factor is the agreement between *values* and *attitudes* on the one hand and the *actual roles* family members assume in daily life. This finding applies to adults and children. I am talking about sex-role attitudes. When parents have young children, we found the incongruencies between sex-role attitudes and behavior are related to problems in the marital relation. Specifically, when husbands and wives have traditional sex-role attitudes but the organization of daily life is egalitarian, couples were much more likely to fight, to have lower scores on a measure of love, and to find the relationship less satisfying.

When we looked at children's involvement in household chores, we found additional evidence of the importance of congruence between attitudes and family roles. For example, the more chores boys in dual-earner families perform, the better their adjustment; the reverse was true for boys in single-earner families, however. The mediating factor seems to be the father's sex-role attitudes. In single-earner families, fathers are more traditional and less involved in tasks themselves. Therefore, when sons do a lot of housework, their behavior is out of concordance with their fathers' values. In both kinds of families, dual and single earners, boys whose roles are incongruent with their fathers' values feel less competent and more stressed, and they report less positive relationships with their parents.

The congruence between values and beliefs and the kinds of family roles children and adults assume is what predicts better adjustment. Whether you can change people's attitudes and beliefs or whether it is easier to change family roles is hard to say. Part of the problem is that the work demands in dual-earner families require that family roles change before people feel really comfortable with that.

is useful. Couples who successfully achieve a balance in household tasks avoid getting caught in old definitions of work (men's versus women's jobs). Instead, they concentrate on how to achieve household goals in an effective and efficient way.

Second, families must negotiate chores in an atmosphere of fairness, respect, and open-mindedness. People's preferences are respected and considered in assigning chores. Principles of fairness operate. Families naturally divide household chores into two categories: (1) self-care (making one's bed, picking up clothes or toys) and (2) family care (setting the table, taking out the garbage). Most families assign self-care responsibilities to children as the children become able to do them. Performing self-care chores gives children feelings of independence and competence, because they can care for themselves. As family chores are distributed among family members, children receive their share to promote feelings of being important participants in family life.

With a changing society expressing such varying opinions about family members' household responsibilities, families often feel dissatisfied with what they are doing and

Parents who share the workload at home have more time available to meet children's needs.

want to alter their patterns. Box 8.1 contains suggestions for successfully negotiating dissatisfactions and moving on to a new style of handling such responsibilities. This process has three key components: (1) maintain underlying respect and caring for other family members' needs, seeing changes as ways of giving to people who matter to one another; (2) stay flexible—reassign, reduce, or eliminate jobs; and (3) focus on the positive benefits for all family members of pulling together and contributing to family life.

In brief, parents feel more satisfied with their family life and with their relationships with children when they have more time, do not feel rushed, and can focus on the child.[28] When they feel they have parental support from family and friends and can raise their children as they want, parents feel more successful. The same qualities related to parents' feelings of satisfaction and success are also associated with parents' reporting that their children have fewer problems with anxiety, depression, and inattention.

Spillover from Home to Work

About 70 percent of parents with children under eighteen say that their positive feelings about their children often or very often carry over to work, and about one-third say they often or very often have more energy on the job because of their children.[29] The parents who are more likely to have positive spillover from home to work are those who (1) are fathers, (2) put a higher priority on family life, (3) feel they have support for doing their work—they have day care they trust and parental support at

BOX 8.1

Moving to New Patterns of Household Work

1. *Take a look at what bothers you.* Ask yourself why you are doing this chore. What specifically bothers you about the chore? What is the worst part of the chore for you?

2. *List the alternatives.* Jobs can be changed in many ways—eliminated, reassigned to someone else in the family, reduced (e.g., iron only some things but not everything), moved outside the family.

3. *Look carefully at the way you frame the problem and at the way you talk and negotiate.* Explain what you want, stick to the point in discussing the problem, and frame the issues in terms of practicality, logic, or benefits to all family members. Avoid name calling.

4. *Be prepared for difficulties.* The greatest difficulty is dealing with family members' having different standards for completing chores. Children often do not want to do chores because of criticism. Focus on the effort each person puts in and do not insist on perfect completion.

5. *Remember that there is more than one way to express caring and affection in a family.* Men and women have to give up old beliefs that caring must be shown by being a "good provider" or a "good homemaker." Caring for a family is more than doing housework.

6. *Keep in mind the gains as well as the costs.* Although all family members give up time to do household chores, everyone gains. All family members gain in doing chores and contributing to family functioning. They gain self-respect, skills, and the primary benefit of greater closeness to other family members.

Jacqueline J. Goodnow and Jennifer M. Bowes, *Men, Women and Household Work* (Melbourne, Australia: Oxford University Press, 1994), pp. 197–201.

times of difficulty, (4) work more days per week but feel fewer stresses and strains at work, (5) have better-quality jobs with more autonomy and learning opportunities, and (6) have more workplace supports from coworkers. The fact that fathers more often experience positive feelings at home is similar to the finding of Larson and Richards that fathers have more positive moods at home than mothers.

When mothers want to work, when they feel that their children do not suffer from their working, and when they have husbands' support, they feel increased satisfaction with themselves and with life.[30] Even if they work when they would prefer to be at home, they do not experience depression or decreased well-being, provided they think that what they are doing is important for the family. Women who want to work but who stay at home for fear of adverse effects on their children become depressed.[31] Further, their children do not function as well as those whose mothers are satisfied with their choice. One study found that academic and social performance of kindergartners was related to mothers' satisfaction with their work status.[32] Children of mothers who stayed at home when they wanted to work or thought they should work had lower levels of performance than did their peers whose mothers either worked and enjoyed it or stayed home and enjoyed that.

Men have high self-esteem and morale when wives work, provided that these men have nontraditional attitudes about working. When men have traditional beliefs that wives' working reflects negatively on their ability as a provider, then they show decreased morale.[33] Like mothers, fathers also experience a drop in morale when they are concerned about childcare and children's adjustment to mothers' working.[34]

Parents also feel conflict and role strain—stress in the way they perform in their various roles. A 1993 national study reveals that mothers and fathers feel equal amounts of conflict in balancing work and family commitments. About 20 percent of men and women report a lot of conflict, and an additional 40 percent report some conflict. Men experience about the same level of conflict regardless of whether their wives are employed.[35] In addition, men of all socioeconomic levels experience similar amounts of conflict, so this is not a phenomenon restricted to "yuppie" fathers.

In combining working and parenting, both parents may feel role strain. A study of parents of preschoolers revealed that fathers were most likely to experience role strain if they (1) were highly committed to work but not satisfied with their job performance, (2) felt they were not living up to their own standards of being a husband or father, and (3) felt they got little support from their wives in meeting their responsibilities to children.[36] The sources of mothers' role strain were similar: (1) being highly involved in work activities but dissatisfied with their job, (2) feeling dissatisfied with the level of support from husband and neighbors in meeting all their responsibilities, and (3) feeling they were not living up to their standards of being a wife.

Women with high role strain feel tension in meeting all the demands on them. In addition to role strain, mothers develop anxiety when they feel they have no chance to make things work out satisfactorily, and depression may accompany the anxiety when mothers feel really committed to parenting and are putting their energy into it but things are not working out.

On the basis of interviews conducted throughout a large U.S. corporation, Arlie Hochschild believes that many parents feel more comfortable at work and seek longer hours there because of the stress from family demands that they feel they cannot meet.[37] Even when companies offer family leave, few parents take it.

Hochschild's interviews were conducted at only one company, and her results are not in agreement with data from Galinsky's work, which indicates that parents are less stressed at home. Other research indicates that when stressed at home, men are more likely to have work spillover and argue with coworkers, but women appear able to avoid the spillover of stress from home to work.[38]

Spillover from Work to Home

Whether one or two parents are employed, parents' work shapes family life in many ways. Parents' job classification—professional, business, skilled or unskilled labor—is the main determiner of the family's social status. The family's social status, in turn, influences its social attitudes and childrearing practices. Middle-class parents value self-reliance and independence in children. To encourage these qualities, such parents tend to explain what they want to their children to motivate them to do what is necessary on their own. Working-class parents value obedience and conformity in children and tend to use power-assertive techniques to force compliance. They use physical punishment more than do middle-class parents; they refuse to give explanations, simply stating, "Because I said so." They are less interested in explanations, saying, "Do it now."[39]

Social status also determines the effects of mothers' employment. In a broad range of middle-class children, followed from age one through adolescence, mothers' work status per se had little effect on children's development.[40] The children of employed and nonemployed mothers were equivalent on cognitive, academic, social-emotional, and behavioral development. The quality of the homes and parent-child relationships, regardless of mothers' work status, determined children's growth. In lower-status African American families, however, mothers' employment was related to children's language and achievement.[41]

In another study, children of single working mothers had higher self-esteem and greater academic achievement and academic self-esteem, and they reported greater family cohesiveness than children whose mothers received aid to dependent children. In families with fewer resources, added income may be the main factor, but it may also be the influence of an achieving parent that contributes to the difference.

In addition to providing income for basic support and forming a pattern of family life, work also brings many psychological benefits in terms of advancing parents' social, cognitive, and emotional development.[42] Work helps parents develop a sense of competence and self-esteem. Mothers who worked as volunteers in Head Start programs, for example, became more confident and motivated to go on in school. One of the benefits of this child-centered program has been to empower the parents who have worked there.[43]

Work often helps parents develop interpersonal skills that they then use at home. Workers in a manufacturing plant described how they used democratic work practices in solving problems at home. One man told how he started holding team meetings with his family: "After all, a family is kind of a team."[44] A mother commented to a psychologist, "Well, my daughter was having trouble going to sleep so I decided to handle the problem like we would at work. I asked her what she thought would solve the problem, and she said 'Reading two stories to me.' I did that, and she went to sleep. That cured the problem."[45]

Work also offers a range of friendships and supports. When asked to describe how she handled stress at home, a mother said, "I go to work. At work we are like a family. Friends listen to me, and we have fun even though there is a lot of work."[46] Supervisors also offer support and help at times of trouble. When one father was severely ill, his supervisor organized coworkers to donate vacation hours so he could keep his benefits as long as possible.

About 77 percent of parents report that they often or very often feel successful at work.[47] Success is related to having time to get work done but more importantly to being able to focus on work without interruptions, being able to complete a task without getting job after job. Having a say in how the work is done, positive relationships with coworkers, and feeling the job is a meaningful one also contribute to feeling successful.

Nevertheless, a sizeable proportion of parents also report stress and frustration from work. Sixty-nine percent of parents report that they feel a moderate or large amount of stress, and 55 percent say they feel a moderate or large amount of frustration. Stress appears to be related to job demands—working more hours per day and more days per week, having to take home work, having to travel more, feeling pressured to complete work in short periods of time with little control of how it is done, and feeling that the job is meaningless. Frustration has similar origins but is more related to the daily work schedule than to the total amount of time worked. Inability to focus, feeling unable to make decisions, feeling that the job entails no learning also increase frustration.

Galinsky's study revealed that parents who were most likely to experience negative spillover from work to home were those who (1) put a higher priority on work than family, (2) were more likely to be managers or professionals with relatively large responsibilities at work, (3) had demanding jobs that were difficult to complete on time, (4) had jobs that were too stimulating or not stimulating enough, and (5) had less parenting support than those who did not feel stress.[48]

Couples' diaries concerning work stress and home activities revealed that fathers with work overload were less active, less communicative, and more withdrawn.[49] Mothers compensated and did household chores, but fathers were not likely to reciprocate when mothers experienced overload. When parents had conflicts with supervisors or coworkers, they tended to argue more than before with spouses about home responsibilities. They confined arguments to spouses and did not include children.

A study of mothers and preschool children found that when mothers had stressful workdays, they were more withdrawn and less attentive, caring, and loving with their children.[50] Children tried to please mothers and engage them in activity but sometimes seemed less happy. Job stress was most upsetting to women who already had feelings of anxiety and depression.

Parents who felt positive spillover from work to home (about a third of the parents participating in Galinsky's study) were those who (1) were married, (2) had jobs that demanded more days per week, (3) experienced less stress and more autonomy at work, (4) had more supportive supervisors and coworkers, (5) had more parental support from family and friends, and (6) felt they were raising their children as they wanted.[51]

Strategies for Navigating Work and Family Life

We have moved through the circular flow of work and family life and have seen common threads in feelings of success or stress in both places and in the process of making transitions between the two. Parents feel most successful and least stressed when they have time—time just to be with children and family without feeling rushed, time to engage in activities with them, and time to accomplish tasks at work. They feel successful when they have control of how they raise their children and how they do their work. They feel successful when they have support from family, friends, and coworkers and the work culture and when they can rely on trustworthy day care.[52]

Galinsky makes various specific suggestions for increasing positive feelings and reducing stress.[53] Navigating work consists of keeping job demands reasonable by seeking flextime, prioritizing work, and using problem-solving techniques to accomplish the work. Parents improve their focus at work by finding ways to work without interruptions. They improve the quality of their jobs by learning new skills and gaining meaning from their work. They encourage positive relationships with supervisors and coworkers by appreciating support when given and making requests for reasonable modifications to the work environment to meet family needs.

Parents minimize difficulties in making transitions from work to home and from home to work in several ways. Parents do best in making the transition from work to home when they have some act or ritual that separates work from their home life—some do breathing exercises, some listen to music or books on tape or read on the way home. Parents anticipate that their children are saving their problems until they get home. Parents also develop rituals that allow time with children to meet their needs when they first get home and then time to prepare dinner and do other household tasks. If parents have had a bad day at work, they are advised to tell their children and take extra time to reduce their stress. In making the transition from home to work, parents reduce stress by preparing for the next day (laying out clothes, making lunches) and allowing enough time in the morning to avoid rushing.

To navigate family life, Galinsky believes, parents need to reconsider the way they think about the time they spend with children. Children do not necessarily want more hours with parents. Children want stress-free, focused time with parents. They want parents to be calm and emotionally available to them. Galinsky recommends that parents spend time with children by hanging around and being available for conversation and supporting children's interests and activities. Because children are concerned about parents' control of anger, parents can improve relationships by communicating feelings in ways that encourage children to listen. Summarizing what she learned about promoting positive family life, Galinsky quotes a twelve-year-old:

> Listen. Listen to what your kids say, because you know, sometimes it's very important. And sometimes a kid can have a great idea and it could even affect you. Because, you know, kids are people. Kids have great ideas, as great as you, as great as ideas that adults have.[54]

Galinsky also recommends that parents talk about their work. Children hear little about work, especially from fathers. They often do not understand the positive aspects of their parents' work, and so they have a limited view of the meaning of work in people's lives. One of the reasons children are so concerned about parents' stress is that they hear mostly negative things about parents' work. Parents need to discuss what they do and the importance of their work. Children learn many indirect lessons about work from the way parents discuss coworkers and strategies for getting along.

Parents have to make stress-free, fun times with children a major priority of family life.

At home and at work and at times of transitions, being proactive, seeking ways to have more autonomy in scheduling tasks and rearing children, seeking support from others, and establishing priorities help parents navigate the waters of work and family life.

On the basis of her interviews with parents, Deutsch also recommends that parents be proactive in making daily choices that enable both parents to have careers and be parents.[55] Many believe that the difficulties that prevent equality among men and women occur in the workplace and are due to the nature of work itself; Deutsch insists that "this reasoning is fundamentally flawed, however, because it ignores the role that couples themselves play. The so-called causes of inequality are as likely to be consequences of decisions as they are to be forces driving inequality."[56]

Couples committed to equal careers and parenting make choices at home and at work that support equality. They have to ignore the traditional view of a career that takes almost two full-time people to support—a husband at work and a wife doing backup at home—and turn to careers "that fit primary parenting for two."[57] That means scaling back work—limiting work hours per day, work days per week, travel, overtime—and "allowing family obligations to intrude on work as a significant part of identity."[58] When both parents make adjustments, neither one has the traditional male career.

Mothers also have to be willing to let fathers assume major responsibility for childcare and decisions about children. Many women, Deutsch found, are reluctant to do this and retain all the responsibility for children. Their primary identity is as mothers, and they do not wish to relinquish it, particularly when children are very young. They have to recognize, however, that children benefit when fathers are equal parents, because children can develop closer relationships with them. Marriages benefit as well, because couples share the responsibilities of parenting and work and neither partner feels overburdened.

Types of Day Care

Parents seek childcare in many places. Recent data concerning childcare for children under five reveal that 28 percent are cared for by a nonrelative at home or in another home; 24 percent, in day care or nursery school; 15 percent, by the father; 9 percent, by the mother at her work; 21 percent, by another relative; and 1 percent, in some other form of care.[59]

The most important factor in selecting day care, particularly for a child in the first year, is the quality of the caregiver. For toddlers and preschoolers as well, having a secure attachment with a sensitive caregiver promotes social competence. Once parents have a reliable, sensitive caregiver, they want to focus on the opportunities available for the child to socialize with others and to be involved in stimulating activities.[60] The child's needs will depend somewhat on his or her age and temperament.

Each form of care has certain advantages and possible drawbacks. Care by parents and relatives has the advantage that children know these people and have special ties to them. Although parental care is usually of high quality, a parent may need to sleep after working a shift or may provide childcare to other children. Thus, parental care can be of variable quality.[61]

Substitute care at home is expensive but requires that the child adjust to only the new person; everything else in the environment remains the same. This form of care has the advantage of being available when the child is sick. As children get older, home care is often supplemented with nursery school attendance or other group activities so the child can be with peers.

Family day care—that is, care in the home of another family with other children— is cheaper than home care and has some advantages. A family day care setting provides a more varied environment for children in the toddler years than does a day care center.[62] In family day care, children can engage in many of the same activities of home care with a mother or father figure.

Because there are fewer children, family day care is sometimes more flexible than a center in meeting children's individual needs. Family day care homes are licensed; some are part of a larger umbrella organization that supplies toys and training to home caregivers. Day caregivers who are part of such a network can give higher-quality care than can untrained caregivers. Guidelines for making a choice of a family day care home are similar to those for choosing a day care program. Parents should make one visit with the child and one visit alone when gathering information to help them choose a childcare provider.

Day care centers provide care for children from infancy and may provide after-school care for children in the elementary grades. In most states, such centers must meet specific standards intended to ensure the health and safety of the children. The parent whose child goes to a day care center is sure of having childcare available every day—at some centers from 7 a.m. until 7 p.m. Many centers have credentialed personnel who have been trained to work with children, and many centers have play equipment and supplies not found in most home care situations. All centers provide opportunities for contact with same-age children.

When children start elementary school, they receive care there for 3 to 6 hours per day and require special provision only before or after school and over holidays. Approximately 2 to 10 million children ages six to eleven are unsupervised after school.[63] Diaries of 1,500 children in 1997 indicate that about 12 to 14 percent of American children ages five to twelve are home alone for, on average, an hour after school.[64] The older the child, the larger the percentage in self-care—1 percent of children five to seven, 8 percent of children eight to ten, and 23 percent of children eleven to twelve.

Most children come straight home from school, eat, watch television, or read. They are less likely to be engaged in sports than are children in afterschool programs. Older, better-educated mothers are more likely to have children in self-care, perhaps because they are more available by phone than are less-educated mothers, who may have jobs where phone access is limited. Quiet children who are not aggressive and children living in stable neighborhoods are likely to be in self-care. Children from higher-income families are more likely to be involved in sports and other activities after school.

Although problems can arise with self-care, some children describe benefits such as increased independence, responsibility, and time to think and to develop hobbies. In part, some children flourish because of their personalities or the living situation. Some children entertain themselves well, and others have friends or activities in the neighborhood, so they are not really alone. A recurrent theme in children's accounts of successful latchkey experiences is that parents and children have good relationships with one another. These children feel that their parents are supportive, and their parents encourage phone contact and activities during their absence.[65]

Availability and Affordability of Day Care

We have described the kinds of care possible, but how available and affordable are they? The average cost of quality full-time care for a child prior to school age is approximately $3,000 per year. Infant and toddler care can cost close to $5,000 per year. In certain geographical areas, the costs are higher.[66] Childcare takes about 10 percent of an average family's income but about 22 to 25 percent of a poor family's income.[67]

Families receive little governmental support in arranging childcare. A tax credit of $2,400 does not cover the full cost of the care and helps primarily middle-class and upper-middle-class families. Single parents and lower-income parents do not pay sufficient taxes to get a large benefit from the credit. Although federal subsidies provide some block support for childcare expenses of poorer families, only about 10 to 15 percent of those eligible receive such benefits.

Experts disagree about the availability of care. Most agree, however, that shortages in service exist for infants and school-age children. As noted, between 2 and 10 million children ages six to eleven are unsupervised at home before and after school. Further, service is limited for children at certain times of the day—early mornings, early and late evenings—and for sick children.

Even when care is available, the quality of care is uneven. Approximately 70 percent of day care homes are unlicensed. Many day care centers have rapid turnovers of staff and too few staff for the ages and number of children attending.[68] Chapter 11 takes up the question of how to provide affordable and quality childcare.

Impact of Nonparental Care on Children

Psychologist Michael Lamb, reviewing studies on the effects of day care on children, writes

> Arrangements regarding nonparental care do not represent a new set of problems for the world's parents. In fact, decisions and arrangements about children's care and supervision are among the oldest problems faced by human society. Exclusive maternal care throughout the period of dependency was never an option in what Bowlby called "The environment of evolutionary adaptiveness," and there are no societies in the 1990s in which it is the typical practice. Indeed, exclusive maternal care through adulthood was seldom an option in any phase of human society; it emerged as a possibility for a small elite segment of society during one small portion of human history.[69]

As we look at the effects of nonparental care at different ages, we should keep clearly in mind Lamb's comment on the effects of nonparental care:

> Although it seldom receives the amount of attention it deserves, there is clear evidence that the quality of children's interactions and relationships with their parents and family members and the quality of care children receive at home continue to be the most important sources of influence on the development of young children, even when they receive substantial amounts of care outside the home.[70]

In evaluating research, we must keep in mind first that a selection process related to mothers' education, personality, and interests determines who, in fact, chooses to return to work once children are born.[71] Second, maternal employment is not a unitary phenomenon, and its meaning in a child's life depends on (1) the child's characteristics (age, sex, temperament), (2) family characteristics (education and socioeconomic level, father's involvement in the home, mother's satisfaction with working), (3) work characteristics (the number of hours the mother works, the level of her stress at work), and, perhaps most important, (4) the nature of the child's substitute care. Because researchers cannot control all these factors, we have to interpret findings from several studies and draw our own conclusions. In discussing the research, we will focus on children's social-emotional and cognitive functioning.

Nonparental Care during Infancy and Early Childhood

Quality of care is a major determiner of the effects of nonparental childcare on children. There are two kinds of indices of quality of care—process measures and structural measures.[72] *Process measures* examine appropriate caregiving for children—that is, appropriate activities in a safe, stimulating setting. *Structural measures* look at the amount of teacher or caregiver training/experience, appropriate group sizes, and staff turnover. These two kinds of measures are usually correlated. The adult-child ratio and the extent of teacher training are thought to be the best structural measures of quality in day care centers; in family day care, group size, safety, and caregiver appropriateness are the best measures. Caregivers' salaries are good measures of caregiver stability; when salaries are high, caregivers stay.

Children who enter high-quality day care in the first year develop many positive social qualities seen later in preschool and elementary school: they are well controlled, popular, and considerate of peers in preschool and socially competent and able to focus and stay on task in kindergarten. In grade school, they are outgoing, affectionate, nonhostile children who perform well in school.[73] In Europe, high-quality care in the first year is associated with cognitive and social maturity through childhood and into early adolescence.[74] So, although children may be at risk for insecure attachment and noncompliance when mothers return to work for extended hours in the first year, there appears to be no risk and many benefits if they go into high-quality day care.

What is high-quality care? The National Academy of Sciences Panel on Child Care Policy uses six criteria to describe quality care:[75]

1. Minimum child-staff ratios that vary according to the child's age—1:4 for infants to 1:7 for preschoolers

2. Caregiver training that includes courses in child development

3. Organized activities programs that are varied enough to permit choice on the child's part

4. Structured space so that activities and groups of children of different ages are separated

5. For family day care, a moderate range of ages of children

6. For day care centers, maximum group sizes ranging from 6 to 8 for infants and 16 to 20 for preschoolers

In high-quality day care settings, children build secure attachments to teachers and develop the many positive social qualities associated with early secure attachment to parents.[76] Clearly, secure attachment to a teacher requires the same qualities in the teacher as those qualities in parents that promote attachment. This adult must be an available, stable, sensitive, responsive caregiver who provides stimulating activities and monitors the child's behavior to increase self-regulation. The child uses this figure as a safe base for exploring the world, just as he or she uses the secure attachment with the mother or father. In the child's first thirty months, it is important for the teacher to remain the same; otherwise, the child-teacher relationship becomes unstable. After thirty months, however, the teacher can change and the child-teacher relationship will still remain stable.[77]

Secure teacher attachment in the first year has a powerful impact on a child's development. It is teacher attachment and day care qualities, not family socialization practices, that predict later childhood competence for children entering day care in the

Interview

with Jay Belsky

Jay Belsky is a professor of human development at Pennsylvania State University in University Park. He is the initiator and director of the Pennsylvania Infant and Family Development Project, an ongoing study of 250 firstborn children whose parents were enrolled for study when the mothers were pregnant in 1981. He has done systematic research on the effects of day care.

What advice would you give to parents in the first two years about day care?

For working parents I say again and again that nothing matters as much as the person who cares for your baby. All too often parents don't look "under the hood" of the childcare situation. They walk in, the walls are painted nicely, the toys are bright, the lunches are nutritious. Especially with a baby, once the minimal safety standards are met, what matters more than anything else psychologically is to find out about this person who'll care for the baby. So, who is this person, and what is his or her capacity to give individualized care? Because babies need individualized care, this issue matters above all else.

The second thing to consider is whether the caregiver and parent can talk together easily. Each person spends less than full time with the baby. The time factor is not necessarily handicapping them, but it can if information is not being communicated back and forth. So the trick then is, "If the caregiver gets to know my baby during the day, what can she tell me in the afternoon, and if I have the baby in the evening and the morning, what can I tell her when I drop the baby off?" There has to be an effective two-way flow of information.

The third thing to consider in selecting care is that the arrangement has to last a decent interval of time. That doesn't mean that you must take the child to the same center for a year's time; it means that the same *person*, or *persons*, takes care of him or her for a year or so. If you find a great person who treats the child as an individual and communicates well with the parent but stays for only a few months, you are not buying yourself a lot. In a baby's life, changing caregivers more than once a year will be stressful. If a baby goes through three or four changes in a year, it may not matter what kind of caregiver he or she gets. Even though the caregivers may get to know the child, the child won't know them. Each has to know the other.

first year.[78] For children entering day care at later ages, it is the family socialization in the first year and the child's characteristics that predict later childhood competence.

There are, of course, confounding factors. Highly motivated, stable parents seek out high-quality care for children.[79] Those infants who go into low-quality care often have parents who are less organized and use less appropriate socialization practices. A vicious cycle may develop for the infant in low-quality care. Highly stressed families give less attention to the child, and the child goes into a day care setting with few adults to interact with and little to do. These children have less contact with adults and receive less stimulation both at home and in day care than do children of motivated parents. Thus, they have cumulative risks for problems in development.

Early and continuing programs that stimulate cognitive development, such as the Abecedarian intervention program, promote intellectual growth during the school years as well.[80] Such programs have reduced grade retention and the need for special programs in the first three years of elementary school. These programs stimulate intellectual growth in children from economically disadvantaged families. However, even controlling for effects of social class and family background, high-quality care in infancy is related to academic performance and verbal skills at age eleven.

Early research raised concerns that early and extensive day care could have negative effects on attachment and children's social-emotional and cognitive functioning. In the early 1990s, the National Institute of Child Health and Human Development (NICHD) initiated studies of 1,281 children from birth to age seven at ten sites around the country. The studies have looked at a number of questions and begun to provide answers.

1. *Does early and extensive childcare affect the child's attachment with the mother?* The studies found that the mother's qualities of warmth, sensitivity, and responsiveness determined the child's attachment to the mother. "Child care by itself constitutes neither a risk or benefit for the development of the infant-mother attachment relationship."[81] When mothers were low in responsiveness and sensitivity, then poor-quality care, unstable care, or extensive amounts of childcare added to the risk of insecure attachment. High-quality childcare seemed to compensate for effects of low maternal sensitivity and reduce the risk of insecure attachment to the mother.

2. *What are the most important predictors of children's cognitive and social-emotional functioning at twenty-four and thirty-six months?*[82] When measures of childcare (quality, stability, type, and age of entry) and measures of family background and parenting were used to predict toddlers' cognitive and social competence, qualities of mothering were stronger and more consistent predictors of outcome than were childcare measures. Of all childcare measures, quality of care was the most consistent predictor.

3. *Are family factors less predictive of childhood outcomes for children in full-time childcare since four months of age than for children in full-time maternal care?*[83] The answer was generally no. Family characteristics predicted children's social-emotional and cognitive functioning assessed at twenty-four and thirty-six months as well as they did for children in full-time maternal care. For both samples, mothers' sensitivity, nonauthoritarian childrearing, and lack of depression predicted social and intellectual competence. There was a slight tendency for mothers' characteristics such as single-parent status to predict certain childhood behaviors more effectively when children were in full-time maternal care. In line with previous research, agreement between mothers' attitudes about working and their actual work status was a significant factor. Children whose mothers were employed and believed working was beneficial for children had fewer problems than children whose mothers worked but did not consider it beneficial. Children whose mothers did not work and thought not working was beneficial for children had fewer problems than children whose mothers stayed home but did not consider it beneficial.

The association between early, extensive nonparental care in the first year of life and negative behavior continues in the elementary school years. Extensive care in the first year of life is related to hitting, kicking, and conflictful interactions in the first three years of elementary school.[84] Contemporaneous afterschool day care that is not high quality is also related to children's being rated as noncompliant by teachers and less well liked by peers.[85] As in the early years, quality afterschool care is related to effective functioning.[86]

Research suggests that low-income third-graders in formal afterschool programs receive better grades in math, reading, and conduct than do children in other forms of care, including maternal care. From about the fifth grade on, children in self-care behave and perform similarly whether an adult is present or not.[87] Nevertheless, lack of supervision and monitoring of early adolescents is related to increased use of alcohol, cigarettes, and marijuana.[88] Eighth-graders in self-care for more than 11 hours a week—whether from dual- or single-earner families, from high- or low-income families, with good or poor grades, or active or nonactive in sports—were more likely than those not in self-care to use these substances. Self-care leads to feelings of greater autonomy and puts early teens at risk of being influenced by peers who are substance abusers.

In adolescence, however, maternal employment is also associated with self-confidence and independence. The benefits are more pronounced for girls who obtain good grades and think of careers for themselves, most likely because their mothers serve as role models of competence.[89]

Boys of employed mothers may not do as well in school, but that has not been a consistent finding in more recent research.[90] Because fathers' involvement in the home is found to stimulate cognitive performance, it may be that fathers' increasing participation reduces that problem.

Gender Differences in Response to Nonparental Care

In several studies, boys were found to be more vulnerable than girls when their mothers worked during the boys' early childhood. It is not clear whether boys require more attention, nurturance, and supervision; whether they are more sensitive to deficiencies in childcare settings; or whether they make more demands on parents who are stressed from working, have less patience with them, and see them more negatively.

Lois Hoffman concludes that boys may have a more difficult time in dual-earner families, and girls more problems in single-earner families.[91] In single-earner families, girls are more at risk for insecure attachments, their behavior is viewed more negatively by mothers, they have less time with fathers, and they receive less encouragement for independence. So, girls profit from living in dual-earner families (that is, having more time with fathers), but boys may not. It is possible, however, to combine the best of both forms of family life so boys and girls get an optimal balance of nurturance, attention, supervision, and independence.

The Effects of Economic Hardship on Parenting

Work provides material resources for daily life, and nothing is more stressful to families than job demotions, layoffs, or firings. We saw in Chapter 1 in our discussion of the Rochester longitudinal study that poverty is one of several events that decrease parents' effectiveness with children and increase children's problem behaviors.

Parenting difficulties occur even under milder conditions of economic hardship. In contemporary society, layoffs, demotions, and economic strain in paying bills lead to a pattern similar to that found when parents live in poverty.[92] When parents experience economic hardship, they become more irritable and more easily frustrated. Their psychological tension has a direct impact on parenting and on their children. They do not communicate with children as openly or share power as much as in less stressful times; this tension can affect children's schoolwork and behavior. When economic conditions improve, parenting skills improve, as does children's behavior.

Economic strain also has an indirect effect on children's behavior. When parents are upset and frustrated, they argue with each other and give each other less support, so parenting declines because parents are not working together.[93] When fathers remain supportive of mothers during economic hardship, mothers' parenting skills do not decrease at all.[94] Although social support from outside the family helps to reduce parents' low moods, it is support from the other parent that maintains parenting effectiveness.

Who Are the Poor?

The most common measure of poverty is the official federal index of poverty developed in the 1960s and based on pretax, cash income and the number of people in the family.[95] The index is determined by the estimated cost of food multiplied by 3, as food was found in surveys to absorb about one-third of the family income. For example, the 1995 poverty threshold for a single person was $7,929 and for a family of four (two adults and two children) $15,455.[96]

In addition to the poverty index, a measure of duration of poverty yields important information for understanding the effects of poverty.[97] One-third of all children in the United States will be poor for least one year before they reach age eighteen, and two-thirds of those who are poor spend less than five years in poverty. Fifteen percent of poor children, however, are poor for more than ten years of childhood, and these children experience the most severe poverty, because their family cash income is half that required to exceed the poverty index.

A measure of neighborhood poverty is significant as well, because it conveys information on services available to children and families. High-poverty neighborhoods are those with more than 40 percent of residents living in poverty. Such residents are less likely to have good health care, schools, parks, community organizations, and informal social support.[98] Neighborhoods with fewer than 20 percent of residents living in poverty are considered low-poverty neighborhoods.[99]

Children, particularly the youngest, are the poorest individuals in the United States. In 1960, about 27 percent of children under eighteen were poor.[100] That figure dropped to a low of 14 percent in 1969. Then, the rate began to rise slowly, with a sharp increase between 1979 and 1984, resulting in 22 percent of children being poor in 1984. The figure dropped briefly but remained at about this level for a decade. In 1998, the rate of poverty for children under eighteen was 19 percent.[101]

Not only are more children poor, but the disparity between the incomes of those children in families with the lowest and highest incomes has increased.[102] Between 1973 and 1990, the adjusted mean cash income for children in families with the lowest fifth of income dropped 30 percent at the same time the mean cash income for children in families with the highest fifth of income rose 13 percent. The disparity has increased over the past ten years as more income has become concentrated in the wealthiest families.

Rates of poverty are higher for children in certain ethnic groups.[103] In 1996 40 percent of African American and 40 percent of Hispanic American children were living in poverty, as compared with 16 percent of European American children. Studies on the persistence of poverty have to be carried out over many years; those reported in the 1980s focused primarily on comparisons between African American and European American children. Ninety percent of persistently poor children are African American.[104]

African American children are also more likely to live in poor neighborhoods. From 1980 to 1990, the percentage of African American children living in such areas increased from 37 to 45 percent. In contrast, about two-thirds of European American poor children live in neighborhoods with low poverty rates.

Rates of poverty vary according to family structure, with children in single-parent families more likely to be poor than those in two-parent families.[105] Still, in one study, almost half the years children spent in poverty were when they were living with two parents. Although African American children are more likely to be living in single-parent families and are thus more at risk for poverty, living in two-parent families does not protect these children against higher rates of poverty. In one study, European American children in two-parent families averaged six months in poverty, whereas African American children in two-parent families averaged three years. In another study, European American children who spent their entire childhoods in single-parent families had the same rate of poverty as African American children in two-parent families.[106]

Many factors influence rates of poverty. Declines in the number of children per family and increases in parental education generally decrease poverty.[107] Vonnie McLoyd points to three factors that push more children into poverty: decreases in the number of skilled jobs that can support families, increases in the number of single-parent families, and reductions in government benefits to families.[108]

The Effects of Poverty on Children's and Adolescents' Development

Jeanne Brooks-Gunn and Greg Duncan describe the effects of poverty on various aspects of children's functioning.[109]

Birth Outcomes and Physical Health

Low birth weight (less than 2,500 grams) and infant mortality are almost twice as common among poor infants as among nonpoor infants. Further, growth stunting (being less than fifth percentile in height for one's age), often considered a measure of nutritional status, is twice as common in poor children as in nonpoor children. Lead poisoning, often related to many physical and cognitive impairments, is 3.5 times more common among poor children than among nonpoor children. It is not surprising that poor children are less often characterized as having excellent health than are nonpoor children and more often described as having fair or poor health.

Cognitive Development and School Achievement

Table 8.2 reveals that poor children are more likely to experience cognitive delays and learning disabilities than are nonpoor children. The poorer the child, the greater the delay. The poorest children, who live below half the poverty level of income, score between 6 and 13 points below poor children who live at 1.5 to 2 times the poverty income level on such measures as IQ, verbal ability, and achievement. These differences appear on children's ability measures as early as age two and persist into the elementary school years. These differences persist even when mothers' age, marital status, education, and ethnicity are controlled for.

Poor children are twice as likely as nonpoor children to repeat a school grade and to drop out of school. After controlling for relevant variables, the effects of low income per se on school attainment are small unless low income occurred in the first five years.

Duration and timing of poverty influence its effects on children's functioning. Those children who live in poverty thirteen years or longer have significantly lower scores on cognitive measures than those who experience short-term poverty in the year of the study. Poverty in the first five years of life is negatively associated with high school graduation, whereas poverty in the adolescent years is not.

Emotional and Behavioral Development

Poverty is less clearly related to emotional outcomes than to physical and cognitive development. Parents of poor and nonpoor children report the same number of behavioral problems, but nonpoor children are almost twice as likely to get treatment for them (see Table 8.2). Persistent poverty, however, is related to emotional problems such as dependency, anxiety, and feelings of unhappiness. Current poverty is related to such behaviors as hyperactivity and peer problems. These differences are found even when mothers' age, education, and mental status are controlled for.

In addition to differences in health and cognitive skills, poor children are more likely to experience hunger, abuse, and neglect. They are more likely to experience violent crimes and to be afraid to go out in their neighborhoods. As teens, they are more likely to bear a child out of wedlock.

Pathways Accounting for the Effects of Poverty

Brooks-Gunn and Duncan identify five ways that poverty may influence children's development—health, home environment, style of parental interactions with children, parents' mental health, and neighborhood characteristics.[110] Although health status itself is, in part, a consequence of poverty, it can influence subsequent development.

TABLE 8.2 Selected Population-Based Indicators of Well-Being for Poor and Nonpoor Children in the United States

Indicator	Percentage of Poor Children (unless noted)	Percentage of Nonpoor Children (unless noted)	Ratio of Poor to Nonpoor Children
Cognitive Outcomes			
Developmental delay (includes both limited and long-term developmental deficits) (0 to 17 years)	5.0	3.8	1.3
Learning disability (defined as having exceptional difficulty in learning to read, write, and do arithmetic) (3 to 17 years)	8.3	6.1	1.4
School Achievement Outcomes (5 to 17 years)			
Grade repetition (reported to have ever repeated a grade)	28.8	14.1	2.0
Ever expelled or suspended	11.9	6.1	2.0
High school dropout (percentage 16- to 24-year-olds who were not in school or did not finish high school in 1994)	21.0	9.6	2.2
Emotional or Behavioral Outcomes (3 to 17 years unless noted)			
Parent reports child has ever had an emotional or behavioral problem that lasted three months or more	16.4	12.7	1.3
Parent reports child ever being treated for an emotional problem or behavioral problem	2.5	4.5	0.6
Parent reports child has experienced one or more of a list of typical child behavioral problems in the last three months (5 to 17 years)	57.4	57.3	1.0
Other			
Female teens who had an out-of-wedlock birth	11.0	3.6	3.1
Economically inactive at age 24 (not employed or in school)	15.9	8.3	1.9
Experienced hunger (food insufficiency) at least once in past year	15.9	1.6	9.9
Reported cases of child abuse and neglect	5.4	0.8	6.8
Violent crimes (experienced by poor families and nonpoor families)	5.4	2.6	2.1
Afraid to go out (percentage of family heads in poor and nonpoor families who report they are afraid to go out in their neighborhood)	19.5	8.7	2.2

Jeanne Brooks-Gunn and Greg J. Duncan, 1997, "The Effects of Poverty on Children," *Future of Children* 7 (2): 58–59. Reprinted with permission of the David and Lucille Packard Foundation.

Note: This list of child outcomes reflects findings from large, nationally representative surveys that collect data on child outcomes and family income. While most data come from the 1988 National Health Interview Survey Child Health Supplement, data from other nationally representative surveys are included. The rates presented are from simple cross-tabulations. In most cases, the data do not reflect factors that might be important to child outcomes other than poverty status at the time of data collection. The ratios reflect rounding.

Low birth weight is associated with increases in learning disabilities, grade retention, and school dropout; and, as noted earlier, lead poisoning is associated with reduced IQ and reduced scores on cognitive measures.

The home environment of poor families provides less stimulation and fewer opportunities for learning. The HOME scale, a measure of household resources, toys, and reading materials, differentiates the homes of children with lower and higher family incomes. The lack of stimulation available in poor homes appears to account for up to half the effect of poverty on the IQs of five-year-old children.

Harsh parental interactions with children are more characteristic of poor families; poor mothers, for instance, spank children more often than do nonpoor mothers. The increases in children's emotional problems and poor school achievement may be related to such harsh practices. These findings have occurred in smaller studies, and a larger study has found only weak relationships between ineffective parenting and poverty status.

When parents are poor, they are more likely to be irritable and depressed and less able to control the expression of these feelings. Poor control of parents' feelings is directly related to increased conflict with children and indirectly related to difficult relationships. Parents with emotional problems are less stimulating with their children, and they use less effective parenting practices.

Family income dictates where families can afford to live and thereby affects children's development. Poor children are more likely to live in neighborhoods with poor schools and fewer parks, playgrounds, and community activities. Further, unsafe neighborhoods often do not permit exploration or play outside.

Brooks-Gunn and Duncan refute the argument that the problems of the poor result from parents' genetic endowment or their work ethic. They report that siblings reared in the same family with the same parental attitudes can differ in the age and duration of poverty in their lives and thus serve to control for the effects of parental characteristics on poverty. That sibling differences in income were related to siblings' years of completed schooling suggests that income does matter even when genes and work ethic are controlled for.

Ways to Intervene

Two general kinds of programs exist for poor children and their families.[111] First are cash-transfer programs that directly give poor families money, such as Aid to Families with Dependent Children (AFDC) or Earned Income Tax Credit (EITC), which gives low-wage earners a refundable credit against their income tax.

Second are programs that provide services, such as food stamps and subsidized lunches, housing supplements, health care, and early childhood education. Food stamps and AFDC, available to all families with a certain level of income, are termed *entitlement programs.* Other programs, such as Head Start and housing supplements, are available to only a portion of those who are eligible.

Although it is beyond the scope of this section to review the effectiveness of the variety of programs available, a 1997 issue of *The Future of Children* focused on the causes and effects of poverty and contained detailed analyses of interventions to deal with the problems. Summarizing the journal's findings, Eugene Lewit, Donna Terman, and Richard Behrman write,

> Contrary to much current rhetoric claiming that public programs for children do not work well, the evidence presented in this journal issue suggests that existing policies do alleviate hardships for a number of families with children and that it is possible to identify specific programs that produce important benefits for children.[112]

Clearly, the United States has markedly reduced poverty among those over sixty-five. In 1960, 35 percent of those over sixty-five were poor; in 1998, the comparable figure was 10 percent.[113] This low figure has existed for over a decade and is half the poverty rate of children. We must ask ourselves, "If it is important to provide adequate income and living for those who are fully developed, how much more important is it to provide adequate life experiences for those in the process of development?"

The Care of Both Partners

In the excitement and busyness of family life and work, parents forget that the family started with the primacy of the couple. Further, the satisfaction that the couple have with each other and their ways of doing things make solutions effective. The continuance of a strong, loving bond between parents is a primary factor in the success of combining working and parenting.

Further, more than anything else in the world, children want the family to stay together. To do this, parents need a strong relationship. Their relationship, however, usually gets put aside during childrearing, especially in the earliest years.

James Levine and Todd Pittinsky suggest that parents make a weekly date to do something without the children.[114] If money is a problem, set aside some special time at home—rent a video, have a special dinner. (Baby-sitting can be an expensive proposition, but baby-sitting cooperatives offer a cost-free way for parents to swap childcare hours with other parents.) The date should be exclusive time with the spouse to reconnect and share what is happening. Parents can also organize daily rituals that give them special time together—reading the paper together, sitting close to each other while listening to music, talking after dinner, or just being physically close while watching television. Telephone calls during the day also help parents stay connected.

Working parents who take care of themselves can take better care of their children and each other. Couples who exercise regularly, eat a balanced diet, and make sure they have private time for thinking and pursuing interests are less likely to be tense and tired and more likely to enjoy their job and family. Gloria Norris and JoAnn Miller suggest the following ways for parents to be good to themselves:[115]

1. Keep up friendships—exercising with a friend several times a week is ideal.

2. Develop ways of easing the transition from office to home—walk the last block or two, take a quick shower before dinner, rest for ten minutes after arriving home.

3. Learn personal signs of stress, and do not ignore them; get rest and spend time relaxing.

4. Discover the most stressful times of the day, and find ways of relieving tension; a different morning or evening routine can reduce stress.

5. Develop a quick tension reliever, such as yoga exercises, deep breathing, or meditation.

The life of the working parent is challenging and demanding. But most working parents find the challenges worth the efforts required, as work makes life richer and more exciting for the whole family.

Main Points

Work

- influences social values in childrearing and the social life and status of families
- develops adults' skills and provides many supports
- creates stress that disrupts parenting skills

Among the many strategies they use to navigate the flow of work and family parents

- place primary importance on spending time with children to meet their needs
- create time for children and family by sharing the workload at home
- maintain control of work demands through problem-solving methods
- build supportive systems at work and use high-quality care

Nonparental care of children

- must meet established criteria to be considered quality care—specified child-staff ratios that vary according to the age of the child, staff training, safety, structure, organized activities programs
- does not interfere with secure mother-infant attachments unless mothers are low in sensitivity and responsiveness; in that case, poor-quality care, unstable care, or extensive amounts of care add to the risk of insecure attachments
- when of high quality, can compensate for the effects of low maternal sensitivity and responsiveness
- is not as predictive of children's development at twenty-four and thirty-six months as parental qualities
- in early childhood promotes competence when children have secure attachments to sensitive teachers who provide stimulating activities and monitor them
- in the elementary school years and adolescence is associated with social and intellectual competence if children are supervised
- sometimes includes self-care by older children who enjoy independence but also require some form of monitoring

Poor children

- are more likely to suffer both complications, cognitive delays, abuse, and neglect than nonpoor children

- lack income that affects quality of health care, home environment, and neighborhoods
- benefit from government programs

Effectively combining working and parenting

- requires that parents make daily decisions to share the workload at home
- means that parents devote time to sustaining their relationship

Exercises

1. Break into small groups, and discuss the research finding that the effect of mothers' working seems to depend on the sex of the child. (See Susan McHale's interview earlier in this chapter.) Discuss the finding that boys may experience more negative effects because they need more monitoring. How can parents take action to optimize effects for both boys and girls?

2. Imagine you had a child under age five—infant, toddler, or preschooler. Investigate day care options in the community for a child of that age. You might form groups to investigate care for a child of a particular age, with each student visiting at least one center to get information and summarize impressions. One group might investigate family day care in the area and compare the quality and the cost of care with that available in a center.

3. Design an ideal day care program for infants or toddlers, specifying the number of caregivers, their qualities, the physical facilities, and the daily routine.

4. Imagine what your family and work life will be like in ten years. Write diary entries for a day during the week and for a day on the weekend about your life at home and at work.

5. Write a short paper containing advice you could give to a parent of the same sex as you who feels frustrated and pressured trying to incorporate an infant and the care of the infant into his or her work life.

Additional Readings

Booth, Alan, ed. *Child Care in the 1990s: Trends and Consequences.* Hillsdale, NJ: Erlbaum, 1992.

Deutsch, Francine M. *Halving It All: How Equally Shared Parenting Works.* Cambridge, MA: Harvard University Press, 1999.

Galinsky, Ellen. *Ask the Children: What America's Children Really Think about Working Parents.* New York: Morrow, 1999.

Goodnow, Jacqueline J., and Jennifer M. Bowes. *Men, Women, and Household Work.* Melbourne, Australia: Oxford University Press, 1994.

Levine, James A., and Todd L. Pittinsky. *Working Fathers: New Strategies for Balancing Work and Family.* Reading, MA: Addison-Wesley, 1997.

9

Nontraditional Families

ALTHOUGH THE CHAPTER IS TITLED "NONTRADI-tional Families," the families described here, when to-taled, outnumber what we consider the traditional family of two biological parents and their children. Biologically speaking, it takes two parents to create a new life. In our society, family has traditionally meant a mother and father and their biological children. But now, more children are born to single mothers, and a sizeable number of children experience divorce of their parents or the death of a parent with subsequent remarriage. How is life different for children in single-parent households? in households with gay or lesbian parents? How does life change when parents remarry? How can parents help children cope with all the special circumstances of living in a nontraditional family?

As we noted in the first chapter, 68 percent of children in the United States live with two parents, one of whom may be a stepparent, 27 percent live in households headed by women, and 5 percent live in households headed by men.[1] Single women raising children may be widowed, divorced, or separated from husbands, but a sizeable number are never-married mothers. The rate of births to unmarried women has been increasing in recent years, and in 1998, 33 percent of babies were born to unmarried mothers.[2]

It is estimated that 50 percent of all children will experience the divorce of their parents and spend an average of five years in a single-parent family. Because one-third of children are born to unmarried mothers and because half of those children living with married parents will live in single-parent families as a result of divorce, living in a single-parent family will be a normative experience in our society, that is, an experience of the majority of children. About 75 percent of divorced mothers and 80 percent of divorced fathers marry again, so a sizeable number of children will live in stepfamilies. Many experience a second divorce, as approximately 50 percent of remarriages end in divorce.[3] This chapter describes the challenges both parents and children face as they experience these changes.

The Heterogeneity of Single-Parent Families

Both numbers and proportions of single-parent families have increased in all Western countries and in all ethnic groups in the United States. African American families have a somewhat higher rate of single-parent families than do other groups; this does not appear to be the result of increased sexual activity among young women but rather of the fact that birthrates have remained the same in this group while rates of marriage have dropped. Thus, more children are born to unmarried mothers.[4]

Single-parent families not only have grown from 9 percent of families in 1960 to 31 percent of families in 1995; they have also become more diverse in form.[5] In 1970, 73 percent of children in single-parent families lived with a separated or divorced parent, 20 percent with a widowed parent, and only 7 percent with a never-married parent. In 1990, 31 percent lived with a never-married parent, 62 percent with a separated or divorced parent, and only 7 percent with a widowed parent. And, as we will see, never-married parents have a variety of lifestyles.

Because the child's experience depends on the specific conditions in his or her family, it is difficult to generalize about the effects of being reared in a single-parent family. Many studies suggest, however, that children in single-parent families are at greater risk for developing emotional and academic problems.[6] This should not be surprising, as it is more difficult for one parent to provide as much nurturance, monitoring, and supervision as two parents, who have the additional benefits of greater resources and support from each other.

A major reason for the difficulties of single-parent families may be the increased rate of poverty. In 1996, the average income of female householders with children under age eighteen was $21,564; for male householders, $35,658; and for two-parent families, $49,858.[7] Half of all single parents are poor, and "no other major demographic group is so poor and stays poor for so long."[8] As we noted in Chapters 1 and 8, economic hardship and poverty bring stress, which decreases parents' abilities to be nurturant and effective in setting limits.

However, economic factors are not the only difficulties. In studies of single mothers committed to raising their children alone, single mothers reported more stress than did mothers in two-parent families, even when families were matched on education, income, and area of residence.[9] The single mothers had to work longer hours and were more worried about finances than were their married counterparts. The greatest difference between these two groups of mothers, however, was that single mothers had fewer social and emotional supports when their children were young. And it was precisely this kind of support that predicted optimal parent-child interactions in both single- and two-parent families. When single mothers had social-emotional support, their children's behavior was similar to that of children in two-parent families. Stressful life events such as poverty, which occurs more frequently in single-parent families, reduced overall parent effectiveness. Mobilizing both economic and social-emotional resources can help single-parent families function as effectively as two-parent families.

The Experiences of Unmarried Mothers and Their Children

Never-married parents are a heterogeneous group. Research has focused primarily on unmarried mothers, which include (1) young and older women who marry after the child's birth, (2) young and older women who do not marry, though some may live with the child's father, (3) single women who adopt a child, and (4) single women who bear a child from assisted reproductive technology, such as artificial insemination.

We look at the women and their lifestyles at the time of the child's birth and in the years following the birth and at the effects of their lifestyles on the child. Before we begin, let us note that this is not a well-studied area. The research comes from several national longitudinal surveys and studies that have gathered data on individuals for decades, such as, The National Survey of Families and Households and The Panel Study of Income Dynamics.

Unmarried Mothers at the Time of the Child's Birth

Four forces are considered to have influenced the rise of births to unmarried women: women's improved economic status, available benefits from welfare and public assistance, decreasing earning power of potential husbands and fathers, and greater social acceptance of births to unmarried women.[10] As we will see, unmarried mothers as a group have few economic advantages, and welfare benefits are shrinking; thus, economic sources of support to these mothers are reduced. Births to unmarried mothers can presage the child's development in compromised circumstances.

People think of unmarried mothers as being teenagers, but two-thirds of births to unmarried mothers are to women in their twenties and thirties, many of whom had their first child as an unmarried teen. African Americans and Hispanic Americans have higher rates of births to unmarried women than do European Americans.[11] Births to unmarried women are more likely for women of lower socioeconomic status, for women growing up in mother-only families, and for women in disadvantaged neighborhoods, in metropolitan areas, and in areas outside the South.

Some believe that over the past decade, more economically advantaged, unmarried women had children alone, but statistics through 1993 indicate that most often it continues to be poor, unmarried women in their thirties who have children and that the conditions of these women are much like those of teen mothers. Although almost half of these mothers worked 500 hours in the year prior to the birth of a child, about half were on welfare and not economically self-sufficient prior to the birth.[12]

Unmarried Mothers in the Years following the Birth

Those women who marry following the child's birth have family incomes that parallel those of children born to married parents. "This pattern suggests that the order of these two events—birth and marriage—[is] not as critical for demographic and economic outcomes as whether both events do occur."[13]

One study found that other actions mothers took after birth also had an impact on their economic self-sufficiency when the child was ages five to seven.[14] Those mothers who shared housing with relatives and got more education were more likely to be economically self-sufficient than were those who received welfare after the birth. Those who got valuable work experience and those who postponed an additional birth increased their chances of economic self-sufficiency.

As we noted, living arrangements for children born to never-married mothers are varied. In one sample about two-thirds of children born to unmarried mothers started out in a single-mother family, and about one-third reported not living in a single-parent family in the first year.[15] Many of this latter group of children were formally adopted or informally adopted by another family member, lived with their biological mother and father, or lived in a three-generation family (that is, with their mother and her parent or parents). Nearly half the sample lived with grandparents at some point during their childhood, often with but sometimes without the mother. Only 20 percent lived exclusively in a single-parent home through the first fifteen years.

Outcomes of Children Born to Unmarried Mothers

Children born to unmarried mothers take many paths to adulthood, and there is no one outcome characteristic of them all. One study found that living with two legal parents through adoption had a positive impact on children's high school completion, which in turn predicted their economic self-sufficiency in adulthood.[16] Living in a stepfamily with two parents did not produce such positive benefits and was associated with lower educational attainment and leaving home early. Living in a stable single-parent family, however, seemed to provide a secure base for children, who as adults did as well as or better than children living in other arrangements. They had more education and had slower transitions to independence. The stability of legally adopted children and the consistency children experienced in a stable single-parent home may have reduced the stress experienced by children in stepfamilies, who had many transitions to make.

Living with grandparents without the mother was related to lower educational attainment and to a higher probability of leaving home by age eighteen. Children who lived with their grandparents and mother in a three-generation family, in contrast, appeared to experience greater stability and achieve higher education than those who lived with their grandparents but not their mother.

Protective factors in the child, the mother, the parent-child relationship, and the larger social context buttress children from stress and predict positive outcomes for children.[17] In one study, eight protective factors were divided into four categories: the child's characteristics (positive sociability and attentiveness), maternal qualities (efficacy and low risk of depression), parenting qualities (positive parent-child relationship and the father's involvement), and qualities of the larger social context (social support and few difficult life experiences). In a sample of disadvantaged mothers, 95 percent of

When single mothers provide stable living arrangements and rely on positive, supportive parenting strategies, their children function effectively.

whom were never married, families averaged three out of the eight protective factors, and 20 percent of families had five or more protective factors.

Protective factors assessed when children were eighteen and twenty-one months of age predicted measures of cognitive and social functioning at forty-two months of age. All protective factors except the father's involvement predicted competent psychological functioning, as measured by low scores on a behavior problem index covering aggressive, anxious, depressed, hyperactive, dependent, and withdrawn behaviors. Only the child's characteristics and positive parent-child relationship predicted cognitive competence, as measured by higher scores on a school-readiness test. The most important aspect of the parent-child relationship for later well-being was the absence of harsh discipline. Economic disadvantage may have its greatest impact on families by intensifying maternal distress that leads to harsh discipline. The more protective factors in the child's family, the better the child functioned. Nevertheless, even the children with the greatest number of protective factors scored below average at the thirty-second percentile on the measure of school readiness.

The evidence from many studies, then, suggests that there is not a single outcome for children of never-married mothers. When children (1) have stable living arrangements through legal adoption, living in a three-generation family, or living with a stable single mother and (2) experience positive parenting, they have greater social and cognitive competence. As we can see, the same qualities that predict effective functioning in children in two-parent households predict positive outcomes for children of never-married mothers.

Marital or Partner Conflict

We have seen in earlier chapters that marital or partner satisfaction and intimacy are positive supports that contribute to parents' sense of well-being, their confidence, and their skills as parents. Nonetheless, even when parents are happily married, they argue. As we noted in Chapter 3, parents' disagreements need not distress children. When parents argue in moderate emotional tones and resolve their conflicts in mutually agreeable ways, children respond in the same way they do to friendly interactions. In fact, children can learn valuable negotiating skills. Even when anger is unresolved, children feel no ill effects if parents encapsulate the anger and confine it to the marital or partner relationship and refuse to allow it to spill over to the parent-child relationship.[18]

But unresolved conflicts affect children in two ways. Observed anger that goes unresolved directly affects children's physiological and social functioning in negative ways, as noted in Chapter 3. Second, marital conflict affects children indirectly by impairing parents' skills and behavior with children. When parents are unhappy with each other, they experience more anger, sadness, and guilt and frequently express these emotions in the family, becoming more negative and intrusive with children.[19]

Other aspects of conflict determine its effects on children as well. When conflicts are intense, center on child-related issues, and imply that the child is to blame, the child feels more upset. If parents directly explain to the child that he or she is not at fault in the argument, the child feels less distress, even when the conflict is intense and is associated with childrearing issues.[20]

In a negative atmosphere, children develop behavior problems. Children from high-conflict homes are at risk for developing (1) externalizing problems such as increased aggressiveness, noncompliance, and unacceptable conduct; (2) internalizing problems such as depression, anxiety, and social withdrawal; (3) problems in school such as poor grades; and (4) an angry, negative view of themselves and the world.[21] These problems persist, and in adolescence, both boys and girls who experienced parental disagreements in the preschool years are poorly controlled and interpersonally less skilled.[22] Boys also show difficulties in intellectual functioning. So, boys whose parents later divorce are already impulsive and poorly controlled ten years before the divorce.[23]

Again, the keys to minimizing the impact of conflict on children are to resolve the conflicts in mutually agreeable ways and to remove any feelings of self-blame the child may have about the conflict.

The Process of Divorce

When parents cannot resolve their conflicts, they often seek a divorce. Mavis Hetherington, who has carried out longitudinal studies of intact, divorced, and remarried families, describes four considerations that underlie all her research: (1) divorce is not a single event but an event that triggers many changes for children and parents over time; (2) changes associated with marital transitions have to be viewed as changes in the entire family system; (3) the entire social milieu—peer group, neighborhood, school, friendship network—will influence an individual's response to the transition; and (4) there is great diversity in the ways children and parents respond to marital transitions.[24] Most studies of families in transition focus on European American middle-class families, and we do not know how widely we can generalize these findings.

Hetherington and Kathleen Camara emphasize that divorce is a parental solution to parental problems.[25] Children often view divorce as the cause of all their problems. For both parent and child, however, divorce brings many related stresses. Financial problems arise; there is no way two families can live as cheaply as one. Often, mothers must go to work or increase their hours at work; as a result, children may see not only much less of their father, who is no longer living with them, but also less of their mother, who must work more. Reduced income means many families must move, so the child has a new neighborhood, new school, and new friends to deal with. As resources grow more limited, parents may become more irritable, discouraged, and impatient with children.

As the divorce rate has risen, society has begun to accommodate the needs of divorcing families. The legal system has changed, making it easier for both parents to continue to be involved in the care of children. With joint legal custody, mothers and fathers, though divorced, continue to make decisions about children, with each parent taking an equal part. Some have joint physical custody, in which children spend significant amounts of time with both parents. When parents have difficulty coming to agreement about custody issues, many states now provide court mediation services. Professional counselors help parents explore children's and parents' needs and reach agreement on reasonable living arrangements.

Further, laws have been passed to make it easier for single mothers to obtain child support payments decreed by the court. This is imperative because, as noted, mothers who are single heads of household have incomes far below those of other family units.

Telling Children about Divorce

When a couple decide to divorce, it is best if both parents together tell the children about the divorce before one parent leaves the home. Judith Wallerstein suggests wording like this: "We married fully hoping and expecting to love each other forever, but we have discovered that one (or both) of us is unhappy. One (or both) of us does

When a couple decide to divorce, it is best if both parents tell
the child before a parent leaves the home, even though doing so
is difficult and painful.

not love the other anymore. We fight with each other. The divorce is going to stop the
fighting and restore peace."[26] Parents present the decision as a rational, sad one:

> The goal is to present the child with models of parents who admit they made a serious
> mistake, tried to rectify the mistake, and are now embarking on a moral, socially
> acceptable remedy. The parents are responsible people who remain committed to the
> family and to the children even though they have decided to go their separate ways.[27]

When parents express their sadness at the solution, then children have permission
to mourn without hiding their feelings from adults. It is also important to express re-
luctance at the solution, because children need to hear that parents know how upsetting this will be for them: "Put simply, parents should tell the children they are sorry
for all the hurt they are causing."[28]

There are many things, however, divorcing parents should *not* say. First, they
should not burden their children with their own negative views of each other. Second,

they should not blame the other parent for all the problems. Third, they should not ask children to take sides—children usually need and want to be loyal to both parents. Parents may be surprised at the loyalty that children feel to both parents, to the marriage, and to the family. Even when one parent has abused the other spouse or the children, children often want the abusive parent present in the family. Moreover, when children are willing to accept a parent's absence, they often do not want anything negative said about him or her.

Wallerstein comments on how little support most children get as they go through the initial turmoil of divorce. Often, no one talks to them, no one listens to them talk about their feelings or answers their questions, and few relatives give added help and support. Children frequently are left on their own to manage as best they can.

To keep communication going, each parent should permit children to express their feelings and should guide the children into acceptable forms of behavior that remedy what can be changed. Parents need to hear that children may be angry at them or the other parent. Using active listening and sending I-messages are appropriate ways to keep channels of communication open.

Children's Reactions to Divorce

Emotional reactions to divorce, common to children of all ages, include sadness, fear, depression, anger, confusion, and sometimes relief; the predominant emotions vary with the child's age and require somewhat different reactions from parents.[29] In the preschool years, children often feel abandoned and overwhelmed; they worry that they may have caused the divorce. Although they usually try hard to handle their feelings with denial, they need parents who will talk to them and explain what is happening, not once but many times. Children may regress, begin wetting their bed, have temper tantrums, and develop fears. Parents can help most by providing emotional support. Outside interventions are not as useful as interventions by parents. Parents are urged to (1) communicate with the child about the divorce and the new adjustments, explaining in simple language the reasons for each change that occurs, and (2) reduce the child's suffering, where possible, by giving reassurance that the child's needs will be met and by doing concrete things such as arranging visits with the absent parent.

Preschool children are often protected initially by their ability to deny what is happening. Five- to seven-year-olds are vulnerable because they understand more but do not have the maturity to cope with what they see and hear. The most outstanding reaction of a child this age is sadness and grief. The child is not yet old enough or independent enough to arrange activities that will bring pleasure and some relief from the worry. The divorce dominates the thoughts of a child this age. One little girl, whose parents had just divorced, was asked what she would like if she could have just three wishes. Her reply: "First, that my daddy would come home. Second, that my parents would get back together. And third, that they would never, ever divorce again."[30]

Fear is another frequent response. Children worry that no one will love them or care for them. Their world has fallen apart and is no longer safe. Many children feel that only a father can maintain discipline in the family.

Children ages five and older may find outside intervention useful, and several weeks of counseling may help them sort out their feelings about the divorce, custody, and visitation. Counseling provides a neutral third party to validate children's feelings. When children are depressed, angry, and worried, it is reassuring for them to hear a professional person say, "Yes, this is a very difficult time, and it is understandable that you feel upset and sad." Children can then accept their feelings more easily.

In helping older children handle divorce, parents need to keep in mind that these children may feel responsible—they may believe they have done something that has brought about the divorce or that they could have fixed the marital difficulties. Parents need to say clearly and often, when opportunities arise, that the divorce *was not* caused by the children but that it was caused by difficulties between the parents. In addition, parents need to remember that children worry about them and how they are doing. It is not always possible for parents to confine their grief and distress to times when the children are not there, but parents can help children by trying to wait until they are alone to express sadness or anger.

The children of a divorcing or divorced couple need, perhaps more than anything else, to be able to talk with their parents about what is happening. Parents can encourage children to ask questions and to express their feelings. And they should respond to questions with clear statements. Children need to know what the practical arrangements for their lives are—where they will be living and with whom. And they need to know that their parents continue to care about their welfare and about their feelings.

Thus far, we have described the reactions of children who regret their parents' divorce, but some children, about 10 percent, feel relieved when their parents divorce.[31] Often, they are older children who have witnessed violence or severe psychological suffering on the part of a parent or other family member. These children feel that dissolution of the marriage is the best solution, and progressing from a conflict-ridden home to a more stable environment with one parent helps these children's overall level of adjustment and functioning.

From a follow-up of children fifteen years after the divorce, Wallerstein and Blakeslee conclude that it is very difficult to determine the long-term adjustment of the child based on the child's reactions at the time of the divorce.[32] Some children who seemed to have had very strong, disorganizing reactions were, nevertheless, doing well many years later, whereas others who seemed to have made a good initial adjustment had long-standing problems.

Parents' Reactions to Divorce

Parents' reactions to divorce are many and varied, but almost all are intense. They often suffer many symptoms—headaches, rapid heartbeat, fatigue, dizziness.[33] Their moods and behavior change at the time of the divorce, and these mood changes may be one of the most upsetting aspects of the divorce process for their children. Each parent may respond differently at different times, and both may show similar behavior only when they are angry with each other. Children are helpless in the face of their parents' extreme moods. One parent may be sad, depressed, and lacking in energy; the other may be busy, agitated, and preoccupied with his or her concerns. Both often lack self-esteem and seek out people or experiences to make them feel good again.

Divorced men and women both start dating again, though men date in larger numbers and older women tend to remain isolated and alone. Heterosexual relationships now become a source of anxiety and tension. Women wonder how to respond to sexual advances, and men worry about sexual performance. Nevertheless, new intimate relationships after divorce tend to boost parents' self-esteem.

Parents must deal with the intense feelings that arise during the divorce process, even if those feelings were not there in the beginning. They feel sad at the end of their marriage, even if the dissolution was necessary. They feel pain as the divorce becomes real—material possessions are divided, money is dispersed, and custody and visiting rights are arranged. Anger keeps the relationship alive for a time, but gradually detachment and distance signal that the marital relationship has truly ended. The loss is real.

Long-term emotional reactions to the divorce are diverse. Seventy-five percent of divorced custodial mothers report that at the end of two years, they feel happier than they did in the last year of the marriage. Many of these women go on to develop independent lives and careers that increase their self-esteem. Some divorced women, however, report depression, loneliness, and health problems six to eleven years after the divorce. Still, they do not have as many problems as nondivorced women in high-conflict marriages, who are more depressed and anxious and have more physical problems.[34]

Factors Affecting Adjustment to Divorce

Several factors influence how well a family adapts to divorce:[35] (1) the amount of conflict among family members, (2) the availability of both parents to their children, (3) the nature of the relationship changes in the family, (4) the responsibilities family members take, and (5) the defensibility of the divorce from the child's point of view.[36]

Moving from a household with two parents always in conflict to a stable household with one parent can lead to better adjustment for children.[37] Parents often continue the fighting when they live separately, however, and this is harmful to children; boys tend to react with undercontrolled behavior and girls with overcontrolled behavior.[38] It is possible that the increased conflict children witness during divorce, not the divorce itself, leads to their poorer adjustment. Increased conflicts can also occur between parents and children in a one-parent household in which the second parent is not available as a buffering agent. In addition, a parent may find the child a convenient target for feelings aroused by the other parent. In the midst of this raging conflict, the child feels very alone. Minimizing the fighting in all arenas aids everyone's adjustment.

Parents can help insulate their children from the conflict that accompanies a divorce. Box 9.1 lists some behavior characteristics of parents who work to protect their children from the parents' own conflicts.

When children have continuing relationships with both parents, they are more likely to adjust well following the divorce process.[39] It is impossible to predict how fathers, who are usually the ones to move out of the home, will respond after the divorce. Some previously devoted fathers find not living with their children so painful

BOX 9.1

Out of Harm's Way: Protecting Children from Parental Conflict

Children can continue to grow and thrive even through a divorce if their parents insulate them from intense or prolonged hostilities. Parents who are able to accomplish this share some important qualities:

1. They make it clear that they value their child's relationship and time both with them *and* with the other parent.
2. They work out a fair and practical time-sharing schedule, either temporary or long-term, as soon as possible.
3. Once that agreement is reached, they make every effort to live up to its terms.
4. They tell each other in advance about necessary changes in plans.
5. They are reasonably flexible in "trading off" to accommodate the other parent's needs.
6. They prepare the child, in a positive way, for each upcoming stay with the other parent.
7. They *do not* conduct adult business when they meet to transfer the child.
8. They refrain from using the child as a confidant, messenger, bill collector, or spy.
9. They listen caringly but encourage their child to work out problems with the other parent directly.
10. They work on their problems with each other in private.

Robert Adler, *Sharing the Children* (New York: Adler & Adler, 1988). Used with permission of the author.

that they withdraw and see less of the children. Some previously uninvolved fathers discover that caring for children alone on visits deepens their attachment, and so they increase their contact with their children. Fathers are more likely to maintain relationships with their sons than with their daughters. In fact, many mothers relinquish custody of older sons to fathers because they feel sons need a male role model.

Not only do children need relationships with both parents; they also need to be able to relate to each separately as a parent.[40] Recently divorced parents, however, often find it difficult to direct their energy to parenting. Thus, at this time of great need in the first year following divorce, when they actually need *more* attention, children receive less attention from their parents. Frequently, children's behavior goes unmonitored, and rules are not enforced. The parent outside the home often becomes highly indulgent and permissive with children; seeing so little of them, he or she hates to spend precious time disciplining them. But children function most effectively when both parents take time to monitor their behavior and enforce the usual rules, as in the past.

In the family with two households and both parents working, the need is greater for children to take on more responsibilities.[41] When demands are not excessive and are tailored to the abilities of children, then children may feel pleased by contributing to the family and developing greater competence. When the demands are too great, however—when they are given too much responsibility for caring for younger children or doing chores—then children become resentful, feeling they are being robbed of their childhood. Realistic demands for responsibility can help children grow in this situation.

Children seem better able to cope with divorce and its aftermath when the divorce is a carefully thought out, reasonable response to a specific problem.[42] When the problem improves after the divorce, children are better able to accept it. They are less able to deal with the impulsive divorce that may have had little to do with the marriage but was related to other problems in the parents' life. For example, one woman divorced her husband following the death of her mother. She later regretted the decision but could not undo what had hurt four people.

Protective Factors for Children

Protective factors for children as they adjust to divorce include qualities of the child, supportive aspects of the family system, and external social supports.[43] The child's age, sex, and intelligence serve as protection. Younger children appear less affected than elementary school children or early adolescents at the time of the divorce or remarriage. Because they are becoming increasingly independent of the family, late adolescents seem less affected than younger children. Boys appear to suffer more difficulties at the time of the divorce, and girls appear to have more problems at the time of the mother's remarriage. Intelligence can help children cope with all the stress.

The child's temperament also influences the process of divorce. An easy, adaptable temperament is a protective factor. In contrast, children with a difficult temperament are more sensitive and less adaptable to change; they can become a focal point for parental anger. In part, they elicit the anger with their reactive behavior; in part, they provide a convenient target for parental anger that may belong elsewhere.

For difficult children, the more stress they experience, the more problems they have. For easy children, the relationship is different. With moderate amounts of stress, easy children actually develop increased coping skills and become more competent than when stress is either low or high.

We have already touched on some forms of family interaction that are protective—reduced conflict between the parents, structure and organization in daily life, and reasonable assignment of responsibilities within the family. Mothers must be especially firm and fair in establishing limits with boys, as their tendency is to develop a vicious repetitive cycle of complaining and fighting.

Researchers point to siblings and grandparents as potential supports.[44] When family life is harmonious after divorce, then sibling relationships resemble those in intact families.[45] When there is conflict between parents, siblings fight, with the greatest difficulty occurring between older brothers and younger sisters.

Grandparents can support grandchildren directly with time, attention, and special outings and privileges that help ease the pain of the divorce. As one girl said, "If it weren't for my grandparents, I don't think I could have made it past sixteen."[46] Grandparents provide support indirectly by helping one of the parents. In fact, returning to live in the home of one's parents is a solution many young parents choose when they do not have the resources to live on their own. Grandparents can be loving, stable baby-sitters who enrich children's lives in ways that no one else can. The mother can work and carry on a social life, knowing that her child is well cared for in her absence. And this arrangement usually reduces living expenses. When the mother and grandparents agree on childrearing techniques and the mother is respected in the household as a mature adult, this solution may be attractive.

Such an arrangement, however, can reflect the neurotic needs of both the mother and the grandparents, and when this is the case, it is likely to create additional problems for the child. If the grandmother was a protective mother who refused to allow the daughter to become independent, that relationship may continue. The daughter may have tried to escape into a marriage that did not last. If the daughter returns to her parents' home, she may have to start again to develop her independence. She will have to establish new supports that will enable her to become more independent and to continue her growth as an individual.

School is another major source of support for children. Authoritative, kind teachers and peer friendships give pleasure and a sense of esteem to children. Educational and athletic accomplishments contribute to feelings of competence that stimulate resilience.

Some protective factors lie beyond a parent's control, including age, sex, and temperament of the child, but many lie within it, such as setting aside anger, establishing structure, monitoring behavior, and seeking out external supports for children.

Family Changes over Time

Previous sections have discussed children's and parents' reactions to divorce and factors affecting their adjustment to this major life change. In this section, we examine how these factors affect interaction among family members over time.

Right after a divorce, *custodial mothers* are under pressure because of all the changes occurring in their lives.[47] Many of these parents become more negative with their children than they were earlier, particularly with boys, and less involved in monitoring their behavior; a small group of these mothers, however, become too lenient and permissive. In response, both boys and girls become more anxious, demanding, aggressive, and noncompliant with peers and adults. As time passes, however, custodial mothers adjust and become more nurturant and more consistent in behavior management. Girls' behavior improves, and mother-daughter relationships often are very close. Relationships with boys improve somewhat, but many boys continue to have some behavior problems.

Custodial fathers initially complain of feeling overwhelmed, angry, confused, and isolated, but after two years, they report better adjustment, perhaps because they generally have greater financial resources and better support than mothers or because they typically get custody of older children.[48]

After the divorce, *noncustodial fathers* tend to become either permissive and indulgent or disengaged. They are less likely to be disciplinarians and more likely to play the role of recreational companion than are custodial mothers.[49] Many times, however, noncustodial fathers do not stay involved. One study reported that two years after the divorce, 25 percent of children had not seen their fathers in the past year; eleven years after the divorce, the number had risen to 50 percent.[50] More recent work indicates, however, that three and a half years after the divorce, two-thirds of adolescents still have contact with their fathers, even if only at holidays and over summer vacation.[51] Noncustodial fathers are most likely to stay involved when they feel they play an important role in their children's lives and their long-term development.

Noncustodial mothers of adolescents are more likely to stay involved than noncustodial fathers. Noncustodial mothers are more active and involved with and supportive of children than are noncustodial fathers, who often continue their role of recreational companion.[52]

Children's Behavior over Time

Children's behavior problems do improve over the first two years, but boys continue to have some difficulties six to eleven years after the divorce. Beginning at age ten, girls, especially early-maturing girls, show behavior problems as well. Both boys and girls are less competent in school, more defiant and noncompliant with rules, and more negative in mood—anxious, depressed, sometimes suicidal—as compared with children of nondivorced parents.[53]

Early adolescents' rule breaking and resistance to custodial parents' authority may result from the early autonomy and independence many experienced during the family adjustment period immediately after the divorce. They have been joint decision makers with their custodial parents, and parents have been less insistent and demanding that children meet family rules. Therefore, they feel entitled to pursue their own ends.[54]

In intact families, parents exert more constraint on early adolescents. They insist that teens do chores and follow the rules. These parents monitor carefully; there are more arguments and less harmony in intact families than in divorced families. Divorced custodial mothers, however, become careful monitors in mid-adolescence, especially with daughters. So, at a time when parents in intact families are disengaging and trusting children's judgment in mid-adolescence (age fifteen), divorced mothers are often becoming more authoritative.[55]

Children in divorced families resist custodial mothers' authority; these mothers are more successful and the children have fewer problems when another adult (such as a grandparent, *not* a stepparent) lives in the home and reinforces the mother's authority.[56]

Feeling caught between divorced parents who are in conflict intensifies adolescents' anxiety, depression, and poor adjustment.[57] Even when parents have high conflict with each other, adolescents can do well, provided parents do not put them in the middle. The feeling of being caught between parents contributes to these children's problems.

Again, we find great diversity in children's adjustment.[58] Although many children of divorce show aggressive and insecure behaviors in adolescence, others are caring, competent teenagers who cooperate with divorced parents and make significant contributions to family functioning. Still others are caring, responsible teenagers whose autonomy and maturity are accompanied by feelings of depression and low self-esteem. They appear to worry that they will be unable to meet the demands placed on them. Those children who have the most difficulty with externalizing behaviors do not have a single caring adult in their lives. Their parents are neglectful, disengaged, and authoritarian, and the children cannot find support outside the family.

Hetherington and her coworkers found in their studies of children in remarriages that one of the biggest stresses in the remarriage was children's experiences during the divorce.[59] Divorce, with all its changes and losses—changes in economic resources, schools, friends, neighborhoods, and the exposure to parental fighting—affects children in fundamental ways. "Witnessing parents demean and criticize one another in an environment of hostility may diminish the capacity of parents in two ways, as effective role models for and as socializers of their children."[60] The fighting may well destroy trust in the hierarchy of rational authority that two parents working together creates for children.

Paul Amato and Brian Keith reviewed ninety-two studies to determine the degree of difficulty children of divorce experience.[61] They concluded that divorce is associated with increased risk for problems in cognitive and social competence. But recent, better-controlled studies reveal that the differences between children of divorce and children in intact families are small and that there is much overlap in the functioning of the two groups.

Amato and Keith examined three possible sources of increased difficulties for children: parental loss, economic deprivation, and family conflict. Parental loss—whether as a result of divorce or the death of a parent—is a significant contributor to problems. Children who lose a parent through death experience difficulties similar to those of children whose parents divorce—shown by lower levels of well-being, poorer academic achievement, and conduct problems, as compared with children in intact families—however, they do score significantly higher on measures of well-being, academic achievement, and conduct than do children in divorced families. Further, when custodial parents remarry, the children's behavior and functioning generally do not improve. Finally, involvement of the noncustodial parent brings only modest improvement. So, although parental loss is an important factor, it is not the only cause of difficulties in children of divorce.

Similar findings occur with economic disadvantage. When studies control for income, children of divorce still appear to have more problems than do children in intact families, and when parents remarry and income increases, children's behavior problems continue.

The third factor, family conflict, appears to be the main contributor to children's difficulties. Children in high-conflict, intact marriages have greater difficulties in self-esteem and adjustment than do children in divorced families in which such conflict is reduced. The level of family conflict and family conflict resolution styles are more powerful predictors of children's overall adjustment status than is family status (intact, divorced, or remarried). Further, longitudinal studies indicate that as time passes after the divorce and, presumably, the conflict, the children's adjustment improves (except when a developmental stage such as adolescence increases problems for all families). Finally, when postdivorce conflict is low, children function more effectively. Thus, living in conflict—whether in an intact or a divorced family—appears to be the most powerful contributor to children's adjustment problems.

We now find that the effects of divorce do not necessarily end with childhood.[62] Young adults whose parents divorced when they were children (1) have lower educational attainment than adults from intact families, (2) earn less money, (3) are more likely to have a child out of wedlock, (4) are more likely to get divorced, and (5) are more likely to be alienated from one parent. Again, there is diversity of outcome. Most adult children of divorce function well within the normal range on most measures of adjustment. The only exception is in having poor relations with the father. Later in the chapter, we will examine general guidelines for parenting at times of marital transitions.

Should Parents Stay Together for the Sake of the Children?

Hetherington has conducted studies on divorce and remarriage and seeks to provide an answer to the often-asked question, "Should parents stay together for the sake of the children?"[63] The answer depends on the nature of the conflict in the marriage, the various changes that follow the divorce, the quality of the postdivorce family relationships, and the degree to which the custodial parent relies on authoritative parenting.

Before the Divorce

Research comparing children in low-conflict nondivorced families with children in high-conflict nondivorced families and with children whose parents later divorce indicates that (1) children in low-conflict nondivorced families are the most socially and psychologically competent children and have the fewest problems and (2) children whose parents later divorce fall between children from low-conflict and high-conflict nondivorced families and are not generally significantly different from either group with the exception that they score higher than children in low-conflict nondivorced families on measures of aggressiveness and lower than that group on cognitive agency. So, children are more disadvantaged in a highly conflictual family atmosphere than in one in which parents will later divorce. The reason may be that in high-conflict nondivorced families, parenting is less effective than in low-conflict nondivorced families. Parents are less positive and more negative. There is more conflict between parent and child and less effective monitoring of the child's behavior. Again, parents who will later divorce fall between the two groups, with only slight differences between the low-conflict nondivorced mothers and later-divorcing mothers. Later-divorcing mothers are more negative and less effective in control before the divorce. Hetherington concludes, "Before the divorce the family dynamics leading to divorce are less deleterious than those associated with extremely high levels of overt marital conflict."

In the first two years following divorce, a greater number of girls in both high-conflict and low-conflict divorced families scored in the range of clinical problems on a child behavior checklist than did girls in high-conflict and low-conflict nondivorcing families. A greater number of boys in high-conflict divorced families and a smaller number of boys in low-conflict divorced families scored in the range of clinical problems on the same checklist than did boys from low-conflict nondivorcing families. Boys in low-conflict divorced families and boys from high-conflict nondivorcing families did not differ from each other. Boys from low-conflict nondivorcing families had the smallest percentage of boys scoring in the clinical range.

Two years after the divorce, children from high-conflict families—whether divorced or nondivorced—had the greatest number scoring in the range of clinical problems. Girls from low-conflict families—whether divorced or nondivorced—had small numbers of girls scoring in the range of clinical problems. Although more boys in low-conflict divorced families than boys in low-conflict nondivorced families had clinical problems, the number was well below that of the number of boys from high-conflict families—whether divorced or nondivorced.

So, if conflict continues after the divorce, children might as well remain in a high-conflict nondivorced family and avoid all the trauma and changes of divorce. If, however, the divorce leads to a harmonious divorced family, then both boys and girls benefit, though girls appear to benefit more.

> The answer to our question about staying together for the sake of the children appears to be that if the stresses and disruptions in family processes, associated with an unhappy conflictual marriage and that erode the well being of children, are reduced by the move to a divorced single-parent family, divorce may be advantageous. If the diminished resources and increased risks associated with divorce also are accompanied by inept parenting and sustained or increased conflict, not only between the divorced couple but also between parents and children and siblings, it is better for children if parents remain in an unhappy marriage. Unfortunately, these "ifs" are difficult to determine when parents are considering divorce.[64]

Fathers' Role in Children's Lives

We saw in Chapter 8 that fathers' increased role in dual-earner families benefits children as well as mothers who are both working and rearing children. The question arises as to the effects on children of fathers' diminished role in the families of single mothers.

Father Absence

Using data from several national longitudinal samples, Sara McLanahan and Julien Teitler report the consequences of father absence for children's development and the factors underlying the consequences.[65] They report that in comparison with children growing up in two-parent families, children growing up apart from their biological fathers had lower grades, achieved less education, were more likely to drop out of school, and were less likely to get and keep a job. Adolescent girls in father-absent homes were far more likely to initiate sexual activity at an early age and to have a teen birth or a birth outside of marriage. In one study, 11 percent of adolescent girls in two-parent families had a teen birth, as compared with 27 percent of girls in father-absent families.

Youth in one-parent homes were also less likely to make an easy transition from school to work, and 12 to 25 percent were considered idle because they were neither in school nor at work. Even when ability levels were controlled for, family structure had a significant effect on the transition.

The effects of father absence on educational attainment did not vary as a result of gender or racial or ethnic status of the family. Boys and girls of all ethnic groups had reduced educational attainment when fathers were absent. Boys from families with higher educational levels had higher dropout rates when families were disrupted than did boys from families with less education. Father absence had a greater effect on the risk for teen births for European American and Hispanic American teens than for African American teens.

It did not seem to matter when father absence occurred or how long it lasted. Nor did it matter what family structure the child lived in, with one exception; children in homes with widowed mothers did nearly as well as children in two-parent families. Being born into a never-married family with more years of father absence did not increase the risk of problem behaviors, but the number of years living in a stepfamily without contact with the biological father had a negative effect and seemed to offset the benefits of marriage. In general, father absence matters more than the circumstances causing it, except in the case of widowhood.

Fathers' Contributions to Children's Lives

McLanahan and Teitler looked at fathers' contributions in three ways but cautioned that these three features—financial, social, and community—may be the result of another, as yet unidentified, factor. They point to fathers' financial contribution, which improves the resources available for childrearing. Without the additional resources, families may not have services such as health care and may live in poorer neighborhoods with poorer schools and fewer community services. They estimate that reduced income accounts for approximately 50 percent of the effects of father absence.

These researchers estimate that about half the disadvantage of father-absent homes results from a loss of social capital, seen in poorer parent-child relationships and poorer relationships with adults, and resources in the community. As we have noted, it is extremely difficult for one parent to provide as much time, attention, and balance in parenting as two parents; nevertheless, some single-parent mothers are able to establish low-conflict homes in which children's functioning improves.

In contrast to McLanahan and Teitler, who have used large sociological surveys to support their views, Paul Amato has examined the psychological literature and con-

ducted new analyses of data to determine fathers' contributions to children's lives.[66]
He looks at both mothers' and fathers' contributions in terms of human, financial, and
social capital. *Human capital* refers to parents' skills, abilities, and knowledge that contribute to achievement in our culture. A useful measure of human capital is parent's
education. *Financial capital* refers to the economic resources available to the family to
purchase needed goods and services. *Social capital* refers to family and social relationships available to promote children's development.

Amato distinguishes between the benefits of the coparental relationship and those
of the parent-child relationship. In a positive coparental relationship, the child views a
model of how two people relate, cooperate, negotiate, and compromise. Children who
learn these skills are likely to get along better with peers and later partners. In providing a unified authority structure to children, two parents teach that authority is consistent and rational. Amato writes,

> Social closure between parents helps children to learn and internalize social norms
> and moral values. Also, a respect for hierarchical authority, first learned in the family,
> makes it easier for young people to adjust to social institutions that are hierarchically
> organized, such as schools and the workplace.[67]

As we have noted in earlier chapters, marital satisfaction and spousal support help
parents to be effective in their individual relationships with children. The parent-child
relationship provides many benefits to children in terms of affection, support, and
help in learning regulated behaviors.

Looking at many studies, Amato demonstrates that children's well-being is positively associated with (1) the father's education, (2) the father's income, (3) the quality
of the coparental relationship, and (4) the quality of the parent-child relationship.
These relationships hold in two-parent and one-parent families as well, even in studies
where mothers' contributions are controlled for.

In his own longitudinal study, Amato interviewed individuals originally studied as
children and followed up to early adulthood. Unfortunately, the percentage of children living with single-parent families was insufficient for a comparison group, so all
the children studied were reared in two-parent families. There was, however, sufficient
information on mothers' contributions to control for them and look at fathers' contributions alone.

Amato finds that fathers' education and income are related to children's education
and that children's education has positive implications for such areas as friendships,
self-esteem, and life satisfaction. Fathers' characteristics appear to account for more
variance in children's education, self-esteem, and lack of psychological distress than
mothers' characteristics. Mothers' characteristics account for more variance in children's developing kin ties and close friends than fathers' characteristics. Fathers' and
mothers' characteristics account for equal amounts of variance in life satisfaction.
Amato summarizes,

> Current research suggests that fathers continue to be important for their contribu-
> tions of human and financial capital. Current research also suggests, however, that
> children benefit when fathers are involved in socioemotional aspects of family life . . .

the current trend for fathers to be less involved in their children's lives (due to shifts in family structure) represents a net decline in the level of resources available for children.[68]

Examining a host of studies, Amato believes that nonresidential fathers who see their children for fun activities but do not take an active parenting role contribute minimally to their child's development. He concludes that fathers matter "to the extent that they are able to provide appropriate support, guidance, and monitoring—especially if this occurs in the context of cooperation between the parents."[69]

Encouraging Fathers' Participation

James Levine, the founder of the Fatherhood Project in 1981 at the Bank Street College of Education in New York, has written extensively on the advantages for children and fathers of fathers' increased involvement regardless of whether fathers are married to mothers.[70] He identifies three lessons he has learned over the years.

The first important ingredient in successfully involving fathers is the recognition that fathers want to be involved and can be effective parents with preparation and help. Second, single fathers need a support network that guides their behavior. Third, women play a key role in supporting men as fathers.

Figure 9.1 describes the "on-ramps" that facilitate men's connections with their children and families. Such on-ramps come from those in the community who interact with fathers—at the hospital, at doctors' visits, at schools. Levine writes,

> Our model does not absolve any man from primary responsibility; indeed, it holds that all fathers—whether unmarried, married, or divorced—are responsible for establishing and maintaining connection to their children. But it broadens that responsibility so it is also shared appropriately by all those in the community who, in their everyday work, have the opportunity and the capacity to build—or influence the building of—the on-ramps to connection.[71]

As Levine mentioned in his interview in Chapter 5, the context of interactions with fathers can help involve them. One example is the Hospital Paternity Establishment Program in West Virginia, which has increased the number of unwed fathers who establish paternity from 600 per year to 3,000 per year. Recall that changing expectations emphasize that new fathers need education about establishing paternity and that they need to be approached in terms of the benefits to the father and the child rather than to the state. Hospital staff were educated to involve fathers when they visited their newborns. Fathers then met with professionals, such as a child psychologist, who could explain the psychological importance of the father to the child; a doctor, who could explain the medical importance; and a lawyer, who could discuss the legal benefits to the child of having a father who is known. "Public education is the key," says Gary Kreps, who designed the program. "We need to start educating both moms and dads about the importance of fathers. And we need to educate teachers, counselors, coaches, the clergy, parents, and anybody who works with kids. And we need to educate our politicians."[72]

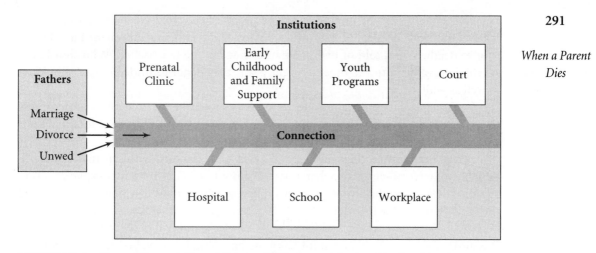

FIGURE 9.1   Connection—A Shared Responsibility. James A. Levine with Edward W. Pitt, *New Expectations: Community Strategies for Responsible Fatherhood* (New York: Families and Work Institute, 1995), p. 41. Reprinted with permission from the author.

When a Parent Dies

According to Earl Grollman,

> One of the greatest crises in the life of a child is the death of a parent. Never again will the world be as secure a place as it was before. The familiar design of family life is completely disrupted. The child suffers not only the loss of the parent, but is deprived of the attention he needs at a time when he craves that extra reassurance that he is cared for.[73]

Many of the changes in the family that occur at the time of a divorce occur in the family that experiences the death of a parent. The whole family must come to terms with a profound loss that brings with it many changes. One parent assumes all the responsibility for childrearing, there may be financial changes, and, certainly, there will be changes as one parent takes on both roles without relief. But there are important differences, too. A surviving spouse usually has greater financial support from insurance. Sympathetic support from both sides of the family is usually available. And conflict is reduced because the death is most often seen as no one's fault. Still, it is a very traumatic experience for all involved.

Telling Children

How does one tell a child a parent has died? Exactly what is said depends on the age of the child and the family's view of death.[74] Very young children (below age five) have a limited conception of death and may consider it a reversible condition—one dies but comes back to life at a later time. Between ages six and eight or nine, children recognize that death happens and is irreversible, but they believe it happens mainly to other people. Because logical thinking is not yet established, children may associate unrelated events with death. For example, one boy had heard that Abraham Lincoln was shot to death. When told of his grandfather's death, the boy asked, "Who shot him?" As children move into the preadolescent years, they begin to understand death about as well as adults do.

In giving explanations about death, parents should be truthful and should phrase the information in a way that makes sense to the child. The child's questions will indicate the need for more information, which the parent can then give.

Because each situation is unique and needs to be handled with sensitivity, it is impossible to determine exactly what a parent should say. Grollman lists explanations to avoid. If they do not believe it themselves, parents should not describe heaven and tell the child that the dead parent is happy for eternity. A child will sense the discrepancy between what a parent says and how the parent feels and will become more confused. It is also unwise to say that a parent has gone on a long journey, because the child may focus on the return or feel angry at being abandoned. One child, told that his mother had gone on a journey, cursed every time he heard her name until he was told she had died and was shown her grave. When he understood his mother's absence, the boy was sad but no longer felt abandoned or rejected by her. It is unwise as well to say that the parent died "because God loves good people and wants them in heaven." If goodness is rewarded with death, the child may shun good behavior or assume that those who live long lives are, in some undetectable way, bad. Finally, when death is equated with sleep, some children begin to fear sleep and are unwilling to go to bed.

Dealing with Children's Reactions

Once the information about a parent's death is given, how will the child experience the grief? John Bowlby describes three phases similar to those experienced by adults: (1) protest, when the child cannot accept the death and tries to regain the parent, (2) pain and despair, as the child gradually accepts the death, and (3) acceptance and hope that life goes on.[75]

Experts agree that after the child has been told of the parent's death, the child should be included in as much of the funeral and formal mourning process as seems comfortable to parent and child. Experts also agree that unless the child protests he or she should view the body to understand that the parent is truly gone. This is not a rigid rule, however, and is not recommended if either parent or child feels upset or if the body of the dead parent has been disfigured by disease or injury. During the mourning period surrounding the funeral and burial, family members may be surprised when young children, although devastated with grief, scamper away to play, only to cry bitter tears an hour later. Parents should not hold back their own tears, and they should not discourage children from crying. Tears are a healthy release of emotion, and many books on grief and mourning recognize the healing quality of tears. Also, parents should not encourage children to "Be brave!" or "Be a little man!" Rather, they should say realistically, "Yes, this is a hard time for you. Life is very sad now." Such statements acknowledge grief without minimizing it. Parents, however, should not insist on a display of grief.

responses.[76]

1. *Denial:* "I dreamt it! Mommy is coming home tomorrow." The child cannot accept the death because it is too painful.

2. *Anxiety expressed in bodily symptoms:* The child develops symptoms the dead parent had or symptoms expressing tension and sadness—"I can't eat" or "I have stomach pains."

3. *Hostile reactions:* "Why did Mommy leave me like this?" These reactions may be very upsetting to the surviving parent.

4. *Guilt:* "Daddy died because I didn't wash the dishes right. I killed him."

5. *Anger:* The child shows anger at such people as doctors, nurses, or the surviving parent, who did not do what they should have to save the parent.

6. *Panic:* "Who will love me now?" The child anticipates being abandoned by the remaining parent through death or remarriage.

7. *Replacement:* The child looks for a family member or friend who will move in and take the parent's place.

8. *Taking on mannerisms or habits of the deceased parent:* The child tries to be like the dead person in interests, activities, and personal traits as a way of replacing the person who died.

9. *Idealization:* "No one can say anything against Mommy. She was wonderful."

Healthy mourning may include some or all of these reactions. Mourning becomes unhealthy when such reactions persist many months after the death and interfere with a return to satisfying activities. It is important to note that some children and adults may react so strongly during the grieving period that they hallucinate about the dead person.

A frequent reaction to the death of a parent, and one that has to be handled carefully, is guilt. Young children in particular often assume they are personally responsible for what happened even though they are in no way involved. The surviving parent must be very alert to pick up on statements suggesting guilt and should introduce the possibility that the child feels guilt, even if the child has not mentioned it. For example, a parent might say, "Sometimes when a person dies, those close to her wonder if something they did was related to the death. I sometimes think, 'Would things have been different if I had called the doctor sooner?' But I know everything was done that could be done. Do you ever wonder or have thoughts like that?"

Thomas Gordon gives the example of a mother who actively listened as her three-year-old asked such painful questions as, "When is Daddy coming home?" and "Where did they put him?"[77] One night, two months after the father's death, the boy awoke and began sobbing that his daddy was dead. As the mother reflected his distress, the boy was able to talk about how much he missed his father and wanted him back. The mother thought that after this expression of feeling, her son seemed less anxious about the death. The child continued to ask many questions that were hard for the mother to answer, but she responded as well as she could, without criticism or complaint.

When parents understand and accept their child's feelings and respond with empathy and love, they help the child move through the grief process. As memories of the parent are recalled and relived, the death gradually becomes real. At times, the child may want to express unbearable pain or anger by striking at pillows or engaging in some physical activity. This can be encouraged. The child's individual reaction to death always should be respected. Grollman sums up the most helpful parental responses:

> Demonstrate in word and touch how much he [the child] is truly loved. A stable and emotionally mature adult who accepts the fact of death with courage and wisdom will bring the truth to the youngster that the business of life is life. Emotional energy formerly directed toward the absent person must now be directed toward the living. This does not mean wiping out the memories of the deceased. Even in death, the absent member can and should remain a constructive force in family life and be remembered in love without constant bitterness or morbidity.[78]

Remarriage

As many as 35 percent of children, 54 percent of women, and 60 percent of men live in second marriages.[79] Remarriage provides many benefits to parents. First, it provides emotional closeness, intimacy, and sexual satisfaction. In caring relationships, parents feel greater self-esteem, contentment, and happiness. Second, parents have someone with whom they can share both the financial and caregiving responsibilities. Wallerstein and Blakeslee find that many parents do not repeat the mistakes of the first marriage.[80] Although remarried parents report feelings of stress and depression related to the many demands they experience, the marriages still are as happy as those in nondivorced families, perhaps because the couples are more pragmatic in their expectations and in seeking solutions to problems.[81]

We know most about remarried families that consist of the custodial mother, her children, and the stepfather, who may or may not have children. There are fewer studies of stepmothers. Few studies focus on marriages of single mothers with children, even though these may have many characteristics of stepfamilies.

Challenges of Stepfamilies

Stepparenting is more demanding than parenting in intact families for several reasons.[82] First, a stepparent does not have long-standing emotional bonds with the children to help all of them overcome the feelings of frustration and stress that occur as a result of remarriage.

Second, stepfamilies include more people than does a nuclear family, and all have different needs and interests to consider. There are husbands and wives, their biological children, ex-spouses, stepbrothers and stepsisters, half-brothers and half-sisters, and stepgrandparents. Parents have the multiple tasks of solidifying and maintaining marital ties while sustaining relationships with their biological children and promoting positive sibling relationships.

Third, members of stepfamilies may have deep feelings of jealousy and ambivalence. Because so many more people are involved and the newly married parents want to devote time to their relationship, stepparents may have less time to give to individual children. Children may feel that the new marriage is depriving them of their parent. Parents must accept those feelings as realistic—there *is* less time for each child. Conversely, the parents may feel that the children are intruding on the marriage.

Fourth, both parents and children are haunted by the earlier marriage. Stepparents may feel insecure, as they live with children who are constant proof that the spouse loved another person. Further, the biological parent usually continues to have contact with the former spouse because of the children.

Fifth, former spouses may use the children and their needs to attack the biological parent and the stepparent. One father and stepmother reported that the mother never bought the children clothes, and when the father did this in addition to making the monthly child support payment, the mother would not launder them. Conversely, one mother reported that the father and stepmother, rather than providing money for clothes for the children, instead bought the children fancy clothes that were appropriate for the lifestyle of the father and stepmother but not for the children's needs at school and play.

Sixth, there are no clear guidelines for being a stepparent. There are few enough for biological parents, but the role of stepparent remains even more vague. The stepparent must create his or her role according to his or her individual personality, the ages and sexes of the children, and the family's living arrangements. Stepparents who are forewarned about the problems of stepparenting and who think and talk in advance about how to cope with these problems can find their new roles rewarding and exciting.

Family Changes over Time

Just as parents' behavior changes after a divorce, *remarried custodial mothers'* behavior changes as well at the time of the remarriage.[83] These mothers become more negative and less controlling, and there is much conflict between mother and children, particularly with daughters. If children are eight or younger when parents remarry, improvements occur with time. When children are nine or older, there are slight improvements, but monitoring and control stabilize at lower levels than in intact families. Regardless of the child's age at remarriage, conflicts increase in early adolescence and relationships are more conflictual than in intact families. Even in mid-adolescence, children remain more distant from their custodial, remarried mothers.

When children live with *remarried custodial fathers*, it is again girls who have greater difficulty.[84] Frequent contact with their biological mothers seems to increase the difficulty, but this unusual finding may be the result of biological mothers' having special problems that argued against their having custody. However, the longer girls live in such families, the more positive the relationship grows between the daughter and the stepmother.

There are no differences in how biological parents parent their own children in nondivorced and remarried families. Regardless of family status, mothers and fathers are warmer, more supportive, and closer to their biological children than to their stepchildren, and their children are more often closer to them.[85]

Interview

with Emily Visher and John Visher

Emily Visher, a clinical psychologist, and John Visher, a psychiatrist, are founders of the Stepfamily Association and authors of such books as *Stepfamilies: Myths and Realities* and *Old Loyalties, New Ties: Therapeutic Strategies with Stepfamilies*.

You have worked with stepparents and stepfamilies for many years, so I want to talk to you about what you feel are the important things for parents to do in order to ease the difficulties that can arise in stepfamilies.

E. Visher: We talk about a parenting coalition that is the coalition between all the adults in the child's life. For example, you see, there could be three or four parenting adults—if both parents have remarried, there will be four. If those adults can somehow develop a working relationship around raising the children, the loyalty conflicts of the children will be much less. The adults will get a lot out of it, too, because there is less tension, and better relationships develop between stepparent and stepchild.

We chose the word *coalition* because it means a temporary alliance of separate entities for accomplishing a task. The households and couples are separate, and it is a temporary alliance between all the adults. The task they are working on together is raising the children.

Families can flounder on the basis of the stepparent's trying to be a parent and the children saying basically, "I've got a mother or a father." We have moderated panels of teenagers in stepfamilies, and we always ask them, "What do you want your stepparents to be? What is their role?" I don't think we have ever heard anyone say anything other than "a friend." The difficulty is that by "friend," they mean something very different. They don't mean a pal; it's closer than that.

They are able to talk to the stepparent in a meaningful way that is different from the way they would talk to a parent. They are freer to talk to a stepparent because they are not so involved. One teenager on a panel said she wanted her stepfather to be her friend, and then later she said, "I love my stepfather, and I've never told him." She's saying she wants a friend, but she has very deep feelings for him. He was in the back of the room and heard her.

It is important to take a role that is satisfying to the adult and to the child, and that may be different for children living in the same household and for children in different households. The relationship is different depending on the age of the child—a six-year-old needs something different from a sixteen-year-old. For the young child, the stepparent may well become a parent.

J. Visher: The only power the stepparent has as a parent is delegated from the remarried parent.

E. Visher: The adults need to be supportive of one another. Together they need to decide what the house rules are, and the parent of the children takes care of enforcing the rules until a relationship is set up.

J. Visher: Another major tip is to develop realistic expectations about what it is going to take to make everything work. So many people feel that they have failed after a few weeks or months, that the remarriage has faltered because things are chaotic. It takes four or five years for things to settle down and for people really to get satisfaction out of the whole family relationship.

One of the keys is for people to inform themselves by reading or talking to other people who also are in stepfamilies. They learn that making the stepfamily work takes time and that you shouldn't expect close family relationships quickly.

The most common pattern now is for children to move back and forth and feel part of two households. If all the adults form a parenting coalition, then children are most likely to feel they belong in both places.

Working out the parenting coalition so that it is at least civil makes an enormous difference to everybody. The children can go through the remarriage smoothly if there is not constant warfare. Sometimes parents who divorce or separate are tied together in bonds of anger. The anger can reflect an inadequate separation between the biological parents. They keep together by fighting.

E. Visher: Truman Capote said, "It's easy to lose a good friend, but it's hard to lose a good enemy." The anger ties you together. Hostility eats you up, and you are not free to go on.

J. Visher: Most people don't understand how much damage they are doing to themselves and to the children. Sometimes people say, "How can I work with that S.O.B. when I couldn't even stay married to him?" We say maybe you can split off the part that does not want to be married to him and share the parenting experience.

E. Visher: What the children need from that parent is different from what the spouse needed.

What can you do to decrease the hostility?

J. Visher: One thing is to trade assurances between the households that you are not trying to take the child away from them or trying to get the child to like you better. Often, in a single-parent household, the parent is afraid of further loss, afraid that the ex-spouse and his or her new spouse will encourage the child to stay there and the child will want to because it is a more attractive place or there is more money. This fear fuels the anger and makes the parent cling to the child more and try to influence the child to turn against the other parent.

E. Visher: So we think that sometimes the anger is not left over from the former marriage but has to do with the fear that builds up between the two households, the fear of more loss. The other household becomes a threat, and the ex-spouses become like enemies rather than like people trying to raise a child. The parents are afraid of each other, and they are not aware that the anger substitutes for fear. If they are more aware of it, they can deal with it.

Also important is the guilt the remarried parent feels. He or she feels guilty that the children have been unhappy through the death or divorce and then the remarriage. That parent has a real investment in its being a big, happy family right away. Yet they have difficulty setting limits for the children who live there or visit there. The stepparent goes up the wall.

(continued)

(*continued*)

Sometimes they feel that to form a good couple relationship and make that primary is a betrayal of their relationship with their child. The parent-child relationship is different from the relationship with the spouse.

J. Visher: There may be an unusually strong bond between parent and child; perhaps it has lasted for many years, and the new spouse is a rival. It becomes a power struggle between spouse and child for the loyalty of the biological parent. The child is sometimes suddenly out of a job as confidant.

E. Visher: I don't think people realize the change for the children, that now they have to share. One mother described that she and her daughter had lived together for five years. When she came home from work, she talked to her daughter. Now that she is remarried, she talks to her husband. That one little thing is not so little, as the daughter has to share her mother.

No matter what the age of a child at a parent's remarriage, *stepfathers* initially feel less close to their stepchildren than to their biological children, and they do not monitor behavior as well as fathers do in intact families. When children are relatively young at the time of the remarriage, stepfathers may be able to build relationships with stepchildren by taking on the role of a warm and supportive figure and foregoing the role of disciplinarian until a relationship is established. Preadolescent boys may settle down in a relationship with a stepfather, but preadolescent girls usually resist stepfathers' overtures and direct angry, negative behavior to the custodial mother.[86]

When children are early adolescents at the time of the remarriage, there appears to be little adaptation to the new family over a two-year period.[87] Children are negative and resistant even when stepfathers attempt to spend time with them and establish a relationship. As a result, stepfathers remain disengaged, critical, and distanced from the day-to-day monitoring of children. The negative behavior of the children shapes stepparents' behavior more than stepparents shape children's behavior. When, however, stepparents can be authoritative parenting figures—warm, positive, appropriate in monitoring—then children's adjustment improves. With adolescents, stepparents fare better when they are authoritative from the start.

Adolescents at the time of the remarriage are often resistant, withdrawn, and unwilling to become involved with stepparents. They frequently retreat from the families and establish strong relationships with families of friends. At the same time, they become more argumentative with the biological parents, both the custodial and noncustodial parent. Their emotional attachment to the parent is shown in a negative rather than a positive way. As noted, adolescents feel closer to noncustodial mothers than to noncustodial fathers.[88]

In stepfamilies, marital happiness has a different relation to children's behavior than it has in intact families.[89] In nondivorced families, marital happiness is related to children's competent functioning and positive relationships with parents. In stepfami-

If people are aware of the losses for the children in the new structure, they can acknowledge those changes with the children and do things differently—sit down with the children alone and talk. When children sense their feelings are accepted, they will talk about them. One stepmother commented to her stepson that when the father talked to the son, she felt left out, and she wondered if he felt left out when the father talked to her. He agreed he did, and they talked about it. There was not a lot they could change, but after they had the talk, they got along better.

J. Visher: We hope that as people are more informed, they will be able to deal more effectively with the situation.

lies, marital happiness is related to children's negativistic and resistant behavior with parents. Girls may be especially resentful of the loss of the close relationship with their custodial mother. Boys, having less to lose, may settle more easily into a relationship with a stepfather. Nevertheless, adolescent daughters respond positively to the satisfying marital relationship, perhaps because it serves as a protective buffer to an inappropriate relationship between stepfather and stepdaughter.

Relationships with siblings are less positive and more negative in remarried families than in nondivorced families.[90] Sibling relationships in divorced families fall between these two groups and do not differ significantly from either of them. Although girls tend to be warmer and more empathetic than boys, they are almost equally aggressive. As siblings become adolescents, they become more separated from each other. Interestingly, relationships with their stepsiblings appear less negative than relationships with their own siblings.

Children's Behavior over Time

Children's adjustment in stepfamilies varies. There are often initial declines in cognitive and social competence after the remarriage, but when boys are young and stepparents are warm and authoritative, problem behaviors improve, and boys in these stepfamilies have levels of adjustment similar to those of boys in nondivorced families. Young girls continue to have more acting-out and defiant behavior problems than do girls in intact or divorced families.[91]

Most gender differences in adjustment disappear at early adolescence, when both boys and girls have more problems. At all ages, children in remarried families, like children in divorced families, have poorer school performance, problems in social responsibility, and more rule-breaking behaviors than do children in intact families. Parenting by the same-sex parent, whether custodial or noncustodial, is positively related to the child's adjustment.[92]

BOX 9.2

Eight-Step Program for Strengthening Ties in Stepfamilies

STEP 1: NURTURING THE COUPLE'S RELATIONSHIPS

  a. Plan something you like away from home once a week.

  b. Arrange 20 minutes of relaxed time alone each day.

  c. Talk together about the running of the household at least 30 minutes each week.

STEP 2: FINDING PERSONAL SPACE AND TIME

  a. Create a special "private" place for parents and for each child who lives or visits there.

  b. Take at least 2 hours a week to engage in personally enriching activities—reading, television, hobby, sports.

STEP 3: NOURISHING FAMILY RELATIONSHIPS

  a. Share with one another every day something each family member appreciates about the others—perhaps at dinner or in less formal settings.

  b. When expressing appreciation, avoid discussing negative feelings or problems.

STEP 4: MAINTAINING CLOSE PARENT-CHILD RELATIONSHIPS

  a. Have parent and child do something fun together for at least 20 minutes once or twice a week.

  b. Provide these times no matter what, and do not make them dependent on good behavior.

Although some children in remarried families have adjustment problems, the majority do well. Between two-thirds and three-quarters score within the average range on assessment instruments. Although this falls below the comparable figure of 90 percent for children of nondivorced parents, it indicates that most children in remarried families are doing well.[93]

As with children of divorced families, children of remarried families are at a disadvantage in early adulthood.[94] Compared with children of nondivorced parents, they are more likely to leave home at an early age, less likely to continue in school, and more likely to leave home as a result of conflict. As adults, they feel they can rely less on their families. Still, there is diversity of response, and many of these children feel close and supported in stepfamilies.

Many of the difficulties stepfamilies encounter can be avoided or lessened if they are anticipated and prepared for. Box 9.2 lists eight steps that stepfamilies can take to strengthen their ties.

STEP 5: DEVELOPING STEPPARENT-STEPCHILD RELATIONSHIPS

a. Do something fun together 15 or 20 minutes a week—if a child visits only occasionally, make this a longer time.

b. Accept a child's refusal, and offer to do something at a later time.

STEP 6: BUILDING FAMILY TRUST

a. Schedule a family event once a month, and give each member a chance to choose what to do.

b. Begin special traditions in the remarried family.

c. Do not always schedule events when nonresident children are visiting, because resident children may believe they are less important.

STEP 7: STRENGTHENING STEPFAMILY TIES WITH REGULAR FAMILY MEETINGS

STEP 8: WORKING WITH THE CHILD'S OTHER HOUSEHOLD

a. Give adults in the other household positive feedback once a month.

b. Give positive messages without expectation of reciprocation.

Adapted from Emily Visher, "The Stepping Ahead Program," in *Stepfamilies Stepping Ahead*, ed. Mala Burt (Baltimore: Stepfamilies Press, 1989), pp. 57–89. Used with permission from the Stepfamily Association of America.

Typologies of Stepfamilies

Based on his ten-year study of 100 stepfamilies made up of custodial mothers, stepfathers, and young children and a controlled sample of 100 nondivorcing families, James Bray has provided a basic understanding of developmental issues facing stepfamilies.[95] His major findings include:

1. A stepfamily has a natural cycle of changes and transition points.

2. A stepfamily takes many years to form a basic family unit.

3. The greatest risk to the stepfamily occurs in the first two years, when about 25 percent of remarriages fail.

4. In a stepfamily, there is no honeymoon period of high satisfaction followed by a gradual decrease, as there is in a first marriage; in a stepfamily, marital satisfaction starts at a moderate level and builds up from there or decreases to the point of divorce.

5. A stepfamily has four basic tasks to achieve cohesion:
   a. integrating the stepfather into the family,
   b. creating a satisfying second marriage,
   c. separating from the ghosts of the past, and
   d. managing all the changes.

6. A stepfamily eventually takes one of three forms: *neotraditional, matriarchal,* or *romantic*—neotraditionals almost always succeed, matriarchals succeed much of the time, and romantics are at great risk for divorce.

The neotraditional family is described as a "contemporary version of the 1950s, white-picket fence; it is close-knit, loving, and works very well for a couple with compatible values."[96] The matriarchal family is one in which the wife-mother is a highly competent woman who directs and manages all the family activities. The romantic family seeks everything the neotraditional family does but wants it all immediately, as soon as the marriage occurs. The romantic family is at great risk for not surviving the conflicts and changes of the first two years. The three types of families do not differ in the crises and turning points they face, but they do differ in their expectations and their willingness to change their expectations and their behaviors to solve the problems they confront.

The first cycle of change stepfamilies experience in the process of their formation occurs in the first two years of the remarriage. It is a stressful period for all members of the family as they find ways to live together, deal with ex-spouses and noncustodial parents, and form a stable unit that brings everyone happiness. Parents' adjustments are often complicated by their unrealistic expectations about how well everyone will get along and how quickly love will form between family members. Such expectations are natural, but they have to be revised in the light of experience.

By the end of two years, the second cycle begins; family members find mutually satisfying ways of getting along, and a family unit is established. Tensions are reduced, and happy stepfamilies resemble nondivorced families. A third cycle of change occurs when children move into adolescence, become more insistent on independence and individuality, and often seek new relationships with noncustodial parents, stepparents, and custodial parents.

Neotraditional families are successful in navigating the changes because they give up unrealistic expectations and because they communicate feelings and solve problems. Bray describes the neotraditional family as having the ability to (1) identify and express feelings clearly, (2) identify and understand other family members' thoughts, feelings, and values so differences are bridged, (3) resolve conflicts, (4) state a complaint so the other person feels empathy for the complaint, (5) establish new rituals that help define the family as a unit, and (6) feel acceptance of other family members.

Matriarchal families are organized with the mother as the leading decision maker. If the spouse or children resist at any point, then difficulties occur. These women, however, are highly resourceful and competent; they often recognize when they themselves must change to meet the demands of the situation.

Romantic families seek the same cohesiveness and close ties that neotraditional families do, but they find it very difficult to give up unrealistic expectations and solve the problems at hand. They deny there are special difficulties in a stepfamily and expect everyone to behave as though this is a first marriage. For example, they are unprepared for the divided loyalties children feel and their attachments to noncustodial parents, and they feel hurt when children do not transfer all their affections to the stepfamily. They get stuck in their hopes and desires and do not develop strategies to deal with the realities of everyone's feelings. Thus, in the second cycle, when other families feel less stress, these families are rehashing the unresolved issues of the first cycle.

Bray reports that despite the crises and difficulties of remarriage, many stepfamilies succeed and form stable, cohesive family units that give all members a sense of warmth and accomplishment. A significant number of stepfamilies do not succeed, however, and dissolve the marriages because the parents do not have the commitment to work through the problems to reach a joint resolution. Because these parents have already survived the unhappiness of one divorce, they know they can survive another and may be quicker to seek it in order to end the stress of the remarriage. A third group of families stay together and seem happy enough, but they lack a sense of vitality and seem to "just get by." These families do not want open communication or to really understand each other and instead choose habitual ways of relating to each other.

Bray asked successful families what got them through all the stressful periods. "The consistent answer was commitment. Commitment to a life together, not just getting by but living and loving fully, communicating about issues, building a stable family, and enjoying a good life together."[97]

Lesbian and Gay Parents

Lesbian and gay parents are a heterogeneous group.[98] The majority of lesbian and gay parents have children in the context of heterosexual marriages and later divorce, adopt a lesbian or gay identity, and rear children with partners of the same sex. These families have all the stresses of remarried families with the additional pressure of prejudice against lesbian and gay parents. Much of the initial research done on lesbian and gay parents and their children has been conducted in order to prevent their being denied custody of and visitation with their children.

A growing segment of lesbian and gay parents are those who choose parenthood after the adoption of a lesbian or gay identity. They are usually living with partners and choose to have a child through assisted reproductive technology or surrogate parenthood. The child may have a biological relationship with one parent, and the other parent becomes a coparent through legal adoption of the child; or the child may have no biological relationship with either parent. A single lesbian or gay person may have a child in the same way.

Divorced Lesbian and Gay Parents

The largest group studied has been divorced lesbian mothers. Concerns have focused on their mental health and on their sex-role behavior and its effects on children. Most studies have compared lesbian and heterosexual mothers and find no differences between them on self-concept, overall psychological adjustment, psychiatric status, sex-role behavior, or interest in children and childrearing. Divorced lesbian mothers are more worried about custody issues than are divorced heterosexual mothers. They are more likely to be living with romantic partners. Studies reveal no differences between biological fathers of children of lesbian mothers and fathers divorced from heterosexual mothers in terms of paying child support, but fathers in the former group are more likely to have frequent visitation.

Research is just beginning on such topics as when and how lesbian mothers should reveal their sexual identity to children. Although there is no firm agreement, it is thought best to avoid doing this during the child's adolescence so that the child's own sexual identity and identity formation can occur without distraction.

Much less is known about divorced gay fathers. There is no research comparing the psychological stability of gay and heterosexual divorced fathers, perhaps because men do not often seek physical custody. Comparing gay and heterosexual divorced fathers' parenting behaviors suggests that gay fathers are more responsive, more careful about monitoring, and more likely to rely on authoritative parenting strategies than are heterosexual divorced fathers. Studies of the family lives of gay fathers, teen sons, and fathers' partners indicate greater family happiness when the partner has a good relationship with the adolescent boy. Comparisons of divorced lesbian mothers and gay divorced fathers reveal that gay fathers report more income and more frequent sex-stereotypic toy play.

Lesbian and Gay Couples' Transition to Parenthood

In the 1990s, many lesbian and gay individuals in committed partnerships chose to have children either through assisted reproductive technology or through adoption, but such couples often faced prejudice and added difficulty in a situation that is stressful enough. Little research has addressed the questions of how and when lesbian and gay couples decide to have children. Research has focused instead on how lesbian and gay couples make the transition to parenthood and divide the responsibilities of childcare and household work.

In lesbian partnerships, the biological mother takes primary care of the child in the earliest months, but nonbiological parents often report an immediate attachment to the child and take a larger role when the child is twelve months or older. When compared with heterosexual couples, there was more equal sharing of childcare and household work in lesbian partnerships than in heterosexual marriages. Lesbian partners, when compared to heterosexual couples, report a high level of relationship satisfaction and greater satisfaction with the division of labor. Nonbiological mothers were seen as more knowledgeable about childcare and more willing to assume equal care of the child than were heterosexual fathers.

A study comparing single and coupled lesbian mothers with single and coupled heterosexual mothers found that (1) single heterosexual and lesbian mothers were warmer and more positive with their children than were coupled heterosexual mothers, and all lesbian mothers were more interactive with their children than were single heterosexual mothers; and (2) single heterosexual and lesbian mothers reported more serious, though not more frequent, disputes with children than coupled heterosexual mothers.

In a study of gay fathers choosing parenthood, gay fathers reported higher self-esteem and fewer negative attitudes about homosexuality than did gay men who elected not to become fathers.[99] There are few other differences between the two groups of men, and the author speculates that higher self-esteem may result from parenthood rather than be a determiner of it.

Children of Lesbian and Gay Parents

A major question of research has been whether lesbian and gay parents influence the gender identity of their children in the direction of lesbian/gay gender identity and same-sex sexual orientation (choice of partner). There is no evidence that children of lesbian and gay parents have an increased likelihood of having a lesbian/gay gender identity or same-sex sexual orientation. Nor is there evidence that they are at increased risk of sexual abuse in lesbian or gay homes.

Children living with lesbian and gay parents are as well adjusted and socially competent as are children living with heterosexual parents. Children of lesbian parents show no special problems with self-concept, gender identity, or sexual orientation. The results of research on lesbian and gay parents and their children indicate that the sexual adjustment of the parent is not predictive of the child's adjustment and that family process variables operate in much the same way in lesbian and gay families as in heterosexual families—that is, when parents are warm and involved, as many lesbian and gay parents are, their children do well.

Parenting Tasks at Times of Partner and Marital Transitions

Research suggests several things parents going through family breakups or transitions can do. First, these parents should maintain positive emotional relationships with children. Even if there is pronounced conflict between parents, parent-child relationships can be satisfying if parents make a special effort to keep children out of the conflict. Parents need to make time for the open communication of feelings, for asking and answering questions, and for sharing enjoyable activities. These same rules apply to relationships with stepchildren.

Second, parents must learn effective ways of resolving conflicts, regardless of who is involved. (See Box 9.1, which lists suggestions for minimizing harm from conflict between parents, and Chapter 3 for a discussion on effective ways of dealing with anger between parents and children.) According to Amato, the most important thing society can do to promote safe and secure environments for children is to encourage parents to learn ways to resolve conflicts within marriages and to settle disputes if they get divorced so children are not put in the middle.[100] It is children's feelings of self-blame, whether parents are married or divorced, that contribute to children's poor adjustment to life.

Third, parents need to model and encourage positive relationships with all family members—siblings, grandparents, and all the relatives involved in stepfamilies. (See Box 9.2, which lists many suggestions for stepfamilies.)

Fourth, parents need to help children seek positive experiences in their own social milieu—with friends, relatives, schoolmates, and teachers. These supports help children cope in times of change.

Finally, parents need to recall that at times of marital transition, they need to do all the things that are beneficial in nondivorced families, but they need to do more of them to buffer children from the stress of change. It is harder to do these things when parents themselves are under stress. Still, parents promote children's growth and competence in all times of change when they foster close, positive emotional relationships with children and monitor their behavior carefully to ensure that it falls within appropriate limits.

The Power of Authoritative Parenting

Hetherington's work,[101] as well as that of other researchers,[102] reveals that regardless of family structure (one or two parents, biological parent or stepparent, lesbian or gay parents), regardless of ethnic background or age or gender, children do well with authoritative parenting. When parents are able to be responsive to children's needs and individuality and also monitor and control behavior, children function well. Similarly, regardless of family structure, children do poorly with authoritarian and harsh, demanding parenting. Authoritative parenting not only contributes to positive parent-child relationships but also builds positive sibling relationships, which increase child competence.

Main Points

Single parents are

- a heterogeneous group made up of never-married, separated or divorced, and widowed adults with children
- more frequently women than men, with 27 percent of families with children headed by women and 5 percent headed by men
- most effective when they organize stable living environments and use authoritative parenting

The process of divorce

- is often preceded by marital conflict, which upsets children and arouses their feelings of self-blame
- is a major disruption for all family members
- involves many changes that affect economic resources, neighborhood, school, friends
- places stress on children and parents, which can be reversed if parents establish low-conflict divorced homes

Protective factors for children at the time of divorce include

- a child's age, sex, intelligence, and temperament
- manageable amounts of stress and appropriate support from grandparents and other relatives
- educational and athletic accomplishments that contribute to children's feelings of competence and stimulate resilience

Children's behavior

- becomes more problematic at the time of divorce but improves as time passes
- is less carefully monitored in single-parent homes in early adolescence
- improves when parents resolve their anger and use authoritative parenting

Men make positive contributions to children's development when

- they provide their human, financial, and social capital to the family
- the social context encourages their involvement

Parents' role in helping children cope with a parent's death is to

- include children as active participants in the funeral and formal mourning process
- offer children many opportunities to express their feelings
- accept children's feelings as they go through stages of grief
- provide a model of an adult who grieves but who goes on with life

When parents remarry, they

- experience many emotional benefits such as closeness, intimacy, and sexual satisfaction
- do not necessarily repeat the mistakes of the first marriage
- experience stress as they integrate everyone into a new family with few guidelines

When parents remarry, children

- differ in their reactions, with girls having more difficulty in adjusting to parents' remarriage than do boys
- show initial declines in social and cognitive competence
- show improvements in behavior, following an initial decline, when parenting figures are warm and authoritative

Stepfamilies

- often have unrealistic expectations about how quickly closeness and cohesiveness of family members develop
- need empathy and communication skills to work through the crises and conflicts that occur in the first two years

Lesbian and gay parents

- are as effective as parents in heterosexual marriages
- have children who function as well as children of heterosexual parents
- have more equal sharing of childcare and household work

Parenting tasks at times of partner and marital transition include

- maintaining positive emotional relationships with children
- learning effective conflict resolution skills
- relying on authoritative parenting strategies
- modeling positive relationships with the extended family
- encouraging children to have positive experiences in their own social world

Exercises

1. Suppose your friend's parents divorced when he or she was a small child and now your friend fears intimacy and commitment. What could you do to help him or her be less fearful? What advice could you offer your friend to lessen such fears? In a class discussion, share your ideas on how to advise your friend.

2. Imagine that your married brother, sister, or friend came to you and said he or she was getting a divorce and wanted help in making arrangements so his or her eight-year-old daughter and six-year-old son would experience the fewest negative effects. What guidelines would you give your relative or friend?

3. Pair off with a classmate, preferably of the same sex. Imagine one of you is eight and the other fifteen years old. One of your parents has just married your partner's parent; you are now stepbrothers or stepsisters. Discuss how you feel now that you are going to be living intimately with each other—perhaps sharing a room, having your time with your biological parent reduced so the parent can spend time with this stranger, having the amount of money available to you dependent on the needs of these new people. Would being older or younger make a difference in your reactions? Describe what your parents could do to ease the adjustment process.

4. Attend divorce court for a morning, and summarize the cases presented there. What issues do parents argue about? What issues about children arise? Describe whether you agree with the judge's ruling, and state why.

5. Write a script for what a mother and stepfather might say to the mother's two children (ages nine and thirteen) and the stepfather's two children (ages six and nine), who visit every other weekend, about their expectations of how they hope the children will get along and how the parents will handle arguments as they arise. What rules can parents set for children of these ages? What will the stepfather's role be?

Additional Readings

Bray, James H., and John Kelly. *Stepfamilies: Love, Marriage, and Parenting in the First Decade.* New York: Broadway Books, 1998.

Cummings, E. Mark, and Patrick Davies. *Children and Marital Conflict: The Impact of Family Disputes and Resolution.* New York: Guilford, 1998.

Hetherington, E. Mavis, ed. *Coping with Divorce, Single Parenting, and Remarriage.* Mahwah, NJ: Erlbaum, 1999.

Lamb, Michael E., ed. *Parenting and Child Development in Nontraditional Families.* Mahwah, NJ: Erlbaum, 1999.

Levine, James A., and Edward W. Pitt. *New Expectations: Community Strategies for Responsible Fatherhood.* New York: Families and Work Institute, 1995.

Visher, Emily B., and John S. Visher. *Stepfamilies: Myths and Realities.* New York: Ticknor & Fields, 1989.

10

Parenting at Times of Trauma

WHEN TRAUMATIC EVENTS OCCUR, PARENTS FACE enormous challenges. What reactions can parents expect from children? What can parents do to help children cope? Which children are more likely to suffer long-term effects from traumatic events? What can parents do to protect children from violence and enable them to feel secure in a world that is sometimes unsafe?

This chapter focuses on various forms of violence and maltreatment children may experience: exposure to family violence, sexual abuse, physical abuse, neglect, and violence in the community. We look at definitions and the incidence and prevalence of such behaviors, ways children react to such experiences, and ways to help them deal with their experiences. We also focus on how parents can help children take actions to minimize their risk of violent encounters.

Victimization of Children

The discussion of violence and abuse in this chapter is divided into five areas for clearer comprehension. However, David Finkelhor and Jennifer Dziuba-Leatherman[1] caution that fragmenting the study of violence against and abuse of children into separate areas has prevented social scientists from recognizing and developing a general field of victimology of children to "highlight more clearly the true vulnerability of children to victimization, the overlap and co-occurrence of different types of victimization, and the common risk factors and effects."[2]

Children are more prone to victimization than are adults. Throughout childhood, they are more often subject to family violence, and adults report beating them harder than they beat spouses. Children are also at greater risk for sexual abuse.

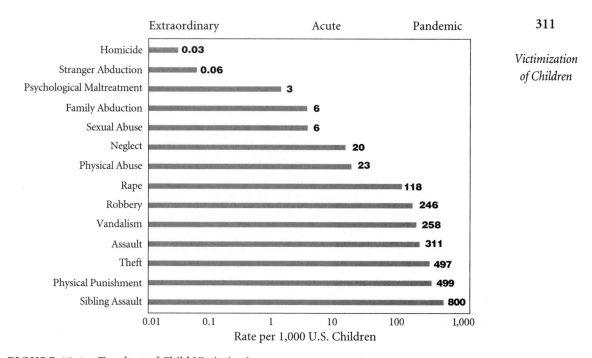

FIGURE 10.1 Typology of Child Victimization. David Finkelhor and Jennifer Dziuba-Leatherman, "Victimization of Children," *American Psychologist* 49 (1994): 176. © 1994 American Psychological Association. Used with permission.

Teenagers are more subject than adults to all the crimes reported by adults, and both children and teenagers experience forms of assault that adults do not—such as sibling assault.

Figure 10.1 shows the rates per 1,000 children for various kinds of violence and abuse and serves to highlight the many dangers with which children live. Finkelhor and Dziuba-Leatherman group forms of victimization into three categories: (1) the *pandemic* (frequent events affecting most children, such as sibling fights), (2) the *acute* (events that affect a small but significant percentage of children, for example, neglect and sexual and physical abuse), and (3) the *extraordinary* (events such as kidnapping and homicide). The most frequent events, experienced by five to eight of every ten children, are sibling assault, physical punishment (usually by parents), and theft. These events are rarely studied, but they should be, because so many children experience them and report fears about them.

Children are more at risk for victimization than are adults for several reasons. First, children are more dependent on others for care. The concept of neglect, for example, has no meaning in regard to independent adults. Second, children are small and less cognitively mature and cannot easily protect themselves from older children and adults. Third, children have less choice about their surroundings and associates than do adults. They have to live at home and have to go to school, so they are forced into contact with abusive people. They cannot leave.

It may be not only unwise but also difficult to separate the various kinds of abuse, because there is considerable co-occurrence of the different types. In one sample, all 70 children experienced more than one form of abuse; in another, 90 percent of 160 children experienced more than one form.[3] Maltreatment of a single kind may be quite rare in reality.

Over time, research in these areas has become more sophisticated; samples are better controlled, several different measures of children's functioning are used, and more longitudinal studies are being carried out. There is concerted effort to delineate the specific effects of abuse separately from the effects of low socioeconomic status or accumulated stress from negative life events. Even so, more controls are needed. Children are often described as either abused or not abused. They are not described in terms of the severity or frequency of abuse or by the closeness of their relationship with the perpetrator. These factors make a difference.[4] As such, researchers are exerting an increasingly greater effort to control them. As we get more information on these topics, our understanding of the effects of abuse and violence will become more refined.

A major conclusion from the more sophisticated studies of both physical and sexual abuse is that there is no one path, no one set of risk factors, and no definite set of characteristics that qualify as "the effects" of abuse.[5] Jay Belsky wrote in 1993, "All too sadly, there are many pathways to child abuse and neglect."[6] And, we can add, there are many effects triggered by the abuse. In the following section, we will examine a model that describes the many factors that lead to abuse and violence and their potential consequences, but first let us look at the criteria of violence.

In 1994, approximately three million children were reported to Children's Protective Services (CPS) for suspected abuse. About a third—one million cases—were substantiated.[7] Of this million, 54 percent were cases of neglect, many of which may have been associated with poverty. About one-quarter involved physical abuse, 11 percent were primarily sexual abuse, 3 percent were emotional neglect, and 6 percent were outside of these categories.

Population surveys result in higher figures.[8] A Gallup poll of a representative sample of one thousand American families reported in 1995 that 5 percent of children met the criteria of physical abuse, and approximately 2 percent met the criteria for sexual abuse. These are ten to sixteen times higher than the rates reported to official agencies.

The criteria for establishing abuse must be specified. For example, because Finkelhor and Dziuba-Leatherman consider spanking as physically violent, they categorized far more children as being victimized than does Gallup's poll, which defined physical abuse as being hit with an object (reported for only 5 percent of the children).

Robert Emery and Lisa Laumann-Billings believe it might be useful to distinguish between family *maltreatment,* characterized by minimal physical, sexual, or psychological harm, and family *violence,* characterized by serious physical injury, sexual exploitation, or psychological trauma.[9] This distinction is made not to minimize the physical and psychological effects of maltreatment but to separate cases that need supportive services from those that require serious coercive intervention, such as the removal of the child from the home. At present, so many resources go into investigating cases and making sure violence exists that little remains for the larger number of families in which maltreatment is the problem. At present, these families receive little treatment, guidance, or support to help them learn to manage aggressive feelings more appropriately.

An Ecological/Transactional Model of Community Violence and Child Maltreatment

Dante Cicchetti and Michael Lynch propose a model of how community violence and child maltreatment affect children's development.[10] Although this model was not applied to sexual abuse, it is relevant in that area. This transactional/ecological model describes how the child's characteristics and the characteristics of the caregiver and the environment interact to shape the child's development. Risk factors for development are those events or people that increase the possibility of a negative outcome; protective factors serve to buffer children from the impact of negative events and promote a positive outcome.

Risk factors can be divided into two groups: (1) enduring, or ongoing, factors and (2) transient, or fluctuating, factors. An enduring risk factor for child maltreatment might be a parent's history of being abused, and a transient risk factor might be a parent's loss of a job. An enduring protective factor might be a child's easygoing temperament, and a transient protective factor might be a sudden improvement in the family's financial status. When risk factors outweigh protective ones, child maltreatment is likelier to occur.

Using Urie Bronfenbrenner's ecological model of development described in Chapter 1, we can envision child maltreatment and community violence at several levels. At the *macrosystemic level*, cultural beliefs promote violence and abuse. For example, as a society, we believe in spanking, in the acceptability of force to settle disagreements, in the importance of sexual gratification for potency or manliness, and in the rights of adults to treat children as property and to do with them what they want. All of these beliefs at the macrosystemic level contribute to a climate that encourages violence toward and maltreatment of children.

At the *exosystemic level* are the social structures that influence children's development. Because young children are no longer primarily in the care of mothers or close relatives, they have more exposure to male figures who are not related to them and who may view them as sexual objects. The economic structure is such that many families with children live in poverty, a risk factor for both community violence and child maltreatment. Community structures sometimes lack the supports that enable parents to be more nurturant and caring with children, such as good schools that provide afterschool recreational programs for children, easy availability of immunization programs and other preventive health services, and parenting programs. Neighborhoods with a high degree of social isolation among residents are at greater risk for child maltreatment. In some instances, supports may be there, but maltreating parents move so often that they do not get connected to support systems.

Factors at the community level can interact with factors at the family level. For example, a neighborhood with high unemployment and drug addiction may have a higher rate of violent crime than a less-stressed community; the prevalence of violent crime can in turn add to the distress of an unemployed father, who then becomes more physically punishing with his son. Unemployed parents lack the resources needed to move out of such neighborhoods and have to deal with the ongoing frustrations that interfere with their parenting.

Children also experience violence at the *microsystemic level* in daily interactions with siblings, parents, peers, and teachers. Both parents and children bring their individual characteristics to these interactions. Parents who maltreat children, as compared with those who do not, are more likely to have experienced abuse in their own childhood. Still, the majority of adults who have been abused do not abuse their children. Abusive parents tend to form unstable, conflictful adult-adult relationships,[11] and they interact with children in many negative ways besides the actual abuse. They are less satisfied with their children and use more disciplinary techniques than do nonmaltreating parents. They want their children to be independent but insist that they meet unrealistically high standards. Abusive parents quite often reverse roles and expect children to act as their caregivers.

Children's individual characteristics also can influence the likelihood of abuse. There is the child's sex; in several studies, boys were found to be more likely to experience physical abuse[12] and girls more likely to experience sexual abuse.[13] The child's age is a factor; the median age for sexual abuse is about eight,[14] but approximately one-third of sexually abused children are under six.[15] Physical abuse peaks between the ages of three and eight. Although children appear to be less at risk after age eight, recent data show that adolescents are subject to significant abuse as well.[16] This finding may be a function of more careful reporting of adolescent injuries. Children who are physically abused may be noncompliant and difficult to care for, but this behavior most likely results from rather than causes negative caregiving.

Finally, children experience violence at the *ontogenic level*—that is, in how they develop as an individual. Cicchetti and Lynch identify five areas that may be problematic for children's development following abuse: the attachment relationship with the parent, regulation of emotion, self-concept, peer relationships, and adaptation to school and learning.

Children who have been either physically or sexually abused by parents may develop an insecure attachment to that parent and internalize a negative working model of relationships. Abuse suggests to children that they are basically unlovable, unacceptable, and unworthy of being cared for, and so they internalize a working model in which they are unworthy and the other person is undependable and unavailable. These working models are carried over into other relationships, and unless intervention occurs, they create lifelong problems in relating to others. Violence experienced in the community might have no demonstrable effect on children's attachment to parents, though it can serve to strengthen attachment if parents are seen as especially supportive.

As a result of abuse and violence, children may be unable to regulate their own emotions. Their feelings of anxiety, anger, or sadness may overwhelm them. Or they may handle the emotions by blunting them and suppressing feelings. If their caregivers are not reliable figures who can help them process the feelings or if, in fact, a caregiver

315

*An Ecological/
Transactional
Model of
Community
Violence and
Child
Maltreatment*

is the *cause* of the feelings, then children have an added burden: they have very intense feelings and little external help in coping with them. Some studies even suggest that abused children have fewer words for feelings than nonabused children and are less skilled in identifying the feelings of others.

Children who experience both physical and sexual abuse tend to have negative attitudes about themselves. When they are older, they see themselves as less competent and less worthy than their peers. Their self-descriptions contain mostly negative terms.

In view of their insecure attachments, their difficulties in regulating their feelings, and their negative self-perceptions, it is not surprising that many abused children have problems with peer relationships. They are more likely than nonabused children to be aggressive with their peers and less positive and caring in interactions. Even more sadly, abused children are in special need of positive peer relations because of their negative family atmosphere, yet they have the greatest difficulty forming them. Finally, their capacity for learning and for adjusting to school may be compromised, because they cannot regulate their feelings and are quick to feel frustrated with tasks and with peers.

The model developed by Cicchetti and Lynch describes risk factors that exist at the cultural, societal, and familial levels and the many ways that abuse may affect an individual's development in several areas. This model also has implications for interventions. First, there are interventions at the microsystemic level, with the individual and the family—helping them deal with the situation, the feelings that arise from it, and the problems that ensue.

Then there are interventions at the exosystemic level—helping parents and children reach out to social agencies and social structures such as schools and community organizations to get support to enable the family to cope. Community and state agencies offer a variety of programs to train parents in anger management, stress reduction, and effective disciplinary techniques. Comprehensive programs seek to preserve the family by meeting its many needs for such services as financial and household management, help in finding employment, and alcohol abuse treatment. They provide broad-based services while the family stabilizes and becomes involved in a network of agencies that can continue to meet these needs.[17] These services reduce the need for social agencies to provide out-of-home living arrangements for abused children.

Community agencies also identify high-risk parents who because of their own characteristics (for example, substance abuse) or characteristics of their children (physical injuries or conditions that make care very difficult) are in need of special services to prevent possible abuse.[18] These agencies provide, often in the home, training and modeling in appropriate caregiving and help parents adopt effective problem-solving skills.

Finally, there are interventions at the macrosystemic level—changing the societal views of violence and sexuality that permit victimization of children. Although this is a complicated process, giving all parents training in effective caregiving and childrearing strategies makes abuse less likely.[19] Requiring parent training as part of a junior high or high school education not only provides needed skills but also sends a strong social message about the importance of parenting skills. Abuse of children affects the entire society; we all must live and interact with those who are hurt by abuse and, additionally, must provide services to deal with the hurt.

Currently, there is only limited research on the most effective forms of intervention. But all levels of intervention appear necessary to help children and prevent the recurrence of abuse.[20]

Dealing with Child Abuse and Violence

As noted by Finkelhor and Dziuba-Leatherman, children in U.S. society are at risk for a variety of traumatic experiences. Among them are exposure to family violence, sexual abuse, physical abuse, neglect, and community violence. Because all have the potential to cause lasting physical and psychological harm, parents must handle such situations with care.

Exposure to Family Violence

Although concerns about family violence between intimate partners have increased over the past three decades, children's exposure to family violence was not discussed in the research literature until the 1980s, and even now, the body of knowledge in this area is limited.[21] The term *domestic violence* encompasses many behaviors and can vary in meaning depending on who uses the term. Legal definitions emphasize acts of physical harm (including forced sexual acts and threats of harm) carried out against intimate partners. Clinical definitions are broader and, in addition to physical and sexual attacks, include economic coercion and psychological attacks against intimate partners. The term *exposure* (to domestic or family violence) is used rather than *witness* to include children who hear the violence, see the effects of the violence, or are involved in interrupting the violence by calling the police. Although exposure to family violence refers to violence between adults, one suspects that children who are exposed to parent-child abuse of a sibling suffer many of the same problems.

Most studies focus on male abusers and female victims, yet a review of several studies suggests that men and women are equally likely to be victimized, but it is women who sustain the more serious injuries. Domestic violence occurs in many different kinds of families.[22] One study identified five different patterns: (1) ongoing/episodic male battering, (2) female-initiated violence, (3) male-controlling violence, (4) separation/divorce violence, and (5) psychotic/paranoid violence.

Children are involved in domestic violence in various ways. In one study, children were involved in the onset of the violence in 20 percent of the incidents.[23] They were involved in making 10 percent of the 911 calls. In a review of several studies, 40 to 70 percent of children from violent homes were also physically abused, and 40 percent of physically abused children came from violent homes.

PREVALENCE   There are no reliable national statistics on the prevalence of domestic violence, though it is estimated that 3 to 10 million children are exposed to domestic violence.[24] Exposure to domestic violence begins in utero, as attested by the fact that 16 percent of women questioned in prenatal clinics reported spousal abuse, and half of them reported several incidents.[25] Severe abuse during pregnancy was also correlated with drug and alcohol use, smoking, low maternal weight gain, and delay in getting prenatal care. An intensive, five-city research project found that children, particularly young children, were more likely to be in homes with domestic violence.[26] Homes with domestic violence also included other risk factors such as poverty, substance abuse, single-female heads of household, and heads of household with limited education.

EFFECTS ON CHILDREN   Children may have a range of reactions to domestic violence, depending on their age and temperament, the specific nature of the violence, its severity and chronicity, and their involvement in it.[27] Children's emotional responses to the events include terror, fear of death, and fear of loss of the parent. As a result of the violence, children may experience the world as a hostile, unpredictable place, where disaster may strike suddenly. There is growing evidence that young children who witness extensive partner conflict and violence are at risk for neurobiological changes in brain structure, which in turn affect later neurological development.[28] The nature of the violent arguing determines how the brain will internalize the experience. If the child is terrified, the brain may be in a constant state of hyperarousal, which will make it difficult for the child to absorb cognitive stimulation and information.

Children suffer a variety of symptoms. When compared with children from nonviolent homes, children exposed to domestic violence are at higher risk for physical symptoms of insomnia, nightmares, tics, and bed wetting.[29] They are more likely to have increased externalizing behavior problems (aggressiveness, temper tantrums, fighting with peers) and increased internalizing problems (anxiety, fear, depression, loss of self-esteem). They also score lower on measures of verbal, motor, and cognitive skills and have poorer concentration and attention for schoolwork.

INTERVENTIONS   The first form of intervention is to help the nonviolent parent establish a safe and stable home.[30] Parents who live with domestic violence sometimes develop *posttraumatic stress disorder* (psychological symptoms in response to an unusual, dramatic event); as part of this disorder, they may become desensitized to violence in the home and minimize the events and thus fail to protect the child as the situation would warrant. Feeling hopeless, helpless, and depressed, the victimized parent may not be available to the child as a caregiver or as a source of help in coping with the events. Thus, outside help to the family is first directed to the parent and to efforts to stabilize the home so that the parent can serve as the primary source of help for the child.

Second, the child needs an explanation of the violent events and an opportunity to express the feelings triggered by the violence. Third, parents provide honest answers to their child's fears and worries and offer as much reassurance as is possible and realistic given the circumstances.

Crisis counseling in homes or in shelters can help children adapt to what has happened.[31] Group therapy programs give children an opportunity to talk about the violence, improve their self-esteem as they realize this happens to other children, reduce their feelings of guilt, and develop safety skills.

In addition to services provided to the child and family, there are community interventions such as educating teachers to help children cope with violence. Sometimes young children spontaneously talk about domestic violence or write about it. Teachers must be prepared to deal with these situations sensitively and effectively so that problems do not continue. Community interventions also educate health care, legal, and law enforcement professionals on ways to respond to victims of domestic violence in sensitive and effective ways. Broader community action includes preventive programs designed by health care and educational systems to make the public aware of the necessity of reducing domestic violence.[32] A major stumbling block, however, is the cultural belief that domestic violence is not wrong or harmful but a personal matter between two adults. Educating the public as to the negative effects of such violence on adults and children and providing opportunities for learning more effective ways of solving conflict are primary tasks of prevention.

> Although evaluative data are limited, early results point to promising strategies and theories that can be applied to the prevention of domestic violence. They include: home visitation, collaborative efforts among child protection agency personnel and domestic violence service providers, prevention efforts that address violence both in homes and in communities, school-based programs, and public education programs and public education campaigns tailored to address the unique perspectives of specific segments of the population.[33]

Sexual Abuse

The National Center on Child Abuse and Neglect defines child sexual abuse as

> contacts or interactions between a child and an adult when the child is being used for the sexual stimulation of the perpetrator or another person. Sexual abuse may also be committed by a person under the age of 18 when the person is either significantly older [five years or more] than the abuse victim or when the perpetrator is in a position of power or control over another child.[34]

Abusive experiences can range from intercourse to touching to viewing an exhibitionist. Abuse can occur within the family (incest or intrafamilial) or outside the family (extrafamilial). Although much of the research on abuse has focused on girls, we are increasingly aware of abuse perpetrated on boys.

PREVALENCE   Determining the incidence and prevalence of sexual abuse in childhood is extremely difficult, as the acts are taboo and most are not reported. In a sample of 1,800 college students, one-third of both men and women reported experiencing sexual abuse in childhood. Only half of the women and a tenth of the men had reported the incident to an adult. Estimates are that one in four girls and one in six boys has experienced some form of sexual abuse by age eighteen.[35]

Diana Russell interviewed a random sample of San Francisco women concerning childhood sexual abuse.[36] Her definition of abuse included only actual sexual contact and not exhibitionism. She found that by the age of eighteen, 16 percent of women had been abused by a family member and 31 percent by a person outside the family. When intrafamilial and extrafamilial abuse were combined, 38 percent of 930 women reported at least one experience of abuse by age eighteen and 28 percent by age fourteen. Only 2 percent of intrafamilial abuse and 6 percent of extrafamilial abuse were ever reported to police.

In intrafamilial abuse, 38 percent of the abusers were members of the nuclear family (parents or siblings). Other relatives identified as abusers were most frequently uncles, male first cousins, and grandfathers. Of extrafamilial abusers, only 15 percent were strangers; 42 percent were acquaintances, and 43 percent were friends of the victim or family.

Karen Meiselman describes the family at high risk for incest as having one or more of the following components: (1) an alcoholic and violent father; (2) a mother who is away from home, physically ill, depressed, or passive; (3) an older daughter who has had to act as a surrogate mother (doing most of the chores, caring for younger siblings or for her father); (4) parents who have failed to establish a satisfying sexual relationship; (5) fathers and daughters who spend much time alone with each other; (6) any condition, such as psychosis or below-average intelligence, that reduces an individual's capacity for self-control; (7) previous incest in a parent's family; and (8) a romantic attachment with an unusual amount of physical affection between adult and child.[37]

EFFECTS ON CHILDREN   The impact of sexual abuse depends very much on the child and the specific circumstances of the abuse—the nature, duration, and frequency of the physical contact and the identity of the perpetrator. Further, it is difficult to disentangle the effects of the family conflict prior to the abuse, the abuse itself, and the events around the disclosure of the abuse. A broad review of studies[38] suggests that sexual abuse that is likely to produce a greater number of symptoms involves (1) a close relationship with the perpetrator; (2) sexual acts of oral, anal, or vaginal penetration; (3) frequent occurrences; (4) a long duration; and (5) lack of maternal support at the time of disclosure. These separate aspects of abuse, however, are related to one another. A close family member often has greater opportunity for frequent contact with the victim over a long period of time.

Sexually abused children report many different symptoms following the abuse, and no one symptom characterizes the majority of sexually abused children.[39] The most frequently reported symptoms are fears, nightmares, sexualized behaviors (sexualized play with dolls or toys, putting things in the vagina or anus, public or inappropriate masturbation) that suggest sexual stimulation from adults or peers, depression, aggression, withdrawal, school problems, poor self-esteem, acting out, regression of behavior, and symptoms of posttraumatic stress (reliving the experience, dread of dire consequences to the victim). These symptoms generally follow the patterns of difficulties that Cicchetti and Lynch proposed in their transactional/ecological model of maltreatment: difficulties in attachment, regulation of emotion, self-concept, peer relationships, and school performance. Although there is no clear-cut evidence of insecure attachment relationships, the symptoms reported reflect all the other difficulties in development.

Preschoolers most often report fears, nightmares, sexualized behaviors, withdrawal, and aggressive and uncontrolled behaviors. School-age children report all these symptoms, as well as school problems, hyperactivity, and regressive behaviors. Adolescents most often report depression, suicidal acting out, anger, running away, and antisocial behavior. Depression is the most commonly reported symptom in adults who have been sexually abused.

Interview
with Jill Waterman

Jill Waterman is an adjunct professor of psychology at the University of California in Los Angeles. She has coauthored *Sexual Abuse of Young Children: Evaluation and Treatment* and *Behind the Playground Wall: Sexual Abuse in Preschools.*

Parents worry that their children may be sexually abused. Do you think there is a greater risk for children, or is the increase in reports of child abuse a function of greater sensitivity to the problem?

I think the increase in the number of reports is due to the awareness of the problem and breaking the taboos about telling. There is more support for children who do tell.

Some parents fear sending their children to preschool because of the possibility of abuse there. Is this a valid concern?

For preschoolers, the likelihood of being abused in day care, including preschool, is less than the risk of being abused at home. Currently, 5.5 children per 10,000 are abused at day care, whereas 8.9 per 10,000 are abused at home. To reduce the risk at preschool, parents need to be sure that (1) they are welcome at the school at any time (there should be no time when they are barred from the school), (2) the school is an open environment where all personnel are easily observed (avoid schools with isolated areas or classrooms), (3) they can observe and feel confident about the way the adults in the school interact with children.

In the past, girls were more at risk for abuse than boys. Now, however, at the preschool level, the risk is about equal for boys and girls. Boys' experiences were underreported, perhaps because boys worried about being victims or being seen as wimpy, but now there is an increase in reporting of boys being abused. Still, in the latency and adolescent years, more girls than boys are abused.

There is more awareness now that women may also be molesters. When women are molesters, they are more likely to be part of a team with a man rather than be a solo molester—an aunt and an uncle, for example. Still the great majority of molesters are males.

There is a real increase in those identified as juvenile offenders or older children who molest other children. In almost all cases, they are repeating abuse done to them by adults.

How can a parent minimize the likelihood that the child will be abused?

First, teach children that their bodies are their own and no one has the right to touch them. Children have a right to stop whoever does touch or tries to touch their bodies. Second, teach children the concept of private parts of the body—that area that is covered by a bathing suit—and teach the concept of good touch and bad touch. When parents are comfortable with affection and have children who feel comfortable with giving and receiving affection, then children have a sense of what feels good and is good touch. Those children are more likely to identify bad touches quickly. Third, help children identify an adult they can go to if bad touching occurs. Teach them which adults can help—teachers, principals, group leaders. Role-play with them how they would tell someone.

Whom are children most likely to tell about abuse?

Whether the abuse is inside or outside the home, the child is most likely to tell the mother. An adolescent may tell a friend, who then tells her mother, who then reports. Most molesters never admit what they have done. Often, there is no way to prove it because much abuse does not involve penile intercourse. Touching and oral sex may leave no evidence at all.

In the event a child does not tell a parent, what are signs by which a parent might tell whether a child has been sexually abused?

In most cases, there are no blatant behavioral indicators of sexual abuse. Rarely, the child may have genital bruising or bleeding. If the child begins sexual play with other children repeatedly, I would be concerned. If a child becomes preoccupied by masturbation to the extent of preferring to masturbate rather than interact with family or other children, I would also be concerned. More commonly, a sexually abused child may shows signs of distress that could be due to a variety of causes, not just abuse. Some of these distress signs are nightmares, sudden fears, withdrawal, or depression. However, these signs would alert a parent only to distress in a child, not necessarily sexual abuse.

If a child has been abused, how can parents act to minimize the impact of the event on the child?

The most important factor is how the parents respond. When parents believe the child and act to protect the child from the molester and get therapy and help for the child, then the child is best able to handle what has happened. When parents do not believe the child or support the perpetrator, the child does least well. This may seem counter to what you would expect, but mothers are more likely to believe a daughter if she is reporting the biological father than if she reports a stepfather. The explanation may be that the mothers have a greater stake in a relationship with a boyfriend or stepfather—it is a newer relationship—than with the biological father and are therefore more likely to support the newer man in their life.

A mother may not support her daughter because she has been abused herself and has not yet resolved that issue in her mind. To support her daughter, she would have to face what has happened to herself as well. Or the mother may have blocked from her mind the experience of her own abuse with only occasional flashbacks. Since these trigger a lot of internal conflict, she needs to deny her child's abuse.

The worst outcomes for abused children occur when a close family member has abused the child, so the child has difficulty developing trust in other relationships. There is mixed evidence concerning how much the severity (frequency, length of time, types of acts) of the abuse affects the outcome for the child. Sometimes, the

(continued)

(*continued*)

severity seems to have great impact, sometimes not. Still, the response of the parents is the most important determiner.

Research shows that sexual abuse of a child is a family trauma and has a major impact on parents. In a study of children abused outside the home, many couples found it difficult to have sex in the first nine months. The parents got images of the child in a sexual situation and could not continue. A small but significant number of couples developed alcohol and drug problems, and a significant number of parents reported they were depressed. They had a decreased trust in all societal institutions—the law, religions, schools, police, media. They lost their belief in a fair, just world.

In another follow-up study we did of children, 46 percent of abused children had scores in the clinical range on behavior problem checklists at the time of the disclosure. Five years later, only 17 percent had scores in that range. Remember, though, that only 2½ percent of a representative sample score in that range. All the abused children received treatment, but many still experienced internal distress several years later. These children are more likely to have symptoms of anxiety and somatic concerns than acting-out, aggressive problems.

What kinds of therapy are most helpful for children who have been abused?

Well, everyone in the family needs some form of individual therapy. Each member needs someone to talk to, to explain what the experience is like for them and to express their feelings. Groups are helpful for children of all ages, even for little children. Linda Damon of the San Fernando Valley Child Guidance Clinic developed parallel groups

Between a third and a half of children who have been sexually abused report no symptoms initially.[40] These may be the children who experienced the least damaging abuse or received the most supportive response at the time of disclosure, and they may be the most resilient children. It is possible, however, that they have suppressed their feelings and may experience difficulties later. Evidence from longitudinal work suggests that between 10 and 24 percent of children report an increasing number of symptoms over a two-year period. In most cases, though, symptoms decrease over an eighteen-month period, with fears, nightmares, and anxiety disappearing first and anger and aggressiveness with peers and siblings tending to remain longer. Follow-up from one to five years later reveals that a small percentage of children—6 to 19 percent—are abused again. This is lower than the reabuse rate for physical abuse and neglect.

Four mechanisms are believed to account for the variety of symptoms sexually abused children experience:[41] (1) traumatic sexualization (the child's learning inappropriate sexual responses as well as faulty beliefs and ideas about sexual behavior), (2) betrayal, (3) stigmatization, and (4) powerlessness. "Traumatic sexualization is the process by which a child's sexuality is shaped in developmentally inappropriate and interpersonally dysfunctional ways."[42] The child learns sexually inappropriate responses through rewards of attention and affection, or the child's anatomy is fetishized, or the

for mothers and children in therapy. Some therapists work with the mothers on a series of topics, and other therapists work with the children on the same topics. The therapists talk to the mothers about what to expect from the children on that week's topic. For example, on the topic that it is okay to say "No," the therapists tell mothers that this week they might expect the children to say a lot of no's. Moms, instead of getting angry at them, should help children see the situations in which it is appropriate to say "No" and those in which, like going to bed, you have to do it anyhow.

Groups for all children over age four have the advantage of reducing children's feelings of being weird. They don't feel like "damaged goods," because they see other children who have gone through the same thing and are doing well. So, the group helps to take the stigma away from being abused.

Family therapy has a place down the road, I think, only when the perpetrator admits what he has done and the family has made a decision to stay together. Then you really need family therapy.

How long does it take for the child to come to terms with the abuse?

It depends on what happened as well as the age of the child. Some people argue that if the child is really young, he or she does not truly understand the meaning of the events and is less likely to experience negative outcomes. The research data are mixed about the age at which children are most or least affected. As children get older—in midlatency—they may feel they are responsible for what happened, that it is their fault. Adolescents may feel guilty as well. Treatment helps them to deal with these feelings.

child associates pain and fear with sexual activity. A child too young to understand the sexual implications of the activity may be less traumatized.

Children may experience the pain of betrayal, the feeling that someone they trusted or depended on has harmed them. Feelings of betrayal may come from the abuse itself or from the way the family responds to the abuse. When the adult is a trusted family member or when a family member knows about the abuse but does not act to protect the child, the child feels betrayed. The family's response to disclosure can also trigger a sense of betrayal. If the focus of concern is on the perpetrator or on the consequences to other family members, or if the child is blamed or rejected, then the abused child may feel betrayed.

Children also feel powerless and helpless when someone has completely disregarded their feelings and forced them to perform or experience unwanted acts. If the child is threatened or feels trapped or is not believed or supported at the time of disclosure, then the child experiences powerlessness. If the child can act to end the abuse and is supported, these feelings decrease.

When a child is stigmatized for the sexual activity, the experience of abuse then may become part of the child's self-image. Sometimes, the abuser blames the child or makes the child feel shameful for the activity. Others in the family or community may blame the child or feel the child is now "damaged goods" because he or she has had such experiences. Keeping the abuse a secret may heighten the child's sense of shame. When a child learns that abuse happens to other children and that the children are not at fault, he or she may feel less stigmatized.

Traumatic sexualization can account for the increased sexualized behavior some children show. Stigmatization may account for depression and poor self-esteem. Powerlessness can be related to fears, feelings of dread, and a sense of imminent disaster; and feelings of betrayal may account for the anger, aggressiveness, and antisocial acting out that abused children display.

An agreed-on finding is that the family plays a powerful role in helping the child deal with the effects of abuse.[43] Family support, particularly from the mother, is the key to the child's improvement. When mothers believe the child and take action to protect him or her, the child has the fewest symptoms over time. Conversely, a maltreating, dysfunctional family, unable to focus on the needs of the child, no doubt contributes to the impact of the abuse.

Court involvement may slow a child's recovery.[44] If the child has to make numerous court appearances, if the legal process extends over time, and if the child is afraid of the perpetrator, then negative effects and symptoms of the abuse may be prolonged. If the case is settled quickly and if the child has to testify only once and can testify by closed-circuit television, then risks to his or her recovery are reduced.

Recent studies of school-age children including adolescents suggest that abuse may push such children's development along distinctive pathways that can create additional problems.[45] Sexual abuse in childhood may result in reduced learning and in poorer social competence at school, in poorer overall academic performance, and in school avoidance. These behaviors have profound consequences for later occupational success. Similarly, problems with a negative self-image and self-concept can lead to a broad spectrum of problems for these children in schoolwork and with peers.

INTERVENTIONS   We have looked at the prevalence of sexual abuse and its effects on children. What should be done when abuse has occurred and has been reported? First, the security of the child should immediately be arranged. Second, the child should have the opportunity to vent with a therapist feelings of anger, fear, guilt, and shame about the act. Although some children may initially resist, the experienced therapist can encourage the child to talk and can offer reassurances that help the child deal with the feelings of betrayal and powerlessness. In play, the child regains feelings of personal power and confidence. Support of these feelings helps the child rebuild trust. The child learns to control his or her world again, and healing and growth proceed.[46]

Group therapy for children helps them deal with the experience of abuse, and participation in such a group may do even more than a therapist can to help children talk about and handle what has occurred and what they are feeling. For example, when a young girl hears that others have had a similar experience, when she realizes that she has not been singled out for some inexplicable reason, it may be easier for her to accept her own victimization.

Family therapy helps all members cope with their reactions to the abuse. Parents and siblings may have strong feelings of sadness, anger, and guilt. They, too, need help in coming to terms with what has happened.

Physical Abuse

There is no commonly agreed-on definition of physical child abuse. In defining an act as physically abusive, consideration is given to the nature of the act, its intensity and frequency, its impact on the victim, the intent of the perpetrator, and community standards. Some acts are so clearly abusive that everyone would label them as such (for example, physical discipline that resulted in a broken bone or severe injury), and some acts are clearly not abusive (for example, talking to a child calmly and respectfully about a misdeed). But between the two extremes, abuse becomes a matter of interpretation. Some define abuse as any physical act that the recipient does not want; others, as extreme yelling and pushing; others, as any spanking; and still others, as any spanking that results in a bruise or injury. Robert Emery suggests that the same standards of violence that apply to acts between strangers in public be used to define violence in the home with family members.[47]

The question arises as to whether violence toward children is a single continuum, varying from no physical punishment at the low end, through varying degrees of abuse, to homicide at the high end.[48] If one believes in a single continuum, one would search for mechanisms that underlie all aspects of violence. Another theory is that physical punishment, mild abuse, severe abuse, and homicide represent different categories of behavior. The search, then, is for mechanisms that underlie each category and that may differ from category to category. Evidence from the Second National Family Violence Survey supports a distinction between physical punishment and severe abuse, as the predictors are somewhat different.[49]

PREVALENCE   Depending on their source, statistics on abuse vary. In 1985, a national probability sample was surveyed by telephone. Of the 6,002 households contacted, 3,232 included a child under eighteen. The caregivers for 60 percent of children reported that they used physical punishment and minor violence (pushing, grabbing, shoving, and slapping) with children. The caregivers for 10 percent of children reported one or more instances of physical abuse or severe violence, consisting of kicking, biting, hitting with a fist or object, or burning.[50]

These were self-reports of punishment and abuse. In 1994, three million agency reports of suspected child abuse were made.[51] The number of reports of abuse to social agencies falls far below the self-report rate of 10 percent. Had caregivers for 10 percent of all children been reported as abusers, the number of reports would have been about 6 million. It is estimated that between 1,200 and 5,000 children die from abuse each year.[52]

Certain characteristics of parent, child, and living setting that are related to physical abuse have been identified. In the National Family Violence Survey, female caregivers most frequently reported physical punishment and minor violence, but there were no sex differences in reported physical abuse or severe violence.[53] Younger

Sibling violence is the most common form of victimization experienced by children.

parents with many children were more likely than others to be abusive. Although abuse occurs at all socioeconomic levels, it was most frequently reported when fathers were unemployed or underemployed and when families lived below the poverty line. Abusive parents also were more likely to report drug use. For example, state agencies reported in a survey that substance abuse was the major issue in 68 percent of child protection cases being followed.[54]

Other studies have shown that 30 percent of parents who have been abused abuse children, but still, the majority who experienced abuse do not repeat it.[55] Abusive parents, as compared with nonabusive parents, are, however, more likely to form families in which spousal abuse and domestic violence occur.[56] More demanding and more negative with children, these parents are more likely to view childrearing as a burden. They believe in strict, firm, physical discipline. Although in the past there has been mention of an "abusive personality," research has not identified one. A maltreating individual is associated with being especially reactive to negative events and with having low self-esteem, poor impulse control, and impaired capacity for empathy.

Characteristics of the physically abused child include (1) age—most are between three and eight years of age, with an increasing number of teenagers who are reported to be abused—and (2) sex, with boys being more often physically abused.[57] Any negative qualities of abused children prior to the abuse are thought to result from parents' generally negative childrearing behaviors.

Abused parents who do not abuse their children have higher IQs, greater emotional stability, and less anxiety and depression than do abused parents who abuse their children. They are also more likely to have a supportive partner.[58]

Glenn Wolfner and Richard Gelles, who have studied family violence extensively, believe that violence to children is the result of parents' predispositions to violence in combination with stressful life conditions.[59] The potential for violence is present in everyone in varying degrees as a result of social learning. Those individuals who have learned to respond to stress with violence are those most likely to abuse children when they experience stressors such as job loss or financial problems.

EFFECTS ON CHILDREN   Children react to physical abuse in many ways. As we saw in discussing Cicchetti and Lynch's transactional/ecological model, five main areas of development are affected: attachment relationships, regulation of emotion, self-concept, peer relationships, and school adjustment.[60]

When children are maltreated in infancy and early childhood, they often develop insecure or disorganized/disoriented attachments. In one study, 80 percent of maltreated infants were classified as disorganized/disoriented in their attachments to their mother, as compared with 20 percent of nonmaltreated infants. Further, these disorganized attachments were stable, as 90 percent of these infants were classified in the same way a year later. When children are between ages seven and thirteen at the time of abuse, about 30 percent report confused patterns of relationships to their mother, so age appears to reduce the impact on this attachment.

Abused children's internal working models of relationships based on experiences with abusive parents may generalize to other relationships, leading these children to have negative views of how others will treat them and how reliable and predictable others are. Thus, not surprisingly, abused children often have problems with peers. Some abused children are fearful and insecure with peers, often withdrawing from or avoiding them. Others are physically and verbally aggressive and find it difficult to be positive and considerate.

Children's ability to regulate their feelings affects all aspects of their functioning. Abused children have difficulty controlling their emotions, in part because these emotions are so intense. The children are likely to feel chronic stress, anxiety, depression, and helplessness. They tend to be inflexible and inappropriate in expressing their feelings. They also have difficulty in communicating their feelings verbally and in identifying the feelings of others. They lack the cognitive control of feelings that children their age usually have. Emotional dysregulation is related to peer difficulties as well, because peers find it hard to be with children who lack control of their feelings.

In view of their poor attachment relationships and intense amounts of uncontrolled feelings, it is not surprising that abused children often have unrealistic self-concepts. When young, they may inflate their sense of competence, feeling overly confident, but as they get older, they describe themselves as less able than and less accepted by others.

Emery states that it is not clear whether the many symptoms come from the abuse itself or from family interactions leading up to the abuse.[61] He notes (as described in Chapter 3) that angry episodes, even those not involving the child, distress the child. Children's distress motivates them to get involved in parental conflicts in order to end them. Because their misbehavior distracts parents from their quarrels, children are likely to repeat misbehavior to stop conflicts even if doing so causes them to become victims.

Despite the abuse they experience, a sizeable number of maltreated children develop competence and caring and are resilient and resourceful in surmounting problems. The most competent and best-functioning children are those who have developed ego control, ego resilience, and self-esteem.[62] The capacity for a more reserved, controlled, and rational way of interacting with others predicts overall competence in maltreated children. This factor does not predict competence in nonmaltreated children, perhaps because control is not as central to competence in nonmaltreated children.

INTERVENTIONS   Just as with child sexual abuse, there are two forms of intervention for physical abuse: (1) providing security and safety for the child and (2) getting psychological services. There is some indication that, at least with spousal abuse, having the perpetrator arrested prevents recurrence more effectively than mediating the dispute informally or having the perpetrator leave the property for 48 hours. In child abuse cases, children deserve at least as much physical protection as they would get if a stranger attacked them. Gelles believes some parents are so abusive on a single occasion that family reunification should never be considered.[63]

Physically abused children need the same form of therapy as sexually abused children. They need the opportunity to vent and understand their intense feelings, to learn to express them appropriately, and to control them when they are very intense. They need help forming positive, trusting relationships with both adults and peers, and they need help in developing the self-esteem that will enable them to explore their world actively.

Interventions are also directed toward the abusing parent. When appropriate, perpetrators are referred to abuse treatment programs. They are taught parenting skills and other ways to manage their anger. Sometimes, home visitors are sent to teach and monitor parenting skills. In a sense, these interventions help provide the community resources that parents had earlier failed to or been unable to access.

Neglect

Families have major responsibilities for caring for and protecting children, but some are unable to perform these tasks. Neglect is defined as a parent's or caregiver's act of omission that involves refusal or delay in meeting health needs; needs for food, clothing, and shelter; psychological needs for affection, attention, and supervision; and educational needs.[64]

PREVALENCE   The National Incidence Study of 1994 found that neglect was the most frequent form of child maltreatment and estimated that 879,000 children were victims of neglect in that year.[65] Although prevalent, neglect is less often studied. So, less is known about neglect and the children who experience it than is known about physical and sexual abuse.

Child neglect occurs most frequently in the context of poverty, even after taking into account the fact that inadequate care due to limited resources is not considered neglect.[66] When families are poor, they lack health care benefits and face increased hazards such as lead exposure and dangerous neighborhoods, as well as poor educational facilities. Nevertheless, most poor families do not neglect their children. Neglect is not associated with any racial group when socioeconomic status is controlled for, but it is associated with the stress of unemployment, illness, and frequent moves.

A second major family risk factor for neglect is parental substance abuse.[67] In one review of studies, substance and alcohol abuse were a factor in 80 to 90 percent of the cases of physical abuse and neglect. A question has been raised as to whether mothers should be cited as physically abusing or neglecting their babies when they engage in prenatal drug use.

Few child characteristics have been consistently associated with neglect. We do know, however, that neglect occurs primarily in young children. In one study, one-third of reports concerned children under four years of age.

EFFECTS ON CHILDREN Neglected children have a greater likelihood of attachment problems, low self-esteem, increased dependency, and anger as compared with physically abused or nonmaltreated children.[68] Neglected children also have more language problems and slower academic and cognitive development. They are often passive and withdrawn in social behavior. Longitudinal follow-ups of neglected children indicate that they are at risk for delinquent behavior. Physical and medical problems are also associated with neglect; half of the fatalities in swimming pools and fires are attributed to lack of appropriate supervision.

INTERVENTIONS Interventions focus on two areas: prevention of neglect and care of the child once neglect has occurred.[69] Many of the interventions described here apply to the prevention and treatment of physical abuse as well. Prevention takes the forms of increased services to families at risk during infancy and early childhood to (1) provide information and access to additional sources of assistance such as home health nurses, (2) model appropriate care, and (3) connect families to community services. Community services include youth athletic programs and afterschool and church programs that help children develop feelings of competence and self-esteem; community programs aimed at adults include parenting programs and parent support groups.

Once neglect has occurred, there must be provision of care for the child, either in the home through increased services to the family or through the removal of the child from the family. One study of suspected neglect found that one-third of children could be cared for in the home with increased money for food and housing.[70] When neglect occurs as a result of substance abuse, however, the child may have to be removed from the home.

Douglas Besharov, the first director of the National Center for Child Abuse and Neglect, has made several recommendations that center on two areas in need of reform: the reporting process and the child protective decision-making process.[71] He believes that, first, the child abuse laws need to be clarified to state specifically the parenting behaviors that require reporting. At present, the laws are so vague and so many reports are made that endless hours go into investigating cases that turn out not to be cases of abuse or neglect. Second, once laws are clarified, all professionals making such reports should be educated so that they can make accurate reports. Third, all the reports must be screened carefully so that all are acted upon in appropriate ways. Finally, those individuals and agencies making reports need feedback about their accuracy.

With regard to reforming the child protective decision-making process, Besharov directs his recommendations to families with drug-addicted, particularly crack-addicted, parents, as he believes drug addiction underlies much physical abuse and neglect and will continue to endanger children in the future. His recommendations are

1. Recognize that "wishful thinking about parents and the efficacy of treatment" are major hurdles to reasonable decisions about children.

2. Assume that parental crack-addiction cannot be cured.

3. Provide intensive and years-long child protective supervision for any child who is permitted to remain with the parents.

4. Carefully structure and assess the kinship care programs, as relatives may need extensive and prolonged help to rear the children.

5. Increase adoptions, especially those of abandoned infants—too many children wait for years for adoption.

6. Create stable and nurturing long-term care arrangements for children who are not adopted.

7. Permit child welfare service agencies to help families plan children, as many women are having children they do not want.

Although Besharov does not believe that better reporting and more realistic and long-term responses to neglect and abuse cases will eliminate child abuse deaths, he does believe that there will be no progress without these kinds of reforms.

Leroy Pelton, director of the University of Nevada School of Social Work, strongly urges separating the investigative work from the preventive and supportive services of welfare agencies. This would enable parents to come for help and support in times of need without fearing that children will be removed from the home.[72] Michael Weber has served as the associative director of the National Committee to Prevent Child Abuse and as president of the National Association of Public Child Welfare Administrators.[73] He believes that no one agency can take responsibility for preventing and treating maltreatment. He recommends that partnership-oriented, community-based child protection networks be formed to focus on (1) the prevention of problems, (2) early intervention when trouble first starts, (3) the provision of treatment and services to families, and (4) sufficient treatment so children do not grow up to repeat the maltreatment.

All these suggestions basically provide ways maltreatment can be prevented, more quickly identified, and treated. To both prevent maltreatment and provide services for maltreated children and their families is a task requiring clear definitions and the resources and personnel of all the community agencies involved.

Other Forms of Personal Abuse

Emotional abuse includes terrorizing, exploiting, and missocializing children.[74] Defined as acts of omission or commission that damage the behavioral, cognitive, affective, and physical functioning of the child, emotional abuse is hard to prove. Emotional abuse is associated with a child's withdrawal, loss of self-esteem, aggressiveness, and failure to trust others.

Moral-legal-educational maltreatment involves failure to help the child develop appropriate social and moral values. Behaviors include such acts as exposing the child to illegal drugs or giving them to the child, involving the child in illegal activity, and failing to intervene when the child is involved in such activity.

Because the majority of abused children experience more than one form of abuse, pure subtypes of abuse rarely exist, but some differences among parents who commit different types of abuse are beginning to be identified.[75] For example, physically abusive parents may be more likely to have insecure adult attachments to their own parents in which they dismiss or deny painful experiences and so are less likely to appreciate their own child's pain. Neglectful parents appear to have insecure adult attachments in which they are preoccupied with feelings and are less available to monitor and care for children.

Community Violence

We have seen that in any form, exposure to unresolved anger and aggression harms children, whether they witness it or experience it. Children do not meet aggression only in their personal lives. Our society has become increasingly violent, with many children exposed to traumatic events. Although a large proportion of violence occurs in lower socioeconomic areas, people are exposed to violence in restaurants, schools, and middle-class communities. No child is immune to the effects of community violence. Even if it does not touch a child personally, he or she may be acquainted with someone who has had a family member die or experience harm.

PREVALENCE   Children are more likely to witness violence than to experience it. In a study in a low-income, moderately violent neighborhood in Washington, D.C., 19 percent of children in grades one and two had been physically threatened, chased, mugged, or shot, and 61 percent had witnessed such acts as muggings, stabbings, and illegal drug use, not once but several times per year.[76] By grades five and six, 32 percent of children had been victims, and 72 percent had witnessed violence.

When questioned, older children reported that none of the victimizations took place at home. Nonetheless, 48 percent occurred near home, and 55 percent took place at or near school. Thus, the violence the children witnessed took place in their immediate environment. Although it occurred outside the home, children knew about two-thirds of the perpetrators; only about a third were strangers to them.

Parents report that their children experience or witness less violence than the children report. However, children may not tell parents all they see. Anecdotal reports suggest that parents may discourage children from talking about the violence they see.[77] This is unfortunate in that it prevents children from dealing with their feelings and parents from helping their children cope with the violence.

EFFECTS ON CHILDREN   Exposure to community violence by itself does not predict personal problems and school difficulties. Even in combination with many other stressors, such as low income, many family moves, and the father's absence, it does not predict difficulty.[78] To have a negative effect, community violence must impact family life. When this violence erodes the safety and stability of the child's home, such as when drug dealing and guns are in the home, then the child is affected. Thus, the child experiences community violence at the level of the microsystem—in day-to-day interactions with his or her parents. When parents can somehow prevent the stressors from disrupting the stability of the home and not allow the violence in the community to influence parent-child relationships, children can then function successfully. John Richters and Pedro Martinez write,

> It seems reasonable to assume that family stability and safety are ultimately the
> products of choices made by children's caretakers about how they will cope with
> and/or react to the circumstances within which they find themselves. We have much
> to learn about how, why, and in what ways such choices are made, but in advance of
> those answers it seems self-evident that these are factors over which caretakers have
> and must exercise control.[79]

Children exposed to community violence develop many of the symptoms of children who have been physically or sexually abused. They have difficulty sleeping, remembering, and concentrating, and they exhibit anxious attachment to parents (not wanting them to leave), aggressive play, severe limitation of activities and exploration, and regressive behavior.[80] Lenore Terr describes the denial and numbing children use to block out frightening reality.[81] Children also experience feelings of grief and loss when a significant loved one dies as a result of violence.

All these reactions make it hard for children to develop intellectually and socially. They come to expect violence and develop a sense of fatalism about their lives, a feeling that they have no future. They believe that planning is not important because they could be crippled or killed before their plans are fulfilled.

Even in adverse circumstances, a significant number of children function well at school and appear to have few behavior problems. Such children are active individuals who seek to surmount obstacles. The main agent for helping them is their family and the stability it provides.[82] A second source of help is their own internal sense that life can improve, that they can influence what happens to them and make life better in the future.[83] Children who live in difficult circumstances but still maintain positive expectations of the future are more successful later on. But again, it is most likely the immediate family members who help children build positive expectations about the future. James Garbarino and his colleagues summarize the parents' role and its dangers:

> If parents, or other significant caregivers, can sustain a strong attachment to their children, can maintain a positive sense of self, and can have access to basic resources, children will manage, although it may be at great cost to the psychic and physical welfare of those parents, who may be "used up" caring for their children.[84]

COPING RESOURCES   Several factors influence how children cope with the experience of violence.[85] Intelligence, self-confidence, self-esteem, sociability, an easygoing attitude, and affectionate nature all increase children's coping ability. Such children demand little, yet they relate positively and happily to others and tend to receive support. Environmental factors include the presence of at least one stable emotional relationship with a caregiver who serves as a model of coping, as well as social relationships outside the family with relatives and family friends. The community can give support in many ways; friends, neighbors, teachers, and members of religious groups can provide support and encourage the competence of parents and children.

The school is a major refuge for children who confront difficult experiences. After the family, the school is the most important social institution in children's lives. Many resilient children find school activities to be a source of self-esteem and competence. They make friends with and get support from schoolmates and from teachers who take an interest in them.

In *Children in Danger*, James Garbarino and his associates describe the schools as a major unit of intervention to counteract the community violence in children's lives. He outlines a school-based intervention program in which teachers form close emotional attachments with students to promote their development. The researchers believe that these relationships serve as the basis for learning in all areas. Teachers and programs provide structure and control for these children, who adopt the values, behavior, and attitudes of a significant other person.

In Garbarino's plan, day care centers can be included in programs to reach children below school age. An attachment teacher is assigned to every six or seven students, and a consistent substitute attachment and subgroup are assigned to each child. Children have an unvarying placement in small groups. Formal teaching programs stimulate the child's curiosity and level of development.

The organized school environment, with familiar teachers and programs, provides security and predictability in a changing world. Teachers are specially trained to work with these children, taking courses in child development and in understanding children's reactions to stress, violence, and loss. Teachers remain available to students who exhibit fluctuating or changing emotions and help the children deal with them.

Therapy can help children cope with their emotional reactions to trauma.[86] All major personality shifts resulting from trauma require treatment. Such personality changes occur in almost all physically and sexually abused children, as well as those who experience some form of trauma.

Parents should arrange for psychiatric treatment for a child as soon after a trauma as possible. If several children are involved, participants can be seen in a mini-marathon group session with a highly trained professional. When each member shares his or her experiences, the possibility of anyone's denying the situation (and thus prolonging traumatization) is lessened. Schools serve as the familiar setting appropriate for such group sessions. If a family has been traumatized, then it can be treated as a unit. However, family therapy is not recommended when a parent has physically or sexually abused a child, because the child is not really free to express the anger he or she feels in the presence of the abuser.

Behavioral therapy is useful for children who have developed fears as a result of the trauma. Deconditioning is useful as an addition to individual treatment designed to deal with the emotional reactions, but behavioral therapy by itself is limited.

A person should begin treatment as soon as possible after the trauma. However, treatment is useful any time a person recognizes that he or she is suffering the effects of a trauma, even if therapy cannot reverse all the effects of the experience.

Parents want to know what to do to prevent violence and trauma in their children's lives. Nothing can completely prevent violence, but children who receive support are most likely to recover from the experience.

Common Themes in Abuse and Violence

Several general themes emerge in the study of abuse and violence. First, no one set of circumstances leads inevitably to abuse and violence; rather, many risk factors increase the likelihood of abuse and violence and increase the traumatic effects on children.

Second, children respond in many ways to trauma, and several different kinds of trauma lead to similar problems in children. For example, all forms of abuse are associated with difficulties in emotional control, in relationships with adults and peers, in self-concept, and in school adjustment. Further, problems are similar to those seen in children when their parents lose their jobs or suffer from prolonged unemployment, get divorced, or remarry and blend families. Sexualized behavior seems to be the one form of reaction that is most frequently linked with sexual abuse.

A question arises as to whether abuse and violence contribute significant difficulties beyond those related to low income or negative life stress. A recent study statistically disentangled the contributions of these factors—physical abuse, low income, and life stress events.[87] Indeed, physical abuse made a significant contribution to children's behavior problems beyond that related to economic disadvantage and stress as a result of negative life events.

Physical abuse was associated with additional problems in relationships with peers, and peer problems occurred after physical abuse, regardless of the sex, socioeconomic status, or stress level of the abused person. The abusive experience in the family appears to lead to distortions in how people relate to each other and what is required to get along. As noted earlier, this is especially sad because children then lose a major source of support in coping with other problems. Other stressors such as low income and negative life events produce few changes in self-perceptions or behavior problems unless they are unusually severe.

Therefore, other difficulties in life appear to produce less marked changes in children's moods and behaviors. Abuse and violence damage children's trust in their peers and decrease their capacity for positive relationships, thus removing an important resource for such children.

In all these difficult situations, the family remains the main source of support for children. Agencies and therapies can help, but it is individuals who are close and have a sense of the child's individuality who are truly helpful. If parents cannot do this, other relatives or family friends, teachers, or day care workers can step in.

Prevention of Violence

From October 1, 1997, to April 1, 1998, five dramatic school-based shootings by adolescents claimed the lives of twenty-four students and two teachers and focused our attention on the amount of violence that children experience, witness, or fear on an ongoing basis.[88] In a chapter concerning the neurobiological effects of experiencing and witnessing trauma, Bruce Perry writes,

> The ultimate solution to the problems of violence, whether from the remorseless predator or the reactive, impulsive youth, is primary prevention. Our society is creating violent children and youth at a rate far faster than we could ever treat, rehabilitate, or even lock them away. No single intervention strategy will solve these heterogeneous problems. No set of intervention strategies will solve these transgenerational problems. In order to solve the problems of violence, we need to transform our culture.[89]

Where can we start? Katherine Christoffel describes the necessity of viewing violence in the form of firearm injuries and deaths as a public health problem rather than a criminal one.[90] Once we do that, the main goal becomes decreasing injuries, and we can search for a variety of strategies to do this.

By describing how we reduced motor vehicle injury deaths, Christoffel illustrates how we might reduce violence. In the late 1960s, motor vehicle injury deaths were redefined as a public health problem, and a variety of actions were taken to decrease them. Car manufacturers improved the safety of cars, passenger restraints were developed, road construction improved, and changes in the driving laws to increase penalties for driving while intoxicated and failure to use seat belts were passed. The number of deaths dropped from 55,000 in 1968 to 45,000 per year in 1990, though the number of cars and drivers had increased.

Using a public health model, one can make the public aware of the risk we all face from firearms. While deaths from motor vehicles are dropping, deaths from firearms are rising. In 1995, 36,000 individuals died from injuries caused by firearms and 43,360 from injuries caused by automobile accidents.[91] It is estimated that in the near future, deaths from firearms will exceed deaths from car accidents.

By recognizing the lethality of guns and their risk to the general population, the public can shift the focus from crime, law enforcement, and civil liberties to a focus on preventing and reducing injuries and deaths from firearms. The emphasis is then placed on having handgun-free homes and neighborhoods, restricting handgun sales and ownership, and developing other self- and home-protection devices. For example, we can emphasize the safe storage of guns and ammunition in locked and separated areas, push for firearm manufacturers to install safety locks on guns, and urge state representatives to pass laws making owners responsible for others' use of their guns.

Although we have taken some action to regulate the purchase of guns, we have paid little attention to gun manufacturers and distributors. Licenses to distribute handguns are cheap and can be obtained through the mail. In 1990, there were more firearm licenses than gas stations in the United States. Many of these distributors, unknown to local officials, operate out of their homes. Thus, their compliance with existing laws may be minimal and could no doubt be improved if all distributors were known.

Another form of prevention is to encourage health professionals to advise and counsel all families on the danger of handguns and the need to have them locked away. They can track the number of injuries and deaths from handguns carefully and educate the public on the importance of reforms to control handgun use and storage.

We can also work to change the content of the media.[92] Research indicates that media violence contributes to violent behavior in three ways: (1) it increases aggressive behavior and willingness to use violence, (2) it desensitizes viewers so that they accept violence as a normal part of life, and (3) it creates a belief in a "mean world syndrome" that makes people more fearful of a world they see as dangerous.

John Murray suggests that families need to act in three ways to counteract media violence. First, they need to change their behavior at home. So that children can become informed consumers of television fare, parents need to watch television with children and talk about what they see. Parents and children can learn from each other in these discussions.

Second, parents can lobby for the inclusion of media literacy courses, so, again, children learn critical viewing habits. Third, parents can begin to lobby the government and industries to make children's television less violent. For example, they might lobby the industry to reduce the amount of time allocated to violent programs during prime time. There are encouraging signs that the chairman of the Federal Communications Commission is ready to make changes. These are just a few of the actions that parents can pursue as they seek to make the world a safer place for children.

The Challenge Model

Therapy can help children deal with the effects of certain traumatic events and troubled family situations. Some therapists have become concerned, however, that certain forms of intervention so emphasize the pain and damaging effects of these difficulties that children and adults believe they are doomed to emotionally impoverished lives as a result of the trauma.

Children cope best with community disasters when family members are supportive.

Steven Wolin and Sybil Wolin term this the *damage model* of human development, in that it focuses on the harmful effects produced by traumas; therapy in this model can only help individuals understand the damage and how it occurred. Drawing on clinical insights and on the research of such people as Ruth Smith and Emmy Werner (see the interview with Emmy Werner in Chapter 3), Wolin and Wolin have developed a *challenge model* of development.[93] Although adversity brings stress, harm, and vulnerability to the individual, Wolin and Wolin believe it also stimulates the person to branch out, to take measures to protect himself or herself and find other sources of strength that promote development. So, the individual experiences pain but develops resiliencies that can limit the pain and promote accomplishment and satisfaction.

In their book *The Resilient Self,* Wolin and Wolin identify seven resiliencies that help individuals rebound in the face of difficult circumstances:

1. *Insight*—developing the habit of asking tough questions and giving honest answers

2. *Independence*—drawing boundaries between oneself and one's troubled parents; keeping emotional distance while satisfying the demands of one's conscience

3. *Relationships*—building intimate and fulfilling ties to other people that balance a mature regard for one's own needs with empathy and the capacity to give to someone else.

4. *Initiative*—taking charge of problems; exerting control; acquiring a taste for stretching and testing oneself in demanding tasks

5. *Creativity*—imposing order, beauty, and purpose on the chaos of one's troubling experiences and painful feelings

6. *Humor*—finding the comic in the tragic

7. *Morality*—developing an informed conscience that extends one's wish for a good personal life to all of humankind[94]

Their book describes the many ways resiliencies grow in childhood, adolescence, and adulthood and offers an optimistic approach that encourages survivors of traumas and difficult childhood experiences to review their lives in terms of the strengths they have developed. As a result, people experience pride in their ability to overcome hardships—whether as a result of violence or abuse or even natural disasters such as floods and earthquakes—and confidence in their capacity to make further changes as needed. In focusing on pain and the sources of pain in the past, the damage model tends to discourage individuals because the past cannot be changed and the pain undone. In contrast, the challenge model asserts that life can be satisfying and productive even with the scars of the past.

Keeping Children Safe

As children spend more time away from parents and home, going to and from school or to friends' homes, parents become concerned about their safety. They want to help children be independent and safe in the world, yet they do not want to frighten them and make them afraid of strangers and new experiences. Grace Hechinger, an education consultant, has interviewed police officials, school safety officials, individuals involved in neighborhood safety programs, and victims of crime and assaults.[95] From this research, she has organized information to help parents prepare their children to be safe as they spend more time on their own.

Fostering children's awareness of danger, sense of caution, and preparedness for unsafe situations does not mean making children live in fear. Children can learn that even though most people in the world are good and helpful and most situations are safe, some people and experiences are not, and everyone must learn to protect himself or herself from dangers that arise. Parents can help by putting this knowledge in perspective for children. Life has always involved danger of some sort, and many objects or experiences that are positive also have dangerous aspects. Cars are useful—they get us to work, to stores, to hospitals—but they can be dangerous if they hit us while we are crossing the street. The answer lies not in eliminating cars, because before we had cars, there were dangers from horses and horse-drawn vehicles. The solution is to take precautions to minimize dangers and enjoy the benefits.

Families need to develop a set of instructions in the event of certain dangerous situations, to be discussed and revised as necessary. A one-time discussion is not enough; periodically, parents must review instructions with children. Children can learn these safety rules gradually—for example, when and where they may go alone or what they should do if bothered by someone on the street or in a store, even when parents are nearby. Learning safety rules can become as natural to children as learning to brush

---

BOX 10.1

Some "What If?" Questions for Young Children

Parents ask children what they would do if the following situations arose. If children give the wrong answers, parents can calmly tell them more practical alternative responses. What if:

1. We were separated in a shopping center, in the movies, at the beach?
2. You were lost in a department store, in the park, at a parade?
3. A stranger offered you candy or presents to leave the playground?
4. A stranger wanted you to get into his car?
5. A stranger started fussing with your clothing?
6. Your friends wanted to play with matches?
7. Someone you did not know asked your name and phone number?

Grace Hechinger, *How to Raise a Street-Smart Child* (New York: Ballantine Books, 1984), p. 59.

---

their teeth. The emphasis is on teaching children the skills to deal with the environment, to make them competent and independent.

Although parents worry that talk of possible fearful events will damage the child, the risks that come with ignorance are much greater. Parents can begin with simple discussions of traffic safety—where, when, and how to cross the street. They can move from that topic to others of importance for the child. Television may prompt some discussion. Hechinger recommends playing the game "What If?" Parents ask a variety of questions and give children chances to develop solutions to difficult situations. Parents should not be upset if their children's initial answers are impractical, because they can guide their children in learning more reasonable responses. Box 10.1 gives some sample "What If?" questions.

Parents should have clear safety rules on (1) behavior for a fire at home, (2) traffic behavior, whether on foot or on a bicycle, (3) boundaries within which the child can come and go freely and outside of which an adult or parent must be present, (4) behavior in public with strangers, (5) behavior at home if strangers telephone or come to the house, (6) behavior when the child is a victim or witness of muggings by peers or adults, and (7) behavior when sexual misconduct occurs.

If children are victimized—their bike is stolen, their money is taken, a stranger approaches them—parents' reactions can help speed the healing process. When parents listen to children's reactions and help children take constructive action, such as notifying the police, they help children cope. When parents' responses are exaggerated ("This is horrible!") or detached ("I cannot deal with this"), children get no help in coping with their feelings. If they cannot talk about how they feel, they will find it difficult to work out their feelings. Active listening and simple I-messages ("If that happened to me, I'd be really upset") give children a chance to say what the experience meant to them. Sometimes, children need to describe the event several times. Each time, more details emerge, as do more feelings. Gradually, after the incident, children will regain their self-confidence. If a child's eating, sleeping, or play habits change or if marked changes in schoolwork or personality continue for some time, professional help should be sought.

An important step in promoting children's safety is working with people in the community. Developing community awareness and programs gives everyone a positive feeling of working together, which does much to banish fear. Promoting public safety programs with school and police officials and organizing block-parent programs to help children in the neighborhood are useful steps. In block-parent programs, one house in the neighborhood is designated as a house where children may come if they need help or reassurance when no one is home.

Family members grow stronger when they face problems and work together to deal with them. Sense of community is strengthened when families and agencies cooperate to make the environment safe for children.

Main Points

Victimization

- can be classified as pandemic, acute, or extraordinary
- is more common for children than for adults
- occurs mainly because children are more dependent on adults, are less able to protect themselves, and have less control of associates and surroundings

An ecological/transactional model of community violence and child maltreatment

- focuses on risk and protective factors
- describes characteristics of the child, parent, and environment that increase the risk of violence
- describes violence at several ecological levels: the macrosystem, the exosystem, the microsystem, and the ontogenic, or personal, level
- emphasizes that factors at different levels interact to increase the likelihood of violence
- describes the effects of violence in five areas of a child's behavior: attachment relationships, regulation of emotions, self-concept, peer relationships, and school adjustment
- has implications for types of intervention at the various ecological levels

Exposure to family violence

- occurs in many different kinds of families
- affects a child's physical, psychological, and cognitive functioning
- requires interventions aimed at helping the nonabusing parent as well as the child
- requires organized community interventions to prevent family violence

Sexual child abuse

- is estimated to be experienced by one in four girls and one in six boys by the age of eighteen
- affects children in different ways, depending on the specific act, its duration, its frequency, and the identity of the perpetrator
- appears most traumatic when it involves someone close who frequently engages in forceful sexual acts of penetration over a long time period and when mothers provide little support
- results in behavior changes such as sexualized behavior and changes in emotional regulation, in attachment relations, in self-concept, in relations with peers, and in school adjustment
- does not always produce symptoms; about one-third to one-half of children show no symptoms at the time they are studied
- victims require protection from the abuser
- victims can profit from individual, group, and family therapy

Physical child abuse

- is difficult to define precisely
- results from a variety of factors, including characteristics of the parents, the family, and the environment
- is learned in the context of the family
- results in a wide variety of symptoms relating to self-concept, emotional control, relations with peers and adults, and adjustment in school
- victims can be resourceful and surmount problems
- requires therapy for the victim, perpetrator, and family
- may be so severe on a single occasion that the child should not live with the person again

Neglect

- is a common but little-studied form of abuse
- occurs in families with other risk factors such as poverty and substance abuse
- can be prevented with increased services to children and families
- requires community-wide programs to prevent it and treat its victims

Community violence

- affects all children but most particularly those in lower socioeconomic areas
- is more often witnessed than experienced
- has a negative impact when it erodes the safety and stability of family life
- results in many symptoms that hinder children's development

- requires interventions at the community level to decrease the violence and provide support for children who experience such violence
- victims can be helped with individual, group, and family therapy

The challenge model

- focuses on strengths people develop to cope with negative family experiences or other traumas
- identifies seven resiliencies: insight, independence, relationships, initiative, creativity, humor, and morality
- presents an optimistic view of people's capacity to create satisfying lives despite the scars of painful experiences

Keeping children safe

- requires that parents teach children about potential dangers and ways to minimize them
- requires that parents teach children coping techniques for dangerous situations
- means that parents and society as a whole have to work to provide a safer community for everyone

Exercises

1. Imagine that a close friend told you that her four-year-old had just showed her how a twenty-five-year-old male relative had touched her genitals. The daughter said he told her it was a secret between them, but she decided to tell her mother because they do not keep secrets from each other. How would you advise your friend to help her daughter after she has reported the event to the authorities? What would you advise her to do to help herself?

2. Divide into groups of four, and describe the general information you would choose to include in an eight-session parenting course for men and women who have physically abused their children. Share your group's results with the entire class. What elements were chosen by only one or two groups? Combine the best information from all groups and come up with one eight-session program. If possible, compare it with a program offered in your area, such as Parental Stress or another such agency.

3. Divide into groups of four, and describe a parenting program for adolescent mothers and fathers to prevent physical child abuse. Is it identical to the program designed for those who have already committed abuse? In what ways does it differ?

4. Imagine that you had unlimited money to go into a low-income housing project in a high-crime area. What kinds of programs would you devise to help children cope with the violence they witness around them?

5. Think about what you most feared as a young child. What would you tell a nine-year-old brother or sister who was afraid of being kidnapped on the street? of experiencing an earthquake or hurricane or flood? of being shot?

Additional Readings

Adams, Caren, and Jennifer Fay. *Helping Your Child Recover from Sexual Abuse.* Seattle: University of Washington Press, 1992.

Garbarino, James, Nancy Dubrow, Kathleen Kostelny, and Carole Pardo. *Children in Danger.* San Francisco: Jossey-Bass, 1992.

Kraizer, Sherryll. *The Safe Child Book.* New York: Fireside, 1996.

Melton, Gary B., and Frank D. Barry, eds. *Protecting Children from Abuse and Neglect.* New York: Guilford Press, 1994.

Osofsky, Joy D., ed. *Children in a Violent Society.* New York: Guilford, 1997.

11

Supports for Parents and Children

SUPPORTS FOR PARENTS AND CHILDREN MAKE PARENT-ing easier and more effective. What support is available for parents in the United States? What family rituals and traditions help foster the child's sense of belonging? What individuals within and outside the extended family contribute to a child's development and a parent's sense of well-being? What community resources **are** *currently available and what kinds of programs are proposed to help children develop and to assist parents with their task?*

In looking at different aspects of parenting—understanding children's needs, forming relationships with them, setting limits, responding to problem behaviors, stimulating positive growth—we have focused on what parents can do to accomplish these formidable tasks. The parent-child relationship is nested in a social context that can hinder or help parents as they strive to achieve their childrearing goals. This is what Urie Bronfenbrenner's ecological model (described in Chapter 1) terms the microsystemic level.[1] At the mesosystemic level, parents interact with other adults who also care for children—teachers, school authorities, day care providers, coaches. Ongoing exchange of information, mutual accommodation, and respect among all caregivers provide support for parents and children. At the exosystemic level, parents' work can establish patterns of behavior that enable parents to be more effective. At the macrosystemic level, society can establish public policies and programs that support not only parents and children but all caregivers, teachers, and institutions that foster children's growth. In this chapter, we examine all four levels of supports.

Social Supports

Social supports are those people, activities, organizations, and environmental resources that provide emotional, instrumental, and informational benefits to children and parents. *Emotional benefits* include feelings of being cared for, valued, encouraged, understood, and validated as a person. *Instrumental benefits* include help with certain tasks such as housework and specific aid such as financial assistance or childcare. *Informational benefits* include advice about childcare, referral to resources, and specific guidance about tasks.[2]

Children and adults have different roles and activities in life; nevertheless, the same general categories of support are useful to both. Supports are divided into those within the family and those outside the family. Supports encompass *people* (relatives and nonrelatives such as neighbors and friends), *activities* (hobbies, recreations), and *organizations* (work, churches, government). Finally, the *environment*—a composite of people, activities, and organizations that are supportive, such as neighborhoods—offers support.

What will be most supportive varies with the age and the stage of life of each individual. For example, as we will see, activities with adult relatives are most supportive to young children, but adult nonrelatives may be most supportive to adolescents as they move away from the family. Single mothers who work may get the most support from nonrelatives in the workplace; nonemployed single mothers may get the most support from relatives.[3]

We like to think that *all* parents and children have equal access to social supports and that only personal initiative and effort are required to get support, yet research suggests that this is not so. There are constraints on access to social supports. People who have education, employment, income, and congenial neighborhoods receive more supports than those who do not.[4] Approximately 40 to 50 percent of nonrelative support is affected by these variables. More than any other variable, education determines the number of social contacts a person has and the depth and breadth of the social support network. Education appears to increase confidence and skills in social interaction as well as to enhance opportunities for meeting new people.[5] Income enables participation in activities and allows for a stable lifestyle in a safe neighborhood. When people live in lower socioeconomic areas that are not safe, they socialize with neighbors less often. Thus, schooling, income, and neighborhood are interacting factors that influence the amount and kind of support people get.

Although these social constraints exist, people are "biologically wired" for social relationships and seek others out.[6] But the development of their social networks is influenced by cultural, ethnic, socioeconomic, and gender-related factors.[7] Middle-class families have larger social networks than do working-class families, primarily because the former include many nonfamily members with whom they engage in many social and leisure activities.[8] Working-class families' social networks are smaller, more family-oriented, and centered on activities that are practical and child related.

Regardless of culture or class, two-parent families have larger social networks than do single-parent families.[9] Married mothers have slightly larger networks than do married fathers, and both groups have larger networks than do single mothers, primarily because married parents are involved with more relatives. It is not known whether this is due to a single mother's having less access to a spouse's relatives or less time in which to engage in activities with relatives. Although single mothers have fewer people in their networks, they rely more heavily on those they consider to form their primary networks. Through community programs, single mothers can be encouraged to enlarge their support networks.

One study compared the social networks of ethnic white mothers (those who affirm an Irish or eastern European heritage) with nonethnic white mothers (those who affirm a western European heritage exclusive of Irish ancestry) and African American mothers.[10] The study revealed that ethnic white mothers have larger family and friend networks than do nonethnic white or African American mothers. There are few differences between nonethnic white and African American mothers except that the latter are less likely to have friends outside the neighborhood.

Regardless of the number available to families, supportive social ties operate generally to improve children's social-emotional functioning[11] and their academic work,[12] to increase parents' self-confidence and well-being, and to enhance their perceptions of their children.[13] Next, we examine in more detail the different kinds of supports available.

Support within the Family

The family environment is the most immediate source of support for both children and parents. This support comes from people within the family and from family rituals.

Supportive Family Members

Potential support within the family comes from siblings, grandparents, and other relatives.

SIBLINGS Positive relationships can develop between siblings. The older sibling may be a model for the younger one, stimulating more advanced play and verbalization and increasing the younger child's empathy and understanding of others. The younger child gives the older one a chance to be a protective caregiver. So, parents have allies in siblings.

Emmy Werner and Ruth Smith point to the strong role siblings play in helping children overcome the effects of family instability and turmoil.[14] Many of the resilient adults in their study mentioned sibling relationships as an important positive feature of their childhood years. The emotional closeness and shared activities with siblings helped compensate for other difficulties.

Even in well-ordered families, close sibling relationships begun in childhood are maintained and valued in middle and old age, even when there is little contact. Sibling relationships appear to gain their power by giving people a sense of intimacy, closeness, and security: "Contact with siblings in late adulthood provides not necessarily deep intimacy, but a sense of belonging, security, attachment to a family."[15]

GRANDPARENTS   In U.S. society, many grandparents function as the primary care-givers for children, with all the responsibilities and tasks of parents. Here, however, we focus on grandparents as supports to parents. As psychologists turn their attention to important people outside the child's nuclear family, they look to grandparents, who exert influence in direct and indirect ways.[16] Grandparents influence grandchildren directly when they serve as caregivers, playmates, and family historians who pass on information that solidifies a sense of generational continuity. They are a direct influence when they act as mentors to their grandchildren and when they negotiate between parent and child. They influence grandchildren indirectly when they provide both psychological and material support to parents, who then have more resources for parenting.

Because minority families interact more with extended family members, more information on the role of grandparents in such families is available than for other families. For example, in 1984, 31 percent of African American children lived in extended families with one or both parents.[17] The extended family often includes one or both grandparents. Grandmothers help families nurture and care for children in a less structured, more spontaneous way than is possible when only two generations are present. The grandparents' role depends on whether one or both parents live in the home. For example, grandmothers are less involved in parenting when both parents are present.[18]

In general, contacts between grandparents and grandchildren vary depending on the age, health, and proximity of grandparents.[19] Grandparents typically see their grandchildren once or a few times a month. Although a few studies suggest that only a small percentage of grandparents enjoy close, satisfying relationships with their grandchildren, many other studies indicate that young adults generally feel close to grandparents (averaging 4 on a 5-point scale of emotional closeness) and that "the grandchild/grandparent bond continues with surprising strength into adulthood."[20]

Geographic proximity is the most important predictor of the nature of the relationship.[21] When grandparents live close by, contact naturally increases. When grandparents are young and healthy enough to share activities, grandchildren feel close because of the shared fun. But at the same time, when grandparents are older and in poorer health, grandchildren feel close because they can help them.

When grandchildren are very young, they see grandparents as sources of treats and gifts. When grandchildren are in elementary school, they look to grandparents to share fun activities with them, and in early adolescence, they also take pleasure in sharing a variety of activities with them. Grandchildren often see grandparents as more patient and understanding than their parents, and contemporary grandparents try to live up to this expectation.[22] They seek to be "supportive" to grandchildren—being their advocates, mediators, and sources of support, rather than being intrusive, critical, over-protective, and "old-fashioned." As noted in Chapter 19, a grandparent can become particularly close at times of family change and serve as confidant and advocate for the child who may become lost in the chaos of events.

OTHER RELATIVES   Other relatives include aunts, uncles, cousins, and in-laws. Support from these relatives appears especially helpful to parents in their parenting role. Relatives baby-sit, give advice, provide financial help, and offer emotional support. Such support increases parents' positive view of their children and of themselves as parents. As noted, such support is also related to children's improved school performance.[23]

Although relatives can be sources of support, they can also add stress when their comments to parents are negative and critical. Still, parents do better with relatives' support.[24] Single mothers appear less likely to have the support of relatives but can increase such support when they feel more confident and reach out for help.[25]

For children, extended family members are like grandparents, who convey a sense that the child is special, important, and capable. In one study, joint activities with relatives—such as washing cars or gardening—were found to predict better performance in school. Outings with adult male relatives (but not with nonrelative adults) were especially helpful for boys living in single-mother homes.[26]

Family Rituals

Steven Wolin and Linda Bennett describe the positive force of family rituals in everyday life and in the long-term development of children.[27] They divide rituals into three categories: (1) *family celebrations* (Thanksgiving, Christmas), (2) *family traditions* (vacations, birthday activities), and (3) *patterned family interactions* (dinnertime, bedtime). They believe these rituals provide a sense of rhythm and continuity to life that increases children's feelings of security and their capacity to communicate with adults.

Rituals provide stability by ensuring predictability in family life—no matter what else happens, the family eats dinner together, decorates the Christmas tree, and serves special meals on birthdays. Rituals also provide stability by linking the present family with the past and the future. Families carry on certain traditions from grandparents, and children grow up planning to carry out the same activities with their children.

The drama and excitement of rituals and traditions encourage communication among family members. Family members are more affectionate and more involved with one another at celebrations and holidays. In addition, rituals reduce the gap between parents and children, because everyone engages in the rituals as equals—everyone in the family hits the piñata at a birthday, everyone gets stuffed at Thanksgiving.

Children who grow up in alcoholic families who nevertheless maintain their family celebrations and rituals are less likely to become alcoholics themselves than are children who grow up with an alcoholic parent who does not maintain traditions.[28] The rituals serve as protective, positive forces at times of stress, giving children added feelings of security and closeness to others.

Family therapist William Doherty describes the importance of rituals for today's families, who

> now live in the best and worst time for families. The worst of times because families have historically followed the guidance of their community and culture in shaping marriage, childrearing, and the countless other elements of family living; and now the community and culture are unable to provide a coherent vision or set of tools and supports. Families are left to struggle on their own. We also live in the best of times because we understand better what makes families work, and because now we have unprecedented freedom to shape the kind of family life we want, to be *intentional* about our families.[29]

Family rituals, such as dinners and holiday celebrations, give members feelings of security.

Doherty uses the term *intentional family* to refer to "one whose members create a working plan for maintaining and building family ties, and then implement the plan as best they can."[30] Without a plan, families become victims of the two drains that sap families' energy—"the time demands outside the home and electronic technology inside the home."[31]

Like Wolin and Bennett, Doherty believes that rituals provide ways of connecting family members to one another and to the larger community. Through rituals, families maintain connections, establish predictability and identity, and enact values. Doherty's categorization of rituals differs from Wolin and Bennett's, however, as his focuses on the purpose of the ritual rather than on the form. He divides rituals into (1) *connection rituals* that promote bonding between family members (family outings, vacations), (2) *love rituals* for showing love to each member (birthdays, Mother's Day, Father's Day), and (3) *community rituals* that connect members to the larger community (weddings, religious activities).

Families are closer and happier when they form rituals that bond members at certain times of the day—when eating meals, going to bed and getting up in the morning, leaving the house and arriving home. In organizing the various rituals, family members

Interview

with Steven Wolin

Steven Wolin is a professor of clinical psychiatry at George Washington University and a researcher at the Center for Family Research. He has published several articles on the importance of rituals and, with his wife, psychologist Sybil Wolin, coauthored *The Resilient Self.*

I have read about your belief in the importance of rituals in family life and their protective value when families experience chronic problems. How did you get on to the importance of rituals?

I am a psychiatrist, and I have a long-standing interest in research on families. I was studying alcoholism back in 1980, examining interactions in marriages in which one partner was an alcoholic. I was mainly interested in ways family life was destroyed by alcohol and was, at that time, what I now call "a damage model" thinker.

I got a grant from the Institute on Alcohol Abuse and Alcoholism to study the transmission of alcoholism across generations. I decided to use family rituals as the variable for study. I have always been interested in culture as a powerful factor in family life, with family members expressing their shared beliefs through their rituals. I learned a lot about rituals from anthropology and hired a young anthropologist, Linda Bennett, who became my coinvestigator. I had the hypothesis that those families whose regular rituals were destroyed by alcohol would have a greater likelihood of transmitting alcoholism to their children.

We compared those families who had two generations of alcoholics (transmitters) with families who only had a parent who was an alcoholic (nontransmitters). The severity of the alcoholic parent was the same in both kinds of families in terms of years of drinking, hospitalizations, etc. We then systematically compared the most important rituals in these two kinds of families. We looked at holiday celebrations, traditions (like family vacations or visits to extended family members), and routines (like dinnertime rituals, greeting rituals, parties). Sure enough, we demonstrated that when alcoholism destroyed the family rituals, then transmission of alcoholism to a child occurred more frequently.

At this point, I became more interested in those families that did *not* transmit alcoholism and, for the first time in my life, asked a strength-based question: "How did you do this thing that succeeded? How did you prevent transmission from occurring?" And families were in fact doing something very deliberate. Nontransmitters were protecting their cherished, nonalcoholic rituals. For example, they made certain that Christmas was protected from the alcohol abuse of a parent. They determined that certain of their routines persisted in the face of trouble, and they kept their healthy holidays alive. Nontransmitter families actually were working to keep their families healthy, in spite of the chronic illness process of the alcoholism.

The second project focused on couples from this type of troubled background. How did they negotiate the construction of rituals of the new generation? Since they come from such troubled families, we know that many of the rituals of the family were destroyed or taken over by the alcohol or substance abuse. How do they decide what is the family of heritage in the new generation?

We selected a group of sixty-eight couples, all of whom had one alcoholic parent. The couples were around thirty years of age and often had young children themselves. We did extensive interviews regarding the ritual process in the couple as well as the rituals in each of the families they had come from. Coders did not know whether the adult children became alcoholics themselves. In half the couples, alcoholism was transmitted to the second generation, and in half not. Sure enough, once again a clear pattern emerged. When rituals were protected in the family of origin and carefully selected in the present generation, alcoholism was not passed on to the children. Couples used a process we came to call deliberateness—the careful planning and carrying out of plans for ritual maintenance and rejection.

I became more interested in the notion that individuals acted in a resilient way to prevent themselves from repeating the past even if they are at risk. When you look at the children-of-alcoholics literature, it is not all so bleak. Sometimes, people worry a lot and are afraid they are going to repeat the past. In fact, they often do not. Most children of alcoholics do not become alcoholics.

We are now describing resilience in general, and the ways individuals and couples remain strong in the face of an at-risk past situation. We did a third project that looked at little children; we examined families in which there was an alcoholic parent or grandparent in the previous generation and the adult children who may or may not have gotten into trouble. We looked at their children. Those couples who acted most deliberately, who used this careful planning and carrying out of plans, and who were most conscious and aware of what the task was in the new generation, did the best, and their children did the best. They are grandchildren of alcoholics, and they are often doing well. Like Emmy Werner's sample of resilient children, they have mastered the problems of the previous generation.

What helps couples act in a deliberate way?

They practice healthy styles of communication. They are aware of the task in front of them. A lot of couples talk about knowing exactly what to do in the new generation because it is exactly the opposite of what happened when they were kids. Healthy families will have flexibility; they can be chaotic for a while without damaging a child. But the family that is fragmented and has problems really needs healthy rituals.

Would you say the dinner rituals are most important?

We studied dinner and holiday rituals because they are so different. We found dinner rituals disappear first in the alcoholic family. We felt that holiday rituals were the most important because when they went, the family seemed to be in the most trouble. Those families who could not carry out Thanksgiving and Christmas had their identity as a family destroyed by the alcohol. Perhaps mother was so drunk she could not come down for dinner or she lit the tree on fire or there was

(continued)

(continued)

no money left for gifts. Although holidays are less frequent, they have positive importance and are the more highly valued rituals because everyone in the culture celebrates them. Family traditions like birthdays are more individual; the family defines itself by the way it does the tradition—how much importance it gives to birthdays or vacations.

Our current work is taking kids who are partially resilient and strengthening those clusters of strength in them. We want to focus on their strengths and apply the strengths to the areas that are not so strong. For example, if a child happens to use

work together to structure activities and events that are especially meaningful to each member. Rituals also help families cope with unexpected trauma and times of change such as divorce and remarriage.

Doherty lists seven major principles for establishing rewarding family rituals:

1. Get agreement between adults in the family.
2. Expect that cooperation from children will emerge gradually.
3. Have as much participation as possible from all family members.
4. Have clear expectations of what will happen and who will do what.
5. Reduce conflict through open communication and respect for others' feelings.
6. Protect rituals from the demands of other activities.
7. Be willing to change or modify the rituals as needed.

In his book *The Intentional Family*, Doherty provides numerous examples of how families overcome the stumbling blocks of lack of time and conflicting views to establish rituals that bring closeness and a sense of meaning to all family members.

Support outside the Family

Support outside the family includes neighbors, friends, and coworkers, as well as such institutions as churches, community groups, and the government.

People outside the Family

A variety of individuals outside the family serve as supports to children and to parents. Often, supportive individuals for children, such as teachers, support parents as well, conveying information and guidelines on caring for children. Parents' supports indirectly affect children when they help parents feel better about themselves and encourage a more positive view of the children.

TEACHERS   Most of us can recall a teacher who played a positive role in our school years. The teacher may have identified a special talent or skill and encouraged its devel-

initiative and becomes a good problem solver but has poor peer relationships, then the child has to learn to apply those same skills to relationship building that he uses to solve problems.

Similarly, children have to learn to do things differently than their parents. They have to see that what their parents did is not necessarily what they have to do. By recruiting "parent substitutes," children can help themselves have new kinds of relationships so they avoid the past. They will see the various hurdles in front of them as challenges and use initiative to continue to work at their problems.

opment or directed us to an area of study that proved important or motivated us to achieve our very best.

Systematic research also has identified teachers as major sources of support to both children and parents. Werner and Smith write,

> During adolescence, a caring teacher was an important protective factor for boys and girls who succeeded against the odds. This teacher served not only as an academic instructor but also as a confidant and an important role model with whom a student could identify.[32]

Even teachers of very young children have a lasting positive impact on children. Innovative research documented the long-term impact of an acknowledged effective first-grade teacher.[33] Not only were the achievement scores of her students higher in first and second grades, but their achievement as adults (twenty-five years later) was rated much higher than that of students from other classes involved in the study. Statistical analysis revealed that the teacher's influence was stronger than any other background factor—including father's occupation, family economic situation, and number of children—in predicting the adult status of her students. Pupils described the attention, kindness, and confidence she gave to them. "Her secret of success was summarized by one of her colleagues this way: 'How did she teach? With a lot of love!' "[34]

School organization and atmosphere have a positive impact on children, too. Schools that serve as protective factors against the development of delinquency have structured classrooms; emphasize homework, preparation, and competence; and encourage students to take responsibility for their behavior.[35]

OTHER NONRELATIVES   This group includes neighbors, coworkers, and community residents. Parents and children are most likely to reach out to neighbors when neighborhoods are safe. Neighbors can and do provide many of the benefits of relatives for families who have little support from relatives. They baby-sit, give advice, and lend or provide material resources. Mothers who work are especially likely to reach out to coworkers as additional sources of support.

Teachers can play a powerful role in a child's development of competence and self-esteem.

Whereas young children tend to get more support from adult relatives, adolescents appear to get support from nonrelatives. Male adolescents who interact with adult nonrelatives generally perform better in school than do other boys.[36]

Parenting Programs

Organizations and agencies provide formal and informal support for parents and children. Of special interest here are programs for parents at various stages of the parenting process.

When extended family members are not readily available for advice, parents may seek support from other parents. They may continue parent groups begun during pregnancy, or they may form or join parenting groups organized around a particular theme—parents of infants and toddlers, parents of adolescents, parents of hyperactive children, parents of children with learning disabilities.

Carolyn Cowan and Philip Cowan have found that parenting groups for mothers and fathers beginning in the last trimester of the pregnancy provide ongoing support for parents as they create new families.[37] In their study, six groups of four couples each met for six months. Couples discussed the stresses of adjusting to parenthood and found reassurance in learning that others had similar problems. The parents discussed what reduced stress and what produced well-being and closeness between parents. In following the families over a five-year period, the Cowans found that all the couples who were in the parenting groups were still together when the child was three years old, whereas 15 percent of couples who had not participated in the groups were divorced. When children were five years old, however, the divorce rate was the same for the two groups of parents.

Impressed that the six-month groups had a positive effect for three years, the Cowans have begun a new intervention study, offering such parenting groups at the time of the child's entrance into elementary school. They hope to increase parents' coping skills and their satisfaction in their marriages.

A variety of organized parenting programs are available. These programs usually last from six to twelve weeks and consist of two-hour sessions geared toward giving parents new skills and new approaches to parenting. Thomas Gordon has organized Parent Effectiveness Training (P.E.T.) sessions lasting from three to six months. A meta-analysis of twenty-six studies reveals that P.E.T. has a significant effect on parents' knowledge of the course material and a small-to-moderate effect on parenting attitudes and behavior toward children and on children's self-esteem.[38]

A review of twenty-one studies of Rudolf Dreikurs's method (discussed in Chapters 3 and 4) and the STEP (Systematic Training for Effective Parenting) program reveals that parents' attitudes change as a result of these parenting programs.[39] They are less strict and less intrusive with children than before; they listen more and encourage children more; and they are more supportive and trusting of the child. There is slight evidence that children's behavior improves as well.

Studies of parent behavioral training indicate that such training has its greatest success in decreasing such problem behaviors as bed wetting, bedtime fears, infant crying, and noncompliant behavior.[40] Parents learn specific management skills and enhance their parenting skills through active modeling and role-playing.

Gerald Patterson and Carla Narrett point out that the benefits of behavioral training for parents are greatest with young, defiant children and are limited with older, more severely disturbed adolescents.[41] Even when defiant children improve at home, the benefits of the training do not always generalize to the school setting, where children continue to have difficulty. Patterson and Narrett consider children's behavioral change to be the most important marker for parent effectiveness. Parents report overall improvement at home even when the child's specific behavior has not changed.

The parenting courses just described can last from six weeks to several months. A recent study found, however, that even a brief intervention with parents can be useful for both parents and infants.[42] First-time parents attending childbirth classes were routinely assigned to one of two groups. During pregnancy, one group received four sessions of behavioral training in helping their newborn develop healthy sleep patterns. The control group had equal discussion time with instructors but no behavioral training. When infants were six to nine weeks old, investigators collected six measures of sleep patterns over several weeks. Infants of trained parents had longer sleep episodes, fewer night awakenings, and fewer night feedings. Trained parents experienced less difficulty with their babies and felt more competent and confident in managing babies' sleep patterns. In contrast, nontrained parents reported a greater number of hassles in caring for their infants.

In a detailed review, Philip Cowan, Douglas Powell, and Carolyn Cowan categorize parenting programs in terms of whether they focus on the child, the parent, or the parent-child relationship.[43] Parenting programs, however, are often difficult to classify, because they can affect more behaviors than the one in question. For example, teaching parents how to improve a child's behavior includes teaching parents new behaviors that, in turn, can affect the parent-child relationship. Indeed, this seems to have happened in the study just described. Parents who established healthy sleep patterns for infants had fewer hassles with babies and felt more competent in caring for them.

Cowan, Powell, and Cowan point out that interventions can target families at high risk for problems—such as those with adolescent mothers or aggressive children—and families at low risk for problems, such as the general population. These researchers cite several examples of programs designed to help parents manage their responses to normative transitions such as becoming parents or to help parents deal with children's special problems such as aggressiveness or attention deficit–hyperactivity disorder.

Some of these programs include interventions at home, at school, and on the playground. Programs designed to improve children's behavior have greater effectiveness when time is devoted to improving parents' abilities to work together. Improving parents' communication and problem-solving skills increases parents' satisfaction with the program and their effectiveness with their children.

As these researchers point out, many of the programs available for families are not well validated. Those with the most evidence to support them have been developed at university and research centers and are not widely available to the public. Further, there remain many unanswered questions about parenting interventions. Is work with parents essential, or is it more effective to change children's behavior, which then triggers changes in parents' behavior? Is it important which parent participates and changes? What are the important ingredients for change?

Further, although millions of children experience cognitive, social, and emotional difficulties, the political forces in the United States are reducing programs for children and parents. Cowan, Powell, and Cowan write, "It is clear that many parents need more assistance than is currently available. The question is whether we as a society are willing to devote energy and resources toward the creation of comprehensive programs for families all along the continuum from low risk to high distress."[44] See Box 1.5 (page 32), which presents the Parents' Bill of Rights developed by Sylvia Hewlett and Cornel West, which outlines the many ways in which society can give parents necessary support in rearing children.

Workplace Supports

As noted in Chapter 8, workplaces can ease the pressures of parenting.[45] More companies today are making various kinds of programmatic changes to help parents coordinate work and family life. First, they can make it possible for parents to spend time with their children in the early years of children's lives; extended parental leave at birth or the adoption of a child can help parents bond with the child and provide the sensitive caregiving that enhances the child's development. Second, providing day care at work in the early years of childhood relieves parents' worries about the care children are receiving while they are at work. Third, flexible work schedules permit parents to

be at home when children return each day from school, when they are on holiday from
school, or when they need to stay home due to illness.

Equally important to parents is a family-friendly work climate.[46] When supervisors sympathize with the needs of parents, there is less spillover of work tension to the
home. Urie Bronfenbrenner and Peter Neville suggest that companies establish a family resources office or specialist.[47] Such an office or individual would serve as an advocate for parents and children in family-work issues. They would collect information on
family services in the community and on child development and parenting concerns.
They would provide referrals for services as needed and promote work practices that
reduce stress for parents. Studies indicate that when parents feel that their employer is
sympathetic to their needs, they are happier, more stable employees, as well as better
parents.

Governmental Supports

Psychologist Edward Zigler and freelance writer Mary Lang emphasize that governmental supports are not available for all U.S. families, as they are in Europe and many
parts of the world. All families in Canada, for example, receive a family allowance
based on the number of children under eighteen in the family. France also provides
many services for parents. For example, a young-child allowance begins in the fifth
month of pregnancy and lasts for nine months. An additional tax-free allowance is
available when a family has subsequent children, provided the mother gets prenatal
care and the infant gets regular medical care. Low-income families receive additional
aid. France also provides low-cost day care for infants and toddlers. Child care givers
are trained and licensed and included in the social security system.[48]

In the United States, one must be sick, handicapped, or poor to qualify for services
available through local, state, and federal agencies. David Hamburg describes the variety of programs available for children and parents in *Today's Children*.[49] Initially,
many programs are available in conjunction with the health care system. Some private
and public hospitals, for example, offer prenatal care, supplementary nutrition for
women and children, and home visits by nurses to demonstrate well-baby care and
healthy parenting practices. Nurses can identify high-risk parents who need more services due to a baby's medical condition or other difficulties in the family.

States provide for single mothers and families who demonstrate financial need.
The amount of financial assistance may vary from state to state, but even in the most
generous states, a family receives less than the amount considered adequate to exceed
the poverty level.

Several intervention programs have targeted families of infants. For example, in
the 1970s and 1980s, federally funded Parent Child Development Centers involved the
family from the birth of the child to age three. This program (1) provided information
for parents on home management and childrearing techniques; (2) offered preschool
education for children; (3) connected families with services for health care, nutrition,
and employment; and (4) provided an array of services for low-income families of different ethnic backgrounds. Assessments of children and parents over an eight-year

period showed that children in the program were more advanced in intellectual and social behavior and that parents and children were more positive toward each other, more affectionate, and better able to work out problems. This program ended because of lack of funds.

Federal funds support early childhood education for low-income children through the Head Start program. However, because funds are limited, only a small percentage of children are eligible for the program. As children approach adolescence, government programs exist for discouraging teenage pregnancies and increasing school attendance and academic performance.

Summarizing the programs necessary to promote children's healthy growth, David Hamburg writes,

> The approach taken here has been to recommend fostering early interventions that offer support similar to that of the traditional family. The pivotal institutions are schools, churches, community organizations, the media, and the health-care systems. A developmental sequence of interventions starts with prenatal care and goes to preventive pediatric care, parent education, social supports for young families, high-quality child care, preschool education, a constructive transition to elementary school, a reformulated middle school. Beyond that lies the possibility of further growth in high school in the transition to work and to higher education, drawing on the principles elucidated here.[50]

Hamburg believes that coordinated health- and growth-fostering programs might well be cheaper to finance than all the programs geared to problems once they have occurred. For example, universal prenatal care likely would cost less than variable care for compromised babies, who require expensive neonatal care and prolonged programs of compensatory care.

Zigler's comprehensive plan for childcare illustrates the kind of coordinated program Hamburg envisions. Zigler's plan could be implemented in modules or as separate programs, depending on the needs and resources of the individual community. Zigler, the first director of the Office of Child Development and the chief of the Children's Bureau from 1970 to 1972, outlines seven basic principles for childcare in the United States.[51]

1. *All* children must have access to high-quality childcare when needed.

2. The caregiver is the single most important determinant of the quality of the childcare—caregivers must have adequate training and supervision so they perceive and attend to the child's needs.

3. Childcare must meet the child's needs in all areas of development—health, nutrition, education—so the child's physical, social, emotional, and intellectual growth flourishes.

4. Childcare should be well integrated with other social systems such as health and education and must involve parents as active participants.

5. Childcare programs must offer options to the great variety of children and families in society, and parents should play a role in evaluating different programs.

6. Quality childcare requires a permanent commitment of resources to children and families.

7. A childcare system must be responsive to larger social demands as these change—for example, the childcare system must support healthy growth that permits individuals to contribute to society.

Because the school system is a permanent part of the social fabric and schools are dispersed throughout communities, Zigler would center his program in local schools. As a result, communities could be sensitive to local preferences, and parents would not need to go far to get services. All proposed programs would be optional for parents; no one would be required to participate.

Zigler proposes that afterschool and vacation care for the many unsupervised children ages six to eleven be available at school sites. Parents would pay, on a sliding scale, for the hiring of additional personnel, who would use the school facilities before and after regular school hours. A second proposed program at the school site would provide year-round, all-day care for preschoolers from three to five years of age. This program would promote all aspects of the child's development. Parents again would pay a sliding-scale fee, and local private and public agencies could contribute to its funding.

As Zigler suggests, schools could serve as a central network for neighborhood family day care providers for infants and toddlers in that area. Schools would provide caregiver training and supervision and make the providers part of the larger community network. Schools would also serve as a resource and referral system, directing parents to needed community services, and would be the sites of such services as well. Further, schools would provide a base for outreach services to parents, beginning in the last trimester of pregnancy. Parent education and screening programs would ensure that parents and children got the care they required.

Like Hamburg, Zigler argues that it might be cheaper to provide preventive services than to pay for problems that develop when families do not have the supports they need. He has outlined funding for such services.

Community Programs

Many existing programs serve as examples of what communities can do to provide support to parents and children. Norman Rice, writing as mayor of Seattle, summarizes in Box 11.1 what a city supportive of families and children would look like. Local government would serve as the catalyst to build coalitions of government agencies, private organizations, and individuals who lived in the neighborhoods where services were provided.[52] These partnerships of government and private resources would address issues of the most immediate interest to residents, such as schools, parks, day care services, and programs for adolescents. When possible, high-quality community programs would be supported. When this was not feasible, city government would target specific problems and pilot innovative programs to meet needs.

In a 1993 report, the U.S. Advisory Board on Child Abuse and Neglect proposed a neighborhood-based program to prevent child abuse and neglect.[53] Community

---

BOX 11.1

A Family-Friendly City

What would a family-supportive city look like? Every city can set a vision that is truly family-focused: a city where neighborhoods would feel and be safe, and everyone would have access to open space, dynamic community centers, and a wide array of cultural, artistic, and recreational activities; a place where people could easily use public transportation and could work and play in environments that supported a mix of individual and family needs. The workplace would be flexible and family friendly. People would be able to find housing they could afford, and building and land-use codes would encourage development with families in mind.

In this community, all people would share responsibility for protecting the natural environment, and business involvement in human development would be consistent and supportive. All families would have others who visited and supported them in their efforts to grow and thrive. When family members needed additional help, affordable health care and social services would be readily available.

School and city facilities would be open for community use after school and on weekends. Taking into account the many ways people learn, schools would support the development of every learner. Everyone would have the opportunity to learn skills for entering and returning to the job market. All families would have access to high-quality early childhood development programs, child care, and elder care, as necessary.

In this thriving community, all segments of the population—people of every age, both genders, all levels of ability, and every sexual orientation, race, and cultural background—would participate fully in the decision-making process and would work together to build a caring community.

Norman B. Rice, "Local Initiatives in Support of Families," in *Putting Families First*, ed. Sharon L. Kagan and Bernice Weissbourd (San Francisco: Jossey-Bass, 1994), pp. 324–325. Copyright © 1994 Jossey-Bass Publishers, Inc. Reprinted with permission of the publisher.

---

programs are especially important in this area, because socially isolated, unstable neighborhoods offering little support to families are at high risk for increased incidence of child abuse and neglect. The board's proposals focused on ways to provide physically safe and socially supportive neighborhoods in which "people care about, watch, and support each other's families."[54]

To strengthen neighborhoods, residents must become involved in positive actions to improve the quality of life in their area.[55] Several principal guidelines are used in organizing services. Comprehensive community services such as medical care, education, and employment become geographically accessible to area residents. Neighborhood-based programs coordinate services that focus on the needs of recipients, not providers. One-stop locations, referrals, and follow-up are organized to meet recipients' needs. Neighborhood residents and organizations participate at all levels of decision making and eventually may come to control the services. Many benefits accrue to residents in the course of planning and implementing services, and the neighborhood or community becomes closer and more effective in dealing with problems.

In general, these programs work best when individuals begin with a single issue of concern and then go on to other issues. For example, Irene Johnson, a mother living in a low-cost housing project in Chicago, was concerned about the safety of her children in the project because of gangs, drug dealing, and gambling.[56] With the help of her friends and social workers, Johnson formed the LeClaire Residents Committee and researched ways to manage the housing project more effectively. The group selected resident management, in which the tenants would form a corporation to run the project. After several years, the Housing Authority agreed to a trial of such management. Tenants took courses to learn how to perform all the services required, and the annual funds for running the project were turned over to residents.

Tenants organized a neighborhood watch, hired a security firm, and met with police to explore ways to decrease violence and crime. Crime dropped 50 percent in the project. Residents began to organize new services such as a laundry and convenience store on the premises. As a result, tenants' income and skills level rose, their children enjoyed a safer environment, and their hopes for the future improved.

Roger Weissberg and Mark Greenberg review school and community programs designed (1) to enhance children's competence in all areas of functioning and (2) to prevent the development of problems.[57] Like parenting programs, these school and community programs can target all neighborhoods of the community. Programs are designed to improve several aspects of functioning—health, school performance, and social and psychological functioning.

Community programs target children from birth through the adolescent years. They include a wide variety of services such as home-visiting programs (see Chapter 5), which involve parents actively, and school-based programs, which work primarily with children and may never involve parents.

These programs are most effective when implemented for several years and include many forms of intervention by a multidisciplinary team. For example, in Baltimore, Johns Hopkins Medical Center worked with the school system to provide school-based reproductive health services to an inner-city junior high school and senior high school. The university provided a nurse and a social worker to give sex education presentations once each semester; they were also available two and half hours a day in a school health suite, providing individual counseling, reproductive health care, and education. The staff also trained and supervised students to be peer leaders in discussion groups.

In the first two years of the program, students' knowledge and use of contraceptives improved. Fewer than 20 percent of girls had unprotected sex, as compared with 44 to 49 percent in schools without the program. After 28 months of the program, the pregnancy rate dropped 30 percent, whereas it increased 57 percent in comparison schools. For those in the program three years, the initiation of sexual activity was postponed seven months.

Other programs have targeted several areas of functioning. The New Haven, Connecticut, school district set up a comprehensive program to decrease high-risk behaviors such as drug use, teen pregnancy, AIDS, delinquency, and school failure. They believed that poor social skills underlay all these behaviors.

Administrators set up a multifaceted program extending from kindergarten through twelfth grade. In the early years, students learned self-monitoring, problem solving, and communication skills. They also learned about taking responsibility for healthy behaviors. As students got older, educational and recreational activities at school and in the community reinforced what they were learning at school. The Extended Day Academy was established; it included afterschool clubs, health services, and an adventure club.

Evaluations of the program revealed improvements in students' social skills, with decreases in acting-out behaviors. Students felt safer at school and in the neighborhood and more positive about their prospects. Decreases in adolescent high-risk behaviors were not found after five years in the program; however, such interventions may require longer involvement to decrease such behavior.

Church Support

In their study of resilient children who overcame the difficulties of growing up in troubled families, Werner and Smith point to the importance of faith:

> A potent protective factor among high-risk individuals who grew into successful adulthood was a faith that life made sense, that the odds could be overcome. This faith was tied to active involvement in church activities, whether Buddhist, Catholic, mainstream Protestant, or fundamentalist.[58]

When parents attend church themselves, it is easy to incorporate the children into that religious life; however, when parents have no religious affiliation, they may wonder what to do. One such father of a young child wrote to Joan Beck, author of *Effective Parenting*, to ask for her advice.[59] He could not pretend a belief he did not have in God, but he wanted his daughter to have the freedom to make her own decision as she matured.

Beck suggests that families must find their own answer. Parents have three options: (1) ignore the whole question, (2) send children for religious instruction without parents' participation, or (3) develop an inquiring attitude about religion that can be shared with children as they grow.

Church attendance is relatively low in the United States today; as a result, it has been increasingly easy to raise a child without religious instruction. Such children, however, may have many questions that remain unanswered: Who is God? What happens when we die? Will God punish me? As such children see the involvement of grandparents and of other families in religious activities, and as they encounter religious references in the media, they may feel a void in their own experiences. This void may be intensified if they lack a source of comfort or solace when a painful loss occurs.

Sending a child for religious instruction without parental participation, however, seems hypocritical. The most reasonable alternative for some parents is to develop an individual belief system that they share with children as they grow. Parents can explore different conceptions of God, convey to children what they accept and do not accept in each conception, and discuss the meanings of rituals and symbols and the reasons others may find them important. In investigating the ideas of different churches, parents may discover a group they can join wholeheartedly, rediscover the religion of their parents, or find they want to join a group devoted to social action rather than worship. The process of searching for an agreed-on source of spiritual or secular meaning can enrich the entire family.

In fostering children's faith, parents have a natural ally in children themselves. Robert Coles reviewed his interactions and interviews with children concerning crises in their lives and their moral and political views of life. He concluded that the area he ignored for too many years of his professional life was children's intense engagement in religious concerns—the meaning of life, the purpose of their individual lives, their goodness and/or badness, and their duties and obligations to themselves, to their families, and to others.[60]

Seeking to understand their spiritual lives, Coles interviewed children around the world about their conceptions of God and the meaning of God in their lives. His book *The Spiritual Life of Children* summarizes numerous poignant interviews and conversations with children, individually and in groups. Religious concerns are not dry intellectual matters to many children but emotionally intense concerns strongly integrated into their personalities and understanding of themselves and life. Cole states,

> I began to realize that psychologically God can take almost any shape for children. He can be a friend or a potential enemy; an admirer or a critic; an ally or an interference; a source of encouragement or a source of anxiety, fear, or even panic. . . . Often, children whose sternly Christian, Jewish, or Moslem parents don't hesitate to threaten them with the most severe of religious strictures (and thus who do likewise with respect to themselves) can construct in their thoughts or dreams a God who is exemplary yet lenient, forgiving, encouraging, capable of confessing a moment's weakness or exhaustion now and then.[61]

Like Werner and Smith, Coles finds that religious beliefs give children a feeling of security that life is predictable and understandable—God knows and understands and controls all. In conversations with God, children experience an emotional closeness— God is "a companion who won't leave."[62] God provides strength and help as needed, though how and when are often difficult questions. With benefits come obligations of moral behavior in interactions with others. Children's conception of God sometimes adds security to life by providing fallible parents with a backup expert who helps them. "God is my parents' parent and mine too,"[63] stated one girl.

Church programs help both parents and children. Many churches offer general parenting classes and classes in teaching values. Churches also provide recreational and family activities that bring pleasure and feelings of belonging and security to all family members.

A Catholic church leadership project in Harlem illustrates the powerful support church activities can provide for adolescent boys.[64] Several decades ago, the church selected fourteen boys on the basis of academic and personal potential for participation

Interview
with Andrew Billingsley

Andrew Billingsley is a professor in the Department of Family Studies at the University of Maryland. He is the author of many books, including *Black Families in White America*, *The Evolution of Black Families*, and *Climbing Jacob's Ladder: The Enduring Legacy of African-American Families*.

You have talked about the strengths in people's lives, particularly the church, so I wanted to talk to you in more detail about that. What role do you see the church playing in people's lives?

The church is a major community support, particularly in African American communities. The churches are increasingly developing programs that support and help young people. Not all churches have embraced this mission. In a large-scale study, about a third of all churches were not involved in supportive programs, a third were moderately involved, and a third were actively involved in elaborate programs for people from cradle to the grave.

In Washington, D.C., an enlightened minister, the Reverend Henry C. Gregor III, came to the men in the church and said, "We have to develop a program to rescue the young boys in our community. Many are in danger of losing their way. They are vulnerable, and there are many snares waiting for them. You men are strong. You must lend some of your strength to these boys." Now, there is a program at the church involving young boys from nine to fifteen. They are at church every afternoon, getting a snack, tutoring. These men stay in touch with the boys' parents, their teachers. They organize activities for them; they focus on the kids to help them get what they need to do well. There is a saying that it takes a whole village to raise a child. A child needs more than parents to grow up well; the child needs community support.

The church can be an agent of reform. On its 100th anniversary, the Friendship Baptist Church in Columbus, Georgia, decided to do a survey to identify community needs. The survey identified needs for day-long affordable childcare and for an afterschool program for older children. First, it organized a high-quality childcare program for parents in the neighborhood so they did not have to go far to get good care for their children. Professional teachers give intellectually stimulating material and spiritually enriching lessons. The church also established an afterschool program that involves children from six to thirteen in constructive activities, including lessons on African American history and culture.

For example, Robert Smalls was a slave who worked on a Confederate warship during the Civil War. In the middle of the night, after the captain and the crew left the ship, Smalls and the other slaves took it over. The next day, dressed correctly,

in a two-year program. The boys attended cultural events, listened to speakers, and went on weekend retreats that combined fun and discussion of serious issues. Although the program designers hoped to recruit some boys for the priesthood, almost all married, some became fathers, and only one became a priest. In large part, they are professional men.

standing on the deck, he and the other slaves sailed the ship out of Charleston harbor, giving all the correct signals so that no one realized who they were. They stopped to pick up their families and then sailed to freedom past Fort Sumter. So then you say to youth, "What do you want to be? These people achieved against great odds. Now, what do you want? What are you going to be?"

The church takes a positive approach to people and says, "You might have made a lot of mistakes, but God loves you." When the church gets into action, it says, "We love you too, and we will help you accomplish what you can." The church can have dramatic results.

I was visiting the oldest continuous black church in America. Scholars think that it is in Philadelphia, but the oldest is the First African Baptist Church in Savannah, founded in 1773 and still functioning. There, about ten teenage boys told me a story. In April of 1993, a bunch of black teenagers got into a fight at the high school. No weapons or blood, just pushing and shoving. The school was integrated, but the fight was only among blacks. The school had an overwhelming need to punish violence. The boys were arrested and taken to court. The school had decided there would be zero tolerance for violence, and the boys were sentenced to thirty days in jail. Now if the boys missed ten days of classes, the school required they repeat the entire grade. The judge and the school were not aware of the long-term consequences of these actions for the boys. They would be out of school and could get into trouble.

A minister, the Reverend Thurman Tillman, went into action and talked to the judge. The boys had no previous trouble and all were passing their classes, so the judge agreed to take another look at the cases. After one week in jail, the boys were assigned to the minister, and he supervised their community activities and reported back to the judge every few days as to how they were doing. At first, the school would not accept them back, so the minister organized a school so they could keep up with their grade. He got them special T-shirts, and overall the boys became more responsible citizens. Last April, at the end of probation, the minister took them all for a treat. Six of the boys have now graduated from high school. The schools need to be more sensitive, and the legal system needs to be more flexible instead of just sending these teenagers away. If left to their own devices, the boys may not have done it right. But the church stepped in.

The church holds out hope and can be an affirming experience for people who don't get that elsewhere. Little children sing, "I am a promise, I am a possibility, I can be anything God wants me to be."

In looking back at what they gained from the experience, the men made such comments as "My whole life I owe to it. It made me realize my self-worth. Growing up where I did, you never saw the outside world for what it was. I learned that you can be successful by giving it your all." "It was taking this group with a bunch of energy and a bunch of mouth and channeling it into something positive. It helped me stand up and formulate some thoughts in an intelligent way." This project is now open to boys and girls.

The Power of a Single Individual

Most of the support programs mentioned in the preceding pages have involved large organizations. It seems fitting to conclude our discussion with an example of what a single person with a clear goal can accomplish when she gathers community resources to provide support for children and parents.

Barbara Barlow, a pediatric surgeon at Harlem Hospital in New York, became concerned at the growing number of preventable injuries she was treating. Children fell from open windows, were hit by automobiles while playing in the street, or were victims of violence.[65]

In 1988, she started Harlem Hospital's Injury Prevention Program (IPP) with a grant from the Robert Wood Johnson Foundation. With a staff of three, Barlow first set out to rebuild playgrounds and parks in the community, because there were no safe places for children to play. She photographed all of the neglected parks and playgrounds and took the information to the Parks Department and the Board of Education. The Parks Department has since made nearly all the parks in the area safe. Barlow then sought private funding for the construction of new playgrounds; at the suggestion of teachers and students, two new playgrounds were built and six more planned.

The IPP has expanded to include activities that foster children's competence, such as an in-hospital art program, begun so patients could express their feelings about illness and hospitalization. Children have exhibited and sold their work, with half the profits going to the children and half to the art program. The IPP also sponsors a dance program, baseball teams, a soccer team, and a "greening program," in which children can grow flowers and vegetables.

Major injuries to children in Harlem have decreased by 37 percent, motor vehicle accidents have decreased by 50 percent, and fewer children have fallen from windows. In addition, the young dancers, athletes, artists, and gardeners have developed skills they may not have learned without the programs.

The high number of violent injuries to children also led Barlow to start the Anti-Violence Project, which contains several specific programs for (1) teaching children how to stay safe, (2) helping children deal with violence after they experience it, and (3) teaching children, their parents, and educators conflict resolution techniques and other ways to avoid violence.

Funding for these programs comes from individuals, corporations, foundations, and fees from Barlow's speaking engagements. She concludes,

> You have to give to get in this world, and we give a lot. We put in lots of hard work, but it's immensely satisfying. There is no such thing as not being able to make things better. In any community, every individual can make a tremendous difference if they truly care, if they look around to see what needs to be done.[66]

Social supports

- provide emotional, instrumental, and informational benefits to children and parents
- are divided into people, activities, organizations, and environments
- vary according to the individual's age and life stage
- are constrained by socioeconomic, cultural, ethnic, and gender-related factors

Supportive family members

- include siblings, grandparents, aunts, uncles, cousins, and in-laws
- increase feelings of closeness and belonging
- serve as companions in activities
- can help carry out parenting activities and nourish and protect children
- teach children new skills

Family rituals

- provide stability by ensuring predictability in family life
- encourage communication among family members
- link family members with the past and the future
- serve as a protective factor in times of difficulty

Teachers and nonrelatives

- serve as models and mentors to children
- provide encouragement for children
- promote responsibility and competence in children

Parenting programs

- can provide support groups for parents
- teach specific skills to parents
- enable parents to reduce children's behavioral difficulties
- reduce the stress of parenting
- increase parents' self-confidence and feelings of competence

Workplace supports for parents

- enable parents to spend more time with children
- can provide quality care for children
- help parents integrate the demands of work and family life

In the United States, government and community programs supportive of parents

- are available only for parents with some special difficulty
- often have too limited funding to help all who are eligible

- can be operated in conjunction with the health care and educational systems
- may be cheaper when funded to prevent rather than treat problems
- can, according to Zigler, be operated through schools and provide quality care for children of all ages

Churches

- help children make sense of life and provide them with a sense of security
- provide emotional closeness and feelings of belonging to all family members
- offer guidelines for daily conduct and can provide programs that help children develop competence

Individuals

- can mobilize resources to support parents and children
- can make an enormous difference in the lives of children and parents

Exercises

1. List activities, people, and organizations that provided you with positive support when you were growing up. Looking back, what supports did your parents rely on when they were raising you?

2. Describe family traditions in your family of origin. What feelings did these traditions create in family members? How will you incorporate these traditions in your own family?

3. Think about the positive supports your school provided for you and your parents. Were there teachers who gave you special encouragement? Did you develop any lifelong interests at that time?

4. Investigate the supports a large company in your area provides its employees. Do they have on-site day care? flex time? family-leave policies?

5. Investigate the services your community provides for parents and children. Does it offer parenting programs? recreational programs? summer day programs for children? joint parent-child activities? How friendly is your community to families and young children?

Additional Readings

Coles, Robert. *The Spiritual Life of Children*. Boston: Houghton Mifflin, 1990.

Doherty, William J. *The Intentional Family*. New York: Avon Books, 1997.

Hamburg, David A. *Today's Children*. New York: Times Books, 1992.

Werner, Emmy E., and Ruth S. Smith. *Overcoming the Odds*. Ithaca, NY: Cornell University Press, 1992.

Wolin, Steven J., and Sybil Wolin. *The Resilient Self*. New York: Villard, 1993.

Zigler, Edward F., and Mary E. Lang. *Child Care Choices*. New York: Free Press, 1991.

Notes

Chapter 1

1. U.S. Bureau of the Census, *Statistical Abstract of the United States: 1998*, 118th ed. (Washington, DC: U.S. Government Printing Office, 1998).
2. William Morris, ed., *The American Heritage Dictionary of the English Language* (Boston: American Heritage Publishing and Houghton Mifflin, 1969).
3. Ellen Goodman, "Why Jaycee Is Parentless," *San Francisco Chronicle*, 16 September 1997, p. A21.
4. Morris, *American Heritage Dictionary*.
5. Jay Belsky, "The Determinants of Parenting: A Process Model," *Child Development* 55 (1984): 83–96.
6. Urie Bronfenbrenner and Pamela A. Morris, "The Ecology of Developmental Processes," in *Handbook of Child Psychology*, ed. in chief William Damon and vol. ed. Richard Lerner, vol. 1, *Theoretical Models of Human Development*, 5th ed. (New York: Wiley, 1998), pp. 996, 1015.
7. Mark Mellman, Edward Lazarus, and Allan Rivlin, "Family Time, Family Values," in *Rebuilding the Nest*, ed. David Blankenhorn, Steven Bayme, and Jean Bethke Elshtain (Milwaukee: Family Service of America, 1990), pp. 73–92.
8. Lois Wladis Hoffman and Jean Denby Manis, "The Values of Children in the United States: A New Approach to the Study of Fertility," *Journal of Marriage and the Family* 41 (1979): 583–596.
9. Bronfenbrenner and Morris, "Ecology of Developmental Processes," p. 1015.
10. *People*, 10 November 1997.
11. Hoffman and Manis, "Values of Children."
12. Ross D. Parke and Raymond Buriel, "Socialization in the Family: Ethnic and Ecological Perspectives," in *Handbook of Child Psychology*, ed. in chief William Damon and vol. ed. Nancy Eisenberg, vol. 3, *Social, Emotional, and Personality Development*, 5th ed. (New York: Wiley, 1998), pp. 463–552.
13. Barbara J. Tinsley and Nancy B. Lees, "Health Promotion for Parents," in *Handbook of Parenting*, ed. Marc H. Bornstein, vol. 4, *Applied and Practical Parenting* (Mahwah, NJ: Erlbaum, 1995), pp. 187–204.
14. Wendy Haight and Katherine Sachs, "The Portrayal of Negative Emotions during Mother-Child Pretend Play," in *Exploring Young Children's Concepts of Self and Other through Conversation*, New Directions for Child Development, ed. Linda J. Sperry and Patricia A. Smiley, no. 69 (San Francisco: Jossey-Bass, 1995), pp. 33–46.
15. Betty Hart and Todd R. Risley, *Meaningful Differences in the Everyday Experience of Young American Children* (Baltimore: Brookes, 1995).
16. Belsky, "Determinants of Parenting."
17. Urie Bronfenbrenner, *The Ecology of Human Development: Experiments by Nature and Design* (Cambridge, MA: Harvard University Press, 1979); Urie Bronfenbrenner, "Ecology of the Family as a Context for Human Development," *Developmental Psychology* 22 (1986): 723–742.
18. Parke and Buriel, "Socialization in the Family."
19. Ibid., p. 496.
20. John D. Coie et al., "The Science of Prevention: A Conceptual Framework and Some Directives for a National Research Program," *American Psychologist* 48 (1993): 1013–1022.
21. Arnold J. Sameroff et al., "Family and Social Influences on the Development of Child Competence," in *Families, Risk, and Competence*, ed. Michael Lewis and Can-

dice Fearing (Mahwah, NJ: Erlbaum, 1998), pp. 161–185.

22. Ibid.

23. Ibid., pp. 178–179.

24. Arnold Sameroff, "Democratic and Republican Models of Development: Paradigms or Perspectives," *APA Division 7 Newsletter* (fall 1996): 8.

25. Ronald Seifer et al., "Child and Family Factors That Ameliorate Risk between 4 and 13 Years of Age," *Journal of the American Academy of Child and Adolescent Psychiatry* 31 (1992): 893–303.

26. Bronfenbrenner and Morris, "Ecology of Developmental Processes."

27. Jay Belsky, Elliot Robins, and Wendy Gamble, "The Determinants of Parental Competence: Toward a Contextual Theory," in *Beyond the Dyad*, ed. Michael Lewis (New York: Plenum, 1984), pp. 251–280.

28. Tamara Hareven, "Themes in the Historical Development of the Family," in *A Review of Child Development Research*, vol. 7, ed. Ross D. Parke et al. (Chicago: University of Chicago Press, 1984), pp. 137–178.

29. Ibid.

30. Stephanie Coontz, *The Way We Really Are: Coming to Terms with America's Changing Families* (New York: Basic Books, 1997).

31. Ibid.

32. Ibid.

33. Louis Uchitelle, "The American Middle Class, Just Getting By," *New York Times*, 1 August 1999, sec. 3, p. 1.

34. U.S. Bureau of the Census, *Statistical Abstract of the United States: 1998*.

35. John P. Robinson and Geoffrey Godbey, *Time for Life: The Surprising Ways Americans Use Their Time* (University Park, PA: Pennsylvania State University Press, 1997).

36. Daniel Yankelovich, *New Rules: Searching for Fulfillment in a World Turned Upside Down* (New York: Random House, 1981).

37. U.S. Bureau of the Census, *Statistical Abstract of the United States: 1998*.

38. Christoph N. Heinicke, "Determinants of the Transition to Parenting," in *Handbook of Parenting*, ed. Marc H. Bornstein, vol. 3, *Status and Social Conditions of Parenting* (Mahwah, NJ: Erlbaum), pp. 277–303.

39. Gerald Y. Michaels, "Motivational Factors in the Decision and Timing of Pregnancy," in *The Transition to Parenthood*, ed. Gerald Y. Michaels and Wendy A. Goldberg (New York: Cambridge University Press, 1988), pp. 23–61.

40. Lisa A. Serbin et al., "Intergenerational Transfer of Psychosocial Risk in Women with Childhood Histories of Aggression, Withdrawal, or Aggression and Withdrawal," *Developmental Psychology* 34 (1998): 1242–1262.

41. Joy D. Osofsky, Della M. Hann, and Claire Peebles, "Adolescent Parenthood: Risks and Opportunities for Mothers and Infants," in *Handbook of Infant Mental Health*, ed. Charles H. Zeanah, Jr. (New York: Guilford Press, 1993), pp. 106–119.

42. Judith Musick, "The Special Role of Parenting in the Context of Poverty: The Case of Adolescent Motherhood," in *Threats to Optimal Development: Integrating Biological, Psychological and Social Risk Factors*, ed. Charles A. Nelson (Hillsdale, NJ: Erlbaum, 1994), pp. 179–216.

43. Osofsky, Hann, and Peebles, "Adolescent Parenthood."

44. Beverly I. Fagot et al., "Becoming an Adolescent Father: Precursors and Parenting," *Developmental Psychology* 34 (1998): 1209–1219.

45. Terrence P. Thornberry, Carolyn A. Smith, and Gregory J. Howard, "Risk Factors for Teenage Fatherhood," *Journal of Marriage and the Family* 59 (1997): 505–522.

46. Laura V. Scaramella et al., "Predicting Risk for Pregnancy by Late Adolescence: A Social Contextual Perspective," *Developmental Psychology* 34 (1998): 1233–1245.

47. Nancy J. Cobb, *Adolescence: Continuity, Change, and Diversity* (Mountain View, CA: Mayfield, 1992).

48. Brenda W. Donnelly and Patricia Voydanoff, "Factors Associated with Releasing for Adoption among Adolescent Mothers," *Family Relations* 40 (1990): 404–410.

49. Carolyn Pape Cowan and Philip A. Cowan, *When Partners Become Parents* (New York: Basic Books, 1992).

50. Melissa Ludtke, *On Our Own: Unmarried Motherhood in America* (New York: Random House, 1997).

51. Marsha Weinraub and Marcy B. Gringlas, "Single Parenthood," in *Handbook of Parenting*, vol. 3, pp. 65–87.

52. Ludtke, *On Our Own.*

53. Jane Mattes, *Single Mothers by Choice*, 2d ed. (New York: Times Books, 1997).

54. Marilyn Fabe and Norma Wikler, *Up against the Clock* (New York: Random House, 1979).

55. Cowan and Cowan, *When Partners Become Parents.*

56. Henry P. David, "Developmental Effects of Compulsory Pregnancy," *Child, Youth, and Family Services Quarterly* (spring 1992).

57. James McCarthy and Janet Hardy, "Age at First Birth and Birth Outcomes," *Journal of Research on Adolescence* 3 (1993): 373–392.

58. Ibid.

59. U.S. Bureau of the Census, *Statistical Abstract of the United States: 1998.*

60. Robert R. Franklin and Dorothy Kay Brockman, *In Pursuit of Fertility*, 2d ed. (New York: Holt, 1995).

61. Lisa Belkin, "Pregnant with Complications," *New York Times Magazine*, 26 October 1997.

62. Carol Harkness, *The Infertility Book*, 2d ed. (Berkeley, CA: Celestial Arts, 1992).

63. Christine A. Bachrach, Clifford C. Clogg, and Karen Carver, "Outcomes of Early Childbearing: Summary of a Conference," *Journal of Research on Adolescence* 3 (1993): 337–348.

64. Osofsky, Hann, and Peebles, "Adolescent Parenthood."

65. Nan Marie Astone, "Are Adolescent Mothers Just Single Mothers?" *Journal of Research on Adolescence* 3 (1993): 353–371.

66. Ibid.

67. Jeanne Brooks-Gunn and P. Lindsay Chase-Lansdale, "Adolescent Parenthood," in *Handbook of Parenting*, vol. 3, pp. 113–149.

68. Lisa A. Serbin, Patricia L. Peters, and Alexander E. Schwartzman, "Longitudinal Study of Early Childhood Injuries and Acute Illnesses in the Offspring of Adolescent Mothers Who Were Aggressive, Withdrawn or Aggressive-Withdrawn in Childhood," *Journal of Abnormal Psychology* 105 (1996): 500–507.

69. Brooks-Gunn and Chase-Lansdale, "Adolescent Parenthood."

70. Janet B. Hardy et al., "Like Mother, Like Child: Intergenerational Patterns of Age at First Birth and Associations with Childhood and Adolescent Characteristics and Adult Outcomes in the Second Generation," *Developmental Psychology* 34 (1998): 1220–1232.

71. Frank F. Furstenberg, J. Brooks-Gunn, and S. Philip Morgan, *Adolescent Mothers in Later Life* (Cambridge: Cambridge University Press, 1990), pp. 145–146.

72. Andrew Yarrow, *Latecomers: Children of Parents over 35* (New York: Free Press, 1991).

73. Ibid.

74. Jane B. Brooks, *The Process of Parenting*, 5th ed. (Mountain View, CA: Mayfield, 1999).

75. Susan Golombok et al., "Families Created by the New Reproductive Technologies: Quality of Parenting and Social and Emotional Development of the Children," *Child Development* 66 (1995): 285–298.

76. Ibid.

77. Raymond W. Chan, Barbara Raboy, and Charlotte J. Patterson, "Psychosocial Adjustment among Children Conceived via Donor and Heterosexual Mothers," *Child Development* 69 (1998): 443–457.

78. Peggy Orenstein, "Looking for a Donor to Call Dad," *New York Times Magazine*, 18 June, 1995, p. 28.

79. Ibid.

80. Brooks, *Process of Parenting.*

81. Harkness, *Infertility Book*, p. 327.

82. Judith Rich Harris, *The Nurture Assumption: Why Children Turn Out the Way They Do* (New York: Free Press, 1998), p. 351.

83. Lynn Singer et al., "Relationship of Prenatal Cocaine Exposure and Maternal Postpartum Psychological Distress to Child Development Outcome," *Development and Psychopathology* 9 (1997): 473–489.

84. Gurney Williams III, "Toxic Dads," *Parenting*, October 1998, p. 94.

85. Bronfenbrenner and Morris, "Ecology of Developmental Processes."

86. Jerome Kagan, Doreen Arcus, and Nancy Snidman, "The Idea of Temperament: Where Do We Go from Here?" in *Nature,*

Nurture and Psychology, ed. Robert Plomin and Gerald E. McClearn (Washington, DC: American Psychological Association, 1993), pp. 197–210.

87. Seong-Yeon Park et al., "Emotionality, Parenting, and 3-Year Inhibition: Exploring Stability and Lawful Discontinuity in a Male Sample," *Developmental Psychology* 33 (1997): 218–227.

88. G. R. Patterson and D. M. Capaldi, "Antisocial Parents: Unskilled and Vulnerable," in *Family Transitions*, ed. Philip A. Cowan and Mavis Hetherington (Hillsdale, NJ: Erlbaum, 1991), pp. 195–218.

89. Roger P. Weissberg and Mark T. Greenberg, "School and Community Competence-Enhancement and Prevention," in *Handbook of Child Psychology*, ed. in chief William Damon and vol. ed. Irving E. Sigel and K. Ann Renninger, vol. 4, *Child Psychology in Practice*, 5th ed. (New York: Wiley, 1998), pp. 877–954.

90. Deborah A. Phillips, "Socialization of Perceived Academic Competence among Highly Competent Children," *Child Development* 58 (1987): 1308–1320.

91. Benjamin S. Bloom, ed., *Developing Talent in Young People* (New York: Ballantine, 1985).

92. Ross D. Parke et al., "Family-Peer Relationships: Cognitive, Emotional, and Ecological Determinants," in *Families, Risk, and Competence*, ed. Lewis and Fearing, pp. 89–112.

93. David M. Buss, Jeanne H. Block, and Jack Block, "Preschool Activity Level: Personality Correlates and Developmental Implications," *Child Development* 51 (1980): 401–408.

94. Carol Tavris, "Peer Pressure," *New York Times Book Review*, 13 September 1998, p. 14.

95. John Leo, "Parenting without a Care," *U.S. News & World Report*, 21 September 1998, p. 14.

96. Urie Bronfenbrenner and Peter R. Neville, "America's Children and Families: An International Perspective," in *Putting Families First*, ed. Sharon L. Kagan and Bernice Weissbourd (San Francisco: Jossey-Bass, 1994), pp. 3–27.

97. Elizabeth Olson, "U.N. Surveys Paid Leave for Mothers," *New York Times*, 16 February 1998, p. A5.

98. Peter Edelman, "Clinton's Cosmetic Poverty Tour," *New York Times*, 8 July 1999, p. A25.

99. Jeanne Brooks-Gunn and Greg J. Duncan, "The Effects of Poverty on Children," *The Future of Children* 7 (1997): 113–131.

100. Sylvia Ann Hewlett and Cornel West, *The War against Parents* (Boston: Houghton Mifflin, 1998).

101. "Rich Nation, Poor Children," *New York Times*, 5 August 1995.

102. Jay Belsky and John Kelly, *The Transition to Parenthood* (New York: Delacorte, 1994), p. 23.

103. Steve Farkas et al., *Kids These Days: What Americans Really Think about the Next Generation* (New York: Public Agenda, 1997).

104. Hewlett and West, *The War against Parents*.

105. E. J. Dionne, Jr., "New Efforts to Mend Tattered Health System," *San Francsico Chronicle*, 14 August 1999, p. A27.

106. Elizabeth Gleick, "The Children's Crusade," *Time*, 3 June 1996.

Chapter 2

1. David Blankenhorn, introduction to *Rebuilding the Nest*, ed. David Blankenhorn, Steven Bayme, and Jean Bethke Elshtain (Milwaukee, WI: Family Service of America, 1990), pp. xi–xv; Lynn Okagaki and Diana Johnson Divecha, "Development of Parental Beliefs," in *Parenting: An Ecological Perspective*, ed. Tom Luster and Lynn Okagaki (Hillsdale, NJ: Erlbaum, 1993), pp. 35–67.

2. Barbara A. Mowdar et al., "Parent-Role Questionnaire: Psychometric Qualities," *Psychology in the Schools* 30 (1993): 205–211.

3. Okagaki and Divecha, "Development of Parental Beliefs," pp. 35–67.

4. Barbara J. Tinsley and Nancy B. Lees, "Health Promotion for Parents," in *Handbook of Parenting*, ed. Marc H. Bornstein, vol. 4, *Applied and Practical*

Parenting (Mahwah, NJ: Erlbaum, 1995), pp. 187–204.

5. Ibid.

6. Ibid.; Nancy Eisenberg and Bridget Murphy, "Parenting and Children's Moral Development," in *Handbook of Parenting*, vol. 4, pp. 227–257; Patricia Chamberlain and Gerald R. Patterson, "Discipline and Child Compliance," in *Handbook of Parenting*, vol. 4, pp. 205–225; Gary W. Ladd and Karen D. LeSieur, "Parents and Children's Peer Relationships," in *Handbook of Parenting*, vol. 4, pp. 377–409.

7. Nancy Eisenberg, introduction to *Handbook of Child Psychology*, ed. in chief William Damon and vol. ed. Nancy Eisenberg, vol. 3, *Social, Emotional, and Personality Development*, 5th ed. (New York: Wiley, 1998), pp. 1–24.

8. Ibid.

9. Tinsley and Lees, "Health Promotion for Parents."

10. Esther Thelen, "Motor Development: A New Synthesis," *American Psychologist* 50 (1995): 79–95.

11. Ibid.

12. Ibid., p. 94.

13. Jean Piaget and Barbel Inhelder, *The Psychology of the Child* (New York: Basic Books, 1969); Herbert Ginsburg and Sylvia Opper, *Piaget's Theory of Intellectual Development* (Englewood Cliffs, NJ: Prentice-Hall, 1969).

14. John M. Belmont, "Cognitive Strategies and Strategic Learning," *American Psychologist* 44 (1989): 142–148; Laboratory of Comparative Human Cognition, "Culture and Cognitive Development," in *Handbook of Child Psychology*, ed. William Kessen, vol. 1, *History, Theory, and Methods* (New York: Wiley, 1982), pp. 295–356; James V. Wertsch and Peeter Tulviste, "L. S. Vygotsky and Contemporary Developmental Psychology,"*Developmental Psychology* 28 (1992): 548–557.

15. Daniel Goleman, *Emotional Intelligence* (New York: Bantam Books, 1995).

16. Pamela M. Cole, Margaret K. Michel, and Lawrence O'Donnell Teti, "The Development of Emotion Regulation and Dysregulation: A Clinical Perspective," in *The Development of Emotion Regulation*, ed. Nathan A. Fox, Monographs of the Society for Research in Child Development 59, serial no. 240 (1994), p. 76.

17. Robert N. Emde et al., "The Moral Self of Infancy: Affective Core and Procedural Knowledge," *Developmental Review* 11 (1991): 251–270.

18. Tiffany Field, "The Effects of Mother's Physical and Emotional Unavailability on Emotion Regulation," in *The Development of Emotion Regulation*, pp. 208–227.

19. Myron A. Hofer, "Hidden Regulators in Attachment, Separation, and Loss," in *The Development of Emotion Regulation*, pp. 208–227.

20. Ross A. Thompson, "Emotion Regulation: A Theme in Search of Definition," in *The Development of Emotion Regulation*, pp. 25–52.

21. Ibid.

22. Goleman, *Emotional Intelligence*; Allan N. Schore, *Affect Regulation and the Origin of the Self* (Hillsdale, NJ: Erlbaum, 1994).

23. Susan Harter, "Causes, Correlates, and the Functional Role of Global Self-Worth: A Life-Span Perspective," in *Competence Considered*, ed. J. Kolligian and Robert Sternberg (New Haven, CT: Yale University Press, 1990), pp. 67–97.

24. Ibid.

25. Susan Harter, "Visions of Self: Beyond the Me in the Mirror," University Lecture, University of Denver, 1990.

26. Ladd and LeSieur, "Parents and Children's Peer Relationships."

27. Ross D. Parke and Raymond Buriel, "Socialization in the Family: Ethnic and Ecological Perspectives," in *Handbook of Child Psychology*, vol. 3, pp. 463–552.

28. Eisenberg and Murphy, "Parenting and Children's Moral Development."

29. James Q. Wilson, *The Moral Sense* (New York: Free Press, 1993), p. 226.

30. Eisenberg and Murphy, "Parenting and Children's Moral Development."

31. Nancy Eisenberg and Richard Fabes, "Prosocial Development," in *Handbook of Child Psychology*, vol. 3, pp. 701–770.

32. Eisenberg and Murphy, "Parenting and Children's Moral Development."

33. Ibid.

34. Diana Baumrind, "The Development of Instrumental Competence through Socialization" in *Minnesota Symposium on Child Psychology*, vol. 2, ed. Ann D. Pick (Minneapolis: University of Minnesota Press, 1973), pp. 3–46.

35. U.S. Bureau of the Census, *Statistical Abstract of the United States: 1998*, 118th ed. (Washington, DC: U.S. Government Printing Office, 1998).

36. Chuansheng Chen et al., "A Cross-Cultural Study of Family and Peer Correlates of Adolescent Misconduct," *Developmental Psychology* 34 (1998): 770–781.

37. Sara Harkness and Charles Super, "Culture and Parenting," in *Handbook of Parenting*, ed. Marc H. Bornstein, vol. 2, *Biology and Ecology of Parenting* (Mahwah, NJ: Erlbaum, 1995), pp. 211–234.

38. Rebecca I. New and Amy L. Richman, "Maternal Beliefs and Infant Care Practices in Italy and the United States," in *Parents' Cultural Belief Systems: Their Origins, Expressions, and Consequences*, ed. Sara Harkness and Charles M. Super (New York: Guilford, 1996), pp. 385–404.

39. Patricia M. Greenfield and Lalita K. Suzuki, "Culture and Human Development: Implications for Parenting, Education, Pediatrics, and Mental Health," in *Handbook of Child Psychology*, ed. in chief William Damon and vol. ed. Irving E. Sigel and K. Ann Renninger, vol. 4, *Child Psychology in Practice*, 5th ed. (New York: Wiley, 1998), pp. 1059–1109.

40. Jean L. Briggs, "Mazes of Meaning: How a Child and a Culture Create Each Other," in *Interpretive Approaches to Socialization*, ed. William A. Corsaro and Peggy J. Miller, New Directions for Child Development, no. 58 (San Francisco: Jossey-Bass, 1992), p. 25.

41. James Youniss, "Rearing Children for Society," in *Beliefs about Parenting: Origins and Developmental Implications*, ed. Judith G. Smetana, New Directions for Child Development, no. 66 (San Francisco: Jossey-Bass, 1994), pp. 37–50.

42. Parke and Buriel, "Socialization in the Family."

43. Greenfield and Suzuki, "Culture and Human Development."

44. Erika Hoff-Ginsberg and Twila Tardif, "Socioeconomic Status and Parenting," in *Handbook of Parenting*, vol. 2, pp. 161–188.

45. Melvin L. Kohn, *Class and Conformity: A Study of Values* (Homewood, IL: Dorsey, 1969).

46. Betty Hart and Todd R. Risley, *Meaningful Differences in the Everyday Experiences of Young American Children* (Baltimore: Brookes, 1995).

47. G. R. Patterson and D. M. Capaldi, "Antisocial Parents: Unskilled and Vulnerable," in *Family Transitions*, ed. Philip A. Cowan and Mavis Hetherington (Hillsdale, NJ: Erlbaum, 1991), pp. 195–218.

48. Erik H. Erikson, "Human Strength and the Cycle of Generations," in *Insight and Responsibility*, ed. Erik Erikson (New York: Norton, 1964), pp. 109–157.

49. Joan E. Grusec, Paul Hastings, and Norma Mammone, "Parenting Cognitions and Relationship Schemes," in *Beliefs about Parenting*, pp. 5–19.

50. June Lichtenstein Phelps, Jay Belsky, and Keith Crnic, "Earned Security, Daily Stress, and Parenting: A Comparison of Five Alternative Models," *Development and Psychopathology* 10 (1998): 21–38.

51. Keith S. Kendler, "Parenting: A Genetic-Epidemiologic Perspective," *American Journal of Psychiatry* 153 (1996): 11–20.

52. Marinus H. van IJzendoorn, "Intergenerational Transmission of Parenting: A Review of Studies in Nonclinical Populations," *Developmental Review* 12 (1992): 76–99.

53. Rima Shore, *Rethinking the Brain* (New York: Families and Work Institute, 1997).

54. Ibid., p. 15.

55. Daniel J. Siegel, *The Developing Mind* (New York: Guilford, 1999), p. 14.

56. *Newsweek*, spring/summer 1997.

57. William Greenough, "We Can't Focus Just on Ages Zero to Three," *American Psychological Association Monitor* (November 1997): 19.

58. Siegel, *The Developing Mind*.

59. Carl T. Hall, "And This Is Your Brain without Gravity," *San Francisco Chronicle*, 25 October 1999, p. A1.

60. Frank R. Wilson, *The Hand* (New York: Vintage Books, 1999), p. 291.

61. Jane B. Brooks, *The Process of Parenting*, 5th ed. (Mountain View, CA: Mayfield, 1999).

62. Field, "The Effects of Mother's Physical and Emotional Unavailability."

63. Urs A. Hunziker and Ronald G. Barr, "Increased Carrying Reduces Crying: A Randomized Controlled Trial," *Pediatrics* 77 (1986): 641–647.

64. Field, "The Effects of Mother's Physical and Emotional Unavailability."

65. Jerome Kagan, Doreen Arcus, and Nancy Snidman, "The Idea of Temperament: Where Do We Go from Here?" in *Nature, Nurture, and Psychology*, ed. Robert Plomin and Gerald E. McClearn (Washington, DC: American Psychological Association, 1993), pp. 197–210.

66. Ross A. Thompson, "Early Sociopersonality Development," in *Handbook of Child Psychology*, vol. 3, pp. 25–104.

67. L. Alan Sroufe, Byron Egeland, and Terri Kreutzer, "The Fate of Early Experience following Developmental Change: Longitudinal Approaches to Individual Adaptation in Childhood," *Child Development* 61 (1990): 1363–1373.

68. Marjorie P. Honzik, "Environmental Correlates of Mental Growth: Prediction from the Family Setting at Twenty-One Months," *Child Development* 38 (1967): 337–364.

69. Hart and Risley, *Meaningful Differences*, p. 180.

70. Ibid., p. 182.

71. Geraldine Dawson et al., "Frontal Brain Electrical Activity in Infants of Depressed and Nondepressed Mothers: Relation to Variations in Infant Behavior," *Development and Psychopathology* 11 (1999): 589–605.

72. Siegel, *The Developing Mind*.

73. Michael Lewis, *Altering Fate: Why the Past Does Not Predict the Future* (New York: Guilford, 1997).

74. Ibid., p. 23.

75. Arnold J. Sameroff et al., "Family and Social Influences on the Development of Child Competence," in *Families, Risk, and Competence*, ed. Michael Lewis and Candice Fearing (Mahwah, NJ: Erlbaum, 1998), pp. 161–185.

76. Alison Gopnik, Andrew N. Meltzoff, and Patricia K. Kuhl, *The Scientist in the Crib* (New York: Morrow, 1999), p. 202.

77. Ibid.

78. John T. Bruer, *The Myth of the First Three Years* (New York: Free Press, 1999), pp. 108–109.

79. Thompson, "Early Sociopersonality Development."

80. Douglas M. Teti et al., "And Baby Makes Four: Predictors of Attachment Security among Pre–School Age Firstborns during the Transition to Siblinghood," *Child Development* 67 (1996): 579–596.

81. Bruer, *The Myth of the First Three Years*.

82. Sandra Blakeslee, "Old Brains Can Learn New Language Tricks," *New York Times*, 20 April 1999, p. D3.

83. Peter Marks, "Long Island Program Turns Around Troubled Students," *New York Times*, 14 April 1994.

84. Bruer, *The Myth of the First Three Years*.

85. Dorothy H. Eichorn, Jane V. Hunt, and Marjorie P. Honzik, "Experience, Personality, and IQ: Adolescence to Middle Age," in *Present and Past in Middle Life*, ed. Dorothy H. Eichorn et al. (New York: Academic Press, 1981), pp. 89–116.

86. Ellen Galinsky, *Between Generations: The Six Stages of Parenthood* (New York: Times Books, 1981).

87. Ibid., p. 317.

Chapter 3

1. Lois Wladis Hoffman and Jean Denby Manis, "The Value of Children in the United States: A New Approach to the Study of Fertility," *Journal of Marriage and the Family* 41 (1979): 583–596.

2. Urie Bronfenbrenner and Pamela A. Morris, "The Ecology of Developmental Processes," in *Handbook of Child Psychology*, ed. in chief William Damon and vol. ed. Richard Lerner, vol. 1, *Theoretical*

Models of Human Development, 5th ed. (New York: Wiley, 1998), pp. 993–1028.

3. Dorothy C. Briggs, *Your Child's Self-Esteem* (Garden City, NY: Doubleday, 1970), pp. 61–62.

4. Ibid., p. 64.

5. Alexander Luria, *Language and Cognition* (New York: Wiley, 1981).

6. Jay D. Schvaneveldt, Marguerite Fryer, and Renee Ostler, "Concepts of 'Badness' and 'Goodness' of Parents as Perceived by Nursery School Children," *The Family Coordinator* 19 (1970): 98–103.

7. John R. Weisz, "Autonomy, Control and Other Reasons Why 'Mom Is the Greatest': A Content Analysis of Children's Mother's Day Letters," *Child Development* 51 (1980): 801–807.

8. Eleanor E. Maccoby and John A. Martin, "Socialization in the Context of the Family: Parent-Child Interaction," in *Handbook of Child Psychology*, ed. Paul H. Mussen and E. Mavis Hetherington, vol. 4, *Socialization, Personality, and Social Development*, 4th ed. (New York: Wiley, 1983), pp. 1–101.

9. J. Kirk Felsman and George E. Vaillant, "Resilient Children as Adults," in *The Invulnerable Child*, ed. E. James Anthony and Bertram J. Cohler (New York: Guilford Press, 1987), p. 298.

10. Charles R. Carlson and John C. Masters, "Inoculation by Emotion: Effects of Positive Emotional States on Children's Reactions to Social Comparison," *Developmental Psychology* 22 (1986): 760–765.

11. Jane B. Brooks and Doris M. Elliott, "Prediction of Psychological Adjustment at Age Thirty from Leisure Time Activities and Satisfactions in Childhood," *Human Development* 14 (1971): 61–71.

12. Anita Weiner, Haggai Kuppermintz, and David Guttmann, "Video Home Training (The Orion Project): A Short-Term Preventive and Treatment Intervention for Families of Young Children," *Family Process* 33 (1994): 441–453.

13. John A. Clausen, Paul H. Mussen, and Joseph Kuypers, "Involvement, Warmth, and Parent-Child Resemblance in Three Generations," in *Present and Past in Middle Life*, ed. Dorothy H. Eichorn et al.

(New York: Academic Press, 1981), pp. 299–319.

14. Mark Mellman, Edward Lazarus, and Allan Rivlin, "Family Time, Family Values," in *Rebuilding the Nest*, ed. David Blankenhorn, Steven Bayme, and Jean Bethke Elshtain (Milwaukee, WI: Family Service of America, 1990), pp. 73–92.

15. John P. Robinson and Geoffrey Godbey, *Time for Life* (University Park, PA: Pennsylvania State University Press, 1997).

16. Ibid., p. 55.

17. Sandra L. Hofferth, "Changes in American Children's Time, 1981–1997," *The Brown University Child and Adolescent Behavior Letter*, March 1999, p. 1.

18. Keith Crnic and Marcela Acevedo, "Everyday Stresses and Parenting," in *Handbook of Parenting*, ed. Marc H. Bornstein, vol. 4, *Applied and Practical Parenting* (Mahwah, NJ: Erlbaum, 1995), pp. 277–297; Theodore Dix, "The Affective Organization of Parenting: Adaptive and Maladaptive Processes," *Psychological Bulletin* 110 (1991): 3–25.

19. Ernest N. Jouriles, Christopher M. Murphy, and K. Daniel O'Leary, "Effects of Maternal Mood on Mother-Son Interaction Patterns," *Journal of Abnormal Child Psychology* 17 (1989): 513–525.

20. John U. Zussman, "Situational Determinants of Parenting Behavior: Effects of Competing Cognitive Activity," *Child Development* 51 (1980): 772–780.

21. Keith A. Crnic and Mark T. Greenberg, "Minor Parenting Stresses with Young Children," *Child Development* 61 (1990): 1628–1637.

22. Crnic and Acevedo, "Everyday Stresses and Parenting"; Jay Belsky, Keith Crnic, and Sharon Woodworth, "Personality and Parenting: Exploring the Mediating Role of Transient Mood and Daily Hassles," *Journal of Personality* 63 (1995): 905–929.

23. Mona El-Sheikh, E. Mark Cummings, and Virginia Goetsch, "Coping with Adults' Angry Behavior: Behavioral, Physiological, and Verbal Responses in Preschoolers," *Developmental Psychology* 25 (1989): 490–498.

24. John M. Gottman and Lynn F. Katz, "Effects of Marital Discord on Young Children's Peer Interaction and Health,"

Developmental Psychology 25 (1989): 373–381.

25. E. Mark Cummings, "Coping with Background Anger in Early Childhood," *Child Development* 58 (1987): 976–984.

26. Jennifer S. Cummings et al., "Children's Responses to Adult Behavior as a Function of Marital Distress and History of Interparent Hostility," *Child Development* 60 (1989): 1035–1043.

27. John H. Grych and Frank D. Fincham, "Children's Appraisals of Marital Conflict: Initial Investigation of the Cognitive-Contextual Framework," *Child Development* 64 (1993): 215–230.

28. Katherine Covell and Brenda Miles, "Children's Beliefs about Strategies to Reduce Parental Anger," *Child Development* 63 (1992): 381–390.

29. E. Mark Cummings et al., "Resolution and Children's Responses to Interadult Anger," *Developmental Psychology* 27 (1991): 462–470.

30. Katherine Covell and Rona Abramovitch, "Understanding Emotion in the Family: Children's and Parents' Attributions of Happiness, Sadness, and Anger," *Child Development* 57 (1987): 985–991.

31. Dix, "The Affective Organization of Parenting."

32. Ibid.

33. Ibid., p. 4.

34. Mellman, Lazarus, and Rivlin, "Family Time, Family Values."

35. Haim G. Ginott, *Between Parent and Child* (New York: Avon Books, 1969), pp. 39–40.

36. Thomas Gordon, *P.E.T.: Parent Effectiveness Training* (New York: New American Library, 1975); Thomas Gordon with Judith G. Sands, *P.E.T. in Action* (New York: Bantam Books, 1978); Thomas Gordon, *Teaching Children Self-Discipline* (New York: Random House, 1989).

37. Gordon with Sands, *P.E.T. in Action*, p. 47.

38. Judy Dunn, Jane Brown, and Lynn Beardsall, "Family Talk about Feeling States and Children's Later Understanding of Others' Emotions," *Developmental Psychology* 27 (1991): 448–455.

39. Adele Faber and Elaine Mazlish, *Liberated Parents/Liberated Children* (New York: Avon Books, 1975);

40. Gordon, *Teaching Children Self-Discipline*.

41. Rudolf Dreikurs with Vicki Soltz, *Children: The Challenge* (New York: Hawthorn, 1964).

42. Dreikurs with Soltz, *Children*.

43. Ibid., p. 39.

44. Ibid., p. 108.

45. Gail D. Heyman, Carol S. Dweck, and Kathleen M. Cain, "Young Children's Vulnerability to Self-Blame and Helplessness: Relationship to Beliefs about Goodness," *Child Development* 63 (1992): 401–415; Martin E. P. Seligman, *Learned Optimism* (New York: Pocket Books, 1990).

46. Seligman, *Learned Optimism*.

47. Ibid., pp. 221–222.

48. Ibid., p. 222.

49. Gregory S. Pettit, John E. Bates, and Kenneth A. Dodge, "Supportive Parenting, Ecological Context, and Children's Adjustment: A Seven-Year Longitudinal Study," *Child Development* 68 (1997): 908–923.

50. Brooks and Elliott, "Prediction of Psychological Adjustment."

51. John M. Gottman, Lynn Fainsilber Katz, and Carole Hooven, "Parental Meta-Emotion Philosophy and the Emotional Life of Families: Theoretical Models and Preliminary Data," *Journal of Family Psychology* 10 (1996): 243–268.

52. John Gottman with Joan DeClaire, *The Heart of Parenting: Raising an Emotionally Intelligent Child* (New York: Simon & Schuster, 1997).

53. Ibid.

54. Nancy Eisenberg et al., "Parental Reactions to Children's Negative Emotions: Longitudinal Relations to Quality of Children's Social Functioning," *Child Development* 70 (1999): 513–534.

55. Robinson and Godbey, *Time for Life*.

56. Ibid., p. 295.

57. Ibid., p. 149.

58. Ibid., p. 316.

59. Carolyn Pape Cowan and Philip A. Cowan, *When Partners Become Parents* (New York: Basic Books, 1992).

60. Joseph Procaccini and Mark Kiefaber, *Parent Burnout* (New York: New American Library, 1984), p. 41.

61. Rex L. Forehand, Page B. Walley, and William M. Furey, "Prevention in the Home: Parent and Family," in *Prevention of Problems in Childhood: Psychological Research and Application*, ed. Michael C. Roberts and Lizette Peterson (New York: Wiley, 1984), pp. 342–368.

62. Crnic and Acevedo, "Everyday Stresses and Parenting."

63. Ibid.

64. Nancy Samalin with Catherine Whitney, *Love and Anger: The Parental Dilemma* (New York: Penguin Books, 1992).

65. Jane Nelson, *Positive Discipline* (New York: Ballantine Books, 1981).

66. Dreikurs with Soltz, *Children*, pp. 55–56.

67. Arthur T. Jersild et al., *Joys and Problems of Child Rearing* (New York: Bureau of Publications, Teachers College, Columbia University, 1949), pp. 1–2.

68. Ibid., p. 122.

Chapter 4

1. Patricia Chamberlain and Gerald R. Patterson, "Discipline and Child Compliance in Parenting," in *Handbook of Parenting*, ed. Marc H. Bornstein, vol. 4, *Applied and Practical Parenting* (Mahwah, NJ: Erlbaum, 1995), pp. 205–225.

2. Diana Baumrind, "The Discipline Controversy Revisited," *Family Relations* 45 (1996): 405–414.

3. Eleanor E. Maccoby and John A. Martin, "Socialization in the Context of the Family: Parent-Child Interaction," in *Handbook of Child Psychology*, eds. Paul H. Mussen and E. Mavis Hetherington, vol. 4, *Socialization, Personality and Social Development*, 4th ed. (New York: Wiley, 1983), pp. 1–101.

4. Daphne Blunt Bugental and Jacqueline J. Goodnow, "Socialization Processes," in *Handbook of Child Psychology*, ed. in chief William Damon and vol. ed. Nancy Eisenberg, vol. 3, *Social, Emotional, and Personality Development*, 5th ed. (New York: Wiley, 1998), pp. 389–462.

5. Barbara Rogoff, "Cognition as Collaborative Process," in *Handbook of Child Psychology*, ed. in chief William Damon and vol. ed. Deanna Kuhn and Robert S. Siegler, vol. 2, *Cognition, Perception, and Language*, 5th ed. (New York: Wiley, 1998), pp. 679–744.

6. Jean V. Carew, *Experience and the Development of Intelligence in Young Children at Home and in Day Care,* Monographs of the Society for Research in Child Development 45, no. 187 (1980).

7. Maccoby and Martin, "Socialization in the Context of the Family," p. 65.

8. Joan E. Grusec and Jacqueline J. Goodnow, "Impact of Parental Discipline Methods on the Child's Internalization of Values: A Reconceptualization of Current Points of View," *Developmental Psychology* 30 (1994): 4–19.

9. Larry P. Nucci and Elliot Turiel, "Social Interactions and the Development of Social Concepts in Preschool Children," *Child Development* 49 (1978): 400–407.

10. Thomas Gordon, *P.E.T.: Parent Effectiveness Training* (New York: New American Library, 1975).

11. Rudolf Dreikurs with Vicki Soltz, *Children: The Challenge* (New York: Hawthorn, 1964).

12. Chamberlain and Patterson, "Discipline and Child Compliance in Parenting."

13. Diana Baumrind, "Necessary Distinctions," *Psychological Inquiry* 8 (1997): 176–182.

14. Anthony M. Graziano, Jessica L. Hamblen, and Wendy A. Plante, "Subabusive Violence in Child Rearing in Middle-Class American Families," *Pediatrics* 98 (1996): 845–848.

15. Diana Baumrind, "The Development of Instrumental Competence through Socialization," in *Minnesota Symposium on Child Psychology*, vol. 7, ed. Ann D. Pick (Minneapolis: University of Minnesota Press, 1973), pp. 3–46.

16. Ray Guarendi with David Eich, *Back to the Family* (New York: Simon & Schuster, 1991).

17. Lawrence S. Wissow, "What Clinicians Want to Know About Teaching Families New Disciplinary Tools," *Pediatrics* 98 (1996): 815–817.

18. Graziano, Hamblen, and Plante, "Subabusive Violence."

19. Thomas F. Catron and John C. Masters, "Mothers' and Children's Conceptualizations of Corporal Punishment," *Child Development* 64 (1993): 1815–1828.

20. Murray A. Straus, "Spanking and the Making of a Violent Society," *Pediatrics* 98 (1996): 837–844.

21. Diana Baumrind, "A Blanket Injunction against Disciplinary Use of Spanking Is Not Warranted by the Data," *Pediatrics* 98 (1996): 828–831.

22. Baumrind, "The Discipline Controversy Revisited," p. 413.

23. Robert E. Larzelare, "A Review of the Outcomes of Parental Use of Nonabusive or Customary Physical Punishment," *Pediatrics* 98 (1996): 824–828.

24. Kirby Deater-Deckard and Kenneth A. Dodge, "Externalizing Behavior Problems and Discipline Revisited: Nonlinear Effects and Variation by Culture, Context, and Gender," *Psychological Inquiry* 8 (1997): 161–175.

25. Hugh Lytton, "Physical Punishment Is a Problem, Whether Conduct Disorder Is Endogenous or Not, "*Psychological Inquiry* 8 (1997): 214.

26. Robert W. Chamberlin, "'It Takes a Whole Village' Working with Community Coalitions to Promote Positive Parenting and Strengthen Families," *Pediatrics* 98 (1996): 805.

27. Baumrind, "The Discipline Controversy Revisited," p. 413.

28. Mary K. Rothbart and John E. Bates, "Temperament," in *Handbook of Child Psychology*, vol. 3, p. 109.

29. Anneliese F. Korner, "Individual Differences at Birth: Implications for Early Experience and Later Development," *American Journal of Orthopsychiatry* 41 (1971): 608–619.

30. Rudolph Schaffer and Peggy E. Emerson, *The Development of Social Attachments in Infancy*, Monographs of the Society for Research in Child Development 29, whole no. 94 (1964).

31. Rothbart and Bates, "Temperament."

32. Anneliese F. Korner et al., "The Relation between Neonatal and Later Activity and Temperament," *Child Development* 56 (1985): 38–42.

33. Rothbart and Bates, "Temperament."

34. Carl E. Schwartz, Nancy Snidman, and Jerome Kagan, "Early Childhood Temperament as a Determinant of Externalizing Behavior," *Development and Psychopathology* 8 (1996): 527–537; Jerome Kagan, Doreen Arcus, and Nancy Snidman, "The Idea of Temperament: Where Do We Go from Here?" in *Nature and Nurture and Psychology*, ed. Robert Plomin and Gerald E. McClearn (Washington, DC: American Psychological Association, 1993), pp. 197–210.

35. John E. Bates, Christine A. Maslin, and Karen H. Frankel, "Attachment Security, Mother-Child Interaction and Temperament as Predictors of Behavior Problem Ratings at Age Three Years," in *Growing Points of Attachment Theory and Research*, ed. Inge Bretherton and Everett Waters, Monographs of the Society for Research in Child Development 50, serial no. 109 (1985): 167–193.

36. Ann Sanson and Mary K. Rothbart, "Child Temperament and Parenting," in *Handbook of Parenting*, vol. 4, pp. 299–321.

37. Avshalom Caspi and Phil A. Silva, "Temperamental Qualities at Age Three Predict Personality Traits in Young Adulthood: Longitudinal Evidence from a Birth Cohort," *Child Development* 66 (1995): 486–498.

38. Sanson and Rothbart, "Child Temperament and Parenting."

39. Kagan, Arcus, and Snidman, "The Idea of Temperament."

40. Sanson and Rothbart, "Child Temperament and Parenting."

41. Cynthia A. Stifter, Tracy L. Spinrad, and Julia M. Braungart-Rieker, "Toward a Developmental Model of Child Compliance: The Role of Emotion Regulation in Infancy," *Child Development* 70 (1999): 21–32.

42. Grazyna Kochanska, Terri L. Tjebkes, and David R. Forman, "Children's Emerging Regulation of Conduct: Restraint, Compliance, and Internalization from Infancy to

the Second Year," *Child Development* 69 (1998): 1378–1389.

43. Sanson and Rothbart, "Child Temperament and Parenting."

44. Kagan, Arcus, and Snidman, "The Idea of Temperament."

45. Sybil Escalona, *The Roots of Individuality: Normal Patterns of Development in Infancy* (Chicago: Aldine, 1968).

46. Beverly I. Fagot, "Parenting Boys and Girls," in *Handbook of Parenting*, ed. Marc H. Bornstein, vol. 1, *Children and Parenting* (Mahwah, NJ: Erlbaum, 1995), pp. 163–183.

47. Diane N. Ruble and Carol Lynn Martin, "Gender Development," in *Handbook of Child Psychology*, vol. 3, pp. 933–1016.

48. Ibid.

49. Fagot, "Parenting Boys and Girls."

50. Ibid.

51. Carolyn Zahn-Waxler, "Warriors and Worriers: Gender and Psychopathology," *Development and Psychopathology* 5 (1993): 79–89.

52. Jack Block cited in Jane B. Brooks, *The Process of Parenting*, 3rd ed. (Mountain View, CA: Mayfield, 1991), pp. 356–357.

53. Ibid., p. 357.

54. Mary Pipher, *Reviving Ophelia* (New York: Ballantine Books, 1994), p. 283.

55. Ibid., p. 357.

56. William Pollack, *Real Boys* (New York: Henry Holt, 1998).

57. Ibid., p. xxiv.

58. Ibid., p. 391.

59. Ibid., p. 398.

60. Rosemary S. L. Mills and Kenneth H. Rubin, "Parental Beliefs about Problematic Social Behaviors in Early Childhood," *Child Development* 61 (1990): 138–151.

61. Ann V. McGillicuddy-De Lisi, "Parental Beliefs within the Family Context: Development of a Research Program," in *Methods of Family Research: Biographies of Research Projects*, ed. Irving E. Sigel and Gene H. Brody, vol. 1, *Normal Families* (Hillsdale, NJ: Erlbaum, 1990), pp. 53–85.

62. Grazyna Kochanska, "Maternal Beliefs as Long-Term Predictors of Mother-Child Interactions and Report," *Child Development* 61 (1990): 1934–1943.

63. Jane Loevinger, "Patterns of Parenthood as Theories of Learning," *Journal of Abnormal and Social Psychology* 59 (1959): 148–150.

64. Ibid., p. 150.

65. Arnold Gesell and Frances L. Ilg, *The Child from Five to Ten* (New York: Harper & Row, 1946), p. 308.

Chapter 5

1. Myra Leifer, "Psychological Changes Accompanying Motherhood and Pregnancy," *Genetic Psychology Monographs* 95 (1977): 55–96.

2. Carolyn Pape Cowan and Philip A. Cowan, *When Partners Become Parents* (New York: Basic Books, 1992); Jay Belsky and John Kelly, *The Transition to Parenthood* (New York: Delacorte, 1994).

3. Ibid.

4. Ross A. Thompson, "Early Sociopersonality Development," in *Handbook of Child Psychology*, ed. in chief William Damon and vol. ed. Nancy Eisenberg, vol. 3, *Social, Emotional, and Personality Development*, 5th ed. (New York: Wiley, 1998), p. 35.

5. Thompson, "Early Sociopersonality Development," pp. 25–104.

6. Marshall H. Klaus and John H. Kennell, *Maternal-Infant Bonding* (St. Louis: Mosby, 1976).

7. Michael Rutter, "Continuities and Discontinuities from Infancy," in *Handbook of Infant Development*, 2d ed., ed. Joy Doniger Osofsky (New York: Wiley, 1987), pp. 1256–1297.

8. Daphne Blunt Bugental and Jacqueline J. Goodnow, "Socialization Processes," in *Handbook of Child Psychology*, vol. 3, pp. 389–462.

9. Tiffany Field, "The Effects of Mother's Physical and Emotional Unavailability on Emotion Regulation," in *The Development of Emotion Regulation: Biological and Behavioral Considerations*, ed. Nathan A. Fox, Monographs of the Society for Research in

Child Development 59, serial no. 240 (1994): 208–227.

10. Carol Zander Malatesta and Jeannette M. Haviland, "Learning Display Rules: The Socialization of Emotion Expression in Infancy," *Child Development* 53 (1982): 991–1003.

11. Jeannette M. Haviland and Mary Lelwica, "The Induced-Affect Response: 10-Week-Old Infants' Responses to Three Emotion Expressions," *Developmental Psychology* 23 (1987): 97–104.

12. Carol Z. Malatesta et al., "Emotion Socialization and Expression Development in Preterm and Full Term Infants," *Child Development* 57 (1986): 316–330.

13. Thompson, "Early Sociopersonality Development."

14. Ibid.

15. Ibid.

16. Robin Hornick, Nancy Risenhoover, and Megan Gunnar, "The Effects of Maternal Positive, Neutral, and Negative Affect Communication on Infant Responses to New Toys," *Child Development* 58 (1987): 936–944.

17. Thompson, "Early Sociopersonality Development."

18. Ibid.

19. Karlen Lyons-Ruth et al., "Infants at Social Risk: Maternal Depression and Family Support Services as Moderators of Infant Development and Security of Attachment," *Child Development* 61 (1990): 85–98.

20. Thompson, "Early Sociopersonality Development."

21. Marianne S. De Wolff and Marinus van IJzendoorn, "Sensitivity and Attachment: A Meta-Analysis on Parental Antecedents of Infant Attachment," *Child Development* 68 (1997): 571–591.

22. Thompson, "Early Sociopersonality Development."

23. Jutta Heckhausen, "Balancing for Weaknesses and Challenging Developmental Potential: A Longitudinal Study of Mother-Infant Dyads in Apprenticeship Interactions," *Developmental Psychology* 23 (1987): 762–770.

24. Mary Jane Gandour, "Activity Level as a Dimension of Temperament in Toddlers: Its Relevance for the Organismic Specificity Hypotheses," *Child Development* 60 (1989): 1092–1098.

25. Thompson, "Early Sociopersonality Development."

26. Ibid.

27. Edward Mueller and Elizabeth Tingley, "The Bears' Picnic: Children's Representations of Themselves and Their Families," in *Children's Perspectives on the Family*, ed. Inge Bretherton and Michael W. Watson, New Directions for Child Development, no. 48 (San Francisco: Jossey-Bass, 1992), pp. 47–65.

28. Thompson, "Early Sociopersonality Development."

29. Abraham Sagi et al., "Sleeping out of Home in a Kibbutz Communal Arrangement: It Makes a Difference for Infant-Mother Attachment," *Child Development* 65, (1994): 992–1004.

30. Thompson, "Early Sociopersonality Development."

31. Ibid.

32. Ibid.

33. Nathan A. Fox, Nancy L. Kimmerly, and William D. Schafer, "Attachment to Mother/Attachment to Father: A Meta-Analysis," *Child Development* 62 (1991): 210–225.

34. Susan Golombok and Robyn Fivush, *Gender Development* (New York: Cambridge University Press, 1994).

35. Ibid.

36. Jay Belsky, Bonnie Gilstrap, and Michael Rovine, "The Pennsylvania Infant and Family Development Project I: Stability and Change in Mother-Infant and Father-Infant Interaction in a Family Setting at One, Three and Nine Months," *Child Development* 55 (1984): 692–705.

37. Ibid.

38. Thompson, "Early Sociopersonality Development."

39. Jay Belsky et al., "Instability of Infant-Parent Attachment Security," *Developmental Psychology* 32 (1996): 921–924.

40. Susan Harter, "The Development of Self-Representations," in *Handbook of Child Psychology*, vol. 3, pp. 553–617.

41. Ibid.

42. Elizabeth Anisfeld et al., "Does Infant Carrying Promote Attachment? An Experimental

Study of the Effects of Increased Physical Contact on the Development of Attachment," *Child Development* 61 (1990): 1617–1627.

43. Kathryn E. Barnard, Colleen E. Morisset, and Susan Spieker, "Preventive Interventions: Enhancing Parent-Infant Relationships," in *Handbook of Infant Mental Health*, ed. Charles H. Zeanah, Jr. (New York: Guilford Press, 1993), pp. 386–401.

44. Ibid.

45. Dymphna C. van den Boom, "The Influence of Temperament and Mothering on Attachment and Exploration: An Experimental Manipulation of Sensitive Responsiveness among Lower-Class Mothers with Irritable Infants," *Child Development* 65 (1994): 1457–1477.

46. Barnard, Morisset, and Spieker, "Preventive Interventions"; Samuel J. Meisels, Margo Dichtemiller, and Fong-ruey Liaw, "A Multidimensional Analysis of Early Childhood Intervention Programs," in *Handbook of Infant Mental Health*, pp. 361–385.

47. Marinus H. van IJzendoorn, Femmie Juffer, and Marja G. C. Duyvesteyn, "Breaking the Intergenerational Cycle of Insecure Attachment: A Review of the Effects of Attachment-Based Interventions on Maternal Sensitivity and Infant Security," *Journal of Child Psychology and Psychiatry* 36 (1995): 225–248.

48. Deborah J. Stipek, J. Heidi Gralinski, and Claire B. Kopp, "Self-Concept Development in the Toddler Years," *Developmental Psychology* 26 (1990): 972–977; Pamela M. Cole, Karen Caplovitz-Barrett, and Carolyn Zahn-Waxler, "Emotion Displays in Two-Year-Olds during Mishaps," *Child Development* 63 (1992): 314–324.

49. Harter, "The Development of Self-Representations."

50. Deborah J. Stipek, Theresa A. Roberts, and Mary E. Sanborn, "Preschool-Age Children's Performance Expectations for Themselves and Another Child as a Function of the Incentive Value of Success and the Salience of Past Performance," *Child Development* 55 (1984): 1983–1989.

51. Golombok and Fivush, *Gender Development*.

52. Kay Bussey and Albert Bandura, "Self-Regulatory Mechanisms Governing Gender Development," *Child Development* 63 (1992): 1236–1250.

53. John Money, "Human Hermaphroditism" in *Human Sexuality in Four Perspectives*, ed. Frank A. Beach (Baltimore: Johns Hopkins University Press, 1976), pp. 62–86.

54. Sandra Lipsitz Bem, "Genital Knowledge and Gender Constancy in Preschool Children, *Child Development* 60 (1989): 649–662; Michael Siegal and Judith Robinson, "Order Effects in Children's Gender Constancy Responses," *Developmental Psychology* 23 (1987): 283–286.

55. Golombok and Fivush, *Gender Development*.

56. Bussey and Bandura, "Self-Regulatory Mechanisms Governing Gender Development."

57. Ibid., p. 1247.

58. Golombok and Fivush, *Gender Development*, p. 111.

59. Margaret Beale Spencer and Carol Markstrom-Adams, "Identity Processes among Racial and Ethnic Minority Children in America," *Child Development* 61 (1990): 290–310.

60. Frances E. Aboud, "The Development of Ethnic Identification and Attitudes," in *Children's Ethnic Socialization*, ed. Jean S. Phinney and Mary Jane Rotheram (Beverly Hills, CA: Sage, 1987).

61. L. Alan Sroufe, "Socioemotional Development," in *Handbook of Infant Development*, ed. Joy D. Osofsky (New York: John Wiley, 1979), pp. 462–506; Michael Lewis et al., "Self-Development and Self-Conscious Emotions," *Child Development* 60 (1989): 146–156.

62. Claire B. Kopp, "Regulation of Distress and Negative Emotions: A Developmental View," *Developmental Psychology* 25 (1989): 343–354; Edward Z. Tronick, "Emotions and Emotional Communications in Infants," *American Psychologist* 44 (1989): 112–119.

63. Carroll E. Izard and Carol Z. Malatesta, "Perspectives on Emotional Development I: Differential Emotions Theory of Early Emotional Development," in *Handbook of Infant Development*, 2d ed., pp. 494–554.

64. Tronick, "Emotions and Emotional Communication in Infants."

65. John S. Watson, "Smiling, Cooing and 'the Game,'" *Merrill-Palmer Quarterly* 18 (1972): 323–339.

66. Inge Bretherton et al., "Learning to Talk about Emotions: A Functionalist Perspective," *Child Development* 57 (1986): 529–548; Kopp, "Regulation of Distress and Negative Emotions."

67. Kopp, "Regulation of Distress and Negative Emotions."

68. Ibid.

69. Bretherton et al., "Learning to Talk about Emotions."

70. Sally K. Donaldson and Michael A. Westerman, "Development of Children's Understanding of Ambivalent and Causal Theories of Emotions," *Developmental Psychology* 22 (1986): 655–662.

71. Richard A. Fabes et al., "Preschoolers' Attributions of the Situational Determinants of Others' Naturally Occurring Emotions," *Developmental Psychology* 24 (1988): 376–385.

72. Marc Weissbluth, *Crybabies* (New York: Arbor House, 1984).

73. Sylvia M. Bell and Mary D. Salter Ainsworth, "Infant Crying and Maternal Responsiveness," *Child Development* 43 (1972): 1171–1190.

74. Judy Dunn, *Distress and Comfort* (Cambridge, MA: Harvard University Press, 1977), p. 23.

75. Urs A. Hunziker and Ronald G. Barr, "Increased Carrying Reduces Crying: A Randomized Controlled Trial," *Pediatrics* 77 (1986): 641–647.

76. William A. H. Sammons, *The Self-Calmed Baby* (Boston: Little, Brown, 1989).

77. Florence L. Goodenough, *Anger in Young Children* (Minneapolis: University of Minnesota Press, 1931).

78. Haim G. Ginott, *Between Parent and Child* (New York: Avon Books, 1969).

79. Adele Faber and Elaine Mazlish, *Liberated Parents/Liberated Children* (New York: Avon Books, 1975).

80. Thomas Gordon, *P.E.T.: Parent Effectiveness Training* (New York: New American Library, 1975).

81. Rudolf Dreikurs with Vicki Soltz, *Children: The Challenge* (New York: Hawthorn, 1964).

82. John D. Krumboltz and Helen B. Krumboltz, *Changing Children's Behavior* (Englewood Cliffs, N.J.: Prentice-Hall, 1972).

83. Stanley Turecki and Leslie Tonner, *The Difficult Child* (New York: Bantam Books, 1985).

84. Marion Radke-Yarrow et al., "Learning Concern for Others," *Developmental Psychology* 8 (1973): 240–260; Herbert Wray, *Emotions in the Lives of Young Children*, Department of Health, Education, and Welfare Publication no. 78-644 (Rockville, Md., 1978).

85. Fabes et al., "Preschoolers' Attributions of the Situational Determinants of Others' Naturally Occurring Emotions."

86. David Matsumoto et al., "Preschoolers' Moral Actions and Emotions in Prisoner's Dilemma," *Developmental Psychology* 22 (1986): 663–670.

87. Claire B. Kopp, "Antecedents of Self-Regulation: A Developmental Perspective," *Developmental Psychology* 18 (1982): 199–214.

88. Eleanor E. Maccoby and John A. Martin, "Socialization in the Context of the Family: Parent-Child Interaction," in *Handbook of Child Psychology*, ed. Paul H. Mussen and E. Mavis Hetherington, vol. 4, *Socialization, Personality, and Social Development*, 4th ed. (New York: Wiley, 1983), pp. 1–101.

89. Susan Crockenberg and Cindy Litman, "Autonomy as Competence in Two-Year-Olds: Maternal Correlates of Child Defiance, Compliance, and Self-Assertion," *Developmental Psychology* 26 (1990): 961–971.

90. George Holden, "Avoiding Conflicts: Mothers as Tacticians in the Supermarket," *Child Development* 54 (1983): 233–240; Thomas G. Power and M. Lynne Chapieski, "Childrearing and Impulsive Control in Toddlers: A Naturalistic Investigation," *Developmental Psychology* 22 (1986): 271–275; George W. Holden and Meredith J. West, "Proximate Regulation by Mothers: A Demonstration of How Differing Styles Affect Young Children's Behavior," *Child Development* 60 (1989): 64–69.

91. J. Heidi Gralinski and Claire B. Kopp, "Everyday Rules for Behavior: Mothers' Requests to Young Children," *Developmental Psychology* 29 (1993): 573–584.

92. Ibid.

93. Leon Kuczynski and Grazyna Kochanska, "Development of Children's Noncompliance Strategies from Toddlerhood to Age 5," *Developmental Psychology* 26 (1990): 398–408.

94. Maccoby and Martin, "Socialization in the Context of the Family"; Crockenberg and Litman, "Autonomy as Competence in Two-Year-Olds."

95. Sandra R. Kaler and Claire B. Kopp, "Compliance and Comprehension in Very Young Toddlers," *Child Development*, 61 (1990): 1997–2003.

96. Cheryl Minton, Jerome Kagan, and Janet A. Levine, "Maternal Control and Obedience in the Two-Year-Old," *Child Development* 42 (1971): 1873–1894.

97. Harriet L. Rheingold, Kay V. Cook, and Vicki Kolowitz, "Commands Cultivate the Behavioral Pleasure of 2-Year-Old Children," *Developmental Psychology* 23 (1987): 146–151.

98. Keng-Ling Lay, Everett Waters, and Kathryn A. Park, "Maternal Responsiveness and Child Compliance: The Role of Mood as Mediator," *Child Development* 60 (1989): 1405–1411.

99. Patricia M. Greenfield and Lalita K. Suzuki, "Culture and Human Development: Implications for Parenting, Education, Pediatrics, and Mental Health," in *Handbook of Child Psychology*, ed. in chief William Damon and vol. ed. Irving E. Sigel and K. Ann Renninger, vol. 4, *Child Psychology in Practice*, 5th ed. (New York: Wiley, 1998), pp. 1059–1109.

100. Marc H. Bornstein, "Parenting Infants," in *Handbook of Parenting*, ed. Marc H. Bornstein, vol. 1, *Children and Parenting* (Mahwah, NJ: Erlbaum, 1995), pp. 3–39.

101. Gilda A. Morelli et al., "Cultural Variations in Infants' Sleeping Arrangements: Questions of Independence," *Developmental Psychology* 28 (1992): 604–613.

102. Klaus Minde, "The Sleep of Infants and Why Parents Matter," *Zero to Three* 19 (October/November 1998): 9–14.

103. Richard Ferber, *Solve Your Child's Sleep Problems* (New York: Simon & Schuster, 1985).

104. Athleen B. Godfrey and Anne Kilgore, "An Approach to Help Very Young Infants Sleep through the Night," *Zero to Three* 19 (October/November 1998): 15–18.

105. Morelli et al., "Cultural Variations in Infants' Sleeping Arrangements."

106. Suad Nakamura, "Adult Beds Are Unsafe Places for Children under Age Two to Sleep," American Medical Association media briefing on children's health, New York, September 29, 1999.

107. James J. McKenna, Sarah S. Mosko, and Christopher A. Richard, "Bedsharing Promotes Breastfeeding," *Pediatrics* 100 (1997): 214–219

108. Nakamura, "Adult Beds Are Unsafe for Children under Age Two to Sleep."

109. John Seabrook, "Sleeping with the Baby," *New Yorker*, 8 November 1999.

110. James J. McKenna, "Cultural Influences on Infant and Childhood Sleep Biology, and the Science That Studies It: Toward a More Inclusive Paradigm," *Zero to Three* 20 (December 1999/January 2000): 17.

111. William Sears, introduction to *Attachment Parenting*, by Katie Allison Granju with Betsy Kennedy (New York: Pocket Books, 1999).

112. Granju with Kennedy, *Attachment Parenting*.

113. Ibid., p. 9.

114. Ibid., p. 10.

115. Jeanne Brooks-Gunn and P. Lindsay Chase-Lansdale, "Adolescent Parenthood," in *Handbook of Parenting*, ed. Marc H. Bornstein, vol. 3, *Status and Social Conditions of Parenting* (Mahwah, NJ: Erlbaum, 1995), pp. 113–149.

116. Joy D. Osofsky, Della M. Hann, and Claire Peebles, "Adolescent Parenthood: Risks and Opportunities for Mothers and Infants," in *Handbook of Infant Mental Health*, pp. 106–119.

117. Brooks-Gunn and Chase-Lansdale, "Adolescent Parenthood."

118. Osofsky, Hann, and Peebles, "Adolescent Parenthood."

119. Brooks-Gunn and Chase-Lansdale, "Adolescent Parenthood."

120. Osofsky, Hann, and Peebles, "Adolescent Parenthood."

121. Judith Musick, "The Special Role of Parenting in the Context of Poverty: The Case of Adolescent Motherhood," in *Threats to Optimal Development: Integrating Biological, Psychological and Social Risk Factors*, ed. Charles A. Nelson (Hillsdale, NJ: Erlbaum, 1994), pp. 179–216.

122. Brooks-Gunn and Chase-Lansdale, "Adolescent Parenthood."

123. Frank F. Furstenberg, J. Brooks-Gunn, and S. Philip Morgan, *Adolescent Mothers in Later Life* (Cambridge: Cambridge University Press, 1990), pp. 145–146.

124. Ross D. Parke and Raymond Buriel, "Socialization in the Family: Ethnic and Ecological Perspectives," in *Handbook of Child Psychology*, vol. 3, pp. 463–552.

125. Ibid.

126. Beverly I. Fagot et al., "Becoming an Adolescent Father: Precursors and Parenting," *Developmental Psychology* 34 (1998): 1217.

127. Furstenberg, Brooks-Gunn, and Morgan, *Adolescent Mothers in Later Life*.

128. Osofsky, Hann, and Peebles, "Adolescent Parenthood."

129. Ibid., p. 116.

130. Al Santoli, "They Turn Young Men with Children into Fathers," *Parade Magazine*, 29 May 1994.

131. Ibid.

132. Tiffany Field, "Psychologically Depressed Parents," in *Handbook of Parenting*, ed. Marc H. Bornstein, vol. 4, *Applied and Practical Parenting* (Mahwah, NJ: Erlbaum, 1995), pp. 85–99.

133. Ibid.

134. Linda C. Mayes, "Substance Abuse and Parenting," in *Handbook of Parenting*, vol. 4, pp. 101–125.

135. Ibid.

136. Ibid.

137. Rina Das Eiden, Felipa Chavez, and Kenneth E. Leonard, "Parent-Infant Interactions among Families with Alcoholic Fathers," *Development and Psychopathology* 11 (1999): 745–762.

138. Mayes, "Substance Abuse and Parenting."

139. Linda C. Mayes, "Developing Brain and In Utero Cocaine Exposure: Effects on Neural Ontogeny," *Development and Psychopathology* 11 (1999): 685–714.

140. Ibid., p. 706.

141. Carolyn Pape Cowan and Philip A. Cowan, *When Partners Become Parents* (New York: Basic Books, 1992).

142. Ibid.

143. Jay Belsky, Sharon Woodworth, and Keith Crnic, "Troubled Family Interaction during Toddlerhood," *Development and Psychopathology* 8 (1996): 477–495.

144. Jay Belsky, Kuang-Hua Hsieh, and Keith Crnic, "Mothering, Fathering, and Infant Negativity as Antecedents of Boys' Externalizing Problems and Inhibition at Age 3 Years: Differential Susceptibility to Rearing Experience," *Development and Psychopathology* 10 (1998): 301–319.

145. Robert B. Stewart et al., "The Firstborn's Adjustment to the Birth of a Sibling: A Longitudinal Assessment," *Child Development* 58 (1987): 341–355.

146. Wyndol Furman, "Parenting Siblings," in *Handbook of Parenting*, vol. 1, pp. 143–162.

147. Radke-Yarrow et al., "Learning Concern for Others."

148. Susan Engel, *Stories Children Tell* (New York: Freeman, 1999), p. 4.

149. Ibid.

150. Ibid.

151. Philip A. Cowan, "What We Talk About When We Talk about Families," in *The Stories Families Tell: Narrative Coherence, Narrative Interaction, and Relationship Beliefs*, ed. Barbara H. Fiese et al., Monographs of the Society for Research in Child Development, serial no. 257 (1999): 163.

152. Barbara H. Fiese and Kathleen A. T. Marjinsky, "Dinnertime Stories: Connecting Family Practices with Relationship Beliefs and Child Adjustment," in *The Stories Families Tell*, pp. 52–68.

153. Engel, *Stories Children Tell*.

154. Arnold J. Sameroff and Barbara H. Fiese, "Narrative Connections in the Family Context: Summary and Conclusions," in *The Stories Families Tell*, p. 122.

155. Ellen Galinsky, *Between Generations: The Six Stages of Parenthood* (New York: Times Books, 1981).

156. Ibid., pp. 136–137.

Notes

1. W. Andrew Collins, Michael L. Harris, and Amy Susman, "Parenting during Middle Childhood," in *Handbook of Parenting*, ed. Marc H. Bornstein, vol. 1, *Children and Parenting* (Mahwah, NJ: Erlbaum, 1995), pp. 65–89.
2. Ibid.
3. Judith G. Smetana, "Adolescents' and Parents' Reasoning about Actual Family Conflict," *Child Development* 60 (1989): 1052–1067.
4. Graeme Russell and Alan Russell, "Mother-Child and Father-Child in Middle Childhood," *Child Development* 58 (1987): 1573–1585.
5. Frances K. Grossman, William S. Pollack, and Ellen Golding, "Fathers and Children: Predicting the Quality and Quantity of Fathering," *Developmental Psychology* 24 (1988): 822–891.
6. Russell and Russell, "Mother-Child and Father-Child in Middle Childhood."
7. Molly Reid, Sharon Landesman Ramey, and Margaret Burchinal, "Dialogues with Children about Their Families," in *Children's Perspectives on the Family*, ed. Inge Bretherton and Malcolm W. Watson, New Directions for Child Development, no. 48 (San Francisco: Jossey-Bass, 1990), pp. 5–28.
8. Collins, Harris, and Susman, "Parenting during Middle Childhood."
9. Kenneth H. Rubin, William Bukowski, and Jeffrey G. Parker, "Peer Interactions, Relationships, and Groups," in *Handbook of Child Psychology*, ed. in chief William Damon and vol. ed. Nancy Eisenberg, vol. 3, *Social, Emotional, and Personality Development*, 5th ed. (New York: Wiley, 1998), pp. 619–700.
10. Ronald Seifer et al., "Child and Family Factors That Ameliorate Risk between 4 and 13 Years of Age," *Journal of the American Academy of Child and Adolescent Psychiatry* 31 (1992): 893–903.
11. Robert L. Nix et al., "The Relation between Mothers' Hostile Attribution Tendencies and Children's Externalizing Problems: The Mediating Role of Mothers' Harsh Discipline Practices," *Child Development* 70 (1999): 896–909.
12. Thomas G. O'Connor et al., "Genotype-Environment Correlations in Late Childhood and Early Adolescence: Asocial Behavioral Problems and Coercive Parenting," *Developmental Psychology* 34 (1998): 970–981.
13. Susan Harter, "The Development of Self-Representations," in *Handbook of Child Psychology*, vol. 3, pp. 553–617.
14. Phyllis A. Katz and Keith R. Ksansnak, "Developmental Aspects of Gender Role Flexibility and Traditionality in Middle Childhood and Adolescence," *Developmental Psychology* 30 (1994): 272–282.
15. Frances E. Aboud, "The Development of Ethnic Self-Identification and Attitudes," in *Children's Ethnic Socialization*, ed. Jean S. Phinney and Mary Jane Rotheram (Beverly Hills, CA: Sage, 1987), pp. 32–55.
16. Mary Jane Rotheram-Borus and Jean S. Phinney, "Patterns of Social Expectations among Black and Mexican-American Children," *Child Development* 61 (1990): 542–556.
17. Michael C. Thornton et al., "Sociodemographic and Environmental Correlates of Racial Socialization by Black Parents," *Child Development* 61 (1990): 401–409.
18. Ibid.
19. Algea O. Harrison et al., "Family Ecologies of Ethnic Minority Children," *Child Development* 61 (1990): 347–362; Margaret Beale Spencer and Carol Markstrom-Adams, "Identity Processes among Racial and Ethnic Minority Children in America," *Child Development* 61 (1990): 290–310.
20. James P. Connell and Barbara C. Ilardi, "Self System Concomitants of Discrepancies between Children's and Teachers' Evaluations of Academic Competence," *Child Development* 58 (1987): 1297–1307.
21. Albert Bandura, "Regulation of Cognitive Processes through Perceived Self-Efficacy," *Developmental Psychology* 25 (1989): 729–735.
22. Mariellen Fischer and Harold Leitenberg, "Optimism and Pessimism in Elementary School–Aged Children," *Child Development* 57 (1986): 241–248.
23. Deborah J. Stipek and Karen M. DeCotis,

"Children's Understanding of the Implications of Causal Attributions for Emotional Experiences," *Child Development* 59 (1988): 1601–1616.

24. Dayna Fuchs and Mark H. Thelen, "Children's Expected Interpersonal Consequences of Communicating Their Affective State and Reported Likelihood of Expression," *Child Development* 59 (1988): 1314–1322.

25. Nancy Eisenberg et al., "The Relations of Children's Dispositional Prosocial Behavior to Emotionality, Regulation, and Social Functioning," *Child Development* 67 (1996): 974–992.

26. Charles L. McCoy and John C. Masters, "The Development of Children's Strategies for the Social Control of Emotion," *Child Development* 56 (1985): 1214–1222.

27. Nancy Eisenberg and Paul H. Mussen, *The Roots of Prosocial Behavior in Children* (Cambridge, England: Cambridge University Press, 1989).

28. Steven R. Asher et al., "Peer Rejection and Loneliness in Childhood," in *Peer Rejection in Childhood*, ed. Steven R. Asher and John D. Coie (Cambridge, England: Cambridge University Press, 1990), 253–273.

29. Michael Rutter, Jack Tizard, and Kingsley Whitmore, eds., *Education, Health and Behavior* (Huntington, NY: Kruger, 1981).

30. Kaoru Yamamoto et al., "Voices in Unison: Stressful Events in the Lives of Children in Six Countries," *Journal of Child Psychology and Psychiatry* 28 (1987): 855–864.

31. Elaine Shaw Sorensen, *Children's Stress and Coping* (New York: Guilford, 1993).

32. Eve Brotman-Band and John R. Weisz, "How to Feel Better When It Feels Bad," *Developmental Psychology* 24 (1998): 247–253.

33. Jennifer L. Altshuler and Diane N. Ruble, "Developmental Changes in Children's Awareness of Strategies for Coping with Uncontrollable Stress," *Child Development* 60 (1989): 1337–1349.

34. Denise F. Hardy, Thomas G. Power, and Susan Jaedicke, "Examining the Relation of Parenting to Children's Coping with Everyday Stress," *Child Development* 64 (1993): 1829–1841.

35. Sorensen, *Children's Stress and Coping.*

36. Molly Reid et al., "My Family and Friends: Six- to Twelve-Year-Old Children's Perceptions of Social Support," *Child Development* 60 (1989): 907.

37. Mary J. Levitt, Nathalie Guacci-Franco, and Jerome L. Levitt, "Convoys of Social Support in Childhood and Early Adolescence," *Developmental Psychology* 29 (1993): 811–818.

38. Martin E. P. Seligman, *Learned Optimism* (New York: Pocket Books, 1990).

39. Hazel J. Markus and Paula S. Nurius, "Self-Understanding and Self-Regulation in Middle Childhood," in *Development during Middle Childhood*, ed. W. Andrew Collins (Washington, DC: National Academy Press, 1984), pp. 147–183.

40. Tamara J. Ferguson, Hedy Stegge, and Ilse Damhuis, "Children's Understanding of Guilt and Shame," *Child Development* 62 (1991): 827–839.

41. Markus and Nurius, "Self-Understanding and Self-Regulation in Middle Childhood."

42. Susan Harter, "Developmental Perspectives on the Self-System," in *Handbook of Child Psychology*, ed. Paul H. Mussen and E. Mavis Hetherington, vol. 4, *Socialization, Personality and Social Development*, 4th ed. (New York: Wiley, 1983), pp. 275–385.

43. Grazyna Kochanska, "Socialization and Temperament in the Development of Guilt and Conscience," *Child Development* 62 (1991): 1379–1392.

44. Judith G. Smetana, Melanie Killen, and Elliot Turiel, "Children's Reasoning about Interpersonal and Moral Conflicts," *Child Development* 62 (1991): 629–644.

45. Lawrence Kohlberg, "The Development of Children's Orientations toward a Moral Order: I Sequence in the Development of Moral Thought," *Vita Humana* 6 (1963): 11–33.

46. David C. Rowe, *The Limits of Family Influence* (New York: Guilford, 1994).

47. Benjamin S. Bloom, ed., *Developing Talent in Young People* (New York: Ballantine, 1985).

48. J. David Hawkins, "Academic Performance and School Success: Sources and Consequences," in *Enhancing Children's Wellness,*

ed. Roger P. Weissberg et al. (Thousand Oaks, CA: Sage, 1997), pp. 278–305.

49. Jacquelynne S. Eccles, Allan Wigfield, and Ulrich Schiefele, "Motivation to Succeed," in *Handbook of Child Psychology*, vol. 3, pp. 1017–1095.

50. Ben Carson with Gregg Lewis, *The Big Picture* (Grand Rapids, MI: Zondervan, 1999).

51. Ibid., p. 10.

52. Deborah A. Phillips, "Socialization of Perceived Academic Competence among Highly Competent Children," *Child Development* 58 (1987): 1308–1320.

53. Peter Ernest Haiman, "How Children Manage Frustration Affects Ability to Focus and Learn," *Brown University Child and Adolescent Newsletter* 16 (February 2000), p. 1.

54. Theodore D. Wachs, *The Nature of Nurture* (Newbury Park, CA: Sage, 1992).

55. Sheppard G. Kellam et al., "The Effect of the Level of Aggression in the First Grade Classroom on the Course and Malleability of Aggressive Behavior in Middle School," *Development and Psychopathology* 10 (1998): 165–185.

56. Hawkins, "Academic Performance and School Success."

57. Ibid.

58. Lori J. Connors and Joyce L. Epstein, "Parent and School partnerships," in *Handbook of Parenting*, ed. Marc H. Bornstein, vol. 4, *Applied and Practical Parenting* (Mahwah, NJ: Erlbaum, 1995), pp. 437–458.

59. Karen Klein Burhans and Carol S. Dweck, "Helplessness in Early Childhood: The Role of Contingent Worth," *Child Development* 66 (1995): 1719–1738.

60. Eccles, Wigfield, and Schiefele, "Motivation to Succeed."

61. Patricia M. Greenfield and Lalita K. Suzuki, "Culture and Human Development: Implications for Parenting, Education, Pediatrics, and Mental Health," in *Handbook of Child Psychology*, ed. in chief William Damon and vol. ed. Irving E. Sigel and K. Ann Renninger, vol. 4, *Child Psychology in Practice*, 5th ed. (New York: Wiley, 1998), pp. 1059–1109.

62. Harold W. Stevenson, Chuansheng Chen, and David H. Uttal, "Beliefs and Achievements: A Study of Black, White, and Hispanic Children," *Child Development* 61 (1990).

63. Rubin, Bukowski, and Parker, "Peer Interactions, Relationships, and Groups."

64. Ibid., p. 676.

65. Ibid.

66. Ibid.

67. Willard W. Hartup, "The Company They Keep: Friendships and Their Developmental Significance," *Child Development* 67 (1996): 1–13.

68. Rubin, Bukowski, and Parker, "Peer Interactions, Relationships, and Groups."

69. Nancy Eisenberg and Richard A. Fabes, "Prosocial Development," in *Handbook of Child Psychology*, vol. 3, pp. 701–778.

70. John D. Coie and Kenneth A. Dodge, "Aggression and Antisocial Behavior," in *Handbook of Child Psychology*, vol. 3, pp. 779–862.

71. Ibid., p. 815.

72. Rubin, Bukowski, and Parker, "Peer Interactions, Relationships, and Groups."

73. Philip G. Zimbardo and Shirley Radl, *The Shy Child* (Garden City, NY: Doubleday, 1982).

74. Sherri Oden and Steven R. Asher, "Coaching Children in Social Skills for Friendship Making," *Child Development* 48 (1977): 495–506.

75. Marlene Jacobs Sandstrom and John D. Coie, "A Developmental Perspective on Peer Rejection: Mechanisms of Stability and Change," *Child Development* 70 (1999): 955–966.

76. Nicki R. Crick and Jennifer K. Grotpeter, "Relational Aggression, Gender, and Social-Psychological Adjustment," *Child Development* 66 (1995): 710–722.

77. Ibid.

78. John D. Coie and Gina Krehbiel Koeppl, "Adapting Intervention to the Problems of Aggressive and Disruptive Children," in *Peer Rejection in Childhood*, pp. 309–337.

79. Gerald R. Patterson et al., *A Social Learning Approach to Family Intervention*, vol. 1, *Families with Aggressive Children* (Eugene, OR: Castalia, 1975).

80. Gerald R. Patterson, *Families: Applications of Social Learning to Family Life*, rev. ed. (Champaign, IL: Research Press, 1975).

81. Gerald R. Patterson, *Living with Children*, rev. ed. (Champaign, IL: Research Press, 1976).

82. Dan Olweus, "Annotation: Bullying at School: Basic Facts and Effects of a School

Based Intervention Program," *Journal of Child Psychology and Psychiatry* 35 (1994): 1171–1190.

83. Nicki R. Crick and Jennifer K. Grotpeter, "Children's Treatment of Peers: Victims of Relational and Overt Aggression," *Development and Psychopathology* 8 (1996): 367–380.

84. David Schwartz et al., "Peer Group Victimization as a Predictor of Children's Behavior Problems at Home and at School," *Development and Psychopathology* 10 (1998): 87–99.

85. Susan K. Egan and David G. Perry, "Does Low Self-Regard Invite Victimization?" *Developmental Psychology* 34 (1998): 299–309.

86. Olweus, "Annotation: Bullying at School," p. 1183.

87. Aletha C. Huston and John C. Wright, "Mass Media and Children's Development," in *Handbook of Child Psychology*, vol. 4, pp. 1042–1043.

88. Patricia Marks Greenfield, *Mind and Media: The Effects of Television, Video Games, and Computers* (Cambridge, MA: Harvard University Press, 1984), p. 51.

89. Huston and Wright, "Mass Media and Children's Development," p. 1043.

90. Ibid., p. 1027.

91. Ibid.

92. Marites F. Pinon, Aletha C. Huston, and John C. Wright, "Family Ecology and Child Characteristics That Predict Young Children's Educational Television Viewing," *Child Development* 60 (1989): 846–856.

93. Robert Kubey, "Media Implications for the Quality of Family Life," in *Media, Children and the Family: Social Scientific, Psychodynamic and Clinical Perspectives*, ed. Dolf Zillmann, Jennings Bryant, and Aletha C. Huston (Hillsdale, NJ: Erlbaum, 1994), pp. 61–69.

94. Ibid, p. 64.

95. Coie and Dodge, "Aggression and Antisocial Behavior," p. 799.

96. Ibid.

97. Aletha C. Huston, Dolf Zillmann, and Jennings Bryant, "Media Influence, Public Policy and the Family," in *Media, Children and the Family: Social Scientific, Psychodynamic and Clinical Perspectives*, pp. 3–18.

98. Aimee Dorr and Beth E. Rabin, "Parents, Children, and Television," in *Handbook of Parenting*, vol. 4, pp. 323–351.

99. Ellen Galinsky, *Between Generations: The Six Stages of Parenthood* (New York: Time Books, 1981).

Chapter 7

1. Jeanne Brooks-Gunn and Edward O. Reiter, "The Role of Pubertal Processes," in *At the Threshold: The Developing Adolescent*, ed. S. Shirley Feldman and Glen R. Elliott (Cambridge, MA: Harvard University Press, 1990), pp. 16–53.

2. Christy Miller Buchanan, Jacquelynne S. Eccles, and Jill B. Becker, "Are Adolescents the Victims of Raging Hormones? Evidence for Activational Effects of Hormones on Mood and Behavior at Adolescence," *Psychological Bulletin* 3 (1992): 62–107.

3. Susan G. Millstein and Iris F. Litt, "Adolescent Health" in *At the Threshold*, pp. 431–456.

4. Cathy Schoen et al., "The Commonwealth Fund Survey of the Health of Adolescent Girls" (New York: Commonwealth Fund, 1997).

5. Millstein and Litt, "Adolescent Health."

6. Susan Harter, "The Development of Self-Representations," in *Handbook of Child Psychology*, ed. in chief William Damon and vol. ed. Nancy Eisenberg, vol. 3, *Social, Emotional, and Personality Development*, 5th ed. (New York: Wiley, 1998), pp. 553–617.

7. Herant Katchadourian, "Sexuality," in *At the Threshold*, pp. 330–351.

8. Joseph Lee Rodgers, "Sexual Transitions in Adolescence," in *Transitions through Adolescence: Interpersonal Domains and Context*, ed. Julie A. Graber, Jeanne Brooks-Gunn, and Ann C. Petersen (Mahwah, NJ: Erlbaum, 1996), pp. 85–110.

9. Roger P. Weissberg and Mark T. Greenberg, "School and Community Competence-Enhancement and Prevention Programs," in *Handbook of Child Psychol-*

ogy, ed. in chief William Damon and vol. ed. Irving E. Sigel and K. Ann Renninger, vol. 4, *Child Psychology in Practice*, 5th ed. (New York: Wiley, 1997), pp. 877–954.

10. Nancy J. Cobb, *Adolescence: Continuity, Change, and Diversity* (Mountain View, CA: Mayfield, 1992).

11. Rodgers, "Sexual Transitions in Adolescence."

12. Daniel P. Keating, "Adolescent Thinking," in *At the Threshold*, pp. 54–89.

13. Karen Bartsch, "Adolescents' Theoretical Thinking," in *Early Adolescence: Perspectives on Research, Policy, and Intervention,* ed. Richard M. Lerner (Hillsdale, NJ: Erlbaum, 1993), pp. 143–157.

14. Reed Larson and Mark Ham, "Stress and 'Storm Stress' in Early Adolescence: The Relationship of Negative Events and Dysphoric Affect," *Developmental Psychology* 29 (1993): 130–140.

15. Reed Larson and Maryse H. Richards, *Divergent Realities: The Emotional Lives of Mothers, Fathers, and Adolescents* (New York: Basic Books, 1994).

16. Buchanan, Eccles, and Becker, "Are Adolescents the Victims of Raging Hormones?"

17. David Elkind, *Children and Adolescents*, 2d ed. (New York: Oxford University Press, 1974), p. 91.

18. Larson and Ham, "Stress and 'Storm Stress' in Early Adolescence."

19. Anne C. Petersen et al., "Depression in Adolescence," *American Psychologist* 48 (1993): 155–168.

20. Ibid.

21. Roberta G. Simmons et al., "The Impact of Cumulative Changes in Early Adolescence," *Child Development* 58 (1987): 1220–1234.

22. Mary J. Levitt, Nathalie Guacci-Franco, and Jerome L. Levitt, "Convoys of Social Support in Childhood and Early Adolescence: Structure and Function," *Developmental Psychology* 29 (1993): 811–818.

23. Susan Harter et al., "The Development of Multiple Role-Related Selves," *Development and Psychopathology* 9 (1997): 835–853.

24. Ibid., 838.

25. Kenneth H. Rubin, William Bukowski, and Jeffrey G. Parker, "Peer Interactions, Relationships, and Groups," in *Handbook of Child Psychology*, vol. 3, pp. 619–700.

26. Lynne Zarbatany, Donald P. Hartmann, and D. Bruce Rankin, "The Psychological Functions of Preadolescent Peer Activities," *Child Development* 61 (1990): 1067–1080.

27. Mihaly Csikszentmihalyi and Reed Larson, *Being Adolescent* (New York: Basic Books, 1984).

28. B. Bradford Brown, "Peer Groups and Peer Culture," in *At the Threshold*, pp. 171–196.

29. Ibid.

30. Duane Buhrmester, "Intimacy and Friendship, Interpersonal Competence, and Adjustment during Preadolescence and Adolescence," *Child Development* 61 (1990): 1101–1111.

31. Jane Norman and Myron Harris, *The Private Life of the American Teenager* (New York: Rawson Wade, 1981).

32. Brown, "Peer Groups and Peer Culture."

33. Aaron Hogue and Laurence Steinberg, "Homophily of Internalized Distress in Adolescent Peer Groups," *Developmental Psychology* 31 (1995): 897–906.

34. Reed W. Larson, "The Emergence of Solitude as a Constructive Domain of Experience in Early Adolescence," *Child Development* 68 (1997): 80–93.

35. John Janeway Conger and Anne C. Petersen, *Adolescence and Youth*, 3d ed. (New York: Harper & Row, 1984).

36. Ibid.

37. Ibid.

38. Ibid.

39. Jacquelynne Eccles et al., "Development during Adolescence: The Impact of Stage-Environment Fit on Young Adolescents' Experiences in Schools and in Families," *American Psychologist* 48 (1993): 90–101.

40. Robert W. Roeser, Jacquelynne S. Eccles, and Arnold J. Sameroff, "Academic and Emotional Functioning in Early Adolescence: Longitudinal Relations, Patterns, and Prediction by Experience in Middle School," *Development and Psychopathology* 10 (1998): 321–352.

41. Erik H. Erikson, *Childhood and Society*, 2d ed. (New York: Norton, 1963).

42. James E. Marcia, "Identity in Adolescence," in *Handbook of Adolescent Psychology*, ed.

Joseph Adelson (New York: Wiley, 1980), pp. 159–187.

43. Harold D. Grotevant, "Adolescent Development in Family Contexts," in *Handbook of Child Psychology*," vol. 3, pp. 1097–1149.

44. Jack Block and Richard W. Robins, "A Longitudinal Study of Consistency and Change in Self-Esteem from Early Adolescence to Early Adulthood," *Child Development* 64 (1993): 909–923.

45. Jack Block, "Some Relationships Regarding the Self from the Block and Block Longitudinal Study" (paper presented at the Social Science Research Council Conference on Selfhood, Stanford, CA, October 1985).

46. Susan Harter, "Self and Identity Development," in *At the Threshold*, pp. 352–387.

47. Patricia Barthalow Koch, "Promoting Healthy Sexual Development during Early Adolescence," in *Early Adolescence: Perspectives on Research, Policy, and Intervention*, pp. 293–307.

48. Katchadourian, "Sexuality."

49. Koch, "Promoting Healthy Sexual Development during Early Adolescence."

50. Jean S. Phinney, "Stages of Ethnic Identity Development in Minority Group Adolescents," *Journal of Early Adolescence* 9 (1989): 34–49.

51. Jean S. Phinney and Victoria Chavira, "Ethnic Identity and Self-Esteem," *Journal of Adolescence* 15 (1992): 271–281.

52. Jean S. Phinney and Mona Devich-Navarro, "Variations in Bicultural Identification among African-American and Mexican-American Adolescents," *Journal of Research on Adolescence* 7 (1997): 3–32.

53. Norman and Harris, *The Private Life of the American Teenager.*

54. Larson and Richards, *Divergent Realities*, p. 189.

55. Judith G. Smetana, "Concepts of Self and Social Convention: Adolescents' and Parents' Reasoning about Hypothetical and Actual Family Conflicts," in *Development during the Transition to Adolescence: Minnesota Symposia on Child Psychology*, vol. 21, ed. Megan R. Gunnar and W. Andrew Collins (Hillsdale, NJ: Erlbaum, 1988), pp. 79–122; Judith G. Smetana, "Adolescents' and Parents' Reasoning about Actual Family Conflict," *Child Development* 60 (1989): 1052–1067.

56. Smetana, "Concepts of Self and Social Convention."

57. Laurence Steinberg, "Impact of Puberty on Family Relations: Effects of Pubertal Status and Pubertal Timing," *Developmental Psychology* 23 (1987): 451–460.

58. Per F. Gjerde, "The Interpersonal Structure of Family Interaction Settings: Parent-Adolescent Relations in Dyads and Triads," *Developmental Psychology* 22 (1986): 297–304.

59. Laurence Steinberg et al., "Authoritative Parenting and Adolescent Adjustment: An Ecological Perspective," in *Examining Lives in Context*, ed. Phyllis Moen, Glen H. Elder, Jr., and Kurt Lusher (Washington, DC: American Psychological Association, 1995), pp. 423–466.

60. Anne C. Fletcher, Laurence Steinberg, and Elizabeth B. Sellers, "Adolescents' Well Being as a Function of Perceived Interparental Consistency," *Journal of Marriage and the Family* 61 (1999): 599–610.

61. Marjory R. Gray and Laurence Steinberg, "Unpacking Authoritative Parenting: Reassessing a Multidimensional Construct," *Journal of Marriage and the Family* 61 (1999): 574–587.

62. Ibid., p. 584.

63. Brian K. Barber, "Introduction: Adolescent Socialization in Context—The Role of Connection, Regulation, and Autonomy in the Family," *Journal of Adolescent Research* 12 (1997): 5–11.

64. Brian K. Barber and Joseph A. Olsen, "Socialization in Context: Connection, Regulation, and Autonomy in the Family, School, and Neighborhood and with Peers," *Journal of Adolescent Research* 12 (1997): p. 310.

65. Carolyn Zahn-Waxler, "Warriors and Worriers: Gender and Psychopathology," *Development and Psychopathology* 5 (1993): 79–89.

66. Les B. Whitbeck et al., "Intergenerational Continuity of Parental Rejection and Depressed Affect," *Journal of Personality and Social Psychology* 63 (1992): 1036–1045.

67. Cheryl Buehler et al., "Interparental Conflict Styles and Youth Problem Behaviors: A Two-Sample Replication Study," *Journal of*

Marriage and the Family 60 (1998): 119–132.

68. Patrick T. Davis, Levent Dumenci, and Michael Windle, "The Interplay between Maternal Depressive Symptoms and Marital Distress in the Prediction of Adolescent Adjustment," *Journal of Marriage and the Family* 61 (1999): 238–254.

69. Lori L. D'Angelo, Daniel Weinberger, and S. Shirley Feldman, "Like Father, Like Son? Predicting Male Adolescents' Adjustment from Parents' Distress and Self-Restraint," *Developmental Psychology* 31 (1995): 615–622.

70. James Garbarino, *Lost Boys: Why Our Sons Turn Violent and How We Can Save Them* (New York: Free Press, 1999).

71. Ibid., p. 74.

72. Ibid., p. 75.

73. Ibid., p. 149.

74. Deborah M. Capaldi and Mike Stoolmiller, "Co-occurrence of Conduct Problems and Depressive Symptoms in Early Adolescent Boys: III. Prediction to Young-Adult Adjustment," *Development and Psychopathology* 11 (1999): 59–84.

75. Ibid., p. 78.

76. Alice W. Pope and Karen L. Bierman, "Predicting Adolescent Peer Problems and Antisocial Activities: The Relative Roles of Aggression and Dysregulation," *Developmental Psychology* 35 (1999): 335–346.

77. Capaldi and Stoolmiller, "Co-occurrence of Conduct Problems and Depressive Symptoms in Early Adolescent Boys."

78. Sara Shandler, *Ophelia Speaks* (New York: HarperCollins, 1999), p. 232.

79. Ibid., p. 233.

80. Dante Cicchetti and Sheree L. Toth, "The Development of Depression in Children and Adolescents," *American Psychologist* 53 (1998): 221–241.

81. Ibid.

82. Ibid.

83. Donald H. McKnew, Leon Cytryn, and Herbert Yahraes, *Why Isn't Johnny Crying?* (New York: Norton, 1983).

84. Anne C. Petersen et al., "Depression in Adolescence," *American Psychologist* 48 (1993): 155–168.

85. Cicchetti and Toth, "The Development of Depression."

86. Petersen et al., "Depression in Adolescence."

87. Ibid.

88. W. Brian Barr, "Child Behavior Professionals Are Not Untouched by Family Suicides," *Brown University Child and Adolescent Behavior Newsletter* (March 1998), p. 1.

89. Millstein and Litt, "Adolescent Health."

90. Pam Belluck, "Black Youths' Rate of Suicide Rising Sharply," *New York Times*, March 20, 1998, p. 1.

91. Weissberg and Greenberg, "School and Community Competence-Enhancement and Prevention Programs," in *Handbook of Child Psychology*, vol. 4.

92. Susan Harter, "Visions of Self beyond the Me in the Mirror" (university lecture, University of Denver, 1990).

93. Ibid., p. 16.

94. Petersen et al., "Depression in Adolescence."

95. Martin E. P. Seligman, *The Optimistic Child* (New York: Houghton Mifflin, 1995).

96. Michael D. Resnick et al., "Protecting Adolescents from Harm," *Journal of the American Medical Association* 278 (1997): 823–832.

97. Schoen et al, "The Commonwealth Fund Survey."

98. Jerald G. Bachman et al., "Transition in Drug Use during Late Adolescence and Young Adulthood," in *Transitions through Adolescence*, pp. 111–140.

99. Schoen et al., "The Commonwealth Fund Survey."

100. Barbara J. Tinsley and Nancy B. Lees, "Health Promotion for Parents," in *Handbook of Parenting*, ed. Marc H. Bornstein, vol. 4, *Applied and Practical Parenting* (Mahwah, NJ: Erlbaum, 1995), pp. 187–204.

101. Judy A. Andrews, Hyman Hops, and Susan C. Duncan, "Adolescent Modeling of Parent Substance Use: The Moderating Effect of the Relationship with the Parent," *Journal of Family Psychology* 11 (1997): 259–270.

102. Diana Baumrind, "The Influence of Parenting Style on Adolescent Competence and Problem Behavior," (paper presented at the American Psychological Association Meetings, New Orleans, LA, August 1989); Jonathan Shedler and Jack Block, "Adoles-

cent Drug Use and Psychological Health: A Longitudinal Inquiry," *American Psychologist* 45 (1990): 612–630.

103. Resnick, "Protecting Adolescents from Harm."

104. Melissa R. Herman et al., "The Influence of Family Regulation, Connection, and Psychological Autonomy on Six Measures of Adolescent Functioning," *Journal of Adolescent Research* 12 (1997): 34–67.

105. Grace M. Barnes and Michael P. Farrell, "Parental Support and Control as Predictors of Adolescent Drinking, Delinquency, and Related Problem Behaviors," *Journal of Marriage and the Family* 54 (1992): 763–776; Grace M. Barnes et al., "The Effects of Parenting on the Development of Adolescent Alcohol Misuse: A Six-Wave Latent Growth Model," *Journal of Marriage and the Family* 62 (2000): 175–186.

106. Resnick, "Protecting Adolescents from Harm."

107. Richard Jessor et al., "Protective Factors in Adolescent Problem Behavior: Moderation Effects and Developmental Change," *Developmental Psychology* 31 (1995): 923–933.

108. Resnick, "Protecting Adolescents from Harm."

109. Ibid.

110. Ibid.

111. Ibid.

112. James Jaccard, Patricia J. Dittus, and Vivian V. Gordon, "Parent-Adolescent Congruency in Reports of Adolescent Sexual Behavior and Communications about Sexual Behavior," *Child Development* 69 (1998): 247–261.

113. "Teen Sex Rates Level Off, but Pregnancy and STD Rates Remain High," *Brown University Child and Adolescent Newsletter* 15 (August 1998), p. 1.

114. Karen Bogenschneider et al., "'Other Teens Drink, but Not My Kid': Does Parental Awareness of Adolescent Alcohol Use Protect Adolescents from Risky Consequences?" *Journal of Marriage and the Family* 60 (1998): 356–373.

115. Ibid.

116. Resnick, "Protecting Adolescents from Harm."

117. Beth Polson and Miller Newton, *Not My Kid: A Parent's Guide to Kids and Drugs* (New York: Avon, 1985).

118. Michael Windle et al., "Adolescent Perceptions of Help-Seeking Resources for Substance Abuse," *Child Development* 62 (1991): 179–189.

119. Renee E. Sieving, Cheryl L. Perry, and Carolyn L. Williams, "Do Friendships Change Behaviors, or Do Behaviors Change Friendships? Examining Paths of Influence in Young Adolescents' Alcohol Use," *Journal of Adolescent Health* 26 (2000): 27–35.

120. W. Andrew Collins et al., "Conflict Processes and Transitions in Parent and Peer Relationships," *Journal of Adolescent Research* 12 (1997): 178–198.

121. Andrew J. Fuligni and Jacquelynne S. Eccles, "Perceived Parent-Child Relationships and Early Adolescents' Orientation toward Peers," *Developmental Psychology* 29 (1993): 622–632.

122. Collins et al., "Conflict Processes and Transitions in Parent and Peer Relationships."

123. B. Bradford Brown et al., "Parenting Practices and Peer Group Affiliation in Adolescence," *Child Development* 64 (1993): 467–482.

124. Smetana, "Concepts of Self and Social Convention"; Smetana, "Adolescents' and Parents' Reasoning about Actual Family Conflict."

125. Joseph P. Allen et al., "Longitudinal Assessment of Autonomy and Relatedness in Adolescent-Family Interactions as Predictors of Adolescent Ego Development and Self-Esteem," *Child Development* 65 (1994): 1179–1194.

126. R. Rogers Kobak et al., "Attachment and Emotion Regulation during Mother-Teen Problem Solving: A Control Theory Analysis," *Child Development* 64 (1993): 231–245.

127. DeWayne Moore, "Parent-Adolescent Separation: The Construction of Adulthood by Late Adolescents," *Developmental Psychology* 23 (1987): 298–307.

128. S. Shirley Feldman and Thomas M. Gehring, "Changing Perceptions of Family Cohesion and Power across Adolescence," *Child Development* 59 (1988): 1034–1045.

129. David Elkind, "Growing Up Faster," *Psychology Today*, February 1979.

130. Ellen Galinsky, *Between Generations: The Six Stages of Parenthood* (New York: Times Books, 1981).

131. Laurence Steinberg with Wendy Steinberg, *Crossing Paths: How Your Child's Adolescence Triggers Your Own Crisis* (New York: Simon & Schuster, 1994).

132. William Damon, *The Youth Charter: How Communities Can Work Together to Raise Standards for All Our Children* (New York: Free Press, 1997).

133. Ibid., p. ix.

Chapter 8

1. Urie Bronfenbrenner, "Ecology of the Family as a Context for Human Development," *Developmental Psychology* 22 (1986): 723–742.

2. Ann C. Crouter et al., "Conditions Underlying Parents' Knowledge about Children's Daily Lives in Middle Childhood: Between- and Within-Family Comparisons," *Child Development* 70 (1999): 246–259.

3. U.S. Bureau of the Census, *Statistical Abstract of the United States: 1998*, 118th ed. (Washington, DC: Government Printing Office, 1998).

4. Graeme Russell, "Primary Caregiving Fathers," in *Parenting and Child Development in Nontraditional Families*, ed. Michael E. Lamb (Mahwah, NJ: Erlbaum, 1999), pp. 57–81.

5. James A. Levine and Todd L. Pittinsky, *Working Fathers: New Strategies for Balancing Work and Family* (Reading, MA: Addison-Wesley, 1997).

6. Ann C. Crouter and Beth Manke, "Development of a Typology of Dual-Earner Families: A Window into Differences between and within Families in Relationships, Roles, and Activities," *Journal of Family Psychology* 11 (1997): 62–75.

7. Francine M. Deutsch, *Halving It All: How Equally Shared Parenting Works* (Cambridge, MA: Harvard University Press, 1999).

8. Penny Edgell Becker and Phyllis Moen, "Scaling Back: Dual-Earner Couples' Working Family Strategies," *Journal of Marriage and the Family* 61 (1999): 995–1007.

9. Ellen Galinsky, *Ask the Children: What America's Children Really Think about Working Parents* (New York: Morrow, 1999).

10. Reed Larson and Maryse H. Richards, *Divergent Realities: The Emotional Lives of Mothers, Fathers, and Adolescents* (New York: Basic Books, 1994).

11. Galinsky, *Ask the Children*.

12. Ibid., p. 205.

13. Adele Eskeles Gottfried, Allen W. Gottfried, and Kay Bathurst, "Maternal and Dual-Earner Employment Status and Parenting," in *Handbook of Parenting*, ed. Marc H. Bornstein, vol. 2, *Biology and Ecology of Parenting* (Mahwah, NJ: Erlbaum, 1995), pp. 139–160.

14. Ann C. Crouter and Susan M. McHale, "The Long Arm of the Job: Influences of Parental Work on Child Rearing," in *Parenting: An Ecological Perspective*, ed. Tom Luster and Lynn Okagaki (Hillsdale, NJ: Erlbaum, 1993), pp. 179–202.

15. Cynthia A. Stifter, Colleen M. Coulehan, and Margaret Fish, "Linking Employment to Attachment: The Mediating Effects of Maternal Separation Anxiety and Interactive Behavior," *Child Development* 64 (1993): 1451–1460.

16. Cheryl D. Hayes, John L. Palmer, and Martha J. Zaslow, eds., *Who Cares for America's Children?* (Washington, DC: National Academy Press, 1990).

17. Crouter and McHale, "The Long Arm of the Job."

18. Ann C. Crouter and Susan M. McHale, "Temporal Rhythms in Family Life: Seasonal Variation in the Relation between Parental Work and Family Processes," *Developmental Psychology* 29 (1993): 198–205.

19. Martha J. Moorehouse, "Linking Maternal Employment Patterns to Mother-Child Activities and Children's School Competence," *Developmental Psychology* 27 (1991): 295–303.

20. Maryse H. Richards and Elena Duckett, "The Relationship of Maternal Employment to Early Adolescent Daily Experience with and without Parents," *Child Development* 65 (1994): 225–236.

21. Ann C. Crouter, "Processes Linking Families and Work: Implications for Behavior and Development in Both Settings," in *Exploring Family Relationships with Other Contexts*, ed. Ross D. Parke and Sheppard G. Kellam (Hillsdale, NJ: Erlbaum, 1994), pp. 29–47.

22. Gregory Pettit, "After-School Experience and Social Adjustment in Early Adolescence: Individual, Family, and Neighborhood Risk Factors" (paper presented at the Meetings of the Society for Research in Child Development, Washington, DC, April 11, 1997).

23. Jean L. Richardson et al., "Substance Use among Eighth-Grade Students Who Take Care of Themselves after School," *Pediatrics* 84 (1989): 556–566.

24. Galinsky, *Ask the Children.*

25. Grace G. Baruch and Rosalind C. Barnett, "Fathers' Participation in Family Work and Children's Sex Role Attitudes," *Child Development* 57 (1986): 1210–1223.

26. Joan E. Grusec, Jacqueline J. Goodnow, and Lorenzo Cohen, "Household Work and the Development of Concern for Others," *Developmental Psychology* 32 (1996): 999–1007.

27. Jacqueline J. Goodnow and Jennifer M. Bowes, *Men, Women and Household Work* (Melbourne, Australia: Oxford University Press, 1994).

28. Galinsky, *Ask the Children.*

29. Ibid.

30. Ellen Greenberger and Robin O'Neil, "Spouse, Parent, Worker: Role Commitments and Role-Related Experiences in the Construction of Adults' Well Being," *Developmental Psychology* 29 (1993): 181–197; Ellen Greenberger and Robin O'Neil, "Parents' Concerns about Their Child's Development: Implications for Fathers' and Mothers' Well Being and Attitudes toward Work," *Journal of Marriage and the Family* 52 (1990): 621–635.

31. Ellen Hock and Debra K. DeMeis, "Depression in Mothers of Infants: The Role of Maternal Employment," *Developmental Psychology* 26 (1990): 285–291.

32. Anita M. Farel, "Effects of Preferred Maternal Roles, Maternal Employment and Sociodemographic Status on School Adjustment and Competence," *Child Development* 50 (1980): 1179–1186.

33. Lois Wladis Hoffman, "Effects of Maternal Employment in the Two-Parent Family," *American Psychologist* 44 (1989): 283–292.

34. Greenberger and O'Neil, "Spouse, Parent, Worker"; Greenberger and O'Neil, "Parents' Concerns about Their Child's Development."

35. Levine and Pittinsky, *Working Fathers.*

36. Greenberger and O'Neil, "Spouse, Parent, Worker"; Greenberger and O'Neil, "Parents' Concerns about Their Child's Development."

37. Arlie Russell Hochschild, *The Time Bind: When Work Becomes Home and Home Becomes Work* (New York: Holt, 1997).

38. Niall Bolger et al., "The Contagion of Stress across Multiple Roles," *Journal of Marriage and the Family* 51 (1989): 175–183.

39. Melvin L. Kohn, *Class and Conformity: A Study in Values* (Homewood, IL: Dorsey Press, 1969).

40. Crouter, "Processes Linking Families and Work."

41. Ibid.

42. Elizabeth Menaghan and Toby Parcel, "Parental Employment and Family Life: Research in the 1980s," *Journal of Marriage and the Family* 52 (1990): 1079–1098.

43. Crouter, "Processes Linking Families and Work."

44. Ibid., p. 21.

45. Personal communication to author.

46. Ibid.

47. Galinsky, *Ask the Children.*

48. Ibid.

49. Niall Bolger et al., "The Contagion of Stress across Multiple Roles."

50. Rena L. Repetti and Jennifer Wood, "Effects of Daily Stress at Work on Mothers' Interactions with Preschoolers," *Journal of Family Psychology* 11 (1997): 90–108.

51. Galinsky, *Ask the Children.*

52. Ibid.

53. Ibid.

54. Ibid., p. 330

55. Deutsch, *Halving It All.*

56. Ibid., p. 231.

57. Ibid., p. 232.

58. Ibid., p. 232.

59. Ramon G. McLeod, "U.S. Study Finds Big Shift in Child Care," *San Francisco Chronicle*, 15 August 1990.

60. Carollee Howes, Deborah A. Phillips, and Marcy Whitebook, "Thresholds of Quality: Implications for the Social Development of Children in Center-Based Child Care," *Child Development* 63 (1992): 449–460.

61. Harriet B. Presser, "Child Care Supply and Demand: What Do We Really Know?" in *Child Care in the 1990s: Trends and Consequences*, ed. Alan Booth (Hillsdale, NJ: Erlbaum, 1992), pp. 26–32.

62. Sally Provence, Audrey Naylor, and June Patterson, *The Challenge of Daycare* (New Haven, CT: Yale University Press, 1977).

63. Edward F. Zigler and Mary E. Lang, *Child Care Choices* (New York: Free Press, 1991).

64. Leslie Berger, "What Children Do When Home and Alone," *New York Times*, 11 April 2000, p. D8.

65. Lynette Long and Thomas Long, *The Handbook for Latchkey Children and Their Parents* (New York: Arbor House, 1983).

66. Zigler and Lang, *Child Care Choices.*

67. Sandra L. Hofferth, "The Demand for and Supply of Child Care in the 1990s," in *Child Care in the 1990s*, pp. 3–25.

68. Zigler and Lang, *Child Care Choices.*

69. Michael E. Lamb, "Nonparental Child Care," in *Parenting and Child Development in Nontraditional Families*, p. 39.

70. Michael E. Lamb, "Nonparental Child Care: Context, Quality, Correlates," in *Handbook of Child Psychology*, ed. in chief William Damon and vol. ed. Irving E. Sigel and K. Ann Renninger, vol. 4, *Child Psychology in Practice*, 5th ed. (New York: Wiley 1998), p. 116.

71. Crouter, "Processes Linking Families and Work."

72. Lamb, "Nonparental Child Care," in *Handbook of Child Psychology*, vol. 4.

73. Tiffany Field, "Quality Infant Day-Care and Grade School Behavior and Performance," *Child Development* 62 (1991): 863–870.

74. Bengst-Erik Andersson, "Effects of Day Care on Cognitive and Socioemotional Competence of Thirteen-Year-Old Swedish Schoolchildren," *Child Development* 63 (1992): 20–36.

75. Rebecca Maynard and Eileen McGinnis, "Policies to Enhance Access for High-Quality Child Care," in *Child Care in the 1990s*, pp. 189–208;

76. Hayes, Palmer, and Zaslow, *Who Cares for America's Children?*

77. Carollee Howes, Claire E. Hamilton, and Catherine C. Matheson, "Children's Relationships with Peers: Differential Associations with Aspects of the Teacher-Child Relationship," *Child Development* 65 (1994): 253–263.

78. Carollee Howes and Claire E. Hamilton, "Children's Relationships with Child Care Teachers: Stability and Concordance with Parental Attachments," *Child Development* 63 (1992): 867–878.

79. Carollee Howes, Catherine C. Matheson, and Claire E. Hamilton, "Maternal, Teacher, and Child Care History Correlates of Children's Relationships with Peers," *Child Development* 65 (1994): 264–273.

80. Lamb, "Nonparental Child Care," in *Handbook of Child Psychology*, vol. 4.

81. NICHD Early Child Care Research Network, "The Effects of Infant Child Care on Infant-Mother Attachment Security: Results of the NICHD Study of Early Child Care," *Child Development* 68 (1997): 876.

82. NICHD Early Child Care Research Network, "Early Child Care and Self-Control, Compliance, and Problem Behavior at Twenty-Four and Thirty-Six Months," *Child Development* 69 (1998): 1145–1170.

83. NICHD Early Child Care Research Network, "Relations between Family Predictors and Child Outcomes: Are They Weaker for Children in Child Care?" *Developmental Psychology* 34 (1998): 1119–1128.

84. Ron Haskins, "Public School Aggression among Children with Varying Day-Care Experience," *Child Development* 56 (1985): 689–703.

85. Deborah Lowe Vandell and Mary Ann Corasaniti, "The Relation between Third-Graders' After-School Care and Social, Academic, and Emotional Func-

tioning," *Child Development* 59 (1988): 868–875.

86. Hayes, Palmer, and Zaslow, *Who Cares for America's Children?*

87. Lamb, "Nonparental Child Care," in *Parenting and Child Development in Nontraditional Families.*

88. Richardson et al., "Substance Use among Eighth-Grade Students."

89. Hoffman, "Effects of Maternal Employment."

90. Ibid.

91. Ibid.

92. Rand D. Conger et al., "A Family Process Model of Economic Hardship and Adjustment of Early Adolescent Boys," *Child Development* 63 (1992): 526–541; Rand D. Conger et al., "Family Economic Stress and Adjustment of Early Adolescent Girls," *Developmental Psychology* 29 (1993): 206–219; Constance A. Flanagan, "Change in Family Work Status: Effects on Parent-Adolescent Decision-Making," *Child Development* 61 (1990): 163–177; Constance A. Flanagan and Jacquelynne S. Eccles, "Changes in Parents' Work Status and Adolescents' Adjustment at School," *Child Development* 64 (1993): 246–257.

93. Ronald L. Simons et al., "Support from Spouse as Mediator and Moderator of the Disruptive Influence of Economic Strain on Parenting," *Child Development* 63 (1992): 1282–1301.

94. Ronald L. Simons et al, "Social Network and Marital Support as Mediators and Moderators of the Impact of Stress and Depression on Parental Behavior," *Developmental Psychology* 29 (1993): 368–381.

95. Vonnie C. McLoyd, "Children in Poverty: Development, Public Policy, and Practice," in *Handbook of Child Psychology*, vol. 4. pp. 135–208.

96. David M. Betson and Robert T. Michael, "Why So Many Children Are Poor," *Future of Children* 7, no. 2 (1997): 25–39.

97. Mary E. Corcoran and Ajay Chaudry, "The Dynamics of Childhood Poverty," *Future of Children* 7, no. 2 (1997): 40–54.

98. Ibid.

99. McLoyd, "Children in Poverty."

100. Ibid.

101. "Study Finds Fewer Kids Living in Poverty," *San Francisco Chronicle*, August 11, 2000, p. A12.

102. McLoyd, "Children in Poverty."

103. U.S. Bureau of the Census, *Statistical Abstract of the United States: 1998.*

104. Corcoran and Chaudry, "The Dynamics of Childhood Poverty."

105. Ibid.

106. McLoyd, "Children in Poverty."

107. Corcoran and Chaudry, "The Dynamics of Childhood Poverty."

108. McLoyd, "Children in Poverty."

109. Jeanne Brooks-Gunn and Greg J. Duncan, "The Effects of Poverty on Children," *Future of Children* 7, no. 2 (1997): 55–71.

110. Ibid.

111. Janet M. Currie, "Choosing among Alternative Programs for Poor Children," *Future of Children* 7, no. 2 (1997): 113–131.

112. Eugene M. Lewit, Donna L. Terman, and Richard E. Behrman, "Children and Poverty: Analysis and Recommendations," *Future of Children* 7, no. 2 (1997): 11.

113. Larry Lipman, "Americans Thriving in Old Age," *San Francisco Chronicle*, August 10, 2000, p. A7.

114. Levine and Pittinsky, *Working Fathers.*

115. Gloria Norris and JoAnn Miller, *The Working Mother's Complete Handbook* (New York: Dutton, 1979).

Chapter 9

1. U.S. Bureau of the Census, *Statistical Abstract of the United States: 1998*, 118th ed. (Washington, DC: Government Printing Office, 1998).

2. "Women in Their 20s Create a Baby Boomlet," *San Francisco Chronicle*, 27 March 2000, p. A8.

3. E. Mavis Hetherington and W. Glenn Clingempeel, *Coping with Marital Transitions: A Family Systems Perspective*, Monographs of the Society for Research in Child Development 57, serial no. 227 (1992): 2–3.

4. Marsha Weinraub and Marcy B. Gringlas, "Single Parenthood," in *Handbook of Par-*

enting, ed. Marc H. Bornstein, vol. 3, *Status and Social Conditions of Parenting* (Mahwah, NJ: Erlbaum, 1995), pp. 65–87.

5. Ibid.

6. Ibid.

7. U.S. Bureau of the Census, *Statistical Abstract: 1998.*

8. Weinraub and Gringlas, "Single Parenthood," p. 66.

9. Ibid.

10. E. Michael Foster, Damon Jones, and Saul D. Hoffman, "The Economic Impact of Nonmarital Childbearing: How Are Older, Single Mothers Faring?" *Journal of Marriage and the Family* 60 (1998): 163–174.

11. Scott J. South, "Historical Change and Life Course Variation in the Determinants of Premarital Childbearing," *Journal of Marriage and the Family* 61 (1999): 752–763.

12. Foster, Jones, and Hoffman, "The Economic Impact of Nonmarital Childbearing."

13. Anne K. Driscoll et al., "Nonmarital Childbearing among Adult Women," *Journal of Marriage and the Family* 61 (1999): 178–187.

14. Jodi R. Sandfort and Martha S. Hill, "Assisting Young, Unmarried Mothers to Become Self-Sufficient: The Effects of Different Types of Early Economic Support," *Journal of Marriage and the Family* 58 (1996): 311–326.

15. William S. Aquilino, "The Life Course of Children Born to Unmarried Mothers: Child Living Arrangements and Young Adult Outcomes," *Journal of Marriage and the Family* 58 (1996): 293–310.

16. Ibid.

17. Martha J. Zaslow et al., "Protective Factors in the Development of Preschool-Age Children of Young Mothers Receiving Welfare," in *Coping with Divorce, Single Parenting, and Remarriage*, ed. E. Mavis Hetherington (Mahwah, NJ: Erlbaum, 1999), pp. 193–223.

18. E. Mavis Hetherington, "Should We Stay Together for the Sake of the Children?" in *Coping with Divorce, Single Parenting, and Remarriage*, pp. 93–116.

19. Robert Fauber et al., "A Mediational Model of the Impact of Marital Conflict on Adolescent Adjustment in Intact and Divorced Families: The Role of Disrupted Parenting," *Child Development* 61 (1990): 1112–1123.

20. John H. Grych and Frank D. Fincham, "Children's Appraisals of Marital Conflict: Initial Investigation of the Cognitive-Contextual Framework," *Child Development* 64 (1993): 215–230; John H. Grych, Michael Seid, and Frank D. Fincham, "Assessing Marital Conflict from the Child's Perspective," *Child Development* 63 (1992): 558–572.

21. E. Mark Cummings and Patrick Davies, *Children and Marital Conflict: The Impact of Family Disputes and Resolution* (New York: Guilford Press, 1994).

22. Brian E. Vaughn, Jeanne H. Block, and Jack Block, "Parenting Agreement on Child Rearing during Early Childhood and the Psychological Characteristics of Adolescents," *Child Development* 59 (1988): 1020–1033.

23. Jeanne H. Block, Jack Block, and Per F. Gjerde, "The Personality of Children prior to Divorce: A Prospective Study," *Child Development* 57 (1986): 827–840.

24. E. Mavis Hetherington, "An Overview of the Virginia Longitudinal Study of Divorce and Remarriage with a Focus on Early Adolescence," *Journal of Family Psychology* 1 (1993): 39–56.

25. E. Mavis Hetherington and Kathleen A. Camara, "Families in Transition: The Process of Dissolution and Reconstruction," in *A Review of Child Development Research*, vol. 7, ed. Ross D. Parke (Chicago: University of Chicago Press, 1984), pp. 398–439.

26. Judith S. Wallerstein and Sandra Blakeslee, *Second Chances* (New York: Ticknor & Fields, 1989), p. 286.

27. Ibid.

28. Ibid., p. 287.

29. Judith S. Wallerstein and Joan B. Kelly, *Surviving the Breakup* (New York: Basic Books, 1980).

30. Ibid., p. 66.

31. Ibid.

32. Wallerstein and Blakeslee, *Second Chances.*

33. M. Janice Hogan, Cheryl Buehler, and Beatrice Robinson, "Single Parenting: Transitioning Alone," in *Stress and the Family*, vol. 1, *Coping with Normative Transitions*, ed. Hamilton I. McCubbin and Charles R. Figley (New York: Brunner/Mazel, 1983), pp. 116–132.

34. Hetherington, "An Overview of the Virginia Longitudinal Study."

35. Hetherington and Camara, "Families in Transition."

36. Wallerstein and Kelly, *Surviving the Breakup.*

37. Ibid.

38. Hetherington and Camara, "Families in Transition."

39. Hetherington and Camara, "Families in Transition"; Wallerstein and Kelly, *Surviving the Breakup.*

40. Ibid.

41. Ibid.

42. Wallerstein and Kelly, *Surviving the Breakup.*

43. E. Mavis Hetherington, "Coping with Family Transitions: Winners, Losers, and Survivors," *Child Development* 60 (1989): 1–14.

44. Wallerstein and Blakeslee, *Second Chances.*

45. Carol E. MacKinnon, "An Observational Investigation of Sibling Interactions in Married and Divorced Families," *Developmental Psychology* 25 (1989): 36–44.

46. Wallerstein and Blakeslee, *Second Chances*, p. 110.

47. Hetherington, "An Overview of the Virginia Longitudinal Study."

48. James H. Bray and E. Mavis Hetherington, "Families in Transition: Introduction and Overview," *Journal of Family Psychology* 7 (1993): 3–8.

49. Sanford L. Braver et al., "A Longitudinal Study of Noncustodial Parents: Parents without Children," *Journal of Family Psychology* 7 (1993): 9–23.

50. Hetherington, "An Overview of the Virginia Longitudinal Study."

51. Eleanor E. Maccoby et al., "Postdivorce Roles of Mothers and Fathers in the Lives of Their Children," *Journal of Family Psychology* 7 (1993): 24–38.

52. E. Mavis Hetherington and Kathleen M. Jodl, "Stepfamilies as Settings for Child Development," in *Stepfamilies: Who Benefits? Who Does Not?* ed. Alan Booth and Judy Dunn (Hillsdale, NJ: Erlbaum, 1994), pp. 55–79.

53. Hetherington, "An Overview of the Virginia Longitudinal Study."

54. Sanford M. Dornbusch et al., "Single Parents, Extended Households and the Control of Adolescents," *Child Development* 56 (1985): 326–341; Judith G. Smetana et al., "Adolescent-Parent Conflict in Married and Divorced Families," *Developmental Psychology* 27 (1991): 1000–1010.

55. Hetherington and Clingempeel, *Coping with Marital Transitions.*

56. Dornbusch et al., "Single Parents."

57. Christy M. Buchanan, Eleanor E. Maccoby, and Sanford M. Dornbusch, "Caught between Parents: Adolescents' Experience in Divorced Homes," *Child Development* 62 (1991): 1008–1029.

58. Hetherington, "An Overview of the Virginia Longitudinal Study."

59. Edward R. Anderson et al., "The Dynamics of Parental Remarriage: Adolescent, Parent, and Sibling Influences," in *Coping with Divorce, Single Parenting, and Sibling Influences*, pp. 295–319.

60. Ibid., p. 316.

61. Paul R. Amato and Brian Keith, "Parental Divorce and the Well Being of Children: A Meta-Analysis," *Psychological Bulletin* 110 (1991): 26046; Dornbusch et al., "Single Parents."

62. Nicholas Zill, Donna Ruane Morrison, and Mary Jo Coiro, "Long-Term Effects of Parental Divorce on Parent-Child Relationships, Adjustment, and Achievement in Young Adulthood," *Journal of Family Psychology* 7 (1993): 91–103.

63. Hetherington, "Should We Stay Together for the Sake of the Children?"

64. Ibid., p. 115.

65. Sara McLanahan and Julien Teitler, "The Consequence of Father Absence," in *Parenting and Child Development in Nontraditional Families*, ed. Michael E. Lamb (Mahwah, NJ: Erlbaum, 1999), pp. 83–102.

66. Paul R. Amato, "More Than Money? Men's Contributions to Their Children's Lives," in *Men in Families: When Do They Get Involved? What Difference Does It Make?* ed. Alan Booth and Ann C. Crouter (Mahwah, NJ: Erlbaum, 1998), pp. 241–278.

67. Ibid., p. 244.

68. Ibid., pp. 271–272.

69. Ibid., p. 257.

70. James A. Levine with Edward W. Pitt, *New Expectations: Community Strategies for Re-*

sponsible Fatherhood (New York: Families and Work Institute, 1995).

71. Ibid., p. 41.
72. Ibid., p. 108.
73. Earl Grollman, prologue to *Explaining Death to Children*, ed. Earl A. Grollman (Boston: Beacon Press, 1967), p. 15.
74. Ibid.
75. John Bowlby, "Childhood Mourning and Its Implications for Psychiatry," *American Journal of Psychiatry* 118 (1961): 481–498.
76. Grollman, prologue to *Explaining Death to Children*.
77. Thomas Gordon with Judith Gordon Sands, *P.E.T. in Action* (New York: Bantam Books, 1978).
78. Grollman, prologue to *Explaining Death to Children*, p. 27.
79. Monica McGoldrick and Betty Carter, "Forming a Remarried Family," in *The Changing Family Life Cycle*, ed. Betty Carter and Monica McGoldrick, 2d ed. (New York: Gardner Press, 1988), pp. 399–429.
80. Wallerstein and Blakeslee, *Second Chances*.
81. Hetherington and Clingempeel, "Coping with Marital Transitions."
82. Fitzhugh Dodson, *How to Discipline with Love* (New York: Rawson Associates, 1977).
83. Hetherington and Jodl, "Stepfamilies as Settings for Child Development."
84. W. Glenn Clingempeel and Sion Segal, "Stepparent-Stepchild Relationships and the Psychological Adjustment of Children in Stepmother and Stepfather Families," *Child Development* 57 (1986): 474–484.
85. Hetherington and Jodl, "Stepfamilies as Settings for Child Development."
86. Ibid.
87. Hetherington, "An Overview of the Virginia Longitudinal Study."

88. Hetherington and Clingempeel, "Coping with Marital Transitions."
89. Hetherington and Jodl, "Stepfamilies as Settings for Child Development."
90. Hetherington and Clingempeel, "Coping with Marital Transitions."
91. Hetherington and Jodl, "Stepfamilies as Settings for Child Development."
92. Ibid.
93. Ibid.
94. Lynn White, "Stepfamilies over the Life Course: Social Support," in *Stepfamilies*, pp. 109–137.
95. James H. Bray and John Kelly, *Stepfamilies: Love, Marriage, and Parenting in the First Decade* (New York: Broadway Books, 1998).
96. Ibid., p. 16.
97. Ibid., p. 265.
98. Charlotte J. Patterson and Raymond W. Chan, "Families Headed by Lesbian and Gay Parents," in *Parenting and Child Development in Nontraditional Families*, pp. 191–219.
99. Ibid.
100. Paul R. Amato, "The Implications of Research Findings on Children in Stepfamilies," in *Stepfamilies*, pp. 81–87.
101. Hetherington, "Should We Stay Together for the Sake of the Children?"
102. Shelli Avenevoli, Frances M. Sessa, and Laurence Steinberg, "Family Structure, Parenting Practices, and Adolescent Adjustment: An Ecological Examination," in *Coping with Divorce, Single Parenting, and Remarriage*, pp. 65–90; Kirby Deater-Deckard and Judy Dunn, "Multiple Risks and Adjustment in Young Children Growing Up in Different Settings," in *Coping with Divorce, Single Parenting, and Remarriage*, pp. 47–64.

Chapter 10

1. David Finkelhor and Jennifer Dziuba-Leatherman, "Victimization of Children," *American Psychologist* 49 (1994): 173–183.
2. Ibid., p. 173.
3. Jay Belsky, "Etiology of Child Maltreatment: A Developmental-Ecological Analysis," *Psychological Bulletin* 114 (1993): 413–434.

4. Jody Todd Manly, Dante Cicchetti, and Douglas Barnett, "The Impact of Subtype, Frequency, Chronicity, and Severity of Child Maltreatment on Social Competence and Behavior Problems," *Development and Psychopathology* 6 (1994): 121–143.

5. Kathleen A. Kendall-Tackett, Linda Meyer Williams, and David Finkelhor, "Impact of Sex Abuse on Children: A Review and Synthesis of Recent Empirical Studies," *Psychological Bulletin* 113 (1993): 164–180.

6. Belsky, "Etiology of Child Maltreatment," p. 413.

7. Robert E. Emery and Lisa Laumann-Billings, "An Overview of the Nature, Causes, and Consequences of Abusive Family Relationships: Toward Differentiating Maltreatment and Violence," *American Psychologist* 53 (1998): 121–135.

8. Ibid.

9. Ibid.

10. Dante Cicchetti and Michael Lynch, "Toward an Ecological/Transactional Model of Community Violence and Child Maltreatment: Consequences for Child Development," *Psychiatry* 56 (1993): 96–118.

11. Fred A. Rogosch et al., "Parenting Dysfunction in Child Maltreatment," in *Handbook of Parenting*, ed. Marc H. Bornstein, vol. 4, *Applied and Practical Parenting* (Mahwah, NJ: Erlbaum, 1995), pp. 127–159.

12. Glenn D. Wolfner and Richard J. Gelles, "A Profile of Violence toward Children: A National Study," *Child Abuse and Neglect* 17 (1993): 199–214.

13. Finkelhor and Dziuba-Leatherman, "Victimization of Children."

14. Penelope K. Trickett, Catherine McBride-Chang, and Frank W. Putnam, "The Classroom Performance and Behavior of Sexually Abused Females," *Development and Psychopathology* 6 (1994): 183–194.

15. Patricia J. Mrazek, "Maltreatment and Infant Development," in *Handbook of Infant Development*, ed. Charles H. Zeanah, Jr. (New York: Guilford Press, 1993), pp. 159–170.

16. Belsky, "Etiology of Child Maltreatment."

17. David A. Wolfe, "The Role of Intervention and Treatment Services in the Prevention of Child Abuse and Neglect," in *Protecting Children from Abuse and Neglect*, ed. Gary B. Melton and Frank D. Barry (New York: Guilford Press, 1994), pp. 224–303.

18. Ibid.

19. Ibid.

20. Ibid.

21. John W. Fantuzzo and Wanda K. Mohr, "Prevalence and Effects of Child Exposure to Domestic Violence," *The Future of Children* 9, no. 3 (1999): 21–32.

22. Kathleen J. Sternberg and Michael E. Lamb, "Violent Families," in *Parenting and Child Development in Nontraditional Families*, ed. Michael E. Lamb (Mahwah, NJ: Erlbaum, 1999), pp. 305–325.

23. Fantuzzo and Mohr, "Prevalence and Effects of Child Exposure to Domestic Violence."

24. Lucy Salcido Carter, Lois A. Weithorn, and Richard E. Behrman, "Domestic Violence and Children: Analysis and Recommendations," *The Future of Children* 9, no. 3 (1999): 4–20.

25. Sternberg and Lamb, "Violent Families."

26. Fantuzzo and Mohr, "Prevalence and Effects of Child Exposure to Domestic Violence."

27. Betsy McAlister Groves, "Mental Health Services for Children Who Witness Domestic Violence," *The Future of Children* 9, no. 3 (1999): 122–133.

28. Bruce D. Perry, "Incubated in Terror: Neurodevelopmental Factors in the 'Cycle of Violence,'" in *Children in a Violent Society*, ed. Joy D. Osofsky (New York: Guilford, 1997), pp. 124–149.

29. Fantuzzo and Mohr, "Prevalence and Effects of Child Exposure to Domestic Violence."

30. Betsy McAlister Groves and Barry Zuckerman, "Interventions with Parents and Caregivers of Children Who Are Exposed to Violence," in *Children in a Violent Society*, pp. 183–201.

31. Ibid.

32. David A. Wolfe and Peter G. Jaffe, "Emerging Strategies in the Prevention of Domestic Violence," in *The Future of Children* 9, no. 3 (1999): 133–144.

33. Ibid., p. 141.

34. Sally Zierler, "Studies Confirm Long-Term Consequences of Childhood Sexual Abuse," *Brown University Child and Adolescent Behavior Newsletter* 8, November 1992, p. 3.

35. Ibid.

36. Diana E. H. Russell, "The Incidence and Prevalence of Intrafamilial and Extrafamilial Sexual Abuse of Female Children," in *Handbook on Sexual Abuse of Children*, ed. Leonore E. Auerbach Walker (New York: Springer, 1988), pp. 19–36.

37. Karin C. Meiselman, *Resolving the Trauma of Incest* (San Francisco: Jossey-Bass, 1990).

38. Kendall-Tackett, Williams, and Finkelhor, "Impact of Sex Abuse on Children."

39. Ibid.

40. Ibid.

41. David Finkelhor and Angela Browne, "Assessing the Long-Term Impact of Child Sexual Abuse: A Review and Conceptualization," in *Handbook on Sexual Abuse of Children*, p. 62.

42. Ibid., pp. 62–63.

43. Kendall-Tackett, Williams, and Finkelhor, "Impact of Sex Abuse on Children."

44. Ibid.

45. Trickett, McBride-Chang, and Putnam, "Classroom Performance and Behavior of Sexually Abused Females."

46. Leonore E. A. Walker and Mary Ann Bolkovatz, "Play Therapy with Children Who Have Experienced Sexual Assault," in *Handbook on Sexual Abuse of Children*, pp. 249–269.

47. Robert E. Emery, "Family Violence," *American Psychologist* 44 (1989): 321–328.

48. Richard J. Gelles, "Physical Violence, Child Abuse, and Child Homicide: A Continuum of Violence or Distinct Behaviors?" *Human Nature* 2 (1991): 59–72.

49. Wolfner and Gelles, "A Profile of Violence toward Children."

50. Ibid.

51. Emery and Laumann-Billings, "An Overview of the Nature, Causes, and Consequences of Abusive Family Relationships."

52. David A. Hamburg, *Today's Children* (New York: Times Books, 1992).

53. Wolfner and Gelles, "A Profile of Violence toward Children."

54. Rogosch et al., "Parenting Dysfunction in Child Maltreatment."

55. Gail S. Goodman, Robert E. Emery, and Jeffrey J. Haugaard, "Developmental Psychology and Law: Divorce, Child Maltreatment, Foster Care, and Adoption," in *Handbook of Child Psychology*, ed. in chief William Damon and vol. ed. Irving E. Sigel and K. Ann Renninger, vol. 4, *Child Psychology in Practice*, 5th ed. (New York: Wiley, 1998), pp. 775–874.

56. Rogosch et al., "Parenting Dysfunction in Child Maltreatment."

57. Belsky, "Etiology of Child Maltreatment."

58. Goodman, Emery, and Haugaard, "Developmental Psychology and Law."

59. Wolfner and Gelles, "A Profile of Violence toward Children."

60. Cicchetti and Lynch, "Toward an Ecological/Transactional Model."

61. Emery, "Family Violence."

62. Dante Cicchetti et al., "Resilience in Maltreated Children: Processes Leading to Adaptive Outcome," *Development and Psychopathology* 5 (1993): 629–647.

63. Richard J. Gelles, "Abandon Reunification Goal for Abusive Families and Replace with Child Protection," *Brown University Child and Adolescent Behavior Newsletter* 8, June 1992, p. 1

64. Diana J. English, "The Extent and Consequences of Child Maltreatment," *The Future of Children* 8, no. 1 (1998): 39–53.

65. Ibid.

66. Howard J. Dubowitz, "The Families of Neglected Children," in *Parenting and Child Development in Nontraditional Families*, pp. 327–345.

67. Ibid.

68. Ibid.

69. Douglas J. Besharov et al., "Four Commentaries: How We Can Better Protect Children from Abuse and Neglect," *The Future of Children* 8, no. 1 (1998): 120–132.

70. Richard Wexler, "Beware the Pitfalls of Foster Care," *New York Times*, 21 January 1996.

71. Besharov, "Four Commentaries."

72. Ibid.

73. Ibid.

74. Goodman, Emery, and Haugaard, "Developmental Psychology and Law."

75. Rogosch et al., "Parenting Dysfunction in Child Maltreatment."

76. John E. Richters and Pedro Martinez, "The NIMH Community Violence Project: I. Children as Victims of and Witnesses to Violence," *Psychiatry* 56 (1993): 7–21.

77. Pedro Martinez and John E. Richters, "The NIMH Community Violence Project: II. Children's Distress Symptoms Associated with Violence Exposure," *Psychiatry* 56 (1993): 22–35.

78. John E. Richters and Pedro Martinez, "Violent Communities, Family Choices, and

Children's Choices: An Algorithm for Improving the Odds," *Development and Psychopathology* 5 (1993): 609–627.

79. Ibid., pp. 622–623.

80. Ibid.

81. Lenore Terr, *Too Scared to Cry* (New York: Harper & Row, 1990).

82. James Garbarino et al., *Children in Danger* (San Francisco: Jossey-Bass, 1992).

83. Peter A. Wyman et al., "The Role of Children's Future Expectations in Self System Functioning and Adjustment to Life Stress: A Prospective Study of Urban At-Risk Children," *Development and Psychopathology* 5 (1993): 646–666.

84. Garbarino et al., *Children in Danger*, p. 110.

85. Ibid.

86. Terr, *Too Scared to Cry*.

87. Alexandra Okun, Jeffrey G. Parker, and Alytia A. Levendosky, "Distinct and Interactive Contributions of Physical Abuse, Socioeconomic Disadvantage, and Negative Life Events to Children's Social, Cognitive and Affective Adjustment," *Development and Psychopathology* 6 (1994): 77–98.

88. Sam Howe Verhovek, "In Arkansas Jail, One Boy Cries and the Other Studies the Bible," *New York Times*, 27 March 1998, p. 1.

89. Perry, "Incubated in Terror," p. 144.

90. Katherine Kaufer Christoffel, "Firearm Injuries Affecting United States Children and Adolescents," in *Children in a Violent Society*, pp. 42–71.

91. U.S. Bureau of the Census, *Statistical Abstract of the United States: 1998*, 118th ed. (Washington, DC: (U.S. Government Printing Office, 1998).

92. John P. Murray, "Media Violence and Youth," in *Children in a Violent Society*, pp. 72–96.

93. Steven J. Wolin and Sybil Wolin, *The Resilient Self* (New York: Villard Books, 1993).

94. Ibid., pp. 5–6.

95. Grace Hechinger, *How to Raise a Street-Smart Child* (New York: Ballantine Books, 1984).

Chapter 11

1. Urie Bronfenbrenner, "Ecology of the Family as a Context for Human Development," *Developmental Psychology* 22 (1986): 723–742.

2. Moncrieff Cochran, "Parenting and Personal Social Networks," in *Parenting: An Ecological Perspective*, ed. Tom Luster and Lynn Okagaki (Hillsdale, NJ: Erlbaum, 1993), pp. 149–178.

3. Ibid.

4. Moncrieff Cochran et al., "Personal Networks and Public Policy," in *Extending Families: The Social Networks of Parents and Their Children*, ed. Moncrieff Cochran et al. (New York: Cambridge University Press, 1990), pp. 307–314.

5. Moncrieff Cochran, "Factors Influencing Personal Social Initiative," in *Extending Families*, pp. 297–306.

6. Ibid., p. 297.

7. Cochran, "Parenting and Personal Social Networks."

8. Moncrieff Cochran and Charles R. Henderson, Jr., "Illustrations," in *Extending Families*, pp. 58–64.

9. Moncrieff Cochran and Starr Niego, "Parenting and Social Networks," in *Handbook of Parenting*, ed. Marc H. Bornstein, vol. 3, *Status and Social Conditions of Parenting* (Mahwah, NJ: Erlbaum, 1995), pp. 393–418.

10. William E. Cross, Jr., "Race and Ethnicity: Effects on Social Networks," in *Extending Families*, pp. 67–85.

11. Brenda K. Bryant, *The Neighborhood Walks: Sources of Support in Middle Childhood*, Monographs of the Society for Research in Child Development 50, whole no. 210 (1985).

12. Moncrieff Cochran and David Riley, "The Social Networks of Six-Year-Olds: Context, Content, and Consequence," in *Extending Families*, pp. 154–177.

13. Cochran, "Parenting and Personal Social Networks."

14. Emmy E. Werner and Ruth S. Smith, *Overcoming the Odds* (Ithaca, NY: Cornell University Press, 1992).

15. Judy Dunn, *Sisters and Brothers* (Cambridge, MA: Harvard University Press, 1985), p. 163.

16. Barbara J. Tinsley and Ross D. Parke, "Grandparents as Support and Socialization Agents," in *Beyond the Dyad*, ed. Michael Lewis (New York: Plenum, 1984), pp. 161–194.

17. Timothy F. J. Tolson and Melvin N. Wilson, "The Impact of Two- and Three-Generational Family Structure on Perceived Family Style," *Child Development* 61 (1990): 416–428.

18. Jane L. Pearson et al., "Black Grandmothers in Multigenerational Households: Diversity in Family Structures on Parenting in the Woodlawn Community," *Child Development* 61 (1990): 434–442.

19. Peter K. Smith, "Grandparenthood," in *Handbook of Parenting*, vol. 3, pp. 89–112.

20. Ibid., p. 96.

21. Ibid.

22. Ibid.

23. Cochran, "Parenting and Personal Social Networks."

24. Moncrieff Cochran and Charles R. Henderson, Jr., "Formal Supports and Informal Social Ties: A Case Study," in *Extending Families*, pp. 230–261.

25. Cochran, "Parenting and Personal Social Networks."

26. Cochran and Riley, "The Social Networks of Six-Year-Olds."

27. Steven J. Wolin and Linda A. Bennett, "Family Rituals," *Family Process* 23 (1984): 401–420.

28. Linda A. Bennett et al., "Couples at Risk for Transmission of Alcoholism: Protective Influences," *Family Process* 26 (1987): 111–129.

29. William J. Doherty, *The Intentional Family* (New York: Avon, 1997), p. 7.

30. Ibid., p. 8.

31. Ibid., p. 14.

32. Werner and Smith, *Overcoming the Odds*, p. 178.

33. Eigel Pedersen and Theresa Annette Faucher with William W. Eaton, "A New Perspective on the Effects of First-Grade Teachers on Children's Subsequent Adult Status," *Harvard Educational Review* 48 (1978): 1–31.

34. Ibid., p. 20.

35. Michael Rutter et al., *Fifteen Thousand Hours: Secondary Schools and Their Effects on Children* (New York: Cambridge University Press, 1979).

36. Cochran, "Parenting and Personal Social Networks."

37. Carolyn Pape Cowan and Philip A. Cowan, *When Partners Become Parents* (New York: Basic Books, 1992).

38. Bruce Cedar and Ronald F. Levant, "A Meta-Analysis of the Effects of Parent Effectiveness Training," *American Journal of Family Therapy* 18 (1990): 373–384.

39. Paul C. Burnett, "Evaluation of Adlerian Parenting Programs," *Individual Psychology* 44 (1988): 63–76.

40. Anthony M. Graziano and David M. Diament, "Parent Behavior Training: An Examination of the Paradigm," *Behavior Modification* 16 (1992): 3–39.

41. Gerald R. Patterson and Carla M. Narrett, "The Development of a Reliable and Valid Treatment Program for Aggressive Young Children," *International Journal of Mental Health* 19 (1990): 19–26.

42. Amy Wolfson, Patricia Lacks, and Andrew Futterman, "Effects of Parent Training on Infant Sleeping Patterns, Parents' Stress, and Perceived Parental Competence," *Journal of Consulting and Clinical Psychology* 60 (1992): 41–48.

43. Philip A. Cowan, Douglas Powell, and Carolyn Pape Cowan, "Parenting Interventions: A Family Systems Perspective," in *Handbook of Child Psychology*, ed. in chief William Damon and vol. ed. Irving E. Sigel and K. Ann Renninger, vol. 4, *Child Psychology in Practice*, 5th ed. (New York: Wiley, 1998), 3–72.

44. Ibid., pp. 59–60.

45. Deborah Stipek and Jacquelyn McCroskey, "Investing in Children: Government and Workplace Policies for Parents," *American Psychologist* 44 (1989): 416–423.

46. Ellen Galinsky, "Families and Work: The Importance of the Quality of the Work Environment," in *Putting Families First*, ed. Sharon L. Kagan and Bernice Weissbourd (San Francisco: Jossey-Bass, 1994), pp. 112–136.

47. Urie Bronfenbrenner and Peter R. Neville, "America's Children and Families: An International Perspective," in *Putting Families First*, pp. 3–27.

48. Edward F. Zigler and Mary E. Lang, *Child Care Choices* (New York: Free Press, 1991).

49. David A. Hamburg, *Today's Children* (New York: Times Books, 1992).

50. Ibid., p. 331.

51. Zigler and Lang, *Child Care Choices*.

52. Norman B. Rice, "Local Initiatives in Support of Families," in *Putting Families First*, pp. 321–337.

53. Gary B. Melton and Frank D. Barry, "Neighbors Helping Neighbors: The Vision of the U.S. Advisory Board on Child Abuse and Neglect," in *Protecting Children from Abuse and Neglect: Foundations for a New National Strategy*, ed. Gary B. Melton and Frank D. Barry (New York: Guilford Press, 1994), pp. 1–13.

54. Ibid., p. 8.

55. Frank D. Barry, "A Neighborhood-Based Approach: What Is It?" in *Protecting Children from Abuse and Neglect*, pp. 14–39.

56. Claudia Dreifus, "We Have a Future Now," *Parade Magazine*, 2 June 1992, p. 20.

57. Roger P. Weissberg and Mark T. Greenberg, "School and Community Competence-Enhancement and Prevention," in *Handbook of Child Psychology*, vol. 4, pp. 877–954.

58. Werner and Smith, *Overcoming the Odds*, p. 177.

59. Joan Beck, *Effective Parenting* (New York: Simon & Schuster, 1976).

60. Robert Coles, *The Spiritual Life of Children* (Boston: Houghton Mifflin, 1990).

61. Ibid., pp. 119–120.

62. Ibid., p. 128.

63. Ibid., p. 127.

64. Felicia R. Lee, "Memories of Youths in Harlem," *New York Times*, 10 July 1993, p. 16.

65. Amy Arner Sgarro, "A Surgeon and Her Community," *Vassar Quarterly* (spring 1993): 10–13.

66. Ibid., p. 13.

Index

AARP (Association of Retired Persons), 31
ABCDE method, 91
Aboud, F. E., 382, 386
Abramovitch, R., 377
abuse
    ecological/transactional model of, 313–316
    emotional, 331
    exposure to family violence, 316–318
    neglect, 328–330
    physical, 325–328, 334–335
    sexual, 318–325
    victimization of children, 310–13
    substance. *See* substance abuse
    See also community violence; domestic violence
acceptance of fate couples, 17
accommodation, 43
Acevedo, M., 376, 378
achievement, 28
active listening, 84–86
activity level, 28–29
Adams, C., 343
Adelson, J., 391
Adler, A., 281
adolescence
    changes during, 203–210
    dating, 208–209
    and divorce, 284, 295, 298
    emotional regulation during, 216–224
    identity formation during, 210–213
    independence during, 231–232
    parent-child relationships, 213–216, 224–232
    parents' experiences during, 232–234
    peer relations, 206–209, 230–231
    promoting healthy behaviors during, 224–230
    self, 206, 210–213
    sexual activity during, 203–204, 227–228
    substance use, 224–226, 228–230
    and working parents, 261
adolescent parents
    fathers, 16–17, 154–156
    mothers, 16–17, 20–21, 153–154, 155–156
adoptive parents, 22–24

African Americans, 12, 19, 20, 30, 51, 56, 116, 140, 151–152, 154, 155, 156, 170–173, 195, 204, 205, 211–213, 214, 221, 231, 263, 270, 271, 272, 288, 346, 347
age
    and parenting, 20–22
    and pregnancy, 18–19
aggression
    in adolescence, 217–219
    in early childhood, 144–146
    in elementary school years, 175, 190–193
    gender differences in, 121–122
AIDS, 228
Aid to Families with Dependent Children (AFDC), 266
Ainsworth, M. D. S., 383
alcohol
    adolescent use, 224–226, 228–230
    parent use, 225–226
    See also substance abuse
Allen, J. P., 394
alloparenting, 74
Altshuler, J. L., 387
Amato, P. R., 285, 289, 290, 400, 401
ambivalent couples, 17
American Association of Retired Persons (AARP), 31
American Indians, 51, 140
Anderson, E. R., 400
Andersson, B. E., 396
Andrews, J. A., 393
Angelou, M., 219
anger
    in adolescence, 217–220, 222–223
    in depressed adolescents, 219, 223
    in early childhood, 144–146
    in elementary school, 175
    high-powered learning strategies and, 106
    low-powered learning strategies and, 105–106
    parental, 80–82
    at parents' fighting, 81–82
Anisfeld, E., 381

406

Anthony, E. J., 376
Anti-Violence Project, 366
anxious avoidant attachments, 131, 133, 136–137
anxious resistant attachments, 131, 133, 136–137
Aquilino, W. S., 398
Arcus, D., 372, 375, 379, 380
Armstrong, T., 201
artificial insemination, 19, 23–24
Asher, S. R., 191, 387, 388
Asian Americans, 51, 170, 181, 205, 214, 231
assimilation, 43
assisted reproductive technology (ART), 2, 16, 19, 23–24
Astone, N. M., 371
attachment
    and child abuse, 314–327
    and childhood behaviors, 45–46, 62, 63–64
    and day care, 257–260
    defined, 129, 130–131
    encouraging secure, 129–133, 138–139
    forms of, 130–131
    infants' contribution to, 130
    parents' contribution to, 134–137
    parents' history of, 57–58
    and peer relationships, 190
    process of forming, 131–133
    social and cultural influences on, 133, 136
    stability of, 137
    value of early positive, 131–133
attachment parenting, 152
attention, 91
authoritarian parenting, 50–51
authoritative parenting, 50–51
authority stage of parenting, 67, 163
Avenevoli, S., 401

babies. *See* infancy
Bachman, J. G., 393
Bachrach, C. A., 371
Ballard, C., 155
Bandura, A., 174, 382, 387
Barber, B. K., 215, 392
Barlow, B., 366
Barnard, K. E., 382
Barnes, G. M., 393
Barnett, D., 401
Barnett, R. C., 395
Barr, R. G., 375, 383
Barr, W. B., 392
Barry, F. D., 343, 401, 405
Bartsch, K., 390
Baruch, G. G., 395

Bates, J. E., 377, 379
Bathurst, K., 394
Baumrind, D., 50, 115, 116, 181, 374, 378, 379, 393
Bayme, S., 369, 372, 376
Beach, F. A., 382
Beardsall, L., 377
Beck, J., 362, 405
Becker, J. B., 389, 390
Becker, P. E., 239, 394
becoming parents
    adolescent parents, 16–17, 20–21, 153–156
    decision to parent, 16–18, 72–73
    infertility, 19, 23–25
    older parents, 21, 22
    pregnancy, 18–19
    reasons for having children, 72–73
    single women, 14, 16–18, 271–275
    timing of children, 16–22
    transition to parenting, 127–128
    unplanned children, 18
behavior geneticists, 26–27
Behrman, R. E., 267, 398, 402
Belkin, L., 371
Bell, S. M., 383
Belluck, P., 392
Belmont, J. M., 373
Belsky, J., 2, 9, 10, 30, 128, 259, 312, 369, 370, 372, 374, 376, 380, 381, 385, 401, 403
Bem, S. L., 382
Bennett, L. A., 348, 349, 350, 404
Berger, L., 396
Bernard, C., 124
Besharov, D. J., 329, 330, 403
Betson, D. M., 397
bicultural identification, 54, 211–213
Bierman, J., 74
Bierman, K. L., 392
Billingsley, A., 364–365
Bing, E., 166
biological parents, 22–25
Blakeslee, S., 279, 292, 375, 399, 400
Blankenhorn, D., 369, 372, 376
Block, J., 121, 372, 380, 391, 393, 399
Block, J. H., 372, 399
Bloom, B. S., 28, 372, 388
Bogenschneider, B., 393
Bolger, N., 396
Bolkovatz, M. A., 402
Bombardieri, M., 18
bonding, 129
Booth, A., 269, 396, 399, 400

Bornstein, M. H., 369, 370, 372, 374, 376, 378, 380, 384, 385, 386, 388, 393, 394, 398, 401, 404

Bowes, J. M., 246, 249, 269, 395

Bowlby, J., 131, 292, 400

boys. *See* gender

Braungart-Rieker, J. M., 379

Braver, S. L., 399

Bray, J. H., 301, 302, 303, 309, 399, 400

Bretherton, I., 379, 381, 383, 386

Briggs, D. C., 73, 103, 376

Briggs, J. L., 54, 374

Brockman, D. K., 371

Brody, G., 380

Bronfenbrenner, U., 2, 4, 6, 9, 27, 72, 236, 313, 357, 369, 370, 371, 372, 375, 394, 404, 405

Brooks, J. B., 371, 375, 376, 377, 380

Brooks-Gunn, J., 263, 264, 265, 266, 371, 372, 384, 385, 389, 390, 397

Brotman-Band, E., 387

Brown, B. B., 207, 390, 394

Brown, J., 377

Browne, A., 402

Bruer, J. T., 64, 375

Bryant, B. K., 404

Bryant, J., 389

Buchanan, C. M., 389, 390, 400

Buehler, C., 392, 399

Bugental, D. B., 378, 380

Buhrmester, D., 390

Bukowski, W., 386, 388, 390

bullying, 193–194

Burchinal, M., 386

Burhans, K. K., 388

Buriel, R., 4, 54, 369, 373, 374, 385

Burnett, P. C., 405

Buss, D. M., 372

Bussey, K., 382

Buzzanca, J. L., 2

Cain, K. M., 377

Camara, K. A., 276, 399

Capaldi, D. M., 27, 56, 59, 372, 374, 392

Caplovitz-Barrett, K., 382

Capote, T., 297

Carew, J., 378

Carlson, C. R., 376

Carson, B., 181, 388

Carter, B., 400

Carter, L. S., 402

Carver, K., 371

cash transfer programs, 266

Caspi, A., 379

Catron, T. F., 379

Cedar, B., 405

challenge model, of dealing with adversity, 336–338

Chamberlain, P., 373, 378

Chamberlin, R. W., 116, 379

Chan, R. W., 371, 400

Chapieski, M. L., 384

Chase-Lansdale, P. L., 371, 384, 385

Chaudry, A., 397, 398

Chavez, F., 385

Chavira, V., 391

Chen, C., 373, 388

Chess, S., 126

child abuse. *See* abuse

childcare. *See* day care

child proofing the house, 108

children

    contemporary families with, 14–15

    and divorce, 276–287

    needs of, 2

    parental qualities valued by, 76, 240–241

    in poverty, 262–267

    role of, 2–3

    temperament of, 117, 120

    and violence, 310–340

    working parents' time with, 242–243

Children's Educational Television Act of 1990, 197

chores. *See* housework

Christoffel, K. K., 335, 403

chronosystem, 6

church supports for families, 362–366

Cicchetti, D., 313, 314, 315, 319, 392, 401, 403

Clausen, J. A., 376

Clingempeel, W. G., 398, 399, 400

Clogg, C. C., 371

close emotional relationships

    affective processes in parenting, 82–83

    dealing with negative feelings, 95–99

    disruptive negative feelings, 78–82

    family atmosphere, 73–82

    increasing joys of parenting, 99–100

    power of positive feelings, 76–77

    promoting harmonious family atmosphere, 84–100

Cobb, N. J., 370, 390

Cochran, M., 404, 405

Cohen, L., 395

Cohler, B. J., 376

Coie, J. D., 8, 369, 387, 388, 389

Coiro, M. J., 400
Cole, P. M., 373, 382
Coles, R., 363, 368, 405
collaborative learning, 106
Collins, W. A., 386, 387, 391, 393
Colman, L., 166
Comer, J. P., 201
communication
    active listening, 84–86
    with adolescents, 228, 231–232
    with children about divorce, 276–278
    coaching, 93–95
    of feelings, 84–87
    I-messages, 86–87
    positive parent-child, 77–78
community
    as support for families, 352–366
    violence in, 331–334
competence
    boyhood, 76
    children's, 9–10
    emotional, 44–45
    intellectual, 43–44
    model for predicting, 9–10
    moral, 49–50
    parents' influences on, 42–49
    physical, 42–43
    self-esteem, 45–48
    social, 48–49
compliance
    and self-regulation, 129–130, 133, 146–150
    ways of achieving, 106–120
conception, 16–19
concrete operations, 43
Conger, J. J., 390
Conger, R. D., 397
Connell, J. P., 387
Connors, L. J., 388
consequences
    learning from, 110
    natural vs. logical, 111
    as punishment, 111–116
contemporary family life, 14–15, 29–33
contraception, 227–228
contracting, 111
Cook, K. V., 384
Coontz, S., 370
Corasaniti, M. A., 397
Corcoran, M. E., 397, 398
Corsaro, W. A., 374
Coulehan, C. M., 395
Covell, K., 377

Cowan, C. P., 17, 96, 128, 354, 355, 356, 370,
    371, 378, 380, 385, 405
Cowan, P. A., 17, 96, 128, 354, 355, 356, 370,
    371, 372, 374, 378, 380, 385, 405
Crack addiction, 330–331
Crick, N. R., 388, 389
Crnic, K. A., 374, 376, 378, 385
Crockenberg, S., 383, 384
Cross, W. E., 404
Crouter, A. C., 394, 395, 396, 400
crying, infancy and, 143–144. *See also* temper
    tantrums
Csikzentmihalyi, M., 390
cultural models, 53–54, 150–152, 311–316
culture
    attachment to parents, 133–136
    importance of, 6, 7, 11–16
    infancy, 150–152
    influence on school behaviors, 181, 188
    parenting beliefs and, 51–56
Cummings, E. M., 81, 376, 377, 398
Cummings, J. S., 377
Currie, J. M., 398
Cytryn, L., 392

damage model of development, 336–338
Damhuis, I., 387
Damon, W., 201, 369, 372, 373, 374, 375, 378,
    380, 384, 386, 388, 389, 390, 394, 396,
    402, 405
D'Angelo, L. L., 392
dating, 208–209
David, J., 371
Davies, P., 309, 398
Davis, P. T., 392
Dawson, G., 375
day care
    availability, 256–257
    high-quality, 258–260
    impact of, on children, 257–261
    self-care, 256, 261
    types of, 255–256
Deater-Deckard, K., 379
death of parent
    dealing with children's reactions, 292–294
    telling children, 291–292
decision to parent, 16–18
DeClaire, J., 103, 377
DeCotis, K. M., 387
DeMeis, D. K., 395
democratic families, 87–89
departure stage of parenting, 67

depression
  in adolescents, 121–122, 219–224
  causes, 220–221
  in children, 220
  gender differences, 121–122
  in mothers, 63, 156–157
  and parenting, 156–157
Deutsch, F. M., 238, 239, 254, 269, 394, 396
Devich-Navarro, M., 391
DeWolff, M. S., 381
Diament, D. M., 405
Dichtemiller, M., 382
difficult children, 145–146
Dinkmeyer, D., 126
Dionne, E. J., Jr., 372
disapproving parents, 95
discipline
  harsh, 169
  high-power, 106, 148
  ineffective forms, 113
  low-power, 105–106
  transmission of styles of, 27, 58–59
  Se also limits
dismissive parents, 58, 93
disorganized/disoriented attachment, 131
Dittus, P J., 393
Divecha, D. J., 372
divorce
  adjustment to, 280–282, 285–286
  children's behavior over time, 284–287
  children's reactions, 278–279
  family changes over time, 283–284
  financial and legal issues, 276
  parents' reactions to, 279–280
  protective factors, 282–283
  telling children, 276–278
Dix, T., 82, 83, 101, 123, 376, 377
Dodge, K. A., 377, 379, 388, 389
Dodson, F., 400
Doherty, W. J., 348, 349, 352, 368, 404
domestic violence, 316–318
Donaldson, S. K., 383
Donnelly, B. W., 370
Dornbusch, S. M., 399, 400
Dorr, A., 389
Dreifus, C., 405
Dreikurs, R., 87, 88, 89, 90, 91, 92, 98, 145, 355, 377, 378, 383
Driscoll, A. K., 398
drugs. *See* substance abuse
dual-earner families. *See* employment
Dubowitz, H. J., 403

Duckett, E., 395
Dumenci, L., 392
Duncan, G. J., 263, 264, 265, 266, 372, 397
Duncan, S. C., 393
Dunn, J., 143, 201, 377, 383, 399, 404
Duyvesteyn, M. G. C., 382
Dweck, C. S., 377, 388
Dziuba-Leatherman, J., 310, 311, 312, 401

early childhood
  attachment, 133
  day care in, 255–260
  emotions in, 141–143, 144–146
  ethnic identity, 140–141
  gender identity formation, 140
  parenting in, 29, 132–133, 141–162
  self-regulation, 146–150
  sense of self, 137–140
  sibling relationships, 160–161
early maturation, 203
Eaton, W. W., 404
Eccles, J., 180, 209, 388, 389, 390, 391, 393, 397
ecological environment, 4, 6
  See also culture; society
ecological/transactional model of abuse, 313–316
Edelman, P., 372
Egeland, B., 375
Ehrensaft, D., 201
Eich, D., 378
Eichorn, D. H., 375, 376
Eiden, R. D., 385
Eisenberg, N., 166, 369, 373, 377, 378, 380, 386, 387, 388, 390
Elder, G. H., 391
elementary school years
  day care in, 246–247
  emotions in, 174–176
  ethnic identity, 170–173
  gender identity, 170, 181
  parent-child relationships, 167–170
  parents' experiences during, 197–198
  partnership of parents/schools, 183–188
  peer relationships in, 188–194
  school experience in, 179–188
  self, 170–174
  self-regulation, 174–179
  television, 194–197
  and working parents, 244–245, 261
Elkind, D., 205, 232, 390, 394
Elliott, D. M., 376, 377
Elliott, G. R., 204, 389
El-Sheikh, M., 376

Elshtain, J. B., 369, 372, 376
Emde, R., 45, 49, 373
Emerson, P. E., 379
Emery, R., 312, 325, 401, 402, 403
emotional abuse, 331
emotional benefits, 345
emotional coaching, 93–95
emotional competence, 44–45
emotional regulation, 45, 141–146, 174–179
emotions
    and child abuse, 314–315
    and close parent-child relationships, 73–75
    communicating, 84–87
    and divorce, 276–287
    negative, 78–82, 95–99
    parents', and parenting, 82–83
    positive, 76–78, 149–150
    regulation of, 45, 49, 130, 141–146, 174–179
    with sibling rivalry, 160–161
empathy
    early childhood, 146
    elementary school years, 174–175
employment
    changing nature of, 31–37, 237–240
    and contemporary families, 34–37
    day care, 255–261
    and economic hardship, 262–267
    and family life, 238–255
    and housework, 246–249
    impact of nonparental care, 257–261
    job stress, 250–252
    marital relationship, 248–250, 267–268
    monitoring children's activities, 245
    navigating family and work life, 243–252
    strategies for successful navigation, 252–255
    support from families, 250
    and time spent with children, 242–245, 253
    typologies of dual-earner families, 238–240
encouragement, 88
encouraging growth. *See* competencies
Engel, S., 162, 385, 386
English, D. J., 403
Epstein, J. L., 388
equilibration, 43
Erikson, E. H., 56, 57, 210, 374, 391
Escalona, S., 120, 380
ethnic diversity, 51–54
ethnic identity, 7, 140–141, 170–173
ethnicity, 7. *See also* culture
European Americans, 19, 20, 30, 51–53, 56, 116,
    150, 181, 195, 204, 205, 221, 231, 263, 270,
    271, 272, 288

exosystem, 6, 313–314, 315
expectations, 97–98, 106–107
external rewards, 107–109

Fabe, M., 371
Faber, A., 377, 383
Fabes, R. A., 373, 383, 388
Fagot, B. I., 370, 380, 385
family
    atmosphere, 73–93, 133, 160–162
    celebrations, 348–352
    changing nature of, 11–15
    rituals, 161–162, 348–352
    time, 79–80, 95–96
    values, 15
    violence, 316–318
Family and Medical Leave Act, 29
Fantuzzo, J. W., 401, 402
Farel, A. M., 395
Farkas, S., 372
Farrell, M. P., 393
fathers
    adolescent, 16–17, 154–156
    and adolescent children, 213–214
    contributions to children's lives, 134, 287–290
    and elementary school children, 168
    encouraging participation of, 134–135, 290
    and family life after divorce, 279–284
    and family life after remarriage, 295–299
    and infants, 136
Fauber, R., 398
Faucher, T. A., 404
Fay, J., 343
fear, 175
Fearing, C., 370, 372, 375
feelings. *See* emotions
Feldman, S. S., 201, 204, 389, 392, 394
Felsman, K., 76, 376
Ferber, R., 151, 384
Ferguson, T. I., 387
Fetal Alcohol Syndrome (FAS), 158
Field, T., 373, 375, 380, 385, 396
Fiese, B. H., 385, 386
Figley, C. R., 399
Fincham, F. D., 377, 398
Finkelhor, D., 310, 311, 312, 401, 402
firearms, 335–336
Fischer, M., 387
Fish, M., 395
Fivush, R., 381, 382
Flanagan, C. A., 397
Fletcher, A. C., 391

Forehand, R. L., 378
formal operations, 43
Forman, D. R., 379
Foster, E. M., 398
Fox, N. A., 373, 380, 381
Frankel, K. H., 379
Franklin, R. R., 371
French, F., 74
Freud, S., 56, 178
friends. *See* peers
Fryer, M., 376
Fuchs, D., 387
Fuligni, A. J., 393
Furey, W. M., 378
Furman, W., 385
Furstenberg, F. F., 371, 385
Futterman, A., 405

Galinsky, E., 67, 71, 162, 163, 197, 232, 240, 242,
       243, 244, 245, 250, 252, 253, 269, 375, 386,
       389, 394, 395, 396, 405
Gamble, W. C., 10, 370
Gandour, M. J., 381
Garbarino, J., 217, 218, 235, 333, 343, 392, 403
Gelles, R. J., 327, 401, 402, 403
gender
    identity, 140, 170, 181
    parenting strategies by, of child, 120–122
genetic influences, 25–29, 41–42, 58–59,
       190–191
Gesell, A., 124, 380
gestational mothers, 2
gifted children, 28–29
Gilstrap, B., 381
Ginott, H., 84, 85, 86, 93, 103, 144, 145, 377, 383
Ginsburg, H., 373
Gjerde, P. F., 391, 399
Gleick, E., 372
Godbey, G., 79, 95, 96, 103, 370, 376, 377
Godfrey, A. B., 151, 384
Goetsch, V., 376
going steady, 208–209
Gold, T., 3
Goldberg, W. A., 370
Golding, E., 386
Goleman, D., 44, 71, 373
Golombok, S., 371, 381, 382
Goodenough, F. L., 144, 383
Goodman, E., 369
Goodman, G. S., 402, 403
Goodnow, J. J., 246, 247, 269, 378, 380, 395
Gopnik, A., 64, 375

Gordon, T., 84, 85, 86, 87, 93, 103, 123, 144, 145,
       293, 355, 377, 378, 383, 400
Gordon, V. V., 393
Gottfried, A. E., 394
Gottfried, A. W., 394
Gottman, J. M., 93, 94, 103, 377
government supports, 13, 29–37, 357–359
Graber, J., 390
Gralinski, J. H., 149, 382, 384
grandparents, 273, 282–283, 347
Granju, A., 384
Gray, M. R., 214, 215, 391
Graziano, A. M., 378, 379, 405
Greenberg, M. T., 361, 372, 376, 390, 392, 405
Greenberger, E., 395
Greenfield, P. M., 53, 374, 384, 388, 389
Greenough, W., 374
Greenspan, A., 35
Greenspan, S., 36
Gringlas, M. B., 371, 398
Grollman, E., 291, 292, 293, 294, 400
Grossman, F. K., 386
Grotevant, H. D., 391
Grotpeter, J. K., 388, 389, 402
Groves, B. M., 402
Grusec, J. E., 374, 378, 395
Grych, J. H., 377, 398
Guacci-Franco, N., 177, 387, 390
Guarendi, R., 71, 378
Gunnar, M. R., 381, 391
guns, 335–336
Guttmann, D., 78, 376

Haight, W., 369
Haiman, P. E., 388
Hall, C. T., 374
Ham, M., 390
Hamblen, J. L., 378, 379
Hamburg, D. A., 38, 357, 358, 359, 368,
       402, 405
Hamilton, C. E., 396, 397
Hann, D. M., 21, 370, 371, 385
happy feelings, 149–150
Hardy, D. F., 371, 387
Hareven, T., 370
Harkness, C., 371
Harkness, S., 51, 374
Harris, J. R., 25, 26, 27, 29, 38, 371
Harris, M., 390, 391
Harris, M. L., 386
Harrison, A. O., 386
Hart, B., 55, 63, 369, 374, 375

Harter, S., 45, 46, 47, 70, 73, 221, 222–223, 224, 373, 382, 386, 387, 390, 391, 392
Hartmann, D. P., 390
Hartup, W. W., 388
Haskins R., 397
hassles, 80
Hastings, P., 374
Haugaard, J. J., 402, 403
Haviland, J. M., 381
Hawkins, J. D., 388
Hayes, C. D., 395, 396, 397
healthy behaviors, 4, 224–230
Hechinger, G., 338, 339, 403
Heckhausen, J., 133, 381
Heinicke, C. N., 16, 370
helplessness, 187–188
Henderson, C. R., 404
Herman, M. R., 393
Hetherington, E. M., 276, 285, 286, 306, 309, 372, 374, 376, 378, 383, 387, 398, 399, 400, 401
Hewlett, S. A., 30, 31, 32, 34–37, 38, 372
Heyman, G. D., 377
high activity level, 117, 118
Hill, M. S., 398
Hispanic Americans, 30, 51, 151–152, 155, 156, 170–171, 195, 205, 211–213, 214, 263, 272, 288
historical time, 11–15
Hochschild, A. R., 250, 395
Hock, E., 395
Hofer, M. A., 373
Hofferth, S. L., 376, 396
Hoff-Ginsberg, E., 54, 55, 374
Hoffman, L. W., 73, 261, 369, 375, 395, 397
Hoffman, S. D., 398
Hogan, M. J., 399
Hogue, A., 390
Holden, G., 383, 384
homosexuality/lesbianism
    adolescence, 211
    parenting, 303–306
Honzik, M. P., 375
Hooven, C., 377
Hops, H., 393
Hornick, R., 381
housework, 246–249
Howard, G. J., 370
Howes, C., 396, 397
Hsieh, K. H., 385
Hunt, J. V., 375
Hunziker, U. A., 375, 383

Huston, A. C., 389
hyperactive children, 28–29, 133

identity
    in adolescence, 210–211
    ethnic, 140–141, 211–214
    gender, 140
    See also self
ignoring, 112–113
Ilardi, B. C., 387
Ilg, F. L., 124, 380
I-messages, 86–87
image-making stage of parenting, 67
inadequacy, 92
industrial revolution, 12–13
ineffective forms of discipline, 113
infancy
    development in, 137–143, 144–150
    individual differences among babies, 117–118
    parents' responses, 129–137, 142–150
    parents' working during, 255–260
    social influences on parenting in, 133, 136, 150–152
infertility, 19, 23–25
informational benefits, 345
Inhelder, B., 373
Injury Prevention Program, 366
insecure attachment, 131
instrumental benefits, 345
intellectual competence, 43–44
intellectual development
    adolescence, 65–66
    adulthood, 66
    early childhood, 59–66
    elementary school years, 179–188
    infancy, 62, 64
intentional parenting, 245, 348–349, 352
interdependent stage of parenting, 67, 232
interpretive stage of parenting, 67, 197
intersubjectivity, 130
in vitro fertilization, 19
irritable distress, 117, 143–144
Italian mothers, 51–53
Izard, C. E., 383

Jaccard, J., 393
Jaedicke, S., 387
Jaffe, P. G., 402
Japanese mothers, 150–151
Jersild, A., 99–100, 378
Jessor, R., 393
Jodl, K. M., 399, 400

Jones, D., 398

Jouriles, E. N., 376

joys children bring
  adolescence, 215
  elementary school years, 198–199
  family generations, 5
  infancy and early childhood, 132
  parenthood, 68
joys of parenting, 99–100
Juffer, F., 382

Kagan, J., 27, 372, 375, 379, 380, 384
Kagan, S. L., 360, 372, 405
Kaler, S. R., 384
Katchadourian, H., 201, 390, 391
Katz, L. F., 377
Katz, P. A., 386
Keating, D. P., 390
Keith, B., 285, 400
Kellam, S. G., 388, 395
Kelly, J., 30, 309, 372, 380, 400
Kelly, J. B., 399
Kendall-Tackett, K. A., 401, 402
Kendler, K. S., 374
Kennedy, B., 384
Kennell, J. H., 380
Keogh, B. K., 184–185
Kessen, W., 373
Kiefaber, M., 96, 97, 378
Kilgore, A., 151, 384
Killen, M., 387
Kimmerly, N. L., 381
Klaus, M. H., 380
Kobak, R. R., 394
Koch, P. B., 391
Kochanska, G., 379, 380, 384, 387
Koeppl, G. K., 389
Kohlberg, L., 179, 388
Kohn, M. L., 55, 374, 396
Kolligian, J., 46, 373
Kolowitz, V., 384
Konner, M., 38
Kopp, C., 149, 382, 383, 384
Korner, A. F., 379
Kraizer, S., 343
Kreutzer, T., 375
Krumboltz, H. B., 145, 383
Krumboltz, J. D., 145, 383
Ksansnak, K. R., 386
Kubey, R., 389
Kuczynski, L., 384
Kuhl, P. K., 64, 375

Kuhn, D., 378
Kuppermintz, H., 78, 376
Kuypers, J., 376

Lacks, P., 405
Ladd, G. W., 373
laissez-faire parents, 93
Lamb, M. E., 257, 309, 394, 396, 397, 400, 402
Lang, M. E., 357, 397, 405
language development, 55–56, 63, 65, 75–76
Larson, R., 213, 235, 249, 390, 391, 394
Larzelare, R. B., 379
late maturation, 203
Laumann-Billings, L., 312, 401, 402
Lay, K.-L., 384
Lazarus, E., 369, 376, 377
learning process, 104–116
Lee, F. R., 405
Lees, N., 13, 369, 372, 373, 393
Leifer, M., 380
Leitenberg, H., 387
Lelwica, M., 381
Leo, J., 372
Leonard, K. E., 385
Lerner, J. V., 118–119
Lerner, R. M., 118–119, 369, 375, 390
lesbianism. *See* homosexuality/lesbianism
Lesieur, K. D., 373
Levant, R. F., 405
Levendosky, A. A., 403
Levine, A., 235
Levine, J. A. (James A.), 134–135, 155, 166, 267, 269, 290, 291, 309, 394, 395, 398, 400
Levine, J. A. (Janet A.), 384
Levitt, J. L., 177, 387, 390
Levitt, M. J., 177, 387, 390
Lewis, G., 388
Lewis, M., 10, 63, 370, 372, 375, 382, 404
Lewit, E. M., 267, 398
Liaw, F., 382
lifespan developmental theory, 56–57
likeability, 189, 208
limits, 109–116, 148–150
Lipman, L., 398
Litman, C., 383, 384
Litt, I. F., 389, 392
Loevinger, J., 123, 380
logical consequences, 111
loneliness, 175
Long, L., 396
Long, T., 396
Louv, R., 38

love, 73–74. *See also* attachment; parenting
Ludtke, M., 371
Luria, A., 75, 376
Lusher, K., 391
Luster, T., 372, 395, 404
Lynch, M., 313, 314, 315, 319, 401, 403
Lyons-Ruth, K., 381
Lytton, H., 116, 379

Maccoby, E. E., 376, 378, 383, 384, 399, 400
MacKinnon, C. E., 399
macrosystem, 6, 313, 315
Malatesta, C. Z., 381, 383
Mammone, N., 374
manipulative tantrum, 145–146
Manis, J. D., 73, 369, 375
Manke, B., 394
Manly, J. T., 401
Marcia, J. E., 210, 391
marital relationship
    conflict, 17, 275–276
    support, 127–128, 164
marital transitions, 305–306. *See also* single-
    parent families
Marjinsky, K. A. T., 385
Marks, P., 375
Markstrom-Adams, C., 212, 382, 386
Markus, H. J., 387
marriage
    domestic violence, 316–318
    parenting during transition in, 305–306
    planning for baby in, 17
    positive relationship, 127–128
    of working parents, 238–243
Martin, C. L., 380
Martin, J. A., 376, 378, 383, 384
Martinez, P., 332, 403
Maslin, C. A., 379
Masters, J. C., 376, 379, 387
Matheson, C. C., 396, 397
Matsumoto, D., 383
Mattes, J., 371
Mayes, L. C., 385
Maynard, R., 396
Mazlish, E., 377, 383
McBride-Chang, C., 401, 402
McCarthy, J., 371
McClearn, G. E., 372, 375, 379
McCoy, C. L., 387
McGoldrick, M. 400
McCubbin, H. I., 399
McGillicuddy-De Lisi, A. V., 380

McGinnis, E., 396
McCroskey, J., 405
McHale, S. M., 246–247, 395
McKay, G. D., 126
McKenna, J. J., 151, 384
McKnew, D. H., 392
McLanahan, S., 287, 288, 400
McLeod, R. G., 396
McLoyd, V., 397
Meiselman, K. C., 319, 402
Meisels, S. J., 382
Mellman, M., 369, 376, 377
Melton, G. B., 343, 401, 405
Meltzoff, A., 64, 375
Menaghan, F., 396
mesosystem, 6
Michael, R. T., 397
Michaels, G. Y., 370
Michel, M. K., 373
microsystem, 6, 314, 315
Miles, B., 377
Miller, J., 267, 398
Miller, P. J., 374
Mills, R. S. L., 380
Millstein, S. G., 389, 392
Minde, K., 384
minorities. *See* ethnic groups
Minton, C., 384
mistakes, 89–92
modeling
    emotional regulation, 130, 141, 144
    by parents, 105
modifiability of early experiences, 64–66
modifying children's behavior
    enforcing limits, 110–116
    helping children meet parents' expectations, 107
    learning process, 104–116
    parental expectations, 107
    problem-solving approach, 123–124
    rewards, 107–108
    stating limits, 109–110
    teaching new behaviors, 109
Moen, P., 239, 391, 394
Mohr, W. K., 401, 402
Money, J., 140, 382
Moore, D., 394
Moorehouse, M. J., 395
moral competence, 45, 49–50
Morelli, G. A., 384
Morgan, S. P., 371, 385
Morisset, C. E., 382
Morris, P. A., 2, 9, 27, 72, 369, 370, 371, 375

Morris, W., 369
Morrison, D. R., 400
Mosco, S. S., 384
mothers
    adolescent, 16–17, 20–21, 153–154, 155–156
    and adolescent children, 213–214
    depressed, 156–157
    and elementary school children, 168–169
    and family life after divorce, 279–284, 286–287
    and infants, 153–154, 155–157
    new, complaints of, 127
    single, 14–15, 18, 272–275
    surrogate, 2
motor competence, 42
Mowdar, B. A., 372
Mrasek, P. J., 401
Mueller, E., 381
Murphy, B., 373
Murphy, C. M., 376
Murray, J. P., 336, 403
Musick, J., 154, 370, 385
Mussen, P. H., 376, 378, 383, 387
mutual problem-solving technique, 110–111

Nakamura, S., 384
Narrett, C. M., 355, 405
National Academy of Sciences Panel on Child
    Care, quality care criteria of, 258
National Center on Child Abuse and Neglect,
    sexual abuse definition of, 318
National Family Violence Survey, 325
National Institute of Child Health and
    Development (NICHD) Research Network,
    260, 397
National Parenting Association, 31, 34
Native Americans, *See* American Indians
natural consequences, 111
Naylor, A., 396
neglect
    consequences, 329
    defined, 328
    interventions, 329–331
Nelson, C. A., 370, 385
Nelson, J., 98, 126, 378
neuroscientific research, 42, 59–61
never-married parents, 272–275
Neville, P. R., 357, 372, 405
New, R. I., 374
Newton, M., 229, 293
Niego, S., 404
Nix, R. L., 386
nonparents, 17

Norman, J., 390, 391
Norris, G., 267, 398
Nucci, L. P., 378
Nurius, P. S., 387
nurturing stage of parenting, 67, 162–163

O'Connor, T. G., 386
Oden, S., 191, 388
Okagaki, L., 372, 395, 404
Okun, A., 403
older parents, 21–22
O'Leary, K. D., 376
Olson, E., 372
Olson, J. A., 392
Olweus, D., 193, 194, 389
O'Neil, R., 395
Opper, S., 373
optimism
    and children's dealing with stress, 174
    in family life, 90–91
    in view of self, 139–140, 174
Oregon Research Institute, on decreasing
    aggression, 193
Orenstein, P., 371
Osofsky, J. D., 21, 153, 155, 343, 370, 371, 380,
    382, 385, 402
Ostler, R., 376

Palmer, J. L., 395, 396, 397
Parcel, T., 396
parent burnout, 96
Parent Child Development Centers, 357–358
parent-child relationships
    in adolescence, 213–216, 224–232
    in elementary school years, 167–170
    in infancy and early childhood, 129–162
Parent Effectiveness Training (P.E.T.), 355
parenthood
    adjustment to, 127–128
    decision for, 16–18
    reasons for, 72
    stages of, 67
    stress of, 127–128
    supports for, 96–97, 128
    timing of, 16–22
    transition to, 128
parenting
    in adolescence, 16–17, 18–19, 153–156
    alloparenting, 74
    attachment, 152
    authoritarian, 50
    authoritative, 50

defined, 2
in different cultures, 51–54, 150–152
during marital/partner transitions, 305–306
effects of social changes on, 11–15
in elementary school years, 167–170,
    176–194
and gender of child, 120–122
historical time and, 11–15
importance of first three years, 59–66
in infancy and early childhood, 129–162
influence of temperament on, 117–120, 130,
    139, 154
intentional, 245, 348–349, 352
optimal environment for, 16
and parents' childhood experiences, 56–59
and parents' emotions, 76–83
permissive, 50–51
as process, 2
stages of, 67
supportive, 92
transition to, 127–128
parenting groups, 354–356
parents
    adolescent, 16–17
    age of, 16–22
    and attachment, 57–58, 129–137
    burnout, 96–97
    children's views of, 76, 133
    death of, 291–294
    defined, 2
    depressed, 65, 156–157
    and emotions, 76–83
    functions of, 14–15
    goals, 40–50, 52–54
    identification of, 2
    importance of, 9–10, 25–29
    influence on children, 4, 25–29, 41–42, 61–66
    influences on, 4, 11–15, 56–59
    job description, 39–40
    lesbian and gay, 303–306
    main tasks of, 39
    means of becoming, 22–25
    needs from children, 3
    over 35, 19, 22–23
    and parenting process, 2, 10–11
    preparenting characteristics of, 16, 57, 58
    reactions of, to divorce, 279–284
    role of, 3, 4, 14–15
    single, 14–15, 18, 272–275, 286–287
    staying together for children, 286–287
    substance-abusing, 157–159
    support system,

Parents' Bill of Rights, 31–32, 34–35
parents' experiences
    adolescence, 232–234
    elementary school years, 197–198
    infancy and early childhood, 162–164
Park, K. A., 384
Park, S.-Y., 372
Parke, R. D., 4, 54, 134, 369, 370, 372, 373, 374,
    385, 395, 399, 404
Parker, J. G., 386, 388, 390, 403
Patterson, C. J., 371, 400
Patterson, G. R., 27, 56, 59, 192, 355, 372, 373,
    374, 378, 389, 405
Patterson, J., 396
Pearson, J. L., 404
Pedersen, E., 404
Peebles, C., 21, 370, 371, 385
peer relations
    adolescent, 206–209, 230–231
    biological influences on, 190
    elementary school years, 188–194
    importance of, 25–26, 188–189
    parents' influence on, 190–194
    See also bullying; dating
Pelton, L., 330
permissive parents, 51–52
Perry, B. D., 335, 402, 403
Perry, C. L., 393
pessimism
    and children's dealing with stress, 177–178
    in family life, 90
Peters, P. L., 371
Petersen, A. C., 390, 392
Peterson, L., 378
Pettit, G. S., 245, 377, 395
Phelps, J. L., 374
Phillips, D. A., 372, 388, 396
Phinney, J. S., 171, 172, 382, 386, 391
physical abuse
    consequences, 7, 327–328, 334–335
    defined, 325
    interventions, 328
    prevalence of, 325–327
physical competence, 42–43
physical punishment, 113–116
Piaget, J., 43, 44, 106, 373
Pick, A. D., 374, 378
Pinon, M. F., 389
Pipher, M., 121, 122, 126, 380
Pitt, E., 291, 400
Pittinsky, T., 267, 269, 394, 395, 398
planning parents, 17

Plante, W. A., 378, 379
plasticity of the brain, 59–61, 64–66
Plomin, R., 372, 375, 379
Pollack, W. S., 122, 126, 380, 386
Polson, B., 229, 393
Pope, A. W., 392
positive family atmosphere, 76–78, 92–96,
     160–162
poverty
   children in, 262–263
   and contemporary families, 29–30
   effects of, on children, 263–266
   forms of intervention, 266–267
   of single-parent families, 263
   of teenage mothers, 20
Powell, D., 405
power, 91
Power, T. G., 384, 387
preconceptual period, 43
pregnancy
   substance use during, 157–158
   unplanned vs. planned, 17–18
Presser, H. B., 396
problem solving
   contracting for, 111
   mutual, 110
   seven-step approach to, 123–124
Procaccini, J., 96, 97, 378
protective factors, 7–9, 21
Provence, S., 396
psychological development. *See* competencies
punishment
   vs. logical consequences, 110–111
   physical, 113–116
   See also spanking
Putnam, F. W., 401, 402

Rabin, B. E., 389
Raboy, B., 371
Radke-Yarrow, M., 383, 385
Radl, S., 191, 388
Ramey, S. L., 386
Rankin, D. B., 390
realistic expectations, 106–107
receptive compliance, 106, 147
regulatory processes. *See* regulation
Reid, M., 386, 387
religious values, 227–228, 362–366
remarriage. *See* stepparenting
Renninger, K. A., 372, 374, 384, 388, 389, 390,
     396, 402, 405
Repetti, R. L., 396

Resnick, M. D., 392, 393
respect, 88–89
revenge, 91
rewards, 105, 107–109
Rheingold, H. L., 384
rhythmicity, 117–120
Rice, N. B., 359, 360, 405
Richard, C. A., 384
Richards, M. H., 213, 235, 249, 390, 391,
     394, 395
Richardson, J. L., 395, 397
Richman, A. L., 374
Richters, J. E., 332, 403
Riley, D., 404
Risenhoover, N., 381
risk factors, 7–9, 21
Risley, T. R., 55, 63, 369, 374, 375
rituals, 348–352
Rivlin, A., 369, 376, 377
Roberts, M. C., 378
Roberts, T. A., 382
Robins, E., 10, 370
Robins, R. W., 391
Robinson, B., 399
Robinson, J., 382
Robinson, J. P., 79, 95, 96, 103, 370, 376, 377
Rochester Longitudinal Study, 7–9, 64
Rodgers, J. L., 390
Roesser, R. W., 391
Rogoff, B., 378
Rogosch, F. A., 401, 402, 403
Rothbart, M. K., 379, 380
Rotheram, M. J., 382, 386
Rotheram-Boris, M. J., 171, 172, 386
Rovine, M., 381
Rowe, D. C., 388
Rubin, K. H, 380, 386, 388, 390
Ruble, D. N., 380, 387
rules, 148–150, 338–340
Russell, A., 386
Russell, D. E. H., 318, 402
Russell, G., 237, 386, 394
Rutter, M., 129, 380, 387, 405

Sachs, K., 369
safety
   rules about, 148–150
   safety proofing home, 108
   teaching children about, 338–340
Sagi, A., 381
Samalin, N., 98, 99, 378
Sameroff, A. J., 7, 9, 369, 370, 375, 386, 391

Sammons, W. A. H., 144, 383
Sanborn, M. E., 382
Sandfort, J. R., 398
Sands, J. G., 377, 400
Sandstrom, M. J., 388
Sanson, A., 379, 380
Santoli, A., 385
scaffolding, 95, 133
Scaramella, L. V., 370
Schafer, W. D., 381
Schaffer, R., 379
Schvaneveldt, J. D., 376
Schatz, M., 166
schemes, 43
Schiefele, U., 180, 388
Schoen, C., 225, 389, 393
school
    adolescents, 209–210
    child care, and, 357–359
    community violence, and, 333
    elementary school years, 179–188
    health service, 361–362
    parents' partnership with, 183–188
    promoting success at, 179–183
    qualities of effective, 183
    as support, 352
Schore, A. N., 379
Schwartz, C. E., 379
Schwartzman, A. E., 371
Seabrook, J., 384
Sears, W., 152, 384
secure attachment, 131
Segal, S., 400
Seid, M., 398
Seifer, R., 370, 386
self
    in adolescence, 206, 210–213
    in elementary school years, 170–174
    in infancy and early childhood, 132, 137–141
    sense of when abused, 315
    See also identity
self-care, by children, 256, 261
self-esteem, 45–48
    and cultural identity of minority children,
        211–213
    and teenage depression, 222–223
self-expression, 92–93
self-regulation
    in elementary school years, 174–179
    in infancy and early childhood, 129–130,
        146–150
    promotion of, 129–130, 133

Seligman, M. E. P., 91, 92, 102, 103, 177, 201,
    224, 377, 387, 392
Sellers, E. B., 391
sense of identity, 210–211
sensorimotor stage, 43
Serbin, L., 370, 371
Sessa, F. M., 401
sexual behavior
    adolescents', 203–204
    postponing, 227–228
    promoting healthy behavior, 227
sexual child abuse
    community preventive programs, 315, 359
    consequences, 319–324
    defined, 318
    interventions, 324–325
    prevalence of, 318–319
sexually transmitted diseases (STDs), 203, 228
Sgarro, A. A., 405
Shandler, S., 219, 235, 392
shaping behavior, 109
shared intentions, 130
Shedler, J., 393
Shore, R., 374
shyness, 191, 193–194
siblings, 160–161, 346–347
Siegal, M., 382
Siegel, D. J., 59, 374, 375
Siegler, R. S., 378
Sieving, R. E., 393
Sigel, I. E., 372, 374, 380, 384, 388, 389, 390, 396,
    402, 405
Silva, P. A., 379
Simmons, R. G., 390
Simons, R. L., 397
Singer, L., 371
single parents
    death of a parent, 291–294
    divorce, 279–284
    fathers, 287–289
    heterogeneity, 14, 18, 271–272
    mothers, 18, 272–275
    in poverty, 263, 271
    statistics, 270–271
Skolnick, A., 38
sleeping, 151–152
Smetana, J. G., 374, 386, 387, 391, 394, 399
Smiley, P. A., 369
Smith, C. A., 370
Smith, P. K., 404
Smith, R. S., 335, 346, 353, 362, 363, 368,
    404, 405

Snidman, N., 372, 375, 379, 380

social competence, 48–49

social development. *See* peers

social disapproval, 113

socialization

    by African American parents, 172–173, 212

    effects of gender on, 120–122

society

    ecological environment, 4

    importance of, to children, 7–10

    importance of, to parents, 29–37

    influence of, 6–15, 133, 136

    interaction effects, 9–11

    protective/risk factors, 7–9

    role of, 4, 51–56

    support for parents, 345–346, 352–366

    view of children and parents, 30–31, 34–37

socioeconomic status (SES), 54–56

Soltz, V., 377, 378, 383

Sorensen, E. S., 387

South, S. J., 398

spanking, 113–116

Spencer, M. B., 212, 382, 386

Sperry, L. J., 369

Spieker, S., 382

Spinrad, T. L., 379

Sroufe, L. A., 375, 382

staying together for the children, 286–287

Stegge, H., 387

Steinberg, L., 214, 215, 235, 390, 391, 394, 401

Steinberg, W., 235, 394

stepfamilies

    challenges of, 294–295

    children's behavior over time, 299–300

    eight-step program to strengthen ties,
        300–301

    family changes over time, 295–299, 301–303

    typologies of, 301–303

Sternberg, K. J., 402

Sternberg, R., 46, 373

Stevenson, H. W., 388

Stewart, R. B., 385

Stifter, C. A., 379, 395

Stipek, D. J., 382, 387, 405

Stoolmiller, M., 392

storytelling, 161–162

Straus, M. A., 115, 379

stress

    in elementary school years, 175–177

    with new parenthood, 127–128

substance use/abuse

    by adolescents, 224–226, 228–230

child abuse with, 158

fetal alcohol syndrome (FAS), 158

interventions for, 158–159

and parenting, 157–159

during pregnancy, 157–158

See also alcoholism

suicide, 221–223

Super, C., 51, 374

support

    to avoid parent burnout, 96–97

    Barlow's individual efforts, 366

    churches as, 362–366

    community programs, 359–362

    family members as, 346–348

    government, 357–359

    kinds of, 345–346

    nonrelatives, 352–354

    parenting programs, 354–356

    rituals as, 348–352

    social, 96–97, 345–366

    teachers as, 352–353

    unconditional, 47, 322–323

    workplace as, 356–357

supportive parenting, 92

surrogate mothers, 2

Sussman, A., 386

Suzuki, L. K., 53, 374, 384, 388

Systematic Training for Effective Parenting
    (STEP), 355

talented children, 28–29

Tardif, T., 54, 55, 374

Tavris, C., 372

teachers

    and children's temperament, 184–185

    and day care, 258–260

    elementary school, 183

    support from, 352–353

    See also school

teaching

    encouraging compliance, 147–150

    household tasks, 246–249

    new behaviors, 109

teenage parents. *See* adolescent parents

teenage pregnancy. *See* adolescent pregnancy

Teitler, J., 287, 288, 400

television, 194–197

temperament

    and child's reaction to divorce, 282–283

    defined, 117

    and early caregiving, 117–118

    and elementary school experience, 184–185,

190–191
   and interaction with infants, 130
   parents' influence on, 120, 190–191
   persistence of qualities, 117–120
temper tantrums, 145–146
Terman, D. L., 267, 398
Terr, L., 332, 403
Teti, D. M., 375
Teti, L. O., 373
Thelen, E., 373
Thelen, M. H., 387
Thomas, A., 126
Thompson, R. A., 373, 375, 380, 381
Thornberry, T. P., 370
Thornton, M. C., 173, 386
time
   with children and employment, 242–248
   limited time, 79–80
   strategies for effective use of, 95–100
time out, 113
Tingley, E., 381
Tinsley, B. J., 369, 372, 373, 393, 404
Tizard, J., 387
Tjebkes, T. L., 379
Tolson, T. F. J., 404
Tonner, L., 145, 166, 383
Toth, S. L., 392
traumatic events. *See* violence
Trickett, P. K., 401, 402
Tronick, E. Z., 382, 383
troubled families, 159–160
Tulviste, P., 373
Turecki, S., 145, 166, 383
Turiel, E., 378, 387

Uchitelle, L., 370
unconditional support, 47
unhappiness, 175–177
unplanned children, 18
U.S. Advisory Board on Child Abuse and
   Neglect, 359
U.S. Bureau of the Census, 369, 370, 371, 374,
   394, 397, 398, 403
Uttal, D., 388

Vaillant, G. E., 76, 376
values of different cultures, 51–54
   See also culture
Vandell, D., 397
van den Boom, D. C., 382
van IJzendoorn, M., 374, 381, 382
Vaughn, B. E., 399

Verhovek, S. H., 403
victimization, 310–313. *See also* violence
violence
   challenge model for dealing with, 336–338
   by children and teenagers, 193–194
   common aspects of, 334–335
   community, 331–334
   ecological/transactional model of, 311–316
   family, 316–318
   neglect, 328–331
   physical abuse, 325–328, 334–335
   prevention of, 335–336, 338–340
   sexual abuse, 318–325
   television, 196
   types of, 310–313, 331
Visher, E. B., 296–299, 301, 309
Visher, J. S., 296–299, 309
Voydanoff, P., 370
Vygotsky, L., 43, 44, 106, 373

Wachs, T. D., 388
Walker, A., 219
Walker, L. E. A., 402
Wallerstein, J., 276, 278, 279, 294, 399, 400
Walley, P. B., 378
Waterman, J., 320–323
Waters, E., 379, 384
Watson, J. S., 383
Watson, M. W. (Malcolm W.), 386
Watson, M. W. (Michael W.), 381
Weber, M., 330
Weinberger, D. L., 392
Weiner, A., 78, 376
Weinraub, M., 371, 398
Weissberg, R. P., 361, 372, 388, 390, 392, 405
Weissbluth, M., 383
Weissbourd, B., 360, 372, 405
Weisz, J. R., 376, 387
Weithorn, L. A., 402
Werner, E. E., 74–75, 337, 346, 353, 362, 363,
   368, 404, 405
Wertsch, J. V., 373
West, C., 30, 31, 32, 34, 38, 372
West, M. J., 384
Westerman, M. A., 383
Wexler, R., 403
What I Wish I Had Known About boxes
   adolescence, 233
   elementary school years, 187
   infancy and early childhood, 142
Whitbeck, L. B., 392
White, L., 400

Whitebook, M., 396
Whitehead, B. D., 15
Whitmore, K., 387
Whitney, C., 99, 378
Wigfield, A., 180, 388
Wikler, N., 371
Williams, C. L., 393
Williams, G., III, 371
Williams, L. M., 401, 402
Wilson, F. R., 61, 375
Wilson, J. Q., 49, 71, 373
Wilson, M. N., 404
Windle, M., 392, 393
Wissow, L. S., 379
Wolfe, D. A., 401, 402
Wolfe, V., 219
Wolfner, G. D., 327, 401, 402, 403
Wolfson, A., 405
Wolin, S., 337, 368, 403
Wolin, S. J., 337, 348, 349, 350–353, 368,
    403, 404
Wood, J., 396
Woodworth, S., 376, 385
work. *See* employment; housework

Wray, H., 383
Wright, J. C., 389
Wyman, P. A., 403

Yahraes, H., 392
Yamamoto, K., 387
Yankelovich, D., 370
Yarrow, A., 21, 22, 371
yes-no couples, 17
Youniss, J., 54, 374
Youth Charters, 233–234

Zahn-Waxler, C., 121, 216, 380, 382, 392
Zarbatany, L., 390
Zaslow, M. J., 395, 396, 397, 398
Zeanah, C. H., Jr., 21, 370, 382, 401
Zierler, S., 402
Zigler, E., 357, 358, 359, 396, 405
Zill, N., 400
Zillmann, D., 389
Zimbardo, P., 191, 388
zone of proximal development, 44
Zuckerman, B., 402
Zussman, J. U., 376